BIBLE READINGS

Straight Answers From God's Word

BIBLE READINGS

REVIEW AND HERALD® PUBLISHING ASSOCIATION
Since 1861 | www.reviewandherald.com

Copyrighted © 1914, 1935, 1942, 1949, 1958, 1963, 2008, Review and Herald®
Publishing Association

Published by Review and Herald® Publishing Association, Hagerstown, MD
21741-1119

Unless otherwise noted, Bible texts in this book are from the King James Version.

Bible texts followed by LXX are from the Septuagint, a Greek version of the Old
Testament.

Scripture quotations marked NASB are from the *New American Standard Bible*,
copyright © 1960, 1962, 1963, 1968, 1971, 1972, 1973, 1975, 1977, 1994 by The Lock-
man Foundation. Used by permission.

Texts credited to NIV are from the *Holy Bible, New International Version*. Copyright © 1973, 1978, 1984, International Bible Society. Used by permission of Zondervan Bible Publishers.

Texts credited to NKJV are from the New King James Version. Copyright © 1979,
1980, 1982 by Thomas Nelson, Inc. Used by permission. All rights reserved.

Bible texts credited to NRSV are from the New Revised Standard Version of the
Bible, copyright © 1989 by the Division of Christian Education of the National Council of the Churches of Christ in the U.S.A. Used by permission.

Bible texts credited to RSV are from the Revised Standard Version of the Bible,
copyright © 1946, 1952, 1971, by the Division of Christian Education of the National
Council of the Churches of Christ in the U.S.A. Used by permission.

Texts credited to Tanakh are from *Tanakh: A New Translation of the Holy Scriptures According to the Traditional Hebrew Text*. Copyright © The Jewish Publication
Society of American, Philadelphia, 1985.

Cover design by Trent Truman
Cover art by istockphoto.com/duckycards
Interior design by Heather Rogers
Typeset: Times New Roman 9/10

Library of Congress Cataloging-in-Publication Data
  Bible readings : straight answers from God's word.
    p. cm.
  1. Bible—Examinations, questions, etc. 2. Bible—Criticism, interpretation, etc.
I. Review and Herald Publishing Association.
BS612.R44 2007
220.6—dc22

                                      2007033925

ISBN 978-0-8280-1728-2

INTRODUCTION
The Most Dangerous Book in the World

The Bible is the best-selling, most studied, and most translated book of all time. Few other books are so dearly loved or so earnestly hated. Because of it millions have died, yet because of it the suffering of millions has been relieved. Its stories can be understood by a simple child, yet its depths tax the intellect of the wise. Much of the world's art and music was inspired by it. It causes proud men to tremble, and fearful men to trust. Hundreds of thousands of books have been written about it, yet its mysteries still tantalize some of the world's greatest minds.

It claims to determine the eternal destiny of man (Matthew 7:24, John 12:48). It consigns those who disagree with it to outer darkness (Isaiah 8:20-22). It claims the power to give everlasting life (John 6:63).

Any book making such claims is bound to be considered extremely dangerous. Indeed, the Bible is the most banned book of all time—it has the longest entry in Anne Haight's *Banned Books*. There are organizations devoted to eradicating the presence of the Bible in public life. There are public schools that will not allow students to bring the Bible into the classroom. And there are still countries in the world that will not allow the Bible to be imported.

In the past the Bible has been suppressed even more than it is today—even in Christendom. The Bible was considered so dangerous that the very institution it created—the church—once made it a capital offense to own one. For more than a thousand years the church would not allow its own members to read the Bible. Only the priests were trusted to interpret the Bible correctly. Laypersons might start thinking for themselves, and realize that some teachings in the Bible didn't jibe with official church dogma.

There must be something extremely unusual about a book that is suppressed by its charter organization. Did America suppress the Constitution? Did Muslims suppress the Koran? Has any other major world religion diligently sought for hundreds of years to restrict access to its sacred writings?

The Bible is the most explosive literature ever published. Mahatma Gandhi said, "You Christians have in your keeping a document with enough dynamite in it to blow the whole of civilization to bits; to turn society upside down; to bring peace to this war-torn world. But you read it as if it were just good literature, and nothing else."

Since Scripture is the most revolutionary tract that can be unleashed on a culture, totalitarian societies often ban it. The Bible always poses a threat to any status quo, because it empowers people. It suggests that the lowly will be lifted up and the high brought down low. It makes the timid brave, and satisfies the longings of the human heart for freedom and significance.

No other book has so molded the world in which we live, and none who lack an acquaintance with it are really educated. It gives us a revelation of the living God. Received by faith, it has power to transform the life. During all its history a divine hand has been over it, and preserved it for the world. Either the Bible is the greatest fraud of all time, or else it is all that it claims to be.

HOW THE BIBLE WAS WRITTEN

The Bible is a compilation—a library, really—written by about 40 authors over a period of some 1,600 years. The first five books of the Bible were written in Hebrew by Moses, around 1500 B.C. Jews still consider this, the Torah, as the most holy of inspired writings. These books served as a standard to which the writings of later prophets were expected to conform. Gradually the prophetic and historical books were added over the next 1,000 years. Isaiah 8:20 mentions "the law [the books of Moses] and . . . the testimony [the later writings]" as the standard of truth in his day. Many of these books were compiled into a single collection by Ezra around 500 B.C. after the Jews had returned from exile in Babylon; later a few more writings were added to this collection.

Then for 400 years the Spirit of prophecy was silent, and there were no inspired writings, although some valuable religious literature (the Apocrypha, pseudepigrapha, Dead Sea scrolls, etc.) was written during this period. The death and resurrection of Christ in A.D. 31 marked a revival of the work of the Holy Spirit in the world. The New Testament was written in Greek within the second half of the first century A.D. It covers the life of Christ and its significance for us today.

In a book that was written over so long a period of time by so many different authors of different cultures and languages, we would expect a great diversity of doctrine. Yet the Bible demonstrates an amazing unity in its teachings that points to a Master Designer behind the whole. If 40 different contractors were asked to manufacture parts for a modern airliner, and when the parts were brought together they were found to fit perfectly into a unified whole, it could only mean there was a single intelligence overseeing the matter. Thus the unity of Scripture bears witness to its divine Author.

THE FIRST TRANSLATIONS OF THE BIBLE

The Old Testament Scriptures were first written upon scrolls, or rolls of parchment, linen, or papyrus. The original languages were Hebrew and Aramaic. These writings were later translated into Greek. The oldest translation into Greek is known as the Septuagint, or "Version of the Seventy," made at Alexandria, for the huge library there, by a company of 70 learned Jews about 285 B.C. According to Josephus (*Antiquities of the Jews* 11. 8. 5), when Alexander the Great visited Jerusalem in 332 B.C., the high priest met him and showed him Daniel's prophecy that Alexander's kingdom—Greece—would overthrow Persia. This so pleased Alexander that he ordered a new translation into Greek of the Hebrew Scriptures. The resulting translation, the Septuagint, became the common version of Jesus' day, and most New Testament authors quote from this version when citing the Old Testament. In scholarly literature the Septuagint is referred to by the abbreviation LXX.

In the third and fourth centuries Latin translations, both of the Septuagint and of the Greek New Testament, were made by several individuals, but a more carefully prepared version of the complete Bible, the Latin Vulgate, was made by Jerome in A.D. 383-405. It was called the Vulgate, or "common" version, because it was in common use among Latin-speaking people.

THE INVENTION OF PRINTING

Since there was no printing, copies of the Bible could be produced only by the slow, laborious, and expensive process of handwriting. This greatly limited its circulation. Worse still, many of its truths were largely hidden for centuries by the errors and superstitions of the Dark Ages. During this time the common people knew little of its contents.

But with the invention of the art of printing about the middle of the fifteenth century, and with the dawn of the Reformation in the century following, the Bible entered upon a new era, preparatory to the final proclamation of the gospel throughout the world.

The first important book printed in Europe from movable type was the Bible in Latin, printed by Johannes Gutenberg, issued at Mainz, Germany, in 1456. The copy of the Gutenberg Bible owned by the Library of Congress is currently the most valuable printed book in the world.

THE BEGINNING OF MODERN TRANSLATIONS

But so far the Bible had been printed only in an ancient tongue, and was largely unavailable to the common people. The translation of the Bible into English by John Wycliffe, in 1380, was one of the main events leading to the Reformation. It also prepared the way for the revival of Christianity in England, and the wide dissemination of the Scriptures that followed in later centuries.

To make such a translation at that time, says Augustus Neander, "required a bold spirit which no danger could appal." In the preface to his translation Wycliffe exhorted everyone to read the Scriptures. For his efforts Wycliffe was attacked from various quarters, because, it was claimed, "he was introducing among the multitude a book reserved exclusively for the use of the priests." In the general denunciation it was declared that "thus was the gospel by him laid more open to the laity, and to women who could read, than it had formerly been to the most learned of the clergy; and in this way the gospel pearl is cast abroad, and trodden underfoot of swine."

A sense of awe and a thrill of joy filled the heart of young Martin Luther, the great German Reformer, when, at the age of 20, while examining the volumes in the library of the University of Erfurt, he held in his hands, for the first time in his life, a complete copy of the Bible. "O God," he murmured, "could I but have one of these books, I would ask no other treasure." A little later he found a chained Bible in a convent.

But these Bibles were in an ancient language, and could be read only by the educated. Why, thought Luther, should the Living Word be confined to dead languages? Like Wycliffe, therefore, he resolved to give his countrymen the Bible in their own tongue. He completed the New Testament in 1522, and the Hebrew Scriptures in 1534.

Impressed with the idea that the people should read the Scriptures in their own tongue, William Tyndale, likewise, in 1525, gave to the English his translation of the New Testament, and later, of portions of the Old Testament Scriptures. He pledged that if God spared his life he would cause any common plowboy to know more of the Scriptures than was commonly known by the religious leaders of his day.

The first complete printed English Bible was that of Miles Coverdale, printed at Zurich, Switzerland, in 1535. Matthew's Bible, the Taverner's Bible, and the Great Bible prepared at the suggestion of Thomas Cromwell, Earl of Essex, appeared soon after. Thus the light of truth began to shine forth once more, but not without opposition.

BURNING THE BIBLE

As Jehoiakim, king of Judah, and the princes under King Zedekiah showed their contempt for God by burning the writings of Jeremiah and confining the prophet in a dungeon (Jeremiah 36:20-23; 38:1-6), so now men sought to stem the rising tide of reform by burning the Bible and its translators.

Bible burning began in England with the destruction of copies of the Antwerp edition of Tyndale's New Testament, at St. Paul's Cross, London, in 1527, followed by the burning of a second edition in 1530. Later there were wholesale burnings of the translations of Wycliffe, Tyndale, Basil, Barnes, Coverdale, and others.

Forty-three years after the death of Wycliffe, in 1428, his bones were dug up and burned by order of the Council of Constance. On October 6, 1536, Tyndale was strangled and burned at the stake at Vilvorde, near Brussels, by order of Charles V of Germany. "If Luther will not retract," wrote Henry VIII of England, "let himself and his writings be committed to the flames."

THE WORD UNBOUND

But the Word of God could not be forever bound by tyranny. Preventing its circulation proved impossible. The Bible had taken deep root in the hearts of the people. What kings and prelates had sought to suppress and destroy, kings and prelates now began to foster and supply.

In his *Stories From English History* Henry P. Warren says: "Henry, by Cromwell's advice, ordered a translation of the Bible to be made in English, and a copy to be placed in every church. There had been English translations before, but they had not been in the hands of the people generally, and had only been read secretly and in fear. . . . Cromwell then appointed Cranmer and the bishops to revise the Bible, and publish it without note or comment; and in the year 1539 a copy of the English Bible was chained to the reading desk of every parish church. From that time the Bible has never ceased to be printed and sold freely" (pp. 196, 197).

In *Story of Liberty* Charles C. Coffin writes: "The people listen to the reading with wonder and delight. They begin to think; and when men begin to think, they take a step toward freedom. They see that the Bible gives them rights which hitherto have been denied them—the right to read, to acquire knowledge. Schools are started. Men and women, who till now have not known a letter of the alphabet, learn to read: children teach their parents. It is the beginning of a new life—a new order of things in the community—the beginning of liberty" (p. 44).

More than 200 years later, after a great revival in the English-speaking world, Bible societies were organized in England, America, and many of the countries of Europe, for the purpose of giving the Bible to the world—to every nation, kindred, tongue, and people in its own language. The British and Foreign Bible Society was organized in 1804. The American Bible Society was organized in 1816. The National Bible Society of Scotland was organized in 1861. These are the three largest Bible societies in the world. Together, these organizations have distributed more than 1 billion copies of the Scriptures in more than 1,000 languages around the world.

So the world is being provided with the Word of God, preparatory to the giving of the closing gospel message to all humanity, the ending of the reign of sin, and the advent of the Lord in glory. "And this gospel of the kingdom will be preached in the whole world as testimony to all nations, and then the end will come" (Matthew 24:14, NIV).

THE VALUE OF BIBLE STUDY

The Bible is a revelation from God to us. It points us to God and to His Son, whom to know is life eternal. As a guide, it is without a rival. It gives a calm peace in believing, and a firm hope of the future. It solves the great problems of life and destiny, and inspires to a life of purity, patience, and well-doing. It fills the heart with love for God and a desire to do good to others, and thus prepares for usefulness here and for a home in heaven. It teaches the value of the soul, by revealing the price that has been paid to redeem it. It makes known the only antidote for sin, and presents the only perfect code of morals ever given. It tells of the future and the preparation necessary to meet it. It makes us bold for the right, and sustains the soul in adversity and affliction. It lights up the dark valley of death, and points to a life unending. It leads to God, and to Christ, whom to know is life eternal. In short, it is the one book to live by and die by.

The Bible is God's great textbook for humanity. It is His lamp to our feet and light to our path in this world of sin. The value of Bible study cannot therefore be overestimated.

As an educating power, the Bible has no equal. Nothing so broadens the vision, strengthens the mind, elevates the thoughts, and ennobles the affections as does the study of the sublime and stupendous truths of revelation. A knowledge of its principles is an essential preparation to every calling. To the extent that it is studied and its teachings are received, it gives strength of character, noble ambition, keenness of perception, and sound judgment. Of all the books ever written, none contains lessons so instructive, precepts so pure, or promises so great as the Bible.

There is nothing that so convinces the mind of the inspiration of the Bible as does the reading of the Bible itself, and especially those portions known as the prophecies. After the resurrection of Christ, when everything else seemed to have failed to convince the disciples that He had risen from the dead, He appealed to the Inspired Word, and "expounded unto them in all the scriptures the things concerning himself" (Luke 24:27), and they believed. On another occasion He said, "If they hear not Moses and the prophets, neither will they be persuaded, though one rose from the dead." Luke 16:31. The king of Israel was instructed to keep a copy of the law and read it "all the days of his life," that he might "fear the Lord," keep His word, and thus prolong his days and the days of his children (Deuteronomy 17:18-20). Those who would do the same today will learn that fear which is the beginning of wisdom, and that knowledge which is unto salvation. As an aid and incentive to this, *Bible Readings* has been prepared and published.

THE USE OF BIBLE READINGS

Briefly stated, a Bible reading consists of questions asked concerning some subject, and answers to them from the Bible. In other words, a Bible reading is a topical study of the Bible by means of questions and answers. Questions are known to be an effective way of stimulating thinking. Even Scripture uses them, asking and often answering its own questions (see Job 38:4, 7; 14:14; Psalms 8:4; 24:3-5; 34:12-14; Proverbs 23:29, 30; Malachi 3:1, 2, 8; Isaiah 33:14-17; Exodus 32:26; 1 Chronicles 29:5).

The Bible itself, therefore, sets the example of giving instruction and of imparting most valuable information by means of asking questions and answering them.

The readings in this book were originally contributed by a large number of Bible instructors, whose experience in giving Bible readings had taught them the most effective methods of presenting the different subjects treated. It has been repeatedly revised to reflect the latest scholarship, and to better present the truths of God's word to modern readers. Several million copies of this book have been sold.

As a help in enabling the reader quickly to discover the answer to the questions, the words within the text that provide the answer are often italicized.

We hope you find *Bible Readings* an excellent aid to private, family, and public study of the Word of God.

CHAPTER 1

The Bible:
How to Study and Understand It

THE SACRED SCRIPTURES

By what name are the sacred writings of the Bible commonly known?

"Jesus said to them, 'Have you never read in *the Scriptures*: "The stone which the builders rejected has become the chief cornerstone. This was the Lord's doing, and it is marvelous in our eyes"?' " Matthew 21:42, NKJV.

What other title is given this revelation of God?

"But he answered and said to them, 'My mother and My brothers are these who hear *the word of God* and do it.' " Luke 8:21, NKJV.

NOTE.—Jesus spoke of hearing God's word rather than reading it because in His day and community few people could read. Instead, they heard the Scripture read each week in the synagogue.

The Bible includes 66 books and was written by about 40 authors over a period of some 1,500 years. The books are called the "word of God," or the "Scriptures." "Scriptures" means "writings." Thus "Sacred Scriptures" means "Sacred Writings." The word "Bible" does not occur in the Bible itself. It is derived from the Latin *biblia*, which came from the Greek *biblia*, or "little books." The Greek word *biblia* in turn is derived from *byblus*, or papyrus, which in ancient times served as paper and upon which books were written.

How were the Scriptures given?

"All Scripture is given by *inspiration of God*." 2 Timothy 3:16, NKJV.

Who inspired Scripture?

"For prophecy never had its origin in the will of man, but men spoke from God as they were carried along *by the Holy Spirit*." 2 Peter 1:21, NIV.

What specific instance of inspiration does Peter mention?

"Brothers, the Scripture had to be fulfilled *which the Holy Spirit spoke long ago through the mouth of David concerning Judas*, who served as guide for those who arrested Jesus." Acts 1:16, NIV.

Who thus spoke through them?

"In the past *God* spoke to our forefathers through the prophets at many times and in various ways." Hebrews 1:1, NIV.

Why were the Scriptures written?

"For everything that was written in the past was written *to teach us*, so that through endurance and the encouragement of the Scriptures we might have hope." Romans 15:4, NIV.

Of what practical use is the Bible?

"All Scripture is God-breathed and is useful *for teaching, rebuking, correcting and training in righteousness.*" 2 Timothy 3:16, 17, NIV.

What was God's design in giving the Scriptures?

"So that the man of God may be *thoroughly equipped for every good work.*" Verse 17, NIV.

How does God's word bless us in this world of darkness?

"Your word is *a lamp* to my feet and *a light* to my path." Psalm 119:105, NKJV.

What three general divisions did Jesus refer to in the writings of the Old Testament?

"He said to them, 'This is what I told you while I was still with you: Everything must be fulfilled that is written about me in the *Law of Moses, the Prophets* and *the Psalms.*'" Luke 24:44, NIV.

NOTE. —These divisions are listed in the order they were canonized, or formally included in the Old Testament. The Law of Moses (the first five books of the Bible) is the oldest part of the Scriptures. The prophets wrote later. The third division of the Hebrew Scriptures, which Jesus mentions by naming its largest book, Psalms, includes all the other writings (Job, Proverbs, Esther, etc.) and was the last to be canonized.

Upon what evidence did Jesus base His Messiahship?

"And beginning with *Moses* and all the *Prophets*, he explained to them what was said *in all the Scriptures* concerning himself." Verse 27, NIV.

NOTE.—When Christ spoke of the Scriptures, He meant the Old Testament, for the New Testament had not yet been written. Jesus cited the Old Testament prophecies as proof of His Messiahship.

How is God described in the Scriptures?

"He is the Rock, his works are perfect, and all his ways are just. *A faithful God* who does no wrong, upright and just is he." Deuteronomy 32:4, NIV.

What, therefore, must be the character of His word?

"Sanctify them by the truth; your word is *truth*." John 17:17, NIV.

What test should we apply to every professed teacher of truth?

"*To the law and to the testimony!* If they do not speak according to this word, they have no light of dawn." Isaiah 8:20, NIV.

How did Job value the words of God?

"I have not departed from the commands of his lips; *I have treasured the words of his mouth more than my daily bread*." Job 23:12, NIV.

What inspired David's songs?

"*Your decrees* are the themes of *my song*, wherever I lodge." Psalm 119:54, NIV.

How firm was the faith of the great Isaiah in the word of God?

"The grass withers and the flowers fall, but *the word of our God stands forever*." Isaiah 40:8, NIV.

People Die—The Bible Lives

Jesus said, "Heaven and earth will pass away, but my words will never pass away." Matthew 24:35, NIV. The Word of God is forever. The French skeptic Voltaire said that the Bible was an exploded book. But it was his theory that exploded—not the Bible. Ingersoll said that in another 10 years the Bible would not be read. Ingersoll and Voltaire have been dead many years, but the Bible lives on as the best-selling book of all time. Those who take this Book to heart and live its teachings will live forever (1 John 2:17).

HOW TO UNDERSTAND THE BIBLE

Who did Jesus say the Scriptures point to?

"These are the Scriptures that testify about me." John 5:39, NIV.

Why did Luke praise the Bereans?

"Now the Bereans were of more noble character than the Thessalonians, for *they received the message with great eagerness and examined the Scriptures every day to see if what Paul said was true."* Acts 17:11, NIV.

NOTE. — "If God's Word were studied as it should be, men would have a breadth of mind, a nobility of character, and a stability of purpose that is rarely seen in these times. But there is but little benefit derived from a hasty reading of the Scriptures. One may read the whole Bible through and yet fail to see its beauty or comprehend its deep and hidden meaning. One passage studied until its significance is clear to the mind and its relation to the plan of salvation is evident is of more value than the perusal of many chapters with no definite purpose in view and no positive instruction gained." Ellen G. White, *Steps to Christ*, p. 90.

Are some portions of God's Word more profound than others?

"In fact, though by this time you ought to be teachers, you need someone to teach you *the elementary truths of God's word* all over again. You need *milk*, not *solid food!* Anyone who lives on milk, being still an *infant,* is not acquainted with the teaching about righteousness. But solid food is for the *mature,* who by constant use have trained themselves to distinguish good from evil." Hebrews 5:12-14, NIV.

Are some portions of Scripture difficult to understand?

"Bear in mind that our Lord's patience means salvation, just as our dear brother *Paul* also wrote you with the wisdom that God gave him. He writes the same way in all *his letters,* speaking in them of these matters. *His letters contain some things that are hard to understand,* which ignorant and unstable people distort, as they do the other Scriptures, to their own destruction." 2 Peter 3:15, 16, NIV.

NOTE.—Some scriptures are too plain to be misunderstood, while others cannot so readily be discerned. To obtain a comprehensive knowledge of any Bible truth, scripture must be compared with scripture, and there should be "careful research and prayerful reflection." But all such study will be richly rewarded.

What did Jesus say about the book of Daniel?

"So when you see standing in the holy place 'the abomination that causes desolation,' spoken through the prophet Daniel—*let the reader understand."* Matthew 24:15, NIV.

What other book of the Bible is especially commended for our study?

"Blessed is the one who reads *the words of this prophecy [the book of Revelation],* and blessed are those who hear it and take to heart what is written in it, because the time is near." Revelation 1:3, NIV.

Through whom has God revealed His secrets to us?

"However, as it is written, 'No eye has seen, no ear has heard, no mind has conceived what God has prepared for those who love him'—but *God has revealed it to us by his Spirit. The Spirit searches all things, even the deep things of God.* For who among men knows the thoughts of a man except the man's spirit within him? In the same way no one knows the thoughts of God except the Spirit of God." 1 Corinthians 2:9-11, NIV.

What is one purpose for which God sent the Holy Spirit?

"But the Counselor, the Holy Spirit, whom the Father will send in my name, *will teach you all things and will remind you of everything I have said to you.*" John 14:26, NIV.

How do we comprehend the things of the Spirit?

"The man without the Spirit does not accept the things that come from the Spirit of God, for they are foolishness to him, and he cannot understand them, because *they are spiritually discerned.*" 1 Corinthians 2:14, NIV.

For what spiritual enlightenment should everyone pray?

"*Open my eyes* that I may see wonderful things in your law." Psalm 119:18, NIV.

What spiritual gift did the apostle Paul pray for?

"I keep asking that the God of our Lord Jesus Christ, the glorious Father, may give you *the Spirit of wisdom and revelation, so that you may know him better.*" Ephesians 1:17, NIV.

How can we attain spiritual wisdom?

"*And if you call out for insight and cry aloud for understanding, and if you look for it as for silver and search for it as for hidden treasure,* then you will understand the fear of the Lord and find the knowledge of God." Proverbs 2:3-5, NIV.

"If any of you lacks wisdom, he should ask God, who gives generously to all without finding fault, and it will be given to him." James 1:5, NIV.

What is promised those who surrender to God's will?

"If anyone chooses to do God's will, he will find out whether my teaching comes from God or whether I speak on my own." John 7:17, NIV.

NOTE.—God desires honest-hearted seekers who will follow the truth wherever it may lead.

How did Jesus answer when a rich young man asked Him how to have eternal life?

" 'What is written in the Law?' he replied. 'How do you read it?' " Luke 10:26, NIV.

What effect can Scripture have on the believer?

"And how from infancy you have known the holy Scriptures, which are able to *make you wise for salvation* through faith in Jesus Christ." 2 Timothy 3:15, NIV.

What great blessing did Jesus bestow upon His disciples after His resurrection?

"Then he opened their minds so they could understand the Scriptures." Luke 24:45, NIV.

How did Jesus reprove those who, though familiar with the tenets of the Scriptures, failed to understand them?

"Jesus replied, 'You are in error because you do not know the Scriptures or the power of God.' " Matthew 22:29, NIV.

Whom did Jesus pronounce blessed?

"He replied, 'Blessed rather are those who hear the word of God and obey it.' " Luke 11:28, NIV.

POWER IN THE WORD OF GOD

Through what agency did God create the heavens?

"By the word of the Lord the heavens were made, and all the host of them by the breath of his mouth. . . . For *He spoke,* and it was done; *He commanded,* and it stood fast."* Psalm 33:6-9, NKJV.

By what does Jesus sustain all things?

"The Son is the radiance of God's glory . . . , sustaining all things *by his powerful word."* Hebrews 1:3, NIV.

Why is God worthy of our praise?

"Praise Him, all His angels; praise Him, all His hosts! Praise Him, sun and moon; praise Him, all you stars of light! Praise Him, you heavens of heavens, and you waters above the heavens! Let them praise the name of the Lord, for *He commanded and they were created."* Psalm

148:2-5, NKJV.

How does Jesus change us?

"For Christ's love compels us, because we are convinced that one died for all, and therefore all died. And he died for all, that those who live *should no longer live for themselves but for him who died for them* and was raised again. So from now on we regard no one from a worldly point of view. Though we once regarded Christ in this way, we do so no longer. Therefore, if anyone is in Christ, he is a *new creation; the old has gone, the new has come!*" 2 Corinthians 5:14-17, NIV.

How is this new creation also described?

"In reply Jesus declared, 'I tell you the truth, no one can see the kingdom of God unless he is *born again*.'" John 3:3, NIV.

How is this new creation, or new birth, accomplished?

"For you have been born again, not of perishable seed, but of imperishable, *through the living and enduring word of God*." 1 Peter 1:23, NIV.

What is the first creative act of God's Word recorded in the Bible?

"And God said, *Let there be light:* and *there was light*." Genesis 1:3.

What connects this creation and the gospel?

"For it is the God who commanded light to shine out of darkness who has shone in our hearts to give *the light of the knowledge of the glory of God in the face of Jesus Christ*." 2 Corinthians 4:6, NKJV.

What about Jesus' teaching astonished people?

"And they were astonished at his doctrine: for *his word was with power*." Luke 4:32.

How powerful was the word of Christ?

"In the synagogue there was a man possessed by a demon, an evil spirit. He cried out at the top of his voice, 'Ha! What do you want with us, Jesus of Nazareth? Have you come to destroy us? I know who you are—the Holy One of God!'

" 'Be quiet!' Jesus said sternly. 'Come out of him!' Then the demon threw the man before them all and came out without injuring him.

"All the people were amazed and said to each other, 'What is this teaching? *With authority and power he gives orders to evil spirits and they come out!*'" Luke 4:33-36, NIV.

How did God heal His people in ancient times?

"*He sent forth his word and healed them*; he rescued them from the grave." Psalm 107:20, NIV.

How did the centurion with a suffering servant show his faith in the power of Jesus' Word?

"The centurion replied, 'Lord, I do not deserve to have you come under my roof. But just say the word, and my servant will be healed.' " Matthew 8:8, NIV.

Where should the Word of Christ dwell?

"Let the peace of Christ rule in your hearts, since as members of one body you were called to peace. And be thankful. Let the word of Christ *dwell in you* richly as you teach and admonish one another with all wisdom, and as you sing psalms, hymns and spiritual songs with gratitude in your hearts to God." Colossians 3:15, 16, NIV.

How did Jesus say the scribes and Pharisees fell short spiritually?

"*And you do not have his word abiding in you*, because you do not believe him whom he has sent." John 5:38, NRSV.

How did the Thessalonians respond to the word that Paul shared with them?

"And we also thank God continually because, when you received the word of God, which you heard from us, you accepted it not as the word of men, but as it actually is, the word of God, *which is at work in you who believe*." 1 Thessalonians 2:13, NIV.

What nature is imparted through God's promises?

"He has given us his very great and precious promises, so that through them you may participate in *the divine nature and escape the corruption in the world caused by evil desires*." 2 Peter 1:4, NIV.

What purifies the hearts of believers?

Jesus is speaking to His disciples at the Last Supper:

"I am the true vine, and My Father is the gardener. He cuts off every branch in me that bears no fruit, while every branch that does bear fruit he prunes so that it will be even more fruitful. You are already clean because of *the word I have spoken to you*.

"Remain in me, and I will remain in you. No branch can bear fruit by itself; it must remain in the vine. Neither can you bear fruit unless you remain in me." John 15:1-4, NIV.

What promise does Jesus give to those who remain in Him and keep His word in their hearts?

"I am the vine; you are the branches. *If a man remains in me and I in him, he will bear much fruit; apart from me you can do nothing.* If anyone does not remain in me, he is like a branch that is thrown away and withers; such branches are picked up, thrown into the fire and burned. *If you remain in me and my words remain you, ask whatever you wish, and it will be given you.* This is to my Father's glory, that you bear much fruit, showing yourselves to be my disciples." Verses 5-8, NIV.

How can we live out Jesus' word to us?

"As the Father has loved me, so have I loved you. Now *remain in my love.* If you *obey my commands,* you will remain in my love, just as I have obeyed my Father's commands and remain in His love. I have told you this so that my joy may be in you and that your joy may be complete. My command is this: *Love each other as I have loved you.* Greater love has no one than this, that he lay down his life for his friends. You are my friends if you do what I command. I no longer call you servants, because a servant does not know his master's business. Instead, I have called you friends, for everything that I learned from my Father I have made known to you. You did not choose me, but I chose you and appointed you to go and bear fruit—fruit that will last. Then the Father will give you whatever you ask in my name. This is my command: *Love each other.*" Verses 9-17, NIV.

How can the young keep their way pure?

"How can young people keep their way pure? *By guarding it according to your word.*" Psalm 119:9, NRSV.

How may we guard our hearts from sin?

"I seek you with all my heart; do not let me stray from your commands. I have hidden your word in my heart that I might not sin against you." Psalm 119:10, 11, NIV. (See also Psalm 17:4.)

"I want to know one thing—the way to heaven, how to land on that happy shore. God Himself has condescended to teach the way: for this very end He came from heaven. He hath written it down in a book. O give me that book! At any price give me that book of God! I have it; here is knowledge enough for me. Let me be a man of one book." John Wesley.

THE LIFE-GIVING WORD

What is the nature of the Word of God?

"For the word of God is *living and active.* Sharper *than any dou-*

ble-edged sword, it penetrates even to dividing soul and spirit, joints and marrow; *it judges the thoughts and attitudes of the heart.*" Hebrews 4:12, NIV.

On the day of his martyrdom Stephen preached a stirring sermon on the history of God's work with Israel. How did he describe the messages God sent through Moses?

"This is that Moses who told the Israelites, 'God will send you a prophet like me from your own people.' He was in the assembly in the desert, with the angel who spoke to him on Mount Sinai, and with our fathers; and he received *living words* to pass on to us." Acts 7:37, 38, NIV.

NOTE.—The Bible is not a dead letter. It is alive with the life-changing power of God.

Why did Peter continue to follow Jesus when many were leaving Him?

"From this time many of his disciples turned back and no longer followed him. 'You do not want to leave too, do you?' Jesus asked the Twelve. Simon Peter answered him, 'Lord to whom shall we go? *You have the words of eternal life.* We believe and know that you are the Holy One of God.' " John 6:66-69, NIV.

What power does God's word have?

"Then Jesus cried out, 'When a man believes in me, he does not believe in me only, but in the one who sent me. When he looks at me, he sees the one who sent me. I have come into the world as a light, so that no one who believes in me should stay in darkness.

" 'As for the person who hears my words but does not keep them, I do not judge him. For I did not come to judge the world, but to save it. There is a judge for the one who rejects me and does not accept my words; that very word which I spoke will condemn him at the last day. For I did not speak of my own accord, but the Father who sent me commanded me what to say and how to say it. *I know that his command leads to eternal life.* So whatever I say is just what the Father has told me to say.' " John 12:44-50, NIV.

What lesson did God teach through the miracle of the manna in the wilderness?

"He humbled you, causing you to hunger and then feeding you with manna, which neither you nor your fathers had known, to teach you that *man does not live on bread alone but on every word that comes from the mouth of the Lord.*" Deuteronomy 8:3, NIV.

Jesus quoted this text when tempted by Satan (Matthew 4:4).

How did Jeremiah describe feeding on God's Word?

"Your words were found, and I ate them, and your words became to me a joy and the delight of my heart; for I am called by your name, O Lord God of hosts." Jeremiah 15:16, NRSV.

How did Jesus speak of such spiritual food?

" '*My food,*' said Jesus, '*is to do the will of him who sent me and to finish his work.*' " John 4:34, NIV.

What name of Jesus describes Him as the revelation of the thought of God in the flesh?

"In the beginning was *the Word,* and the Word was with God, and the Word was God." John 1:1. "And He was clothed with a vesture dipped in blood: and His name is called *The Word of God.*" Revelation 19:13.

What did this Word become?

"The Word became *flesh* and made his dwelling among us." John 1:14, NIV.

What was in the Word?

"In Him was *life,* and that life was the light of men." John 1:4, NIV.

What is Jesus therefore also called?

"That which was from the beginning, which we have heard, which we have seen with our eyes, which we have looked at and our hands have touched—this we proclaim concerning *the Word of life.*" 1 John 1:1, NIV.

What did Jesus declare Himself to be in John 6:35?

"Then Jesus declared, 'I am the bread of life. He who comes to me will never go hungry, and he who believes in me will never be thirsty.' " John 6:35, NIV.

If Jesus is the bread of life, what should we do with this bread?

"Just as the living Father sent me and I live because of the Father, so *the one who feeds on me will live because of me.* This is the bread that came down from heaven. Your forefathers ate manna and died, but *he who feeds on this bread will live forever.*" Verses 57, 58, NIV.

What did Jesus really mean by our eating His flesh?

"The Spirit gives life; the flesh counts for nothing. The words I have spoken to you are *spirit* and they are *life.*" Verse 63, NIV.

NOTE.—Thus we clearly understand that to eat the flesh of the Son of God is to live by His words.

What grand privilege do we have as Christians?

"And have *tasted the good word of God*, and the powers of the world to come." Hebrews 6:5. (See also Jeremiah 15:16.)

What glorious invitation is extended to all?

"Oh, *taste* and *see* that the Lord is good; blessed is the man who trusts in Him!" Psalm 34:8, NKJV.

How are we instructed to pray for both physical and spiritual nourishment?

"Give us this day our daily bread." Matthew 6:11.

NOTE.—When "the Word became flesh, and made his dwelling among us" (John 1:14, NIV), the thought of God was revealed in human flesh. When the Bible's writers "spoke as they were moved by the Holy Spirit" (2 Peter 1:21, NKJV), the thought of God was revealed in human language. The union of the divine and human in Jesus is declared to be "the mystery of godliness" (1 Timothy 3:16, NIV); and there is the same mystery in the union of divine thought and human language. The two revelations of God, in human flesh and in human speech, are both called the *Word of God*, and both are the *Word of Life*. Those who fail to find Christ in the Scriptures will not be able to receive the power God seeks to give each of us.

CHRIST IN ALL THE BIBLE

Of whom did Jesus say the Scriptures testify?

"These [the Old Testament books] are the scriptures that testify about *me*." John 5:39, NIV.

NOTE.—"Search the Old Testament Scriptures: for they are they that testify of Christ. To find Him in them is the true and legitimate end of their study. To be able to interpret them as He interpreted them is the best result of all Biblical learning." Dean Alford.

Of whom did Moses and the prophets write?

"Philip found Nathanael and told him, 'We have found the one Moses wrote about in the Law, and about whom the prophets also wrote—*Jesus of Nazareth,* the son of Joseph.' " John 1:45, NIV.

What writers testify of the death and resurrection of Jesus?

"He said to them, 'How foolish you are, and how slow of heart to believe *all that the prophets have spoken!* Did not the Christ have to suffer these things and then enter his glory?' " Luke 24:25, 26, NIV.

How did Jesus show that all the Scriptures testify of Him?

"And beginning with Moses and all the Prophets, *he explained to them what was said in all the Scriptures concerning himself.*" Verse 27, NIV.

Where in the Bible do we find the first promise of a Redeemer?

"So the Lord God said to the serpent, '. . . I will put enmity between you and the woman, and between your offspring and hers; he will crush your head, and you will strike his heel.' " Genesis 3:14, 15.

NOTE.—After Adam and Eve sinned in the Garden of Eden, God pronounced curses, including one on the serpent, which represented Satan (Revelation 12:9).

In what words was this promise renewed to Abraham?

"*In your seed* all the nations of the earth shall be blessed, because you have obeyed My voice." Genesis 22:18, NKJV. (See also Genesis 26:4; 28:14.)

To whom did this promised seed refer?

"The promises were spoken to Abraham and to his seed. The Scripture does not say 'and to seeds,' meaning many people, but 'and to your seed,' meaning one person, *who is Christ.*" Galatians 3:16, NIV.

Who was the Rock that spiritually fed the Israelites during their wilderness journey?

"They all ate the same spiritual food and drank the same spiritual drink; for they drank from the spiritual rock that accompanied them, and *that rock was Christ.*" 1 Corinthians 10:3, 4, NIV.

The Face in the Puzzle Picture

Did you ever see one of those 3-D puzzle pictures that conceal a portrait or landscape? At first it appears to be a meaningless chaos, but suddenly the pattern appears, and you wonder why you had not seen it before! The great face in the Bible is that of Jesus. Like the scarlet thread that runs through every inch of rope in the British Navy, like the melody of a beautiful song, like the theme of a great masterpiece, so is Jesus in the Scriptures. They testify of Him. He is the author and the hero, the beginning and the ending of your Holy Bible.

CHAPTER 2

Sin: Our Problem, God's Answer

CREATION AND THE CREATOR

How does Genesis describe God and creation in the beginning?

"In the beginning *God* created the heavens and the earth. Now the earth was formless and empty, darkness was over the surface of the deep, and the Spirit of God was hovering over the waters." Genesis 1:1, 2, NIV.

NOTE.—Genesis presents a clear contrast to the prevailing theologies of the ancient world. Mesopotamian religion saw the gods as dependent on nature, as pantheistic personifications of the elements with no inherent eternalness. Genesis presents God as both eternal and distinct from His creation.

"The first verse of Genesis not only reveals a lot about God, but also attacks the common ancient view about religion. In doing this, it sets the trend of the creation account as a whole, which takes every opportunity available to confound the conventional wisdom of its time. In more recent years, the ways in which Genesis disagrees with modern humanistic atheism have been emphasized. The assumption has often been that as an ancient work, Genesis simply reflects the general views of its own time. This is not the case. Genesis has always been out of step, not only with the prevailing views of its own time, but also with ours today. It was radical then. It is radical now." Laurence Turner, *Back to the Present: Encountering Genesis in the 21st Century* (Grantham, Eng.: Autumn House, 2004), p. 19.

How did God begin His acts of creation?

"And God said, 'Let there be light,' and there was light. God saw that the light was good, and he separated the light from the darkness. God called the light 'day,' and the darkness he called 'night.' And there was evening, and there was morning—the first day." Verses 3-5, NIV.

NOTE.—God is sovereign. While ancient religions depicted creation as the result of struggle between gods, God creates by merely speaking His word.

How did God shape the world and create an environment suitable for living creatures?

"And God said, 'Let there be an expanse between the waters to separate water from water.' So God made the expanse and separated the water under the expanse from the water above it. And it was so. God called the expanse 'sky.' And there was evening, and there was morning—the second day.

"And God said, 'Let the water under the sky be gathered to one place, and let dry ground appear.' And it was so. God called the dry ground 'land,' and the gathered waters he called 'seas.' And God saw that it was good.

"Then God said, 'Let the land produce vegetation: seed-bearing plants and trees on the land that bear fruit with seed in it, according to their various kinds.' And it was so. The land produced vegetation: plants bearing seed according to their kinds and trees bearing fruit with seed in it according to their kinds. And God saw that it was good. And there was evening, and there was morning—the third day.

"And God said, 'Let there be lights in the expanse of the sky to separate the day from the night, and let them serve as signs to mark seasons and days and years, and let them be lights in the expanse of the sky to give light on the earth.' And it was so. God made two great lights—the greater light to govern the day and the lesser light to govern the night. He also made the stars. God set them in the expanse of the sky to give light on the earth, to govern the day and the night, and to separate light from darkness. And God saw that it was good. And there was evening, and there was morning—the fourth day." Verses 6-19, NIV.

NOTE.—Ancient astrology viewed the sun and the moon as gods impacting events on earth, yet Genesis depicts them as mere "lights" under God's control, doing His will. "So, implicitly the account is inviting its readers to reject any form of sun or moon worship, and all forms of astrology that claim to predict the future of individuals based on their sign of the zodiac. It rejects a fatalistic view of human existence.

"This significant point is driven home by two other features. First, many readers of Genesis are puzzled as to why God creates light on the first day but creates the heavenly luminaries only on the fourth day. Actually, this is neither an oversight nor a problem. On the first day the word 'light' is used five times. On the corresponding fourth day, the word 'lights' is used five times. Through this repetition the text underlines the connection between the two days in order to say something significant about God and the heavenly bodies: God is the source of light. The heavenly bodies are simply the means he chooses later to fulfill that role. In other words, worship God the source of light, not the sun, moon, or stars that are part of this creation. To make this point even clearer, note how the account does not use the words 'sun' or 'moon' to describe what God created. Rather, it uses the terms 'the greater light' and 'the lesser light.' Apparently, Genesis does this so that there can be no ambiguity at all that the heavenly bodies are not to be worshipped. For the Hebrew words for 'sun' and 'moon' were also the names of the sun-god and moon-goddess in some ancient near eastern languages. So it does not even use these words in case there is any misunderstanding. For similar reasons, the 'stars' are placed last after sun and moon, almost as an afterthought, because they were usually accorded pride of place in astrological texts.

"Genesis is adamant. The heavenly lights are merely lights, placed there by God to fulfill certain functions. But since they are merely lights, their function is not to control or indicate human destiny. That lies in the hand of God, the creator of 'the heavens and the earth.' The point is made more explicit elsewhere, for example when God judges any Israelite who, 'contrary to my command has worshipped other gods, bowing down to them or to the sun or the moon or the stars of the sky' (Deuteronomy 17:3, NIV). The wisdom of Genesis might be just as offensive to modern readers as it was to its ancient ones. To those who view astrology as giving valid insights into their personal destinies, the account asserts that the heavenly bodies are lights, and nothing more. On the other hand, to those who view the universe as being run merely by the 'laws of physics,' the account points to the creator God, who transcends physical laws." Laurence Turner, *Back to the Present: Encountering Genesis in the 21st Century* (Grantham, Eng.: Autumn House, 2004), pp. 24, 25.

How does Genesis describe God's creation of living creatures?

"And God said, 'Let the water teem with living creatures, and let birds fly above the earth across the expanse of the sky.' So God created the great creatures of the sea and every living and moving thing with which the water teems, according to their kinds, and every winged bird according to its kind. And God saw that it was good. God blessed them and said, 'Be fruitful and increase in number and fill the water in the seas, and let the birds increase on the earth.' And there was evening, and there was morning—the fifth day.

"And God said, 'Let the land produce living creatures according to their kinds: livestock, creatures that move along the ground, and wild animals, each according to its kind.' And it was so. God made the wild animals according to their kinds, the livestock according to their kinds, and all the creatures that move along the ground according to their kinds. And God saw that it was good." Verses 20-25, NIV.

What distinguishes God's creation of humans from that of animals?

"Then God said, '*Let us make man in our image, in our likeness,* and let them rule over the fish of the sea and the birds of the air, over the livestock, over all the earth, and over all the creatures that move along the ground.'

"So God created man in his own image,
"in the image of God he created him;
"male and female he created them.

"God blessed them and said to them, 'Be fruitful and increase in number; fill the earth and subdue it. Rule over the fish of the sea and the birds of the air and over every living creature that moves on the ground.'

"Then God said, 'I give you every seed-bearing plant on the face of the whole earth and every tree that has fruit with seed in it. They will be yours for food. And to all the beasts of the earth and all the birds of the air and all the creatures that move on the ground—everything that has the breath of life in it—I give every green plant for food.' And it was so.

"God saw all that he had made, and it was very good. And there was evening, and there was morning—the sixth day. Thus the heavens and the earth were completed in all their vast array." Genesis 1:1-2:1, NIV.

NOTE.—God established humans as His rulers on earth, as stewards over His creation. We were not created to be mere afterthoughts, but unique creations, God's representatives exercising dominion over His world.

How did God bring the heavens and earth into existence?

"By the word of the Lord were the heavens made, their starry host by the breath of his mouth. . . . For He spoke, and it came to be; he *commanded,* and it stood firm." Psalm 33:6-9, NIV.

Through whom did God create all things?

"For by him [Jesus] all things were created: things in heaven and on earth, visible and invisible, whether thrones or powers or rulers or authorities; *all things were created by him and for him."* Colossians 1:16, NIV.

"In the beginning was the Word, and the Word was with God, and the Word was God. He was with God in the beginning. Through him [Jesus] all things were made; without him nothing was made that has been made." John 1:1-3, NIV. (See also Hebrews 1:1, 2.)

Why did God make the world?

"For this is what the Lord says—he who created the heavens, he is God; he who fashioned and made the earth, he founded it; he did not create it to be empty, but *formed it to be inhabited."* Isaiah 45:18, NIV.

What did God establish as a weekly reminder to us of His act of creation?

"By the seventh day God had finished the work he had been doing; so on the seventh day he rested from all his work. And God blessed the seventh day and made it holy, because on it he rested from all the work of creating he had done." Genesis 2:2, 3, NIV.

NOTE.—According to Genesis 1 and 2, God created the world in six days. He then rested on the seventh day, and established the Sabbath as a weekly memorial to His creative work. The Sabbath is unique in all of God's creation, as it alone is sanctified—declared holy.

"The significance of this seventh day of rest is not spelled out in detail at this point. But enough is said to anticipate what the rest of Scripture says. On days 1-3, God names his creation. On days 5 and 6 He blesses it. But on the seventh day He both blesses and sanctifies the day itself. By contrast, no physical object in the 'heavens and earth' is sanctified, not even human beings who were created in the image of God. Why should the seventh day be distinguished like this? It is God's final act of separation. Previously God had separated the light from the darkness (1:4); waters above from waters beneath (1:7); dry land from seas (1:9, 10.) He now separates the seventh day from all other days, setting it apart for holy use. All days are God's days, but this day is God's day *par excellence*, advertising that the heartbeat of God's creation is blessing, holiness and spirituality." Laurence Turner, *Back to the Present: Encountering Genesis in the 21st Century*, (Grantham, Eng.: Autumn House, 2004), pp. 30, 31.

"This seventh day is not a theological appendix to the creation account, just to bring closure now that the main event of creating people has been reported. Rather, it intimates the purpose of creation and of the cosmos. God does not set up the cosmos so that only people will have a place. He also sets up the cosmos to serve as his temple in which he will find rest in the order and equilibrium that he has established." J. H. Walton, "Creation," in T. Desmond Alexander and David W. Baker, eds., *Dictionary of the Old Testament: Pentateuch* (Downers Grove, Ill.: InterVarsity Press, 2003), p. 161.

"Among many other matters, Genesis 1 makes clear that whatever exists was created by God, effortlessly. He is the eternal God of order who brings order out of chaos. He is the lord of time and space, who has control over matter, making a fertile and richly varied world. He creates human beings with whom he can have a relationship, whose destiny is in his hands and not decided by the random position of the sun, moon or stars. And he concludes his creation with holy Sabbath rest, building it into the rhythm of history, to indicate that life needs spiritual nurture if it is to be lived as God intended it." Laurence Turner, *Back to the Present: Encountering Genesis in the 21st Century* (Grantham, Eng.: Autumn House, 2004), p. 32.

How does Genesis describe God's creation of the first man and woman and their original garden home?

"This is the account of the heavens and the earth when they were created. When the Lord God made the earth and the heaven—and no shrub of the field had yet appeared on the earth and no plant of the field had yet sprung up, for the Lord God had not sent rain on earth and there was no man to work the ground, but streams came up from the earth and watered the whole surface of the ground—the Lord God formed the man from the dust of the ground and breathed into his nostrils the breath of life, and the man became a living being.

"Now the Lord God had planted a garden in the east, in Eden; and there he put the man he had formed. . . . The Lord God took the man and put him in the Garden of Eden to work it and take care of it. . . . The Lord God said, 'It is not good for the man to be alone. I will make a helper suitable for him.' Now the Lord God had formed out of the ground all the beasts of the field and all the birds of the air. He brought them to the man to see what he would name them; and whatever the man called each living creature, that was its name. So the man gave names to all the livestock, the birds of the air and all the beasts of the field. But for Adam no suitable helper was found. So the Lord God caused the man to fall into a deep sleep; and while he was sleeping, he took one of the man's ribs and closed up the place with flesh. Then the Lord God made a woman from the rib he had taken out of the man, and he brought her to the man. The man said, 'This is now bone of my bones and flesh of my flesh; she shall be called 'woman,' for she was taken out of man.' " Genesis 2:4-23, NIV.

"Adam named his wife Eve, because she would become the mother of all the living." Genesis 3:20, NIV.

In whose image were human beings created?

"So God created humankind *in his image*, in the image of God he created them; male and female he created them." Genesis 1:27, NRSV.

To what glorious position did God assign human beings?

"*Let them have dominion* over the fish of the sea, and over the birds of the air, and over the cattle, and over all the wild animals of the earth, and over every creeping thing that creeps upon the earth." Verse 26, NRSV. "What is man that you are mindful of him, the son of man that you care for him? *You made him a little lower than the angels*; you crowned him with glory and honor and put everything under his feet." Hebrews 2:6-8, NIV.

What is the true basis of the kinship of humanity?

"*Have we not all one Father? Did not one God create us?* Why do we profane the covenant of our fathers by breaking faith with one another?" Malachi 2:10, NIV. "From one man he made every nation of men, that they should inhabit the whole earth; and he determined the times set for them and the exact places where they should live." Acts 17:26, NIV.

How did God provide for the perpetuation of life?

"And the Lord God made all kinds of trees grow out of the ground—trees that were pleasing to the eye and good for food. In the middle of the garden were *the tree of life* and the tree of the knowledge of good and evil." Genesis 2:9, NIV.

What power upholds all things?

"The Son is the radiance of God's glory and the exact representation of his being, sustaining all things *by his powerful word*." Hebrews 1:3, NIV.

What do the heavens declare?

"The heavens declare *the glory of God*; the skies proclaim the work of his hands. Day after day they pour forth speech; night after night they display knowledge." Psalm 19:1, 2, NIV.

What truths about God do the visible things of nature reveal?

"For since the creation of the world God's invisible qualities—*his eternal power and divine nature*—have been clearly seen, being understood from what has been made, so that men are without excuse." Romans 1:20, NIV.

What do the stars tell us about the Creator?

"When I consider your heavens, the work of your fingers, the moon and the stars, which you have set in place, *what is man that you are mindful of him,* the son of man that you care for him?" Psalm 8:3, 4, NIV.

NOTE.—General Mitchell, the astronomer, said, "If there is anything which can lead the mind upward to the omnipotent Ruler of the Universe, and give to it approximate knowledge of His incomprehensible attributes, it is to be found in the grandeur and beauty of His works." Theodore Roosevelt used to say, after a long search of the night sky, "Now I think we are small enough! Let's go to bed."

What effect will sin ultimately have on this creation?

"In the beginning you laid the foundations of the earth, and the heavens are the works of your hands. *They will perish,* but you will remain; *they will all wear out like a garment.* Like clothing you will change them and they will be discarded." Psalm 102:25, 26, NIV.

What will happen after the old cosmos has been destroyed?

"Behold, *I will create new heavens and a new earth.* The former things will not be remembered, nor will they come to mind." Isaiah 65:17, NIV. (See Revelation 21:1.)

How can this new creation begin for us now?

"Therefore, *if anyone is in Christ, he is a new creation*; the old has gone, the new has come!" 2 Corinthians 5:17, NIV.

NOTE.—Someday God is going to renew the cosmos, but He wants to start with us. If we surrender our lives to the Creator, He will create in us a new heart (Psalm 51:10).

For what purpose are we created?

"For we are God's workmanship, created in Christ Jesus *to do good works,* which God prepared in advance for us to do." Ephesians 2:10, NIV.

What do we owe God, who created us?

"Come, let us bow down in *worship,* let us kneel before the Lord our maker." Psalm 95:6, NIV. "*Worship him who made the heavens, the earth, the sea and the springs of water.*" Revelation 14:7, NIV.

THE FALL OF HUMANITY

What simple test of loyalty did God impose upon Adam and Eve?

"And the Lord God commanded the man, 'You are free to eat from any tree in the garden; but *you must not eat from the tree of the knowledge of good and evil,* for when you eat of it you will surely die.' " Genesis 2:16, 17, NIV.

How did the serpent in Eden tempt Eve?

"Now the serpent was more crafty than any of the wild animals the Lord God had made. He said to the woman, 'Did God really say, "You must not eat from any tree in the garden"?' " Genesis 3:1, NIV.

Who is this serpent?

"And there was war in heaven. Michael and his angels fought

against the dragon, and the dragon and his angels fought back. But he was not strong enough, and they lost their place in heaven. The great dragon was hurled down—*that ancient serpent called the devil, or Satan, who leads the whole world astray*. He was hurled to the earth, and his angels with him." Revelation 12:7-9, NIV.

NOTE.—The fall of Satan is covered in chapter 11. Satan approached Eve in the guise of a serpent.

How did Eve answer the serpent?

"The woman said to the serpent, 'We may eat fruit from the trees in the garden, but God did say, "You must not eat fruit from the tree that is in the middle of the garden, and you must not touch it, or you will die." ' " Genesis 3:2, 3, NIV.

How did the serpent cast doubt on God's word?

" 'You will not surely die,' the serpent said to the woman. 'For God knows that when you eat of it your eyes will be opened, and you will be like God, knowing good and evil.' " Verses 4, 5, NIV.

NOTE.—Why would Eve doubt God and believe this creature? Perhaps because there was evidence to support its claims: if this fruit could give a serpent the power of speech, think what godlike powers it might bestow upon human beings! It is never safe to doubt God's word in the light of evidence to the contrary.

Satan is the master of the half-truth. His enticements to Eve were not outright lies. When Adam and Eve ate the fruit, their eyes *were* opened (verse 7) and they *did* become like God in knowing good and evil (verse 22). But they also lost their innocence and brought upon themselves pain, suffering, and death. Those who covet that which is not rightfully theirs end up losing even what they already have. Satan lost heaven, and Adam and Eve lost Eden (verse 23).

What did Adam and Eve do?

"When the woman saw that the fruit of the tree was good food and pleasing to the eye, and also desirable for gaining wisdom, she took some and ate it. She also gave some to her husband, who was with her, and he ate it." Verse 6, NIV.

NOTE.—There is no sin in eating a piece of fruit, but this fruit was forbidden. Adam and Eve disobeyed a command of God and desired something that was not rightfully theirs.

What was the immediate result of Adam and Eve's disobedience?

"Then the eyes of both of them were opened, and they realized they were naked; so they sewed fig leaves together and made coverings for themselves. Then the man and his wife heard the sound of the Lord God as he was walking in the garden in the cool of the day, and they hid from the Lord God among the trees of the garden. But the Lord God called to the man, 'Where are you?' He answered, 'I heard you in the garden, and I was afraid because I was naked; so I hid.' " Verses 7-10, NIV.

NOTE.—Disobedience brings guilt and shame. Sin creates a rift in our companionship with God. But even when we run away from God, He still loves us, and takes the initiative in seeking out His estranged children.

What curse did God place on His creation?

"To Adam he said, 'Because you listened to your wife and ate from the tree about which I commanded you, "You must not eat of it," cursed is the ground because of you; through painful toil you will eat of it all the days of your life. It will produce thorns and thistles for you, and you will eat the plants of the field. By the sweat of your brow you will eat your food until you return to the ground, since from it you were taken; for dust you are and to dust you will return.' " Verses 17-19, NIV.

What has been the condition of creation ever since?

"We know that the whole creation has been groaning as in the pains of childbirth right up to the present time." Romans 8:22, NIV.

How did God show grace to Adam and Eve?

"The Lord God made garments of skin for Adam and his wife and clothed them." Genesis 3:21, NIV.

NOTE.—This suggests that an animal had to die on behalf of Adam and Eve, the first sacrifice for sin. Even though they had brought their predicament upon themselves, God in His mercy and love provided for their needs, and provided an atonement, but only at the cost of shed blood.

Why did death come upon the human race?

"And the Lord God said, 'The man has now become like one of us, knowing good and evil. He must not be allowed to reach out his hand and take also from the tree of life and eat, and live forever.' So the Lord God banished him from the Garden of Eden to work the ground from which he had been taken. After he drove the man out, he placed on the east side of the Garden of Eden cherubim and a flaming sword flashing back and forth to guard the way to the tree of life." Verses 22-24, NIV.

NOTE.—As long as Adam and Eve kept eating the fruit of the tree of life, they would never have died. God knew that it would not be safe to allow sinners to live forever. Therefore He cut them off from the source of their longevity.

What happened to Adam's descendants as a result of his transgression?

"Therefore, just as sin entered the world through one man, and death through sin, and in this way *death came to all men,* because all sinned—for before the law was given, sin was in the world." Romans 5:12, 13, NIV. "In Adam all die." 1 Corinthians 15:22, NIV.

What curse did God place on the serpent which amounted to a promise to Adam and Eve of deliverance from sin?

"And I will put enmity between you and the woman, and between your offspring and hers; he will crush your head, and you will strike his heel." Genesis 3:15, NIV.

NOTE.—This is a veiled promise that someday God would take vengeance on the serpent and deliver Adam and Eve's descendants from the power of sin. Jesus would "bruise the head" of Satan.

What does God promise those who turn to Him?

"Rid yourselves of all the offenses you have committed, and get *a new heart and a new spirit.* Why will you die, O house of Israel? For I take no pleasure in the death of anyone, declares the Sovereign Lord. Repent and live!" Ezekiel 18:31, 32, NIV.

Can human beings free themselves from the dominion of sin?

"Can the Ethiopian change his skin or the leopard its spots? *Neither can you do good who are accustomed to doing evil.*" Jeremiah 13:23, NIV.

How many of Adam's descendents are sinners?

"For *all* have sinned and fall short of the glory of God." Romans 3:23, NIV.

What provision has God made for sinners?

"For the wages of sin is death; but the *gift of God is eternal life in Christ Jesus our Lord.*" Romans 6:23, NIV.

Who may take advantage of this gift?

"The Spirit and the bride say, 'Come!' And let him who hears say, 'Come!' *Whoever is thirsty*, let him come; and *whoever wishes, let him take the free gift of the water of life*." Revelation 22:17, NIV.

What is the basis for this gift?

"But he was *pierced* for our transgressions, he was *crushed* for our iniquities; the *punishment* that brought us peace was upon him, and by his *wounds* we are healed." Isaiah 53:5, NIV.

What does Jesus' sacrifice do for us?

"But God demonstrated his own love for us in this: While we were still sinners, Christ died for us. Since we have now been *justified* by his blood, how much more shall we *be saved* from God's wrath through him!" Romans 5:8, 9, NIV.

How do we receive God's forgiveness?

"'Sirs, what must I do to be saved?' They replied, '*Believe in the Lord Jesus, and you will be saved*—you and your household.' " Acts 16:30, 31, NIV.

For what purpose did Jesus come?

"But you know that he appeared *so that he might take away our sins*. . . . The reason the Son of God appeared was *to destroy the devil's work*." 1 John 3:5-8, NIV. "Since the children have flesh and blood, he too shared in their humanity so that by his death he might destroy him who holds the power of death—that is, the devil." Hebrews 2:14, NIV.

What explains God's apparent delay in dealing with sin?

"The Lord is not slow in keeping his promise, as some understand slowness. He is patient with you, *not wanting anyone to perish*, but everyone to come to repentance." 2 Peter 3:9, NIV.

How thoroughly will God remove the effects of sin?

"He will *wipe every tear* from their eyes. There will be no more death or mourning or crying of pain, for the old order of things has passed away." Revelation 21:4, NIV. "*No longer will there be any curse*. The throne of God and of the Lamb will be in the city, and his servants will serve him." Revelation 22:3, NIV.

Will sin and its evil results ever appear again?

"There shall *be no more death*." Revelation 21:4. "And there shall be *no more curse*." Revelation 22:3.

CREATION AND REDEMPTION

What does the first verse of the Bible say about God?

"In the beginning *God created the heavens and the earth*." Genesis 1:1, NIV.

What contrast is drawn between the true God and false gods?

"Tell them this: '*These gods, who did not make the heavens and the earth, will perish from the earth* and from under the heavens.' . . . He who is the Portion of Jacob is not like these, *for he is the Maker of all things*, including Israel, the tribe of his inheritance—the Lord Almighty is his name." Jeremiah 10:11-16, NIV. (See Jeremiah 14:22; Acts 17:22-29; Revelation 14:6-10.)

Through whom did God work in creating all things?

"God . . . has spoken to us by his Son, . . . through whom he made the universe." Hebrews 1:1, 2, NIV. (See also John 1:1-3.)

What scripture shows that the Creator is also the Savior?

"Declare what is to be, present it—let them take counsel together. Who foretold this long ago, who declared it from the distant past? Was it not I, the Lord? And there is no God apart from me, a righteous God and a Savior; there is none but me. Turn to me and be saved, all you ends of the earth; for I am God, and there is no other." Isaiah 45:21, 22, NIV.

What prayer of David's shows that he regarded redemption as a creative work?

"Create in me a pure heart, O God; and renew a steadfast spirit within me." Psalm 51:10, NIV.

Besides being the Creator, what other office does Christ hold?

"For by him all things were created: things in heaven and on earth, visible and invisible, whether thrones or powers or rulers or authorities; all things were created by him and for him. He is before all things, and in him all things hold together. And *he is the head of the body, the church*; he is the beginning and the firstborn from among the dead, so that in everything he might have the supremacy." Colossians 1:16-18, NIV.

Whose creative power transforms the believer?

"For we are God's workmanship, *created in Christ Jesus to do good works,* which God prepared in advance for us to do." Ephesians 2:10, NIV.

Who keeps the heavenly bodies in their places?

" 'To whom will you compare me? Or who is my equal?' says *the Holy One*. Lift your eyes and look to the heavens: Who created all these? *He who brings out the starry host one by one,* and calls them each by name. Because of his great power and mighty strength, not one of them is missing." Isaiah 40:25, 26, NIV.

What can the same Holy One do for the believer?

"To him who is able *to keep you from falling and to present you before his glorious presence without fault and with great joy*—to the only God our Savior be glory, majesty, power and authority, through Jesus Christ our Lord, before all ages, now and forevermore! Amen." Jude 24, 25.

What power to help the believer is available?

"I keep asking that the God of our Lord Jesus Christ, the glorious Father, may give you the Spirit of wisdom and revelation, so that you may know him better. I pray also that the eyes of your heart may be enlightened in order that you may know the hope to which he has called you, the riches of his glorious inheritance in the saints, and *his incomparably great power for us who believe. That power is like the working of his mighty strength,* which he exerted in Christ when he raised him from the dead and seated him at his right hand in the heavenly realms." Ephesians 1:17-20, NIV.

Who is declared to be the source of power to the weak?

"Do you not know? Have you not heard? *The Lord* is the everlasting God, *the Creator* of the ends of the earth. He will not grow tired or weary, and his understanding no one can fathom. He gives strength to the weary and increases the power of the weak." Isaiah 40:28, 29, NIV.

What did God set up as a memorial of His creation?

"*Remember the Sabbath day* by keeping it holy. Six days you shall labor and do all your work, but the seventh day is a Sabbath to the Lord your God. On it you shall not do any work, neither you, nor your son or daughter, nor your manservant or maidservant, nor your animals, nor the alien within your gates. *For in six days the Lord made the heavens and the earth, the sea, and all that is in them, but he rested on the seventh day.* Therefore the Lord blessed the Sabbath day and made it holy." Exodus 20:8-11, NIV. "It will be a sign between me and the Israelites forever, *for in six days the Lord made the heavens and the earth*, and on the seventh day he abstained from work and rested." Exodus 31:17, NIV.

Since God is both the Creator and Redeemer, what else is the Sabbath a sign of?

"Also I gave them my Sabbath as a sign between us, *so they would know that I the Lord made them holy.*" Ezekiel 20:12, NIV.

Why is God worthy to receive glory and honor?

"You are worthy, our Lord and God, to receive glory and honor and power, *for you created all things*, and by your will they were created and have their being." Revelation 4:11, NIV.

NOTE.—Theories of evolution are based on human research to the exclusion of divine revelation. Substituting impersonal forces for a personal Creator, evolution opposes the very foundation of the gospel. If human life evolved from bacteria, then there was no fall into sin, no need for the atoning sacrifice of Christ, and no need to become new creatures through faith in the saving power of Christ. By explaining away creation we do away with redemption, for redemption is simply the new creation, and the Creator is the Redeemer.

THE CHARACTER AND ATTRIBUTES OF GOD

What basic characteristics are part of God's nature?

"*Righteousness* and *justice* are the foundation of your throne; steadfast *love* and *faithfulness* go before you." Psalm 89:14, NRSV. (See also Exodus 34:5-7.)

In what language is the justice of God described?

"He is the Rock, his works are perfect, and *all his ways are just*. A faithful God, who does no wrong, *upright and just is he*." Deuteronomy 32:4, NIV.

What is said of the strength and steadfastness of God?

"God is mighty, but does not despise men; *he is mighty, and firm in his purpose*." Job 36:5, NIV.

What treasures are hid in Christ?

Paul wrote the Colossians, "I want you to know how much I am struggling for you and for those at Laodicea, and for all who have not met me personally. My purpose is that they may be encouraged in heart and united in love, so that they may have the full riches of complete understanding, in order that they may know the mystery of God, namely, Christ, in whom are hidden all the treasures of *wisdom* and *knowledge*." Colossians 2:1-3, NIV.

What is said of God's faithfulness in keeping His promises?

"Know therefore that the Lord your God is God; he is the faithful God, *keeping his covenant of love to a thousand generations of those who love him and keep his commands.*" Deuteronomy 7:9, NIV.

In what one word is the character of God expressed?

"Whoever does not love does not know God, because God is *love.*" 1 John 4:8, NIV.

What is said of the tender compassion of God?

"But you, O Lord, are a *compassionate and gracious* God, slow to anger, abounding in love and faithfulness." Psalm 86:15, NIV.

Is God impartial?

"For the Lord your God is God of gods and Lord of lords, the great God, mighty and awesome, who *shows no partiality,* and accepts no bribes." Deuteronomy 10:17, NIV. "Then Peter began to speak to them: 'I truly understand that God *shows no partiality,* but in every nation anyone who fears him and does what is right is acceptable to him.'" Acts 10:34, 35, NRSV.

To how many is the Lord good?

"The Lord is *good to all*; he has compassion on all he has made." Psalm 145:9, NIV.

Why did Christ tell us to love our enemies?

"If you love those who love you, what credit is that to you? Even 'sinners' love those who love them. And if you do good to those who are good to you, what credit is that to you? Even 'sinners' do that. And if you lend to those from whom you expect repayment, what credit is that to you? Even 'sinners' lend to 'sinners,' expecting to be repaid in full. But love your enemies, do good to them, and lend to them without expecting to get anything back. Then your reward will be great, and *you will be sons of the Most High, because he is kind to the ungrateful and wicked.* Be merciful, just as your Father is merciful." Luke 6:32-36, NIV.

THE LOVE OF GOD

What is God declared to be?

"God is love." 1 John 4:16.

How great is God's love for the world?

"For God so loved the world *that he gave his one and only Son,* that whoever believes in him shall not perish but have eternal life." John 3:16, NIV.

In what special way did God show His love?

"This is how God showed his love among us: He sent his one and only Son into the world that we might live through him." 1 John 4:9, NIV.

What does God delight in?

"Who is a God like you, who pardons sin and forgives the transgression of the remnant of his inheritance? You do not stay angry forever but *delight to show mercy*." Micah 7:18, NIV.

How are His mercies continually manifested?

"Because of the Lord's great love we are not consumed, for his compassions never fail. *They are new every morning*; great is your faithfulness." Lamentations 3:22, 23, NIV.

Does God restrict His blessings?

"He causes his sun to rise on the evil and the good, and sends rain on the righteous and the unrighteous." Matthew 5:45, NIV.

What may we, in view of God's great love, confidently expect?

"He who did not withhold his own Son, but gave him up for all of us, will he not with him also give us *everything* else?" Romans 8:32, NRSV.

What did Jesus say of the one who loves Him?

"Whoever has my commands and obeys them, he is the one who loves me. *He who loves me will be loved by my Father, and I too will love him and show myself to him*." John 14:21, NIV.

What is our relationship to God as a result of His love?

"How great is the love the Father has lavished on us, that we should be called *children of God!* And that is what we are!" 1 John 3:1, NIV.

How may we become God's children?

"Yet to all who received him, to those who *believed in his name,* he gave the right to become children of God." John 1:12, NIV.

What is the evidence that a believer is part of God's family?

"Because *those who are led by the Spirit of God* are sons of God. . . . *The Spirit himself testifies with our spirit* that we are God's children." Romans 8:14-16, NIV.

How is the love of God supplied to the believer?

"And hope does not disappoint us, because God has poured out his love into our hearts *by the Holy Spirit,* whom he has given us." Romans 5:5, NIV.

When people appreciate God's love, what will they do?

"How priceless is your unfailing love! Both high and low among men *find refuge in the shadow of your wings.*" Psalm 36:7, NIV.

In view of God's great love to us, what ought we to do?

"Beloved, if God so loved us, *we also ought to love one another.*" 1 John 4:11, NKJV.

With what measure of love should we serve others?

"This is how we know what love is: Jesus Christ laid down his life for us. And *we ought to lay down our lives for our brothers.*" 1 John 3:16, NIV.

How should Jesus' example inspire us?

"Be imitators of God, therefore, as dearly loved children and *live a life of love,* just as Christ loved us and gave himself up for us as a fragrant offering and sacrifice to God." Ephesians 5:2, NIV.

What is the basis of God's work for sinners?

"But because of his great love for us, God, who is rich in mercy, made us alive with Christ even when we were dead in transgressions—*it is by grace you have been saved.*" Ephesians 2:4-6, NIV. (See Titus 3:5, 6.)

What does God do for those He loves?

"However, the Lord your God would not listen to Balaam but *turned the curse into a blessing* for you, because the Lord your God loves you." Deuteronomy 23:5, NIV.

In what other way is God's love sometimes shown?

"My son, do not despise the Lord's discipline and do not resent his rebuke, because *the Lord disciplines those he loves,* as a father the son he delights in." Proverbs 3:11, 12, NIV.

How enduring is God's love for us?

"The Lord appeared to us in the past, saying: '*I have loved you with an everlasting love*; I have drawn you with loving-kindness.' " Jeremiah 31:3, NIV.

Can anything separate us from God's love?

"For I am convinced that neither death nor life, neither angels nor demons, neither the present nor the future, nor any powers, neither height nor depth, nor anything else in all creation, will be able to separate us from the love of God that is in Christ Jesus our Lord." Romans 8:38, 39, NIV.

How shall we honor our Savior in the ages to come?

"To him who loves us and has freed us from our sins by his blood, and has made us to be a kingdom and priests to serve his God and Father—*to him be glory and power for ever and ever!* Amen." Revelation 1:5, 6, NIV.

THE DEITY OF CHRIST

In what form did Jesus exist prior to His humanity?

"Your attitude should be the same as that of Christ Jesus: who, being in very nature God, did not consider equality with God something to be grasped, but made himself nothing, taking the very nature of a servant, being made in human likeness." Philippians 2:5-7, NIV. "The Son is *the radiance of God's glory and the exact representation of his being,* sustaining all things by his powerful word." Hebrews 1:3, NIV.

Where was Christ prior to His incarnation?

"For *I have come down from heaven* not to do my will but to do the will of him who sent me." John 6:38, NIV. "Aware that his disciples were grumbling about this, Jesus said to them, 'Does this offend you? What if you see the Son of Man ascend to *where he was before*?' " Verses 61, 62, NIV.

What was Christ's situation before He came to earth?

"For you know the grace of our Lord Jesus Christ, that *though he was rich,* yet for your sakes he became poor, so that you through his poverty might become rich." 2 Corinthians 8:9, NIV.

In what way did Jesus claim to exist before Abraham?

" 'Your father Abraham rejoiced at the thought of seeing my day; he saw it and was glad.'

" 'You are not yet fifty years old,' the Jews said to him, 'and you have seen Abraham!'

" 'I tell you the truth,' Jesus answered, '*before Abraham was born, I am*!' " John 8:56-58, NIV.

NOTE.—In the Old Testament "I AM" is the name of God (Exodus 3:14). Jesus was applying that name to Himself.

How do the Scriptures refer to the eternity of Christ?

"And now, Father, glorify me in your presence with the glory I had with you *before the world began*." John 17:5, NIV.

"But you, Bethlehem Ephrathah, though you are small among the clans of Judah, out of you will come for me one who will be ruler over Israel, *whose origins are from of old, from ancient times*." Micah 5:2, NIV.

"For to us a child is born, to us a son is given, and the government will be on his shoulders. And he will be called Wonderful Counselor, Mighty God, *Everlasting Father,* Prince of Peace." Isaiah 9:6, NIV.

How does the Father show that His Son is a member of the Godhead?

"But *about the Son he says,* 'Your throne, *O God,* will last for ever and ever, and righteousness will be the scepter of your kingdom.' " Hebrews 1:8, NIV.

How did God affirm His Son while Jesus was on earth?

"And a voice from heaven said, '*This is my Son, whom I love; with him I am well pleased*.' " Matthew 3:17, NIV.

Who else claimed that Jesus was the Son of God?

[Jesus said,] "What about the one whom the Father set apart as his very own and sent into the world? Why then do you accuse me of blasphemy because I said, 'I am God's Son'?" John 10:36, NIV.

"When he arrived at the other side in the region of the Gadarenes, two demon-possessed men coming from the tombs met him. They were so violent that no one could pass that way. 'What do you want with us, Son of God?' they shouted. 'Have you come here to torture us before the appointed time?' " Matthew 8:29, NIV.

How did the Jewish religious leaders understand the claims of Jesus?

"For this reason the Jews tried all the harder to kill him; not only was he breaking the Sabbath, but he was even calling God his own Father, *making himself equal with God*." John 5:18, NIV.
" 'We are not stoning you for any of these,' replied the Jews, 'but for blasphemy, because you, a mere man, *claim to be God*.' " John 10:33, NIV.

What does Christ say is His relation to the Father?

"I and My Father are *one*." John 10:30.

To whom do the angels belong?

"*Praise the Lord, you his angels,* you mighty ones who do his bidding, who obey his word." Psalm 103:20. "He who overcomes will, like them, be dressed in white. I will never blot out his name from the book of life, but will acknowledge his name before *my Father and his angels*." Revelation 3:5, NIV.

Who holds the same position in relation to the angels as does the Father?

"The Son of Man will send out *his angels*, and they will weed out of his kingdom everything that causes sin and all who do evil." Matthew 13:41, NIV.

NOTE.—In other words, the angels belong to Jesus just as they belong to God.

To whom do the chosen belong?

"And will not God bring about justice for *his chosen ones*, who cry out to him day and night? Will he keep putting them off?" Luke 18:7, NIV.

To whom also do God's chosen—the "elect" —belong?

"They will see the Son of Man coming on the clouds of the sky, with power and great glory. And he will send his angels with a loud trumpet call, and they will gather *his elect* from the four winds, from one end of the heavens to the other." Matthew 24:30, 31, NIV.

NOTE.—In other words, the chosen belong to Jesus just as they belong to God.

Who rewards the seeker?

"And without faith it is impossible to please *God*, because anyone who comes to him must believe that he exists and that *he rewards* those who earnestly seek him." Hebrews 11:6, NIV.

Who likewise bestows the final rewards?

"For the Son of Man is going to come in his Father's glory with his angels, and then *he will reward each person* according to what he has done." Matthew 16:27, NIV.

NOTE.—In other words, Jesus, like God, gives us our final reward. Calling Himself the Son of Man, Christ refers to the angels as "His angels" and to the kingdom as "His kingdom" and to the elect as "His elect" (Matthew 16:27; 13:41; 24:31). It appears that while He was on earth as a man, He recognized His equality with His Father in heaven. This is why the Jewish leaders sought to kill him for blasphemy, according to John 5:18.

What does God declare Himself to be?

"This is what the Lord says—Israel's King and Redeemer, the Lord Almighty: *I am the first and I am the last*; apart from me there is no God." Isaiah 44:6, NIV.

Where does Christ make the same claims?

"Behold, I am coming soon! My reward is with me, and I will give to everyone according to what he has done. I am the Alpha and the Omega, *the First and the Last,* the Beginning and the End." Revelation 22:12, 13, NIV.

What scripture calls Jesus God?

"In the beginning was the Word, and the Word was with God, and *the Word was God*. . . . The Word became flesh and made his dwelling among us. We have seen his glory, the glory of the One and Only, who came from the Father, full of grace and truth." John 1:1-14, NIV.

What fullness dwells in Christ?

"For in Christ *all the fullness of the Deity lives in bodily form.*" Colossians 2:9, NIV.

How was He manifested on earth as a Savior?

"Today in the town of David a Savior has been *born* to you; he is Christ the Lord." Luke 2:11, NIV.

How was Jesus born?

"In the sixth month, God sent the angel Gabriel to Nazareth, a town in Galilee, to a virgin pledged to be married to a man named Joseph, a descendant of David. The virgin's name was Mary. The angel went to her and said, 'Greetings, you who are highly favored! The Lord is with you.' . . . 'You will be with child and give birth to a son, and you are to give him the name Jesus.' . . .

" 'How will this be,' Mary asked the angel, 'since I am a virgin?'

"The angel answered, '*The Holy Spirit will come upon you, and the power of the Most High will overshadow you. So the holy one to be born will be called the Son of God.*' " Luke 1:26-35, NIV.

Why was it necessary for Jesus to have a human nature?

"For this reason he had to be made like his brothers in every way, in order *that he might become a merciful and faithful high priest in service to God,* and that he might make atonement for the sins of the people." Hebrews 2:17, NIV.

With such a wonderful Savior, what then should we do?

"Therefore, since we have a great high priest who has gone through the heavens, Jesus the Son of God, *let us hold firmly to the faith we profess.* For we do not have a high priest who is unable to sympathize with our weaknesses, but we have one who has been tempted in every way, just as we are—yet was without sin." Hebrews 4:14, 15, NIV.

PROPHECIES RELATING TO CHRIST

What did the Old Testament prophets foretell about Christ?

"Concerning this salvation, the prophets, who spoke of *the grace that was to come to you,* searched intently and with the greatest care, trying to find out the time and circumstances to which the Spirit of Christ in them was pointing when he predicted *the sufferings of Christ and the glories that would follow.*" 1 Peter 1:10, 11, NIV.

Whom did Moses, in his farewell message to the Israelites, say the Lord would raise up?

"The Lord your God will raise up for you a *prophet* like me from among your own brothers. You must listen to him." Deuteronomy 18:15, NIV. (See also verse 18.)

To whom did the apostle Peter apply this prophecy?

"Repent, then, and turn to God, so that your sins may be wiped out, that times of refreshing may come from the Lord, and that he may send the *Christ,* who has been appointed for you—even *Jesus.* He must remain in heaven until the time comes for God to restore everything, as he promised long ago through his holy prophets. For Moses said, 'The Lord will raise up for you a prophet like me from among your own people; you must listen to everything he tells you. Anyone who does not listen to him will be completely cut off from among his people.' Indeed, all the prophets from Samuel on, as many as have spoken, have foretold these days. . . . When *God raised up his servant,* he sent him first to you to bless you by turning each of you from your wicked ways." Acts 3:19-26, NIV.

What metaphoric emblem did Balaam use to describe Jesus in his prophecy?

"A star will come out of Jacob; a *scepter* will rise out of Israel." Numbers 24:17, NIV.

In what scripture does Christ apply the same emblem to Himself?

"I am the Root and the Offspring of David, and *the bright Morning Star*." Revelation 22:16, NIV. (See also 2 Peter 1:19; Revelation 2:28.)

What prophecy of Isaiah's did Matthew apply to Jesus' birth?

"All this [the birth of Jesus of the virgin Mary] took place to fulfill what the Lord had said through the prophet: *'The virgin will be with child and will give birth to a son,* and they will call him Immanuel'—which means, 'God with us.' " Matthew 1:22, 23, NIV.

Where was the Messiah to be born?

"But you, *Bethlehem Ephrathah,* though you are small among the clans of Judah, out of you will come for me one who will be ruler over Israel, *whose origins are from of old, from ancient times*." Micah 5:2, NIV.

When was Jesus born?

"Jesus was born in Bethlehem of Judaea *in the days of Herod the king*." Matthew 2:1.

What prophecy was fulfilled in the slaughter of the children of Bethlehem?

"When Herod realized that he had been outwitted by the Magi, he was furious, and he gave orders to kill all the boys in Bethlehem and its vicinity who were two years old and under, in accordance with the time he had learned from the Magi. Then *what was said through the prophet Jeremiah* was fulfilled: 'A voice is heard in Ramah, weeping and great mourning, Rachel weeping for her children and refusing to be comforted, because they are no more.' " Matthew 2:16-18, NIV.

How was Christ's first coming to be proclaimed?

"A voice of one calling: 'In the desert prepare the way for the Lord; make straight in the wilderness a highway for our God.' " Isaiah 40:3, NIV.

By whom was this fulfilled?

"Now this was John's testimony when the Jews of Jerusalem sent priests and Levites to ask him who he was. . . . John replied in the words of Isaiah the prophet, 'I am the voice of one calling in the desert, "Make straight the way of the Lord." ' " John 1:19-23, NIV.

What was predicted of Jesus' preaching?

"The Spirit of the Sovereign Lord is on me, because *the Lord has anointed me to preach good news to the poor*." Isaiah 61:1, NIV.

What application did Jesus make of this prophecy?

"He went to Nazareth, where he had been brought up, and on the Sabbath day he went into the synagogue, as was his custom. And he stood up to read. The scroll of the prophet Isaiah was handed to him. Unrolling it, he found the place where it is written: 'The Spirit of the Lord is on me, because he has anointed me to preach good news to the poor. He has sent me to proclaim freedom for the prisoners and recovery of sight for the blind, to release the oppressed, to proclaim the year of the Lord's favor.' Then he rolled up the scroll, gave it back to the attendant and sat down. The eyes of everyone in the synagogue were fastened on him, and he began by saying to them, *'Today this scripture is fulfilled in your hearing.'* " Luke 4:16-21, NIV. (See Luke 7:19-22.)

How was Christ to be received?

"He was *despised* and *rejected* by men, a man of sorrows, and familiar with suffering. Like one from whom men hide their faces he was *despised*, and *we esteemed him not*." Isaiah 53:3, NIV.

How is the fulfillment of this prophecy recorded?

"He was in the world, and though the world was made through him, the world did not recognize him. *He came to that which was his own, but his own did not receive him*." John 1:10, 11.

What prophecy described Christ's demeanor under persecution?

"He was oppressed and afflicted, *yet he did not open his mouth*; he was led like a lamb to the slaughter, and as a sheep before her shearers is silent, so *he did not open his mouth*." Isaiah 53:7, NIV.

What was Christ's demeanor under accusation during His trial?

"Then Pilate asked him, 'Don't you hear the testimony they are bringing against you?' But *Jesus made no reply*, not even to a single charge—to the great amazement of the governor." Matthew 27:13, 14, NIV.

With whom did the prophet Isaiah say Jesus would be buried?

"He was assigned a grave with the *wicked*, and with the *rich* in his death." Isaiah 53:9, NIV.

With whom was Jesus crucified?

"*Two robbers* were crucified with him, one on his right and one on his left." Matthew 27:38, NIV.

Who took charge of Jesus' body after it was taken down from the cross?

"As evening approached, there came *a rich man* from Arimathea, named Joseph, who had himself become a disciple of Jesus. Going to Pilate, he asked for Jesus' body, and Pilate ordered that it be given to him. Joseph took the body, wrapped it in a clean linen cloth, and placed it in his own new tomb that he had cut out of rock. He rolled a big stone in front of the entrance to the tomb and went away." Verses 57-60, NIV.

What experience in the life of the prophet Jonah symbolically parallels Jesus' death?

"Then some of the Pharisees and teachers of the law said to him, 'Teacher, we want to see a miraculous sign from you.' He answered, 'A wicked and adulterous generation asks for a miraculous sign! But none will be given it except the sign of the prophet Jonah. For as *Jonah was three days and three nights in the belly of a huge fish,* so the Son of Man will be three days and three nights in the heart of the earth.' " Matthew 12:38-40, NIV.

CHRIST, THE WAY OF LIFE

What does Jesus declare Himself to be?

"Jesus answered, *'I am the way and the truth and the life.* No one comes to the Father except through me.' " John 14:6, NIV.

What condition are we all in?

"But the Scripture declares that the whole world is *a prisoner of sin*, so that what was promised, being given through faith in Jesus Christ, might be given to those who believe." Galatians 3:22, NIV. "For *all have sinned, and fall short of the glory of God*, and are justified freely by his grace through the redemption that came by Christ Jesus." Romans 3:23, NIV.

What are the wages of sin?

"The wages of sin is *death*." Romans 6:23.

How many are affected by Adam's transgression?

"Therefore, just as sin entered the world through one man, and death through sin, and in this way death came to all men, because *all* sinned." Romans 5:12, NIV.

What is the gift of God?

"The gift of God is *eternal life* through Jesus Christ our Lord." Romans 6:23.

How many may receive this gift?

"The Spirit and the bride say, 'Come!' And let him who hears say, 'Come!' *Whoever is thirsty*, let him come; and *whoever wishes*, let him take the free gift of the water of life." Revelation 22:17, NIV.

In whom is the gift?

"And this is the testimony: God has given us eternal life, and *this life is in his Son*." 1 John 5:11, NIV.

In receiving the Son, what do we have in Him?

"He who has the Son has *life*." Verse 12, NIV.

What loss do those sustain who do not accept Him?

"He who does not have the Son of God *does not have life*." Verse 12, NIV.

In what other way is this same truth stated?

"*Whoever believes in the Son has eternal life, but whoever rejects the Son will not see life*, for God's wrath remains on him." John 3:36, NIV.

When we truly receive Christ, what is the spiritual effect?

"I have been crucified with Christ and I no longer live, but *Christ lives in me*. The life I live in the body, I live by faith in the Son of God, who loved me and gave himself for me." Galatians 2:20, NIV.

In what condition are we before we receive new life in Christ?

"But because of his great love for us, God, who is rich in mercy, made us alive with Christ even when *we were dead in transgressions*." Ephesians 2:4, 5, NIV.

NOTE.—God "made us alive" with Christ. When Jesus rose from the dead, we rose with Him.

What is this change from death to life called?

"For you have been *born again*, not of perishable seed, but of imperishable, through the living and enduring word of God." 1 Peter 1:23, NIV.

What is one purpose of Jesus' death?

"Since the children have flesh and blood, he too shared in their *humanity so that by his death he might destroy him who holds the power of death—that is, the devil*—and free those who all their lives were held in slavery by their fear of death." Hebrews 2:14, NIV.

What would make the death of Christ in vain?

"I do not set aside the grace of God, for *if righteousness could be gained by the law*, Christ dies for nothing!" Galatians 2:21, NIV.

NOTE.—Attempting to earn God's salvation by works is an insult to His grace, just as it would be an insult for a guest to attempt to pay a gracious host for a freely offered meal.

How may we receive what was promised?

"But the Scripture declares that the whole world is a prisoner of sin, *so that what was promised, being given through faith in Jesus Christ, might be given to those who believe*." Galatians 3:22, NIV.

How then do all become children of God?

"You are all sons of God *through faith in Christ Jesus*, for all of you who were baptized into Christ have clothed yourselves with Christ. There is neither Jew nor Greek, slave nor free, male nor female, for you are all one in Christ Jesus." Verses 26-28, NIV.

With whom are the children of God joint heirs?

"The Spirit himself testifies with our spirit that we are God's children. Now if we are children, then we are heirs—heirs of God and co-heirs *with Christ*, if indeed we share in his sufferings in order that we may also share in his glory." Romans 8:16, 17, NIV.

The Prince of Orange Makes a Pledge

When William, Prince of Orange, handed a chosen man a written pledge for a high position in his kingdom if the man would support him, the man declined it, saying, "Your Majesty's word is sufficient. I would not serve a king if I could not trust his word."

"Peter answered him, 'We have left everything to follow you! What then will there be for us?' Jesus said to them, 'I tell you the truth, at the renewal of all things, when the Son of Man sits on his glorious throne, you who have followed me will also sit on twelve thrones, judging the twelve tribes of Israel. And everyone who has left houses or brothers or sisters or father or mother or children or fields for my sake will receives a hundred times as much and will inherit eternal life.' " Matthew 19:27-29, NIV.

Jesus wrote no pledge. He pledged His word, and we may rely upon it. His word is good, and will be fulfilled. The question is, "Shall we follow Him?"

SALVATION ONLY THROUGH CHRIST

Why did Jesus come to earth?

"Here is a trustworthy saying that deserves full acceptance: Christ Jesus came into the world *to save sinners*." 1 Timothy 1:15, NIV.

Why was He to be named "Jesus"?

"You are to give him the name Jesus, *because he will save his people from their sins*." Matthew 1:21, NIV.

NOTE.—The Greek name "Jesus" is equivalent to the Jewish name "Joshua," and means "Savior."

Is salvation available through any other?

"Salvation is found in no one else, for *there is no other name* under heaven given to men by *which we must be saved*." Acts 4:12, NIV.

Through whom only may we come to God?

"For there is one God and *one mediator between God and men, the man Christ Jesus*, who gave himself as a ransom for all men—the testimony given in its proper time." 1 Timothy 2:5, 6, NIV.

What effect does Jesus' sacrifice have on us?

"God made him who had no sin to be sin for us, *so that in him we might become the righteousness of God*." 2 Corinthians 5:21, NIV.

How dependent are we upon Jesus for salvation?

"I am the vine; you are the branches. If a man remains in me and I in him, he will bear much fruit; *apart from me you can do nothing*." John 15:5, NIV.

What three essentials for a Savior are found in Christ?

Deity. "But about the Son he says, 'Your throne, *O God*, will last for ever and ever.' " Hebrews 1:8, NIV.

Humanity. "But when the time had fully come, God sent his Son, *born of a woman*, born under law." Galatians 4:4, NIV.

Sinlessness. "To this you were called, because Christ suffered for you, leaving you an example that you should follow in his steps. 'He committed no sin, and no deceit was found in his mouth.' " 1 Peter 2:22, NIV.

How did Jesus show from the Scriptures that the promised Savior of the world must be both human and divine?

"While the Pharisees were gathered together, Jesus asked them, 'What do you think about the Christ? Whose son is he?'

" '*The son of David,*' they replied.

"He said to them, '*How is it then that David, speaking by the Spirit, calls him "Lord"?* For he says, "The Lord said to my Lord: 'Sit at my right hand until I put your enemies under your feet.' " If then David calls him "Lord," how can he be his son?' " Matthew 22:41-45, NIV.

NOTE.—"Divinity needed humanity that humanity might afford a channel of communication between God and man. . . . Man needs a power outside of and beyond himself, to restore him to the likeness of God." Ellen G. White, *The Desire of Ages*, p. 296. "There must be a power working from within, a new life from above, before men can be changed from sin to holiness. That power is Christ." Ellen G. White, *Steps to Christ*, p. 18.

What two facts testify to the union of divinity and humanity in Christ?

"Regarding his Son, who *as to his human nature was a descendant of David, and who through the Spirit of holiness was declared with power to be the Son of God* by his resurrection from the dead: Jesus Christ our Lord." Romans 1:3, 4, NIV.

How complete was Christ's victory over death?

"I am the First and the Last. I am the Living One; I was dead, and behold I am alive for ever and ever! And I hold the keys of death and Hades." Revelation 1:17, 18, NIV. (See Acts 2:24.)

How complete is the salvation obtained in Christ?

"Therefore *he is able to save completely* those who come to God through him, because he always lives to intercede for them." Hebrews 7:25, NIV.

What should we say for such a Savior?

"*Thanks be to God* for his indescribable gift!" 2 Corinthians 9:15, NIV.

CHAPTER 3

The Way to Christ

VICTORIOUS FAITH

What is faith declared to be?

"Faith is the *substance of things hoped for, the evidence of things not seen*." Hebrews 11:1.

NOTE.—Biblical faith has three components:

1. Belief. True faith believes what God says.

2. Trust. The Old Testament uses the word "trust" instead of "faith." Genuine faith not only believes in what God says, but it trusts Him to fulfill His promises and meet the needs of His children.

3. Action. A person of faith trusts God's word and acts upon it even when it is hard to understand (as when God told Abraham to offer up his son Isaac [Genesis 22:2]).

Faith is not an irrational leap into the dark; but a step into the twilight. Faith is not blind; it is based upon evidence. But it does not wait for proof, but follows God's leading even where it cannot fully see the way.

How necessary is faith?

"*Without faith it is impossible to please God*." Hebrews 11:6, NIV.

Is it sufficient to merely agree with divine truth?

"You believe that there is one God. Good! *Even the demons believe that—and shudder*." James 2:19, NIV.

What is required besides a belief in the existence of God?

"Anyone who comes to him must believe that he exists *and that he rewards those who earnestly seek him*." Hebrews 11:6, NIV.

What is necessary in order that the preaching of the gospel may be effective?

"For we also have had the gospel preached to us, just as they did; but the message they heard was of no value to them, because those who heard did not *combine it with faith*." Hebrews 4:2, NIV.

What is the character of any act or service not performed in faith?

"Everything that does not come from faith is *sin*." Romans 14:23, NIV.

How is faith developed?

"*Faith comes from hearing the message,* and the message is heard through the *word of Christ*." Romans 10:17, NIV.

Why did God raise Christ from the dead?

"Through him you believe in God, who raised him from the dead and glorified him, and *so your faith and hope are in God*." 1 Peter 1:21, NIV.

What is Christ's relation to this faith?

"Let us fix our eyes on Jesus, *the author and perfecter* of our faith." Hebrews 12:2, NIV. "But these are written that you may believe that Jesus is the Christ, the Son of God, and that by believing you may have life in his name." John 20:31, NIV.

What principle sets faith in motion?

"But by faith we eagerly await through the Spirit the righteousness for which we hope. For in Christ Jesus neither circumcision nor uncircumcision has any value. The only thing that counts is *faith expressing itself through love*." Galatians 5:5, 6, NIV.

Of what is faith a fruit?

"But *the fruit of the Spirit* is love, joy, peace, longsuffering, gentleness, goodness, *faith*." Verse 22.

What relation does faith bear to knowledge?

"*By faith we understand* that the universe was formed at God's command." Hebrews 11:3, NIV.

What in the early church showed living faith?

"We continually remember before our God and Father your *work produced by faith*, your labor prompted by love, and your endurance inspired by hope in our Lord Jesus Christ." 1 Thessalonians 1:3, NIV.

How does Abraham's experience show that faith and obedience are inseparable?

"*By faith Abraham,* when called to go to a place he would later receive as his inheritance, obeyed and went, even though he did not know where he was going." Hebrews 11:8, NIV.

With what, therefore, is the faith of Jesus joined?

"Here is the patience of the saints; here are those who keep *the commandments of God* and *the faith of Jesus*." Revelation 14:12, NKJV.

In what other statement is the same truth emphasized?

"You foolish man, do you want evidence that *faith without deeds is useless*?" James 2:20, NIV.

How is faith brought to perfection?

"Was not our ancestor Abraham considered righteous for what he did when he offered his son Isaac on the altar? You see that his faith and his actions were working together, and *his faith was made complete by what he did*." Verses 21, 22, NIV.

What is the result of faith's being put to the test?

"The testing of your faith *develops perseverance*." James 1:3, NIV.

What relationship to God is established by faith?

"For in Christ Jesus you are all *children of God through faith*." Galatians 3:26, NRSV.

What guides us in our spiritual journeys?

"We walk by faith, not by sight." 2 Corinthians 5:7, NRSV.

Upon what condition may one expect answers to prayer?

"If any of you is lacking in wisdom, ask God, who gives to all generous and ungrudgingly, and it will be given you. But *ask in faith*, never doubting, for the one who doubts is like a wave of the sea, driven and tossed by the wind." James 1:5, 6, NRSV.

To what ancient armor does Paul compare faith?

"In addition to all this, take up the *shield* of faith, with which you can extinguish all the flaming arrows of the evil one." Ephesians 6:16, NIV. "Putting on faith and love as a *breastplate*." 1 Thessalonians 5:8, NIV.

What chapter in the Bible is devoted to faith?

Hebrews 11. Verses 33-38 summarize the victories of the heroes of faith.

What gives victory in our conflicts with the world?

"This is the victory that has overcome the world, *even our faith*."

1 John 5:4, NIV.

What is the ultimate goal of faith?

"For you are receiving the goal of your faith, *the salvation of your souls*" 1 Peter 1:9, NIV.

The Simplicity of Salvation

The nineteenth-century evangelist Dwight Moody said that God made the offer of salvation so simple that the whole world could grasp it. Everyone can believe. People with disabilities might not be able to visit the sick, but they can believe. Those who cannot see are unable to do many things, but they can believe. A deaf person cannot hear, but can believe. Even the dying can believe. Salvation has been placed within the reach of all, the young and old, the foolish and the brilliant, the rich and the poor, the high and the low. All may have it if they believe.

HOPE IN GOD

What is the relationship between faith and hope?

"Now *faith* is being sure of what we *hope* for and certain of what we do not see." Hebrews 11:1, NIV.

What is hope?

"For in this hope we were saved. But hope that is seen is no hope at all. Who hopes for what he already has? But if we hope for what we do not yet have, we wait for it patiently." Romans 8:24, 25, NIV.

NOTE.—Hope is the glow of the future lighting up the present. Hope looks forward to a bright tomorrow, and borrows from that joy for today.

Why were the Scriptures written?

"For everything that was in the past was written *to teach us, so that* through endurance and the encouragement of the Scriptures *we might have hope*." Romans 15:4, NIV.

Why should God's wonderful works be rehearsed to the children?

"We will not hide them from their children; we will tell the next generation the praiseworthy deeds of the Lord, his power, and the wonders he has done. . . . *Then they would put their trust in God, and would not forget his deeds, but would keep his commands*." Psalm 78:4-7, NIV.

In what condition are those who are without Christ?

"Remember that at that time you were separate from Christ, excluded from citizenship in Israel and foreigners to the covenants of the promise, *without hope and without God in the world.*" Ephesians 2:12, NIV.

What does hope become to the Christian?

"We have this hope as *an anchor for the soul,* firm and secure." Hebrews 6:19, NIV.

Who have hope when they die?

"When calamity comes, the wicked are brought down, but *even in death the righteous have a refuge.*" Proverbs 14:32, NIV.

What comfort in grief may we have as Christians?

"But we do not want you to be uninformed, brothers and sisters, about those who have died, *so that you may not grieve as others do who have no hope.*" 1 Thessalonians 4:13, NRSV.

How has God given us hope in the face of death?

"Praise be to the God and Father of our Lord Jesus Christ! In his great mercy he *has given us new birth into a living hope through the resurrection of Jesus Christ* from the dead." 1 Peter 1:3, NIV.

What did Paul call the Christian's hope?

"While we wait for *the blessed hope*—the glorious appearing of our great God and Savior, Jesus Christ." Titus 2:13, NIV.

When did Paul expect to realize his hope?

"Now there is in store for me the crown of righteousness, which the Lord, the righteous Judge, will award to me *on that day*—and not only to me, but also to all who have longed for *his appearing.*" 2 Timothy 4:8, NIV.

NOTE.—Paul looked forward to the resurrection at Jesus' second coming.

What did the prophet Jeremiah say about patience?

"*It is good to wait quietly* for the salvation of the Lord." Lamentations 3:26, NIV.

What will this hope lead one to do?

"Everyone who has this hope in him *purifies himself,* just as he is pure." 1 John 3:3, NIV.

What is said of the hope of the hypocrite?

"Such is the destiny of all who forget God; so *perishes* the hope of the godless." Job 8:13, 14, NIV.

What is the condition of one whose hope is in God?

"*Blessed* is he whose help is the God of Jacob, whose hope is in the Lord his God." Psalm 146:5, NIV. "*Blessed* is the man who trusts in the Lord, whose confidence is in him." Jeremiah 17:7, NIV.

What are some of the blessings of trusting God?

"May the God of hope fill you with all joy and peace as you trust in him, so that you may *overflow with hope* by the power of the Holy Spirit." Romans 15:13, NIV.

What do Christians rejoice in?

"Through whom we have gained access by faith into this grace in which we now stand. And we rejoice in *the hope of the glory of God.*" Romans 5:2, NIV.

Why does hope not disappoint us?

"Not only so, but we also rejoice in our sufferings, because we know that suffering produces perseverance; perseverance, character; and character, hope. And hope does not disappoint us, *because God has poured out his love into our hearts* by the Holy Spirit, whom he has given us." Verses 3-5, NIV.

Who will be our hope and refuge in earth's last days?

"The Lord will roar from Zion and thunder from Jerusalem; the earth and the sky will tremble. But *the Lord will be a refuge for his people*, a stronghold for the people of Israel." Joel 3:16, NIV.

What inspiring words did David write to God's people?

"*Be strong and take heart*, all you who hope in the Lord." Psalm 31:24, NIV.

How long should our hope endure?

"We want each of you to show this same diligence *to the very end*, in order to make your hope sure." Hebrews 6:11, NIV.

REPENTANCE

Who are called to repentance?

"I have not come to call the righteous, but *sinners* to repentance."

Luke 5:32, NIV.

What accompanies repentance?

"And repentance and *forgiveness of sins* will be preached in his name to all nations." Luke 24:47.

How is sin made known?

"Therefore no one will be declared righteous in his sight by observing the law; rather, *through the law* we become conscious of sin." Romans 3:20, NIV.

What do transgressors bring upon themselves?

"Let no one deceive you with empty words, for because of such things *God's wrath* comes on those who are disobedient." Ephesians 5:6, NIV.

Who awakens the soul to a sense of its sinful condition?

Speaking to His disciples before His death, Jesus said, "Unless I go away, *the Counselor* will not come to you; but if I go, I will send him to you. When he comes, *he will convict the world of guilt in regard to sin* and righteousness and judgment." John 16:7, 8, NIV.

NOTE.—The Counselor is another name for the Holy Spirit.

What is an appropriate question for those convicted of sin?

"Brothers, what shall we do?" Acts 2:37, NIV. "Sirs, *what must I do to be saved?*" Acts 16:30, NIV.

What did Peter, Paul, and Silas reply to these inquiries?

"*Repent and be baptized,* every one of you, in the name of Jesus Christ for the forgiveness of your sins." Acts 2:38, NIV. "They replied, *'Believe in the Lord Jesus, and you will be saved.'*" Acts 16:31, NIV.

What will the truly repentant sinner do?

"I *confess my iniquity*; I am troubled by my sin." Psalm 38:18, NIV.

What is the result of godly sorrow?

"Godly sorrow brings *repentance that leads to salvation* and leaves no regret." 2 Corinthians 7:10, NIV.

What does the sorrow of the world cause?

"Worldly sorrow brings death." Verse 10, NIV.

How do we demonstrate real sorrow for sin?

"See what this godly sorrow has produced in you: what *earnestness,* what *eagerness to clear yourselves,* what indignation, what alarm, what longing, what concern, what readiness to see justice done." Verse 11, NIV.

NOTE.—True sorrow causes us to set things right, and, so far as is possible, undo the wrong that has been done. There is no true repentance without reformation. Repentance is a change of mind; reformation is a change of life.

What did John the Baptist say to the Pharisees and Sadducees when he saw them come to his baptism?

"You brood of vipers! Who warned you to flee from the coming wrath?" Matthew 3:7, NIV.

What did he tell them to do?

"Produce fruit in keeping with repentance." Verse 8, NIV.

NOTE.—Just as apple trees will bear apples, those who are truly penitent will behave in ways appropriate to their remorse. Those who have stolen will repay what they stole (Ezekiel 33:15; Luke 19:8); those who have offended others will apologize (James 5:16). This is the fruit of repentance.

When God sent the Ninevites a warning message, how did they show their repentance, and how did God respond?

"When God saw what they did and how *they turned from their evil ways,* he had compassion and did not bring upon them the destruction he had threatened." Jonah 3:10, NIV.

NOTE.—A human being's repentance implies a change of mind. God's repentance implies a change of circumstances and relationships. A person may change their relation to God by complying with the conditions upon which they may be brought into the divine favor, or they may, by their own action, place themselves outside the favoring condition; but the Lord is the same "yesterday and today and for ever." Hebrews 13:8, NIV.

What leads sinners to repentance?

"Or do you show contempt for the riches of his kindness, tolerance and patience, not realizing that *God's kindness leads you toward repentance?"* Romans 2:4, NIV.

CONFESSION AND FORGIVENESS

What instruction is given concerning confession of sin?

"Say to the Israelites: 'When a man or woman wrongs another in any way and so is unfaithful to the Lord, that person is guilty and *must confess the sin he has committed.*' " Numbers 5:6, 7, NIV.

How futile is it to attempt to hide sin from God?

"But if you fail to do this, you will be sinning against the Lord; and you may *be sure that your sin will find you out.*" Numbers 32:23, NIV. "You have set our iniquities before you, our secret sins in the light of your presence." Psalm 90:8, NIV. "Nothing in all creation is hidden from God's sight. Everything is uncovered and laid bare before the eyes of him to whom we must give account." Hebrews 4:13, NIV.

What are the results of hiding or confessing sins?

"He who conceals his sins *does not prosper,* but whoever confesses and renounces them finds mercy." Proverbs 28:13, NIV.

What promise is made to those who confess their sins?

"If we confess our sins, *he* is faithful and just and *will forgive us our sins and purify us from all unrighteousness.*" 1 John 1:9, NIV.

How definite should we be in confessing our sins?

"When anyone is guilty in any of these ways, he must confess *in what way he has sinned.*" Leviticus 5:5, NIV.

NOTE.—"True confession is always of a specific character, and acknowledges particular sins. They may be of such a nature as to be brought before God only; they may be wrongs that should be confessed to individuals who have suffered injury through them; or they may be of a public character, and should then be as publicly confessed. But all confession should be definite and to the point, acknowledging the very sins of which you are guilty." Ellen G. White, *Steps to Christ,* p. 43.

How fully did the nation of Israel once acknowledge their wrongdoing?

"The people all said to Samuel, 'Pray to the Lord your God for your servants so that we will not die, *for we have added to all our other sins the evil of asking for a king.*" 1 Samuel 12:19, NIV.

What does God do when we confess our sins?

"Then I acknowledged my sin to you and did not cover up my iniquity. I said, 'I will confess my transgressions to the Lord'—and *you forgave the guilt of my sin.*" Psalm 32:5, NIV.

What is God's attitude toward all who seek for forgiveness?

"You are *forgiving* and good, O Lord, abounding in love to all who call to you." Psalm 86:5, NIV.

Upon what did David rest his hope of forgiveness?

"Have mercy on me, O God, according *to your unfailing love; according to your great compassion* blot out my transgressions." Psalm 51:1, NIV.

What is the measure of the greatness of God's mercy?

"For *as high as the heavens are above the earth,* so great is his love for those who fear him." Psalm 103:11, NIV.

How fully does the Lord forgive when one repents?

"Let the wicked forsake his way and the evil man his thoughts. Let him turn to the Lord, and he will have mercy on him, and to our God, for *he will freely pardon.*" Isaiah 55:7, NIV.

What reason is given for God's readiness to forgive sin?

"Who is a God like you, who pardons sin and forgives the transgression of the remnant of his inheritance? You do not stay angry forever but *delight to show mercy.*" Micah 7:18, NIV (See Psalm 78:38.)

Why does God show us such mercy and patience?

"The Lord is not slow in keeping his promise, as some understand slowness. He is patient with you, *not wanting anyone to perish,* but everyone to come to repentance." 2 Peter 3:9, NIV.

In the parable of the prodigal son, how does the father respond when he sees his son coming home?

"But while he was still a long way off, his father saw him and was *filled with compassion* for him; he ran to his son, threw his arms around him and kissed him." Luke 15:20, NIV.

How did the father show his joy at his son's return?

"But the father said to his servants, 'Quick! *Bring the best robe and put it on him. Put a ring on his finger and sandals on his feet. Bring the fattened calf and kill it. Let's have a feast and celebrate.* For this son of mine was dead and is alive again; he was lost and is found.' So they began to celebrate." Verses 22-24, NIV.

How does heaven respond when we return to God?

"In the same way, I tell you, *there is rejoicing in the presence of the angels of God* over one sinner who repents." Verse 10, NIV.

What did Hezekiah say God had done with his sins?

"Surely it was for my benefit that I suffered such anguish. In your love you kept me from the pit of destruction; *you have put all my sins behind your back.*" Isaiah 38:17, NIV.

How completely does God wish to separate sin from us?

"You will again have compassion on us; you will tread our sins underfoot and hurl all our iniquities into the depths of the sea." Micah 7:19, NIV. "As far as the east is from the west, so far has he removed our transgressions from us." Psalm 103:12, NIV.

NOTE.—The deepest part of the ocean (the Marianas Trench) is deeper than the highest mountain (Mount Everest) is high. Even if our sins are piled up to heaven, God's grace is deeper, and covers all of our sin.

How did the people respond to John the Baptist's preaching?

"People went out to him from Jerusalem and all Judea and the whole region of the Jordan. *Confessing their sins,* they were baptized by him in the Jordan River." Matthew 3:5, 6, NIV.

How did the believers at Ephesus give evidence of their sincere repentance?

"Many of those who believed now came and *openly confessed their evil deeds.* A number who had practiced sorcery brought their scrolls together and burned them publicly. When they calculated the value of the scrolls, the total came to fifty thousand drachmas." Acts 19:18, 19, NIV.

NOTE.—In some cases, repentance may involve separating oneself from enticements to evil. This may include destroying occult material, pornography, or anything that separates us from our Savior.

On what basis did Jesus teach us to ask forgiveness?

"And forgive us our debts, *as we forgive our debtors.*" Matthew 6:12, NKJV.

What is the condition of obtaining God's forgiveness?

"For *if you forgive men their trespasses,* your heavenly Father will also forgive you. But if you do not forgive men their trespasses, neither will your Father forgive your trespasses." Verses 14, 15, NKJV.

Since God has forgiven us, how should we treat others?

"Be kind and compassionate to one another, *forgiving each other,* just as in Christ God forgave you." Ephesians 4:32, NIV.

Through whom are repentance and forgiveness granted?

"The God of our fathers raised *Jesus* from the dead—whom you had killed by hanging him on a tree. God exalted him to his own right hand as Prince and Savior that he might *give repentance and forgiveness of sins to Israel*." Acts 5:30, 31, NIV.

In what condition is one whose sins are forgiven?

"*Blessed* is he whose transgressions are forgiven, whose sins are covered. Blessed is the man whose sin the Lord does not count against him and in whose spirit is no deceit." Psalm 32:1, 2, NIV.

CONVERSION, OR THE NEW BIRTH

What must happen to us before we can enter heaven?

"Assuredly, I say to you, *unless you are converted* and become as little children, *you will by no means enter the kingdom of heaven*." Matthew 18:3, NKJV.

What did Jesus say this conversion was like?

"I tell you the truth, no one can see the kingdom of God *unless he is born again*." John 3:3, NIV.

How did Jesus further explain this new birth?

"Jesus answered, 'I tell you the truth, no one can enter the kingdom of God *unless he is born of water and the spirit*.'" Verse 5, NIV.

To what did Jesus, while talking with Nicodemus, compare the Holy Spirit?

"Flesh gives birth to flesh, but the Spirit gives birth to spirit. You should not be surprised at my saying, 'You must be born again.' *The wind* blows where it pleases. You hear its sound, but you cannot tell where it comes from or where it is going. *So it is with everyone born of the Spirit*." Verse 8, NIV.

What takes place when one is converted to Christ?

"Therefore, if anyone is in Christ, *he is a new creation; the old has gone, the new has come!*" 2 Corinthians 5:17, NIV. (See Acts 9:1-22; 22:1-21; 26:1-23.)

Of what value is a mere outside observance of religion?

"*Neither circumcision nor uncircumcision means anything*; what counts is a new creation." Galatians 6:15, NIV.

How did God create the world?

"By the word of the Lord were the heavens made, their starry host by the breath of his mouth." Psalm 33:6, NIV.

What brings about our conversion?

"For you have been born again, not of perishable seed, but of imperishable, *through the living and enduring word of God*." 1 Peter 1:23, NIV.

From what is a converted sinner saved?

"Whoever turns a sinner from the error of his way will save him from *death* and cover over a multitude of sins." James 5:20, NIV. (See Acts 26:14-18.)

What is the sinner's prayer?

"Create in me a pure heart, O God, and renew a steadfast spirit within me. Do not cast me from your presence or take your Holy Spirit from me. Restore to me the joy of your salvation and grant me a willing spirit, to sustain me. Then I will teach transgressors your ways, and sinners will *turn back to you*." Psalm 51:10-13, NIV.

How should we relate to others after our conversion?

"Simon, Simon, Satan has asked to sift you as wheat. But I have prayed for you, Simon, that your faith may not fail. And when you have turned back, *strengthen your brothers*." Luke 22:31, 32, NIV.

What is God willing to do for those who convert to Him?

"For this people's heart has become calloused; they hardly hear with their ears and they have closed their eyes. Otherwise they might see with their eyes, hear with their ears, understand with their hearts and turn, and *I would heal them*." Matthew 13:15, NIV.

What sort of healing does God promise to give His people?

"*I will heal their waywardness* and love them freely, for my anger has turned away from them." Hosea 14:4, NIV.

How are we healed by Jesus' sacrifice?

"But he was pierced for our transgressions, he was crushed for our iniquities; the punishment that brought us peace was upon him, and *by his wounds we are healed*." Isaiah 53:5, NIV.

According to 1 John, what evidence shows that we have been born again?

1. *We love others.* "We know that we have passed from death to life, because we love our brothers. Anyone who does not love remains in death." 1 John 3:14, NIV. "Dear friends, let us love one another, for love comes from God. Everyone who loves has been born of God and knows God." 1 John 4:7, NIV. (See also John 2:29.)

2. *We obey God's commands.* "We know that we have come to know him if we obey his commands. The man who says, 'I know him,' but does not do what he commands is a liar, and the truth is not in him. But if anyone obeys his word, God's love is truly made complete in him. This is how we know we are in him." 1 John 2:3-5, NIV.

3. *We live righteous lives.* "If you know that he is righteous, you know that everyone who does what is right has been born of him." Verse 29, NIV.

What power keeps the believer from habitual sinning?

"No one who is born of God will continue to sin, because *God's seed remains in him*; he cannot go on sinning, because he has been born of God." 1 John 3:9, NIV. (See 1 John 5:4; Genesis 39:9.)

Does this mean that we never again make a mistake?

"*If we claim to be without sin, we deceive ourselves* and the truth is not in us. If we confess our sins, he is faithful and just, and will forgive us our sins and purify us from all unrighteousness. If we claim we have not sinned, we make him out to be a liar and his word has no place in our lives." 1 John 1:8-10, NIV.

Who advocates for us if we do sin?

"My dear children, I write this to you so that you will not sin. But if anybody does sin, *we have one who speaks to the Father in our defense—Jesus Christ*, the Righteous One. He is the atoning sacrifice for our sins, and not only for ours but also for the sins of the whole world." 1 John 2:1, 2, NIV.

What will be the experience of those born of the Spirit?

"Therefore, there is now *no condemnation* for those who are in Christ Jesus." Romans 8:1, NIV.

What happens as we keep our focus on Jesus?

"And we, who with unveiled faces all reflect the Lord's glory, are being *transformed into his likeness* with ever-increasing glory, which from the Lord, who is the Spirit." 2 Corinthians 3:18, NIV.

CHRISTIAN BAPTISM

What rite is associated with the gospel?

"He said to them, 'Go into all the world and preach the good news to all creation. Whoever *believes and is baptized* will be saved, but whoever does not believe will be condemned.' " Mark 16:15, 16, NIV.

What did the apostle Peter tell his conscience-stricken audience to do on the day of Pentecost?

"Peter replied, *'Repent* and be baptized, every one of you, in the name of Jesus Christ for the forgiveness of your sins.' " Acts 2:38, NIV.

When the Philippian jailer asked Paul and Silas how he could be saved, what was their answer?

"They replied, *'Believe in the Lord Jesus*, and you will be saved— you and your household.' " Acts 16:31, NIV.

What happened next?

"Then they spoke the word of the Lord to him and to all the others in his house. At that hour of the night the jailer took them and washed their wounds; then immediately he and his family were *baptized*." Verses 32, 33, NIV.

What does baptism symbolically wash away?

"And now what are you waiting for? Get up, be baptized, and wash your sins away, calling on his name." Acts 22:16, NIV. (See Titus 3:5; 1 Peter 3:21.)

By what means are sins actually washed away?

Through Jesus' blood. "To him who loves us and has freed us from our sins *by his blood*." Revelation 1:5, NIV.

In whose name are believers to be baptized?

"Therefore go and make disciples of all nations, *baptizing them in the name of the Father and of the Son and of the Holy Spirit*." Matthew 28:19, NIV.

Whom are baptized believers symbolically clothed with?

"You are all sons of God, through faith in Christ Jesus, for all of you who were baptized into Christ have *clothed yourself with Christ*." Galatians 3:27, NIV.

Into what experience are Christians baptized?

"Or don't you know that all of us who were baptized into Christ

Jesus were baptized *into his death*?" Romans 6:3, NIV.

NOTE.—Baptism is a gospel ordinance commemorating the *death, burial,* and *resurrection* of Christ. In baptism public testimony is given to the effect that the one baptized has been crucified with Christ, buried with Him, and is raised with Him to walk in newness of life. Only one mode of baptism can rightly represent these facts of experience, and that is immersion—the mode followed by Christ and the primitive church.

How is such a baptism described?

"We were therefore *buried with him* through baptism *into death* in order that, just as Christ was raised from the dead through the glory of the Father, we too may live a new life." Verse 4, NIV.

If we die with Christ, to what honor are we entitled?

"If we have been united with him like this in his death, we will certainly also be *united with him* in his resurrection." Verse 5, NIV. "Now if we died with Christ, we believe that we will also *live with him.*" Verse 8, NIV.

What example did Jesus set for us?

"Then Jesus came from Galilee to the Jordan *to be baptized* by John." Matthew 3:13, NIV.

What remarkable occurrence highlighted the baptism of Jesus?

"As soon as Jesus was baptized, he went up out of the water. At that moment heaven was opened, and he saw *the Spirit of God descending like a dove and lighting on him.* And a voice from heaven said, '*This is my son, whom I love; with him I am well pleased.*'" Verses 16, 17, NIV.

What promise is made to those who repent and are baptized?

"Peter replied, 'Repent and be baptized, every one of you, in the name of Jesus Christ for the forgiveness of your sins. And *you will receive the gift of the Holy Spirit.*" Acts 2:38, NIV.

What instruction did the apostle Peter give regarding certain Gentiles who had received the Holy Spirit?

" 'Can anyone keep these people from being baptized with water? They have received the Holy Spirit just as we have.' So he ordered that *they be baptized in the name of Jesus Christ.*" Acts 10:47, 48, NIV.

What question did an Ethiopian official ask after Philip witnessed to him about Jesus?

"As they traveled along the road, they came to some water and the eunuch said, 'Look, here is water. *Why shouldn't I be baptized?'* And he gave orders to stop the chariot. Then both Philip and the eunuch went down into the water and Philip baptized him." Acts 8:36-38, NIV.

How did the people of Samaria show their faith in the preaching of Philip?

"But when they believed Philip as he preached the good news of the kingdom of God and the name of Jesus Christ, *they were baptized*, both men and women." Verse 12, NIV.

What symbolizes the unity of those who are baptized into Christ?

"*The body is a unit, though it is made up of many parts; and though all its parts are many, they form one body*. So it is with Christ. For *we were all baptized by one Spirit into one body*—whether Jews or Greeks, slave or free—and we were all given the one Spirit to drink." 1 Corinthians 12:12, 13, NIV.

How does baptism make us a part of Christ's death and resurrection?

"Having been buried with him in baptism and raised with him through your faith in the power of God, who raised him from the dead." Colossians 2:12, NIV.

NOTE.—If we are in Christ, God considers that whatever happened to Him also happened to us.

Since this is so, what should the believer do?

"Since, then, you have been raised with Christ, *set your hearts on things above*, where Christ is seated at the right hand of God." Colossians 3:1, NIV.

RECONCILED TO GOD

What plea does God send to us through His appointed messengers?

"We are therefore Christ's ambassadors, as though God were making his appeal through us. We implore you on Christ's behalf: *Be reconciled to God.*" 2 Corinthians 5:20, NIV.

Through whom is this reconciliation made?

"All this is from God, who reconciled us to himself *through Christ* and gave us the ministry of reconciliation." Verse 18, NIV.

What was required in order to effect this reconciliation?

"For if, when we were God's enemies, we were reconciled to him through *the death of his Son*, how much more, having been reconciled, shall we be saved through his life!" Romans 5:10, NIV.

What is the basis for our reconciliation?

"For God was pleased to have all his fullness dwell in him, and through him to reconcile to himself all things, whether things on earth or things in heaven, by making peace through *his blood, shed on the cross*." Colossians 1:19, 20, NIV.

How was Jesus treated?

"But he was *pierced* for our transgressions, he was *crushed* for our iniquities; the *punishment* that brought us peace was upon him, and by his *wounds* we are healed." Isaiah 53:5, NIV.

What did John the Baptist declare about Jesus?

"Look, the Lamb of God, who takes away the sin of the world!" John 1:29, NIV.

For what purpose did Christ bear our sins?

"He himself bore our sins in his body on the tree, *so that we might die to sins and live for righteousness*; by his wounds you have been healed." 1 Peter 2:24, NIV.

What did God, when reconciling the world, do about the sins of humanity?

"God was reconciling the world to himself in Christ, *not counting men's sins against them*." 2 Corinthians 5:19, NIV.

What made it possible for God to treat sinners this way?

"We all, like sheep, have gone astray, each of us has turned to his own way; and the *Lord has laid on him the iniquity of us all*." Isaiah 53:6, NIV.

NOTE.—In other words, God charged the penalty for sin to Jesus instead of to us, who incurred the debt.

How does this act of reconciliation break down racial barriers?

"His purpose was to create in himself one new man out of the two, thus making peace, and *in this one body* to reconcile both of them to God through the cross, by which he put to death their hostility." Ephesians 2:15, 16, NIV.

NOTE.—Since Christ has atoned for the sins of the world, all who accept Christ as their Savior become brothers and sisters in God's family, and all racial barriers are dissolved. Jesus has "put to death the hostility" between the races.

What is the purpose of Christ in His work of reconciliation?

"Once you were alienated from God and were enemies in your minds because of your evil behavior. But now he has reconciled you by Christ's physical body through death to *present you holy in his sight, without blemish and free from accusation*." Colossians 1:21, 22, NIV.

Through whom is the reconciliation received?

"Not only is this so, but we also rejoice in God *through our Lord Jesus Christ*, through whom we have now received reconciliation." Romans 5:11, NIV.

One Choice of Three

To reconcile holy heaven and sinful earth, one of three things was necessary: Either heaven must take up earthly ways, earth must turn to heavenly ways, or both must be merged. There was only one real way—earth must be reconciled to God. To open the door of heaven to humans meant Jesus' sacrifice on Calvary. At Calvary every sinner may find the peace of reconciliation, fellowship with God, and hope of everlasting life.

ACCEPTANCE WITH GOD

In whom has God made us accepted?

"Praise be to the God and Father of our Lord Jesus Christ, who has blessed us in the heavenly realms with every spiritual blessing *in Christ*. For he chose us in him before the creation of the world to be holy and blameless in his sight. In love he predestined us to be adopted as his sons *through Jesus Christ*, in accordance with his pleasure and will—to the praise of his glorious grace, which he has freely given us *in the One he loves*." Ephesians 1:3-6, NIV.

What great gift comes with our acceptance of Christ?

"For my Father's will is that everyone who looks to the son and believes in him shall have *eternal life*, and I will raise him up at the last day." John 6:40, NIV. (See also John 17:2.)

What is the foundation of faith?

"Faith comes by hearing, and hearing by *the word of God*." Romans 10:17, NKJV.

What is the first and primary evidence of our acceptance with God?

"If we receive the witness of men, the *witness of God is greater*; for this is the witness of God *which He has testified of His Son. . . . And this is the testimony: that God has given us eternal life, and this life is in His Son.*" 1 John 5:9-11, NKJV.

NOTE.—The primary basis of all faith and acceptance is God's own Word. To receive and believe what He said is the first essential to salvation—the first evidence of acceptance.

Why did John write his Gospel?

"These are written *that you may believe* that Jesus is the Christ, the Son of God, and that believing you may have life in His name." John 20:31, NKJV. "These things I have written to you who believe in the name of the Son of God, that you may know that you have eternal life, and *that you may continue to believe* in the name of the Son of God." 1 John 5:13, NKJV.

What witness do true believers in Christ have that they are accepted of God?

"He who believes in the Son of God *has the witness in himself*; he who does not believe God has made Him a liar, because he has not believed the *testimony* that God has given of His Son." Verse 10, NKJV.

NOTE.—Faith and feeling should not be confused. Faith is ours to exercise in the Word of God, regardless of our feelings, and often even in opposition to our feelings. Many fail to accept God's pardon and assurance of acceptance because they do not take God at His word, turning instead to their changeable moods and feelings. *Faith* precedes the *joyful feelings* that naturally result from the assurance of forgiveness and acceptance.

What is another evidence of divine acceptance?

"We know that we have passed from death to life, *because we love our brothers*. Anyone who does not love remains in death." 1 John 3:14, NIV.

What three definite witnesses of acceptance are mentioned by John?

"For there are three that testify: *the Spirit, the water and the blood*; and the three are in agreement." 1 John 5:7, 8, NIV.

How does the Spirit witness to our acceptance with God?

"Because you are sons, God sent the Spirit of his Son into our hearts, the Spirit who calls out, *'Abba, Father.'* " Galatians 4:6, NIV. "The Spirit himself testifies with our spirit that we are God's children." Romans 8:16, NIV.

How does the water witness to our acceptance with God?

"As many of you as have been baptized into Christ *have put on Christ.*" Galatians 3:27.

NOTE.—In baptism the water and the Spirit both bear witness of God's acceptance. The same Spirit that, at Christ's baptism, said, "This is my beloved Son, in whom I am well pleased" (Matthew 3:17), witnesses to the acceptance of every sincere believer at their baptism.

How does the blood witness to our acceptance with God?

"If we walk in the light, as he is in the light, we have fellowship with one another, and the blood of Jesus, his Son, purifies us from all sin." 1 John 1:7, NIV. "In him we have redemption through his blood, *the forgiveness of sins.*" Ephesians 1:7, NIV. (See also Revelation 1:5, 6.)

How do we become children of God?

"Ye are all the children of God *by faith in Christ Jesus.*" Galatians 3:26.

When is the best time to find acceptance with God through Christ?

"For he says, 'In the time of my favor I heard you, and in the day of salvation I helped you.' I tell you, *now is the time of God's favor, now is the day of salvation.*" 2 Corinthians 6:2, NIV.

To whom should we thus give glory and honor?

Jesus. "To him who loves us and has freed us from our sins by his blood, and has made us to be a kingdom and priests to serve his God and Father—to him be glory and power for ever and ever! Amen." Revelation 1:5, 6, NIV.

NOTE.—We are heirs of God, and all of God's resources are available to us. Yet some live in self-imposed spiritual poverty, because they do not know how to appropriate from God those spiritual resources that are already theirs. Faith believes the promises and accepts the blessings Heaven offers.

JUSTIFICATION BY FAITH

What does justification by faith include?

"Therefore, my brothers, I want you to know that through Jesus *the forgiveness of sins is proclaimed to you*. Through him everyone who believes is justified from everything you could not be justified from by the law of Moses." Acts 13:38, 39, NIV.

NOTE.—To be justified is to be declared innocent, acquitted, vindicated. It is God's way of restoring us to the status we would have had if we had never sinned.

What is the ground or basis of justification on God's part?

"So that, having been justified *by his grace*, we might become heirs having the hope of eternal life." Titus 3:7, NIV.

Through what means is this grace made available to us?

"Since we have now been justified *by his [Christ's] blood*, how much more shall we be saved from God's wrath through him!" Romans 5:9, NIV.

What plays no part in our justification?

"For we maintain that a man is justified by faith apart from *observing the law*." Romans 3:28, NIV. "Now when a man works, his wages are not credited to him as a gift, but as an obligation. However, to the man who does not work but trusts God who justifies the wicked, his faith is credited as righteousness." Romans 4:4, 5, NIV.

What is the only way sinners may be justified, or made righteous?

"Know that a man is not justified by observing the law, but *by faith in Jesus Christ*. So we, too, have put our faith in Christ Jesus that we may be justified by faith in Christ and not by observing the law, because by observing the law no one will be justified." Galatians 2:16, NIV.

What concrete example makes clear the meaning of this doctrine?

"He took him outside and said, 'Look up at the heavens and count the stars—if indeed you can count them.' Then he said to him, 'So shall your offspring be.' *Abram believed the Lord, and he credited it to him as righteousness*." Genesis 15:5, 6, NIV.

How is the righteousness thus obtained described?

"And be found in him, *not having a righteousness of my own that comes from the law, but that which is through faith in Christ*—the righteousness that comes from God and is by faith." Philippians 3:9, NIV.

Can justification be earned?

No. "For the wages of sin is death; but the *gift* of God is eternal life through Jesus Christ our Lord." Romans 6:23. "Consequently, just as the result of one trespass was condemnation for all men, so also the result of one act of righteousness was justification that brings life for all men." Romans 5:18, NIV.

How does grace, as the ground of justification, exclude righteousness by works?

"And *if by grace, then it is no longer by works; if it were, grace would no longer be grace.*" Romans 11:6, NIV.

In what way did Paul say both Jews and Gentiles are justified?

"Is God the God of Jews only? Is he not the God of Gentiles too? Yes, of Gentiles too, since there is only one God, who will justify the circumcised [Jews] *by faith* and the uncircumcised [Gentiles] *through that same faith.*" Romans 3:29, 30, NIV.

How does Paul describe Abraham's faith in God?

"Yet he did not waver through unbelief regarding the promise of God, but was *strengthened in his faith* and gave glory to God, *being fully persuaded* that God had power to do what he had promised." Romans 4:20, 21, NIV.

What did Abraham's faith bring him?

"This is why 'it was credited to him as *righteousness.*'" Verse 22, NIV.

On what condition may we receive this same imputed righteousness?

"The words 'it was credited to him' were written not for him alone, but also for us, to whom God will credit righteousness—for us *who believe in him who raised Jesus our Lord from the dead.* He was delivered over to death for our sins and was raised to life for our justification." Verses 23-25, NIV. (See 1 Corinthians 15:17.)

NOTE.—The resurrection of Christ is the historical basis for our faith. We are justified by our faith in God's promises just as Abraham was. We look back on the Resurrection by faith, just as Abraham looked forward to the promise of many "offspring." Our faith lays hold on that which makes imputed righteousness (that is, righteousness credited to us from Jesus) possible. (See Hebrews 11:17-19.)

How is it possible for righteousness to be credited to the believer?

"For as by one man's disobedience many are made sinners, so *by the obedience of one* shall many be made righteous." Romans 5:19.

What prophetic declaration foretold this truth?

"But in the Lord all the descendants of Israel will be found righteous and will exult." Isaiah 45:25, NIV.

What other prediction asserts the same great truth?

"By His knowledge my righteous servant will justify many; and he will bear their iniquities." Isaiah 53:11, NIV.

How does the cross enable God to be both merciful and just?

"God presented him as a sacrifice of atonement, through faith in his blood. He did this to demonstrate his justice, because in his forbearance he had left the sins committed beforehand unpunished—he did it to demonstrate his justice at the present time, so as to be just and the one who justifies those who have faith in Jesus." Romans 3:25, 26, NIV.

NOTE.—God could not simply let sin go unpunished, for that would be a travesty of justice in the eyes of all unfallen beings. Justice demands that a penalty be paid for sin. God took the penalty upon Himself in the person of His Son, thus upholding His law and His governing authority. Yet at the same time this sacrifice made it possible to extend mercy to the penitent sinner. Thus God is both just and merciful at the same time.

As our substitute, Jesus bore our sin and penalty so that we could participate in His righteousness.

How is Jesus our substitute?

"God made him who had no sin to be sin for us, so that in him we might become the righteousness of God." 2 Corinthians 5:21, NIV.

By what name is Christ appropriately called?

" 'The days are coming,' declares the Lord, 'when I will raise up to David a righteous Branch, a King who will reign wisely and do what is just and right in the land. In his days Judah will be saved and Israel will live in safety. This is the name by which he will be called: *The Lord Our Righteousness*.' " Jeremiah 23:5, 6, NIV.

What blessed experience follows when we accept Christ as our righteousness?

"Therefore being justified by faith, *we have peace with God* through our Lord Jesus Christ." Romans 5:1. "For he is our peace." Ephesians 2:14.

Is it possible to be justified by keeping the law?

"Therefore no one will be declared righteous in his sight by observing the law; rather, through the law we become conscious of sin." Romans 3:20, NIV.

How does the death of Christ bear testimony to this?

"I do not set aside the grace of God, for *if righteousness could be gained through the law, Christ died for nothing!"* Galatians 2:21, NIV.

What is the result of any attempt to be justified by the law?

"You who are trying to be justified by law have been alienated from Christ; *you have fallen away from grace*." Galatians 5:4, NIV.

NOTE.—Just as a criminal cannot be acquitted in a modern court of law by promising to keep the law in the future, so it is impossible for a sinner to be justified by keeping the law.

Why did Israel fail to attain unto righteousness?

"What then shall we say? That the Gentiles, who did not pursue righteousness, have obtained it, a righteousness that is by faith; but Israel, who pursued a law of righteousness, has not attained it. Why not? *Because they pursued it not by faith but as if it were by works*." Romans 9:30-32, NIV.

What is revealed by the law?

"Through the law *we become conscious of sin*." Romans 3:20, NIV.

What is one valid function of the law?

"Through the law we become conscious of sin." Romans 3:20, NIV. "What shall we say, then? Is the law sin? Certainly not! Indeed I would not have known what sin was except through the law. For I would not have known what coveting really was if the law had not said, 'Do not covet.' " Romans 7:7, NIV. "Everyone who sins breaks the law; in fact, sin is lawlessness." 1 John 3:4, NIV.

NOTE.—One valid function of the law is to define sin. By making us aware of sin in our lives, the law motivates us to seek the remedy for sin, Christ.

Does faith set aside the law of God?

"Do we, then, nullify the law by this faith? Not at all! Rather, we uphold the law." Romans 3:31, NIV.

Does God's grace constitute an excuse for continuing in sin?

"What shall we say, then? *Shall we go on sinning so that grace may increase? By no means!* We died to sin; how can we live in it any longer?" Romans 6:1, 2, NIV.

What is the visible evidence of genuine faith?

"What good is it, my brothers, if a man claims to have faith but has no deeds? Can such faith save him? Suppose a brother or sister is without clothes and daily food. If one of you says to him, 'Go, I wish you well; keep warm and well fed,' but does nothing about his physical needs, what good is it? In the same way, *faith by itself, if it is not accompanied by action, is dead. . . .* You believe that there is one God. Good! Even the demons believe that—and shudder. You foolish man, do you want evidence that *faith without deeds is useless*?" James 2:14-20, NIV.

How did the death of Christ make possible our justification?

"For Christ's love compels us, because we are convinced that *one died for all, and therefore all died.*" 2 Corinthians 5:14, NIV.

NOTE.—If one died for all, then all died. In other words, since Jesus died for us, it is as if we died. When we surrender our lives to God, we are incorporated *into Christ.* To understand what this means, imagine placing a card inside this book. If the book is then thrown into fire or water, the card goes into the water or fire too. Whatever happens to the book also happens to the card within it. So likewise, if we are in Christ, then whatever happened to Him is counted as if it happened to us. When He was crucified, we were crucified, which means that the penalty for our sins has been paid. And when He rose from the dead, we rose with Him.

How should Christ's atoning death affect us?

"And he died for all, that those who live should no longer live for themselves but for him who died for them and was raised again. . . . Therefore, if anyone is in Christ, he is a new creation; *the old has gone, the new has come!*" Verses 15-17, NIV.

NOTE.—We have been reborn as a new creature into a new life— a life that is devoted to the One who died for us. This glorious truth is the motivating force of our lives.

What are the implications of this for someone who is in Christ?

"All this is from God, who reconciled us to himself through Christ and *gave us the ministry of reconciliation*: that God was reconciling the world to himself in Christ, not counting men's sin against them. And *he has committed to us the message of reconciliation. We are therefore Christ's ambassadors, as though God were making his appeal through us. We implore you on Christ's behalf: Be reconciled to God.* God made him who had no sin to be sin for us, so that in him we might become the righteousness of God." Verses 18-21, NIV.

NOTE.—Those who have been reconciled to God will carry on the ministry of reconciliation by inviting others to participate in the same wonderful experience. Christ, our substitute, took our sin and its punishment, that we might receive His righteousness and its reward—the greatest bargain of all time! Now He invites us to become His ambassadors to make this same offer to others.

Martin Luther wrote: "Learn to know Christ and Him crucified. Learn to sing unto Him a new song; to despair of thyself, and say, Thou, O Lord Jesus! Thou art my righteousness, and I am Thy sin! Thou hast taken what is mine, and given me what is Thine. What Thou wert not Thou hast become, in order that what I was not I might become." Letter to Spenlein (1516), Luther's *Sammtliche Schriften* (Walch ed.), vol. 21a, col. 21, as translated by Merle D'Aubigne, *History of the Reformation*, book 2, chap. 8.

RIGHTEOUSNESS AND LIFE

What is assured to the believer in Christ?

"For God so loved the world that he gave his one and only Son, that whoever believes in him shall not perish but have eternal life." John 3:16, NIV.

What is revealed in the gospel?

"For in the gospel *a righteousness from God* is revealed, a righteousness that is by faith from first to last, just as it is written: 'The righteous will live by faith.' " Romans 1:17, NIV.

What has Christ brought to light through the gospel?

"This grace was given us in Christ Jesus before the beginning of time, but it has now been revealed through the appearing of our Savior, Christ Jesus, who has destroyed death and has *brought life and immortality to light through the gospel*." 2 Timothy 1:9, 10, NIV.

NOTE.—The purpose of the gospel is to bring both life and righteousness.

How closely are righteousness and life thus united?

"In the way of righteousness there is life; along that path is immortality" Proverbs 12:28, NIV.

What is the result of righteous living?

"He who pursues righteousness and love finds *life, prosperity and honor.*" Proverbs 21:21, NIV.

What is the ultimate result of grace?

"But where sin increased, grace increased all the more, so that, just as sin reigned in death, so also grace might reign through righteousness to bring *eternal life* through Jesus Christ our Lord." Romans 5:20-21, NIV.

What constitutes righteous living?

"All Your commandments are *righteousness*." Psalm 119:172, NKJV.

What did Jesus declare God's commandment to be?

"And I know that his commandment is *life everlasting*." John 12:50. NOTE.—Life and righteousness are inseparable.

What does Christ declare Himself to be?

"I am the way, the truth, and the life." John 14:6.

What did Christ indicate as essential to eternal life?

"So he said to him, 'Why do you call Me good? No one is good but One, that is, God. But if you want to enter into life, keep the commandments.' " Matthew 19:17, NKJV.

NOTE.—Those who receive the imputed righteousness of Christ as a gift will live holy lives. Without holiness, no one will see the Lord (Hebrews 12:14). However, keeping the commandments is always a *result* of, a response of, never a *basis* for, our salvation.

How is righteousness received?

"For if, by the trespass of the one man, death reigned through that one man, how much more will those who receive God's abundant provision of grace and of the *gift of righteousness* reign in life through the one man, Jesus Christ." Romans 5:17, NIV.

How is eternal life bestowed?

"For the wages of sin is death; but the gift of God is eternal life *through Jesus Christ our Lord.*" Romans 6:23.

CONSECRATION

What offering did King Hezekiah command to be made when he reconsecrated the Temple after a period of apostasy?

"Hezekiah gave the order to sacrifice the *burnt offering* on the altar. As the offering began, singing to the Lord began also, accompanied by trumpets and the instruments of David king of Israel." 2 Chronicles 29:27, NIV.

How did Hezekiah interpret the meaning of this service to the people of Judah?

"Then Hezekiah said, *'You have now dedicated yourselves to the Lord.* Come and bring sacrifices and thank offerings to the temple of the Lord.' So the assembly brought sacrifices and thank offerings, and all whose hearts were willing brought burnt offerings." Verse 31, NIV.

NOTE.—The morning and the evening burnt offering (Exodus 29:38-41) symbolized the daily consecration of the people to the Lord.

How does Peter urge this consecration upon all Christians?

"You also, like living stones, are being built into a spiritual house to be a holy priesthood, *offering spiritual sacrifices* acceptable to God through Jesus Christ." 1 Peter 2:5, NIV.

How should we consecrate ourselves today?

"Therefore, I urge you, brothers, in view of God's mercy, to *offer your bodies as living sacrifices*, holy and pleasing to God—this is your spiritual act of worship." Romans 12:1, NIV.

What is another sort of spiritual sacrifice we can offer?

"Through Jesus, therefore, *let us continually offer to God a sacrifice of praise*—the fruit of lips that confess his name." Hebrews 13:15, NIV.

What example of complete consecration did Jesus set?

"Whoever wants to become great among you must be your servant, and whoever wants to be first must be your slave—just as the Son of Man did not come to be served, but to serve, and to give his life as a ransom for many." Matthew 20:26-28, NIV.

How did Jesus demonstrate His consecration to His disciples?

"For who is greater, the one who is at the table or the one who serves? Is it not the one who is at the table? But *I am among you as one who serves*." Luke 22:27, NIV.

How are we to imitate Christ?

"Your attitude should be the same as that of Christ Jesus: Who, being in very nature God, did not consider equality with God something to be grasped, but made himself nothing, taking the very nature of a servant, being made in human likeness." Philippians 2:5-7, NIV.

To what extent did Christ humble Himself?

"And being found in appearance as a man, he humbled himself and became obedient to death—*even death on a cross*!" Verse 8, NIV.

NOTE.—Death on a cross was as humiliating and horrifically painful a death as one could imagine (the word "excruciating" comes from the same root word as "crucify").

How does He encourage us to the same consecration?

"Take my yoke upon you and learn from me, for I am gentle and humble in heart, and you will find rest for your souls." Matthew 11:29, NIV.

What does He make the condition of discipleship?

"In the same way, any of you who does not give up everything he has cannot be my disciple." Luke 14:33, NIV.

What is proof that one does not belong to Christ?

· "For those who live according to the flesh set their minds on the things of the flesh, but those who live according to the Spirit set their minds on the things of the Spirit. To set the mind on the flesh is death, but to set the mind on the Spirit is life and peace. For the mind that is set on the flesh is hostile to God; it does not submit to God's law, indeed it cannot; and those who are in the flesh cannot please God. But you are not in the flesh; you are in the Spirit, if in fact the Spirit of God dwells in you. *Anyone who does not have the Spirit of Christ* does not belong to Him." Romans 8:5-9, RSV.

NOTE.—About Romans 8:9 George Knight has written, "Paul has been speaking in the previous verses about those who were fleshly minded, those who had their minds focused on the present world. 'But' not everybody is in that camp. Counterposed to those in the flesh are those 'in the Spirit.' The apostle feels so strongly about this topic that he goes on to say that those who do not 'have the Spirit of Christ' do not belong to Him, that they are not Christians.

"We find two important truths about the Holy Spirit in this verse. First, every Christian (rather than church member) has the gift of the

Holy Spirit. That is exactly what Jesus taught during His evening meeting with Nicodemus: 'Truly, truly, I say to you, unless one is born of water *and the Spirit*, he cannot enter the kingdom of God. That which is born of the flesh is flesh, and that which is born of the Spirit is spirit' (John 3:5, 6, RSV).

"According to Paul, indwelling sin characterizes those 'in Adam' (Rom. 7:17, 20), but the indwelling of God's Holy Spirit is the mark of the Christian. Jesus' promise in John 14:16, 17 reflects that spiritual indwelling: 'I will pray the Father' to send the Holy Spirit, 'even the Spirit of truth, whom the world cannot receive, because it neither sees him nor knows him; you know him, for he dwells with you and is in you' (RSV). Because of that indwelling Paul refers to our bodies as 'the temple of the Holy Spirit' (1 Corinthians 6:19, RSV).

"The Holy Spirit is God's gift to every true Christian. Of course, beyond the gift of the Spirit to all Christians are those special gifts or talents bestowed upon individuals for specialized ministries. But we must not confuse them with the Spirit's indwelling in every person who has faith in Christ.

"The second important thing to note about Romans 8:9 as it relates to the Spirit is its implication for the doctrine of the Trinity. . . . The good news is that each Person in the Trinity cooperates with each of the others for our salvation." George Knight, *Walking With Paul Through the Book of Romans* (Hagerstown, Md., Review and Herald, 2002), p. 199.

How does obeying God's word transform us?

"We know that we have come to know him if we obey his commands. The man who says, 'I know him,' but does not do what he commands is a liar, and the truth is not in him. But if anyone obeys his word, *God's love is made complete* in him. Whoever claims to live in him must walk as Jesus did." 1 John 2:3-6, NIV.

How should Christians view their bodies?

"Do you not know that your body is a *temple of the Holy Spirit*, who is in you, whom you have received from God? *You are not your own*; you were bought at a price. Therefore honor God with your body." 1 Corinthians 6:19, 20, NIV.

NOTE.—Our time, strength, skills, and resources are God's, and should be given to His service.

How does a willingness to serve demonstrate true consecration?

"Then I heard the voice of the Lord saying, 'Whom shall I send? And who will go for us?' And I said, 'Here am I. Send me!' " Isaiah 6:8, NIV.

CHOSEN BY GOD

What does the apostle Peter admonish us to do?

"Therefore, my brothers, be all the more eager to make your calling and election sure. For if you do these things, you will never fall, and you will receive a rich welcome into the eternal kingdom of our Lord and Savior Jesus Christ." 2 Peter 1:10, 11, NIV.

NOTE.—This text reveals that we need to reaffirm daily our commitment to God. We are elected to be saved; but we must be diligent to make this election sure. If we are not, we may fall from grace.

What warning given by Christ teaches the same truth?

"I am coming soon. Hold on to what you have, so that no one will take your crown." Revelation 3:11, NIV.

NOTE.—Every soul is a candidate for eternal life, and hence for "the crown of life" (James 1:12). Faith in Jesus and perseverance to the end will make our election sure.

Upon what condition is the crown of life promised?

"*Be faithful* even to the point of death, and I will give you the crown of life." Revelation 2:10, NIV.

Does God have a purpose in calling us?

"And we know that in all things God works for the good of those who love him, who have been called according to his purpose. For those God foreknew he also *predestined to be conformed to the likeness of his Son*, that he might be the firstborn among many brothers. And those he predestined, he also *called*; those he called, he also *justified*; those he justified, he also *glorified*." Romans 8:28-30, NIV.

What is the seal and guarantee of our present and future salvation?

"In him we were also chosen, having been predestined *according to the plan of him* who works out everything in conformity with the purpose of his will, in order that we, who were the first to hope in Christ, might be for the praise of his glory. And you also were included in Christ when you heard the word of truth, the gospel of your salvation. Having believed, you were marked in him with a seal, the promised Holy Spirit, who is a deposit guaranteeing our inheritance until the redemption of those who are God's possession—to the praise of his glory." Ephesians 1:11-14, NIV.

How does the Holy Spirit aid us as we endure the trials of this earthly life?

"I consider that our present sufferings are not worth comparing with the glory that will be revealed in us. The creation waits in eager expectation for the sons of God to be revealed. For the creation was subject to frustration, not by its own choice, but by the will of the one who subjected it, in hope that the creation itself will be liberated from its bondage to decay and brought into the glorious freedom of the children of God.

"We know that the whole creation has been groaning as in the pains of childbirth right up to the present time. Not only so, but we ourselves, who have the firstfruits of the Spirit, groan inwardly as we wait eagerly for our adoption as sons, the redemption of our bodies. For in this hope we were saved. But hope that is seen is no hope at all. Who hopes for what he already has? But if we hope for what we do not yet have, we wait for it patiently.

"In the same way, *the Spirit helps us in our weakness*. We do not know what we ought to pray for, but *the Spirit himself intercedes for us*, with groans that words cannot express. And he who searches our hearts knows the mind of the Spirit, because the Spirit intercedes for the saints in accordance with God's will." Romans 8:18-27, NIV.

What has ever been God's destiny for us?

"For *he chose us* in him [Christ] before the creation of the world *to be holy and blameless in his sight*." Ephesians1:4, NIV.

To what has God predestined those who accept Christ as Savior and Lord?

"In love *he predestined us to be adopted as his sons* through Jesus Christ, in accordance with his pleasure and will." Verses 4, 5, NIV.

Upon what condition is salvation offered?

"Believe on the Lord Jesus Christ, and you will be saved." Acts 16:31, NKJV.

How long must we maintain this faith to be saved?

"But the one who endures *to the end* will be saved." Matthew 24:13, NRSV. (See James 1:12; Revelation 2:10.)

In what fact may every believer rejoice?

"Rejoice *that your names are written in heaven*." Luke 10:20, NRSV.

Whose names are to be retained in the book of life?

"He who overcomes will . . . be dressed in white. I will never blot out his name from the book of life, but will acknowledge his name before my Father and his angels." Revelation 3:5, NIV.

What scripture is sometimes cited as evidence that God is arbitrary in His dealings with human beings?

"Therefore God has mercy on whom he wants to have mercy, and he hardens whom he wants to harden." Romans 9:18, NIV.

What other scripture shows with whom God wills to be merciful, and with whom otherwise?

"To the *faithful* you show yourself *faithful*, to the *blameless* you show yourself *blameless*, to the *pure* you show yourself *pure*, but to the *crooked* you show yourself *shrewd*." Psalm 18:25, 26, NIV.

NOTE.—God wills that all shall be saved, but He does not force anyone to receive Christ and be saved. This is a matter of individual choice. By His mighty acts and judgments in Egypt, God "hardened Pharaoh's heart." Exodus 7:3, 13, 22. But the same manifestations *softened* the hearts of others. The difference was in the hearts and in the way God's message and dealings were received, not in God. The same sun that melts the wax hardens the clay. Exodus 8:32 says that Pharaoh hardened his own heart.

Is God's mercy available to everyone?

Yes. "Let the wicked forsake his way and the evil man his thoughts. Let him turn to the Lord, and he will have mercy on him, and to our God, for he will freely pardon." Isaiah 55:7, NIV.

How many does God desire to save?

"This is right and acceptable in the sight of God our Savior, who desires *everyone* to be saved and to come to the knowledge of the truth." 1 Timothy 2:3, 4, NRSV.

What on our part is essential to salvation?

"Choose for yourselves this day whom you will serve." Joshua 24:15, NIV. "If anyone *chooses to do God's will*, he will find out whether my teaching comes from God or whether I speak on my own." John 7:17, NIV. *"Believe* on the Lord Jesus Christ, and you will be saved." Acts 16:31, NKJV. "Whoever *desires*, let him take the water of life freely." Revelation 22:17, NKJV.

BIBLE SANCTIFICATION

What standard did Paul wish for Christians to reach?

"May God himself, the God of peace, *sanctify you through and through*. May your whole spirit, soul and body, be kept *blameless* at the coming of our Lord Jesus Christ." 1 Thessalonians 5:23, NIV.

NOTE.—The Greek word translated "sanctify" means to set apart for a special purpose, to dedicate or consecrate. Those who are sanctified are set apart for God's special use, and hence are set apart from sin. Those who are sanctified continue to grow in grace throughout the Christian life. Thus sanctification is both a historical change of status (see 1 Corinthians 6:11) and an ongoing process of daily separation from sin.

What did Paul compare sanctification to?

"But in a great house there are not only vessels of gold and silver, but also of wood and clay, some for honor and some for dishonor. Therefore if anyone cleanses himself from the latter, he will be a vessel for honor, sanctified and useful *for the Master, prepared for every good work*." 2 Timothy 2:20, 21, NKJV.

NOTE.—People often set aside a fine set of china for special occasions. This china might be said to be "sanctified," for it is set apart for a special purpose. This is the illustration Paul is using here (as well as in Romans 9:21). We are God's "china," His "vessels for honor." Through His power we are purified from sin, sanctified, and fit for God's use.

How necessary is the experience of sanctification?

"Pursue peace with everyone, and the *holiness* without which no one will see the Lord." Hebrews 12:14, NRSV.

NOTE.—Some translations read "sanctification" instead of "holiness."

What purpose did Christ have in giving Himself for the church?

"Husbands, love your wives, even as Christ also loved the church, and gave Himself for it; *that He might sanctify and cleanse it with the washing of water by the word*." Ephesians 5:25, 26.

What kind of church was He seeking?

"That he might present it to himself *a glorious church, not having spot, or wrinkle, or any such thing*; but that it should be holy and without blemish." Verse 27.

What accomplishes this cleansing from sin?

"The blood of goats and bulls and the ashes of a heifer sprinkled on those who are ceremonially unclean sanctify them so that they are outwardly clean. How much more, then, will the *blood* of Christ, who through the eternal Spirit offered himself unblemished to God, cleanse our consciences from acts that lead to death, so that we may serve the living God!" Hebrews 9:13, 14, NIV. (See also Hebrews 10:29.)

How can this spiritual cleansing change us?

"Do not conform any longer to the pattern of this world, but *be transformed by the renewing of your mind*. Then you will be able to test and approve what God's will is—his good, pleasing and perfect will." Romans 12:2, NIV.

What is God's will for your life?

"It is God's will *that you should be sanctified*." 1 Thessalonians 4:3, NIV.

What two things does God expect from those who have been chosen by Him?

"From the beginning God chose you to be saved *through the sanctifying work of the Spirit and through belief in the truth*." 2 Thessalonians 2:13, NIV.

How is the sanctified life described?

"But *grow in grace*, and in the knowledge of our Lord and Saviour Jesus Christ" 2 Peter 3:18. (See 2 Peter 1:5-7.)

What was Paul's experience in sanctification?

"Not that I have already obtained all this, or have already been made perfect, but I press on to take hold of that for which Christ Jesus took hold of me. Brothers, I do not consider myself yet to have taken hold of it. But one thing I do: Forgetting what is behind and straining toward what is ahead. *I press on toward the goal* to win the prize for which God has called me heavenward in Christ Jesus." Philippians 3:12-14, NIV.

Can anyone boast of sinlessness?

"If we say that we have no sin, we deceive ourselves, and the truth is not in us." 1 John 1:8.

What did the prophet Zephaniah urge the people to seek?

"Seek the Lord, all you humble of the land, you who do what

he commands. *Seek righteousness, seek humility*; perhaps you will be sheltered on the day of the Lord's anger." Zephaniah 2:3, NIV.

In whose name should everything be done?

"And whatever you do, whether in word or deed, *do it all in the name of the Lord Jesus*, giving thanks to God the Father through him." Colossians 3:17, NIV.

What perspective determines the right or wrongness of whatever we do?

"So whether you eat or drink or whatever you do, do it all for the glory of God." 1 Corinthians 10:31, NIV.

What must we eliminate from our lives if we would be holy?

"Put to death, therefore, whatever belongs to your earthly nature: sexual immorality, impurity, lust, evil desires and greed, which is idolatry. Because of these, the wrath of God is coming." Colossians 3:5, 6, NIV.

In light of these texts, how can the sinful find salvation?

"If we confess our sins, he is faithful and just and will forgive us our sins and purify us from all unrighteousness." 1 John 1:9, NIV.

IMPORTANCE OF SOUND DOCTRINE

Does it matter what we believe, so long as we are sincere?

"There is a way that seems right to a man, but in the end it leads to death." Proverbs 16:25, NIV.

NOTE.—Doctrine affects the life. Truth leads to life and God; error to death and destruction. No one would think of saying that it doesn't matter what we eat or drink as long as we enjoy it, or what road we travel, as long as we think we are on the right road. Sincerity is a virtue, but it is not the test of sound doctrine. It is God's will that we know the truth, and He has provided many avenues and opportunities for us to learn it.

Did Joshua think it mattered what god Israel served?

"Now fear the Lord and serve him with all faithfulness. *Throw away the gods your forefathers worshiped beyond the River and in Egypt, and serve the Lord*. But if serving the Lord seems undesirable to you, then choose for yourselves this day whom you will serve, whether the gods your forefathers served beyond the River, or the gods of the Amorites, in whose land you are living. But *as for me and my household, we will serve the Lord.*" Joshua 24:14, 15, NIV.

NOTE.—The influence of all idolatrous worship is degrading (see Romans 1:21-32; Numbers 15; 1 Corinthians 10:20; 1 John 5:21).

What advice did Paul give Timothy to help him prepare for the gospel ministry?

"Until I come, devote yourself to the public reading of Scripture, to preaching and to teaching. . . . *Watch your life and doctrine closely.* Persevere in them, because if you do, you will save both yourself and your hearers." 1 Timothy 4:13-16, NIV.

What solemn charge did Paul give him concerning his public work?

"In the presence of God and of Christ Jesus, who will judge the living and the dead, and in view of his appearing and his kingdom, I give you this charge: *Preach the Word; be prepared in season and out of season; correct, rebuke and encourage*—with great patience and careful instruction." 2 Timothy 4:1, 2, NIV.

What similar instruction did Paul give Titus?

"You must *teach what is in accord with sound doctrine.* . . . In everything set them an example by doing what is good. In your teaching show integrity, seriousness and soundness of speech that cannot be condemned." Titus 2:1-7, NIV.

What should we watch out for as Christians?

"Then we will no longer be infants, tossed back and forth by the waves, and blown here and there by every wind of teaching and by *the cunning and craftiness of men in their deceitful scheming.*" Ephesians 4:14, NIV.

What wind did the prophet Jeremiah warn against?

"The prophets are but wind and the word is not in them." Jeremiah 5:13, NIV.

NOTE.—There are many false doctrines that are not sustained by the Word of God.

What danger attends the teaching of false doctrine?

"Avoid godless chatter, because those who indulge in it will become more and more ungodly. Their teaching will spread like gangrene. Among them are Hymenaeus and Philetus, who have wandered away from the truth. They say that the resurrection has already taken place, and they *destroy the faith* of some." 2 Timothy 2:16-18, NIV.

What kind of worship results from false teaching?

"These people honor me with their lips, but their hearts are far from me. *They worship me in vain*; their teachings are but rules taught by men." Matthew 15:8, 9, NIV.

What doctrines will mislead some in the last days?

"The Spirit clearly says that in later times some will abandon the faith and follow deceiving spirits and *things taught by demons*." 1 Timothy 4:1, NIV. (See 2 Peter 2:1.)

What will some prefer to the truth?

"For the time will come when men will not put up with sound doctrine. Instead, to suit their own desires, they will gather around them a great number of teachers to say what their itching ears want to hear. They will turn their ears away from the truth and *turn aside to myths*." 2 Timothy 4:3, 4, NIV.

By what should we test, or prove, all doctrine?

"To the law and to the testimony! If they do not speak according to *this word*, they have no light of dawn." Isaiah 8:20, NIV.

NOTE—The Bible is the test of all doctrine. Whatever does not harmonize and square with this is not to be received.

What are some proper uses of Scripture?

"All Scripture is God-breathed and is *useful for teaching, rebuking, correcting and training in righteousness*." 2 Timothy 3:16, NIV.

What will sound doctrine enable the faithful teacher to do?

"He must hold firmly to the trustworthy message as it has been taught, so that he can *encourage others by sound doctrine and refute those who oppose it*." Titus 1:9, NIV.

What is one characteristic of Jesus' disciples?

"*If you hold to my teaching*, you are really my disciples. Then you will know the truth, and the truth will set you free." John 8:31, 32, NIV.

Through what are they to be sanctified?

"Sanctify them by *the truth*; your word is truth." John 17:17, NIV.

What happens to those who close their ears to truth?

"If anyone turns a deaf ear to the law, *even his prayers are detestable*." Proverbs 28:9, NIV.

What promise is made to those who determine to do God's will?

"If anyone chooses to do God's will, he will find out whether my teaching comes from God or whether I speak on my own." John 7:17, NIV. (See also Psalm 25:9; John 8:12.)

What will God allow to come to those who reject truth?

"The coming of the lawless one will be in accordance with the work of Satan displayed in all kinds of counterfeit miracles, signs and wonders, and in every sort of evil that deceives those who are perishing. They perish because they refused to love the truth and so be saved. For this reason *God sends them a powerful delusion so that they will believe the lie* and so that all will be condemned who have not believed the truth but have delighted in wickedness." 2 Thessalonians 2:9-12, NIV.

What fate awaits self-absorbed teachers and their followers?

"Leave them; they are blind guides. If a blind man leads a blind man, *both will fall into a pit*." Matthew 15:14, NIV.

To whom will the gates of the heavenly city finally be opened?

"Open the gates, that the *righteous nation* which keeps the truth may enter in." Isaiah 26:2, NKJV.

PRESENT TRUTH

What sanctifies us?

"Sanctify them by *the truth*; your word is truth." John 17:17, NIV.

What knowledge does God want us to have?

"This is good, and pleases God our Savior, who wants all men to be saved and to *come to a knowledge of the truth*." 1 Timothy 2:3, 4, NIV.

What must we do in order to be sanctified by this knowledge?

"From the beginning God chose you to be saved through the sanctifying work of the Spirit and through *belief in the truth*." 2 Thessalonians 2:13, NIV.

And what besides a mere belief in the truth is necessary?

"Who have been chosen according to the foreknowledge of God the Father, through the sanctifying work of the Spirit, for *obedience* to Jesus Christ and sprinkling by his blood." 1 Peter 1:2, NIV.

What effect does obedience to the truth have?

"Now that you have *purified yourselves by obeying the truth* so that you have sincere love for your brothers, love one another deeply, from the heart." Verse 22, NIV.

How should the truth be cherished?

"Buy the truth and do not sell it; get wisdom, discipline and understanding." Proverbs 23:23, NIV.

NOTE.—That is, secure the truth at whatever sacrifice or cost, and do not lose it under any consideration.

What was the special message for Noah's day?

"So God said to Noah, 'I am going to put an end to all people, for the earth is filled with violence because of them. *I am surely going to destroy both them and the earth. So make yourself an ark of cypress wood*.' " Genesis 6:13, 14, NIV.

NOTE.—Some truths are applicable in all ages, and are therefore present truth for every generation; others are of special application to one specific generation. They are no less important, however, because of this; for upon their acceptance depends the salvation of that generation. An example of this would be Noah's message of a coming Flood. To Noah's generation that message was present truth; but not to later generations. Similarly, the message of John the Baptist about a soon-coming Messiah would not have been present truth in the generation before or after John's time. The people of the generation before would not have lived to see it fulfilled, and to those not yet born it would have come too late. God's Word contains many general truths, such as love, faith, hope, repentance, obedience, justice, and mercy, which are always in season, and of a saving nature at all times. But whenever God is about to do something special in the world, such as just before the Flood, or the first advent of Jesus, or the Second Coming, God sends a special message of vital importance to His people. This is present truth.

How did Noah show his faith in this message?

"By faith Noah, when warned about things not yet seen, in holy fear *built an ark* to save his family. By his faith he condemned the world and became heir of the righteousness that comes by faith." Hebrews 11:7, NIV.

How many were saved in the ark?

"God waited patiently in the days of Noah while the ark was being built. In it only a few people, *eight in all*, were saved through water." 1 Peter 3:20, NIV.

NOTE.—Doubtless many who were lost in the Flood held, in a

nominal way, to faith in God; but the test as to the genuineness of this came with Noah's special message; and the difference between their faith and his was made plain when they rejected the saving truth for that time—the warning message concerning a coming flood.

What special message for Nineveh was Jonah given?

"Jonah obeyed the word of the Lord and went to Nineveh. . . . He proclaimed: '*Forty more days and Nineveh will be overturned.*' " Jonah 3:3, 4, NIV.

What saved the people from the predicted overthrow?

"The Ninevites believed God. They declared a fast, and all of them, from the greatest to the least, put on sackcloth. . . . When God saw what they did and how *they turned from their evil ways*, he had compassion and did not bring upon them the destruction he had threatened." Jonah 3:5-10, NIV.

NOTE.—God would have likewise spared the antediluvian world had they received Noah's message and turned from their evil ways.

What was the special message of John the Baptist?

"There came a man who was sent from God; his name was John. He came as a witness *to testify concerning that light*, so that through him all men might believe." John 1:6, 7, NIV.

How did he describe his mission?

"I am the voice of one calling in the desert, 'Make straight the way for the Lord.'" Verse 23, NIV.

What impact did John's message have in preparing the way for Jesus?

"All the people, even the tax collectors, when they heard Jesus' words, *acknowledged that God's way was right*, because they had been baptized by John. But *the Pharisees and experts in the law rejected God's purpose for themselves*, because they had not been baptized by John." Luke 7:29, 30, NIV.

Did the leaders of God's chosen people receive Christ when He came?

"He came to that which was his own, but his own did not receive him." John 1:11, NIV.

What reason did they give for not receiving Him?

"We know that God spoke to Moses, but as for this fellow, we don't even know where he comes from." John 9:29, NIV.

NOTE.—These men had faith in the old, but they had no faith in the new. They knew that God had spoken by Moses; they had been raised in a tradition that revered him. But although Jesus came in fulfillment of the prophecies of Moses and the prophets as their long-looked-for Messiah, they were unwilling to risk accepting Him, because they did not understand the prophecies relating to Him, and time had not worked out to their satisfaction the truthfulness of His claims. It required too much faith to accept Christ. It also called for a change of views in some things, and a reformation in life, and might sever them from their friends and deprive them of their status in society. So they rejected Him. They believed in the old truths—Noah and the Flood, Elijah, Daniel and all the prophets; but when it came to this special truth for their time, they refused to accept it.

How did Christ say those who rejected Him reasoned?

"You build tombs for the prophets and decorate the graves of the righteous. And you say, 'If we had lived in the days of our forefathers, we would not have taken part with them in shedding the blood of the prophets.' " Matthew 23:29, 30, NIV.

NOTE.—While these men condemned their ancestors for slaying the prophets who brought God's messages of reproof and warning in times past, they would soon commit an even worse crime by betraying the Son of God to Roman crucifixion. In reality they were no different than their ancestors. Thus we see that present truths are testing truths.

What was the result of the Jewish leadership not accepting Christ?

"As he approached Jerusalem and saw the city, he wept over it and said, 'If you, even you, had only known on this day what would bring you peace—*but now it is hidden from your eyes.*' " Luke 19:41, 42, NIV. "O Jerusalem, Jerusalem, you who kill the prophets and stone those sent to you, how often I have longed to gather your children together, as a hen gathers her chicks under her wings, but you were not willing. Look, your house is left to you *desolate.*" Matthew 23:37, 38, NIV.

Is there to be a special message for the last days?

"So you also must be ready, because the Son of Man will come at an hour when you do not expect him. Who then is the faithful and wise servant, whom the master has put in charge of the servants in his household to give them *their food at the proper time*?" Matthew 24:44, 45, NIV.

NOTE.—In the last days a message will go forth which will be "*food at the proper time*" to the people. This must be the warning concerning the Lord's soon coming, and the preparation necessary to meet Him. Because such a message was not always preached is no evidence that it is not now to be proclaimed.

What does Christ say of that servant who, when He comes, is found giving "food in due season" (NKJV)?

"*It will be good for that servant* whose master finds him doing so when he returns." Verse 46, NIV.

NOTE.—The coming of Christ in glory has been the hope of the faithful in all ages.

What will be the burden of the closing gospel message?

"Fear God and give him glory, because the hour of his judgment has come. Worship him who made the heavens, the earth, the sea and the springs of water.' . . . 'Fallen! Fallen is Babylon the Great, *which made all the nations drink the maddening wine of her adulteries.*' . . . 'If anyone worships the beast and his image and receives his mark on the forehead or the hand, he, too, will drink of the wine of God's fury.' " Revelation 14:7-10, NIV.

How are those who accept this message described?

"This calls for *patient endurance* on the part of the saints who obey God's commandments and remain faithful to Jesus." Verse 12, NIV.

How earnestly is this work to be prosecuted?

"Then the master told his servant, 'Go out to the roads and country lanes and *make them come in*, so that my house will be full.' " Luke 14:23, NIV.

NOTE.—This work is now going on. In every part of the world the sound of this closing gospel message is being heard, and the people are being urged to accept it and to prepare for Christ's coming and kingdom.

THE OBEDIENCE OF FAITH

What did the Lord command Abraham to do?

"The Lord had said to Abram, 'Leave your country, your people and your father's household, and *go to the land I will show you*.' " Genesis 12:1, NIV.

How did Abraham respond to this command?

"*So Abram left*, as the Lord had told him; and Lot went with him. Abram was seventy-five years old when he set out from Haran." Verse 4, NIV.

How did Abraham's faith relate to his obedience?

"By *faith* Abraham, when called to go to a place he would later receive as an inheritance, obeyed and went, even though he did not know where he was going." Hebrews 11:8, NIV.

What shocking command did the Lord later give to Abraham?

"Then God said, '*Take your son*, your only son, *Isaac*, whom you love, and go to the region of Moriah. *Sacrifice him* there as a burnt offering on one of the mountains I will tell you about.'" Genesis 22:2, NIV.

What happened when Abraham set out to follow this strange command from God?

"Early the next morning Abraham got up and saddled his donkey. He took with him two of his servants and his son Isaac. When he had cut enough wood for the burnt offering, he set out for the place God had told him about. On the third day Abraham looked up and saw the place in the distance. He said to his servants, 'Stay here with the donkey while I and the boy go over there. We will worship and then we will come back to you.'

"Abraham took the wood for the burnt offering and placed it on his son Isaac, and he himself carried the fire and the knife. As the two of them went on together, Isaac spoke up and said to his father Abraham, 'Father?'

" 'Yes, my son?' Abraham replied.

" 'The fire and wood are here,' Isaac said, 'but where is the lamb for the burnt offering?'

"Abraham answered, 'God himself will provide the lamb for the burnt offering, my son.' And the two of them went on together.

"When they reached the place God had told him about, Abraham built an altar there and arranged the wood on it. He bound his son Isaac and laid him on the altar, on top of the wood. Then he reached out his hand and took the knife to slay his son. But the angel of the Lord called out to him from heaven, 'Abraham! Abraham!'

" 'Here I am,' he replied.

" 'Do not lay a hand on the boy,' he said. 'Do not do anything to him. Now I know that you fear God, because you have not withheld from me your son, your only son.'

"Abraham looked up and there in a thicket he saw a ram caught by its horns. He went over and took the ram and sacrificed it as a burnt offering instead of his son. So Abraham called that place The Lord Will Provide. And to this day it is said, 'On the mountain of the Lord it will be provided.' " Genesis 22:3-14, NIV.

Upon what ground were the previous promises then renewed to Abraham?

"The angel of the Lord called to Abraham from heaven a second time and said, 'I swear by myself, declares the Lord, that *because you have done this and have not withheld your son*, your only son, I will surely bless you and make your descendants as numerous as the stars in the sky and as the sand on the seashore. Your descendants will take possession of the cities of their enemies, and through your offspring all nations on earth will be blessed, because you have obeyed me.' " Verses 15-18, NIV.

What enabled Abraham to endure this test?

"By *faith* Abraham, when God tested him, offered Isaac as a sacrifice. He who had received the promises was about to sacrifice his one and only son, even though God had said to him, 'It is through Isaac that your offspring will be reckoned.' Abraham reasoned that God could raise the dead, and figuratively speaking, he did receive Isaac back from death." Hebrews 11:17-19, NIV.

Of what value were the works of Abraham?

"Was not Abraham our father *justified* by works when he offered Isaac his son on the altar?" James 2:21, NKJV.

NOTE.—Works can never be the ground or basis or cause of justification, but they are an essential evidence, proof, and result of it. They are the fruit of God's work in the life. Fruitless trees are cut down, and fruitless vines are cut off (Matthew 3:10; 7:19; Luke 13:7; John 15:2; Hebrews 6:7, 8; Jude 12), because the lack of fruit indicates that the tree is dead. Hence "faith [i.e., mere mental assent] without works is dead." James 2:26. (See also verse 17.)

How did Abraham's works show that his faith was complete?

"You see that *his faith and his actions were working together*, and his faith was made complete by what he did." James 2:22, NIV.

What Old Testament statement showed Abraham's obedience?

"And the scripture was fulfilled that says, *'Abraham believed God*, and it was credited to him as righteousness,' and he was called God's friend." Verse 23, NIV.

NOTE.—James is quoting Genesis 15:6.

What kind of faith has value with God?

"For in Christ Jesus neither circumcision nor uncircumcision has any value. The only thing that counts is *faith expressing itself through love*." Galatians 5:6, NIV.

NOTE.—True justifying faith results in obedience and good works. Those who say but don't do are not people of faith. God-pleasing obedience is the fruit of faith that takes God at His word, and submits to the working of His power. Such faith is fully assured that what God has promised He is able also to perform (see Romans 4:21, 22).

For what purpose is the mystery of the gospel made known?

"Now to him who is able to establish you by my gospel and the proclamation of Jesus Christ, according to the revelation of the mystery hidden for long ages past, but now revealed and made known through the prophetic writings by the command of the eternal God, *so that all nations might believe and obey him*." Romans 16:25, 26, NIV.

For what purpose is the grace of Christ received?

"Through him and for his name's sake, we received grace and apostleship *to call people from among all the Gentiles to the obedience that comes from faith*." Romans 1:5, NIV.

What effect did the apostles' preaching have upon the people of Jerusalem after Pentecost?

"And the word of God increased; and *the number of the disciples multiplied in Jerusalem greatly; and a great company of the priests were obedient to the faith*." Acts 6:7.

What effect did Paul's preaching have upon the Gentiles?

"I will not venture to speak of anything except what Christ has accomplished through me in *leading the Gentiles to obey God* by what I have said and done." Romans 15:18, NIV.

When King Saul disregarded God's instructions, the prophet Samuel told him how highly God regards obedience.

"But Samuel replied: 'Does the Lord delight in burnt offerings and sacrifices as much as obeying the voice of the Lord? *To obey is better than sacrifice*, and to heed is better than the fat of rams.' " 1 Samuel 15:22, NIV.

With what sins are rebellion and stubbornness classed?

"For rebellion is like the sin of *divination*, and arrogance like the evil of *idolatry*. Because you have rejected the word of the Lord, he has rejected you as king." Verse 23, NIV.

NOTE.—In God's eyes, rebellion and arrogance are as wrong as idolatry and sorcery.

Whose voice had more weight with Saul than God's commands?

"Then Saul said to Samuel, 'I have sinned. I violated the Lord's command and your instructions. *I was afraid of the people and so I gave in to them*." Verse 24, NIV.

What example of obedience did Jesus set for us?

"And being found in appearance as a man, he humbled himself and became obedient to death—even death on a cross!" Philippians 2:8, NIV.

At what cost did even Jesus learn the lesson of obedience?

"Although he was a son, he learned obedience from what he *suffered*." Hebrews 5:8, NIV.

To whom did Jesus become the source of salvation?

"And, once made perfect, he became the source of eternal salvation *for all who obey him*." Verse 9, NIV.

How complete should this obedience be?

"We demolish arguments and every pretension that sets itself up against the knowledge of God, and we take captive every thought to make it obedient to Christ." 2 Corinthians 10:5, NIV.

What charge did Jesus bring against the Pharisees?

"And he said to them: *'You have a fine way of setting aside the commands of God in order to observe your own traditions!'* " Mark 7:9, NIV.

NOTE.—Human tradition is simply the voice of humanity preserved in the church. To follow the traditions of individuals instead of obeying the commandments of God is to repeat the sin of Saul.

What will be the fate of those who do not obey the gospel of Christ?

"God is just: He will pay back trouble to those who trouble you and give relief to you who are troubled, and to us as well. This will happen when the Lord Jesus is revealed from heaven in blazing fire with his powerful angels. *He will punish those who do not know God and do not obey the gospel of our Lord Jesus*." 2 Thessalonians 1:6-8, NIV.

Obedience to the truth will lead to what goal?

"Now that you have purified yourselves by obeying the truth so that you have sincere love for your brothers, *love one another deeply*, from the heart." 1 Peter 1:22, NIV.

What promise is made to the obedient?

"If you are willing and obedient, you *will eat the best from the land.*" Isaiah 1:19, NIV.

Whose example are we urged to imitate?

"We do not want you to become lazy, but to *imitate those who through faith and patience inherit what has been promised.*" Hebrews 6:12, NIV.

CHAPTER 4

The Life of Christ

More has been written about Jesus than any other person in history, yet He remains largely misunderstood. Millions view Jesus as kind, caring, and self-sacrificing, yet few study His mission and Messiahship. Too few allow Jesus to guide their lives.

Jim Wallis has written, "The phrases 'Jesus saves' or 'Jesus is Lord' have been so often used in the absence of any visible historical application that most people simply do not know what the words mean anymore. Perhaps never before has Jesus' name been more frequently mentioned and the content of His life and teachings so thoroughly ignored."

May this chapter point you to Jesus as your Savior and Friend, and inspire you to search the Scriptures to better know and follow Him.

BIRTH, CHILDHOOD, AND EARLY LIFE OF CHRIST

Where was Christ to be born?

"After Jesus was born in *Bethlehem* in Judea, during the time of King Herod, Magi from the east came to Jerusalem and asked, 'Where is the one who has been born king of the Jews? We saw his star in the east and have come to worship him.' When Herod heard this he was disturbed, and all Jerusalem with him. When he had called together all the people's chief priests and teachers of the law, he asked them where the Christ was to be born. 'In Bethlehem of Judea,' they replied, 'for this is what the prophet has written: " 'But you, *Bethlehem*, in the land of Judah, are by no means least among the rulers of Judah; for out of you will come a ruler who will be the shepherd of my people Israel.' " Matthew 2:1-6, NIV.

NOTE.—The priests and teachers of the law are here quoting Micah 5:2.

To whom was Christ to be born?

"Behold, *a virgin* shall conceive, and bear a son, and shall call His name Immanuel." Isaiah 7:14.

NOTE.—Immanuel means "God with us" (see Matthew 1:23).

What name did the angel give the child before His birth?

"She will give birth to a son, and you are to give him the name

Jesus, because he will save his people from their sins." Matthew 1:21, NIV.

At Jesus' birth, what did the angel say to the shepherds of Bethlehem?

"But the angel said to them, 'Do not be afraid. I bring you good news of great joy that will be for all the people. *Today* in the town of David *a Savior has been born to you; he is Christ the Lord*. This will be a sign to you: You will find a baby wrapped in cloths and lying in a manger.' " Luke 2:10-12, NIV.

What song did the angels sing in Jesus' honor?

"Suddenly a great company of the heavenly host appeared with the angel, praising God and saying, *'Glory to God in the highest, and on earth peace to men on whom his favor rests.'* " Verses 13, 14, NIV.

What prophecy of Isaiah was fulfilled at Christ's birth?

"*For to us a child is born, to us a son is given*, and the government will be on his shoulders." Isaiah 9:6, NIV.

What did Isaiah say His name should be called?

"And he will be called *Wonderful Counselor, Mighty God, Everlasting Father, Prince of Peace*. Of the increase of his government and peace there will be no end." Verses 6, 7, NIV.

What did the devout Simeon say when he saw the child Jesus?

"Now there was a man in Jerusalem called Simeon, who was righteous and devout. He was waiting for the consolation of Israel, and the Holy Spirit was upon him. It had been revealed to him by the Holy Spirit that he would not die before he had seen the Lord's Christ. Moved by the Spirit, he went into the temple courts. When the parents brought in the child Jesus to do for him what the custom of the Law required, Simeon took him in his arms and praised God, saying: 'Sovereign Lord, as you have promised, you now dismiss your servant in peace. *For my eyes have seen your salvation, which you have prepared in the sight of all people, a light for revelation to the Gentiles and for glory to your people Israel*." Luke 2:25-32, NIV.

What did the aged prophet Anna do at the sight of Jesus?

"Coming up to them at that very moment, *she gave thanks to God* and spoke about the child to all who were looking forward to the redemption of Jerusalem." Verse 38, NIV.

What did the Wise Men of the East do when they found Jesus?

"On coming to the house, they saw the child with his mother Mary, and they *bowed down and worshiped him*. Then they opened their treasures and *presented him with gifts of gold* and of incense and of myrrh." Matthew 2:11, NIV.

How did Jesus come to live for a time in Egypt?

"When they had gone, an angel of the Lord appeared to Joseph in a dream 'Get up,' he said, 'take the child and his mother and escape to Egypt. Stay there until I tell you, for Herod is going to search for the child to kill him.'" Verse 13, NIV.

How does Revelation describe this satanic desire to destroy Christ?

"The dragon stood in front of the woman who was about to give birth, so that he might devour her child the moment it was born." Revelation 12:4, NIV.

By what means did Herod seek to destroy Christ?

"When Herod realized that he had been outwitted by the Magi, he was furious, and *he gave orders to kill all the boys in Bethlehem* and its vicinity who were two years old and under, in accordance with the time he had learned from the Magi." Matthew 2:16, NIV.

After Herod's death, where did Joseph and his family live?

"And *he went and lived in a town called Nazareth*. So was fulfilled what was said through the prophets: 'He will be called a Nazarene.'" Verse 23, NIV.

What is said of Jesus' childhood and early life?

"And the child *grew and became strong; he was filled with wisdom, and the grace of God was upon him*. . . . Then he went down to Nazareth with them and *was obedient to them*." Luke 2:40-51, NIV.

How did Joseph and Mary, upon returning from a feast at Jerusalem, lose Jesus when He was 12 years old?

"*Thinking he was in their company, they traveled on for a day*. Then they began looking for him among their relatives and friends. When they did not find him, they went back to Jerusalem to look for him." Verses 44, 45, NIV.

What was Jesus doing when they found Him?

"After three days they found him in the temple courts, *sitting*

among the teachers, listening to them and asking them questions."
Verse 46, NIV.

How did His questions and answers impress those who heard Him?
"*Everyone who heard him was amazed* at his understanding and
his answers." Verse 47, NIV.

How do the Scriptures sum up the record of Christ's early life?
"*And Jesus grew in wisdom and stature, and in favor with God
and men.*" Verse 52, NIV.

A SINLESS LIFE

How spotless was Christ's life on earth?
"To this you were called, because Christ suffered for you, leaving
you an example, that you should follow in his steps. 'He committed
no sin, and no deceit was found in his mouth.' " 1 Peter 2:21, 22, NIV.

NOTE.—Peter is quoting Isaiah 53:9, from Isaiah's moving "suffering servant" chapter.

What is true of all other members of the human family?
"*For all have sinned*, and come short of the glory of God." Romans 3:23.

What is one question Jesus used to challenge His enemies?
"*Can any of you prove me guilty of sin?* " John 8:46, NIV.

To what extent was Christ tempted?
"For we do not have a high priest who is unable to sympathize
with our weaknesses, but we have one who has been tempted *in every
way*, just as we are—yet was without sin." Hebrews 4:15, NIV.

In His humanity, of what nature did Christ partake?
"Since the children have *flesh and blood*, he too shared in their humanity so that by his death he might destroy him who holds the power
of death—that is, the devil—and free those who all their lives were
held in slavery by their fear of death." Hebrews 2:14, NIV.

How fully did Christ share our common humanity?
"For this reason he had to be made like his brothers *in every way*,
in order that he might become a merciful and faithful high priest in
service to God, and that he might make atonement for the sins of the
people." Verse 17, NIV.

NOTE.—Jesus Christ is both Son of God and Son of man. As a member of the human family he became "like his brothers in every way"—"in the likeness of sinful flesh." Just how far that "likeness" goes is a mystery of the Incarnation that humans have never been able to solve. The Bible clearly teaches that Christ was tempted just as we are tempted—"in all points . . . like as we are." Such temptation must necessarily include the possibility of sinning; but Christ was without sin. There is no Bible support for the teaching that the mother of Christ, by an immaculate conception, was cut off from the sinful inheritance of the race, and therefore her divine Son was incapable of sinning. Concerning this false doctrine Dean F. W. Farrar has well said:

"Some, in a zeal at once intemperate and ignorant, have claimed for Him not only an actual sinlessness but a nature to which sin was divinely and miraculously impossible. What then? If His great conflict were a mere deceptive phantasmagoria, how can the narrative of it profit us? If we have to fight the battle clad in that armor of human free-will, . . . what comfort is it to us if our great Captain fought not only victoriously, but without real danger; not only uninjured, but without even the possibility of a wound. . . . Let us beware of contradicting the express teaching of the Scriptures, . . . by a supposition that He was not liable to real temptation." *The Life of Christ* (1883 ed.), vol. 1, p. 57.

What victory did Christ win for us over temptation and sin?

"For what the law could not do, in that it was weak through the flesh, God sending his own Son in the likeness of sinful flesh, and for sin, *condemned sin in the flesh: that the righteousness of the law might be fulfilled in us*, who walk not after the flesh, but after the Spirit." Romans 8:3, 4.

NOTE.—God, in Christ, condemned sin, not merely by pronouncing against it as a judge, but by coming and living in the flesh, and yet without sinning. In Christ He demonstrated that it is possible, by His grace and power, for the righteousness of the law to be fulfilled in us.

By whose power did Christ live the perfect life?

"By myself I can do nothing." John 5:30, NIV. "The words I say to you are not just my own. Rather, *it is the Father, living in me, who is doing his work*." John 14:10, NIV.

NOTE.—In His humanity Christ was as dependent upon divine power to do the works of God as is any human to do the same thing. He employed no means to live a holy life that are not available to every human being. Through Him we may have God dwelling in us "to will and to act according to his good purpose" (Philippians 2:13, NIV), and we may "participate in the divine nature" (2 Peter 1:4, NIV).

What unselfish purpose did Jesus ever have before Him?

"For I have come down from heaven *not to do my will but to do the will of him who sent me.*" John 6:38, NIV.

OUR PATTERN

In whose steps should we follow?

"To this you were called, because Christ suffered for you, *leaving you an example, that you should follow in his steps.*" 1 Peter 2:21, NIV.

How should the Christian walk?

"Whoever claims to live in him must walk *as Jesus did.*" 1 John 2:6, NIV. (See also Colossians 2:6.)

Whose attitude should we share?

"Your attitude should be the same as *that of Christ Jesus.*" Philippians 2:5, NIV.

NOTE.—The mind of Christ was characterized by humility (verses 6-8); dependence on God (John 5:19, 30); a determination to do only the Father's will (John 5:30; 6:38); thoughtfulness of others (Acts 10:38); and a willingness to sacrifice and suffer, and even to die, for the good of others (2 Corinthians 8:9; Romans 5:6-8; 1 Peter 2:24).

According to Paul, what are some hallmarks of Jesus' attitude?

"Do nothing out of selfish ambition or vain conceit, but in humility consider others better than yourselves. Each of you should look not only to your own interests, but also to the interests of others." Philippians 2:3, 4, NIV.

What example did Jesus set concerning baptism?

"Then Jesus came from Galilee to the Jordan *to be baptized by John.* But John tried to deter him, saying, 'I need to be baptized by you, and do you come to me?' Jesus replied, 'Let it be so now; it is proper for us to do this to fulfill all righteousness.' Then John consented." Matthew 3:13-15, NIV.

How did Jesus show that a life of prayer and devotion was necessary for His followers?

"One of those days Jesus went out to a mountainside to pray, and spent the night praying to God." Luke 6:12, NIV. "He took Peter, John and James with him and went up onto a mountain to pray." Luke 9:28, NIV.

To what kind of work did Jesus devote His life?

"You know . . . how God anointed Jesus of Nazareth with the Holy Spirit and power, and how he went around *doing good* and healing all who were under the power of the devil, because God was with him." Acts 10:37, 38, NIV.

For whom and why did Christ leave the riches of heaven?

"For you know the grace of our Lord Jesus Christ, that though he was rich, yet *for your sakes* he became poor, so that you through his poverty might become rich." 2 Corinthians 8:9, NIV.

When He was reviled and mistreated, what did He do?

"When they hurled their insults at him, *he did not retaliate*; when he suffered, *he made no threats*. Instead, he entrusted himself to him who judges justly." 1 Peter 2:23, NIV.

How did He pray for those who crucified Him?

"Jesus said, *'Father, forgive them*, for they do not know what they are doing.'" Luke 23:34, NIV. (See Acts 3:17.)

What is the inspired testimony about Jesus?

"*You have loved righteousness and hated wickedness*; therefore God, your God, has set you above your companions by anointing you with the oil of joy." Hebrews 1:9, NIV.

NOTE.—The author of Hebrews is quoting Psalm 45:6, 7.

OUR HELPER AND FRIEND

How did the prophet Zechariah represent Jesus' cleansing of our sins?

"On that day *a fountain* will be opened to the house of David and the inhabitants of Jerusalem, to cleanse them from sin and impurity." Zechariah 13:1, NIV.

NOTE.—Jesus' sacrifice provided for us a spiritual fountain of grace in which our stains of sin may be washed away.

For what purpose did Christ come to this world?

"For the Son of Man came *to seek and to save what was lost*." Luke 19:10, NIV. (See also Hebrews 2:9.)

Through what was Christ made a complete and perfect Savior?

"In bringing many sons to glory, it was fitting that God, for whom and through whom everything exists, should make the author of their salvation perfect *through suffering*." Hebrews 2:10, NIV.

Because of this, what is Christ able to do?

"Because he himself suffered when he was tempted, he is able *to help those who are being tempted*." Verse 18, NIV.

How complete a Savior is Jesus?

"Therefore he is able to save *completely* those who come to God through him, because he always lives to intercede for them." Hebrews 7:25, NIV.

What is Jesus able to keep us from?

"To him who is able to keep you *from falling* and *to present you before his glorious presence without fault* and with great joy—to the only God our Savior be glory, majesty, power and authority, through Jesus Christ our Lord, before all ages, now and forevermore! Amen." Jude 24, 25, NIV.

What does Jesus call those who accept Him?

"I no longer call you servants, because a servant does not know his master's business. Instead, I have called you *friends*, for everything that I learned from my Father I have made known to you." John 15:15, NIV.

What kind of friend is He?

"There is a friend *who sticks closer than a brother*." Proverbs 18:24, NIV.

What is the mark of a true friend?

"A friend *loves at all times*." Proverbs 17:17, NIV.

What has God promised those who trust in Christ?

"God has said, *'Never will I leave you; never will I forsake you.'* So we say with confidence, 'The Lord is my helper; I will not be afraid. What can man do to me?'" Hebrews 13:5, 6, NIV.

NOTE.—Hebrews is quoting Deuteronomy 31:6, 8, and Psalm 118:6, 7.

CHRIST'S MINISTRY

With what words did John the Baptist announce Jesus' ministry?

"I baptize you with water for repentance. But after me will come one who is more powerful than I, whose sandals I am not fit to carry. *He will baptize you with the Holy Spirit and with fire.*" Matthew 3:11, NIV.

How old was Jesus when He began His ministry?

"Now Jesus himself was *about thirty years old* when he began his ministry." Luke 3:23, NIV.

By what miraculous manifestations was His ministry opened?

"At that time Jesus came from Nazareth in Galilee and was baptized by John in the Jordan. As Jesus was coming up out of the water, he saw heaven being torn open and *the Spirit descending on him like a dove. And a voice came from heaven: 'You are my Son, whom I love; with you I am well pleased.*' " Mark 1:9-11, NIV.

Before Jesus began His ministry, what difficult experience did He pass through?

"At once the Spirit sent him out into the desert, and he was in the desert forty days, being tempted by Satan. He was with the wild animals, and angels attended him." Verses 12, 13, NIV. (See also Matthew 4:1-11; Luke 4:1-13.)

How was Jesus empowered for His work?

"*How God anointed Jesus of Nazareth with the Holy Spirit and power*, and how he went around doing good and healing all who were under the power of the devil, because God was with him." Acts 10:38, NIV.

Where did Jesus begin His ministry?

"Jesus returned to *Galilee* in the power of the Spirit, and news about him spread through the whole countryside. He taught in their synagogues, and everyone praised him." Luke 4:14, 15, NIV.

How did Jesus announce His mission in Nazareth?

"He went to Nazareth, where he had been brought up, and on the Sabbath day he went into the synagogue, as was his custom. And he stood up to read. The scroll of the prophet Isaiah was handed to him. Unrolling it, he found the place where it is written: 'The Spirit of the Lord is on me, because he has anointed me to preach good news to the poor. He has sent me to proclaim freedom for the prisoners and recovery of sight for the blind, to release the oppressed, to proclaim the year of the Lord's favor.' . . . *He began by saying to them, 'Today this scripture is fulfilled in your hearing.' "* Verses 16-21, NIV.

How were the people impressed with His preaching?

"All spoke well of him and *were amazed at the gracious words that came from his lips.*" Verse 22, NIV.

Why were the people at Capernaum astonished at His teaching?

"Then he went down to Capernaum, a town in Galilee, and on the Sabbath began to teach the people. They were amazed at his teaching, *because his message had authority.*" Verses 31, 32, NIV.

Wherein did His teaching differ from that of the scribes?

"When Jesus had finished saying these things, the crowds were amazed at his teaching, because he taught as one who had authority, and not as their teachers of the law." Matthew 7:28, 29, NIV.

How did the crowds receive Christ?

"The large crowd listened to him *with delight.*" Mark 12:37, NIV.

What did Jesus do besides preach?

"Jesus went throughout Galilee, *teaching* in their synagogues, preaching the good news of the kingdom, and *healing* every disease and sickness among the people." Matthew 4:23, NIV.

NOTE.—In His ministry Jesus combined plain teaching with practical, helpful relief work.

How extensive was His fame, and how many were attracted to Him?

"News about him spread *all over Syria*, and people brought to him all who were ill with various diseases, those suffering severe pain, the demon-possessed, those having seizures, and the paralyzed, and he healed them. Large crowds from *Galilee, the Decapolis, Jerusalem, Judea and the region across the Jordan* followed him." Verses 24, 25, NIV.

What expression shows Christ's deep sympathy with humanity?

"When he saw the crowds, he *had compassion* on them, because they were harassed and helpless, like sheep without a shepherd."

Matthew 9:36, NIV. "When Jesus landed and saw a large crowd, he had *compassion* on them and healed their sick." Matthew 14:14, NIV.

In what few words did Christ sum up His mission?

"For the Son of Man came *to seek and to save what was lost*." Luke 19:10, NIV.

How did Christ feel over Jerusalem's lack of repentance?

"As he approached Jerusalem and saw the city, he wept over it." Verse 41, NIV.

NOTE.—In no other place did Jesus appear so much a reformer as in Jerusalem, the headquarters of the Jewish religion, which, despite having come from Christ Himself, had become mere formalism and a round of ceremony (see, for example, Isaiah 1:13-20; Malachi 2:1-9; John 5). Jesus put His reform into action by cleansing the Temple (Matthew 21:12-16; cf. John 2:13-18).

CHRIST THE GREAT TEACHER

When the chief priests and Pharisees sent officers to arrest Jesus, what report did they bring back?

"No one ever spoke the way this man does." John 7:46, NIV.

How did Christ teach the people?

"He taught *as one who had authority*, and not as their teachers of the law." Matthew 7:29, NIV.

NOTE.—"The teaching of the scribes and elders was cold and formal, like a lesson learned by rote. To them the Word of God possessed no vital power. Their own ideas and traditions were substituted for its teaching. In the accustomed round of service they professed to explain the law, but no inspiration from God stirred their own hearts or the hearts of their hearers." Ellen G. White, *The Desire of Ages*, p. 253.

How freely was the Holy Spirit conferred on Jesus?

"For the one whom God has sent speaks the words of God, *for God gives the Spirit without limit*." John 3:34, NIV.

What question did Jesus' teaching inspire?

"Coming to his hometown, he began teaching the people in their synagogue, and they were amazed. *'Where did this man get this wisdom and these miraculous powers?'* they asked." Matthew 13:54, NIV.

What did Isaiah say Christ would do with the law?

"The Lord is well pleased for His righteousness' sake; He will *exalt the law and make it honorable*." Isaiah 42:21, NKJV.

What did Christ say in response to the idea that He might abolish God's law?

"Do not think that I have come to abolish the Law or the Prophets; *I have not come to abolish them but to fulfill them*. I tell you the truth, *until heaven and earth disappear, not the smallest letter, not the least stroke of a pen, will by any means disappear from the Law* until everything is accomplished. Anyone who breaks one of the least of these commandments and teaches others to do the same will be called least in the kingdom of heaven, but whoever practices and teaches these commands will be called great in the kingdom of heaven. For I tell you that unless your righteousness surpasses that of the Pharisees and the teachers of the law, you will certainly not enter the kingdom of heaven." Matthew 5:17-20, NIV.

How did the Pharisee Nicodemus begin his conversation with Jesus?

"He came to Jesus at night and said, 'Rabbi, *we know you are a teacher who has come from God*. For no one could perform the miraculous signs you are doing if God were not with him." John 3:2, NIV.

How did the Samaritan woman at Jacob's well react to meeting Jesus?

"Then, leaving her water jar, the woman went back to the town and said to the people, 'Come, see a man who told me everything I ever did. *Could this be the Christ?*' " John 4:28, 29, NIV.

How were the two on the road to Emmaus affected by Jesus' conversation with them?

"They asked each other, *'Were not our hearts burning within us as he talked with us on the road* and opened the Scriptures to us?' " Luke 24:32, NIV.

What did Jesus direct their attention to as they traveled?

"And beginning with Moses and all the Prophets, he explained to them *what was said in all the Scriptures concerning himself*. . . . He said to them, 'This is what I told you while I was still with you: Everything must be fulfilled that is written about me in the Law of Moses, the Prophets and the Psalms.' Then he opened their minds so they could understand the Scriptures." Verses 27-45, NIV.

How does the Bible encourage Jesus' followers to look for the fulfillment of prophecy?

"So when you see standing in the holy place 'the abomination that causes desolation,' spoken of through the prophet Daniel—*let the reader understand*—then let those who are in Judea flee to the mountains." Matthew 24:15, 16, NIV.

Jesus and the Bible

Christ was a faithful student, a consistent user, and a perfect expounder of the Scriptures. He met temptation with the Scriptures; He proved His Messiahship by the Scriptures; He taught from the Scriptures; and He told His disciples to look to the Scriptures as their guide for the future.

PARABLES OF CHRIST

What reference does Psalms make to the use of parables?

"I will open my mouth in parables, I will utter hidden things, things from of old." Psalm 78:2, NIV.

NOTE.—A parable is an analogy, a comparison or similitude; specifically it is a short story or narrative drawn from life or nature, by means of which some important lesson is taught, or some moral drawn. Using a story to convey truth can be far more effective than merely stating the truth, for the truth may be disturbing, and the story provides a vehicle by which truth can slip into the heart past the sentinel of prejudice.

Are there examples of parables in the Old Testament Scriptures?

Yes. "The Lord sent Nathan to David. When he came to him, he said, 'There were two men in a certain town, one rich and the other poor. The rich man had a very large number of sheep and cattle, but the poor man had nothing except one little ewe lamb he had bought. He raised it, and it grew up with him and his children. It shared his food, drank from his cup and even slept in his arms. It was like a daughter to him. Now a traveler came to the rich man, but the rich man refrained from taking one of his own sheep or cattle to prepare a meal for the traveler who had come to him. Instead, he took the ewe lamb that belonged to the poor man and prepared it for the one who had come to him.'

"David burned with anger against the man and said to Nathan, 'As surely as the Lord lives, the man who did this deserves to die! He must pay for that lamb four times over, because he did such a thing and had no pity.'

"Then Nathan said to David, 'You are the man!'" 2 Samuel 12:1-7, NIV.

NOTE.—Compare the parable of the trees, Judges 9:8-15; the story of the thistle in 2 Kings 14:9; etc. Jesus adopted this tried-and-true method of conveying truth.

From what sources did Christ usually draw His parables?

From nature and from everyday experiences.

Following one of His parables, what did Jesus say?

"He who has ears, let him hear." Matthew 13:9, NIV.

What question did the disciples then ask?

"The disciples came to him and asked, *'Why do you speak to the people in parables?'* " Verse 10, NIV.

What reply did Jesus give?

"He replied, *'The knowledge of the secrets of the kingdom of heaven has been given to you, but not to them.* Whoever has will be given more, and he will have an abundance. Whoever does not have, even what he has will be taken from him. This is why I speak to them in parables: 'Though seeing, they do not see; though hearing, they do not understand.' " Verses 11-13, NIV.

NOTE.—Christ's object in using parables was to teach the mysteries, or truths, of the kingdom of heaven—truths not necessarily difficult to understand, but that had long been hidden or obscured by sin, apostasy, and tradition—in such a way that the spiritual-minded might understand them, and the worldly-minded would not. When asked the meaning of any parable, Christ readily explained it to His disciples (see Luke 8:9-15; Matthew 13:36-43; Mark 4:33, 34).

After he told a parable, what question did Christ frequently ask His disciples?

" *'Have you understood all these things?'* Jesus asked. 'Yes,' they replied." Matthew 13:51, NIV.

How extensively did Christ make use of parables?

"Jesus spoke all these things to the crowd in parables; *he did not say anything to them without using a parable.*" Verse 34, NIV.

NOTE.—Parables are simply stories. All, young and old, like to hear a story. Storytelling is one of the most successful means of awakening an interest, securing attention, and teaching, illustrating, and enforcing important truths. Christ, the greatest of all teachers, recognized this, and therefore made constant use of this method of instruction.

How did Jesus suggest that His disciples follow His example in teaching gospel truth?

"He said to them, 'Therefore every teacher of the law who has been instructed about the kingdom of heaven is like the owner of a house *who brings out of his storeroom new treasures as well as old*.' " Verse 52, NIV.

What are some of Christ's most touching and important parables?

The parable of the lost sheep, and that of the prodigal son. (See Luke 15:3-7, 11-32.)

"So wide was Christ's view of truth, so extended His teaching, that every phase of nature was employed in illustrating truth. The scenes upon which the eye daily rests were all connected with some spiritual truth, so that nature is clothed with the parables of the Master.

"In the earlier part of His ministry, Christ had spoken to the people in words so plain that all His hearers might have grasped truths which would make them wise unto salvation. But in many hearts the truth had taken no root, and it had been quickly caught away. 'Therefore speak I to them in parables,' He said, 'because they seeing see not; and hearing they hear not, neither do they understand. . . . For this people's heart is waxed gross, and their ears are dull of hearing, and their eyes they have closed.' Matthew 13:13-15.

"Jesus desired to awaken inquiry. He sought to arouse the careless, and impress truth upon the heart. Parable teaching was popular, and commanded the respect and attention, not only of the Jews, but of the people of other nations. No more effective method of instruction could He have employed. If His hearers had desired a knowledge of divine things, they might have understood His words; for He was always willing to explain them to the honest inquirer.

"Again, Christ had truths to present which the people were unprepared to accept or even to understand. For this reason also He taught them in parables. By connecting His teaching with the scenes of life, experience, or nature, He secured their attention and impressed their hearts. Afterward, as they looked upon the objects that illustrated His lessons, they recalled the words of the divine Teacher. To minds that were open to the Holy Spirit, the significance of the Savior's teaching unfolded more and more. Mysteries grew clear, and that which had been hard to grasp became evident.

"Jesus sought an avenue to every heart. By using a variety of illustrations, He not only presented truth in its different phases, but appealed to the different hearers. Their interest was aroused by figures drawn from the surroundings of their daily life. None who listened to the Savior could feel that they were neglected or forgotten. The humblest, the most sinful, heard in His teaching a voice that spoke to them in sympathy and tenderness." Ellen G. White, *Christ's Object Lessons*, pp. 20-22.

MIRACLES OF CHRIST

What testimony did Jesus' enemies bear concerning His work?

"Then the chief priests and the Pharisees called a meeting of the Sanhedrin. 'What are we accomplishing?' they asked. 'Here is this man *performing many miraculous signs*.' " John 11:47, NIV.

NOTE.—Even Jesus' enemies agreed that He worked miracles (compare Mark 3:22). Even the Jewish Talmud admits that Jesus worked miracles, quoting rabbis who lived around the end of the first century, although they called it sorcery. Likewise with the second-century skeptic Celsus.

What proved that Christ had been approved by God?

"Men of Israel, listen to this: Jesus of Nazareth was a man accredited by God to you by *miracles, wonders and signs*, which God did among you through him, as you yourselves know." Acts 2:22, NIV.

By what means did Christ claim to cast out demons?

"But if I drive out demons by *the finger of God*, then the kingdom of God has come to you." Luke 11:20, NIV. Matthew 12:28 says "by the Spirit of God."

NOTE.—Under the third plague in Egypt—that of turning the dust into lice—the magicians, failing to duplicate it, said to Pharaoh, "This is the finger of God." Exodus 8:18, 19, NIV.

What convinced Nicodemus that Jesus was a teacher from God?

"He came to Jesus at night and said, 'Rabbi, we know you are a teacher who has come from God. For *no one could perform the miraculous signs you are doing if God was not with him*.' " John 3:2, NIV.

After Jesus healed a blind man on the Sabbath, how did Pharisees criticize Jesus?

"Some of the Pharisees said, 'This man is not from God, *for he does not keep the Sabbath*.' " John 9:16, NIV.

NOTE.—This was a false charge. Christ did keep the Sabbath, but not according to the Pharisees' idea of Sabbathkeeping (pp. 363-368).

What question did others raise in opposition to this view?

"But others asked, *'How can a sinner do such miraculous signs?'* So they were divided." Verse 16, NIV.

What impact did Jesus' miracles have?

"Now while he was in Jerusalem at the Passover Feast, *many people saw the miraculous signs he was doing and believed in his name*." John 2:23, NIV. "Still, *many in the crowd put their faith in him*. They said, 'When the Christ comes, will he do more miraculous signs than this man?' " John 7:31, NIV.

Why were many attracted to Christ?

"A great crowd of people followed him *because they saw the miraculous signs* he had performed on the sick." John 6:2.

NOTE.—A miracle is the display of divine or superhuman power in some unusual or extraordinary manner; hence its nature to attract attention. Christ fed the 5,000 with the multiplied loaves and fishes, and all wondered. Every day God feeds millions of humanity with the multiplied fruits of the earth, and no one marvels. Christ, by a shortened process, changed water into wine, and everybody was astonished; but every year God does this in the usual way—through the vine—in almost limitless quantities, and no one is astonished. A divine miracle, therefore, whenever performed, is wrought to heal and to save, and to call attention to the source of divine power.

What did the people say when they saw these things?

"People were overwhelmed with amazement. *'He has done everything well,'* they said. 'He even makes the deaf hear and the mute speak.' " Mark 7:37, NIV.

What kinds of disease and sickness did Jesus cure?

"Jesus went throughout Galilee, teaching in their synagogues, preaching the good news of the kingdom, and healing *every disease and sickness among the people*." Matthew 4:23, NIV. "Many followed him, and *he healed their sick*." Matthew 12:15, NIV.

Who were brought to Him for healing?

"News about him spread all over Syria, and people brought to him *all who were ill with various diseases, those suffering severe pain, the demon-possessed, those having seizures, and the paralyzed*, and he healed them." Matthew 4:24, NIV.

What did Christ say to the woman who had been healed by touching His garment?

"*Your faith has healed you.*" Matthew 9:22, NIV.

What did He say to the two blind men as He healed them?

"According to your *faith* will it be done to you." Verse 29, NIV.

To another whose sight He had restored, what did Christ say?

"Your *faith* has healed you." Luke 18:42, NIV.

Why did Christ work so few miracles in His own country?

"And he did not many miracles there *because of their lack of faith*." Matthew 13:58, NIV.

What lesson did Christ design to teach in healing a man sick of the palsy?

" '*But that you may know that the Son of Man has authority on earth to forgive sins. . . .*' He said to the paralyzed man, 'I tell you, get up, take your mat and go home.' " Luke 5:24, NIV.

NOTE.—By His miracles, therefore, Christ designed to teach faith in the power of God not only to *restore the body* but to *heal the soul*.

What effect did Christ's miracles have on His audience?

"Immediately he received his sight and followed Jesus, praising God. When all the people saw it, they also praised God." Luke 18:43, NIV. "The people were delighted with all the wonderful works he was doing." Luke 13:17, NIV.

What message did Christ send to John the Baptist in prison to strengthen his wavering faith?

"Jesus replied, 'Go back and report to John what you hear and see: *The blind receive sight, the lame walk, those who have leprosy are cured, the deaf hear, the dead are raised, and the good news is preached to the poor*. Blessed is the man who does not fall away on account of me.' " Matthew 11:4-6, NIV.

What great miracle did Jesus perform near the end of His life on Earth?

"When he had said this, Jesus called in a loud voice, 'Lazarus, come out!' The dead man came out, his hands and feet wrapped with strips of linen, and a cloth around his face. Jesus said to them, 'Take off the grave clothes and let him go.' " John 11:43, 44, NIV.

What was the result of this miracle?

"Therefore *many of the Jews* who had come to visit Mary, and had seen what Jesus did, *put their faith in him.*" Verse 45, NIV.

Because of the interest created by this miracle, what did the Pharisees say?

"Look how the whole world has gone after him!" John 12:19, NIV.

What evidence did Jesus offer as a basis for confidence in Him?

"Do not believe me unless I do what my Father does. But if I do it, even though you do not believe me, *believe the miracles,* that you may know and understand that the Father is in me, and I in the Father." John 10:37, 38, NIV. "Believe me when I say that I am in the Father and the Father is in me; or at least *believe on the evidence of the miracles themselves.*" John 14:11, NIV.

Did Jesus ever make use of natural materials in His miracles?

"Having said this, he spit on the ground, made some mud with the saliva, and put it on the man's eyes. 'Go,' he told him, 'wash in the pool of Siloam' (this word means Sent). So the man went and washed, and came home seeing." John 9:6, 7, NIV. (See also Mark 7:33-35; 8:23-25; 2 Kings 5:1-14.)

What Old Testament story shows that the use of natural remedies is not contrary to faith in the healing power of God?

"In those days Hezekiah became ill and was at the point of death. The prophet Isaiah son of Amoz went to him and said, 'This is what the Lord says: Put your house in order, because you are going to die; you will not recover.'

"Hezekiah turned his face to the wall and prayed to the Lord, 'Remember, O Lord, how I have walked before you faithfully and with wholehearted devotion and have done what is good in your eyes.' And Hezekiah wept bitterly.

"Before Isaiah had left the middle court, the word of the Lord came to him: 'Go back and tell Hezekiah, the leader of my people, "This is what the Lord, the God of your father David, says: I have heard your prayer and seen your tears; *I will heal you.* On the third day from now you will go up to the temple of the Lord. I will add fifteen years to your life. . . ." '

"Then Isaiah said, *'Prepare a poultice of figs.'They did so and ap-*

plied it to the boil, and he recovered." 2 Kings 20:1-7, NIV.

NOTE.—Notice that even after God had promised to heal Hezekiah, Isaiah still made use of the best medicine of his day. This demonstrates, not a lack of faith in God, but a desire to cooperate with Him in the healing process.

Why did the inspired writers record Jesus' miracles?

"Jesus did many other miraculous signs in the presence of his disciples, which are not recorded in this book. But they are written *that you may believe that Jesus is the Christ, the Son of God, and that by believing you may have life in his name.*" John 20:30, 31, NIV.

SUFFERINGS OF CHRIST

For what purpose did Christ come into the world?

"This is a faithful saying, and worthy of all acceptation, that Christ Jesus came into the world *to save sinners*; of whom I am chief." 1 Timothy 1:15.

Why did God give His Son to die for man?

"For God so loved the world that he gave his one and only Son, that whoever believes in him shall not perish but have eternal life." John 3:16, NIV. (See 1 John 4:9, 10; Romans 5:8.)

What did the prophet Isaiah say the Messiah would be called to endure?

"He was *oppressed and afflicted*, yet he did not open his mouth; he was led like a lamb to the slaughter and as a sheep before her shearers is silent, so he did not open his mouth. By oppression and judgment he was taken away. And who can speak of his descendants? For he was *cut off from the land of the living*; for the transgression of my people he was stricken." Isaiah 53:7, 8, NIV.

Did Christ know beforehand the treatment He would receive?

"Jesus took the Twelve aside and told them, *'We are going up to Jerusalem, and everything that is written by the prophets about the Son of Man will be fulfilled.* He will be handed over to the Gentiles. They will *mock him, insult him, spit on him, flog him and kill him.'*" Luke 18:31-33, NIV.

How heavy was the burden He bore on the night of His betrayal?

"He took Peter and the two sons of Zebedee along with him, and he began to be sorrowful and troubled. Then he said to them, *'My soul is overwhelmed with sorrow to the point of death*. Stay here and keep watch with me.' " Matthew 26:37, 38, NIV.

What trembling prayer did Jesus pray in the Garden of Gethsemane?

"Going a little farther, he fell with his face to the ground and prayed, 'My Father, if it is possible, may this cup be taken from me. Yet not as I will, but as you will.' " Verse 39, NIV.

How great was the agony of His soul?

"And being in anguish, he prayed more earnestly, and his sweat was like drops of blood falling to the ground." Luke 22:44, NIV.

What happened after Jesus repeated this prayer three times?

"While he was still speaking a crowd came up, and the man who was called Judas, one of the Twelve, was leading them. He approached Jesus to kiss him, but Jesus asked him, 'Judas, *are you betraying the Son of Man with a kiss?*' " Verses 47, 48, NIV.

Where was Jesus taken?

"Then seizing him, they led him away and took him into *the house of the high priest*. Peter *followed at a distance*." Verse 54, NIV.

How did Peter deny Jesus at the high priest's house?

"But when they had kindled a fire in the middle of the courtyard and had sat down together, Peter sat down with them. A servant girl saw him seated there in the firelight. She looked closely at him and said, 'This man was with him.' But he denied it. 'Woman, I don't know him,' he said.

"A little later someone else saw him and said, 'You also are one of them.'

" 'Man, I am not!' Peter replied.

"About an hour later another asserted, 'Certainly this fellow was with him, for he is a Galilean.'

"Peter replied, *'Man, I don't know what you're talking about!'* Just as he was speaking, the rooster crowed. The Lord turned and looked straight at Peter. Then Peter remembered the word the Lord had spoken to him: 'Before the rooster crows today, you will disown me three times.' And he went outside and wept bitterly." Verses 55-62, NIV.

To what insults was Jesus subjected at the high priest's house?

"*The men who were guarding Jesus began mocking and beating him*. They blindfolded him and demanded, 'Prophesy! Who hit

you?' And they said many other insulting things to him." Verses
63, 64, NIV.

Where was Jesus taken next?

"At daybreak *the council of the elders* of the people, both the chief
priests and teachers of the law, met together, and *Jesus was led before
them*." Verse 66, NIV.

What acknowledgment did Jesus' accusers secure from Him as the basis for condemning Him?

" 'If you are the Christ,' they said, 'tell us.'

" Jesus answered, 'If I tell you, you will not believe me, and if I
asked you, you would not answer. But from now on, the Son of Man
will be seated at the right hand of the mighty God.'

"They all asked, 'Are you then the Son of God?' He replied, *'You
are right in saying I am.'*

"Then they said, 'Why do we need any more testimony? We have
heard it from his own lips.' " Verses 67-71, NIV.

What was the next step in their plan?

"Then the whole assembly rose and led him off to Pilate." Luke
23:1, NIV.

NOTE.—The Jewish authorities did not have the power to condemn someone to death. Only the Romans could do that.

When Pilate desired that Christ be released, how did they protest?

"But they insisted, 'He stirs up the people all over Judea by his
teaching. He started in Galilee and has come all the way here.' " Verse
5, NIV.

NOTE.—This has always been a favorite accusation against the
work of true reformers. The Romans had a law forbidding the teaching of any new religion "whereby the minds of men may be disturbed."

When Pilate heard that Jesus was from Galilee, what did he do?

"When he learned that Jesus was under Herod's jurisdiction, *he sent
him to Herod*, who was also in Jerusalem at that time." Verse 7, NIV.

Who appeared to accuse Jesus before Herod?

"And *the chief priests and scribes* stood and vehemently accused
him" Verse 10.

To what indignities did Herod subject Jesus?

"Then Herod and his soldiers ridiculed and mocked him. Dressing him in an elegant robe, they sent him back to Pilate." Verse 11, NIV.

What did Pilate propose to do when Christ was again brought before him?

"For the third time he spoke to them: 'Why? What crime has this man committed? I have found in him no grounds for the death penalty. *Therefore I will have him punished and then release him.*' " Verse 22, NIV.

What did Jesus' accusers, instead of consenting to His release, now demand?

"But with loud shouts they insistently demanded that he be crucified, and their shouts prevailed." Verse 23, NIV.

Although Pilate had declared his belief in Christ's innocence, what cruel punishment did he inflict upon Him?

"Then Pilate took Jesus and *had him flogged*." John 19:1, NIV.

What shameful treatment did Jesus receive from the soldiers?

"They stripped him and put a scarlet robe on him, and then *twisted together a crown of thorns and set it on his head*. They put a staff in his right hand and knelt in front of him and mocked him. 'Hail, king of the Jews!' they said. *They spit on him, and took the staff and struck him on the head again and again.*" Matthew 27:28-30, NIV.

In what prayer for those who crucified Him did Christ manifest the true spirit of the gospel—love for sinners?

"Jesus said, *'Father, forgive them, for they do not know what they are doing.'* " Luke 23:34, NIV.

How did the chief priests and others mock Jesus while He was on the cross?

"In the same way the chief priests, the teachers of the law and the elders mocked him. *'He saved others,' they said, 'but he can't save himself!* He's the King of Israel!' Let him come down now from the cross, and we will believe in him." Matthew 27:41, 42, NIV.

NOTE.—In their blindness they could not see that Christ could not save others and save Himself at the same time.

As He cried out in agony on the cross, and said, "I thirst," what was given Him?

"Immediately one of them ran and got a sponge. He filled it with wine *vinegar*, put it on a stick, and offered it to Jesus to drink." Verse 48, NIV. (See John 19:28, 29.)

What closed this terrible scene?

"When he had received the drink, Jesus said, 'It is finished.' With that, *he bowed his head and gave up his spirit*." John 19:30, NIV.

What miraculous phenomena accompanied Jesus' death?

"It was now about the sixth hour, and *darkness came over the whole land* until the ninth hour, *for the sun stopped shining*. And *the curtain of the temple was torn in two*." Luke 23:44, 45, NIV.

"The earth shook and the rocks split. The tombs broke open and *the bodies of many holy people who had died were raised to life*. They came out of the tombs, and after Jesus' resurrection they went into the holy city and appeared to many people." Matthew 27:51-53, NIV.

What divine purpose did Jesus' sufferings fulfill?

"In *bringing many sons to glory*, it was fitting that God, for whom and through whom everything exists, should make the author of their salvation perfect through suffering." Hebrews 2:10, NIV.

How did Jesus act as our substitute?

"For our sake he made him to be sin who knew no sin, so that in him we might become the righteousness of God." 2 Corinthians 5:21, NRSV.

For whom did Christ suffer all these things?

"But he was *pierced for our transgressions*, he was *crushed for our iniquities*; the *punishment that brought us peace was upon him, and by his wounds we are healed*." Isaiah 53:5, NIV.

How much was included in the gift when God gave us Jesus?

"He who did not spare his own Son, but gave him up for us all—how will he not also, along with him, graciously give us *all things*?" Romans 8:32, NIV.

THE RESURRECTION OF CHRIST

In what psalm was the resurrection of Christ foreshadowed?

"You will not abandon me to the grave, nor will you let your Holy One see decay." Psalm 16:10, NIV.

In what way was the prophet Jonah a type of Christ?

"For as Jonah was three days and three nights in the belly of a huge fish, so the Son of Man will be three days and three nights in the heart of the earth." Matthew 12:40, NIV.

In what plain words did Christ foretell His resurrection?

"From that time on Jesus began to explain to his disciples that he must go to Jerusalem and suffer many things at the hands of the elders, chief priests and teachers of the law, and that he must be killed *and on the third day be raised to life.*" Matthew 16:21, NIV. "When they came together in Galilee, he said to them, 'The Son of Man is going to be betrayed into the hands of men. They will kill him, *and on the third day he will be raised to life.*' " Matthew 17:22, 23, NIV. "The Son of Man must suffer many things and be rejected by the elders, chief priests and teachers of the law, and he must be killed *and on the third day be raised to life.*" Luke 9:22, NIV. (See also Matthew 20:17-19; Mark 8:31; 9:31, 32; 10:32-34; Luke 18:31-34.)

What did Jesus say to the Jews who asked for a sign to prove His Messiahship?

"Jesus answered them, *'Destroy this temple, and I will raise it again in three days.*' " John 2:19, NIV.

To what temple did He refer?

"The Jews replied, 'It has taken forty-six years to build this temple, and you are going to raise it in three days?' *But the temple he had spoken of was his body.*" Verses 20, 21, NIV.

After His resurrection, what effect did this prediction have on His disciples?

"After he was raised from the dead, his disciples recalled what he had said. Then *they believed the Scripture and the words that Jesus had spoken.*" Verse 22, NIV.

How did the chief priests and Pharisees seek to prevent the fulfillment of Christ's prophecy of His resurrection?

"The next day, the one after Preparation Day, the chief priests and the Pharisees went to Pilate. 'Sir,' they said, 'we remember that while he was still alive that deceiver said, "After three days I will rise again." *So give the order for the tomb to be made secure until the third day.* Otherwise, his disciples may come and steal the body and tell the people that he has been raised from the dead. This last deception will be worse than the first.' " Matthew 27:62-64, NIV.

How did Pilate comply with their request?

" '*Take a guard*,' Pilate answered. 'Go, *make the tomb as secure as you know how*.' So they went and made the tomb secure by putting a seal on the stone and posting the guard." Verses 65, 66, NIV.

How futile was all this?

"After the Sabbath, at dawn on the first day of the week, Mary Magdalene and the other Mary went to look at the tomb. There was a violent earthquake, for an angel of the Lord came down from heaven and, going to the tomb, rolled back the stone and sat on it. His appearance was like lightning, and his clothes were white as snow. The guards were so afraid of him that they shook and became like dead men. The angel said to the women, 'Do not be afraid, for I know that you are looking for Jesus, who was crucified. He is not here; *he has risen, just as he said*. Come and see the place where he lay. Then go quickly and tell his disciples: "*He has risen from the dead*." ' " Matthew 28:17, NIV. (See also Mark 16:1-16; Luke 24:1-8, 44-46; John 20:1-9.)

Was it possible for death to hold Jesus?

"This man was handed over to you by God's set purpose and fore-knowledge; and you, with the help of wicked men, put him to death by nailing him on the cross. But God raised him from the dead, free-ing him from the agony of death, because *it was impossible for death to keep its hold on him*." Acts 2:23, 24, NIV.

How does Paul speak of the resurrection of Christ?

"For what I received I passed on to you as of first importance: that Christ died for our sins according to the Scriptures, that he was buried, that *he was raised on the third day according to the Scriptures*." 1 Corinthians 15:3, 4, NIV.

Who does the apostle say saw Christ after He was risen?

"He appeared to Peter, and then to the Twelve. After that, he appeared to more than five hundred of the brothers at the same time. . . .Then he appeared to James, then to all the apostles, and last of all he appeared to me also, as to one abnormally born." Verses 5-8, NIV.

What importance is attached to Christ's resurrection?

"And if Christ has not been raised, our preaching is useless and so is your faith. More than that, we are then bound to be false witnesses about God, for we have testified about God that he raised Christ from the dead. But he did not raise him if in fact the dead are not raised. For if the dead are not raised, Christ has not been raised either. And if Christ has not been raised, your faith is futile; you are still in your sins. Then those who have fallen asleep in Christ are lost." Verses 14-18, NIV.

What positive assurance of the Resurrection is given?

"But *Christ has indeed been raised from the dead*, the firstfruits of those who have fallen asleep." Verse 20, NIV.

What great truth therefore follows?

"As in Adam all die, even so *in Christ shall all be made alive.*" Verse 22.

What joyful declaration has Jesus left us regarding His resurrection?

"I am the Living One; I was dead, and behold I am alive for ever and ever! And I hold the keys of death and Hades." Revelation 1:18, NIV.

What is the measure of the power of God that believers may experience in their daily lives?

"I pray also that the eyes of your heart may be enlightened in order that you may know the hope to which he has called you, the riches of his glorious inheritance in the saints, and *his incomparably great power* for us who believe. That power is *like the working of his mighty strength, which he exerted in Christ when he raised him from the dead.*" Ephesians 1:18-20, NIV.

What Christian ordinance has been given as a memorial of Christ's burial and resurrection?

"Or don't you know that all of us who were baptized into Christ Jesus were baptized into his death? We were therefore buried with him through *baptism* into death in order that, just as Christ was raised from the dead through the glory of the Father, we too may live a new life." Romans 6:35, NIV.

CHAPTER 5

The Holy Spirit

THE HOLY SPIRIT AND HIS WORK

What promise did Jesus make to His disciples shortly before His crucifixion?

"And I will ask the Father, *and he will give you another Counselor to be with you forever*—the Spirit of truth." John 14:16, NIV.

Why was it necessary for Jesus to go away?

"But I tell you the truth: It is for your good that I am going away. *Unless I go away, the Counselor will not come to you*; but if I go, I will send him to you." John 16:7, NIV.

Who is the Counselor, and what was He to do?

"But the Counselor, *the Holy Spirit*, whom the Father will send in my name, *will teach you all things and will remind you of everything I have said to you*." John 14:26, NIV.

NOTE.—The Holy Spirit, or Holy Ghost, is a member of the Godhead. He is mentioned alongside God and Jesus in Trinitarian formulas such as Matthew 28:19 and 2 Corinthians 13:14. He has traits of personality (mind, will, emotions, etc.), and Jesus identified Him as *another* like Himself (John 14:16).

What other work was the Counselor to do?

"When he comes, he will *convict the world of guilt in regard to sin and righteousness and judgment*." John 16:8, NIV.

What did Jesus say the Spirit of truth would do?

"But when he, the Spirit of truth, comes, *he will guide you into all truth*. He will not speak on his own; he will speak only what he hears, and *he will tell you what is yet to come*." Verse 13, NIV.

NOTE.—The Spirit *speaks* (1 Timothy 4:1); *teaches* (1 Corinthians 2:3); *testifies* (Romans 8:16, NIV); *makes intercession* (Romans 8:26); *distributes the gifts* (1 Corinthians 12:11); and *invites the sinner* (Revelation 22:17).

Why can't the world receive Him?

"The world cannot accept him, *because it neither sees him nor knows him.*" John 14:17, NIV.

What did Christ say the Holy Spirit would reveal?

"He will bring glory to *me* by taking from *what is mine* and making it known to you." John 16:14, NIV.

How has God revealed to us the hidden things of the kingdom?

"God has revealed it to us *by his Spirit*. The Spirit searches all things, even the deep things of God." 1 Corinthians 2:10, NIV.

Who moved upon the prophets to give their messages?

"For prophecy never had its origin in the will of man, but men spoke from God as they were carried along by *the Holy Spirit*." 2 Peter 1:21, NIV.

After Pentecost, how was the gospel preached?

"It was revealed to them that they were not serving themselves but you, when they spoke of the things that have now been told you by those who have preached the gospel to you *by the Holy Spirit* sent from heaven. Even angels long to look into these things." 1 Peter 1:12, NIV.

How intimate is the Holy Spirit's union with believers?

"But you know him, for *he lives with you* and will be *in you*." John 14:17, NIV.

NOTE.—The same Spirit that inspired the prophets and the apostles will impress us, if we are in tune with Him. "Whether you turn to the right or to the left, your ears will hear a voice behind you, saying, 'This is the way; walk in it'." Isaiah 30:21, NIV. Of course, this does not give us prophetic authority over others, which requires a special commission from God.

Whose presence does the Holy Spirit bring to the believers?

Jesus'. "I will not leave you as orphans; *I will come to you*." John 14:18, NIV.

This is a fulfillment of what promise?

"And surely *I am with you always*, to the very end of the age." Matthew 28:20, NIV. (See also John 14:21-23.)

What threefold union is thus established?

"On that day you will realize that *I am in my Father*, and *you are in me*, and *I am in you*." John 14:20, NIV.

By whom is this union sealed?

"And you also were included in Christ when you heard the word of truth, the gospel of your salvation. Having believed, you were marked in him with a seal, *the promised Holy Spirit*." Ephesians 1:13, NIV.

What warning is given to those who have received the Spirit?

"And *do not grieve the Holy Spirit of God*, with whom you were sealed for the day of redemption." Ephesians 4:30, NIV.

Will there be a limit to the Holy Spirit's work?

"Then the Lord said, 'My Spirit will not contend with man forever.'" Genesis 6:3, NIV.

NOTE.—The limit is determined by the creature rather than by the Creator. It is when there is an utter abandonment to evil, and further appeals would be without avail. God, foreknowing all things, may designate a definite period of probation for us, as in the case of the 120 years before the Flood (Genesis 6:3); but His Spirit never ceases to strive with us as long as there is hope of our salvation.

What did David pray for?

"Do not cast me from your presence or take your Holy Spirit from me." Psalm 51:11, NIV.

How willing is God to give us the Holy Spirit?

"If you then, though you are evil, know how to give good gifts to your children, how much more will your Father in heaven give the Holy Spirit to those who ask him!" Luke 11:13, NIV.

How does Jesus, through the Spirit, seek an entrance to every heart?

"Here I am! *I stand at the door and knock*. If anyone hears my voice and opens the door, I will come in and eat with him, and he with me." Revelation 3:20, NIV.

FRUIT OF THE SPIRIT

What is the fruit of the Spirit?

"The fruit of the Spirit is *love, joy, peace, patience, kindness, goodness, faithfulness, gentleness and self-control.*" Galatians 5:22, 23, NIV.

By way of contrast, what are the works of the flesh?

"The acts of the sinful nature are obvious: sexual immorality, impurity and debauchery; idolatry and witchcraft; hatred, discord, jealousy, fits of rage, selfish ambition, dissensions, factions and envy; drunkenness, orgies, and the like." Verses 19-21, NIV.

NOTE.—The evils here mentioned are a close parallel to the lists found in Matthew 15:18, 19; Mark 7:20-23; Romans 1:29-31; and 2 Timothy 3:1-5.

How may the works of the flesh be avoided?

"So I say, *live by the Spirit*, and you will not gratify the desires of the sinful nature." Galatians 5:16, NIV.

By what is the love of God shed abroad in the heart?

"And hope does not disappoint us, because God has poured out his love into our hearts *by the Holy Spirit*, whom he has given us." Romans 5:5, NIV.

By what does genuine faith work?

"You who are trying to be justified by law have been alienated from Christ; you have fallen away from grace. But by faith we eagerly await through the Spirit the righteousness for which we hope. For in Christ Jesus neither circumcision nor uncircumcision has any value. The only thing that counts is *faith expressing itself through love.*" Galatians 5:4-6, NIV.

How does Paul restate the same truth in different words in another passage?

"Circumcision is nothing and uncircumcision is nothing. *Keeping God's commands is what counts.*" 1 Corinthians 7:19, NIV.

How are "keeping God's commands" and "faith working by love" the same thing?

"The entire law is summed up in a single command: *'Love your neighbor as yourself.'* " Galatians 5:14, NIV.

How does love fulfill the law?

"Let no debt remain outstanding, except the continuing debt to love another, for he who loves his fellowman has fulfilled the law. The commandments, 'Do not commit adultery,' 'Do not murder,' 'Do not steal,' 'Do not covet,' and whatever other commandment there may be, are summed up in this one rule: 'Love your neighbor as yourself.' *Love does no harm to its neighbor. Therefore love is the fulfillment of the law*." Romans 13:8-10, NIV.

In what way does love manifest itself?

"Love is patient, love is kind. It does not envy, it does not boast, it is not proud. It is not rude, it is not self-seeking, it is not easily angered, *it keeps no record of wrongs*." 1 Corinthians 13:4, 5, NIV.

What does love do when it encounters sin?

"Hatred stirs up dissension, but love *covers over all wrongs*." Proverbs 10:12, NIV. "Above all, love each other deeply, because love *covers over a multitude of sins*." 1 Peter 4:8, NIV.

Of what does the kingdom of God consist?

"For the kingdom of God is not a matter of eating and drinking, but of *righteousness, peace and joy* in the Holy Spirit." Romans 14:17, NIV.

NOTE.—It is the Christian's privilege to have righteousness, peace, and joy—a righteousness that is of God by faith (Romans 3:21, 22); a peace that transcends understanding (Philippians 4:7, NIV), which the world can neither give nor take away; and an ever joyful attitude (1 Thessalonians 5:16; Philippians 4:4).

What spirit should we show toward others?

"And the Lord's servant must not quarrel; instead, he must *be kind* to everyone, able to teach, not resentful." 2 Timothy 2:24, NIV.

Does God wish us to judge others, or does He have a better way to transform sinner's hearts?

"You, therefore, have no excuse, you who pass judgment on someone else, for at whatever point you judge the other, you are condemning yourself, because you who pass judgment do the same things. Now we know that God's judgment against those who do such things is based on truth. So when you, a mere man, pass judgment on them and yet do the same things, do you think you will escape God's judgment? Or do you show contempt for the riches of his kindness, tolerance and patience, not realizing that *God's kindness leads you toward repentance*?" Romans 2:1-4, NIV.

"Who are you to judge someone else's servant? To his own master he stands or falls. And he will stand, for the Lord is able to make him stand." Romans 14:4, NIV. "You, then, why do you judge your brother? Or why do you look down on your brother? For we will all stand before God's judgment seat. It is written: ' "As surely as I live," says the Lord, "every knee will bow before me, every tongue will confess to God." ' So then, each of us will give an account of himself to God. Therefore let us stop passing judgment on one another. Instead, make up your mind not to put any stumbling block or obstacle in your brother's way." Verses 10-14, NIV.

NOTE.—*God's kindness leads to repentance.* What better way is there to express God's plan in saving lost souls? Paul calls us to avoid any attitude or action that would distract someone from God's loving-kindness and the patient work of the Holy Spirit.

"Throughout the latter part of Romans 1, Paul has spoken in the third person ('they') *about* the sinners who are subject to God's wrath. Now he turns to the second person ('you') and speaks *to* those who pass judgment upon these obvious sinners.

"Immediately he puts them all in the same boat. In Romans 1 he had said that the Gentile sinners were 'without excuse' (verse 20). Now in Romans 2 he contends that those who pass judgment 'have no excuse' because they do the very same things (verse 1). This is a serious charge. Both groups are without excuse because both groups do the same things.

"Did God's people really do the same things? Probably some of them did. No doubt among God's professed people there were those with secret sins that looked very much like the sins of the obvious sinners. The only difference was that God's people kept such sins under wraps rather than committing them in the open and cheering on those who practiced them (see Romans 1:32).

"On the other hand, certainly there were many who would never have thought of committing such sins as idolatry and sexual immorality. What can Paul possibly mean when he accuses these pious people of 'doing the same things'? Perhaps there is a clue in verse 3. Paul speaks of the 'mere man' (as NIV puts it) passing judgment. Is Paul implicitly pointing to the sin of judging as being the same as the other sins because it usurps God's role and thus becomes a form of idolatry?

"The point is only implicit here [in Romans 2], but Paul makes it more explicitly in Romans 14:4, where he chides those who judge as judging someone else's servant, and in 14:10-12, where he shows from the Old Testament (Isaiah 49:18; 45:23) that God alone has the right to judge. In other words, to judge another person, one of God's children, is to take a role on oneself that belongs only to God. What could be more idolatrous than to usurp God's role and take over His prerogative?

"In verse 4 Paul accuses his readers of showing contempt for God's kindness, since this very kindness is meant to lead to repentance. Apparently a judgmental attitude stands in the way of both a full appreciation of God's kindness and the need to come to God in a spirit of repentance." John C. Brunt, *The Abundant Life Bible Amplifier: Romans* (Boise, Idaho: Pacific Press, 1996), pp. 60, 61.

How should we treat those who have wronged us?

"Do not repay anyone evil for evil. Be careful to do what is right in the eyes of everybody. If it is possible, as far as it depends on you, live at peace with everyone. *Do not take revenge*, my friends, but leave room for God's wrath, for it is written: 'It is mine to avenge, I will repay,' says the Lord. On the contrary: *'If your enemy is hungry, feed him; if he is thirsty, give him something to drink. In doing this, you will heap burning coals on his head.'*" Romans 12:17-20, NIV.

NOTE.—Paul is quoting Deuteronomy 32:35 and Proverbs 25:21, 22.

How should Christians respond to evil?

"Do not be overcome by evil, but overcome evil with good." Romans 12:21, NIV.

How does faith determine our standing with God?

"And *without faith it is impossible to please God*, because anyone who comes to him must believe that he exists and that he rewards those who earnestly seek him." Hebrews 11:6, NIV.

How does God regard the meek and quiet spirit?

"Your beauty" "should be that of your inner self, the unfading beauty of *a gentle and quiet spirit, which is of great worth in God's sight.*" 1 Peter 3:3, 4, NIV.

In our Christian growth and experience, what is to accompany faith, courage, and knowledge?

"For this very reason, make every effort to add to your faith goodness; and to goodness, knowledge; and to knowledge, *self-control*." 2 Peter 1:5, 6.

NOTE.—Self-control means strength or power over passions and addictions of all kinds. It denotes the self-rule that the overcomer or converted person has over the sinful propensities of human nature.

How highly are those with self-control commended?

"Better a patient man than a warrior, a man who controls his temper than one who takes a city." Proverbs 16:32, NIV.

What is said of all these different virtues?

"Against such things there is no law." Galatians 5:23, NIV.

NOTE.—The law condemns sin. But all these qualities, being virtues, are in harmony with the law. When our lives are under the control of the Spirit, we will act in harmony with God's law.

From what condemnation does the Spirit's leading save us?

"But if you are led by the Spirit, *you are not under the law.*" Verse 18, NIV.

What unity does Paul encourage?

"Make every effort to keep the unity of the Spirit through the bond of peace. There is one body and one Spirit—just as you were called to one hope when you were called—one Lord, one faith, one baptism; one God and Father of all, who is over all and through all and in all." Ephesians 4:3-6, NIV.

GIFTS OF THE SPIRIT

What aspect of the Christian life did Paul urge the Corinthians to study?

"Now *about spiritual gifts*, brothers, I do not want you to be ignorant." 1 Corinthians 12:1, NIV.

When Christ ascended to heaven, what did He give us?

"But to each one of us grace has been given as Christ apportioned it. This is why it says: 'When he ascended on high, he led captives in his train and *gave gifts to men*.' " Ephesians 4:7, 8, NIV.

What are some of these gifts that Christ gave us?

"It was he who gave some to be apostles, some to be prophets, some to be evangelists, and some to be pastors and teachers, to prepare God's people for works of service, so that the body of Christ may be built up until we all reach unity in the faith and in the knowledge of the Son of God and become mature, attaining to the whole measure of the fullness of Christ." Verses 11-13, NIV.

Where else are these gifts listed?

"To one there is given through the Spirit the message of wisdom, to another the message of knowledge by means of the same Spirit, to another faith by the same Spirit, to another gifts of healing by that one Spirit, to another miraculous powers, to another prophecy, to another distinguishing between spirits, to another speaking in different kinds of tongues, and to still another the interpretation of tongues." 1 Corinthians 12:8-10, NIV.

"And in the church God has appointed first of all apostles, second prophets, third teachers, then workers of miracles, also those having gifts of healing, those able to help others, those with gifts of administration, and those speaking in different kinds of tongues." Verse 28, NIV.

How many of God's baptized children have a spiritual gift?

"*Each man* has his own gift from God; one has this gift, another that." 1 Corinthians 7:7, NIV. "Now to *each one* the manifestation of the Spirit is given for the common good." 1 Corinthians 12:7, NIV.

Can something like artistic ability, music, and craftsmanship be spiritual gifts?

"Then Moses said to the Israelites, 'See, the Lord has chosen Bezalel son of Uri, the son of Hur, of the tribe of Judah, *and he has filled him with the Spirit of God*, with skill, ability, and knowledge in all kinds of crafts—to make artistic designs for work in gold, silver and bronze, to cut and set stones, to work in wood and to engage in all kinds of artistic craftsmanship. And he has given both him and Oholiab son of Ahisamach, of the tribe of Dan, the ability to teach others. He has filled them with skill to do all kinds of work as craftsmen, designers, embroiderers in blue, purple and scarlet yarn and fine linen, and weavers—all of them master craftsmen and designers.' " Exodus 35:30-35, NIV.

For what purpose were these gifts bestowed upon the church?

"*To prepare God's people for works of service, so that the body of Christ may be built up.* . . . Then we will no longer be infants, tossed back and forth by the waves, and blown here and there by every wind of teaching and by the cunning and craftiness of men in their deceitful scheming. Instead, speaking the truth in love, we will in all things grow up into him who is the Head, that is, Christ." Ephesians 4:12-15, NIV.

What will be the end result of these gifts in the church?

"Until we all reach *unity in the faith* and in the knowledge of the Son of God and become mature, attaining to the whole measure of the fullness of Christ." Verse 13, NIV.

What is the basis for unity in diversity?

"There are different kinds of gifts, but the *same Spirit*." 1 Corinthians 12:4, NIV.

Who controls the distribution of the gifts of the Spirit?

"All these are the work of one and *the same Spirit*, and he gives them to each one, just as he determines." Verse 11, NIV.

Was it God's design that all should possess the same gifts?

"Are all apostles? Are all prophets? Are all teachers? Do all work miracles? Do all have gifts of healing? Do all speak in tongues? Do all interpret?" Verses 29, 30, NIV.

NOTE.—This is a rhetorical question; the expected answer is 'Of course not.' Every believer needs every one of the gifts of the Spirit in his life, but not every believer will have every one of them.

Will the gifts of the Spirit be needed forever?

"But where there are prophecies, *they will cease*; where there are tongues, *they will be stilled*; where there is knowledge, *it will pass away*." 1 Corinthians 13:8, NIV.

When will the gifts of the Spirit no longer be needed?

"But *when that which is perfect has come, then* that which is in part will be done away." Verse 10, NKJV.

NOTE.—That is, at the Second Coming (compare verse 12). First Corinthians 13:8-12 and Ephesians 4:13 both indicate that the gifts of the Spirit are never withdrawn from the church until the end of the world. The view that the supernatural gifts were given only for the first century cannot be sustained from the Scriptures. As long as God's people are not perfect, they need the gifts of the Spirit. This was the belief of the early church. Eusebius, the ancient church historian, mentions many manifestations of genuine prophecy in the second century, and at one point quotes Miltiades: "The apostle shows that the gift of prophecy should be in all the church until the coming of the Lord." *Ecclesiastical History*, book 5, chapter 17.

THE GIFT OF PROPHECY

How did God communicate with Adam and Eve in the Garden of Eden?

"But the Lord God *called to the man*, 'Where are you?' " Genesis 3:9, NIV.

Since the Fall of humanity, what has been one of God's major means of communication with humans?

"I spoke to *the prophets*, gave them many visions and told parables through them." Hosea 12:10, NIV.

What things belong to God, and what to us?

"The secret things belong to the Lord our God, but *the things revealed* belong to us and to our children forever, that we may follow all the words of this law." Deuteronomy 29:29, NIV.

How fully and to whom does God reveal His purposes?

"Surely the Sovereign Lord does nothing without *revealing his plan to his servants the prophets*." Amos 3:7, NIV.

How does the Lord reveal Himself to His prophets?

"When a prophet of the Lord is among you, I reveal myself to him in *visions*, I speak to him in *dreams*." Numbers 12:6, NIV.

Under what influence did the prophets of old speak?

"For prophecy never had its origin in the will of man, but men spoke from God as they were carried along by the Holy Spirit." 2 Peter 1:21. (See 2 Samuel 23:2.)

What is the prophetic chain of command?

"The revelation of Jesus Christ, which God gave him to show his servants what must soon take place. He made it known by sending his angel to his servant John." Revelation 1:1, NIV.

NOTE.—Notice the prophetic chain of command: God, Jesus, angel, prophet.

What angel revealed to Daniel the meaning of his visions and dreams?

"While I was still in prayer, *Gabriel*, the man I had seen in the earlier vision, came to me in swift flight about the time of the evening sacrifice. He instructed me and said to me, 'Daniel, I have now come to give you insight and understanding.' " Daniel 9:21, 22, NIV. (See also Daniel 10 and Revelation 22:9, 10.)

Who is the true author of prophecy?

"Concerning this salvation, the prophets, who spoke of the grace that was to come to you, searched intently and with the greatest care, trying to find out the time and circumstances to which *the Spirit of Christ in them* was pointing when he predicted the sufferings of

Christ and the glories that would follow." 1 Peter 1:10, 11, NIV.

NOTE.—This passage suggests that the prophets did not always understand fully everything that they wrote.

How were the Lord's words to the prophets preserved?

"In the first year of Belshazzar king of Babylon, Daniel had a dream, and visions passed through his mind as he was lying on his bed. He wrote down the substance of his dream." Daniel 7:1, NIV. (See Jeremiah 51:60; Revelation 1:10, 11.)

By whom has God spoken to us in these last days?

"In the past God spoke to our forefathers through the prophets at many times and in various ways, but *in these last days he has spoken to us by his Son.*" Hebrews 1:1, 2, NIV.

What was one of the offices to be filled by the Messiah?

"The Lord your God will raise up for you a *prophet* like me from among your own brothers. You must listen to him." Deuteronomy 18:15, NIV.

Who alone can reveal the future?

"Daniel replied, 'No wise man, enchanter, magician or diviner can explain to the king the mystery he has asked about, but *there is a God in heaven who reveals mysteries.* He has shown King Nebuchadnezzar what will happen in days to come.' " Daniel 2:27, 28, NIV.

How did Daniel acknowledge the insufficiency of human wisdom?

"As for me, *this mystery has been revealed to me, not because I have greater wisdom than other living men*, but so that you, O king, may know the interpretation and that you may understand what went through your mind." Verse 30, NIV.

What did Daniel say after revealing and interpreting the dream?

"The great God has shown the king what will take place in the future. The dream is true and the interpretation is trustworthy." Verse 45, NIV.

How does God show His foreknowledge?

"See, the former things have taken place, and *new things I declare; before they spring into being I announce them to you.*" Isaiah 42:9, NIV.

What were some of the gifts Christ gave to His church?

"When he ascended on high, he led captives in his train and gave gifts to men. . . . It was he who gave some to be *apostles*, some to be *prophets*, some to be *evangelists*, and some to be *pastors* and *teachers*." Ephesians 4:8-11, NIV.

By what means did God deliver and preserve Israel?

"By a prophet the Lord brought Israel out of Egypt, and *by a prophet* was he preserved." Hosea 12:13.

When Moses complained of his poor speaking ability, what assistance did God promise him?

"He [Aaron] will speak to the people for you, and it will be as if he were your mouth and as if you were God to him." Exodus 4:16, NIV. "Then the Lord said to Moses, 'See, I have made you like God to Pharaoh, and your brother Aaron will be your prophet.' " Exodus 7:1, NIV.

NOTE.—In other words, Aaron would be Moses' prophet, and Moses would stand in the place of God to Aaron. Thus Aaron was to Moses as Moses was to God. A prophet is simply a spokesperson for God.

What is one test by which to detect false prophets?

"If what a prophet proclaims in the name of the Lord *does not take place or come true, that is a message the Lord has not spoken.* That prophet has spoken presumptuously. Do not be afraid of him." Deuteronomy 18:22, NIV.

NOTE.—There are, however, certain special exceptions to this rule in situations in which those who are the object of the prophecy change their behavior. See next question.

Can a true prophet ever make a prediction that does not come true?

"If at any time I announce that a nation or kingdom is to be uprooted, torn down and destroyed, and if that nation I warned repents of its evil, then I will relent and not inflict on it the disaster I had planned. And if at another time I announced that a nation or kingdom is to be built up and planted, and if it does evil in my sight and does not obey me, then I will reconsider the good I had intended to do for it." Jeremiah 18:7-10, NIV.

NOTE.—This was demonstrated time and again in the history of Israel and its neighbors.

What is one major example of unfulfilled prophecy?

"On the first day, Jonah started into the city. He proclaimed: 'Forty more days and Nineveh will be overturned.' The Ninevites believed God. They declared a fast, and all of them, from the greatest to the least, put on sackcloth. . . . *When God saw what they did and how they turned from their evil ways, he had compassion and did not bring upon them the destruction he had threatened.*" Jonah 3:4-10, NIV.

What other test should be applied in determining the validity of the claims of a prophet?

"If a prophet, or one who foretells by dreams, appears among you and announces to you a miraculous sign or wonder, and if the sign or wonder of which he has spoken takes place, and he says, *'Let us follow other gods'* (gods you have not known) *'and let us worship them,'* you must not listen to the words of that prophet or dreamer. The Lord your God is testing you to find out whether you love him with all your heart and with all your soul. *It is the Lord your God you must follow, and him you must revere.*" Deuteronomy 13:1-4, NIV.

NOTE.—In other words, if a prophet's words do not prove to be true, it is evidence that God has not sent that prophet. On the other hand, even if the prediction proves true, and the pretended prophet seeks to lead others to break God's commandments, this is positive evidence that the individual is not a true prophet.

What additional rule did Jesus give for distinguishing between true and false prophets?

"Watch out for false prophets. They come to you in sheep's clothing, but inwardly they are ferocious wolves. *By their fruit you will recognize them.* Do people pick grapes from thornbushes, or figs from thistles? Likewise every good tree bears good fruit, but a bad tree bears bad fruit. A good tree cannot bear bad fruit, and a bad tree cannot bear good fruit." Matthew 7:15-18, NIV.

What general rule is laid down for testing all prophets?

"To the law and to the testimony! If they do not speak according to this word, they have no light of dawn." Isaiah 8:20, NIV.

What is the promised result of believing God's prophets?

"Have faith in the Lord your God and you will be upheld; *have faith in his prophets and you will be successful.*" 2 Chronicles 20:20, NIV.

How should we relate to modern prophets?

"Do not put out the Spirit's fire; *do not treat prophecies with contempt*. Test everything. Hold on to the good." 1 Thessalonians 5:19-21, NIV.

What will characterize the last, or remnant, church?

"Then the dragon was enraged at the woman and went off to make war against the rest of her offspring—*those who obey God's commandments and hold to the testimony of Jesus*." Revelation 12:17, NIV.

What is the "testimony of Jesus"?

"For the testimony of Jesus is the *spirit of prophecy*." Revelation 19:10, NIV. (See Revelation 1:9.)

NOTE.—When we compare Revelation 19:10, ("At this I fell at his feet to worship him. But he said to me, 'Do not do it! I am a fellow servant with you and with your brothers *who hold to the testimony of Jesus*' ") with Revelation 22:9 ("But he said to me, 'Do not do it! I am a fellow servant with you and with your brothers *the prophets* and of all who keep the words of this book' "), we see that the testimony of Jesus is equated with the gift of prophecy. Thus Revelation 12:17 says that the remnant of God's people will keep the commandments of God and have the gift of prophecy in their midst.

What results when this gift is absent?

"Where there is no revelation, *the people cast off restraint*; but blessed is he who keeps the law." Proverbs 29:18, NIV. (See also Psalm 74:9.)

THE OUTPOURING OF THE SPIRIT

Just before His ascension, what did Jesus tell His disciples to wait for?

"I am going to send you what my Father has promised; but *stay in the city until you have been clothed with power from on high*." Luke 24:49, NIV.

How were they to receive this power?

"For John baptized with water, but in a few days you will be *baptized with the Holy Spirit*." Acts 1:5, NIV.

NOTE.—John the Baptist had foretold this baptism. He said, "I baptize you with water for repentance. But after me will come one who is more powerful than I, whose sandals I am not fit to

carry. He will baptize you with the Holy Spirit and with fire."
Matthew 3:11, NIV.

For what work was this baptism to prepare them?

"But you will receive power when the Holy Spirit comes on you;
and *you will be my witnesses* in Jerusalem, and in Judea and Samaria,
and to the ends of the earth." Acts 1:8, NIV.

**What were some of the results of the preaching of the gospel
under the outpouring of the Spirit?**

"When the people heard this, *they were cut to the heart* and
said to Peter and the other apostles, 'Brothers, what shall we do?'
Peter replied, 'Repent and be baptized, every one of you, in the
name of Jesus Christ for the forgiveness of your sins. And you
will receive the gift of the Holy Spirit.' . . . Those who accepted
the message were baptized, and *about three thousand were added
to their number that day*." Acts 2:37-41, NIV. "The apostles performed many miraculous signs and wonders among the people.
. . . *More and more men and women believed in the Lord and were
added to their number*." Acts 5:12-14, NIV. "So the word of God
spread. *The number of disciples in Jerusalem increased rapidly*,
and a large number of priests became obedient to the faith." Acts
6:7, NIV.

How did persecution affect the preaching of the gospel?

"On that day a great persecution broke out against the church at
Jerusalem, *and all except the apostles were scattered* throughout
Judea and Samaria. . . . *Those who had been scattered preached the
word wherever they went*." Acts 8:1-4, NIV.

NOTE.—"Persecution has only had a tendency to extend and establish the faith which it was designed to destroy. . . . There is no lesson which men have been so slow to learn as that to oppose and
persecute men is the very way to confirm them in their opinions, and
to spread their doctrines." Albert Barnes, on Acts 4:4.

**What words of Peter seem to indicate another outpouring of the
Spirit yet to come?**

"Repent, then, and turn to God, so that your sins may be wiped
out, *that times of refreshing may come from the Lord, and that he
may send the Christ*, who has been appointed for you—even Jesus.
He must remain in heaven until the time comes for God to restore
everything, as he promised long ago through his holy prophets." Acts
3:19-21, NIV.

What prophecy was fulfilled in the outpouring of the Spirit at Pentecost?

"Then Peter stood up with the Eleven, raised his voice and addressed the crowd: . . . 'These men are not drunk, as you suppose. . . . *This is that which was spoken by the prophet Joel*: "In the last days, God says, *I will pour out my Spirit on all people*. Your sons and daughters will prophesy, your young men will see visions, your old men will dream dreams. Even on my servants, both men and women, I will pour out my Spirit in those days, and they will prophesy." ' " Acts 2:14-18, NIV. (See Joel 2:28, 29.)

NOTE.—In the Old Testament the Holy Spirit was selectively apportioned to anointed leaders, such as prophets, priests, and kings. But the prophets spoke of a time when it would be "poured out" (see Isaiah 32:15; 44:3; Ezekiel 39:29) on *all* people—even the male and female slaves (Joel 2:28, 29). This new era of the Spirit began with the day of Pentecost. In the Old Testament the bestowal of the Spirit is often associated with anointing (1 Samuel 10:1, 6; 16:13; Isaiah 61:1), and only a few leaders were anointed. But in the New Testament the bestowal of the Spirit is associated with baptism, and all Christians are baptized: "Peter replied, 'Repent and be baptized, every one of you, in the name of Jesus Christ for the forgiveness of your sins. And you will receive the gift of the Holy Spirit.' " Acts 2:38. (See also Acts 5:32; 10:47; 19:5, 6.)

What illustration from nature is used of the outpouring of the Spirit?

"Be glad then, you children of Zion, and rejoice in the Lord your God; for He has given you the *former rain* faithfully, and He will cause the rain to come down for you—the former rain, and *the latter rain* in the first month." Joel 2:23, NKJV. (See also Hosea 6:3.)

NOTE.—In Palestine the early rains prepare the soil for the seed sowing, and the latter rains ripen the grain for the harvest. So the early outpouring of the Spirit prepared the world for the extensive sowing of the gospel seed, and the final outpouring will come to ripen the golden grain for the harvest of the earth, which Christ says is "the end of the world" (Matthew 13:37-39; Revelation 14:14, 15).

For what are we told to pray at this time?

"Ask the Lord for rain in the time of the latter rain. The Lord will make flashing clouds; He will give showers of rain, grass in the field for everyone." Zechariah 10:1, NKJV.

NOTE.—Before the apostles received the baptism of the Spirit in the early rain on the day of Pentecost, they all "joined together constantly in prayer" (Acts 1:14, NIV). During this time they confessed their faults, put away their differences, ceased their selfish ambitions and contentions for place and power, so that when the time for the outpouring came, "they were all with one accord in one place" (Acts 2:1), ready for its reception. To prepare for the final outpouring of the Spirit, all sin and selfish ambition must again be put away, and a like work of grace worked upon the hearts of God's people.

How is the closing message of the gospel described in Revelation?

"After this I saw another angel coming down from heaven. He had great authority, and *the earth was illuminated by his splendor*." Revelation 18:1, NIV.

What does this messenger say?

"With a mighty voice he shouted: *'Fallen! Fallen is Babylon the Great!* She has become a home for demons and a haunt for every evil spirit, a haunt for every unclean and detestable bird.' " Verse 2, NIV.

NOTE.—At the end of time the religious world will be in much the same condition as the Jewish nation after it rejected Christ at His first advent (see 2 Timothy 3:1-5).

What did Peter on the day of Pentecost tell his hearers to do?

"With many other words he warned them; and he pleaded with them, *'Save yourselves from this corrupt generation.'* " Acts 2:40, NIV.

What similar appeal will be made under the final outpouring of the Spirit?

"Then I heard another voice from heaven say: *'Come out of her, my people*, so that you will not share in her sins, so that you will not receive any of her plagues; for her sins are piled up to heaven, and God has remembered her crimes.' " Revelation 18:4, 5, NIV.

NOTE.—A great work will be accomplished in a short time under the final outpouring of the Spirit. Many voices all over the earth will sound the warning cry. Signs and wonders will be wrought by the believers, and, as at Pentecost, thousands will be converted in a day.

Those who fail to heed this final gospel call, like the unbelievers of Jesus' day, will be doomed to destruction. The seven last plagues will overtake them, as war, famine, death, and destruction overtook those who, not believing in Christ, failed to heed His call to flee, and shut themselves up in Jerusalem to their doom. Those who heed the call, and separate themselves from sin and from sinners, will be saved.

CHAPTER 6

The Sure Word of Prophecy

WHY PROPHECY WAS GIVEN

Why were the Sacred Writings given?

"For everything that was written in the past was written *to teach us, so that through endurance and the encouragement of the Scriptures we might have hope*." Romans 15:4, NIV.

By what means is all scripture given?

"All scripture is *God-breathed*." 2 Timothy 3:16, NIV.

For what is it useful?

"And is useful for *teaching, rebuking, correcting and training in righteousness*, so that the man of God may be thoroughly equipped for every good work." 2 Timothy 3:16, NIV.

How was the prophecy given?

"For prophecy never had its origin in the will of man, but *men spoke from God as they were carried along by the Holy Spirit*." 2 Peter 1:21, NIV.

What is the Lord able to do regarding the future?

"See, the former things have taken place, and new things I declare; *before they spring into being I announce them to you*." Isaiah 42:9, NIV.

Why does the Lord do this?

"I have told you now before it happens, so that when it does happen you will believe." John 14:29, NIV.

NOTE.—The purpose of prophecy is not merely to satisfy curiosity or even to enable us to know the future in advance, but to assure the righteous, once they see the fulfillment, in knowing that God is in control of human history and is carrying out His purpose and plan in the earth.

How far-reaching is God's ability to reveal the future?

"Remember the former things, those of long ago; I am God, and there is no other; I am God, and there is none like me. *I make known*

the end from the beginning, from ancient times, what is still to come."
Isaiah 46:9, 10, NIV.

NOTE.—God works through history, and speaks to His prophets
of things He will bring to pass. More, perhaps, than any other one
thing, the prophecies of the Bible and their fulfillment bear witness
to its divine inspiration.

To whom does God reveal the secrets of the future?

"Surely the Sovereign Lord does nothing without revealing his
plan to his servants *the prophets*." Amos 3:7, NIV.

To whom do these revealed things belong?

"The secret things belong to the Lord our God, but the things revealed belong *to us and to our children forever*." Deuteronomy 29:29,
NIV.

What did the apostle Peter say about the message he preached?

"We did not follow cleverly invented stories when we told you
about the power and coming of our Lord Jesus Christ, *but we were
eyewitnesses of his majesty*." 2 Peter 1:16, NIV.

How does Peter emphasize the reliability of prophecy?

"And we have the word of the prophets *made more certain*, and
you will do well to pay attention to it, as to a light shining in a dark
place, until the day dawns and the morning star rises in your hearts."
Verse 19, NIV.

**What has always been the theme of God's prophets, and whose
spirit has led them?**

"For you are receiving the goal of your faith, *the salvation of your
souls*. Concerning this salvation, the prophets, who spoke of the grace
that was to come to you, searched intently and with the greatest care,
trying to find out the time and circumstances to which *the Spirit of
Christ* in them was pointing when he predicted the sufferings of
Christ and the glories that would follow." 1 Peter 1:9-11, NIV.

In what prophecy did Jesus recognize Daniel as a prophet?

"So when you see standing in the holy place 'the abomination
that causes desolation,' spoken of *through the prophet Daniel*—let
the reader understand—then let those who are in Judea flee to the
mountains." Matthew 24:15, 16, NIV.

NOTE.—This text confirms that Jesus saw the "abomination of
desolation" as still future in His day.

Until when were the prophecies of Daniel, as a whole, to be sealed?

"But you, Daniel, close up and seal the words of the scroll until *the time of the end*. Many will go here and there to increase knowledge." Daniel 12:4, NIV.

What assurance that these prophecies would be understood in the last days was given by the angel?

"He replied, 'Go your way, Daniel, because the words are closed up and sealed until the time of the end. Many will be purified, made spotless and refined, but the wicked will continue to be wicked. None of the wicked will understand, but *those who are wise will understand.*' " Verses 9, 10, NIV.

What is the last book of the Bible called?

"The Revelation of Jesus Christ, which God gave him." Revelation 1:1, NRSV.

What is said of those who read, hear, and keep the things contained in the book of Revelation?

"*Blessed* is the one who reads aloud the words of the prophecy, and blessed are those who hear and who keep what is written in it; for the time is near." Verse 3, NRSV.

GOD'S PLANS THROUGHOUT SCRIPTURE

What curses did God pronounce to Adam and Eve as a consequence of their sin?

"To the woman he said, *'I will greatly increase your pains in childbearing*; with pain you will give birth to children. Your desire will be for your husband, and he will rule over you.'

"To Adam he said, 'Because you listened to your wife and ate from the tree about which I commanded you, "You must not eat of it," *cursed* is *the ground* because of you; through painful toil you will eat of it all the days of your life. It will produce thorns and thistles for you, and you will eat the plants of the field. By the sweat of your brow you will eat your food until you return to the ground, since from it you were taken; for dust you are and to dust you will return.' " Genesis 3:16-19, NIV.

What did God then do?

"And the Lord God said, 'The man has now become like one of us, knowing good and evil. He must not be allowed to reach out his hand and take also from the tree of life and eat, and live forever.' So *the Lord God banished him from the Garden of Eden* to work the ground from which he had been taken." Verses 22, 23, NIV.

NOTE.—God created a sin-free world in which humanity enjoyed perfect relationships with each other, with nature, and with God. Sin soon corrupted these relationships. The Bible is the story of God's tireless efforts to set things right again.

How did God plan to bless the world through Abraham?

"The Lord had said to Abram, 'Leave your country, your people and your father's household and go to the land I will show you. *I will make you into a great nation* and I will bless you; I will make your name great, and you will be a blessing. I will bless those who bless you, and whoever curses you I will curse; and all peoples on earth will be blessed through you.' " Genesis 12:1-3, NIV.

NOTE.—Here God is beginning to undo the curses of Genesis 3, blessing Abraham with children, land, and a renewed relationship with God. God had separated the peoples at the Tower of Babel, but now He planned to bring the people together again through the children of Abraham.

What covenant did God establish with Abraham?

"As the sun was setting, Abram fell into a deep sleep, and a thick and dreadful darkness came over him. Then the Lord said to him, *'Know for certain that your descendants will be strangers in a country not their own, and they will be enslaved and mistreated four hundred years. But I will punish the nation they serve as slaves, and afterward they will come out with great possessions.* You, however, will go to your fathers in peace and be buried at a good old age. *In the fourth generation your descendants will come back here,* for the sin of the Amorites has not yet reached its full measure." Genesis 15:12-16, NIV.

NOTE.—God's patience with the sinful Canaanites is an early evidence of His grace.

How did God renew this covenant?

"When Abram was ninety-nine years old, the Lord appeared to him and said, 'I am God Almighty; walk before me and be blameless. I will confirm my covenant between me and you and will greatly increase your numbers.' Abram fell facedown, and God said to him, 'As for me, this is my covenant with you: *You will be the father of many nations. No longer will you be called Abram; your name will be Abraham,* for I have made you a father of many nations. *I will make you very fruitful; I will make nations of you, and kings will come from you.* I will establish my covenant as an everlasting covenant between me and you and your descendants after you for the generations to come, to be your God and the God of your descendants after you. The whole land of Canaan, where you are now an alien, I will give as an everlasting possession to you and your descendants after you; and I will be their God.' " Genesis 17:1-8, NIV.

NOTE.—Though humanity had lost Eden, God planned for Canaan to be its new Eden. Had Abraham's descendants been faithful to God, the whole world would have been restored in relationship to Him.

How did God present the Israelites' future as a nation as they at last prepared to enter Canaan?

"If you fully obey the Lord your God and carefully follow all his commands I give you today, the Lord your God will set you high above the all the nations on earth. All these blessings will come upon you and accompany you if you obey the Lord your God.

"You will be blessed in the city and blessed in the country. The fruit of your womb will be blessed, and the crops of your land and the young of your livestock—the calves of your herds and the lambs of your flocks. Your basket and your kneading trough will be blessed. You will be blessed when you come in and blessed when you go out. . . . The Lord will send a blessing on your barns and on everything you put your hand to. The Lord your God will bless you in the land he is giving you. The Lord will establish you as a holy people, as he promised you on oath, if you keep the commands of the Lord your God and walk in his ways. Then all the peoples on earth will see that you are called by the name of the Lord, and they will fear you.

"The Lord will grant you abundant prosperity—in the fruit of your womb, the young of your livestock and the crops of your ground—in the land he swore to your forefathers to give you." Deuteronomy 28:1-11, NIV.

NOTE.—God planned to bless them in the areas humanity had been cursed at the Fall—in childbirth, crops, and land—if they would be faithful to Him. In this way the end of the sinful world would not come all at once, but would instead be a gradual process of restoration.

What would happen if Israel turned away from God?

"However, if you do not obey the Lord your God and do not carefully follow all his commands and decrees I am giving you today, all these curses will come upon you and overtake you: You will be cursed in the city and cursed in the country. Your basket and your kneading trough will be cursed. The fruit of your womb

will be cursed, and the crops of your land, and the calves of your
herds and the lambs of your flocks. You will be cursed when you
come in and cursed when you go out.

"The Lord will send on you curses, confusion and rebuke in
everything you put your hand to, until you are destroyed and come to
sudden ruin because of the evil you have done in forsaking him. . . .
If you do not carefully follow all the words of this law, which are
written in this book, and do not revere this glorious and awesome
name—the Lord your God—the Lord will send fearful plagues on
you and your descendants, harsh and prolonged disasters, and severe
and lingering illnesses. He will bring upon you all the diseases of
Egypt that you dreaded, and they will cling to you. The Lord will also
bring on you every kind of sickness and disaster not recorded in this
Book of the Law, until you are destroyed. You who were as numerous
as the stars in the sky will be left but few in number, because you did
not obey the Lord your God. Just as it pleased the Lord to make you
prosper and increase in number, so it will please him to ruin and destroy you. You will be uprooted from the land you are entering to possess." Verses 15-63, NIV.

NOTE.—God's predictions of prosperity and restoration depended on Israel's keeping of the covenant. If the covenant was forsaken, disaster would result. The Bible tells us that is what happened.

How did God depict Jerusalem's spiritual history to the prophet Ezekiel, exiled in Babylon?

As a woman abandoned at birth whom God rescues and restores
to health, yet who abandons God for other lovers.

"Later I passed by, and when I looked at you and saw that you
were old enough for love, I spread the corner of my garment over
you and covered your nakedness. I gave you my solemn oath and
entered into a covenant with you, declares the Sovereign Lord, and
you became mine. I bathed you with water and washed the blood
from you and put ointments on you. I clothed you with an embroidered dress and put leather sandals on you. I dressed you in fine
linen and covered you with costly garments. I adorned you with
jewelry: I put bracelets on your arms and a necklace around your
neck, and I put a ring on your nose, earrings on your ears and a
beautiful crown on your head. So you were adorned with gold and
silver; your clothes were of fine linen and costly fabric and embroidered cloth. . . . You became very beautiful and rose to be a
queen. And your fame spread among the nations on account of your
beauty, because the splendor I had given you made your beauty perfect, declares the Sovereign Lord.

"But you trusted in your beauty and used your fame to become a prostitute. You lavished your favors on anyone who passed by and your beauty became his. You took some of your garments to make gaudy high places, where you carried on your prostitution. Such things should not happen, nor should they ever occur. You also took the fine jewelry I gave you, the jewelry made of my gold and silver, and you made for yourself male idols and engaged in prostitution with them. And you took your embroidered clothes to put on them, and you offered my oil and incense before them. . . . At the head of every street you built your lofty shrines and degraded your beauty, offering your body with increasing promiscuity to anyone who passed by." Ezekiel 16:8-25, NIV.

NOTE.—God depicts Jerusalem as a woman whom He blesses with great beauty and possessions, yet who turns her spiritual and material blessings into curses through prostitution. It is an allegory of Israel's unfaithfulness to God, turning again and again to idolatry and false gods. The allegory also parallels the experience of King Solomon. God blessed Solomon's kingdom with unparalleled prosperity, yet his multiple marriages to idol worshippers turned his heart from God, and God tore his kingdom in two (1 Kings 11:1-13).

What remedy did God give for Israel's unfaithfulness?

"Therefore say to the house of Israel, 'This is what the Sovereign Lord says: It is not for your sake, O house of Israel, that I am going to do these things, but for the sake of my holy name, which you have profaned among the nations where you have gone. I will show the holiness of my great name, which has been profaned among the nations, the name you have profaned among them. Then the nations will know that I am the Lord, declares the Sovereign Lord, when I show myself holy through you before their eyes.

" 'For I will take you out of the nations; I will gather you back from all the countries and bring you back into your own land. I will sprinkle clean water on you, and you will be clean; I will cleanse you from all your impurities and from all your idols. I will give you a new heart and put a new spirit in you; I will remove from you your heart of stone and give you a heart of flesh. And I will put my Spirit in you and move you to follow my decrees and be careful to keep my laws. You will live in the land I gave your forefathers; you will be my people, and I will be your God. I will save you from all your uncleanness. I will call for the grain and make it plentiful and will not bring famine upon you. I will increase the fruit of the trees and the crops of the field, so that you will no longer suffer disgrace among the nations because of famine. Then you will remember your evil ways and wicked deeds, and you will loathe yourselves for your sins and detestable practices. I want you to know that I am not doing this for your sake, declares the Sovereign Lord. Be ashamed and disgraced for your conduct, O house of Israel!

" 'This is what the Sovereign Lord says: On the day I cleanse you from all your sins, I will resettle your towns, and the ruins will be rebuilt. The desolate land will be cultivated instead of lying desolate in the sight of all who pass through it. They will say, "This land that was laid waste has become like the garden of Eden; the cities that were lying in ruins, desolate and destroyed, are now fortified and inhabited." Then the nations around you that remain will know that I the Lord have rebuilt what was destroyed and have replanted what was desolate. I the Lord have spoken, and I will do it.'

" 'This is what the Sovereign Lord says: Once again I will yield to the plea of the house of Israel and do this for them: I will make their people as numerous as sheep, as numerous as the flocks for offerings at Jerusalem during her appointed times. So will the ruined cities be filled with flocks of people. Then they will know that I am the Lord.' " Ezekiel 36:22-38, NIV.

NOTE.—In these verses, God is offering to renew His covenant promises, despite centuries of spiritual failure. "The most comprehensive picture of Israel's ideal future can be found in Ezekiel 36:22-38, which portrays a threefold transformation of reality. God planned to transform *human society* by restoring Israel to her land and to her witness to the nations (verses 24, 28, 33-36). He would transform *human nature* with a new heart and a new spirit (verses 25-27). And He would eventually transform the *natural world* itself, banishing hunger and violence (verses 30, 35).

"The triple transformation of reality envisioned by the prophets differed somewhat from earlier views of the end. Unlike the Flood story, in which the end involved the full, physical destruction of the planet, *the end that the prophets envisioned would come within history and geography as they understood it*. Unlike Deuteronomy, where the end would come gradually, a little at a time, as Israel obeyed, *the end that the prophets foretold would begin with a sudden, mighty intervention of God*, usually described in the context of the exile to and return from Babylon.

"God's mighty intervention would precipitate the eschatological war, the last battle of earth's history. Not only would God break into history to radically transform *human society*, *human nature*, and *the natural world*, but He would also clear the way for His people on earth through a great final war against their enemies. That war and its results would help set in motion the blessed end that Israel as a whole might have gained gradually by obedience, but did not.

"The move from a gradual to a spectacular view of the end went hand in hand with Israel's failure to live up to God's expectations in Deuteronomy. In Deuteronomy the promise was offered that the world could be transformed by the obedience of God's people. In the prophets, however, the transformation of the world would not come because Israel deserved it, but rather to vindicate the character of God . . . (Ezekiel 36:22, 23).

"Instead of bringing blessing (relationship with God) to the nations, Israel profaned God's name among the nations. The end does not come through Israel's obedience; therefore, *it is purely an act of grace. God intervenes to vindicate His name among the nations.* He does so by elevating His people, even though they have not carried out their part of the bargain. God's transformation of *human society* would serve larger concerns than just the welfare of the Israelites." Jon Paulien, *What the Bible Says About the End-time* (Hagerstown, Md.: Review and Herald, 1994), pp. 56, 57.

How does Ezekiel describe a war at the end of time?

"Therefore, son of man, prophesy and say to Gog: 'This is what the Sovereign Lord says: In that day, when my people Israel are living in safety, will you not take notice of it? You will come from your place in the far north, you and many nations with you, all of them riding on horses, a great horde, a mighty army. You will advance against my people Israel like a cloud that covers the land. In days to come, O Gog, I will bring you against my land, so that the nations may know me when I show myself holy through you before their eyes.

" 'This is what the Sovereign Lord says: Are you not the one I spoke of in former days by my servants the prophets of Israel? At that time they prophesied for years that I would bring you against them. This is what will happen in that day: When Gog attacks the land of Israel, my hot anger will be aroused, declares the Sovereign Lord. In my zeal and fiery wrath I declare that at that time there shall be a great earthquake in the land of Israel. The fish of the sea, the birds of the air, the beasts of the field, every creature that moves along the ground, and all the people on the face of the earth will tremble at my presence. The mountains will be overturned, the cliffs will crumble and every wall will fall to the ground. I will summon a sword against Gog on all my mountains, declares the Sovereign Lord. Every man's sword will be against his brother. I will execute judgment upon him with plague and bloodshed; I will pour down torrents of rain, hailstones and burning sulfur on him and on his troops and on the many nations with him." Ezekiel 38:14-22, NIV.

What was to have been God's purpose in this eschatological war?

"And so I will show my greatness and my holiness, and I will make myself known in the sight of many nations. Then they will know that I am the Lord." Ezekiel 38:23, NIV.

NOTE.—The purpose of this war was to have been God's purpose throughout history: to glorify His name and draw people to Him. This war did not take place, but the prophecy is to be fulfilled at the end of the millennium (see Revelation 20:7-9).

"The war at the end is found in many places, including Zechariah 12 and 14 and Daniel 11. . . . In Joel 2 and 3 the war at the end takes place in the context of the return from the Exile (Joel 3:1, 2)—a time of great spiritual renewal (Joel 2:28, 29). There is a remnant, calling on the name of the Lord, huddled for safety in Jerusalem (verse 32). God does not embark on this war arbitrarily, but He deals with the nation according to how they have treated His people (Joel 3:2-8). *The end-time war is not a battle between secular powers in the Middle East but a battle between God's people and their enemies. It is an act of judgment against spiritual rebellion.*

"God calls the nations to the Valley of Jehoshaphat, the valley around Jerusalem, to sit in judgment on them (verses 12-15). He then acts to protect His people (verse 16). His people don't have to fight in the war themselves. Following this description, comes a beautiful picture of security (verses 17-21). God dwells with His people in Jerusalem. Jerusalem will never again be invaded. The mountains drip new wine and milk, and abundant water flows from the Temple. Judah and Jerusalem are inhabited forever. . . .

"If you compare Joel and Ezekiel . . . the prophets actually described two separate wars at the end. The first (Joel) would take place in the context of the return from Babylonian exile and would involve the nearer nations around Israel resisting the Israelites' return. After that resistance was overcome, there would be a time of settling in and the gradual fulfillment of the restoration promises. At some point, the more distant nations would become jealous and so seek to profit from Israel's prosperity (Ezekiel 38:12-14). Their invasion would precipitate a second and final intervention on the part of God.

"Something similar to the above takes place in Revelation. The most extensively described portion of the battle of Armageddon occurs before the second coming of Christ in Revelation 16:12-16; 17:14; and 19:11-21. But the ultimate battle at the end is repeated once more after the thousand years, at the final end (Revelation 20:17-10). . . .

"Tragically, the end envisioned by the prophets never came true in any literal sense. The Old Testament, therefore, closes with a big question mark. Its view of the end, by itself, is incomplete. The Old Testament looks forward to something outside itself for completion." Jon Paulien, *What the Bible Says about the End-time* (Hagerstown, Md.: Review and Herald, 1994), pp. 62-64.

Thus, if we want to understand the prophecies of the Old Testament, we must do so through the book of Revelation. In turn, if we want to understand Revelation, we must understand how it is grounded in the Old Testament.

NEBUCHADNEZZAR'S DREAM

What did Nebuchadnezzar, king of Babylon, say to the astrologers he assembled after a disturbing dream?

"In the second year of his reign, Nebuchadnezzar had dreams; his mind was troubled and he could not sleep. So the king summoned the magicians, enchanters, sorcerers and astrologers to tell him what he had dreamed. When they came in and stood before the king, he said to them, *'I have had a dream that troubles me and I want to know what it means.'* " Daniel 2:1-3, NIV.

What did the astrologers, after being threatened with death if they did not tell Nebuchadnezzar the dream and its interpretation, say to the king?

"The astrologers answered the king, *'There is not a man on earth who can do what the king asks!* No king, however great and mighty, has ever asked such a thing of any magician or enchanter or astrologer. What the king asks is too difficult. *No one can reveal it to the king except the gods, and they do not live among men.'* " Verses 10, 11, NIV.

After the astrologers confessed their inability to do what the king demanded, who offered to interpret the dream?

"At this, *Daniel* went in to the king and asked for time, so that he might interpret the dream for him." Verse 16, NIV.

After Daniel and his friends had pleaded earnestly in prayer, how were the dream and its interpretation revealed to Daniel?

"During the night the mystery was revealed to Daniel *in a vision*. Then Daniel praised the God of heaven." Verse 19, NIV.

What did Daniel, when brought before the king, say?

"Daniel replied, 'No wise man, enchanter, magician or diviner can explain to the king the mystery he has asked about, but *there is a God in heaven who reveals mysteries*. He has shown King Neb-uchadnezzar what will happen in days to come.'" Verses 27, 28, NIV.

What did Daniel say the king had seen in his dream?

"Your dream and the visions that passed through your mind as you lay on your bed are these: As you were lying there, O king, your mind turned to things to come, and the revealer of mysteries showed you what is going to happen. As for me, this mystery has been re-vealed to me, not because I have greater wisdom than other living men, but so that you, O king, may know the interpretation and that you may understand what went through your mind. You looked, O king, and there before you stood *a large statue*—an enormous, daz-zling statue, awesome in appearance." Verses 28-31, NIV.

Of what were the different parts of the image composed?

"The head of the statue was made of pure *gold*, its chest and arms of *silver*, its belly and thighs of *bronze*, its legs of *iron*, its feet *partly of iron and partly of baked clay*." Verses 32, 33, NIV.

What smashed the image to pieces?

"While you were watching, *a rock* was cut out, but not by human hands. It struck the statue on its feet of iron and clay and smashed them." Verse 34, NIV.

What happened to the various parts of the image?

"Then the iron, the clay, the bronze, the silver and the gold were broken to pieces at the same time and *became like chaff on a thresh-ing floor in the summer. The wind swept them away without leaving a trace*. But the rock that struck the statue became a huge mountain and filled the whole earth." Verse 35, NIV.

What did Daniel say the head of gold represented?

"You, O king, are the king of kings. The God of heaven has given you dominion and power and might and glory; in your hands he has placed mankind and the beasts of the field and the birds of the air. Wherever they live, he has made you ruler over them all. *You are that head of gold*." Verses 37, 38, NIV.

NOTE.—The character of the Neo-Babylonian Empire is fittingly represented by gold. It was "the golden kingdom of a golden age." Enlarged and beautified during the reign of Nebuchadnezzar, Baby-lon reached a height of unrivaled magnificence. The ancient writers, like Herodotus, are found by archaeologists to be generally accurate, except for a tendency to exaggerate, in their enthusiastic descriptions, the size of the great city with its massive fortifications, its lavishly ornamented temples and palaces, its lofty temple-tower, and its "hanging gardens" rising terrace upon terrace, which came to be known among the Greeks as one of the Seven Wonders of the Ancient World.

How does the prophet Jeremiah describe the kingdom of Babylon?

"Babylon was a gold cup in the Lord's hand; she made the whole earth drunk. The nations drank her wine; therefore they have gone mad." Jeremiah 51:7, NIV.

NOTE.—Revelation 14:8 draws on this imagery for its description of spiritual Babylon: "A second angel followed and said, 'Fallen! Fallen is Babylon the Great, which made all the nations drink the maddening wine of her adulteries.'"

What was to be the nature of the next kingdom after Babylon?

"After you, another kingdom will rise, *inferior to yours*." Daniel 2:39, NIV.

Who was the last Babylonian king?

"That very night *Belshazzar*, king of the Babylonians, was slain, and Darius the Mede took over the kingdom, at the age of sixty-two." Daniel 5:30, 31, NIV. (See also verses 1, 2.)

Who conquered Belshazzar's kingdom?

"Your kingdom is divided and given to *the Medes and Persians*." Verse 28, NIV.

What represents the kingdom of the Medes and Persians, generally known as the Persian Empire, in Nebuchadnezzar's dream?

The chest and arms of *silver* (Daniel 2:32).

By what is the Greek, or Macedonian, Empire, which succeeded the kingdom of the Medes and Persians, represented in the image?

"Its belly and thighs of *bronze*." Daniel 2:32, NIV. "Next, *a third kingdom, one of bronze*, will rule over the whole earth." Verse 39, NIV.

NOTE.—That the Greek Empire replaced the Persian is clearly stated in Daniel 8:5-8, 20, 21.

What is said of the fourth kingdom?

"Finally, there will be a fourth kingdom, *strong as iron*—for iron breaks and smashes everything—and as iron breaks things to pieces, *so it will crush and break all the others.*" Daniel 2:40, NIV.

What scripture shows that the Roman emperors ruled the world?

"In those days *a decree went out from Emperor Augustus that all the world should be registered.*" Luke 2:1, NIV.

What did the mixture of clay and iron in the feet and toes of the image represent?

"As you saw the feet and toes partly of potter's clay and partly of iron, it shall be a divided kingdom; but some of the strength of iron shall be in it, as you saw the iron mixed with the clay." Daniel 2:41, NRSV.

NOTE.—Today's world is divided by ethnicity, religion, classes, and more.

In what prophetic language was the varying strength of the 10 kingdoms of the divided empire indicated?

"As the toes of the feet were part iron and part clay, so the kingdom shall be strong and partly brittle." Verse 42, NRSV.

Were any efforts to be made to reunite the divided empire of Rome?

"As you saw the iron mixed with clay, *so will they mix with one another in marriage*, but they will not hold together, just as iron does not mix with clay." Verse 43, NRSV.

NOTE.—Charlemagne, Charles V, Louis XIV, Napoleon, Kaiser Wilhelm, and Hitler all tried to reunite the broken fragments of the Roman Empire and failed. By marriage and intermarriage of royalty ties have been formed with a view to strengthening and cementing together the shattered kingdom, but none have succeeded.

This remarkable dream, as interpreted by Daniel, represents in the briefest form, and yet with unmistakable clearness, a series of world empires from the time of Nebuchadnezzar to the close of earthly history and the setting up of the everlasting kingdom of God. The history confirms the prophecy. Babylon was the leading world power at the time of this dream, 603 B.C. The succeeding Persian Empire, which included the Medes also, began its first year about 538 B.C. The Persian Empire fell to the Greek forces at the Battle of Arbela, in 331 B.C., and the Macedonian Greeks then became the undisputed world power of that time. The Roman takeover of the Greek Empire began in the second half of the fourth century, then crested decisively with the battle of Pydna, in Macedonia, in 168

B.C., and ended in the second half of the second century B.C., when the fourth kingdom was fully established. Today no one empire rules our divided world.

What is to take place in the days of these kingdoms?

"And in the days of those kings *the God of heaven will set up a kingdom that shall never be destroyed*, nor shall this kingdom be left to another people. It shall crush all these kingdoms and bring them to an end, and it shall stand forever." Verse 44, NRSV.

NOTE.—This verse foretells the establishment of another universal kingdom, the kingdom of God, which would overthrow all existing earthly kingdoms, and would stand forever. This kingdom was to be set up "in the days of these kings." This cannot refer to the four preceding empires, or kingdoms; for they were not contemporaneous, but successive; neither can it refer to an establishment of the kingdom at Christ's first advent, for the 10 kingdoms which arose out of the ruins of the Roman Empire were not yet in existence. Therefore, God's eternal kingdom must still be future.

For what have we been taught to pray?

"*Your kingdom come*, your will be done on earth as it is in heaven." Matthew 6:10, NIV.

What is the final announcement, in the New Testament, of the establishment of the kingdom of God?

"Then the seventh angel blew his trumpet, and there were loud voices in heaven, saying, 'The kingdom of the world has become the kingdom of our Lord and of his Messiah, and he will reign forever and ever.' " Revelation 11:15, NRSV.

THE KINGDOMS OF GRACE AND GLORY

Where are we invited to come to find mercy?

"Let us therefore approach the *throne of grace* with boldness, so that we may receive mercy and find grace to help in time of need." Hebrews 4:16, NRSV.

NOTE.—A throne implies a kingdom, and a throne of grace implies a kingdom of grace.

To what other kingdom do the Scriptures call our attention, and when is it to be set up?

"When the Son of Man comes in his glory, and all the angels with him, he will sit on his throne in heavenly glory." Matthew 25:31, NIV.

NOTE.—The kingdom of glory is to be established at the second coming of Christ. Christ said to Pilate, "My kingdom is not of this world." John 18:36, NIV.

What promise does Jesus give to those who overcome the world?

"To him who overcomes, I will give *the right to sit with me on my throne*, just as I overcame and sat down with my Father on his throne." Revelation 3:21, NIV.

How did Jesus seek to correct the false idea that He was about to set up His kingdom of glory?

"He went on to tell them a parable, because he was near Jerusalem and the people thought that the kingdom of God was going to appear at once." Luke 19:11, NIV.

In this parable what did Jesus teach?

"He said: *'A man of noble birth* went to a distant country to have himself appointed king and then to return.' " Verse 12, NIV.

Who is the nobleman?

"In my Father's house are many rooms; if it were not so, I would have told you. I am going there to prepare a place for you. And if I go and prepare a place for you, I will come back and take you to be with me that you also may be where I am." John 14:2, 3, NIV.

NOTE.—The nobleman is Christ Jesus. When He ascended to His Father, He was seated upon His Father's throne, which, while probation lingers, is the throne of grace. Soon He is to receive His kingdom of glory. He has not yet returned, but when He comes it will be to claim His subjects, and to take them to be with Him where He is. The kingdom of glory will be set up at the second coming of Christ, but not on this earth until the close of the 1,000 years (see Revelation 20:6; 15:2, 3, and pp. 298-301).

In what words did Jesus make it clear that the only kingdom God now has on the earth is the kingdom of grace?

"Once, having been asked by the Pharisees when the kingdom of God would come, Jesus replied, 'The kingdom of God does not come with your careful observation, nor will people say, "Here it is," or "There it is," because the kingdom of God *is within you.*' " Luke 17:20, 21, NIV.

NOTE.—Jesus reigns over willing subjects only. His reign now is wholly spiritual. Not until His second coming will He set up His kingdom of glory.

By what are we saved from sin?

"For it is by *grace* you have been saved, through *faith*—and this is not from yourselves, it is the gift of God." Ephesians 2:8, NIV. (See Romans 6:23.)

NOTE.—It follows, then, that only through the grace, or favor, of God can sinners be saved. There is no other way. Abraham, Moses, and David, as well as Peter, Paul, and John, were saved by grace. These all, therefore, were in the kingdom of grace, which must have been in existence as early as there was a lost person who needed grace.

When Christ sent out His disciples, what did He tell them to preach?

"He sent them to preach the *kingdom of God*, and to heal the sick." Luke 9:2.

What did they, in carrying out their commission, preach?

"They departed, and went through the towns, preaching *the gospel*, and healing every where." Verse 6.

NOTE.—Theirs was a gospel not of compulsion, but of persuasion; a gospel not of the sword, but of the love of God; not a political gospel, but the gospel of the Gift of God.

In the parable of the wheat and the weeds, what does the good seed represent?

"The field is the world, and the good seed stands for *the sons of the kingdom*." Matthew 13:38, NIV.

Who sowed the weeds in the kingdom?

"The enemy who sows them is *the devil*." Verse 39, NIV.

To whom did God entrust this earth?

"Then God said, 'Let us make *man* in our image, in our likeness, *and let them rule* over the fish of the sea and the birds of the air, over the livestock, over all the earth, and over all the creatures that move along the ground." Genesis 1:26, NIV.

What did human beings do with this trust?

"*Sin* entered the world through one man, and death through sin. . . . Through the *disobedience* of the one man the many were made sinners." Romans 5:12-19, NIV.

NOTE.—Human beings fell, and the world became the abode of sin. Satan will continue his reign until sin is blotted out. Whoever would become a subject of God's kingdom of grace must now separate from Satan's control. The sinner must yield obedience to God's laws. Those who do this enter into an arrangement made by God, by which they become His subjects, and renounce the service of Satan. They are then in God's kingdom of grace, because they are the subjects of God's favor, or grace (cf. Colossians 1:13).

What did God promise to David, king of Israel?

"You said, 'I have made a covenant with my chosen one, I have sworn to David my servant, "I will establish your line forever and *make your throne firm through all generations*."'" Psalm 89:4, NIV.

Through whom was the throne of David to be perpetuated?

"For to us a child is born, to us a son is given, and *the government will be on his shoulders*. And he will be called Wonderful Counselor, Mighty God, Everlasting Father, Prince of Peace. Of the increase of his government and peace there will be no end. He will reign on David's throne and over his kingdom, establishing and upholding it with justice and righteousness from that time on and forever." Isaiah 9:6, 7, NIV.

Who is this heir to David's throne?

"You will be with child and give birth to a son, and you are to give him the name *Jesus*. He will be great and will be called the Son of the Most High. The Lord *God will give him the throne of his father David*, and he will reign over the house of Jacob forever; his kingdom will never end." Luke 1:31-33, NIV.

Where did Jesus go after His resurrection?

"God has raised this Jesus to life, and we are all witnesses of the fact. *Exalted to the right hand of God*, he has received from the Father the promised Holy Spirit and has poured out what you now see and hear. For David did not ascend to heaven, and yet he said, 'The Lord said to my Lord: *"Sit at my right hand until I make your enemies a footstool for your feet."*' Therefore let all Israel be assured of this: *God has made this Jesus, whom you crucified, both Lord and Christ*." Acts 2:32-36, NIV.

"To him who overcomes, I will give the right to sit with me on my throne, just as I overcame and sat down with my Father on his throne." Revelation 3:21, NIV.

What is He doing at the Father's right hand?

"The God of our fathers raised Jesus from the dead—whom you

had killed by hanging him on a tree. God exalted him to his own right hand as Prince and Savior *that he might give repentance and forgiveness of sins to Israel.*" Acts 5:30, 31, NIV. "The point of what we are saying is this: *We do have such a high priest, who sat down at the right hand of the throne of the Majesty in heaven.*" Hebrews 8:1, NIV.

When His priestly work is finished, what will Christ receive?

"In my vision at night I looked, and there before me was one like a son of man, coming with the clouds of heaven. He approached the Ancient of Days and was led into his presence. *He was given authority, glory and sovereign power; all peoples, nations and men of every language worshiped him.* His dominion is an everlasting dominion that will not pass away, and his kingdom is one that will never be destroyed." Daniel 7:13, 14, NIV.

When He comes in the clouds of glory, on whose throne will He sit?

"When the Son of Man comes in his glory, and all the angels with him, he will sit *on his throne in heavenly glory.*" Matthew 25:31, NIV. (See Revelation 11:15.)

What will He then say to the redeemed?

"Then the King will say to those on his right, 'Come, you who are blessed by my Father; take your inheritance, the kingdom prepared for you since the creation of the world.' " Matthew 25:34, NIV

FOUR GREAT MONARCHIES

At what time was Daniel's second vision given?

"In the first year of Belshazzar king of Babylon, Daniel had a dream, and visions passed through his mind as he was lying on his bed. He wrote down the substance of his dream." Daniel 7:1, NIV.

What effect did this dream have upon Daniel?

"I, Daniel, *was troubled in spirit*, and the visions that passed through my mind disturbed me." Verse 15, NIV.

NOTE.—The effect of Daniel's dream upon him was similar to the effect of Nebuchadnezzar's dreams upon him; it troubled him (see Daniel 2:1).

What did Daniel ask one of the heavenly beings he saw in his dream?

"I approached one of those standing there and *asked him the true meaning of all this*. So he told me and gave me the interpretation of these things." Daniel 7:16, NIV.

What did the prophet see in this vision?

"Daniel said, 'In my vision at night I looked, and there before me were *the four winds of heaven churning up the great sea*.'" Verse 2, NIV.

NOTE.—While the pagan Nebuchadnezzar saw the world's great kingdoms represented by an idol, a symbol he would understand, Daniel's vision recalls scriptural imagery of Creation (see Genesis 1:2), the Flood (see Genesis 8:1), and the Exodus (see Exodus 14:21).

What emerged from the ocean's strife?

"Four great beasts, each different from the others, came up out of the sea." Daniel 7:3, NIV.

What did these four beasts represent?

"The four great beasts are *four kingdoms that will rise from the earth*." Verse 17, NIV.

In symbolic language, what is represented by winds?

Strife, war, commotion (see Jeremiah 25:31-33; 49:36, 37).

NOTE.—That winds denote strife and war is evident from the vision itself. As a result of the striving of the winds, kingdoms rise and fall.

What, in Bible prophecy, is symbolized by waters?

"Then the angel said to me, 'The waters you saw, where the prostitute sits, are *peoples, multitudes, nations* and *languages*." Revelation 17:15, NIV.

NOTE.—In the second chapter of Daniel, under the figure of an image of man, the mere political outline of the rise and fall of earthly kingdoms is given, preceding the setting up of God's everlasting kingdom. In the seventh chapter earthly governments are represented as viewed in the light of Heaven—under the symbols of wild and ferocious beasts—the last, in particular, oppressing and persecuting the saints of the Most High.

How is the first beast described?

"The first was like a lion, and it had the wings of an eagle. I watched until its wings were torn off and it was lifted from the ground that it stood on two feet like a man, and the heart of a man was given to it." Daniel 7:4, NIV.

NOTE.—The lion, the first of these four great beasts, like the golden head of Nebuchadnezzar's dream, represents the Babylonian monarchy; the lion, the king of beasts, standing at the head of his kind, as gold does of metals. The eagle's wings doubtless denote the rapidity with which Babylon rose to its peak of power under Nebuchadnezzar, who reigned from 605 B.C. to 562 B.C. (605 B.C. was his accession year, and the following year was counted his first official year).

What symbolized the second kingdom?

"And there before me was a second beast, which looked like *a bear*. It was raised up on one of its sides, and it had three ribs in its mouth between its teeth. It was told, 'Get up and eat your fill of flesh!' " Verse 5, NIV.

NOTE.—"The Bible characterized the bear by its cruelty (2 Samuel 17:8; Proverbs 28:15; Amos 5:19). The parallel passage of Daniel 2 identifies the bear with the Medes and Persians, a conclusion confirmed by the bear's bizarre posture: 'It was raised up on one of its sides' (Daniel 7:5). The creature is evidently not standing up on its hind paws, because it is later told to 'get up and eat.' More likely the bear has raised on one of its sides, left or right, presenting one part of its body as higher than the other and ready to strike. . . . The image of the 'side,' biblical symbol of aggressiveness (see Ezekiel 34:21, which describes the aggressiveness of the sheep that shoves 'with flank and shoulder'), alludes to the creature's cruelty. In chapter 8 two horns, one bigger than the other (verse 3), depict the power of the Medes and Persians. A bear 'raised up on one of its sides' thus represents a duality of powers, one stronger than the other. . . .

"Another characteristic of the beast is that it carries three ribs in its mouth. A similar passage in Amos mentions three pieces of flesh and bones recovered from the lion's mouth as the sole remains of his meal (Amos 3:12). It is another way to suggest the beast's voracity. The carnivorous character of the meal ('three ribs' or sides) echoes the bear's carnivorous position ('on its side'). The passage then concludes: 'Get up and eat your fill of flesh!'—a passage often understood as alluding to the three main conquests of the Persians: Lydia, Babylonia, and Egypt. But if these three conquests are but the remains, how much more did the conquering power of Cyrus actually devour! One college textbook declares: 'The Persian empire had been created in a single generation by Cyrus the Great. In 559 B.C. he came to the throne of Persia, then a small kingdom well to the east of the lower Mesopotamian valley; unified Persia under his rule; made an alliance with Babylonia; and led a successful rebellion to-

ward the north against the Medes, who were the overlords of Persia.
. . . In succeeding years he expanded his empire in all directions, in
the process defeating Crosesus and occupying Lydia' (Donald Kagen,
Steven Ozment, and Frank M. Turner, *The Western Heritage*, 3rd ed.
[New York: 1987], p. 59)." Jacques B. Doukhan, *Secrets of Daniel*
(Hagerstown, Md.: Review and Herald, 2000), pp. 102-104.

The first year of this kingdom of the Medes and Persians began
in October of 539 B.C., when Babylon fell to the Persians.

What symbolized the third universal empire?

"After that, I looked, and there before me was another beast, one
that looked *like a leopard*. And on its back it had four wings like
those of a bird. This beast had four heads, and it was given authority
to rule." Daniel 7:6, NIV.

NOTE.—If the wings of an eagle on the back of a lion denoted rapidity of movement in the Babylonian Empire (Habakkuk 1:6-8), four
wings on the leopard must denote unparalleled speed in the Greek
Empire. This we find to be historically true.

"In the spring of 334 B.C. Alexander crossed over to Asia Minor
at the head of an army of some thirty-five thousand Macedonians
and Greeks. . . . Four years later—he had overthrown the Persian Empire founded by Cyrus the Great, and set himself up as its ruler by
right of conquest. Another four years were spent in the subjugation
of the wild tribes of the Iranian Plateau and the more civilized peoples of the Indus Valley. In this short space of eight years Alexander
had annexed an area of little less than two million square miles, containing a population of more than twenty million persons. The amazing rapidity of his conquest, a feat all the more remarkable in view
of the small force at his disposal, was due in large part to the superior organization of the Macedonian army, the excellence of Alexander's generals, trained in the school of his father, Philip, and his own
superlative qualities as a general and a leader of men." A.E.R. Boak,
Albert Hyma, and Preston Slosson, *The Growth of European Civilization* (F. S. Crofts & Co., Inc., 1938), vol. 1, pp. 59, 60. Used by
permission of Appleton-Century-Crofts, Inc.

"This beast had four heads." The Greek Empire maintained its
unity only a short time after the death of Alexander in 323 B.C.
Within 22 years after the close of his brilliant career, or by 301 B.C.,
the empire was divided among four of his leading generals.

How was the fourth kingdom represented?

"After that, in my vision at night I looked, and there before me
was *a fourth beast—terrifying and frightening and very powerful*. It

had *large iron teeth*; it crushed and devoured its victims and trampled underfoot whatever was left. It was different from all the former beasts, and *it had ten horns*." Daniel 7:7, NIV.

What was the fourth beast declared to be?

"He gave me this explanation: *'The fourth beast is a fourth kingdom that will appear on earth*. It will be different from all the other kingdoms and will devour the whole earth, trampling it down and crushing it." Verse 23, NIV.

NOTE.—"The fourth beast of Daniel 7:7 is not identified for us by name anywhere in the book of Daniel—not in chapter 2 nor in chapter 8 nor in chapter 11. That leaves us with a historical question: What power succeeded Greece? Historically, the answer is quite simple. It was Rome. . . . Rome first conquered Greece. Then it had Asia Minor willed to it by the king of Pergamum who had no male offspring. Next, Syria, along with Judea, fell to Pompey and his legions. Finally, Egypt, the last of the four, fell to Rome. In this way, Rome made its conquest of the eastern Mediterranean basin complete. The fourth beast that followed the four heads of the leopard can readily be identified as Rome.

"Daniel does not describe the appearance of the fourth beast as completely as he does the third; for that reason it is sometimes called the 'nondescript' beast. Whatever it may have looked like, the fourth beast shocked Daniel by its appearance. It was, he said, 'terrifying and frightening and very powerful' (Daniel 7:7). This power went on and 'crushed its victims and trampled underfoot whatever was left' (verse 7). The picture is one of very, very thorough conquests. Archaeology has shown how thorough Roman engineers were in destroying previously existent cities to make way for the new Roman occupation. Jerusalem itself was an example. When Rome conquered and destroyed Jerusalem in A.D. 70, the debris from that destruction was scraped into a valley on the west side of the city. Today, that valley, the Tyropoean, no longer even exists because it has been completely filled with the Roman debris from the destruction of the city. . . .

"The prophecy gives an interesting detail about this fourth beast; it says it had teeth of iron (Daniel 7:7). These iron teeth further represent the conquering and destructive nature of this kingdom, but it also forms a direct link with the fourth kingdom in Daniel 2, where the fourth kingdom was represented by the iron legs of the image (Daniel 2:33, 40). Iron was connected with the fourth kingdom in each prophecy, indicating that the powers represented were one and the same." William H. Shea, *The Abundant Life Bible Amplifier:*

Daniel 7-12 (Boise, Idaho: Pacific Press Publishing Association, 1996), pp. 132, 133.

What do the 10 horns represent?

"The horns are *ten kings who will come from this kingdom.*" Daniel 7:24, NIV.

NOTE.—"There is a precedent in Daniel for using the word king to mean 'kingdom.'. . . In Daniel 2, the prophet told Nebuchadnezzar, 'You, O king, . . . are that head of gold' (Verses 36-38). He immediately went on to say, 'After you, another kingdom will arise' (Verse 39). This same parallel usage is found in Daniel 7. In his first and more simple explanation, the angel said to Daniel, 'the four great beasts are four kingdoms [literally, "kings"] that will rise from the earth' (Verse 17). Then later in the chapter, the angel tells Daniel, 'The fourth beast is a fourth kingdom that will appear on earth' (Verse 23). Thus in the original Aramaic text of Daniel 7, there is an example of 'king' and 'kingdom' being used with parallel meanings, just as in chapter 2. With this usage in mind, we can see that the ten horns represent not individual kings, but kingdoms that arose out of the political and military turmoil occurring when Imperial Rome broke up under the assaults of the barbarian tribes from the east and the north. This historical process took a couple of centuries to accomplish, beginning in the fifth century A.D. or even before. Gradually the barbarian tribes that had filled the vacuum left by the fall of Imperial Rome settled down to occupy their respective territories, and eventually they evolved into what we now view as the modern nations of Europe." William H. Shea, *The Abundant Life Bible Amplifier: Daniel 7-12* (Pacific Press, 1996), p. 134.

The Roman Empire was broken up into 10 kingdoms by A.D. 476. Because of the uncertainties of the times, religious writers have differed in the enumeration of the exact kingdoms intended by the prophecy. With good show of reason the following list has freely been adopted by interpreters of prophecy: Alamanni, Ostrogoths, Visigoths, Franks, Vandals, Suevi, Burgundians, Heruli, Anglo-Saxons, and Lombards.

"It is not necessary to be adamant about precisely what tribes were involved. There was a flux in the number of tribes migrating through Europe, and so likewise, there has been a flux in the number of modern nations derived from them. We can take the number ten as a representative number for the corporate whole of such tribes and nations." William H. Shea, *The Abundant Life Bible Amplifier: Daniel 7-12* (Pacific Press, 1996), pp. 134-137.

What change did Daniel see take place in these horns?

"While I was thinking about the horns, there before me was *another horn, a little one, which came up among them; and three of the first horns were uprooted before it.* This horn had eyes like the eyes of a man and a mouth that spoke boastfully." Daniel 7:8, NIV.

What words of Daniel suggest that the fourth beast with its little horn is the main feature of this vision?

"Then I *wanted to know the true meaning of the fourth beast,* which was different from all the others and most terrifying, with its iron teeth and bronze claws—the beast that crushed and devoured its victims and trampled underfoot whatever was left. I *also wanted to know about the ten horns on its head and about the other horn that came up, before which three of them fell*—the horn that looked more imposing than the others and that had eyes and a mouth that spoke boastfully." Verses 19, 20, NIV.

When was the little horn to arise?

"The ten horns are ten kings who will come from this kingdom. *After them* another king will arise." Verse 24, NIV.

NOTE.—The 10 horns, as already shown, arose when Rome, the fourth kingdom, was divided into 10 kingdoms. This division was completed by A.D. 476. After this a little horn was to arise, before whom three of the other kingdoms would fall. The three other kingdoms were the Heruli, Vandals, and Ostrogoths; and the little horn represents the medieval church, under the control of the Papacy.

"When Christianity conquered Rome the ecclesiastical structure of the pagan church, the title and vestments of the *pontifex maximus,* the worship of the Great Mother and a multitude of comforting divinities, the sense of supersensible presences everywhere, the joy or solemnity of old festivals, and the pageantry of immemorial ceremony, passed like maternal blood into the new religion, and captive Rome captured her conqueror. The reins and skills of government were handed down by a dying empire to a virile papacy; the lost power of the broken sword was rewon by the magic of the consoling word; the armies of the state were replaced by the missionaries of the Church moving in all directions along the Roman roads; and the revolted provinces, accepting Christianity, again acknowledged the sovereignty of Rome." Will Durant, *Caesar and Christ* (New York: MFJ Books, 1971), pp. 671, 672.

THE LITTLE HORN

What is said of the little horn as compared with the 10 horns of the fourth beast of Daniel 7?

"After them another king will arise, *different* from the earlier ones; he will subdue three kings." Daniel 7:24, NIV.

NOTE.—The medieval church, which arose on the ruins of the Roman Empire, claimed universal dominion over both spiritual and temporal affairs. It was a union of church and state, frequently with the church dominant.

How does Paul describe this same power under the symbol of "the man of sin"?

"Concerning the coming of our Lord Jesus Christ and our being gathered to him, we ask you . . . not to become easily unsettled or alarmed . . . Don't let anyone deceive you in any way, for that day will not come until the rebellion occurs and the man of lawlessness is revealed, the man doomed to destruction. He will oppose and will exalt himself over everything that is called God or is worshiped, so that he sets himself up in God's temple, proclaiming himself to be God." 2 Thessalonians 2:1-4, NIV.

What is the little horn's attitude toward God and His people?

"He will speak against the Most High and *oppress his saints*." Daniel 7:25, NIV.

What else does the prophecy say the little horn would do?

"He will . . . *try to change the set times and the laws*." Daniel 7:25, NIV.

For how long were the saints of the Most High to be given into the hands of the little horn?

"The saints will be handed over to him for *a time, times and half a time*." Verse 25, NIV.

In what other prophecies is this same time period mentioned?

"The woman was given the two wings of a great eagle, so that she might fly to the place prepared for her in the desert, where she would be taken care of for *a time, times and half a time*, out of the serpent's reach." Revelation 12:14, NIV.

"The beast was given a mouth to utter proud words and blasphemies and to exercise his authority for *forty-two months*." Revelation 13:5, NIV. (See also Revelation 11:2.)

"The woman fled into the desert to a place prepared for her by God, where she might be taken care of for *1,260 days*." Revelation 12:6, NIV.

NOTE.—Daniel's expression "a time, times, and half of time" is to be understood as three and a half times. This same prophetic period of great persecution is described in several different ways (three and a half times in Daniel 7:25, 12:7, and Revelation 12:14; 42 months in Revelation 11:2 and 13:5; and 1260 days in Revelation

---

Chiastic Structure in Daniel

Ancient biblical writers structured their writings in ways that gave clues to their meaning, highlighting details of particular importance. One model was what we today call "chiastic structure," or a chiasm, named after the Hebrew letter chi, which parallels the letter X. Reflecting an A, B, C . . . C, B, A pattern, this literary technique may be seen in individual sets of verses, or in an entire book.

An example of a verse written as a chiasm is Genesis 1:27, "(a) God created man (b) in his own image; (b) in the image of God (a) he created him." The books of Lamentations and Revelation are two prominent models of entire books that feature elaborate chiasmic structures. The texts found in the center of the chiasmic structure are seen as containing, literally, the book's central truth.

"The chiastic structure of [Daniel] chapter 7 puts the judgment right at the center. . . . And since chapter 7 is at the middle of the book of Daniel, it follows that the judgment is at the center of the whole work of Daniel. Biblical tradition remembers the prophet in connection with divine judgment. The book of Ezekiel (Ezekiel 14:14-20), the only other book in the Old Testament that refers to Daniel, associates the prophet with Job and Noah, two central figures of the theme of the judgment of God, in a context of judgment (verses 13, 17-22). Likewise, in the New Testament, the only passage referring to Daniel deals with the great day of judgment (Matt. 24:15-21, 28, 39). Finally, Daniel himself testifies to the importance of divine judgment in the very name he bears: 'Daniel'means precisely 'judgment of God.' " Jacques B. Doukhan, *Secrets of Daniel* (Hagerstown, Md.: Review and Herald, 2000), p. 112.

11:3 and 12:6). Forty-two months (of 30 days each) is 1260 days, or three and a half years. These are all symbolic, prophetic time.

In symbolic prophecy, what length of time is represented by a day?

"I have laid on you a day for each year." Ezekiel 4:6, NKJV.

"For forty years—*one year for each of the forty days* you explored the land—you will suffer for your sins and know what it is like to have me against you." Numbers 14:34, NIV.

NOTE.—Daniel and Ezekiel were contemporaries in Babylon.

"The equation of 'day-year' appears throughout the Bible. Narratives often employ the word 'days' *(yamim)* in the sense of years to the point where most versions actually translate it by 'years' (see Exodus 13:10; Judges 11:40; 1 Samuel 1:21; 2:19; 27:7; Numbers 9:22; 1 Kings 11:42; Gen. 47:9, etc.). The poetic passages of the Bible contain many parallelisms between 'days' and 'years': 'Are your days like those of a mortal or your years like those of a man?' (Job 10:5); 'I thought about the former days, the years of long ago' (Psalm 77:5); 'To proclaim the year of the Lord's favor and the day of the vengeance of our God' (Isaiah 61:2).

"This principle also appears in Levitical texts. For six years the Israelite farmer was to work his land, but on the seventh year he had to let it be idle. Scripture calls the seventh year of rest a sabbath, like the seventh day for the week (Leviticus 25:1-7), with the difference that it was a 'Sabbath of years' and not a 'Sabbath of days.' The Bible uses the same language in regard to the jubilee: 'Count off seven sabbaths of years—seven times seven years' (verse 8).

"The principle also applied to prophecy. Hence, the 40 days during which the spies explored Canaan became 40 years of wandering in the desert. . . . Likewise, God commanded the prophet Ezekiel to lie on his left side for so many days, each day symbolizing a year. . . . Both Jewish tradition and Christian tradition have understood the weeks of Daniel as weeks of years. . . . The day-year principle of interpretation is probably the most ancient and the most solid principle in the exegesis of our passage." Jacques B. Doukhan, *Secrets of Daniel* (Hagerstown, Md.: Review and Herald, 2000), pp. 144, 145.

In symbolic prophecy, given in code, a prophetic day represents an entire year of actual history. Just as beasts represent kingdoms, so days represent years. But when does this 1260-year period begin and end? History indicates that it began in the 530s and ended in the 1790s.

As we have seen, the little-horn power was to rise out of the Roman Empire, and the only power that rose out of the collapse of the

Roman Empire was the Holy Roman Empire. The power of the church became complete in the 530s after it had uprooted three of the 10 kingdoms—the Heruli, the Vandals, and the Ostragoths.

The emperor Justinian issued a decree in 533 that recognized the pope as "head of all the holy churches" (*Code Justinianus*, book 1, title 1, sec. 4, in *The Civil Law*, translated by S. P. Scott, vol 12, p. 12). This letter was incorporated into Justinian's Code the following year, which became the law of the land in Europe until Napoleon replaced the code with his own. But important battles had yet to be won. Robert Browning, in his book *Justinian and Theodora* (London: Thames and Hudson, 1987), reviews the conquest of the Heruli by the Byzantine emperor Zeno (pp. 24, 25), then describes the conquest of the Vandals in 534, after which "the Vandals as a people vanished from the face of the earth" (p. 98). He then describes the retaking of Rome from the Ostrogoths in the spring of 538 (p. 111), and states that shortly thereafter, "the Ostrogothic kingdom had ceased to exist" (p. 114). *Encyclopedia Americana* (Danbury, Conn.: Grolier, Inc., 1997) describes the victory of Justinian's general Belisarius over the Ostrogoths when the enemy's siege was raised in March of 538 (vol. 3, p. 502). The defeat of the Ostrogoths in the siege of Rome was a deathblow to the independence of the Arian power then ruling Italy, marking the beginning of the 1260 years of papal supremacy.

The year 1793 was the year of the Reign of Terror in the French Revolution, and the year when the Roman Catholic religion was set aside in France and the worship of reason was established in its stead. As a direct result of the revolt against papal authority in the French Revolution, the French army, under Berthier, entered Rome, and the pope was taken prisoner in February 1798, dying in exile at Valence, France, the following year. This was an apparent death stroke.

The 1260 years of persecution, then, coincide with the rule of the medieval church, when Justinian's code was the law of the land.

What will happen to the dominion exercised by the little horn at the final judgment?

"But the court will sit, and *his power will be taken away and completely destroyed forever.*" Daniel 7:26, NIV.

To whom will the dominion finally be given?

"Then the sovereignty, power and greatness of the kingdoms under the whole heaven will be handed over *to the saints, the people of the Most High.* His kingdom will be an everlasting kingdom, and all rulers will worship and obey him." Verse 27, NIV.

What Does the Bible Mean by "Antichrist"?

The idea of "antichrist" has fascinated and frightened Christians since the first century. But what does it mean? The Bible uses "antichrist" and "antichrists" in just four verses in the books of 1 and 2 John, and the term never appears in the book of Revelation. In 2 Thessalonians 2:3 the Bible uses the term "man of lawlessness" (NIV). These texts reveal that antichrist is anyone or anything that opposes or attempts to replace Christ, His work, and His role.

Let's look at the four verses, in context, that actually use the word "antichrist":

"Do not love the world or anything in the world. If anyone loves the world, the love of the Father is not in him. For everything in the world—the cravings of sinful man, the lust of his eyes, and the boasting of what he has and does—comes not from the Father but from the world. The world and its desires pass away, but the man who does the will of God lives forever.

"Dear children, this is the last hour; and as you have heard that *the antichrist* is coming, even now *many antichrists* have come. This is how we know it is the last hour. They went out from us, but they did not really belong to us. For if they had belonged to us, they would have remained with us; but their going showed that none of them belonged to us.

"But you have an anointing from the Holy One, and all of you know the truth. I do not write to you because you do not know the truth, but because you do know it and because no lie comes from the truth. Who is the liar? It is the man who denies that Jesus is the Christ. Such a man is *the antichrist*—he denies the Father and the Son. No one who denies the Son has the Father; whoever acknowledges the Son has the Father also." 1 John 2:15-23, NIV.

"Dear friends, do not believe every spirit, but test the spirits to see whether they are from God, because many false prophets have gone out into the world. This is how you can recognize the Spirit of God: Every spirit that acknowledges that Jesus Christ has come in the flesh is from God, but every spirit that does not acknowledge Jesus is not from God. This is the

What Does the Bible Mean by "Antichrist"? CONTINUED

spirit of the *antichrist*, which you have heard is coming and
even now is already in the world." 1 John 4:1-3, NIV.

"Many deceivers, who do not acknowledge Jesus Christ as
coming in the flesh, have gone out into the world. Any such
person is the deceiver and the *antichrist*. Watch out that you do
not lose what you have worked for, but that you may be rewarded fully. Anyone who runs ahead and does not continue in
the teaching of Christ does not have God; whoever continues in
the teaching has both the Father and the Son. If anyone comes
to you and does not bring this teaching, do not take him into
your house or welcome him. Anyone who welcomes him shares
in his wicked work." 2 John 7-11, NIV.

Popular thinking often equates "antichrist" with a single diabolical end-time individual, but this does not bear up to scriptural evidence. First John 4:3 tells us that the "spirit of the
antichrist" was already at work among the earliest Christians.
It is not limited to the last days, but has worked through many
people and institutions throughout the centuries.

Let's look at what Paul wrote about the "man of lawlessness," a description that parallels that of the "little horn" of
Daniel 7.

"Concerning the coming of our Lord Jesus Christ and our
being gathered to him, we ask you, brothers, not to become easily unsettled or alarmed by some prophecy, report or letter supposed to have come from us, saying that the day of the Lord
has already come. Don't let anyone deceive you in any way, for
that day will not come until the rebellion occurs and the man of
lawlessness is revealed, the man doomed to destruction. He will
oppose and will exalt himself over everything that is called God
or is worshiped, so that he sets himself up in God's temple, proclaiming himself to be God.

"Don't you remember that when I was with you I used to
tell you these things? And now you know what is holding him
back, so that he may be revealed at the proper time. For the secret power of lawlessness is already at work; but the one who
now holds it back will continue to do so till he is taken out of
the way. And then the lawless one will be revealed, whom the
Lord Jesus will overthrow with the breath of his mouth and destroy by the splendor of his coming. The coming of the lawless

What Does the Bible Mean by "Antichrist"? CONTINUED

one will be in accordance with the work of Satan displayed in all kinds of counterfeit miracles, signs and wonders, and in every sort of evil that deceives those who are perishing. They perish because they refused to love the truth and so be saved. For this reason God sends them a powerful delusion so that they will believe the lie and so that all will be condemned who have not believed the truth but have delighted in wickedness." 2 Thessalonians 2:1-12, NIV.

The word "antichrist" means not just "against Christ" but "in place of Christ." The spirit of antichrist substitutes precepts and efforts for the role, work, and truths of Christ. It substitutes tradition and legalistic dogma for the clear word of God, and gives to human institutions and individuals glory that is Christ's alone. It puts God "in a box." Such doctrines as praying to saints, confession of sins to a human priest, and purgatory for sin instead of trusting in Jesus' all-sufficient sacrifice take the focus off Jesus and put it on human efforts and institutions. By the same token, the spirit of antichrist may exist in any one of us who allows our attention to turn from Christ to self.

THE PROPHETIC SYMBOLS OF DANIEL 8

Where was Daniel at the time of this vision?

"In my vision I saw myself in the citadel of Susa in the province of Elam; in the vision I was beside the Ulai Canal." Daniel 8:2, NIV.

What first appeared to the prophet?

"I looked up, and there before me was *a ram with two horns*, standing beside the canal, and the horns were long. One of the horns was longer than the other but grew up later." Verse 3, NIV.

What next appeared upon the scene?

"As I was thinking about this, suddenly *a goat with a prominent horn between his eyes* came from the west, crossing the whole earth without touching the ground. He came toward the two-horned ram I had seen standing beside the canal and charged at him in great rage. I saw him attack the ram furiously, striking the ram and shattering his two horns. The ram was powerless to stand against him; the goat knocked him to the ground and trampled on him, and none could rescue the ram from his power. The goat became very great." Verses 5-8, NIV.

When the prominent horn was broken, what came up?

"At the height of his power his large horn was broken off, and in its place *four prominent horns* grew up toward the four winds of heaven." Verse 8, NIV.

What came out of one of the winds?

"Out of one of them came *another horn, which started small but grew in power* to the south and to the east and toward the Beautiful Land. It grew until it reached the host of the heavens, and it threw some of the starry host down to the earth and trampled on them." Verses 9, 10, NIV.

What command was given to an angel who stood nearby?

"And I heard a man's voice from the Ulai calling, 'Gabriel, *tell this man the meaning of the vision.*' " Verse 16, NIV.

What were the first words that Gabriel said to the prophet?

"As he came near to the place where I was standing, I was terrified and fell prostrate. 'Son of man,' he said to me, 'understand that the vision concerns the time of the end.' " Verse 17, NIV.

NOTE.—This vision was given a few years before the Persians conquered Babylon. The vision begins with animals that represent Medo-Persia and Greece. Yet the angel claims that the vision pertains to the time of the end. So the 2300 days cannot represent literal days, but must represent prophetic time, or 2300 years; otherwise the prophecy would not reach down to the time of the end.

According to Daniel 12:9, 10, "the time of the end" is when the prophecies of Daniel would be unsealed so that the "wise" would be able to understand them. Evidently Daniel himself did not fully understand this vision, for it made him faint (Daniel 8:27), and it was not until a few years later that the angel finished explaining the matter, in chapter 9.

What powers did Gabriel identify as symbolized by the ram and goat?

"The two-horned ram that you saw represents the *kings of Media and Persia*. The shaggy goat is the *king of Greece*, and the large horn between his eyes is the first king." Daniel 8:20, 21, NIV.

NOTE.—The goat's "prominent horn" is explained in verse 21 to be the first king of the Grecian or Macedonian Empire: Alexander the

Great. We have already read Daniel's description of the fury with which the goat would attack the ram: the "goat came from the west, crossing the whole earth without touching the ground." Greece lay west of Persia and attacked from that direction. So rapid was Alexander's progress that he seemed to fly from point to point with the swiftness of the wind. The same characteristic of speed is indicated by the four wings of the leopard, which also represents Greece in the parallel vision of Daniel 7.

What is represented by the four horns standing up in the place of the one broken?

"The shaggy goat is the king of Greece, and the large horn between his eyes is the first king. The four horns that replaced the one that was broken off represent *four kingdoms that will emerge from his nation* but will not have the same power." Daniel 8:21, 22, NIV.

NOTE.—The great horn that was broken symbolized the first king, Alexander the Great. Alexander died at the age of 33, in the prime of life and at the height of his conquests, in 323 B.C. Afterward his kingdom was divided by fighting among his four generals: Cassander (Macedonia), Lysimachus (Thrace and northwestern Asia Minor), Seleucus (Syria and Babylonia), and Ptolemy (Egypt). However, the kingdom of Lysimachus was conquered by Seleucus in 281 B.C.

What is meant by the little horn that "grew in power" (verse 9)?

"In the latter part of their reign [i.e., the kingdom of Alexander's successors], when rebels have become completely wicked, a stern-faced king, a master of intrigue, will arise." Verse 23, NIV.

NOTE.—The second passage above (Daniel 8:23) is the angel's interpretation of the first (verses 8, 9). Verse 9 says the little horn (representing the "stern-faced king") came "out of one of them"—i.e., out of one of the four winds (verse 8). The construction of the Hebrew sentence and the gender of its nouns and pronouns indicate that the horn came out of the winds, not out of the horns. In other words, it came from a direction of the compass. Notice how this fits exactly with history. Rome came out of the west and conquered the remnants of the Greek Empire.

As Daniel in the previous vision watched the persecuting work of the little horn of Daniel 7, what did he see take place next?

"But the court will sit, and his *power will be taken away* and completely destroyed forever." Daniel 7:26, NIV.

NOTE.—The seventh chapter of Daniel traces the rise and fall of the four great kingdoms, the division of the fourth, as represented by the 10 horns, and the establishment of a religiopolitical power under the symbol of the little horn. As the prophet beheld the persecutions of this power, he saw the Ancient of Days sit and the judgment begin. Following the judgment, the kingdom was to be given to the saints of the Most High.

The eighth chapter of Daniel starts with Medo-Persia and reviews briefly the history of Greece and Rome in both its pagan and papal phases, with emphasis on the final judgment as depicted in the cleansing of the heavenly sanctuary. Thus Daniel 8 parallels the earlier vision of Daniel 7, but with added information.

At what time, according to the prophecy, was the sanctuary to be cleansed?

"Then I heard a holy one speaking, and another holy one said to him, 'How long will it take for the vision to be fulfilled—the vision concerning the daily sacrifice, the rebellion that causes desolation, and the surrender of the sanctuary and of the host that will be trampled underfoot?' He said to me, 'It will take 2,300 evenings and mornings; then the sanctuary will be reconsecrated.' " Daniel 8:14, NIV.

NOTE.—The Jewish Day of Atonement was on the tenth day of the seventh month, at which time the sanctuary was cleansed. This Day of Atonement was looked upon by the Jews as a day of soul-searching and judgment. It was, in fact, a type or symbolic representation of the final judgment (compare the parallel prophecy of Daniel 7:9, 10) that would take place at the end of the 2300-day period (i.e., 2300 years in symbolic prophecy). At the end of this period the sanctuary in heaven would be cleansed. The significance of this "cleansing" will become more clear in the later studies of this section.

To what time did the angel say the vision belongs?

" 'Son of man,' he said to me, 'understand that the vision concerns *the time of the end.'* . . . 'I am going to tell you what will happen later *in the time of wrath, because the vision concerns the appointed time of the end.'* " Daniel 8:17-19, NIV.

What indicates that the 2300 "evenings and mornings" of verse 14 also relates to the time of the end?

"The vision of the evenings and mornings that has been given you is true, but seal up the vision, *for it concerns the distant future.*" Verse 26, NIV.

As Daniel saw the chosen people of God persecuted and scattered, as well as the desolation of the holy city and the sanctuary, how did it affect the prophet?

"I, Daniel, *was exhausted and lay ill* for several days. Then I got up and went about the king's business. I was appalled by the vision; it was beyond understanding." Daniel 8:27, NIV.

NOTE.—The scenes of persecution were too much for the strength of the prophet, who by this time was an old man. Unable to bear the rest of the prophetic interpretation, he collapsed. During this interval between the partial interpretation of the prophecy in the eighth chapter and the final interpretation in the ninth chapter, an important change took place: Babylon was overthrown by the Medes and Persians. It was in the first year of the reign of Darius the Mede that the interpretation of the vision was completed, as recorded in the ninth chapter. The concluding portion of the interpretation is taken up in the next study.

THE HOUR OF GOD'S JUDGMENT

What startling message is given in Revelation 14:7?

"Fear God and give him glory, because *the hour of his judgment has come*. Worship him who made the heavens, the earth, the sea and the springs of water" (NIV).

When is the hour of God's judgment?

"And he answered him, 'For *two thousand three hundred evenings and mornings*; then the sanctuary shall be restored to its rightful state." Daniel 8:14, NRSV.

NOTE.—The cleansing of the sanctuary is a work of judgment. The Jewish people understood it so. This 2300-day period, being 2300 literal years (Ezekiel 4:6), reaches down to the cleansing of the sanctuary in heaven, or, in other words, to the time when the pre-Advent investigative judgment begins, as described in Daniel 7:9, 10.

Does God execute judgment without first investigating the matter?

No. Numerous biblical stories illustrate God's investigation before taking action.

"Then the man and his wife heard the sound of the Lord God as he was walking in the garden in the cool of the day, and they hid from the Lord God among the trees of the garden. But the Lord God called to the man, *'Where are you?'* He answered, 'I heard you in the garden, and I was afraid because I was naked; so I hid.' And he [God] said, *'Who told you that you were naked? Have you eaten from the tree that I commanded you not to eat from?'* " Genesis 3:8-11, NIV.

"Then the Lord said to Cain, *'Where is your brother Abel?'* 'I don't know,' he replied. 'Am I my brother's keeper?' The Lord said, *'What have you done?* Listen! Your brother's blood cries out to me from the ground.' " Genesis 4:9, 10, NIV.

"The Lord *saw* how great man's wickedness on the earth had become, and that every inclination of the thoughts of his heart was only evil all the time." Genesis 6:5, NIV.

"Then they said, 'Come, let us build ourselves a city, with a tower that reaches to the heavens, so that we may make a name for ourselves and not be scattered over the face of the whole earth.' But *the Lord came down to see the city and the tower that the men were building.*" Genesis 11:4, 5, NIV.

"Then the Lord said, 'The outcry against Sodom and Gomorrah is so great and their sin so grievous that *I will go down and see if what they have done is as bad as the outcry that has reached me. If not, I will know.'* " Genesis 18:20, 21, NIV.

"Take a bunch of hyssop, dip it into the blood in the basin and put some of the blood on the top and on both sides of the doorframe. Not one of you shall go out the door of his house until morning. When the Lord goes through the land to strike down the Egyptians, *he will see* the blood on the top and sides of the doorframe and will pass over that doorway, and he will not permit the destroyer to enter your houses and strike you down." Exodus 12:22, 23, NIV.

"You have been weighed on the scales and found wanting. . . . Your kingdom is divided and given to the Medes and Persians." Daniel 5:27, 28, NIV.

"At that time *I will search* Jerusalem with lamps and punish those who are complacent, who are like wine left on its dregs, who think, 'The Lord will do nothing, either good or bad.' " Zephaniah 1:12, NIV.

Why was the time period not fully explained when the angel first appeared to Daniel?

"So I, Daniel, was overcome and lay sick for some days; then I arose and went about the king's business. But I was dismayed by the vision and did not understand it." Daniel 8:27, NRSV.

NOTE.—Daniel was so overwhelmed with worry about the import of this vision that he fainted and became sick. Consequently the angel was unable to finish the interpretation until several years later, after the prophet had recovered and the Medo-Persian power had taken control of Babylon.

After Daniel recovered from his illness, to what did he turn his attention?

"In the first year of Darius . . . I, Daniel, understood from the Scriptures, according to the word of the Lord given to Jeremiah the prophet, that the desolation of Jerusalem would last seventy years." Daniel 9:1, 2, NIV.

To what prophecy does Daniel refer?

"This is what the Lord says: *'When seventy years are completed* for Babylon, I will come to you and fulfill my gracious promises to bring you back to this place. For I know the plans I have for you,' declares the Lord, 'plans to prosper you and not to harm you, plans to give you hope and a future. Then you will call upon me and come and pray to me, and I will listen to you. You will seek me and find me when you seek me with all your heart. I will be found by you,' declares the Lord, 'and will bring you back from captivity. I will gather you from all the nations and places where I have banished you,' declares the Lord, 'and will bring you back to the place from which I carried you into exile.' " Jeremiah 29:10-14, NIV.

NOTE.—Nebuchadnezzar besieged Jerusalem in the third year of Jehoiakim (Daniel 1:1), and Jeremiah announced the 70-year captivity in the fourth year of Jehoiakim (Jeremiah 25:1, 12). The first deportation of Jews to Babylon, when Daniel and his companions were carried away, was in 605 B.C. Shortly before the vision of Daniel 9 occurred, the empire of Babylon had fallen to Medo-Persia (539 B.C.). So the 70 years of Jeremiah's prophecy were due to expire soon, and the restoration was due. Yet at the time of Daniel's prayer, there was still no sign that the Jews would be allowed to return to their homeland. This greatly concerned Daniel.

What did this nearness of the time of restoration from captivity lead Daniel to do?

"So I turned to the Lord God and *pleaded with him in prayer* and petition, in fasting, and in sackcloth and ashes." Daniel 9:3, NIV.

How did Daniel pray for his people?

"I prayed to the Lord my God and confessed: 'O God, the great and awesome God, who keeps his covenant of love with all who love him and obey his commands, we have sinned and done wrong. We have been wicked and have rebelled; we have turned away from your commands and laws. We have not listened to your servants the prophets, who spoke in your name to our kings, our princes and our fathers, and to all the people of the land.

"'Lord, you are righteous, but this day we are covered with shame—the men of Judah and the people of Jerusalem and all Israel, both near and far, in all the countries where you have scattered us because of our unfaithfulness to you. O Lord, we and our kings, our princes and our fathers are covered with shame because we have sinned against you. The Lord our God is merciful and forgiving, even though we have rebelled against him; we have not obeyed the Lord our God or kept the laws he gave us through his servants the prophets. All Israel has transgressed your law and turned away, refusing to obey you.

"'Therefore the curses and sworn judgments written in the Law of Moses, the servant of God, have been poured out on us, because we have sinned against you. You have fulfilled the words spoken against us and against our rulers by bringing upon us great disaster. Under the whole heaven nothing has ever been done like what has been done to Jerusalem. Just as it is written in the Law of Moses, all this disaster has come upon us, yet we have not sought the favor of the Lord our God by turning from our sins, and giving attention to your truth. The Lord did not hesitate to bring the disaster upon us, for the Lord our God is righteous in everything he does; yet we have not obeyed him.

"'Now, O Lord our God, who brought your people out of Egypt with a mighty hand and who made for yourself a name that endures to this day, we have sinned, we have done wrong. O Lord, in keeping with all your righteous acts, turn away your anger and your wrath from Jerusalem, your city, your holy hill. Our sins and the iniquities of our fathers have made Jerusalem and your people an object of scorn to all those around us.

"'Now, our God, hear the prayers and petitions of your servants. For your sake, O Lord, look with favor on your desolate sanctuary. Give ear, O God, and hear; open your eyes and see the desolation of the city that bears your Name. We do not make requests of you because we are righteous, but because of your great mercy. O Lord, listen! O Lord, forgive! O Lord, hear and act! For your sake, O my God, do not delay, because your city and your people bear your Name.'" Verses 4-19, NIV.

NOTE.—Daniel's prayer is a beautiful summation of both Israel's history and the character of God. It points back to the covenants of Deuteronomy, acknowledging that Israel's sins prevented the fulfillment of God's covenant promises, and brought on the disaster so long predicted. Still, Daniel trusts in God's mercy and love, and reminds God of His past mighty acts, asking for restoration that God's name might again be glorified.

In what was the prophet particularly interested?

"For your own sake, Lord, let your face shine upon *your desolated sanctuary.*" Verse 17, NRSV.

What angel appeared to Daniel in response to his prayer?

"While I was still in prayer, *Gabriel,* the man I had seen in the earlier vision, came to me in swift flight about the time of the evening sacrifice." Verse 21, NIV.

NOTE.—While Daniel was praying over the desolate sanctuary in Jerusalem, the angel Gabriel returned to the prophet to explain the portion of the prophecy in Daniel 8 that had been left unexplained: the cleansing of the heavenly sanctuary. The angel not only would open to his understanding the earthly typical sanctuary and its future, but would give him, for the benefit of those living at the time of the end, a view of the true heavenly service.

What did the angel ask the prophet to understand?

"He instructed me and said to me, 'Daniel, I have now come to give you insight and understanding. . . . Therefore, consider the message and understand *the vision.*'" Verses 22, 23, NIV.

NOTE.—It is evident that the angel began just where he had left off in explanation of the prophecy of the eighth chapter, for there is no new symbolic vision in this chapter—that is, there are no more beasts or images. Gabriel invites Daniel to "understand the vision" of Daniel 8. In the Hebrew text the definite article *the* here clearly specifies the vision previously mentioned. Since the 2300-day period was the only part of the former vision left unexplained, the angel would naturally begin with an interpretation of that time period.

What portion of the 2300 days mentioned in the previous vision was allotted to the Jews?

"Seventy 'sevens' are decreed for your people and your holy city." Daniel 9:24, NIV.

NOTE.—The word translated "sevens" is used in Jewish literature to refer to periods of seven days and also to periods of seven years. Jewish and Christian scholars, generally, have concluded that the context here requires that "weeks" of years be understood. "Seventy weeks" of seven years each would be 490 years.

In postbiblical Hebrew the word here translated "decreed" had the meaning "to cut," "to cut off," "to determine." In view of the fact that the 70 weeks of Daniel 9 are a part of the 2300 days of chapter 8, and were cut off from them and assigned particularly to the Jews, the meaning "to cut" here seems especially appropriate.

The 70 weeks, therefore, were cut off. Cut off of what? Evidently, cut off of the longer 2300-day period. Since the vision of Daniel 9 is really a continuation of Gabriel's explanation of Daniel 8, and since no beginning is given in Daniel 8 for the 2300 years, the starting point of the 70 weeks must be the starting point for both. The full restoration of the Jewish laws and government pertaining to the people and their sanctuary took place in 457 B.C., as we shall see later. The 70 weeks, then, were a part of the 2300-year period, and were "cut off" as a period pertaining to the Jewish people and their sanctuary service.

What was to be accomplished near the close of this 70-week period?

"To finish transgression, to put an end to sin, to atone for wickedness, to bring in everlasting righteousness, to seal up vision and prophecy and to anoint the most holy." Daniel 9:24, NIV.

"To finish transgression."—"The two actions that were the responsibility of God's people were 'to finish transgression, [and] to put an end to sin' (Daniel 9:24). The Hebrew language has quite a few words for sin, each with its own shade of meaning. The meaning of 'transgression' (in the phrase 'to finish transgression') is sin as rebellion against God. The second phrase ('to put an end to sin') uses the common word for sin, meaning to miss the mark, the goal, or standard which God has set up. Thus, Gabriel charges the Jewish people with the responsibility of putting away sin and developing a righteous society. Like ancient Israel in the wilderness, they were to purify the camp in order to prepare conditions which would be right for the Messiah to come." William Shea, *The Abundant Life Bible Amplifier: Daniel 7-12* (Boise, Idaho: Pacific Press, 1996), p. 57.

"To put an end to sin."—The best explanation of this clause is given in Hebrews 9:26 ("But now he has appeared once for all to do away with sin by the sacrifice of himself") and in Romans 8:3 ("For what the law was powerless to do in that it was weakened by the sinful nature, God did by sending his own Son in the likeness of sinful man to be a sin offering").

"To atone for wickedness."—This refers to the final once-and-for-all atoning sacrifice for sin offered by Jesus on the cross of Calvary.

"To bring in everlasting righteousness."—This must mean the righteousness of Christ—that saving righteousness that was made possible by His atonement for sin, and which, through faith, may be imputed to the penitent believer.

"To anoint the most holy."—The Hebrew words here used are al-

ways used of the sanctuary, not of persons. The anointing of the "most holy" in the sanctuary is described in Exodus 30:25-29 and 40:9. In antitype, then, this must refer to the anointing of the heavenly sanctuary, when Christ "serves in the sanctuary, the true tabernacle set up by the Lord, not by man." Hebrews 8:2.

When were the 70 weeks (490 years) to begin?

"Know and understand this: *From the issuing of the decree to restore and rebuild Jerusalem* until the Anointed One, the ruler, comes, there will be seven 'sevens,' and sixty-two 'sevens.' It will be rebuilt with streets and a trench, but in times of trouble." Daniel 9:25, NIV.

NOTE.—Seventy weeks are 490 prophetic days (70 x 7), which stand for years (a prophetic day stands for a year [Ezekiel 4:6; Numbers 14:34]. "Seven 'sevens' and sixty-two sevens" are 69 weeks, or 483 years (7 x 69 = 483 days, which stand for years). The 483 years were to reach "until the Anointed One." *Messiah* is the Hebrew word, and *Christ* the Greek word, meaning "anointed one." Exactly 483 years from the command of Artaxerxes in 457 B.C. Jesus was baptized by John and began His public ministry.

How was Jesus anointed?

"God anointed Jesus of Nazareth *with the Holy Spirit and with power*." Acts 10:38, NIV.

At what time did Jesus receive the special anointing of the Holy Spirit?

"When all the people were being baptized, Jesus was baptized too. And as he was praying, heaven was opened and the Holy Spirit descended on him in bodily form like a dove. And a voice came from heaven: 'You are my Son, whom I love; with you I am well pleased.'" Luke 3:21, 22, NIV.

What prophecy did Jesus quote shortly after this as applying to Himself?

"The Spirit of the Lord is on me, because he has anointed me to preach good news to the poor." Luke 4:18, NIV. (See Mark 1:15.)

NOTE.—It is evident that the 69 weeks (483 years) were to reach to the baptism of Christ, as that was the time of His anointing by the Holy Spirit, when He began to preach the gospel. John the Baptist began his work in the fifteenth year of the reign of Tiberius (Luke 3:1-3), and this would put the anointing of Jesus in A.D. 27, at the time of His baptism.

2300 Days (YEARS)
The Most Significant Prophetic Period in the Bible

"SEVENTY WEEKS (490 YEARS) ARE DETERMINED UPON THY PEOPLE"

7 WEEKS — 457 B.C. — 408 B.C. — DECREE TO BUILD JERUSALEM

62 WEEKS

**"THEN SHALL THE SANCTUARY BE CLEANSED"
1810 YEARS**

"WE HAVE A GREAT HIGH PRIEST..... JESUS THE SON OF GOD" HEB. 4:14

1844 A.D.

ONE WEEK — 27 A.D. — 31 A.D. — 34 A.D.

CHRIST BAPTIZED

CHRIST CRUCIFIED

STONING OF STEPHEN

GOSPEL TO THE GENTILES

THE HOUR OF HIS JUDGMENT IS COME

T he 2300 years was to reach, according to Daniel's prophecy, "from the going forth of the commandment to restore and to build Jerusalem," (Daniel 9:25) to the time for the cleansing of the sanctuary.

457 B.C.—Artaxerxes, king of Persia, commanded the restoration and rebuilding of Jerusalem (Daniel 9:25; Ezra 7:11-26; 4:11-16). Beginning of the 2300 years.

408 B.C.—The reconstruction and restoration of Jerusalem carried to completion during the first 49 years of Daniel's long time prophecy. This work was finished in 408 B.C. (Daniel 9:25).

A.D. 27—Jesus, anointed with the Holy Spirit at His baptism, began to preach and to teach (Matthew 3:16; Acts 10:38). From 457 B.C. to Christ the "anointed" was 69 weeks or 483 years (Daniel 9:25).

A.D. 31—Messiah "cut off" "in the midst of the [final] week" (i.e., the last seven years of the 490-year period) after three and one-half years of ministry (Daniel 9:27; Matthew 27:50, 51). The remaining three and a half years of the seventieth week bring us to the close of the 490-year period allotted to the Jewish people.

A.D. 34—Stoning of Stephen. From that time the gospel was preached to the Gentiles (Daniel 9:24; Acts 7:54-60; 8:1; 11:19, 20). From 457 B.C. to "the times of the Gentiles" (Luke 21:24) was 490 years.

A.D. 1844—End of the 2300 years. Cleansing of the heavenly sanctuary in the hour of God's judgment (Daniel 8:14; Revelation 14:7).

A.D. 1844—The threefold message of Revelation 14:6-12 is heralded to all the world, just before Christ's second coming.

When was the decree made to restore and build Jerusalem made?

"This Ezra came up from Babylon. . . . Some of the Israelites, including priests, Levites, singers, gatekeepers and temple servants, also came up to Jerusalem in the seventh year of King Artaxerxes. Ezra arrived in Jerusalem in the fifth month of the seventh year of the king." Ezra 7:6-8, NIV.

NOTE.—Three decrees were issued by Persian monarchs for the restoration of the Jews to their homeland. All three are mentioned in Ezra 6:14: "They finished building the temple according to the command of the God of Israel and the decrees of Cyrus, Darius and Artaxerxes, kings of Persia" (NIV).

This passage (Ezra 6:14) marks a transition from Aramaic, the language of exile, to Hebrew, the language of Israel. This turning point marks the beginning of the national restoration. The singular noun ("commandment," not "commandments") suggests that Ezra considered all of these proclamations as the outworking of a single "commandment" that became finally effective only after the final proclamation. The first decree, of Cyrus, pertained only to the Temple, not to all of Jerusalem. The second decree, of Darius Hystaspes, provided for the completion of the Temple (Ezra 6:1-12, 15), which had been hindered by a short-lived usurper of the Persian throne, Smerdis. But it was the third decree, that of Artaxerxes, that restored the full Jewish government, making provision for the enforcement of their laws. This last decree, therefore, is the one that marks the beginning of the 70 weeks, as well as the 2300 days.

The letter of Artaxerxes to Ezra, conferring upon him authority to do this work, is found in Ezra 7:11-26. This letter included the rebuilding of the city, according to the testimony of the enemies of the Jews (Ezra 4:11-16).

The decree of Artaxerxes was issued in the seventh year of his reign, and according to ancient methods of chronology, went into effect in Jerusalem in the fall of 457 B.C. Reckoning 483 full years (69 "weeks") from 457 B.C. would bring us to A.D. 27 (remember that there is no zero year between 1 B.C. and A.D. 1).

A.D. 27 is the beginning of the seventieth week—that is, the last seven years of the 490. What was to happen in the midst of that week?

"He will confirm a covenant with many for one 'seven.' In the middle of the 'seven' *he will put an end to sacrifice and offering.*" Daniel 9:27, NIV.

NOTE.—As the 69 weeks ended in the fall of A.D. 27, the middle of the seventieth week, or the three and a half years, would end in the spring of A.D. 31, when Christ was crucified, and by His death brought to an end the sacrifices and offerings of the earthly sanctuary. Three and a half years more (the last part of the seventieth week) would end in the autumn of A.D. 34. This brings us to the end of the 490 years that were "cut off" from the 2300. There still remain 1810 years, which, if added to A.D. 34, take us to A.D. 1844.

What did the angel say would then take place?

"And he answered him, 'For two thousand three hundred evenings and mornings; then the sanctuary shall be restored to its rightful state." Daniel 8:14, NRSV.

NOTE.—In other words, the great closing work of Christ for the world, the investigative phase of the judgment, would at that time begin. Already that work has been going on for many years, and will soon close. Israel's Day of Atonement occupied but one day in a year.

What takes place on earth while the investigative judgment is taking place in heaven?

"Then I saw another angel flying in midair, and he had the eternal gospel to proclaim to those who live on the earth—to every nation, tribe, language and people. He said in a loud voice, 'Fear God and give him glory, because the hour of his judgment has come. Worship him who made the heavens, the earth, the sea and the springs of water.'" Revelation 14:6, 7, NIV.

NOTE.—The symbol of an angel is here used to represent God's last warning message of impending judgment and the preaching of the gospel to every people group on earth (nation, kindred, tongue). Since angels preach their messages to us through human agencies, this symbol of an angel flying in midheaven represents a great religious movement proclaiming the last judgment-hour message and the final offer of mercy (the everlasting gospel). The two messages together—judgment and mercy; coming destruction and a way of escape—are far more effective than either one alone.

What are we, in view of the judgment, commanded to do?

"*Fear God and give him glory*, for the hour of his judgment has come; and worship him who made heaven and earth, the sea and the springs of water." Verse 7, NRSV.

How else are we told to prepare for the judgment?

"While God has overlooked the times of human ignorance, now he commands all people everywhere to *repent*, because he has fixed a day on which he will have the world judged in righteousness by a

man whom he has appointed, and of this he has given assurance to all
by raising him from the dead." Acts 17:30, 31, NRSV.

THE ATONEMENT IN TYPE AND ANTITYPE

What did God, through Moses, command Israel to make?

"And let them *make me a sanctuary*; that I may dwell among
them." Exodus 25:8.

What was offered in this sanctuary?

"In which were offered *both gifts and sacrifices*." Hebrews 9:9.

Besides the court, how many parts had this sanctuary?

"The curtain will separate the *Holy Place* and the *Most Holy
Place*." Exodus 26:33, NIV.

What was in the first apartment, or holy place?

"A tabernacle was set up. In its first room were the *lampstand,
the table and the consecrated bread*; this was called the Holy Place."
Hebrews 9:2, NIV. "Moses placed the gold altar in the Tent of Meeting in front of the curtain." Exodus 40:26, NIV. (See also Exodus
30:1-6.)

What was contained in the Second Apartment?

"Behind the second curtain was a room called the Most Holy
Place, which had *the golden altar of incense and the gold-covered
ark of the covenant*. This ark contained the gold jar of manna, Aaron's
staff that had budded, and *the stone tablets of the covenant*." Hebrews
9:3, 4, NIV. See also Exodus 40:20, 21.

By what name was the cover of the ark known?

"You shall put *the mercy seat* on the top of the ark; and in the ark
you shall put the covenant that I shall give you." Exodus 25:21,
NRSV.

Where was God to meet with Moses?

"There I will meet with you, and from above the mercy seat, from
between the two cherubim that are on the ark of the covenant." Verse
22, NRSV.

What was in the ark, under the mercy seat?

"Then he wrote on *the tablets* the same words as before, *the ten
commandments. . . .* So I turned and came down from the mountain,

and *put the tablets in the ark* that I had made; and there they are, as the Lord commanded me." Deuteronomy 10:4, 5, NRSV.

When did the priest minister in the first apartment?

"Such preparations having been made, the priests go *continually* into the first tent to carry out their ritual duties." Hebrews 9:6, NRSV.

Who went into the Second Apartment? When and why?

"But only *the high priest goes into the second, and he but once a year, and not without taking the blood that he offers for himself and for the sins committed unintentionally by the people*." Verse 7, NRSV.

What were sinners desiring pardon instructed to do?

"If a member of the community sins unintentionally and does what is forbidden in any of the Lord's commands, he is guilty. When he is made aware of the sin he committed, he must bring as his offering for the sin he committed a female goat without defect. *He is to lay his hand on the head of the sin offering and slaughter it at the place of the burnt offering.*" Leviticus 4:27-29, NIV.

NOTE.—Israelites who sinned violated one of the commandments that were in the ark under the mercy seat. These commandments are the foundation of God's government. To violate them is to commit sin, and so become subject to death (1 John 3:4; Romans 6:23). But there was a mercy seat reared above these holy and just commandments. In His mercy God grants sinners the privilege of confessing sins and bringing a substitute to meet the demands of the law, and thus of obtaining mercy.

What was done with the blood of the offering?

"Then the priest is to take some of the blood with his finger and put it on the horns of the altar of burnt offering and *pour out the rest of the blood at the base of the altar*. . . . In this way the priest will make atonement for him, and he will be forgiven." Leviticus 4:30, 31, NIV.

NOTE.—Guilty offenders first brought their offering, then confessed their sin while laying their hands on the head of the victim, thus symbolically transferring their sin to the victim; the victim was next slain in the court, or outer part of the sanctuary, and its blood put on the horns of the altar and poured at the foot of the altar. In this way atonement was made. The sins were pardoned, but not obliterated; they were transferred from the sinner to the sanctuary, where they accumulated over the course of the year, awaiting the annual Day of Atonement.

Likewise, in the gospel antitype, sinners who accept Christ's sacrifice and confess their sins are justified and cleansed by the blood of Jesus. Their sins are forgiven and atoned for, and they need not concern themselves with them ever again. God assumes the guilt until such time as the record of those sins is finally dealt with, for Hebrews 9:23 indicates that there is a cleansing of the heavenly sanctuary that is analogous to the cleansing of the earthly sanctuary on the Day of Atonement.

What service to expunge these accumulated sins from the sanctuary took place yearly?

"This is to be a lasting ordinance for you: On the tenth day of the seventh month you must deny yourselves . . . because *on that day atonement will be made for you, to cleanse you. Then, before the Lord, you will be clean from all your sins*." Leviticus 16:29, 30, NIV.

How was the sanctuary itself cleansed, so that the corporate sin of the people was finally disposed of?

"From the Israelite community he [the high priest] is to take two male goats for a sin offering. . . . Then he is to take the two goats and present them before the Lord at the entrance to the Tent of Meeting. He is to cast lots for the two goats—one lot for the Lord and the other for the scapegoat." Verses 5-8, NIV.

NOTE.—The Hebrew word for scapegoat is *Azazel*. It is used as a proper name, and, according to Jewish tradition, refers to Satan, or the angel who revolted and persisted in rebellion and sin. For example, in 1 Enoch, written during the intertestamental period and quoted in the New Testament, Azazel is a fallen angel (1 Enoch 6-8, etc.).

What was done with the blood of the goat upon which the Lord's lot fell?

"He shall slaughter the goat of the sin offering that is for the people and bring its blood inside the curtain, and do with its blood as he did with the blood of the bull, *sprinkling it upon the mercy seat* and before the mercy seat." Leviticus 16:15, NRSV.

Why was it necessary to make this atonement?

"In this way he will make atonement for the Most Holy Place *because of the uncleanness and rebellion of the Israelites, whatever their sins have been*. He is to do the same for the Tent of Meeting, which is among them in the midst of their uncleanness." Verse 16, NIV.

NOTE.—Sins were transferred to the sanctuary during the year by the blood of the sin offerings made daily at the door of the tabernacle. Here they remained until the Day of Atonement. When the high priest went into the Most Holy Place with the blood of the goat on which the Lord's lot fell, he there, in type, atoned for them, and so cleansed the sanctuary.

What did the high priest, after having made atonement for the people in the Most Holy Place, do next?

"When Aaron has finished making atonement for the Most Holy Place, the Tent of Meeting and the altar, he shall bring forward the live goat. *He is to lay both hands on the head of the live goat and confess over it all the wickedness and rebellion of the Israelites—all their sins—and put them on the goat's head. He shall send the goat away into the desert in the care of a man appointed for the task. The goat will carry on itself all their sins to a solitary place*; and the man shall release it in the desert." Verses 20-22, NIV.

NOTE.—The offering of the Lord's goat cleansed the sanctuary. By this offering the sins of the people, transferred there during the year, were, in type, atoned for. The scapegoat, symbolizing Satan, the great tempter and originator of sin, was brought to the sanctuary, and *upon his head* were placed these already-atoned-for sins. The sending away of the goat into the wilderness separates the sins forever from the sanctuary.

Of what sanctuary, or tabernacle, is Christ the minister?

"We do have such a high priest, who sat down at the right hand of the throne of the Majesty in heaven, who serves in the sanctuary, *the true tabernacle set up by the Lord*, not by man." Hebrews 8:1, 2, NIV.

Of what was the blood of all the sacrifices of the former dispensation only a type?

"When Christ came as high priest of the good things that are already here, he went through the greater and more perfect tabernacle that is not man-made, that is to say, not a part of this creation. He did not enter by means of the blood of goats and calves, but he entered the Most Holy Place once for all by his own blood, having obtained eternal redemption." Hebrews 9:11, 12, NIV. (See Ephesians 5:2.)

NOTE.—Through the sacrifices and offerings brought to the altar of the earthly sanctuary, the penitent believer was to lay hold of the merits of Christ, the Savior to come. In this way, and in this way only, was there any virtue connected with them (compare Hebrews 10:4).

At Christ's death what miracle signified that the priestly services of the earthly sanctuary were finished?

"And when Jesus had cried out again in a loud voice, he gave up his spirit. At that moment the curtain of the temple was torn in two from top to bottom." Matthew 27:50, 51, NIV.

NOTE.—Type had met antitype; the shadow had reached the substance. Christ, the great sacrifice, had been slain, and was about to enter upon His final work as our great high priest in the sanctuary in heaven.

The priestly work in the earthly sanctuary was a model of the work of Christ in the heavenly sanctuary. In the earthly sanctuary the atonement was performed on the last day of the ceremonial year. All who did not then have their sins atoned for were "cut off," and the camp was cleansed from sin. For this reason the Day of Atonement was a day of judgment for those who did not participate, and a day of release and freedom from sin for those who did. They could enter upon the services of the new year clean in the sight of God. This work was repeated year after year.

The blood of the sacrifices offered in the earthly sanctuary could not by itself take away the sins of the people (Hebrews 10:4). The service in the earthly sanctuary was ordained by God to provide the people with a way to demonstrate faith in God's grace and His great future sacrifice, to which the sanctuary service was to direct their minds. The work there was a type, or shadow, of Christ's great final atoning work in heaven in the end of time.

How are the heavenly and earthly sanctuaries related?

"They serve as a sanctuary that is *a copy and shadow* of what is in heaven. This is why Moses was warned when he was about to build the tabernacle: 'See to it that you make everything according to the *pattern* shown you on the mountain.' " Hebrews 8:5, NIV.

Does the heavenly sanctuary need cleansing?

"It was necessary, then, for the copies of the heavenly things to be purified with these sacrifices, *but the heavenly things themselves with better sacrifices than these*." Hebrews 9:23, NIV.

NOTE.—Scripture explicitly says that the heavenly sanctuary needs cleansing. In the final cleansing of the heavenly sanctuary the record books are examined and every case is decided. Just as atonement is made again in the earthly Most Holy Place, so the justification of the believer is reaffirmed in the pre-Advent or investigative judgment if the record indicates the believer is still by faith in a growing union with Christ.

What will be the fate of those who, once sanctified, turn their back upon God's grace and live in sin?

"If we deliberately keep on sinning after we have received the knowledge of the truth, no sacrifice for sins is left, but only a fearful expectation of judgment and of raging fire that will consume the enemies of God. Anyone who rejected the law of Moses died without mercy on the testimony of two or three witnesses. How much more severely do you think a man deserves to be punished who has trampled the Son of God under foot, *who has treated as an unholy thing the blood of the covenant that sanctified him,* and who has insulted the Spirit of grace? For we know him who said, 'It is mine to avenge; I will repay,' and again, *'The Lord will judge his people.'* " Hebrews 10:26-30, NIV.

NOTE.—God gives this solemn warning to those who abuse His grace. This passage is not speaking of those who fall into occasional sin, but to those who cease trying to live holy lives and deliberately keep on sinning. God will judge even His own people—those who have been sanctified by the blood—and reject them if they turn away from following Him. (See also Hebrews 6:4-8; John 15:2, 6; Luke 8:13; 12:42-46; 2 Peter 2:20-22.)

What confident assurance can the believer have in Jesus?

"We have been made holy through the sacrifice of the body of Jesus Christ once for all. . . . By one sacrifice he has made perfect forever those who are being made holy." Hebrews 10:10-14, NIV.

NOTE.—No believing Christian need wonder about their status in the judgment. As long as we continue to walk with Jesus, He will finish what He has begun in us (Philippians 1:6). As long as we are being made holy, we are perfect. As long as we are advancing toward the goal, we are considered as if we had already reached it, for the once-and-for-all sacrifice of Jesus paid the price for our sins forever.

What status does the penitent believer enjoy?

"Therefore, there is now *no condemnation* for those who are in Christ Jesus," "who do not live according to the sinful nature but according to the Spirit." Romans 8:1, 4, NIV. "I tell you the truth, whoever hears my word and believes him who sent me has eternal life and *will not be condemned;* he has crossed over from death to life." John 5:24, NIV.

NOTE.—The word translated "condemnation" in these verses is the Greek word for judgment, *krisis,* from which we derive our English word "crisis." These verses do not mean that Christians are exempt from the process of judgment, for that would contradict Ecclesiastes 3:17; Romans 14:10; 2 Corinthians 5:10; and Hebrews 10:30. Rather, those who abide in Christ, and who do not live "according to the sinful nature" need not fear a negative verdict in the judgment. *Krisis* here is not the process but the result, as in John 5:29, which says that the righteous will come forth "unto the resurrection of life; and they that have done evil, unto the resurrection of damnation *[krisis].*" Also, please note that the Greek verbs in John 5:24 are in the present continuous tense, giving the meaning "He who is *hearing* My words and is *believing* on Him that sent Me *is not coming* into condemnation." As long as we keep hearing and believing, we are not condemned. Such persevering Christians, no matter how weak, have been made holy (sanctified) once and for all, and nothing can snatch them away from their Redeemer (John 10:29).

Should Christians fear the judgment?

"In this way, love is made complete among us so that *we will have confidence on the day of judgment*, because in this world we are like him. There is no fear in love. But perfect love drives out fear, because fear has to do with punishment. The one who fears is not made perfect in love." 1 John 4:17, 18, NIV.

NOTE.—Christians do not need to fear the judgment, for they are secure in God's love.

What encouraging picture of an investigative judgment is found in Jeremiah?

" 'In those days, at that time,' declares the Lord, 'search will be made for Israel's guilt, but there will be none, and for the sins of Judah, but none will be found, for I will forgive the remnant I spare.' " Jeremiah 50:20, NIV.

What reassuring judgment scene did the prophet Zechariah see in vision?

"Then he showed me Joshua the high priest standing before the angel of the lord, and Satan standing at his right side to accuse him. The Lord said to Satan, 'The Lord rebuke you, Satan! The Lord, who has chosen Jerusalem, rebuke you! Is not this man a burning stick snatched from the fire?'

"Now Joshua was dressed in filthy clothes as he stood before the angel. The angel said to those who were standing before him, 'Take off his filthy clothes.'

"Then he said to Joshua, 'See, I have taken away your sin, and I will put rich garments on you.'

"Then I said, 'Put a clean turban on his head.' So they put a clean turban on his head and clothed him, while the angel of the Lord stood by.

"The angel of the Lord gave this charge to Joshua: 'This is what the Lord Almighty says: "If you walk in my ways and keep my requirements, then you will govern my house and have charge of my courts, and I will give you a place among these standing here.

" ' "Listen, O high priest Joshua and your associates seated before you, who are men symbolic of things to come: I am going to bring my

The Good News of Judgment

It is appointed for men to die once, but after this the judgment' (Hebrews 9:27, NKJV). Just as death is the lot of humanity, so every human being has to face the final judgment, 'for we must all appear before the judgment seat of Christ' (2 Corinthians 5:10, NKJV). Although we are saved by faith in Christ (Ephesians 2:8), we are still judged by our works (Ecclesiastes 12:14; Matthew 12:36). However, if we have accepted Christ as our Lord and Savior, we have nothing to fear in the judgment because Jesus has taken our sins to the cross and died in our place. Paul says that He was made 'sin for us, that we might become the righteousness of God in Him' (2 Corinthians 5:21, NKJV), and that 'there is therefore now no condemnation to those who are in Christ Jesus' (Romans 8:1, NKJV).

"Zechariah 3 graphically demonstrates this wonderful truth. When Satan opposed Joshua before the Lord, God said to His helpers, 'Take away the filthy garments from him.' Then Joshua received new clothes and a clean turban (verses 4, 5, NKJV). The filthy garments, representing the sins of the individuals, were not burned or sent to the dry cleaners, but Jesus put them on and then went to the cross to pay the penalty (Romans 5:8).

"The pre-Advent judgment in Daniel 7 is the first phase of the final judgment. . . . Then at the Second Coming God will reveal the decisions reached in the pre-Advent judgment, and His saints will receive the kingdom (Daniel 7:27). During the millennium the righteous will judge the wicked (Revelation 20:4; 1 Corinthians 6:2, 3), and after it the wicked and Satan with all his followers will receive the ultimate penalty—eternal death (Revelation 20:11-15). Together these various phases of judgment constitute the final judgment, the climax of which will be the vindication of God's love and righteousness for all eternity."
Gerhard Pfandl, *Daniel: The Seer of Babylon* (Hagerstown, Md.: Review and Herald, 2004), pp. 73, 74.

servant, the Branch. See the stone I have set in front of Joshua! There are seven eyes on that one stone, and I will engrave an inscription on it," says the Lord Almighty, "and I will remove the sin of this land in a single day.

" ' "In that day each of you will invite the neighbor to sit under his vine and fig tree," declares the Lord Almighty.' " Zechariah 3, NIV.

When Christ has finished His priestly mediatorial work in the heavenly sanctuary, what decree will go forth?

"Let him who does wrong continue to do wrong; let him who is vile continue to be vile; let him who does right continue to do right; and let him who is holy continue to be holy." Revelation 22:11, NIV.

What statement immediately following the announcement mentioned in Revelation 22:11 indicates that a judgment work had been in progress before Christ comes?

"Behold, I am coming soon! My reward is with me, and I will give to everyone according to what he has done." Verse 12, NIV.

THE JUDGMENT

What indication do we have that there will be a final judgment?

"God . . . has fixed a day on which he will have the world judged in righteousness by a man whom he has appointed, and of this he has given assurance to all by raising him from the dead." Acts 17:30, 31, NRSV.

Was the judgment still future in Paul's day?

"As Paul discoursed on righteousness, self-control and *the judgment to come, Felix was afraid.*" Acts 24:25, NIV.

How many must meet the test of the judgment?

"I thought in my heart, 'God will bring to judgment *both the righteous and the wicked.*' " Ecclesiastes 3:17, NIV. *"For we must all appear before the judgment seat of Christ,* that each one may receive what is due him for the things done while in the body, whether good or bad." 2 Corinthians 5:10, NIV. (Compare Romans 14:10-12.)

NOTE.—"Judgment is the fulfillment of humanity's hopes and yearnings. In our minds it conveys the ideas of crime and punishment and inspires fear and apprehension. The Bible, however, sees judgment from the viewpoint of the oppressed, the suffering victim, and thus places it in the context of salvation and victory over the oppressor and evil. Israelite culture already recognized that fact on a national level. The judges of Israel were war heroes who would crush the enemy. Scripture also referred to them as saviors, *moshiah* (Judges 3:9, 15; 6:36; 12:3). This two-level aspect of the judgment of God is especially clear in the psalms that describe the judging God as both savior and avenger (Psalm 18:47, 48; 58:11; 94:1-6, 22, 23; 149:4, 7, 9; etc.). Such a depiction of God can shock our modern sensibilities. And yet just coaxing the lion into letting go of the lamb will not work. To save the lamb, one must overcome the lion. That is why the term *tsedaqa*, which means 'justice,' implying the punishment of the oppressor, also means 'love,' as it liberates the oppressed back to life.

"Chapter 7 of Daniel also explicates these two dimensions of divine judgment. The judgment is pronounced 'in favor of the saints of the Most High' (verse 22, NIV) and against their enemies. In fact, the vision views judgment against a background of war and oppression: 'As I watched, this horn was waging war against the saints and defeating them' (verse 21, NIV)." Jacques B. Doukhan, *Secrets of Daniel* (Hagerstown, Md.: Review and Herald, 2000), pp. 112, 113.

What reason did Solomon give for urging all to fear God and keep His commandments?

"For God will bring every deed into judgment, including every hidden thing, whether it is good or evil." Ecclesiastes 12:14, NIV.

What view of the judgment scene was given Daniel?

"As I looked, thrones were set in place, and the Ancient of Days took his seat. His clothing was as white as snow; the hair of his head was white like wool. His throne was flaming with fire, and its wheels were all ablaze. A river of fire was flowing, coming out from before him. Thousands upon thousands attended him; ten thousand times ten thousand stood before him. The court was seated, and the books were opened." Daniel 7:9, 10, NIV.

How does Revelation describe such a scene?

"And I saw the dead, great and small, standing before the throne, and *books were opened*. Another book was opened, which is the book of life. *The dead were judged according to what they had done as recorded in the books*." Revelation 20:12, NIV.

For whom has a book of remembrance been written?

"Then those who revered the Lord spoke with one another. The Lord took note and listened, and a book of remembrance was written before him of those who revered the Lord and thought on his name."

Malachi 3:16, NRSV. (See Revelation 20:12.)

Who opens the judgment and presides over it?

"As I looked, thrones were set in place, and *the Ancient of Days took his seat.*" Daniel 7:9, NIV.

Who minister to God and assist in the judgment?

"Thousands upon thousands attended him; ten thousand times ten thousand stood before him. The court was seated, and the books were opened." Verse 10, NIV. (See Revelation 5:11.)

Who is brought before the Father at this time?

"In my vision at night I looked, and there before me was *one like a son of man*, coming with the clouds of heaven. He approached the Ancient of Days and was led into his presence." Daniel 7:13, NIV.

NOTE.—Jesus is approaching God the Father.

What does Christ as the advocate of His people acknowledge before the Father and His angels?

"He who overcomes will, like them, be dressed in white. I will never blot out his name from the book of life, but *will acknowledge his name before my Father and his angels*." Revelation 3:5, NIV. (See Matthew 10:32, 33; Mark 8:38.)

NOTE.—During this judgment both the righteous and the wicked dead are still in their graves. The record of their lives, however, is in the books of heaven, where the characters and deeds of everyone are recorded. Christ is there to appear in behalf of those who have chosen Him as their advocate (1 John 2:1). He presents His blood as He appeals for their sins to be blotted from the books of record. All are judged by the record of their lives. This work will not only decide forever the cases of the dead but also close the probation of all who are living, after which Christ will come to take to Himself those who have been found loyal to Him.

After the subjects of the kingdom have been determined by the investigative judgment, what is bestowed upon Christ?

"Then to Him was given *dominion and glory and a kingdom*, that all peoples, nations, and languages should serve Him. His dominion is an everlasting dominion, which shall not pass away, and his kingdom the one which shall not be destroyed." Daniel 7:14, NKJV.

When He comes the second time, what title will He bear?

"On his robe and on his thigh he has this name written: *KING OF*

KINGS AND LORD OF LORDS." Revelation 19:16, NIV.

What will He then do for each one?

"For the Son of Man is going to come in his Father's glory with his angels, and then he will *reward* each person according to what he has done." Matthew 16:27, NIV. (See Revelation 22:12.)

Where will Christ then take His people?

"In my Father's house are many rooms; if it were not so, I would have told you. I am going there to prepare a place for you. And if I go and prepare a place for you, *I will come back and take you to be with me that you also may be where I am.*" John 14:2, 3, NIV.

How many of the dead will be raised?

"For a time is coming when *all who are in their graves will hear his voice* and come out—those who have done good will rise to live, and those who have done evil will rise to be condemned." John 5:28, 29, NIV. (See Acts 24:15.)

What time intervenes between the two resurrections?

"I saw thrones on which were seated those who had been given authority to judge. And I saw the souls of those who had been beheaded because of their testimony for Jesus and because of the word of God. They had not worshiped the beast or his image and had not received his mark on their foreheads or their hands. They came to life and reigned with Christ *a thousand years.*" Revelation 20:4, NIV.

When are the wicked dead resurrected?

"The rest of the dead did not come to life until the thousand years were ended." Verse 5, NIV.

What work will the redeemed be engaged in during this 1,000-year period?

"Then I saw thrones, and those seated on them were given authority to judge. . . . They came to life and reigned with Christ a thousand years." Revelation 20:4, NRSV. "Do you not know that the *saints will judge the world*? And if you are to judge the world, are you not competent to judge trivial cases? Do you not know that *we will judge angels*?" 1 Corinthians 6:2, 3, NIV.

What phase of the final judgment will follow this 1,000-year review by the redeemed?

"Then I saw a great white throne and him who was seated on it. Earth and sky fled from his presence, and there was no place for them. And I saw the dead, great and small, standing before the throne, and books were opened. Another book was opened, which is the book of life. *The dead were judged according to what they had done as recorded in the books*." Revelation 20:11, 12, NIV.

NOTE.—The final judgment has three phases:

1. The investigative court trial (Daniel 7:9, 10) preceding the Second Advent decides whose names are to be retained in the book of life (cf. Revelation 3:5). The purpose is to determine, to the satisfaction of the universe, who among the dead are worthy to be raised in the first resurrection, so the judgment must occur prior to that event.

2. The judgment of the lost by the saints during the 1,000 years following the Second Advent gives the redeemed an opportunity to "audit the books," so to speak, and satisfy themselves that God's decisions have been just.

3. The executive, or sentencing, phase of the judgment occurs at the end of the millennium, where punishment is assigned and the sentence is carried out.

Keep in mind that the purpose of the entire judgment process is not to inform God, who already knows who belongs to Him (2 Timothy 2:19), but to assure His creatures of His justice. Therefore, God goes to the trouble of securing the consensus of His servants, who are invited to participate in the investigation, before He executes judgment. This was true with the judgment of Sodom (where God sends angels to investigate and allows Abraham to intervene [Genesis 18:20-33]); it was true with the judgment of Jerusalem in Ezekiel 9:1-10 (the investigative phase, involving Ezekiel, is described in Ezekiel 8); and it is true of the pre-Advent judgment of Daniel 7:9, 10, where "thrones" are set up (cf. Revelation 20:4) and the books are opened before myriads of angels.

In the initial investigative phase of the final judgment, then, God apparently allows angels in on the process of determining which human beings are worthy of joining them in heaven. Then, in the second phase, He lets these approved human beings in on the process of judging the wicked. The judgment is God's way of giving His creatures a say in their future and showing them that He has nothing to hide.

Why is the execution of the judgment given to Christ?

"For as the Father has life in himself, so he has granted the Son to have life in himself. And he has given him authority to judge *be-*

cause he is the Son of Man." John 5:26, 27, NIV.

THE JUDGMENT-HOUR MESSAGE

What message announces that the time for the judgment has arrived?

"Then I saw another angel flying in midair, and he had the eternal gospel to proclaim to those who live on the earth—to every nation, tribe, language and people. He said in a loud voice, *'Fear God and give him glory, because the hour of his judgment has come. Worship him who made the heavens, the earth, the sea and the springs of water.'* " Revelation 14:6, 7, NIV.

In view of the judgment hour, what is proclaimed anew?

"The eternal gospel." Verse 6, NIV.

How extensively is this message to be proclaimed?

"To every nation, tribe, language and people." Verse 6, NIV.

What is the whole world called upon to do?

"Fear God, and give him glory." Verse 7, NIV.

What special reason is given for this?

"Because *the hour of his judgment has come*." Verse 7, NIV.

Upon whom are all called to worship?

"Him who made the heavens, the earth, the sea and the springs of water." Verse 7, NIV.

NOTE.—There is only one gospel (Romans 1:16, 17; Galatians 1:8), first announced in Eden (Genesis 3:15), preached to Abraham (Galatians 3:8) and to the children of Israel (Hebrews 4:1, 2), and proclaimed anew in every generation. In its development the gospel meets the needs of every crisis in the world's history. John the Baptist in his preaching announced the kingdom of heaven at hand (Matthew 3:1, 2), and prepared the way for the First Advent (John 1:22, 23). Christ Himself, in His preaching of the gospel, announced the fulfillment of a definite time prophecy (the 69 weeks, or 483 years, of Daniel 9:25), and called the people to repentance, in view of the coming of the predicted Messiah (Mark 1:14, 15). So when the time for the judgment comes, and Christ's second advent is near, a worldwide announcement of these events and the final appeal of the gospel is to be made.

What prophetic period extends to the time of the cleansing of the sanctuary (i.e., the investigative judgment)?

"And he said to me, *'For two thousand three hundred days; then the sanctuary shall be cleansed.'*" Daniel 8:14, NKJV

When did this long period expire?

In A.D. 1844 (see pp.189-199).

NOTE.—Jesus proclaimed the imminent fulfillment of the first part of the 2300 days—the 490 years (Mark 1:14, 15), which determined the time of the First Advent. The full period extends to the time of the heavenly judgment, which precedes the Second Advent. At the end of the 2300 years a special gospel message is sent to all the world, proclaiming the judgment hour at hand and calling upon all to worship the Creator. And indeed, at this very time (1844) just such a message was being proclaimed in various parts of the world. This was the beginning of the great Second Advent message that is now being proclaimed throughout the world.

How is the true God distinguished from false gods?

"'Tell them this: "These gods, who did not make the heavens and the earth, will perish from the earth and from under the heavens."' But *God made the earth by his power; he founded the world by his wisdom and stretched out the heavens by his understanding.*" Jeremiah 10:11, 12, NIV.

Why is worship due God?

"For the Lord is the great God, the great King above all gods. . . . *The sea is his, for he made it, and his hands formed the dry land.* Come, let us bow down in worship, let us kneel before the Lord our Maker." Psalm 95:3-6, NIV.

Why do the inhabitants of heaven worship God?

"The twenty-four elders fall down before him who sits on the throne, and worship him who lives for ever and ever. They lay their crowns before the throne and say: 'You are worthy, our Lord and God, to receive glory and honor and power, for *you created all things*, and by your will they were created and have their being.'" Revelation 4:10, 11, NIV.

What memorial of His creative power did God establish?

"Remember the Sabbath day by keeping it holy. . . . For in six days the Lord made the heavens and the earth, the sea, and all that is

in them, but he rested on the seventh day. Therefore *the Lord blessed the Sabbath day and made it holy.*" Exodus 20:8-11, NIV.

What place has the Sabbath in the work of salvation?

"Also I gave them my Sabbaths as *a sign* between us, so they would know that I the Lord *made them holy.*" Ezekiel 20:12, NIV.

How many are concerned in the judgment?

"For we must *all* appear before the judgment seat of Christ, that *each one* may *receive what is due him for the things done while in the body, whether good or bad.*" 2 Corinthians 5:10, NIV.

What will be the legal standard against which we will be judged?

"For whoever keeps the whole law and yet stumbles at just one point is guilty of breaking all of it. For he who said, 'Do not commit adultery,' also said, 'Do not murder.' If you do not commit adultery but do commit murder, you have become a lawbreaker. Speak and act as those who are going to be judged by *the law that gives freedom.*" James 2:10-12, NIV.

In view of the judgment, what exhortation is given?

"Now all has been heard; here is the conclusion of the matter: *Fear God and keep his commandments*, for this is the whole duty of man. For God will bring every deed into judgment, including every hidden thing, whether it is good or evil." Ecclesiastes 12:13, 14, NIV.

NOTE.—A comparison of Revelation 14:7 with Ecclesiastes 12:13 suggests that the way to give glory to God is to keep His commandments, and that in giving the judgment-hour message, the duty of keeping the commandments would be emphasized. This is plainly shown in the description given of the people who are gathered out of every nation, kindred, tongue, and people as the result of the preaching of this message, in connection with other messages that immediately follow and accompany it. Of this people it is said, "Here are those who keep the commandments of God and the faith of Jesus." Revelation 14:12, NKJV.

THE FALL OF MODERN BABYLON

Following the judgment-hour message of Revelation 14:6, 7, what second message is given to the world?

"A second angel followed and said, 'Fallen! *Fallen is Babylon the Great*, which made all the nations drink the maddening wine of her adulteries.' " Revelation 14:8, NIV.

NOTE.—This announcement of the spiritual fall of spiritual Babylon is a replay on a larger scale of the fall of the ancient historical empire of Babylon.

What warning was given to God's people prior to the fall of ancient Babylon?

"Flee from Babylon! Run for your lives! Do not be destroyed because of her sins. It is time for the Lord's vengeance; he will pay her what she deserves." Jeremiah 51:6, NIV.

Just before the Babylonian Empire fell, how did Belshazzar and his court defy the true God?

"So they brought in the gold goblets that had been taken from the temple of God in Jerusalem, and the king and his nobles, his wives and his concubines drank from them. As they drank the wine, they praised the gods of gold and silver, of bronze, iron, wood and stone." Daniel 5:3, 4, NIV.

NOTE.—Daniel bore such faithful witness to the truth in Babylon that Nebuchadnezzar was brought to acknowledge and to worship the true God. But after Nebuchadnezzar's death his successors failed to profit by his experience. Belshazzar finally profaned the sacred vessels of the Jewish Temple, which had been consecrated to God, by using them to drink the Babylonian wine of idolatrous worship. That night Babylon fell. Read the story in Daniel 5.

The prophecy of Revelation 17 and 18 indicates that this spiritual history will be repeated in the last days, on a worldwide scale.

Aside from rejecting God's message, what did ancient Babylon do to the nations?

"Babylon was a gold cup in the Lord's hand; she made the whole earth drunk. The nations drank her wine; therefore they have now gone mad." Jeremiah 51:7, NIV.

What symbol did an angel show in vision to John the apostle on Patmos?

"Then the angel carried me away in the Spirit into the desert. There I saw a woman sitting on a scarlet beast that was covered with blasphemous names and had seven heads and ten horns. The woman was dressed in purple and scarlet, and was glittering with gold, precious stones and pearls. She held a golden cup in her hand, filled with abominable things and the filth of her adulteries. This title was written on her forehead: MYSTERY, BABYLON THE GREAT, THE MOTHER OF PROSTITUTES AND OF THE ABOMINATIONS

OF THE EARTH." Revelation 17:3-5, NIV.

NOTE.—This suggests at once a religious power supported by, or deriving its authority from, a political power—in other words, a union of church and state. "End-time Babylon is a worldwide religious confederacy with the satanic trinity—Satan, the sea beast, and the earth beast or false prophet—arrayed against God and his faithful people and supported by the secular and political powers (cf. Revelation 13:12-17)." Ranko Stefanovich, *The Revelation of Jesus Christ: Commentary on the Book of Revelation* (Berrien Springs, Mich.: Andrews University Press, 2002), p. 505.

The word "mystery" indicates a secret code or cryptic riddle. Revelation speaks in symbol; this fallen woman is mystic or symbolic Babylon. The symbol is apt, for the parallels between the medieval church and ancient Babylon are striking. The pagan Babylonian state religion had its wealthy and powerful hierarchy, its elaborate temple ritual, its priestly monopoly of learning, its liturgy performed in an ancient language unknown to the common people, its processions of divine images, its great spring festival in which mourning is followed by rejoicing, and even a virgin mother goddess who interceded for her worshippers.

Throughout the second and third centuries "Christianity was becoming more popular with the people and was gaining steadily in numbers. Christian teachers were listened to with more and more respect, and hope emerged that presently Christianity might take over the community of the world. Therefore, whenever possible, customs of the world were taken over and 'baptized'—given Christian names and garbs. Care was taken to offend the state as little as possible. When the issues were clearly drawn, church leaders and those they led sought to stand firm. But where was the issue to be met? Expediency often postponed the moment of resistance, and more than once the issues were obscured by compromise. It can well be supposed that had the pagan Roman government been more complacent, Christianity would have followed such a program of compromise as to have learned to live content in a pagan environment, and perhaps eventually to have been completely modified by and absorbed into it. Fortunately for the church, the government remained a bitter enemy of the movement and Christianity was compelled to remain distinct, until Constantine led the Roman government into a surrender to the outward forms of Christianity." *The Seventh-day Adventist Bible Commentary* (Washington, D.C.: Review and Herald, 1957), vol. 6, p. 64. "Constantine inaugurated the extraordinary new policy of union of church and state, the effect of which, although materially beneficial to the church, was more adverse spiritually than any persecution it had ever suffered." *Ibid.*, p. 62.

Meanwhile Christian doctrine was shifting. "Under the pressure of anti-Judaism the seventh-day Sabbath fell gradually into disrepute; even more quickly, the distinction between clean and unclean foods was given up completely. With the elaboration of ritual, with the change of the presbyters into priests, and with an overall massive borrowing from paganism, Christianity so lost its original nature and complexion that had the apostles come back to life, they would scarcely have been able to recognize the system they helped to found. Christianity in its official structure and general nature became by A.D. 400 little more than a pagan mystery cult." *Ibid.*, p. 67.

"During and after Constantine's reign the church, relieved of anxiety concerning its relationships with the state, became involved in doctrinal controversies that resulted in the crystallized dogma, and thus Christianity became a creedal system. The church had achieved seeming success in the sight of men, but it had already apostatized in the sight of God. Paganism had been Christianized, but simultaneously Christianity had absorbed a great deal that was pagan. . . . Augustine, the North African theologian, now picked up boldly and expanded the earlier teaching of Origen of Alexandria, that the church need no longer look for its triumph to a cataclysmic end of the world at the second coming of Christ. Instead, he said, it should look to a gradual achievement of success as the victorious 'city of God' on earth, conquering the satanic 'city' of this world. . . . To accomplish this became the hope and objective of the steadily apostatizing church as a great politico-ecclesiastical system, which has guided its policy ever since." *Ibid.*, vol. 7, p. 20.

How did the angel explain "the mystery of the woman and of the beast she rides"?

"When I saw her, I was greatly astonished. Then the angel said to me, 'Why are you astonished? I will explain to you the mystery of the woman and of the beast she rides, which has the seven heads and ten horns. The beast, which you saw, once was, now is not, and will come up out of the Abyss and go to his destruction. The inhabitants of the earth whose names have not been written in the book of life from the creation of the world will be astonished when they see the beast, because he once was, now is not, and yet will come." Revelation 17:6-8, NIV.

NOTE.—The woman riding the beast represents a relationship between religious and political powers. The religious power represented by the woman exercises control over the political powers, yet is also "dependant on them to enforce her plans and purposes" Ranko

Stefanovich, *The Revelation of Jesus Christ: Commentary on the Book of Revelation* (Berrien Springs, Mich.: Andrews University Press, 2002), p. 507.

The description that the beast "once was, now is not, and yet will come" parodies the description of God as one "who was, and is, and is to come." Revelation 4:8, NIV.

What does this symbolic harlot represent?

"The woman you saw is *the great city that rules over the kings of the earth.*" Revelation 17:18, NIV. (See verses 3, 4, 9.)

NOTE.—A woman is used in Scripture as a symbol of God's people (Jeremiah 6:2; 2 Corinthians 11:2). A fallen woman represents a fallen church (compare Ezekiel 16, Jeremiah 2:20). "In the image of a prostitute seducing the people of the world and dragging them into illicit relationships, John portrays the end-time worldwide religious confederacy based on the evil religious system empowered by Satan himself. This religious system is now to be judged. John reverses the metaphor from a prostitute to a great city. . . . Prostitute Babylon and the great city Babylon are the same entity. They symbolize the same end-time religious system that stands in opposition to God. Divine judgment is now set into motion against this end-time religious system. This judgment is described in Revelation 18 in terms of the destruction of the ancient city of Babylon that has grown wealthy through economic trade." Ranko Stefanovich, *The Revelation of Jesus Christ: Commentary on the Book of* Revelation (Berrien Springs, Mich.: Andrews University Press, 2002), pp. 518, 519.

What is the significance of her attire?

"The woman was dressed in purple and scarlet, and was glittering with gold, precious stones and pearls. She held a golden cup in her hand, *filled with abominable things and the filth of her adulteries.*" Revelation 17:4, NIV.

NOTE.—The "gold, precious stones and pearls" that adorn the adulterous woman are a diabolical parallel to the jewels adorning the New Jerusalem (Revelation 21:11, 18-21). The New Jerusalem is described as being dressed like "a bride beautifully dressed for her husband" (Revelation 21:2, NIV). Ezekiel 16 describes God adorning His beloved ancient Jerusalem with fine clothing and precious jewels (verses 10-13). Like unfaithful ancient Jerusalem (verses 15-29), Babylon has turned from God and prostituted itself to false teachings and secular political powers.

By way of contrast, what does God's true bride wear?

"For the wedding of the Lamb has come, and his bride has made herself ready. *Fine linen, bright and clean*, was given her to wear. (Fine linen stands for the righteous acts of the saints.)" Revelation 19:7, 8, NIV.

For what is Babylon indicted?

"I saw that the woman was *drunk with the blood of the saints*, the blood of those who bore testimony to Jesus." Revelation 17:6, NIV.

"In her was found the blood of prophets and of the saints, and of all who have been killed on the earth." Revelation 18:24, NIV.

How have God's persecuted people cried out for justice?

"They called out in a loud voice, 'How long, Sovereign Lord, holy and true, until you judge the inhabitants of the earth and avenge our blood?' " Revelation 6:10, NIV.

For what will Babylon be repaid?

"Hallelujah! Salvation and glory and power belong to our God, for true and just are his judgments. He has condemned the great prostitute who corrupted the earth by her adulteries. He has avenged on her the blood of his servants." Revelation 19:1, 2, NIV.

NOTE.—In Revelation 17 and 18 judgment at last comes. The persecutors are finally judged.

What other actions indicate that "Babylon the Great" symbolizes an apostate Christian power?

"With her the kings of the earth committed adultery and the inhabitants of the earth were intoxicated with the wine of her adulteries." Revelation 17:2, NIV.

NOTE.—Spiritual Babylon commits spiritual fornication, imbibing false teachings and practices from the world and having illicit connections with secular powers, as did ancient Israel, who is described in Ezekiel 16:32: "Adulterous wife, who receives strangers instead of her husband!" (NRSV). In other words, like ancient Israel, spiritual Babylon formed alliances with the kings of the earth instead of remaining true to God.

In contrast to the "wine of fornication" in the hand of the fallen woman, what cup does Jesus offer in the Lord's Supper?

"This cup is the *new covenant* in my blood." Luke 22:20, NIV.

What is the essential teaching of the new covenant?

" 'This is the covenant I will make with the house of Israel after that time, declares the Lord. *I will put my laws in their minds and write them on their hearts.* I will be their God, and they will be my people." Hebrews 8:10, NIV.

NOTE.—Hebrews is quoting Jeremiah 31:33, 34, NIV.

When Christ puts His law in our hearts, what is the result?

"Therefore, there is now no condemnation for those who are in Christ Jesus, because *through Christ Jesus the law of the Spirit of life* set me free from the law of sin and death. For what the law was powerless to do in that it was weakened by the sinful nature, God did by sending his own Son in the likeness of sinful man to be a sin offering. And so he condemned sin in sinful man in order that *the righteous requirements of the law might be fully met in us,* who did not live according to the sinful nature but according to the Spirit." Romans 8:1-4, NIV.

When the law is fulfilled in us, how will we behave toward others?

"Let no debt remain outstanding, except the continuing debt to love one another, for he who loves his fellowman has fulfilled the law. The commandments, 'Do not commit adultery,' 'Do not murder,' 'Do not steal,' 'Do not covet,' and whatever other commandment there may be, are summed up in this one rule: 'Love your neighbor as yourself.' *Love does no harm to its neighbor. Therefore love is the fulfillment of the law*." Romans 13:8-10, NIV.

What kind of teaching has often been substituted for the Word of God?

" ' "They worship me in vain; their teachings are but rules taught by men." *You have let go of the commands of God and are holding on to the traditions of men.*' And he said to them: 'You have a fine way of setting aside the commands of God in order to observe your own traditions!' " Mark 7:7-9, NIV.

NOTE.—Jesus here quotes Isaiah 29:13. He condemns the exaltation of tradition over God's Word.

What will be the final fate of the harlot?

"The beast and the ten horns you saw will hate the prostitute. They will bring her to ruin and leave her naked; they will eat her flesh *and burn her with fire*." Revelation 17:16, NIV.

NOTE.—Revelation 18:21, using different symbolism, says that Babylon would be thrown down and destroyed. Evidently her political patrons will see her for what she really is and turn on her.

NOTE.—"In the final stage the picture suddenly and dramatically changes. The drunken prostitute lovers, the ten horns, and the beast that have loyally supported Babylon now awaken from their drunkenness and turn against their mistress. The very powers that have up to this point loyally supported Babylon now withdraw their support. The river Euphrates upon which Babylon sits dries up (Revelation 16:12). The reason for such a sudden reversal is not explained here. Most likely the deceived governing political powers of the world have become disillusioned with Babylon's impotence to protect herself (cf. Revelation 16:10, 11, 19) and have unitedly withdrawn their loyal support from her. They have turned to such antagonism and hostility that they will hate the prostitute and bring her to ruin. This recalls the Old Testament prophecies according to which, in the eschatological state of turmoil, the enemies of God's people turn against each other (Ezekiel 38:21, NASB; Haggai 2:22, NASB; Zechariah 14:13, NASB).

"The disillusioned worldwide political powers will make Babylon desolate and naked, and will eat her flesh. This savage act is driven by extreme hostility and hatred (cf. Psalm 27:2, NASB; Micah 3:3, NASB). The impassioned lovers have become the hostile haters. They will burn her up with fire. These cruel acts remind one of the prophecies of Ezekiel about judgment falling upon prostitute Jerusalem:

" 'I shall gather all your lovers. . . . So I shall gather them against you from every direction and expose your nakedness to them that they may see all your nakedness. . . . Thus I shall judge you, like women who commit adultery or shed blood are judged; and I shall bring on you the blood of wrath and jealousy. I shall also give you into the hands of your lovers, and they will tear down your shrines, demolish your high places, strip you of your clothing, take away your jewels, and will leave you naked and bare. . . . And they will burn your houses with fire and execute judgments on you in the sight of many women. Then I shall stop you from playing the harlot' (Ezekiel 16:37-41, NASB).

" 'Behold I will arouse your lovers against you. . . . They will remove your nose and your ears. . . . Your survivors will be consumed by the fire. They will also strip you of your clothes and take away your beautiful jewels. . . . And they will deal with you in hatred, take all your property, and leave you naked and bare. And the nakedness of your harlotries shall be uncovered' (Ezekiel 23:22-29, NASB).

"In both Ezekiel and Revelation, former lovers are responsible for the punishment of the prostitute.

"We see in this scene in Revelation the pattern of Satan's kingdom: each power destroys its predecessor (Babylon destroyed Assyria, Persia destroyed Babylon, etc.). Finally the battle of Armageddon "breaks this cycle." God himself steps into the action and brings the history of oppression to its end." Ranko Stefanovich, *The Revelation of Jesus Christ: Commentary on the Book of Revelation* (Berrien Springs, Mich.: Andrews University Press, 2002), pp. 517, 518.

What final call is being given to God's people who are still in Babylon?

"Then I heard another voice from heaven say: *'Come out of her, my people*, so that you will not share in her sins, so that you will not receive any of her plagues; for her sins are piled up to heaven, and God has remembered her crimes.' " Revelation 18:4, 5, NIV.

Does Jesus have faithful followers throughout the religious spectrum?

"I have other sheep that are not of this sheep pen. I must bring them also. They too will listen to my voice, and there shall be one flock and one shepherd." John 10:16, NIV.

How will those who come out of spiritual Babylon be characterized?

"This calls for patient endurance on the part of the saints who obey God's commandments and remain faithful to Jesus." Revelation 14:12, NIV.

THE CLOSING GOSPEL MESSAGE

What indicates that the messages of the judgment hour and the fall of Babylon are two parts of a threefold message?

"A third angel followed them and said in a loud voice: . . ." Revelation 14:9, NIV.

What apostasy from the worship of God is named here?

"If anyone worships the beast and his image and receives his mark on the forehead or on the hand, he, too, will drink of the wine of God's fury, which has been poured full strength into the cup of his wrath. He will be tormented with burning sulfur in the presence of the holy angels and of the Lamb." Verses 9, 10, NIV. (See Isaiah 33:14; 34:1-10; Hebrews 12:29.)

NOTE.—The Greek words for this mark are *charagma* (from which we get the English word "character") and sometimes *stigma*. This was sort of a scarlet letter, a mark of dishonor with which runaway slaves or criminals were branded, though it was usually reserved for the lower classes. Plato provided that slaves or aliens who robbed temples should have their guilt inscribed on their forehead or hands. In the ancient world slaves were often marked on the forehead with the mark of ownership of their master, and imperial Roman soldiers were marked in the hand with the name of the emperor for whom they fought. Caligula even had shameful marks branded on the foreheads of honorable citizens condemned to forced labor in the construction of buildings and roads. Constantine finally outlawed the practice of marking with the *stigma* on the face.

In the religious world the mark was sometimes adopted voluntarily. Devotees of a certain god would consecrate themselves to that god by having a certain symbol tattooed on their hand or forehead. This meant that they belonged to him and came under his protection. For example, devotees of the god Dionysus had an ivy leaf tattooed on their brow. A pagan king by the name of Ptolemy, who lived about two centuries before Christ, tried to force all Jews who lived in Alexandria in Egypt to be branded with the ivy leaf stigma of Dionysus.

In Revelation this is a symbol, not a literal, physical mark. The followers of the beast are marked as his by their obedience to his commands.

What served in place of a literal mark on the hand or forehead to identify God's people?

"This observance will be for you *like a sign on your hand* and a *reminder on your forehead* that the law of the Lord is to be on your lips. For the Lord brought you out of Egypt with his mighty hand." Exodus 13:9, NIV.

"These commandments that I give to you today [the Ten Commandments (Deuteronomy 5)] are to be upon your hearts. Impress them on your children. Talk about them when you sit at home and when you walk along the road, when you lie down and when you get up. Tie them as symbols on your *hands* and bind them on your *foreheads*." Deuteronomy 6:6-8, NIV.

NOTE.—For a believer, then, the mark in the hand or forehead symbolizes allegiance to God's law of 10 commandments. God's people are symbolically marked by keeping His law. The mark was never a literal, visible mark, for the Hebrews were forbidden to tattoo themselves (Leviticus 19:28). The Babylonian Talmud (Megillah 24b) said that whoever placed the tephillin on the brow or on their hand followed the practice of the heretics. Instead, faithful followers of God were identified by their lifestyle of obedience to His law.

How are those who heed the warning against the mark of the beast described?

"This calls for patient endurance on the part of the saints who *obey God's commandments* and remain faithful to Jesus." Revelation 14:12, NIV.

How does Revelation describe the beast from the sea that it warns against?

"And I saw a beast coming out of the sea. He had ten horns and seven heads, with ten crowns on his horns, and on each head a blasphemous name. The beast I saw resembled a leopard, but had feet like those of a bear and a mouth like that of a lion. The dragon gave the beast his power and his throne and great authority." Revelation 13:1, 2, NIV.

NOTE.—In this composite beast from the sea are combined the symbols of the seventh chapter of Daniel. Its blasphemous words, its persecution of the saints, and its allotted time (verses 5-7) show that this beast is identical with the little horn of the vision of Daniel 7, the political power of the Papacy. The composite character of this beast (Revelation 13:2) indicates that this political-religious system combines the Christian faith with elements of pagan Babylon, Medo-Persia, Greece, and Rome.

The crowns on the sea beast's heads parody those of Christ, who is described as wearing "many crowns" (Revelation 19:12). The "blasphemous names" upon his heads indicate that this beast claims divine authority for himself, and further indicate a union of religious and political power.

What challenge is made by those who worship the beast?

"Men worshiped the dragon because he had given authority to the beast, and they also worshiped the beast and asked, 'Who is like the beast? Who can make war against him?' " Revelation 13:4, NIV.

NOTE.—This beast demands homage that is due to God alone. Such language is used in Scripture only of Deity ("Who is like you?" [see Exodus 15:11; Psalm 35:10]). Only God is to be worshipped (Matthew 4:10). The world's question "Who is like the beast?" parodies "Who is like God?" in such texts as Exodus 15:11; Psalm 35:10; and Micah 7:18.

Whose sovereignty is thus challenged?

"Who is like the *Lord* our God, the One who sits enthroned on high, who stoops down to look on the heavens and the earth?" Psalm 113:5, 6, NIV. (See also Psalm 35:10; 71:19; 86:6-8; 89:6, 8.)

What specifications of "the man of lawlessness" are thus met?

"Don't let anyone deceive you in any way, for that day will not come until the rebellion occurs and the man of lawlessness is revealed, the man doomed to destruction. He will oppose and will *exalt himself over everything that is called God or is worshiped, so that he sets himself up in God's temple, proclaiming himself to be God.*" 2 Thessalonians 2:3, 4, NIV.

By what threat is the worship of the image of the beast enforced?

"He was given power to give breath to the image of the first beast, so that it could speak and cause all who refused to worship the image to be killed." Revelation 13:15, NIV.

NOTE.—See pp. 236-243.

What is one Old Testament vision from which Revelation draw its imagery of a mark?

"The the Lord called to the man clothed in linen who had the writing kit at his side and said to him, 'Go throughout the city of Jerusalem and put a mark on the foreheads of those who grieve and lament over all the detestable things that are done in it.' As I listened, he said to the others, 'Follow him through the city and kill, without showing pity or compassion. . . . But do not touch anyone who has the mark." Ezekiel 9:3-6, NIV.

How will the sea beast attempt to compel all to receive his mark?

"He also forced everyone, small and great, rich and poor, free and slave, to receive a mark on his right hand or on his forehead, so that no one could buy or sell unless he had the mark, which is the name of the beast or the number of his name." Revelation 13:16, 17, NIV.

NOTE.—On the mark of the beast, see pp.384-387.

Who is the real power operating through the sea beast?

"The *dragon* gave the beast his power and his throne and his great authority." Verse 2, NIV.

Who is this dragon?

"The great dragon was hurled down—that ancient serpent called *the devil*, or *Satan*, who leads the whole world astray." Revelation 12:9, NIV.

How did the devil seek to induce Jesus to worship him?

"The devil led him up to a high place and showed him in an instant all the kingdoms of the world. And he said to him, 'I will give you all their authority and splendor, for it has been given to me, and I can give it to anyone I want to. So if you worship me, it will all be yours.' " Luke 4:5-7, NIV.

How did Jesus show His loyalty to God?

"Jesus answered, 'It is written: *"Worship the Lord your God and serve him only"* ' " Verse 8, NIV.

NOTE.—Jesus is quoting Deuteronomy 6:13.

The threefold message of Revelation 14:6-12 is proclaimed in connection with the closing scenes of the great controversy between Christ and Satan. Lucifer (Satan) had sought to put himself in the place of God (Isaiah 14:12-14), and to secure to himself the worship that is due God alone. The final test comes over the commandments of God. Those who acknowledge the supremacy of the beast by yielding obedience to its law will receive its mark.

How many will yield to the demand to worship the beast?

"*All inhabitants of the earth* will worship the beast—all whose names have not been written in the book of life belonging to the Lamb that was slain from the creation of the world." Revelation 13:8, NIV.

In the judgment-hour message, upon whom are all called to fear, glorify, and worship?

"Fear *God* and give him glory, because the hour of his judgment has come. Worship him who made the heavens, the earth, the sea and the springs of water." Revelation 14:7, NIV.

Who will sing the victor's song on the sea of glass?

"And I saw what looked like a sea of glass mixed with fire and, standing beside the sea, *those who had been victorious over the beast and his image and over the number of his name*. They held harps given them by God and sang the song of Moses the servant of God and the song of the Lamb: 'Great and marvelous are your deeds, Lord God Almighty. Just and true are your ways, King of the ages. Who will not fear you, O Lord, and bring glory to your name? For you alone are holy. All nations will come and worship before you, for your righteous acts have been revealed.' " Revelation 15:2-4, NIV.

SATAN'S WARFARE AGAINST THE CHURCH

How is God's true church represented in symbol in Revelation?

"A great and wondrous sign appeared in heaven: a *woman* clothed with the sun, with the moon under her feet and a crown of twelve stars on her head." Revelation 12:1, NIV.

NOTE.—Frequently in the Scriptures a woman is used to represent the church (see Jeremiah 6:2; 2 Corinthians 11:2). The sun, moon, and 12 stars in this vision allude to Joseph's vision of the sun, moon, and stars that stood for Jacob, his wife, and his children (Genesis 37:9, 10), the predecessors of the 12 tribes of Israel. We are reminded as well of Solomon's bride (Song of Solomon 6:10), who "appears like the dawn, fair as the moon, bright as the sun, majestic as the stars in procession" (NIV). The woman of Revelation 12:1 wears a crown like that promised to the faithful Christian (Revelation 2:10; 3:11).

To whom does the woman give birth?

"She was pregnant and cried out in pain as she was about to give birth. . . . She gave birth to a son, *a male child, who will rule all the nations with an iron scepter*. And her child was snatched up to God and to his throne." Revelation 12:2-5, NIV.

NOTE.—The prophecy can apply only to Jesus Christ. He will at His return strike the nations with a rod of iron (Revelation 19:15; Psalm 2:6-9). Likewise, the prophecy speaks of Christ's ascension and enthronement at God's right hand (cf. 1 Peter 3:22; Revelation 3:21).

What other sign, or wonder, appeared in heaven?

"Then another sign appeared in heaven: an enormous red dragon with seven heads and ten horns and seven crowns on his heads. His tail swept a third of the stars out of the sky and flung them to the earth. The dragon stood in front of the woman who was about to give birth, so that he might devour her child the moment it was born." Revelation 12:3, 4, NIV.

Who is this dragon said to be?

"The great dragon was thrown down, *that ancient serpent*, who is called the *Devil* and *Satan*, the deceiver of the whole world." Verse 9, NRSV.

NOTE.—The dragon represents Satan, the great enemy and persecutor of the church in all ages. But Satan works through principalities and powers in his efforts to destroy the people of God. It was through a Roman king, King Herod, that he sought to destroy Christ as soon as He was born (Matthew 2:16), and it was a Roman governor who sentenced Him to die. The seven heads of the dragon are said in Revelation 17:10 to be "seven kings," evidently symbolizing earthly powers or kingdoms or agencies through whom Satan works to carry out his purposes.

How is the conflict between Christ and Satan described?

"And there was war in heaven. Michael and his angels fought against the dragon, and the dragon and his angels fought back. But he was not strong enough, and they lost their place in heaven. The great dragon was hurled down—that ancient serpent called the devil, or Satan, who leads the whole world astray. He was hurled to the earth, and his angels with him." Revelation 12:7-9, NIV.

NOTE.—This conflict, begun in heaven, continues on earth. Near the close of Christ's ministry He said, "I saw Satan *fall like lightning from heaven.*" Luke 10:18, NIV. "Now is the time for judgment on this world; now the prince of this world will be *driven out then*" (John 12:31, NIV), and this is linked with Christ's death in the following verse. From the councils of the representatives of the various worlds to which Satan, as the prince of this world, was formerly admitted (Job 1:6, 7; 2:1, 2), he was cast out when he crucified Christ, the Son of God.

"It was at the cross that it became clear to the entire universe who God was and the character of his rule. In the same manner, Satan's character was revealed at the cross. Though he had been a murderer from the beginning (John 8:44), it was at the cross that the entire universe came to realize his true character. As a result, Satan was forever excommunicated from the heavenly places; and since then, there was no longer any place for him and his angels in heaven. Jesus referred to Satan's expulsion as legal action, saying that "now the ruler of this world shall be cast out" (John 12:31, NASB; cf. Luke 10:18; John 14:30; 16:11). This *now* referred to the death of Jesus on the cross. It is the death of Jesus that marks the casting down of Satan as well as the exaltation of Christ on the heavenly throne (cf. John 12:32).

"Revelation 12:10 sheds more light on this *now*. It indicates that at Christ's ascension and subsequent exaltation on the heavenly throne (cf. Revelation 5), 'the kingdom of our God and authority of his Christ' was set up, and Satan was ultimately expelled from heaven. The cross marks the decisive point in human history, with cosmic meaning and significance, 'when God's "direct rule" replaces Satan's abuse of his powers, and *authority* passes to God's Christ.' [John P.M. Sweet, *Revelation*, TPI New Testament Commentaries (Philadelphia: Trinity Press International, 1990), p. 201]. As John Sweet says, 'Christ is now enthroned at God's right hand, but on the earth the usurping *authorities* must still be fought' *[ibid.]* (Revelation 12:17; 1 Corinthians 15:24-26)." Ranko Stefanovich, *The Revelation of Jesus Christ: Commentary on the Book of Revelation* (Berrien Springs, Mich.: Andrews University Press, 2002), p. 388.

What shout of triumph is heard in heaven following the victory gained by Christ at the cross?

"Then I heard a loud voice in heaven say: *'Now have come the salvation and the power and the kingdom of our God, and the authority of his Christ.* For the accuser of our brothers, who accuses them before our God day and night, has been hurled down. They overcame him by the blood of the Lamb and by the word of their testimony; they did not love their lives so much as to shrink from death. Therefore rejoice, you heavens and you who dwell in them!' " Revelation 12:10-12, NIV.

Why was woe proclaimed to the world at this same time?

"But woe to the earth and the sea, *because the devil has gone down to you! He is filled with fury, because he knows his time is short.*" Verse 12, NIV.

NOTE.—This shows that since the crucifixion of Christ Satan knows not only that his doom is sealed, but that now his efforts are largely if not wholly confined to this world, and concentrated upon its inhabitants. Better than many professed Christians, Satan knows that time is short.

What did the dragon do when he was cast to the earth?

"When the dragon saw that he had been hurled to the earth, he pursued the woman who had given birth to the male child." Verse 13, NIV.

NOTE.—The persecution of Christians began under pagan Rome and has continued ever since wherever religious freedom and liberty of conscience are not respected (Matthew 24:21, 22). Recent estimates indicate that more Christians have been martyred in the past 50 years than were killed in the first 300 years under Rome.

What specific period of time was allotted to this great persecution of God's people?

"The woman was given the two wings of a great eagle, so that she might fly to the place prepared for her in the desert, where she would be taken care of for *a time, times and half a time*, out of the serpent's reach." Revelation 12:14, NIV.

NOTE.—This is the same period as that of Daniel 7:25. In Revelation 13:5 this period is referred to as "forty-two months," and in Revelation 12:6 as 1260 days, each representing 1,260 literal years. The woman fleeing into the wilderness fittingly describes the condition of the church during those times of bitter persecution.

How did God describe His rescue of the Israelites from Egypt, leading them into the wilderness?

"You yourselves have seen what I did to Egypt, and how I carried you *on eagle's wings* and brought you to myself." Exodus 19:4, NIV.

"In a desert land he found him, in a barren and howling waste. He shielded him and cared for him; he guarded him as the apple of his eye, like an eagle that stirs up its nest and hovers over its young, that spreads its wings to catch them and carries them on its pinions." Dueteronomy 32:10, 11, NIV.

What was Satan's design in thus persecuting the church?

"Then from his mouth the serpent spewed water like a river, *to overtake the woman and sweep her away with the torrent.*" Revelation 12:15, NIV.

NOTE.—The serpent in Eden ensnared the first woman with a mix of truth and error, and Satan tried to sweep the church away by the same method.

How was the flood stopped, and Satan's design defeated?

"But the earth helped the woman by opening its mouth and swallowing the river that the dragon had spewed out of his mouth." Verse 16, NIV.

NOTE.—The mountainous retreats and secluded valleys of Europe for centuries shielded many who swore allegiance only to God's word in the Bible. Here, too, may be seen the results of the work of the Reformation of the sixteenth century, when some of the governments of Europe came to the help of various reform groups, by staying the hand of persecution and protecting the lives of those who dared to take their stand against a misrepresentation of God.

How did God protect the Israelites in the wilderness?

"You stretched out your right hand and the earth swallowed them." Exodus 15:12, NIV.

What did Christ say would be the result if the days of persecution were not shortened?

"If those days had not been cut short, *no one would survive*, but for the sake of the elect those days will be shortened." Matthew 24:22, NIV.

How does Satan manifest his continued enmity against the

church in the "time of the end"?

"Then the dragon was enraged at the woman and went off to make war against the rest of her offspring—those who obey God's commandments and hold to the testimony of Jesus." Revelation 12:17, NIV.

NOTE.—To the very end Satan will persecute and seek to destroy the people of God. Against the remnant, or last portion, of the church, he is especially to make war. Their obedience to God's commandments, and their possession of the testimony of Jesus, or Spirit of prophecy (Revelation 19:10), are especially offensive to him, and incite his intense fury.

A GREAT PERSECUTING POWER

What is the first symbol of Revelation 13?

"And the dragon stood on the shore of the sea. And I saw *a beast coming out of the sea. He had ten horns and seven heads*, with ten crowns on his horns, and on each head a blasphemous name." Verse 1, NIV.

NOTE.—As we already learned from studying the book of Daniel, a beast in prophecy represents some great earthly power or kingdom. A head or horn represents a governing power as well. Waters represent "peoples, multitudes, nations, and languages." Revelation 17:15)

How is this beast further described?

"The beast I saw *resembled a leopard*, but had *feet like those of a bear* and a *mouth like that of a lion*." Revelation 13:2, NIV.

NOTE.—These are the characteristics of the first three symbols of Daniel 7—the *lion*, *bear*, and *leopard* there representing the kingdoms of *Babylon*, *Persia*, and *Greece*. This beast also shares in the characteristics of the fourth beast of Daniel 7. Both have 10 horns. Both this beast and the "little horn" of the fourth beast of Daniel 7 have "a mouth" speaking great things; both make war upon the saints; both continue for the same period of time (42 months = 1260 days/years = three and a half times). This implies that they both represent the same religiopolitical power that emerged in the wake of the Roman empire.

What did the dragon give this beast?

"The dragon gave the beast his *power* and his *throne* and *great authority*." Revelation 13:2, NIV.

NOTE.—"The removal of the capital of the Empire from Rome

to Constantinople in 330 left the Western Church, practically free from imperial power, to develop its own form of organization. The Bishop of Rome, *in the seat of the Caesars*, was now the greatest man in the West, and was soon [when the barbarians overran the empire] forced to become the political as well as the spiritual head." A. C. Flick, *The Rise of the Mediaeval Church* (New York: Putnam's, 1909), p. 168.

The codex of Justinian that became the legal code of the empire in A.D. 533 gave legal status to the bishop of Rome as "head of all the holy churches" and "corrector of heretics." In this way secular

The Sea Beast Parodies Jesus

Jesus	Sea beast
"The Lamb that was slain" (Rev. 13:8, NIV; cf. 5:6)	Received a fatal wound yet lives (Rev. 13:3)
Ministered 3.5 years	Ruled 42 months (Rev 13:5)
Began ministry out of water (Mark 1:10)	Emerged from sea (Rev. 13:1)
Received authority from Father (Rev. 2:27)	Received authority from dragon (Rev. 13:2)
Wears many crowns (Rev. 19:12)	Wears many crowns (Rev. 13:1)
Carries a sword (Rev. 1:16)	Persecutes with a sword (Rev. 13:10)
Has horns (Rev. 5:6)	Has horns (Rev. 13:1)
Worshiped after resurrection (Matt. 28:17)	Worshiped after wound is healed (Rev. 13:5)
"Michael" ("Who is like God?") (Rev. 12:7)	"Who is like the beast?" (Rev. 13:4, NIV)
Name in followers' foreheads (Rev. 14:1)	Mark on followers' foreheads (Rev. 13:16)
Authority over heaven and earth (Matt. 28:18)	Authority over earth (Rev. 13:7)

Rome gave ecclesiastical Rome its power and authority.

How does the dragon's gift of authority to the sea beast parallel the relationship between God and Jesus?

"To him who overcomes and does my will to the end, I will give authority over the nations—'He will rule them with an iron scepter, he will dash them to pieces like pottery'—just as *I have received authority from my Father*." Revelation 2:26, 27, NIV.

NOTE.—In Revelation's counterfeit trinity, the dragon parallels and parodies God, the beast from the sea is a satanic imitation of Jesus, and the beast from the earth is a false version of the Holy Spirit. As Jesus received His authority from God, so the sea beast gets his authority from the dragon.

How else is the sea beast a counterfeit of Jesus?

"One of the heads of the beast seemed to have had a *fatal wound, but the fatal wound had been healed*. The whole world was astonished and followed the beast." Revelation 13:3, NIV. "The beast was given a mouth to utter proud words and blasphemies and to exercise his authority for *forty-two months*." Verse 5, NIV.

NOTE.—The sea beast's recovery from a "fatal wound" is a counterfeit of Christ's death and resurrection. The 42 months given to the sea beast to exercise his authority, equaling three and a half years, parallels the three and a half years of Christ's earthly ministry. In Revelation 11:2, 3 we read of the "holy city" being trampled for 42 months, as the "two witnesses" prophesy "for 1260 days, clothed in

The Sea Beast
Parallels the Little Horn of Daniel 7

Little horn	Sea beast
Emerges from Roman Empire	Emerges from Roman Empire
Speaks against Most High (Dan. 7:25)	Blasphemes God (Rev. 13:6)
Acts for 3.5 years (Dan. 7:25)	Acts for 42 months (Rev. 13:5)

sackcloth" (NIV). This time period represents the medieval era, when religiopolitical powers oppressed followers of Christ.

The sea beast's 42 months also parallels that of the "little horn" of Daniel 7, who "will speak against the Most High and oppress his saints and try to change the set times and the laws. The saints will be handed over to him for a time, times and half a time." Daniel 7:25, NIV.

How does Revelation describe the reign of the sea beast?

"The beast was given a mouth to utter proud words and blasphemies and to exercise his authority for forty-two months. He opened his mouth to blaspheme God, and to slander his name and his dwelling place and those who live in heaven. He was given power to make war against the saints and to conquer them. And he was given authority over every tribe, people, language and nation." Revelation 13:5-7, NIV.

NOTE.—All these specifications were met in the medieval church, and identify this beast as representing the same power as that represented by the little horn phase of the fourth beast of Daniel 7, and the little horn of Daniel 8 (see Daniel 7:25; 8:11, 12, 24, 25).

What explanation is given for the sea beast's seven heads?

"This calls for a mind with wisdom. The seven heads are seven hills on which the woman sits. They are also seven kings. Five have fallen, one is, the other has not yet come; but when he does come, he must remain for a little while. The beast who once was, and now is not, is an eighth king. He belongs to the seven and is going to his destruction." Revelation 17:9-11, NIV.

NOTE.—The sea beast stands for all the world powers, spiritual and secular, that have persecuted God's people throughout history. These political agencies are represented by the seven heads of the beast and seven mountains. The text identifies the heads as the seven kings or kingdoms that have persecuted God's people throughout history since the beginning of God's church at the Exodus. The first five empires (Egypt, Assyria, Babylon, Persia, and Greece) had come and gone before John's time. The sixth head, Rome, was currently in power. The seventh power was yet to come, and was to receive a fatal wound (Revelation 13:3), and thus "is not" for a period of time. This power returns as the eighth king, the final, end-time religiopolitical power that will misrepresent God and persecute God's people.

What was to happen to one of the heads of the sea beast?

"One of the heads of the beast seemed to have had a fatal wound, but the fatal wound had been healed. The whole world was aston-

ished and followed the beast." Revelation 13:3, NIV.

NOTE.—The medieval church's power began to diminish with the Reformation and the development of modern thought. Writes Stefanovich, "Starting with both the Renaisssance humanist skepticism and the Protestant challenge on theological and political fronts, the ecclesiastical authoritarian rule was being seriously undermined. Furthermore, the rise of the urban class was bringing in a challenge of its own to both the aristocratic and ecclesiastic hierarchies. The ensuing Enlightenment Age attacked the entire rationale behind the existing political and religious governance. Continuing in the tradition of the Renaissance spirit, the new thinkers began to secularize society in earnest. What the philosophers advocated in theory, the American and French revolutionaries would eventually put into practice. The liberal philosophers were demanding a quantity of freedoms which the Church and the monarch were not willing to hand out. The establishment of the republican form of government in North America and in Europe and the gradual secularization of society, ranging from education to governance, was progressively ending the religious and political oppression and intolerance of both the Middle Ages and the post-Medieval period.

"Furthermore, the emancipation of the masses meant freedom from religious superstition and oppression. Nationalism was elevating the masses to the level of the ruling elite; while destroying the monarchial system, it was also effectively incapacitating the Church for its own needs. The events of the French Revolution (including the demise of the papacy under Napoleon) that impacted politics and religious liberty are probably the most apparent manifestation of the 'mortal wound.' But for all practical purposes, it was this long process of political, social, and religious transformation that caused the 'mortal wound' and brought the sea beast to the 'is not' period (cf. Revelation 17:11). Both the authoritarian oppressive religious-political rule and the traditional God-centered theology that dominated the Western world for centuries were brought to an end, and since have been replaced with the human-centered and materialistic (atheistic) philosophy expressed in various forms." Ranko Stefanovich, *The Revelation of Jesus Christ: Commentary on the Book of Revelation* (Berrien Springs, Mich.: Andrews University Press, 2002), pp. 412, 413.

The beast's power has been diminished, but Revelation tells us it will return for a time, as the eighth king that is yet a continuation of the first seven (Revelation 17:11). Religious intolerance will again disguise itself as service to God (see John 16:2). Yet at the end of the world this power will be defeated once and for all, and God will rescue all who respond to Him.

What questions indicate the high position of this beast power?

"Men worshiped the dragon because he had given authority to the beast, and they also worshiped the beast and asked, *'Who is like the beast? Who can make war against him?'* " Revelation 13:4, NIV.

How universal is the worship of this power to become?

"All inhabitants of the earth will worship the beast—all whose names have not been written in the book of life belonging to the Lamb that was slain from the creation of the world." Verse 8, NIV.

Who can make war against the beast, and what did John say will be its end?

"Then I saw the beast and the kings of the earth and their armies gathered together to make war against the rider on the horse and his army. But the beast was captured, and with him the false prophet who had performed the miraculous signs on his behalf. . . . *The two of them were thrown alive into the fiery lake of burning sulfur.*" Revelation 19:19, 20, NIV. (See Isaiah 47:7-15; 2 Thessalonians 2:3-8; Revelation 17:16, 17; 18:4-8.)

How is this like the fate of the fourth beast of Daniel 7?

"I kept looking until *the beast was slain and its body destroyed and thrown into the blazing fire.*" Daniel 7:11, NIV.

MAKING AN IMAGE TO THE BEAST

What is the second symbol of Revelation 13?

"Then I saw another beast, coming out of the earth. He had two horns like a lamb, but he spoke like a dragon." Revelation 13:11, NIV.

NOTE.—John Wesley, in his note on Revelation 13:11, written in 1754, says of the two-horned beast: "He is not yet come: tho' he cannot be far off. For he is to appear at the End of the forty-two Months of the first Beast." *Explanatory Notes Upon the New Testament* (1791 ed.), vol. 3, p. 299.

The United States emerged at the end of the 1260-year prophetic period, after the sea beast had received its fatal wound, and today is a leading world power. "Like a lamb," America has stood for freedom, yet prophecy points to a time when America will, like the sea beast, exercise force in the name of religion.

What is the character of this new power?

"He had *two horns like a lamb.*" Verse 11.

NOTE.—The nations of the past, pictured in the Bible as beasts of prey, were filled with intolerance, persecution, and oppression. The United States was founded on the principles of liberty, equality, and tolerance. The men who had fled the tribulations of the Old World were determined that those trials should not be repeated in the New.

The principles of civil and religious liberty that have made the United States great were incorporated into the law of the nation at its very founding, in the Bill of Rights:

Article I. "Congress shall make no law respecting an establish-ment of religion, or prohibiting the free exercise thereof; or abridg-ing the freedom of speech or of the press; or the right of the people peaceably to assemble, and to petition the government for a redress of grievances."

Article IV. "The right of the people to be secure in their persons, houses, papers, and effects, against unreasonable searches and seizures, shall not be violated."

Article V. "No person shall be . . . subject for the same offense to be twice put in jeopardy of life or limb, nor shall be compelled in any criminal case to be a witness against himself; nor to be deprived of life, liberty, or property, without due process of law; nor shall pri-vate property be taken for public use without just compensation."

Notwithstanding the lamblike appearance of this power, what will ultimately happen?

"He spoke like a dragon." Verse 11, NIV.

NOTE.—The voice of the dragon is the voice of intolerance and persecution. It is repugnant to the American mind to think that reli-gious persecution might mar the fair record of a nation founded on liberty to all. But all through the history of the country, from its very founding, farseeing leaders have recognized that the tendency to en-force religious dogmas by civil law is all too common with human-ity, and will eventually lead to persecution unless specifically guarded against.

At the very beginning of the nation's existence Thomas Jefferson said, "The spirit of the times may alter, will alter. Our rulers will be-come corrupt, our people careless. A single zealot may commence persecution, and better men be his victims." *Notes on Virginia*, Query XVII, in *The Works of Thomas Jefferson* (Ford ed., 1904-1905), vol. 4, pp. 81, 82.

In a letter to Rabbi Mordecai M. Noah, Jefferson wrote: "Your sect by its sufferings has furnished a remarkable proof of the universal spirit of religious intolerance, inherent in every sect. . . . Our laws have applied the only antidote to the vice. . . . But more remains to be done; for although we are free by the law, we are not so in practice; public opinion erects itself into an Inquisition, and exercises its office with as much fanaticism as fans the flames of an auto da fe." Letter to Mordecai M. Noah, May 28, 1818, in *Thomas Jefferson Papers*, vol. 213, p. 37988 (in Manuscript Division, Library of Congress).

Noble leaders have largely held in check the tendency to tyranny that Thomas Jefferson foresaw. Nevertheless, zealous but misguided religious leaders continue to seek civil enforcement of their religious convictions.

How much power will this beast exercise?

"He exercised all the authority of the first beast on his behalf, and made the earth and its inhabitants worship the first beast, whose fatal wound had been healed." Verse 12, NIV.

What is this lamblike creature later called?

"Then I saw three evil spirits that looked like frogs; they came out of the mouth of the dragon [the creature of Revelation 12], out of the mouth of the beast [the creature of Revelation 13:1-10] and out of the mouth of *the false prophet* [the creature of Revelation 13:11-18]." Revelation 16:13, NIV.

NOTE.—These three symbolic creatures form a counterfeit trinity. The dragon, from heaven, is anti-God; the 10-horned beast, from the sea, is anti-Christ; and the lamblike beast, from the earth, is anti-Spirit, bearing the false spirit of prophecy.

Which one of Jesus' parables provides the symbolism for this lamblike false prophet?

"Watch out for false prophets. They come to you in sheep's clothing, but inwardly they are ferocious wolves. . . . Many will say to me on that day, 'Lord, Lord, did we not prophesy in your name, and in your name drive out demons and perform many miracles?' Then I will tell them plainly, 'I never knew you. Away from me, you evildoers!' " Matthew 7:15-23, NIV.

NOTE.—This tells us something about the nature of the lamblike beast. To all outward appearances it is harmless, even pious, and does many wonderful and miraculous works. But appearances are deceiving. It represents a religious movement that appears to be quite different from that represented by the 10-horned beast. But eventually this lamblike coalition comes to support what it once opposed.

How will this beast lead the people back into false worship?

"Because of the signs he was given power to do on behalf of the first beast, he deceived the inhabitants of the earth." Revelation 13:14, NIV.

NOTE.—Miracles are evidence of the working of a supernatural power, whether God or Satan. Whenever the Bible speaks of miracles that occur in the last days, they are always evidence of a demonic power (Matthew 24:24; 2 Thessalonians 2:9; Revelation 13:13; 16:14; 19:20).

What special miracle of deception will the lamblike beast perform?

"And he performed great and miraculous signs, even causing fire to come down from heaven to earth in full view of men." Revelation 13:13, NIV.

NOTE.—As miracles from God prompted belief in Jesus' day and at Pentecost, so false, satanic wonders will deceive at the end of time. In the time of Elijah, in the controversy over Baal worship, the power to make fire fall from heaven was the test as to who was the true God (1 Kings 18:24). The end of time will witness a parallel contest on a global scale, yet this time God's miracle will be counterfeited. Revelation urges us to be discerning lest we be deceived. As the false prophet, this beast is a counterfeit of the prophet Elijah, a herald of deception.

What will this power propose that the people do?

"Because of the signs he was given power to do on behalf of the first beast, he deceived the inhabitants of the earth. He ordered them to set up an image in honor of the beast who was wounded by the sword and yet lived." Revelation 13:14, NIV.

NOTE.—Revelation 13 points us back to two Old Testament "showdowns" of belief: Elijah on Mount Carmel (1 Kings 18), and Nebuchadnezzar's command to bow down to his image or be killed (Daniel 3). Revelation tells us that those stories will be paralleled in the last days.

What is the image to the beast? Revelation speaks in symbols, so this is not about a literal statue, but a replica of the sea beast's power. In the Middle Ages it used civil power to enforce its dogmas. Therefore, the image, or replica, of the beast represents another ecclesiastical organization clothed with civil power—another union of church and state—to enforce religion by law. The image to the beast will be formed when the end-time religiopolitical power forces people to observe its beliefs.

Power corrupts, and religious groups who achieve secular power have a long and dismal history of persecution. America was founded by refugees from such persecution. Whenever any religious entity has achieved absolute political power, it has abandoned persuasion and used force against those who hold different beliefs.

What does this beastlike power attempt to enforce?

"He also forced everyone, small and great, rich and poor, free and slave, to receive a mark on his right hand or on his forehead." Revelation 13:16, NIV.

NOTE.—This mark, called in verse 17 "the mark . . . of the beast," is set over against the seal of God in the book of Revelation. The symbol of a mark in the hand or forehead originates in the books of Moses: "This observance will be for you like *a sign on your hand and a reminder on your forehead* that *the law of the Lord* is to be on your lips." Exodus 13:9, NIV. *"These commandments* that I give you today [the Ten Commandments (Deuteronomy 5)] are to be upon your hearts. . . . Tie them as *symbols on your hands and bind them on your foreheads*." Deuteronomy 6:6-8, NIV. This is not a literal mark on the flesh, but a distinctive ceremony or ritual which sets apart the people of God. Keeping God's ten-commandment law marks God's children as His own. Today God desires to see His law written in our hearts. "I will put my law in their minds and write it on their hearts. I will be their God, and they will be my people." Jeremiah 31:33, NIV. (See also Hebrews 8:10.)

One of the laws in question is the Sabbath commandment of Exodus 20:8-11. In Exodus 31:13-17 the Sabbath is specifically called a sign between God and His people, and a "perpetual covenant" (verse 16). This is what the apostate religiopolitical power of Revelation 13:1-10 and Daniel 7:25 sought to change when it attempted to change "times and laws." The Sabbath commandment has to do with both times and laws.

Jon Paulien writes, "The remnant at the end is made up of people who obey God's commandments. This characterization of the remnant implies that the commandments of God will somehow be an issue between God's faithful people and those who are deceived. But since many of the commandments (such as the prohibition against stealing) are commonly acknowledged, it is pertinent to ask whether Revelation narrows the focus of conflict to one or more commandments in particular.

"This is, in fact, the case. The focus of the conflict between the dragon and the remnant centers on a single word that appears over and over again in Revelation 13 and 14—'worship.' In Revelation 13:4: 'Men *worshiped* the dragon because he had given authority to the beast, and they also *worshiped* the beast' (NIV). In verse 8: 'All inhabitants of the earth will *worship* the beast' (NIV). In verse 12, the inhabitants of the earth are forced to *worship* the first beast, and in verse 15, they are forced to *worship* the image of the beast. And so it goes (cf. Revelation 14:6, 9-11).

"Eight times in chapters 13 and 14 attention is called to worship. It is the crucial word throughout the section of the book. *At the end the testing truth for the world is centered on the matter of proper worship*. This is nothing new. Right from the beginning, the brothers Cain and Abel divided over the issue of worship (Genesis 4:3-9). On Mount Carmel the issue was worship (1 Kings 18:16-46). When Satan tempted Jesus in the desert, the crucial issue was worship (Matthew 4:8-10). Does the focus on worship call our attention to any commandments in particular? Without a doubt. The first four commandments . . . are directly concerned with our relationship to God and with worship.

"It should come as no surprise, therefore, that the unholy trinity described in Revelation 13 not only offers a counterfeit of the persons of the Godhead but of the first four commandments as well. The first commandment says, 'You shall have no other gods before me,' but the sea beast takes the place of God by receiving worship of itself (verses 4, 8). The second commandment warns against the worship of images, yet the land beast raises up an image to be worshiped (verses 14, 15). The third commandment says, 'You shall not misuse the name of the Lord your God,' but the sea beast has the names of blasphemy written all over it (verses 1, 5, 6). The fourth commandment says, 'Remember the Sabbath day.' Ancient covenant tablets (contract documents) were stamped at the center with a seal of ownership and authority. Since the Ten Commandments follow the form of ancient covenant tablets, we should not be startled that they too have a seal of authority in the center, the Sabbath command. . . . This statement is the only place in the Ten Commandments where the basis of God's authority over all creation (He is the Creator) is stated.

"The concept of a seal is important in Revelation as well. The 144,000 are sealed on their foreheads (Revelation 14:1; cf. 7:3, 4; Exodus 31:13, 17). The unholy trinity offers a counterfeit to the seal as well, the mark of the beast (Revelation 13:16, 17). Thus all four commandments in the first table of the law come under attack by the unholy trinity of Revelation 13. *The first table of the law is at the center of the battle between the dragon and the remnant*." Jon Paulien, *What the Bible Says About the End-time* (Hagerstown, Md.: Review and Herald, 1994), pp. 122, 123.

What text in Revelation 14 points to the Sabbath commandment?
"He said in a loud voice, 'Fear God and give him glory, because the

hour of his judgment has come. Worship *him who made the heavens, the earth, the sea* and the springs of water.'" Revelation 14:7, NIV.

"Remember the Sabbath day by keeping it holy. . . . For in six days *the Lord made the heavens and the earth, the sea,* and all that is in them, but he rested on the seventh day." Exodus 20:8-11, NIV.

NOTE.—Though it almost never quotes the Old Testament directly, Revelation is packed with Old Testament references that provide keys to interpreting the text. Rarely, however, does it echo more than two or three key words. Revelation 14:7 is one of the strongest references to an Old Testament text, directly echoing Exodus 20:11. Jon Paulien writes, "Seven times in chapters 13 and 14 the word 'worship' is applied to the unholy trinity. . . . Only one time in the whole section is there a call to worship the true God. If true versus false worship is the central issue at the end, *this passage (Revelation 14:7) is the central text of the section, perhaps of the entire book. When Revelation finally gets around to calling on people to worship the true God, it does so in the context of the fourth commandment, the Sabbath command. In a special sense, therefore, the author of Revelation understood the Sabbath to be* the *crucial issue in the final crisis.*

"In both texts (Revelation 14:7 and Exodus 20:8-11), the call to worship takes place in the context of Creation. . . . As the memorial of creation, the Sabbath points continually to God as the object of worship. The issue in the final crisis, therefore, is not limited to the Sabbath, but the Sabbath is an integral part of the issue." Jon Paulien, *What the Bible Says about the End-time* (Hagerstown, Md.: Review and Herald, 1994), p. 126.

What principle should govern our duty to the state?

"Give to Caesar what is Caesar's, and to God what is God's." Matthew 22:21, NIV.

NOTE.—The Sabbath belongs to God. Its observance, therefore, should be rendered only to Him.

What means will be employed to compel all to receive this mark?

"He also forced everyone, small and great, rich and poor, free and slave, to receive a mark on his right hand or on his forehead, so *that no one could buy or sell* unless he had the mark, which is the name of the beast or the number of his name." Revelation 13:16, 17, NIV.

NOTE.—This may have either a literal or symbolic meaning. If it is symbolic, it may represent the adversity God's people will face when the rest of the world is trafficking in Babylon's spiritual wares. A literal economic penalty for refusing to worship happened in a limited way in the past. In the reign of Roman emperor Decius (A.D. 249-251) any man who did not possess the certificate of sacrifice to Caesar could not pursue ordinary trades, but faced imprisonment, death, or banishment. A person paid his respects to the godhead of Caesar and received the certification.

How will the worship of the beast be enforced?

"He was given power to give breath to the image of the first beast, so that it could speak and cause all who refused to worship the image to be killed." Verse 15, NIV.

NOTE.—In earth's final conflict God's people will demonstrate their allegiance to God by their observance of the Sabbath. As followers of Christ, they follow His example in keeping the seventh-day Sabbath. In contrast, as the end-time religiopolitical authority exercises its power, rejection of the Sabbath demonstrates allegiance to the beast.

Where will those who are victorious over the beast one day stand?

"And I saw what looked like *a sea of glass* mixed with fire and, standing beside the sea, those who had been victorious over the beast and his image and over the number of his name. They held harps given them by God." Revelation 15:2, NIV.

What song will they sing?

"And they sing *the song of Moses* the servant of God, and the song of the Lamb." Verse 3.

NOTE.—The original song of Moses, found in Exodus 15, is a song of deliverance from oppression.

THE SEVEN CHURCHES

What title is given the last book of the Bible?

"The Revelation of Jesus Christ." Revelation 1:1.

To whom do those things that are revealed belong?

"The secret things belong to the Lord our God, but *the things revealed belong to us and to our children forever*." Deuteronomy 29:29, NIV.

For what purpose was the Revelation given?

"The revelation of Jesus Christ, which God gave him to show his servants what must soon take place." Revelation 1:1, NIV.

What great event, according to this book, is imminent?

"Look, he is coming with the clouds, and every eye will see him, even those who pierced him, and all the peoples of the earth will mourn because of him." Verse 7, NIV.

NOTE.—Not only does this book open and close with the subject of Christ's second coming, but its eight lines of prophecy all reach down to this as the great culminating event to the church and the world.

What encouragement is given to study this book?

"*Blessed is the one who reads the words* of this prophecy, and blessed are those who *hear* it and *take to heart* what is written in it, because the time is near." Verse 3, NIV.

To whom was the book dedicated?

"*To the seven churches which are in Asia.*" Verse 4.

What were the names of these seven churches?

"Write on a scroll what you see and send it to the seven churches: to Ephesus, Smyrna, Pergamum, Thyatira, Sardis, Philadelphia and Laodicea." Verse 11, NIV.

NOTE.—The letters to the seven churches in Asia were addressed to actual groups of Christian believers in the Roman province of Asia. These messages describe conditions existing in these churches in John's day and provide counsel appropriate to their particular needs. But why did John choose these particular churches? There were other Christian churches in Asia at the time. Because of this, and the fact that the number 7 occurs repeatedly in Revelation in a symbolic sense, these seven churches are to be understood as representative of the church as a whole. Biblical scholars have also demonstrated parallels between each of the seven churches and specific eras of church history, reaching from the first to the second advent of Christ.

What encouragement was given to the first church?

"To the angel of the church in Ephesus write: These are the words of him who holds the seven stars in his right hand and walks among the seven golden lamp stands: I know your deeds, your hard work and your perseverance. I know that you cannot tolerate wicked men, that you have tested those who claim to be apostles but are not, and have found them false. You have persevered and have endured hardships for my name, and have not grown weary." Revelation 2:1-3, NIV.

NOTE.—Ephesus represents the character and condition of the church in its first state, when its members received the doctrine of Christ in its purity, and enjoyed the benefits and blessings of the gifts of the Holy Spirit. This applies to the first century, or during the lifetime of the apostles.

What charge did the Lord, after commending this church for their good works, bring against them?

"Yet I hold this against you: You have forsaken your first love. Remember the height from which you have fallen! Repent and do the things you did at first." Verses 4, 5, NIV.

NOTE.—The "first love" is the love of the truth, and the desire of making it known to others. The "first works" are the fruit of this love.

What message is given to the second church?

"To the angel of the church in Smyrna write: 'These are the words of him who is the First and the Last, who died and came to life again. I know your afflictions and your poverty—yet you are rich!" Verses 8, 9, NIV.

NOTE.—Smyrna may be related to "myrrh," or sweet-smelling incense. They are not blessed with material goods or an easy life, yet spiritually they are strong. Jesus points to His death and resurrection, an encouraging message to a church suffering persecution. Smyrna's experience has been applied to the period of time when many of the saints of God suffered martyrdom under pagan Rome during the second, third, and early fourth centuries.

What tribulation would be endured by the church during this time?

"Do not be afraid of what you are about to suffer. I tell you, the *devil will put some of you in prison* to test you, and *you will suffer persecution for ten days*. Be faithful, even to the point of death, and I will give you the crown of life." Verse 10, NIV.

NOTE.—When Revelation was written, the church in Smyrna faced persecution forces both religious and political. They were persecuted for refusing to participate in emperor worship.

The most severe of the persecutions under pagan Rome was a 10-year period under the emperor Diocletian, from A.D. 303 to 313.

How does Jesus identify Himself to the third church?

"To the angel of the church in Pergamum write: These are the words of him who has the sharp, double-edged sword." Verse 12, NIV.

NOTE.—The Christians of Pergamum faced persecution from the sword, yet Jesus' message assures that He remains in control. Scholars have applied the legacy of Pergamos to the period that began with Constantine's conversion and ended with Christianity the state religion. During this period the church, which formerly "had not where to lay its head, is raised to sovereign authority in the state, enters into the prerogatives of the pagan priesthood, grows rich and powerful." At the same time, however, the church "received into her bosom vast deposits of foreign material from the world and from heathenism." Philip Schaff, *History of the Christian Church* (New York: Scribner's, 1902), vol. 3, p. 5.

How was the faithfulness of this church commended?

"I know where you live—where Satan has his throne. Yet you remain true to my name. You did not renounce your faith in me, even in the days of Antipas, my faithful witness, who was put to death in your city—where Satan lives." Verse 13, NIV.

What advice and encouragement does Jesus give to members in Pergamum who are beset by idolatry, immorality, and false teachings?

"He who has an ear, let him hear what the Spirit says to the churches. To him who overcomes, I will give him some of the hidden manna. I will also give him a white stone with a new name written on it, known only to him who receives it." Verse 17, NIV.

NOTE.—These words encourage believers to stand fast. The temporary sustenance the world provides if we compromise is nothing compared to the feast and honor awaiting us if we persevere.

What encouragement and admonishment did Jesus give the fourth church?

"To the angel of the church in Thyatira write: These are the words of the Son of God, whose eyes are like the blazing fire, and whose feet are like burnished bronze. I know your deeds, your love and faith, your service and perseverance, and that you are now doing more than you did at first. Nevertheless, I have this against you: You tolerate that woman Jezebel, who calls herself a prophetess. By her teaching she misleads my servants into sexual immorality and the eating of food sacrificed to idols. I have given her time to repent of her immorality, but she is unwilling. So I will cast her on a bed of suffering, and I will make those who commit adultery with her suffer intensely, unless they repent of her ways." Verses 18-22, NIV.

NOTE.—Thyatira's experience parallels the condition of God's people during the long, dark period of persecution connected with the 1260-year prophecy. During that time millions of the saints of God were put to death. Christ referred to this time in His wonderful prophecy recorded in Matthew 24: "For then there will be great distress, unequaled from the beginning of the world until now—and never to be equaled again. If those days had not been cut short, no one would survive, but for the sake of the elect those days will be shortened." Verses 21, 22, NIV. The tribulation of the 1260 years was cut short through the influence of the Reformation.

What promise did God leave for these persecuted ones?

"Only hold on to what you have until I come. To him who overcomes and does my will to the end, *I will give authority over the nations*—'He will rule them with an iron scepter; he will dash them to pieces like pottery'—just as I have received authority from my Father." Revelation 2:25-27, NIV.

NOTE.—Jesus' words in these verses echo those of Psalm 2:8, 9.

What issues troubled Jesus about the fifth church?

"To the angel of the church of Sardis write: These are the words of him who holds the seven spirits of God and the seven stars. I know your deeds; you have a reputation of being alive, but you are dead. Wake up! Strengthen what remains and is about to die, for I have not found your deeds complete in the sight of my God. Remember, therefore, what you have received and heard; obey it, and repent. But if you do not wake up, I will come like a thief, and you will not know at what time I will come to you." Revelation 3:1-3, NIV.

NOTE.—Sardis was admonished to "be watchful, and strengthen the things which remain" (verse 2). Sardis' spiritual state parallels that of Christianity after the Reformation. The energy of the Reformation faded into polemicism, and in too many ways the church became spiritually dead.

What encouraging words does Jesus give to those in Sardis who remain faithful?

"Yet you have a few people in Sardis who have not soiled their clothes. They will walk with me, dressed in white, for they are worthy. He who overcomes will, like them, be dressed in white. I will never blot out his name from the book of life, but will acknowledge his name before my Father and his angels." Verses 4, 5, NIV.

How does Jesus greet the sixth church?

"To the angel of the church in Philadelphia write: These are the words of him who is holy and true, who holds the key of David. What he opens no one can shut, and what he shuts no one can open. I know your deeds. See, I have placed before you an open door that no one can shut." Verses 7, 8, NIV.

NOTE.—Philadelphia means "brotherly love." An "open door" represents an opportunity to spread the good news. Paul spoke of a "great door for effective work" opening for him (1 Corinthians 16:9), and asked his readers to pray "that God may open a door for our message, so that we may proclaim the mystery of Christ" (Colossians 4:3, NIV). Hearts were open to hear God in the First and Second Great Awakenings of the eighteenth and early nineteenth centuries.

How does Jesus encourage Philadelphia to stand firm despite weakness?

"I know that you have little strength, yet you have kept my word and not denied my name. . . . Since you have kept my command to endure patiently, I will also keep you from the hour of trial that is going to come upon the whole world to test those who live on the earth. I am coming soon. Hold on to what you have, so that no one will take your crown. Him who overcomes I will make a pillar in the temple of my God. Never again will he leave it. I will write on him the name of my God and the name of the city of my God, the new Jerusalem, which is coming down out of heaven from my God; and I will also write on him my new name. He who has an ear, let him hear what the Spirit says to the churches." Revelation 3:8-13, NIV.

What is Christ's message to the last church?

"To the angel of the church in Laodicea write . . ." Revelation 3:14, NIV.

NOTE.—Bible scholars particularly apply the message to Laodicea to those who live during the time of the investigative judgment, and the proclamation of the final warning messages (Revelation 14:6-16) preceding Christ's second coming. This is a time of great profession, with but little vital godliness and true piety.

"That John intended to set the message to Laodicea as a model for the church of the last period of earth's history is supported by verbal and conceptual parallels between the message to Laodicea and the final warning to Christians living at the threshold of the battle of Armageddon (Revelation 16:15). This last church appears to be the most troubled one; it goes through the motions of great political, religious, and secular upheavals and faces challenges that no previous generation of Christians did. Yet it is a halfhearted and self-sufficient church, characterized by lukewarmness and a struggle with the issues of its authenticity." Ranko Stefanovich, *The Revelation of Jesus Christ: Commentary on the Book of Revelation* (Berrien Springs, Mich.: Andrews University Press, 2002), p. 151.

What is the sad state of faith in Laodicea?

"I know your deeds, that you are neither cold nor hot. I wish you were either one or the other! So, because you are lukewarm—neither hot nor cold—I am about to spit you out of my mouth." Revelation 3:15, 16, NIV.

NOTE.—Several of the seven churches are rebuked for having problems with false doctrine, but not Laodicea. The problem with the Laodiceans is their lack of fervor. Theirs is a listless religion; they have no enthusiasm, zeal, or zest (from the Greek *zestos*, "hot"). God hates apathy and indifference.

Jesus threatened to "spit you out of my mouth." Every citizen of literal Laodicea would have understood the allusion. Six miles away, in nearby Hierapolis, there were springs of hot water. As the water made its way over the plateau it lost its heat, and finally poured over a nearby cliff that was encrusted with white lime from the waters, and so perpetually visible in Laodicea. The citizens were very familiar with the lukewarm water that would make a person sick if they drank it. One traveler described the water as tasting like a mixture of ginger ale and kerosene.

The reason that Jesus finds Laodicea (the modern Western church in a post-Christian society) so repugnant relates to its complacency, which is a result of its prosperity.

In what condition does Laodicea picture itself?

"You say, 'I am rich; I have acquired wealth and do not need a thing.' But you do not realize that you are wretched, pitiful, poor, blind and naked.' " Verse 17, NIV.

NOTE.—Literal Laodicea was a proud and rich city—so much so that when it was largely destroyed by an earthquake in A.D. 60, it refused to accept the government's offer of financial aid. Modern Laodicea also considers itself to be rich.

John Wesley, founder of the Methodist Church, clearly foresaw the problem of prosperity: "I do not see how it is possible in the nature of things for any revival of religion to continue long," he wrote. "Religion must necessarily produce both industry and frugality, and these cannot but produce riches. But as riches increase, so will pride, anger, and love of the world in all its branches. . . . The Methodists in every place grow diligent and frugal; consequently, they increase in goods. Hence they proportionately increase in pride, in anger, in the desire of the flesh, the desire of the eyes, and the pride of life. So, although the form of religion remains, the spirit is swiftly vanishing away." Scripture warns about this problem (Deuteronomy 8:12-14; Amos 6:1-7; Hosea 10:1, 2; 12:8; 13:6; 14:4).

Arnold J. Toynbee undertook as his life's work to answer the question "What makes great societies come into being and die? Under what conditions do civilizations thrive?" The results of his study are found in his multivolume work *A Study of History*. Here are his conclusions. He rejects the hypothesis that there is an innately superior race, and also the hypothesis that environments that produce easy and comfortable conditions are conducive to the development of great societies. Instead, he finds somewhat the opposite: great societies arise as a response to the challenge of some great difficulty that spurs them on to unprecedented effort. The obstacle may be geographical, political, military, or climatic (a balmy climate does not produce great civilizations), but as long as there is a challenge, as long as there is something to fight against and overcome, as long as there are new frontiers, there is growth and vitality. However, often the successful society becomes lax and lazy and rests on its laurels, and decline sets in.

The church today is faced with a great challenge: the commission to take the gospel to all the world. Only by striving with all its might toward this end will God's church be able to resist decline and continually renew itself.

What solution does Christ propose for Laodicea's poverty?

"I counsel you to buy from me gold refined in the fire, so you can become rich; and white clothes to wear, so you can cover your shameful nakedness; and salve to put on your eyes, so you can see. Those whom I love I rebuke and discipline. So be earnest, and repent." Revelation 3:18, 19, NIV.

NOTE.—Ancient Laodicea was a famous banking center, and transactions in gold occurred daily. Christ offers modern Laodicea gold purified in the fire, as opposed to the often impure gold of Laodicea. Ancient Laodicea manufactured a famous variety of black wool. In contrast, Christ offers the white garments of righteousness (Revelation 19:8). Laodicea was also famous for its eyesalve. Christ offered spiritual eyesight through the ointment or anointing of His Spirit.

The fact that Christ rebukes and chastens His church is the sign that He loves it and has great plans for it.

What promise is made to those who heed this message?

"Here I am! I stand at the door and knock. If anyone hears my voice and opens the door, I will come in and eat with him, and he with me. To him who overcomes, I will give the right to sit with me on my throne, just as I overcame and sat down with my Father on his throne." Revelation 3:20, 21, NIV.

NOTE.—Christ will not break down the door and enter by force, but for those who open to Him, he offers to share table fellowship, and even a seat on His throne—the honor that Lucifer sought but could not obtain (Isaiah 14:12-14).

The pointed, searching messages to the seven churches contain most important lessons of encouragement and warning for all Christians in all ages. The seven promises to the overcomer found in this line of prophecy (Revelation 2:7, 11, 17, 26-28; 3:5, 12, 21), with the eighth or universal promise recorded in Revelation 21:7, form a galaxy of promises as precious, as comforting, and as inspiring as any recorded in the Scriptures. "He who has an ear, let him hear what the Spirit says to the churches" (Revelation 3:22, NIV).

THE SEVEN SEALS

What did John, who wrote the book of Revelation, see in the right hand of God?

"Then I saw in the right hand of him who sat on the throne *a scroll with writing on both sides and sealed with seven seals.*" Revelation 5:1, NIV.

What did the Lamb do with this book?

"He came and took the scroll from the right hand of him who sat on the throne." Verse 7, NIV.

Why was Christ, the Lamb, declared worthy to open these seals?

"You are worthy to take the scroll and to open its seals, *because you were slain, and with your blood you purchased men for God from every tribe and language and people and nation.*" Verse 9, NIV.

What was shown upon the opening of the first seal?

"I watched as the Lamb opened the first of the seven seals. Then I heard one of the four living creatures say in a voice like thunder, 'Come!' I looked, and there before me was *a white horse!* Its rider held a bow, and he was given a crown, and he rode out as a conqueror bent on conquest." Revelation 6:1, 2, NIV.

NOTE.—The events described in the seven seals parallel the seven churches. The white horse, with his rider going forth to conquer, represents the early Christian church in its purity, going into all the world with the gospel message of salvation, a fit emblem of the church triumphant in the first century.

"In Revelation white is associated with purity, heaven, and righteousness. We read of Jesus' white hair, the saints' white stones and white clothes, the 24 elders' white clothing, the white cloud, the white horses of Jesus and His angels, and the white throne. In another reference we read that the fine white linen in which the saints are clothed represented righteousness (Revelation 19:8).

"In light of this information, we assume that the white horse represents the triumphant preaching of the gospel of the righteousness of Jesus. After centuries of Pharisaic legalism and degrading heathenism, the conquests of the preaching of the gospel in the first century are without parallel.

"With the bow of the Spirit to send the arrow of the gospel to the heart of each hearer, dramatic results were seen, and shortly the church numbered in the hundreds of thousands.

"This seal, with its white horse, symbolizes the same historical period as the church of Ephesus, the first century, when the gospel spread quickly and enthusiastically in the Roman world.

"In another sense, the gospel horse still rides and must continue to ride until everyone has the opportunity to respond to its invitation. And each of us is called to participate in that work through our spiritual gifts." Roy C. Naden, *The Lamb Among the Beasts: Finding Jesus in the Book of Revelation* (Hagerstown, Md.: Review and Herald, 1996), p. 107.

What appeared upon the opening of the second seal?

"When the Lamb opened the second seal, I heard the second living creature say, 'Come!' Then *another horse came out, a fiery red one*. Its rider was given power to take peace from the earth and to make men slay each other. To him was given a large sword." Revelation6:3, 4, NIV.

NOTE.—As whiteness in the first horse denoted the purity of the gospel in the Apostolic Age, so the color of the second horse indicates that corruption began to creep into the church thereafter.

"This seal runs parallel to the second church, Smyrna, and covers the persecution during the second and third centuries down to the conversion of Emperor Constantine." Roy C. Naden, *The Lamb Among the Beasts: Finding Jesus in the Book of Revelation* (Hagerstown, Md.: Review and Herald, 1996), p. 108.

What texts indicate that the sword mentioned at the opening of the second seal symbolizes division and opposition caused by the gospel?

"Do not suppose that I have come to bring peace to the earth. I did not come to bring peace, but a sword. For I have come to turn 'a man against his father, a daughter against her mother, a daughter-in-law against her mother-in-law—a man's enemies will be the members of his own household.' " Matthew 10:34-36, NIV.

NOTE.—Jesus is quoting Micah 7:6. See also Luke 12:51-53.

What was the color of the symbol under the third seal?

"When the Lamb opened the third seal, I heard the third living creature say, 'Come!' I looked, and there before me was *a black horse! Its rider was holding a pair of scales in his hand.*" Revelation 6:5, NIV.

NOTE.—"This third seal is parallel to the third church, Pergamos, and describes a period of compromise and spiritual scarcity during which Jesus' teachings were corrupted or lost. The church maintained purity under persecution, but lost it in times of political acceptance." Roy C. Naden, *The Lamb Among the Beasts: Finding Jesus in the Book of Revelation* (Hagerstown, Md.: Review and Herald, 1996), p. 109.

NOTE.—"The black horse follows the red horse, as famine does war. The voice that surges from the midst of the four beings seems to be the voice of the Lamb, since He is also situated 'in the center of the throne, encircled by the four living creatures' (Revelation 5:6). The voice of the judge seated on the throne is thus the voice of the Lamb, tempering justice with grace. . . .

"The more the church prospered materially and politically, the more impoverished it became spiritually. The institution itself and its traditions gradually came to replace the study of God's Word. It is a lesson important even today for churches seeking to establish themselves. Each time the church has sought to embellish its structure, to add to its grandeur and style, it has plunged itself into spiritual poverty. When the form rules in place of the content, the sense for the absolute, what really counts gets lost. But there is even a greater risk. Intoxicated by its political status, the church began to consider itself the criterion of truth. Dogma replaced the Word, creating an open invitation for oppression and intolerance." Jacques B. Doukhan, *Secrets of Revelation* (Hagerstown, Md.: Review and Herald, 2002), pp. 61, 62.

What announcement did John hear as the black horse came out?

"Then I heard what sounded like a voice among the four living creatures, saying, 'A quart of wheat for a day's wages, and three quarts of barley for a day's wages, and do not damage the oil and the wine!" Revelation 6:6, NIV.

NOTE.—"Usually the olive tree and the vine, because of their deeper roots, can resist periods of drought better than wheat and barley. Moreover, grain, oil, and wine usually represent the three main products of the land of Israel. The appearance of the third being, with its human face, already alludes to such an interpretation. It represents the spiritual dimension versus the natural and nonreligious aspects depicted by the other three beasts (see Daniel 4:16, 34; cf. 7:8, 13). The famine therefore symbolizes spiritual drought. Moreover, grain, wine, and oil all have their distinctive connotations in the Bible.

"Grain symbolizes the Word of God (see Deuteronomy 8:3; cf. Matthew 4:4; John 6:46-51; Nehemiah 9:15; Psalm 146:7).

"Oil symbolizes the Holy Spirit (Psalm 45:8; Zechariah 4:1-6).

"Wine symbolizes the blood of Yeshua [the Hebrew name for Jesus] (Luke 22:20; 1 Corinthians 11:25).

"The famine and drought affect only God's Word, sparing the Holy Spirit and the blood of Yeshua. Of the two components of the covenant, the human one—the Word of God—and the divine one—the Holy Spirit and the blood of Yeshua—the famine touches only the human one. On the human level, the church has lost its calling. It does not meet the spiritual and theological needs of its members. The people are not spiritually fed. The church neglects the study of the Word of God, and understanding is limited.

"On the divine level, however, the influence of the Holy Spirit and the grace of the blood of Yeshua remain active among God's people, providing a balm of relief. Interestingly, the ancients traditionally used oil and wine as treatment for wounds. The symbols are rich in connotations, and the two meanings of wine and oil are not mutually exclusive. Biblical symbolism often functions in this way. The wine and the oil represent the redemptive action of the Messiah, and constitute, as such, a balm upon the church's self-inflicted wounds." Jacques B. Doukhan, *Secrets of Revelation* (Hagerstown, Md.: Review and Herald, 2002), p. 61.

What were the color and character of the fourth symbol?

"When the Lamb opened the fourth seal, I heard the voice of the fourth living creature say, 'Come!' I looked, and there before me was a *pale* horse! Its rider was named *Death*, and *Hades* was following closely behind him. They were given power over a fourth of the earth to kill by sword, famine and plague, and by the wild beasts of the earth." Revelation 6:7, 8, NIV.

NOTE.—The Greek word here translated "pale" denotes the sickly yellowish green of blighted plants, an unnatural color for a horse.

"The opening of the fourth seal brings a horse of a pale color (*chloros*), suggestive of death and terror. . . . The church now em-

bodies death to the most murderous degree. Not only does the Apocalypse call the rider 'death,' but another rider described as *Hades* (the
dwelling place of the dead) immediately follows him. . . .

"Its conquest of the world had started with the triumph of peace.
The scene had opened on a white horse, whose rider, Yeshua the Messiah [Jesus], bore an empty bow. From the second horse, however,
the momentum turned into violence. Whereas the Messiah had fought
for the church, the church now considered it its duty to wage war for
the Messiah. The religious wars and Crusades testify to a shift in the
church's mentality. Actions from below replace revelation from
above. The church assumed the prerogative to speak and act on God's
behalf. Intolerance always stems from this type of usurping attitude,
when God's witness comes to identify himself or herself with God;
when success obliterates the revelation from above; when an imperi-
alistic mentality replaces an evangelical concern; when statistics and
the number of baptisms prevail over the genuineness of conversion;
and when the church seeks the answer to its problems in strategies
and marketing plans rather than in spiritual guidance. When humanity replaces God, anything goes. The reason is simple. The need for
security always opts for the visible and concrete versus a humble trust
in the incomprehensible and invisible God. The success of worldly
achievements then lead only to pride and intolerance.

"Violence and oppression are the natural consequences when we
usurp God's role. From the Crusades to the concentration camps,
each time people have hoisted themselves to God's level to fight in
the name of the cross, or for the *'Gott mit uns,'* millions of victims
have suffered, and their shouts to the heavens for justice still ring in
our ears." Jacques B. Doukhan, *Secrets of Revelation* (Hagerstown,
Md.: Review and Herald, 2002), pp. 62-64.

What did John see under the altar as the fifth seal was opened?
"When he opened the fifth seal, I saw under the altar *the souls of
those who had been slain because of the word of God and the testimony they had maintained*. They called out in a loud voice, 'How
long, Sovereign Lord, holy and true, until you judge the inhabitants
of the earth and avenge our blood?' " Verses 9, 10, NIV.

NOTE.—The martyrs depicted here have been persecuted for proclaiming the gospel. Their cruel mistreatment cried for vengeance,
just as the blood of Abel (the first person to die for his allegiance to
God) cried to God from the ground (Genesis 4:10).

"The Old Testament temple had two altars. The altar of sacrifice
was in the outer court outside the temple for the sacrifice of animals
in burnt offering. Inside the temple was the altar of incense. The altar

in view here is most likely the altar of burnt offering rather than the altar of incense. This is clearly seen in the fact that in the Old Testament temple ritual, the blood was poured out at the base of the altar of burnt offering. 'All the blood of the bull he shall pour out at the base of the altar of burnt offering' (Leviticus 4:7, 18, 25, 30-34; 8:15; 9:9, NASB). The phrase 'poured out' is also used in Revelation 16:6 where the blood of saints and prophets is poured out (evidently beneath the altar as verse 7 indicates). Since the altar of sacrifice was not in the temple, but in the outer court, it is clear that the scene portrayed here takes place not in the heavenly temple but on the earth which was symbolized by the outer court of the temple." Ranko Stefanovich, *The Revelation of Jesus Christ: Commentary on the Book of Revelation* (Berrien Springs, Mich.: Andrews University Press, 2002), p. 238.

The apostle Paul, writing from prison, described himself as "poured out like a drink offering on the sacrifice" (Philippians 2:17, NIV). "When Christ's followers die for their faith and loyalty to God, it may very often appear to be a tragedy. The scene of the fifth seal, however, describes the death of Christ's followers as a triumph—a sacrificial offering made to God." Ranko Stefanovich, *The Revelation of Jesus Christ: Commentary on the Book of Revelation* (Berrien Springs, Mich.: Andrews University Press, 2002), p. 240.

What was given these martyrs?

"Then each of them was given *a white robe*, and they were told to wait a little longer, until the number of their fellow servants and brothers who were to be killed as they had been was completed." Revelation 6:11, NIV.

NOTE.—These had been slain during the centuries covered by the preceding seal. Their persecutors had died. (And if they had at death passed into hell, as some suppose, then why should the martyrs still cry for their punishment?)

Scripture sometimes uses personification, in which inanimate things are represented as alive and speaking (compare Genesis 4:10; Judges 9:8-15; Proverbs 1:20). These martyrs had been branded as heretics under the preceding seal, covered with disgrace and shame. Now, in the light of the Reformation, their true character appears, and they are seen to have been righteous, and hence are given "white robes," which represent righteousness (Revelation 19:8). They are told to rest a little longer till all others who are to die for their faith have followed them, then together they will be raised to immortality.

What was first seen on the opening of the sixth seal?

"I watched as he opened the sixth seal. There was a great *earth-*

quake. The sun turned black like sackcloth made of goat hair, *the whole moon turned blood red.*" Revelation 6:12, NIV.

NOTE.—The Old Testament associates earthquakes with the "day of the Lord." See Isaiah 13:13; Ezekiel 38:19, 20; Joel 2:10; Amos 8:8; Haggai 2:6. Joel 2:31 speaks of the sun turning to darkness and "the moon to blood before the coming of the great and dreadful day of the Lord" (NIV).

What other event is mentioned under this seal?

"And *the stars in the sky fell to earth*, as late figs drop from a fig tree when shaken by a strong wind." Revelation 6:13, NIV.

NOTE.—John's description here echoes the words of Isaiah 34:4: "All the stars of the heavens will be dissolved and the sky rolled up like a scroll; all the starry host will fall like withered leaves from the vine, like shriveled figs from the fig tree" (NIV). Jesus quotes such Old Testament verses in Matthew 24:29, in His Mount of Olives sermon about the end-times.

What was the next event mentioned in the prophecy?

"The *sky receded like a scroll*, rolling up, and every mountain and island was removed from its place." Revelation 6:14, NIV.

NOTE.—This event is still future, and will take place in connection with Christ's second coming. We are now standing between the two events—the last of the signs in the heavens, and the parting of the heavens and removal of earthly things out of their places. The great signs here mentioned, which mark the approach of Christ's second coming and the dissolution of all earthly things, are all in the past, and the world awaits the sound of the last trump as the closing scene in earth's drama.

How will this great event affect the world?

"Then the kings of the earth, the princes, the generals, the rich, the mighty, and every slave and every free man hid in caves and among the rocks of the mountains. They called to the mountains and the rocks, 'Fall on us and hide us from the face of him who sits on the throne and from the wrath of the Lamb! For the great day of their wrath has come, and who can stand?'" Verses 15-17, NIV.

NOTE.—Like Adam and Eve hiding in the garden (Genesis 3:8), unconfessed sin will motivate people to run from God at Jesus' return.

After the sealing work in Revelation 7, which takes place under the sixth seal, how is the seventh seal introduced?

"When he opened the seventh seal, *there was silence in heaven* for about half an hour." Revelation 8:1, N IV.

NOTE.—"Some Old Testament texts shed light on the possible meaning of the 'silence' in Revelation 8:1. In the prophecies of Habakkuk (2:20), Zephaniah (1:7), and Zechariah (2:13), the inhabitants of the earth are exhorted to keep silence in view of the coming judgment of God from his temple. The anticipation of God's imminent action dominates the scene and forms the basis for the prophetic appeal." Ranko Stefanovich, *The Revelation of Jesus Christ: Commentary on the Book of Revelation* (Berrien Springs, Mich.: Andrews University Press, 2002), p. 247.

THE SEVEN LAST PLAGUES

What is God's final warning against false worship?

"If anyone worships the beast and his image and receives his mark on the forehead or on the hand, *he, too, will drink of the wine of God's fury, which has been poured full strength into the cup of his wrath*. He will be tormented with burning sulfur in the presence of the holy angels and of the Lamb." Revelation 14:9, 10, NIV.

NOTE.—During probationary time God's wrath is always tempered, or mingled, with mercy. Thus the prophet Habakkuk prays, "In wrath remember mercy." Habakkuk 3:2, NIV. God's wrath, unmixed with mercy, is displayed only when mercy has done its final work, and evil has gone to the limit, so that there is "no remedy" (see Genesis 6:3; 15:16; 19:12, 13; 2 Chronicles 36:16; Matthew 23:37, 38; Luke 19:42-44; 2 Peter 2:6; Jude 7). This point of no return is sometimes referred to as the close of human probation.

In what is the wrath of God filled up?

"I saw in heaven another great and marvelous sign: seven angels with the *seven last plagues*—last, because with them God's wrath is completed." Revelation 15:1, NIV.

How does Joel describe the day of the Lord?

"Alas for that day! For the day of the Lord is near; it will come like destruction from the Almighty." Joel 1:15, NIV. "The Lord thunders at the head of his army; his forces are beyond number, and mighty are those who obey his command. The day of the Lord is great; it is dreadful. Who can endure it?" Joel 2:11, NIV.

What has Daniel said of this time?

"At that time Michael, the great prince who protects your people, will arise. There will be a *time of distress* such as has not happened from the beginning of nations until then. But at that time your people—everyone whose name is found written in the book—will be delivered." Daniel 12:1, NIV.

NOTE.—As Ahab accused Elijah of being the cause of Israel's calamities (1 Kings 18:17, 18), so those who have departed from God will accuse the righteous. They will seek to destroy them as Haman sought to destroy the Jews (see Esther 3:8-14). But God will miraculously deliver His people at this time as He did in Esther's time.

How is the close of probation described in heaven?

"And the temple was filled with smoke from the glory of God and from his power, and *no one could enter the temple* until the seven plagues of the seven angels were completed." Revelation 15:8, NIV.

NOTE.—In other words, the mediatorial work of Christ as our high priest (Hebrews 8:1, 2) is finished, mediation for sinners ceases, and the door of mercy closes.

What is the condition of sinners when probation ceases?

"They were seared by the intense heat and they cursed the name of God, who had control over these plagues, but *they refused to repent* and glorify him. . . . Men gnawed their tongues in agony and cursed the God of heaven because of their pains and their sores, but *they refused to repent* of what they had done." Revelation 16:9-11, NIV.

Since there is no more repentance, what decree will be issued by God just prior to the "seven last plagues"?

"Let him who does wrong continue to do wrong; let him who is vile continue to be vile; let him who is right continue to do right; and let him who is holy continue to be holy." Revelation 22:11, NIV.

NOTE.—This is a very strange thing for God to say, for in the past God's appeal was always "Rid yourselves of all the offenses you have committed, and get a new heart and a new spirit. Why will you die, O house of Israel? For I take no pleasure in the death of anyone, declares the Sovereign Lord. Repent and live!" Ezekiel 18:31-33, NIV. But someday soon God will declare a close to probation, and it will be too late to repent. The plagues are the beginning of the judgment of God against the wicked (see Revelation 18:7, 8; 16:5, 6), poured out unmingled with mercy (Revelation 14:10).

What will be the first plague, and upon whom will it fall?

"Then I heard a loud voice from the temple saying to the seven angels, 'Go, pour out the seven bowls of God's wrath on the earth.' The first angel went and poured out his bowl on the land, and *ugly and painful sores broke out on the people who had the mark of the beast and worshiped his image."* Revelation 16:1, 2, NIV.

NOTE.—The third angel warned the world not to worship the beast and his image, proclaiming that those who do "will drink of the wine of God's fury, which has been poured full strength into the cup of his wrath" (Revelation 14:10, NIV). The plagues are the promised punishment for following the false trinity and persecuting God's true followers (Revelation 13:15-17; 16:5, 6).

How does John describe the second and third plagues?

"The second angel poured out his bowl on the sea, and *it turned into blood like that of a dead man, and every living thing in the sea died.* The third angel poured out his bowl on the rivers and springs of water, and *they became blood."* Revelation 16:3, 4, NIV.

NOTE.—These plagues parallel the first plague of ancient Egypt (Exodus 7:17-21), when the Nile turned to blood, and the second and third trumpets (Revelation 8:8-11), in which a third of the world's waters are desecrated. "In the bowl plagues there is an intensification of the divine wrath executed on the enemies of God's people unlike the trumpet plagues which were just the forewarning and preliminary visitation of God's wrath." Ranko Stefanovich, *The Revelation of Jesus Christ: Commentary on the Book of Revelation* (Berrien Springs, Mich.: Andrews University Press, 2002), p. 482, 483..

How does the angel in charge of the waters describe God's actions in this chapter?

"Then I heard the angel in charge of the waters say: 'You are just in these judgments, you who are and who were, the Holy One, because you have so judged; for they have shed the blood of your saints and prophets, and you have given them blood to drink as they deserve." Revelation 16:5, 6, NIV.

NOTE.—In this is shown God's abhorrence of oppression and persecution. The plagues are God's rebukes against colossal forms of sin.

How does John describe the fourth plague?

"The fourth angel poured out his bowl on the sun, and *the sun was given power to scorch people with fire."* Verse 8, NIV. (See Joel 1:16-20.)

NOTE.—Sun worship is the most ancient and widespread of all forms of idolatry. In this plague God manifests His displeasure at this form of idolatry. That which men have worshipped as a god becomes a plague and a tormentor. Thus it was in the plagues of Egypt. Those things which the Egyptians had worshipped became scourges to them instead of benefactors and blessings.

How does John describe the fifth plague?

"The fifth angel poured out his bowl on the throne of the beast, and *his kingdom was plunged into darkness*." Revelation 16:10, NIV.

NOTE.—This plague strikes at the very seat of the end-time religiopolitical power, and parallels the ninth plague of Egypt. People can now see clearly that the beast is powerless, and that its authority is a sham.

What takes place under the sixth plague?

"The sixth angel poured out his bowl on the great river *Euphrates*, and *its water was dried up* to prepare the way for the kings from the East." Verse 12, NIV.

NOTE.—This symbolizes the divine judgment on the end-time religious apostasy of "Babylon the Great." The narrative parallels the fall of ancient Babylon in 539 B.C., as prophesied by Isaiah. "[I am the Lord] who says to the watery deep, 'Be dry, and I will dry up your streams,' who says of Cyrus, 'He is my shepherd and will accomplish all that I please; he will say of Jerusalem, "Let it be rebuilt," and of the temple, "Let its foundations be laid." ' " Isaiah 44:27, 28, NIV. Cyrus was God's "anointed" (Isaiah 45:1), and thus a type of the Messiah in prophetic history. Cyrus' work of conquering Babylon and delivering God's people from exile, that they may return to Jerusalem, points us to parallel events at the end of time. "The kings of the east" alludes to Cyrus and his armies of Media and Persia, and reminds us of the references to the sun in connection with Jesus and his return (Luke 1:78; Matthew 24:27-31). Revelation 22:16 refers to Jesus as the "Morning Star" (NIV).

"The historical fulfillment of these prophecies was later recorded by the famous Greek historian Herodotus and confirmed in modern times by the Cyrus Cylinder. According to Herodotus, Cyrus the Persian captured Babylon by drying up the Euphrates River which flowed through the city. When he approached Babylon, he discovered that the walls and defenses were too strong and that the city had supplies for many years to come. Cyrus used a section of his soldiers to divert the incoming water flow of the river, when it was low, into a lake. According to Daniel 5, it was that night when Babylon was having a drinking celebration that the Persians entered the city on the dry riverbed beneath the city walls in a surprise attack, conquering the overconfident defenders of Babylon. Later, Cyrus issued the decree allowing Israel to return to their homeland and rebuild Jerusalem and the temple. It seems clear that John used the real historical scene in order to symbolically portray God's final judgment on end-time Babylon which would initiate the deliverance of God's end-time people from their oppressors." Ranko Stefanovich, *The Revelation of*

Jesus Christ: Commentary on the Book of Revelation (Berrien Springs, Mich.: Andrews University Press, 2002), p. 486.

The sixth plague parallels the sixth trumpet plague of Revelation 9:13-21.

What satanic counterfeit parodies the work of God's three angelic messengers?

"Then I saw *three evil spirits that looked like frogs*; they came out of the mouth of the dragon, out of the mouth of the beast and out of the mouth of the false prophet. *They are spirits of demons performing miraculous signs*, and they go out to the kings of the whole world, to gather them for the battle on the great day of God Almighty." Revelation 16:13, 14, NIV.

NOTE.—The plague of frogs upon Egypt was the last one that the pharaoh's satanic magicians were able to emulate. This suggests that the three froglike demons of the sixth plague represent Satan's last-ditch effort to deceive the world. All manner of manifestations will seek to convince the world to unite against God's people. This scripture shows that it is the spirit of Satan that incites people to war.

In light of such deception and peril, what message does Jesus give to His end-time people?

"Behold, I come like a thief! Blessed is he who stays awake and keeps his clothes with him, so that he may not go naked and be shamefully exposed." Verse 15, NIV.

NOTE.—In the midst of this warning we find a message from Jesus: "Behold, I come like a thief! Blessed is he who stays awake." This parallels Jesus' words in such texts as Luke 21:36, "Be always on the watch, and pray that you may be able to escape all that is about to happen, and that you may be able to stand before the Son of Man."

How does Paul describe the end-time work of the "lawless one"?

"For the secret power of lawlessness is already at work; but the one who now holds it back will continue to do so till he is taken out of the way. And then the lawless one will be revealed, whom the Lord Jesus will overthrow with the breath of his mouth and destroy by the splendor of his coming. The coming of the lawless one will be in accordance with the work of Satan displayed in all kinds of counterfeit miracles, signs and wonders, and in every sort of evil that deceives those who are perishing. They perish because they refuse to love the truth and so be saved. For this reason God sends them a powerful delusion so that they will believe the lie and so that all will be condemned who have not believed the truth but have delighted in wickedness." 2 Thessalonians 2:7-12, NIV.

What is the goal of the three evil spirits?

"Then *they gathered the kings together to* the place that in Hebrew is called *Armageddon*." Revelation 16:16, NIV.

NOTE.—Each person must choose whether to follow God or a deception. The term "Armageddon" appears to be the Greek form of the Hebrew "mountain of Megiddo," perhaps pointing us to Elijah's showdown on Mount Carmel (which overlooks the valley of Megiddo) with the prophets of Baal, which decisively demonstrated the sovereignty of God. Revelation suggests a key difference, however. Whereas the prophets of Baal were unable to duplicate the fire God poured down from heaven onto Elijah's altar, in the last days the false trinity will deceive many with supernatural displays of power (Revelation 13:13, 14).

How does Paul describe Christian (spiritual) warfare?

"For though we live in the world, we do not wage war as the world does. The weapons we fight with are not the weapons of the world. On the contrary, they have divine power to demolish strongholds. We demolish arguments and every pretension that sets itself up against the knowledge of God, and we take captive every thought to make it obedient to Christ." 2 Corinthians 10:3-5, NIV.

How does John describe the seventh plague?

"The seventh angel poured out his bowl into the air, and out of the temple came a loud voice from the throne, saying, 'It is done!' Then there came flashes of lightning, rumblings, peals of thunder and a severe earthquake. No earthquake like it has ever occurred since man has been on earth, so tremendous was the quake. The great city split into three parts, and the cities of the nations collapsed. God remembered Babylon the Great and gave her the cup filled with the wine of the fury of his wrath. Every island fled away and the mountains could not be found. From the sky huge hailstones of about a hundred pounds each fell upon men. And they cursed God on account of the plague of hail, because the plague was so terrible." Revelation 16:17-21, NIV.

NOTE.—The voice from God's throne proclaiming "It is done!" echoes Jesus' final words on the cross (John 19:30). On Calvary Jesus proclaimed victory over sin. Now Jesus announces the end of earthly history and victory over the forces of Satan. The destruction of Babylon into three parts symbolizes the shattering of the false trinity, and the fall of the cities the powers that supported her. Meanwhile, the wicked refuse to repent, as the door of probation has closed.

What accompanies the earthquake?

"From the sky *huge hailstones* of about a hundred pounds each *fell upon men*. And they cursed God on account of the plague of hail, because the plague was so terrible." Revelation 16:21, NIV. (See Job 38:22, 23; Psalm 7:11-13.)

What will the Lord be to His people at this time?

"The Lord will roar from Zion and thunder from Jerusalem; the earth and the sky will tremble. But the Lord will be *a refuge for his people, a stronghold for the people of Israel*." Joel 3:16, NIV. (See also Jeremiah 25:30, 31; Haggai 2:21; Hebrews 12:26; Psalm 91:5-10.)

NOTE.—To prepare His people and the world for these terrible judgments, the Lord, as in the days of Noah, sends a warning message to every nation, tribe, language, and people. (See Revelation 14:6-10.)

Just before the pouring out of the plagues, what call does God send to His people still in Babylon?

"Then I heard another voice from heaven say: *'Come out of her, my people*, so that you will not share in her sins, so that you will not receive any of her plagues; for her sins are piled up to heaven, and God has remembered her crimes." Revelation 18:4, 5, NIV. (See Genesis 19:12-17; Jeremiah 51:6.)

How suddenly will the plagues come upon modern Babylon?

"Therefore *in one day* her plagues will overtake her; death, mourning, and famine. She will be consumed by fire, for mighty is the Lord God who judges her. When the kings of the earth who committed adultery with her and shared her luxury see the smoke of her burning, they will weep and mourn over her. Terrified at her torment, they will stand far off and cry: 'Woe! Woe, O great city, O Babylon, city of power! In one hour your doom has come!' " Revelation 18:8-10, NIV.

NOTE.—In other words, it will happen very quickly, evidently within a short period of time.

What kind of "famine" will, at this time, come upon those who have rejected God's messages of mercy?

" 'The days are coming,' declares the Sovereign Lord, 'when I will send a famine through the land—not a famine of food or a thirst for water, but *a famine of hearing the words of the Lord*. Men will stagger from sea to sea and wander from north to east, searching for the word of the Lord, but they will not find it.' " Amos 8:11, 12, NIV. (See Luke 13:25; Proverbs 1:24-26; Hebrews 12:15-17.)

What announcement is made under the seventh plague?

"And there came a great voice out of the temple of heaven, from the throne, saying, *It is done*." Revelation 16:17.

NOTE.—God made us to bless us (Genesis 1:28). When His blessings are abused, He withholds them, to teach us their source and their proper use (Haggai 1:7-11). Judgments are sent that we may "learn righteousness" (Isaiah 25:9; 1 Kings 17:1). That the wicked do not repent under the plagues is no evidence that God has ceased to be merciful and forgiving. They simply demonstrate that even the severest judgments of God will not move the ungodly and impenitent to repentance. Their destiny is fixed by their own choice.

What psalms bring comfort and encouragement for the righteous who live during the time of the seven last plagues?

Psalm 91 and 46. (See also Isaiah 33:13-17.)

THE GOSPEL FINISHED

After his vision of the sixth trumpet, what did John see?

"Then I saw *another mighty angel coming down from heaven*. He was robed in a cloud, with a rainbow above his head; his face was like the sun, and his legs were like fiery pillars. He was holding a little scroll, which lay open in his hand." Revelation 10:1, 2, NIV.

NOTE.—The book of Daniel, which was "sealed" till the time of the end (Daniel 12:4, 9), is pointed to here.

What solemn announcement did this angel make?

"Then the angel I had seen standing on the sea and on the land raised his right hand to heaven. And he swore by him who lives for ever and ever, who created the heavens and all that is in them, the earth and all that is in it, and the sea and all that is in it, and said, *'There will be no more delay!'* " Revelation 10:5, 6, NIV.

NOTE.—In other words, all of the prophetic time periods had run out. The 2300-day period, which ended in 1844, must be alluded to here. (see pp. 189-199.) No prophetic period in the Bible reaches beyond this.

According to this angel, what is finished when the seventh trumpet begins to sound?

"But in the days when the seventh angel is about to sound his trumpet, *the mystery of God* will be accomplished, just as he announced it to his servants the prophets." Verse 7, NIV.

According to Scripture, what is "the mystery of God"?

"Surely you have heard about the administration of God's grace that was given to me for you, that is, the mystery made known to me by revelation, as I have already written briefly. In reading this, then, you will be able to understand my insight into the mystery of Christ, which was not made known to men in other generations as it has now been revealed by the Spirit to God's holy apostles and prophets. This mystery is that through *the gospel* the Gentiles are heirs together with Israel, members together of one body, and sharers together in the promise in Christ Jesus." Ephesians 3:2-6, NIV.

NOTE.—The mystery of God is the gospel. (See also Ephesians 6:19; Galatians 1:11, 12.) The gospel, then, is to be finished as the seventh trumpet begins.

What was John's experience with the little book?

"Then the voice that I had heard from heaven spoke to me once more: 'Go, take the scroll that lies open in the hand of the angel who is standing on the sea and on the land.' So I went to the angel and asked him to give me the little scroll. He said to me, 'Take it and eat it. It will turn your stomach sour, but in your mouth it will be as sweet as honey.' I took the little scroll from the angel's hand and ate it. It tasted as sweet as honey in my mouth, but when I had eaten it, my stomach turned sour." Revelation 10:8-10, NIV.

NOTE.—Revelation 10 is part of an interlude between trumpets 6 and 7, just as Revelation 7 is an interlude between seals 6 and 7. So it relates to the time of the sixth trumpet, and portrays the experience of God's people in the last phase of human history—those who proclaimed the Advent and the judgment-hour message of 1843-1844. The "little book" is Daniel, whose message first brought joy, then disappointment, because it was at first misunderstood. Those who proclaimed the judgment message of Daniel 8 were full of joy at first in the hope that Christ was coming immediately. The message was sweet as honey, but then they were bitterly disappointed—as were the early disciples when they expected Jesus to set up an earthly kingdom (Luke 24:21; Acts 1:6). Just as the disciples, after the death, resurrection, and ascension of Christ, found that there was still a work on earth for them to do, so did those who remained faithful through the Great Disappointment of the Advent movement in 1844. Their disappointment was God's appointment.

John's experience in Revelation 10 parallels that of the prophet

Ezekiel (a contemporary of Daniel's in ancient Babylon) in Ezekiel 3. "Like [John], Ezekiel finds the contents of the scroll 'sweet as honey' (verse 3, NIV; cf. Revelation 10:9, 10). But both experiences have a bitter aftertaste. The book contains 'words of lament and mourning and woe' (Ezekiel 2:10, NIV), part of its dual message of judgment and restoration.

" 'The end! The end has come,' the prophet declares (Ezekiel 7:2, 3, 6, NIV). Ezekiel, prophet in exile, announces God's impending judgment. . . . But at the heart of the summons and threats of destruction lies the promise of hope. Ezekiel is also the prophet of restoration, because the captives are to be set free, the tribes reunited (Ezekiel 37:21), Jerusalem rebuilt (Ezekiel 40-48), and the land to prosper (Ezekiel 47:12). Men and women will receive a new heart (Ezekiel 36:24-48). The prophet foretells the event as a resurrection. The Word of God brings bones back to life (Ezekiel 37). The world once again witnesses the miracle of creation. As in Genesis 2:7, the Spirit changes dust into life (Ezekiel 37:9).

"It is this bittersweet message of judgment and of creation that the book of the Apocalypse here alludes to through its reference to the book of Ezekiel—the message of [the Jewish holiday of Yom] Kippur.

"The insights of Daniel and of the Apocalypse [the book of Revelation] converge into a revelation of the 'time of the end.' Daniel compares it to Kippur, to a time of trembling expectation of judgment and recreation. The Apocalypse [Revelation] portrays this period through the vision of the 'open scroll' with the bittersweet taste, evocative of the dual message of judgment and recreation that characterizes the nature of Kippur.

"The books of Daniel and the Apocalypse [Revelation] complement each other. That the angel asks [John] to eat the book of Daniel further emphasizes their interdependence." Jacques B. Doukhan, *Secrets of Revelation* (Hagerstown, Md.: Review and Herald, 2002), pp. 92, 93.

What shows that literal time was yet to continue and that God had a further message for the world?

"Then I was told, 'You must prophesy again about many peoples, nations, languages and kings.' " Revelation 10:11, NIV.

NOTE.—"Again, the message is a dual one—a message of judgment but also of re-creation. The Apocalypse [the book of Revelation] presents God's people in the time of the end as prophets commissioned to give the message of Daniel, 'digested' by the Apocalypse itself." Jacques B. Doukhan, *Secrets of Revelation* (Hagerstown, Md.: Review and Herald, 2002), pp. 93, 94.

CHAPTER 7

Coming Events and Signs of the Times

OUR LORD'S GREAT PROPHECY

How did Christ feel concerning Jerusalem?

"As he approached Jerusalem and saw the city, *he wept over it* and said, 'If you, even you, had only known on this day what would bring you peace—but now it is hidden from your eyes.'" Luke 19:41, 42, NIV.

In what words did He foretell its destruction?

"The days will come upon you when your enemies will build an embankment against you and encircle you and hem you in on every side. They will dash you to the ground, you and the children within your walls. They will not leave one stone on another, because you did not recognize the time of God's coming to you." Verses 43, 44, NIV.

What compassionate appeal did He make to the impenitent city?

"O Jerusalem, Jerusalem, you who kill the prophets and stone those sent to you, how often have I longed to gather your children together, as a hen gathers her chicks under her wings, but you were not willing." Matthew 23:37, NIV.

As He was about to leave the Temple, what did He say?

"Look, your house is left to you desolate. For I tell you, you will not see me again until you say, 'Blessed is he who comes in the name of the Lord.'" Verses 38, 39, NIV.

What questions did the disciples, upon hearing these words, ask?

"As Jesus was sitting on the Mount of Olives, the disciples came to him privately. 'Tell us,' they said, 'when will this happen, and what will be the sign of your coming and of the end of the age?'" Matthew 24:3, NIV.

NOTE.—The overthrow of Jerusalem and of the Jewish nation is a type of the final destruction of all the cities of the world, and of all nations. Christ's prophetic words were spoken not for the early disciples only, but for those who were to live during the closing scenes of the world's history. Christ gave definite signs, both of the destruction of Jerusalem and of His second coming.

What had to happen first before the end?

"Jesus answered: *'Watch out that no one deceives you.* For many will come in my name, claiming, "I am the Christ," and will deceive many. You will hear of wars and rumors of wars, but see to it that you are not alarmed. *Such things must happen, but the end is still to come.'* " Verses 4-6, NIV.

NOTE.—False messiahs and wars, then, are not unique or special signs of the end; they have occurred throughout history. Josephus describes a number of false messiahs that arose prior to the destruction of Jerusalem in A.D. 70.

What events did Jesus say would begin the final countdown?

"Nation will rise against nation, and kingdom against kingdom. There will be famines and earthquakes in various places. *All these are the beginning of birth pains.*" Verses 7, 8, NIV.

What would be the experiences of His people?

"Then you will be handed over to be persecuted and put to death, and you will be hated by all nations because of me. At that time many will turn away from the faith and will betray and hate each other, and many false prophets will appear and deceive many people. *Because of the increase of wickedness, the love of most will grow cold.*" Verses 9-12, NIV.

Who did He say would be saved?

"But *he who stands firm to the* end will be saved." Verse 13, NIV.

When did Christ say the end would come?

"And *this gospel of the kingdom* will be *preached in the whole world* as a *testimony to all nations, and then the end will come.*" Verse 14, NIV.

NOTE.—Before the fall of Jerusalem, Paul said that the gospel had been "proclaimed to every creature under heaven." Colossians 1:23, NIV. This prophecy will again be fulfilled in the end of the world. When the gospel—the "good news"—of Christ's coming kingdom has been preached in all the world for a witness unto all nations, then the end will come. As the end of the Jewish nation came with overwhelming destruction, so will come the end of the world (Revelation 19:17-21).

What would be a sign that the fall of Jerusalem was imminent?

"When you see Jerusalem being surrounded by armies, you know that its desolation is near." Luke 21:20, NIV.

When the sign appeared, what were the disciples to do?

"So when you see standing in the holy place 'the abomination that causes desolation,' spoken of through the prophet Daniel—let the reader understand—then let those who are in Judea *flee to the mountains*." Matthew 24:15, 16, NIV.

NOTE.—In A.D. 66, when Cestius came against the city, but unaccountably withdrew (Josephus *Wars of the Jews* 2. 19. 7), the Christians discerned in this the sign foretold by Christ, and fled (Eusebius *Church History* 3. 5). More than 1 million Jews were killed in the terrible siege in A.D. 70. Here is a striking lesson on the importance of studying the prophecies and heeding the signs of the times. Those who believed Christ and watched for the sign that He had foretold were saved, while the unbelieving perished. So in the end of the world the watchful and believing will be delivered, while the careless and unbelieving will be snared and taken (see Matthew 24:36-44; Luke 21:34-36; 1 Thessalonians 5:1-6).

When the sign appeared, how immediately were they to flee?

"Let no one on the roof of his house go down to take anything out of the house. Let no one in the field go back to get his cloak." Matthew 24:17, 18, NIV.

How did Christ further show His care for His disciples?

"Pray that your flight will not take place in the winter or on the Sabbath." Verse 20, NIV.

NOTE.—Flight in winter would entail discomfort and hardship; the Sabbath was a sacred day. The prayers of Christ's followers were heard. Events were so overruled that neither Jews nor Romans hindered their flight. When Cestius retreated, the Jews pursued his army, and the Christians thus had an opportunity to leave the city. The country was cleared of enemies, for at the time of this siege, the Jews had assembled at Jerusalem for the Feast of Tabernacles. Thus the Christians of Judea were able to escape unharmed, and in the autumn. (See Josephus *Wars of the Jews* 2. 19. 4; Eusebius *Church History* 3. 5.)

What trying experience did Christ then foretell?

"For then *there will be great distress*, unequaled from the beginning of the world until now—and never to be equaled again." Verse 21, NIV.

NOTE.—In the siege of Jerusalem a prophecy of Moses (Deuteronomy 28:47-53) was literally fulfilled: "Because of the suffering that your enemy will inflict on you during the siege, you will eat the fruit of the womb, the flesh of the sons and daughters the Lord your God has given you." Verse 53, NIV. For the fulfillment, see Josephus *Wars of the Jews* 6. 3. 4. Later this prophecy was again fulfilled in the terrible persecution by the church of the Middle Ages, foretold in Daniel 7:25 and Revelation 12:6.

For whose sake would the period of persecution be shortened?

"If those days had not been cut short, no one would survive, but *for the sake of the elect* those days will be shortened." Matthew 24:22, NIV.

NOTE.—Through the influence of the Reformation of the sixteenth century, and the movements that grew out of it, liberty of conscience was more and more valued in the Western world. Governments became free from religious control, until religious persecution ceased almost wholly by the middle of the eighteenth century, before the 1260 years ended.

Against what deceptions did Christ then warn us?

"At that time if anyone says to you, 'Look, here is the Christ!' or, 'There he is!' do not believe it. For false Christs and false prophets will appear and perform great signs and miracles to deceive even the elect—if that were possible. See, I have told you ahead of time. So if anyone tells you, 'There he is, out in the desert,' do not go out; or 'Here he is, in the inner rooms,' do not believe it." Verses 23, 24, NIV.

NOTE.—It is ever Satan's tactic to substitute something false, a counterfeit, for God's truth.

What signs of the end would be seen in the heavens?

"There will be signs in the *sun, moon* and *stars*." Luke 21:25, NIV.

When were the first of these signs to appear?

"Immediately after the distress of those days 'the sun will be darkened, and the moon will not give its light; the stars will fall from the sky, and the heavenly bodies will be shaken.' " Matthew 24:29, NIV. (Compare Joel 2:30, 31; 3:15; Isaiah 13:10; Amos 8:9.)

NOTE.—Within the 1260 years, but after the persecution (about the middle of the eighteenth century), the signs of Jesus' return began to appear.

1. *The sun and moon darkened.* (See also p. 256.) The remarkable Dark Day of May 19, 1780, is described by Samuel Williams of Harvard. The professor relates that the obscuration approached with the clouds from the southwest "between the hours of ten and eleven a.m., and continued until the middle of the next night," varying in degree and duration in different localities. In some places "persons could

not see to read common print in the open air, for several hours," although "this was not generally the case." "Candles were lighted up in the houses; the birds having sung their evening songs, disappeared, and became silent; the fowls retired to roost; the cocks were crowing all around, as at break of day; objects could not be distinguished but at a very little distance; and everything bore the appearance and gloom of night." See *Memoirs of the American Academy of Arts and Sciences* (through 1783), vol. 1, pp. 234, 235.

"The darkness of *the following evening* was probably as gross as ever has been observed since the Almighty fiat gave birth to light. It wanted only palpability to render it as extraordinary, as that which overspread the land of Egypt in the days of Moses. . . . If every luminous body in the universe had been shrouded in impenetrable shades, or struck out of existence, the darkness could not have been more complete. A sheet of white paper held within a few inches of the eyes was equally invisible with the blackest velvet." Samuel Tenney, letter (1785) in *Collections of the Massachusetts Historical Society* (1792 ed.), part 1, vol. 1, pp. 97, 98.

Timothy Dwight, president of Yale, remembered that "a very general opinion prevailed, that the day of judgment was at hand. The [Connecticut] House of Representatives, being unable to transact their business, adjourned," but the Council lighted candles, preferring, as a member said, to be found at work if the judgment were approaching. See John W. Barber, *Connecticut Historical Collections,* 2nd ed. (1836), p. 403.

Canadian forest fires caused the Dark Day of 1780. Like God's sign the rainbow (Genesis 9:13), it had a natural explanation. God uses natural means to accomplish His will; He used "a strong east wind" to open a path for His people through the sea (Exodus 14:21). But the Dark Day was predicted 17 centuries before it occurred, and this is what gives it value as a sign of the end of time.

2. *Remarkable display of falling stars.* "The morning of November 13th, 1833," says an eyewitness, a Yale astronomer, "was rendered memorable by an exhibition of the phenomenon called shooting stars, which was probably more extensive and magnificent than any similar one hitherto recorded. . . . Probably no celestial phenomenon has ever occurred in this country, since its first settlement, which was viewed with so much admiration and delight by one class of spectators, or with so much astonishment and fear by another class." Denison Olmsted, in *The American Journal of Science and Arts* (1834): 363, 364.

"From the Gulf of Mexico to Halifax, until daylight with some difficulty put an end to the display, the sky was scored in every direction with shining tracks and illuminated with majestic fireballs. At Boston, the frequency of meteors was estimated to be about half that of flakes of snow in an average snowstorm. . . . Traced backwards, their paths were invariably found to converge to a point in the constellation Leo." Agnes M. Clerke, *A Popular History of Astronomy* (1885 ed.), pp. 369, 370.

Frederick Douglass, in reminiscing about his early days in slavery, says: "I witnessed this gorgeous spectacle, and was awe-struck. The air seemed filled with bright descending messengers from the sky. . . . I was not without the suggestion at the moment that it might be the harbinger of the coming of the Son of Man; and in my then state of mind I was prepared to hail Him as my friend and deliverer. I had read that 'the stars shall fall from heaven,' and they were now falling." Frederick Douglass, *Life and Times of Frederick Douglass* (1941 ed.), p. 117.

What were to be the signs on earth of Christ's coming?
"On the earth, *nations will be in anguish and perplexity* at the roaring and tossing of the sea. *Men will faint from terror*, apprehensive of what is coming on the world, for the heavenly bodies will be shaken." Luke 21:25, 26, NIV.

What was to be the next great event after these signs?
"At that time they will see *the Son of Man coming in a cloud with power and great glory*." Verse 27, NIV. (See Matthew 24:30.)

When these things begin to happen, what should we do?
"When these things begin to take place, *stand up and lift up your heads*, because your redemption is drawing near." Luke 21:28, NIV.

What lesson did Jesus teach from the fig tree?
"Now learn this lesson from the fig tree: As soon as its twigs get tender and its leaves come out, *you know that summer is near*. Even so, when you see all these things, *you know that it is near, right at the door*." Matthew 24:32, 33, NIV.

What did Jesus say of the certainty of this prophecy?
"I tell you the truth, this generation will certainly not pass away until all these things have happened. Heaven and earth will pass away, but my words will never pass away." Verses 34, 35, NIV.

NOTE.—What Christ foretold of the destruction of Jerusalem came true to the very letter. Some 40 years after the prophecy was given, Jerusalem was destroyed. A generation in Scripture is often regarded as lasting 40 years (Numbers 32:13; Deuteronomy 1:35 with 2:14; Psalm 95:10; Hebrews 3:9, 10). Likewise what He has said about the end of the world will as certainly and as literally be fulfilled.

Who alone knows when Jesus will return?

"No one knows about that day or hour, not even the angels in heaven, nor the Son, but *only the Father."* Matthew 24:36, NIV.

What moral conditions would precede Christ's second advent?

"As it was in the days of Noah, so it will be at the coming of the Son of Man. For in the days before the flood, *people were eating and drinking, marrying and giving in marriage,* up to the day Noah entered the ark; and they knew nothing about what would happen until the flood came and took them all away. *This is how it will be at the coming of the Son of Man."* Verses 37-39, NIV.

What attitude should we maintain about Jesus' return?

"So *you* also *must be ready,* because the Son of Man will come at an hour when you do not expect him." Verse 44, NIV.

What will be the experience of those who doubt Jesus' soon coming and begin to live carelessly?

"Who then is the faithful and wise servant, whom the master has put in charge of the servants in his household to give them their food at the proper time? It will be good for that servant whose master finds him doing so when he returns. I tell you the truth, he will put him in charge of all his possessions. But suppose that servant is wicked and says to himself, 'My master is staying away a long time,' and he then begins to beat his fellow servants and to eat and drink with drunkards. The master of that servant will come on a day when he does not expect him and at an hour he is not aware of. *He will cut him to pieces and assign him a place with the hypocrites, where there will be weeping and gnashing of teeth."* Verses 45-51, NIV.

INCREASE OF KNOWLEDGE

When might the world look for an increase of knowledge?

"But you, Daniel, close up and seal the words of the scroll until *the time of the end.* Many will go here and there to increase knowledge." Daniel 12:4, NIV.

NOTE.—The book of Daniel was not to be shut up *till the end*— for then there would be no time to develop or utilize knowledge—

but until "the *time of the end*," a period just preceding the end. During this time there was to be a great increase of knowledge concerning the prophecies of Daniel.

Until what time were the saints to be persecuted?

"Some of the wise may stumble, so that they may be refined, purified and made spotless until *the time of the end*, for it will still come at the appointed time." Daniel 11:35, NIV.

NOTE.—Even in the days of Daniel God had an appointed time, "the time of the end," when the age of persecution was to close and knowledge was to increase.

How long were they to be under the power of the little horn?

"He will speak against the Most High and oppress his saints and try to change the set times and the laws. The saints will be handed over to him for *a time, times and half a time*." Daniel 7:25, NIV.

NOTE.—This period is mentioned seven times in the Bible, and always in connection with an oppressive religious power that is in conflict with God, truth, and God's people. The three and a half times (Daniel 7:5; 12:7; Revelation 12:14) are equivalent to the 42 months (Revelation 11:2; 13:5) and the 1260 days (Revelation 11:3; 12:6). In the previous section we established that this period began in 538 and ended in 1798. Daniel 7:25, then, suggests that the time of the end begins at the end of this period of the dominance of the little horn, or in 1798.

After 1798 what happened that resulted in the unsealing of Daniel's prophecy?

"He replied, 'Go your way, Daniel, because the words are closed up and sealed until the time of the end.'" Daniel 12:9, NIV.

NOTE.—The Religious Tract Society of London was organized in 1799, the British and Foreign Bible Society in 1804, the American Bible Society in 1816, and the American Tract Society in 1825. The Bible has been translated into more than 1,000 languages and dialects. Hundreds of millions of copies of the Scriptures, and countless pages of tracts, pamphlets, and religious papers, have gone out. In the nineteenth century an era of missions began; by the end of the twentieth, missionaries had been to almost every country in the world. Thus in this "time of the end" the gospel of the kingdom has literally gone "to every kindred, and tongue, and people, and nation." Revelation 5:9, NIV. As a result, Bible knowledge has greatly increased, and Daniel has been extensively studied and preached.

For what do all these changes pave the way?

"And this gospel of the kingdom will be preached in the whole world as a testimony to all nations, and then the end will come." Matthew 24:14, NIV.

ECONOMIC TENSIONS

What are some sins of the last days?

"People will be *lovers of themselves, lovers of money, boastful, proud,* abusive, disobedient to their parents, ungrateful, unholy, without love, unforgiving, slanderous, without self-control, brutal, not lovers of the good, treacherous, rash, conceited, lovers of pleasure rather than lovers of God—having a form of godliness but denying its power. Have nothing to do with them." 2 Timothy 3:2, NIV.

For what sin did Ezekiel condemn the people of his generation?

"The people of the land practice extortion and commit robbery; they oppress the poor and needy and mistreat the alien, denying them justice." Ezekiel 22:29, NIV.

What does the book of James say about wealth in the last days?

"Now listen, you rich people, weep and wail because of the misery that is coming upon you. Your wealth has rotted, and moths have eaten your clothes. Your gold and silver are corroded. Their corrosion will testify against you and eat your flesh like fire. *You have hoarded wealth* in the last days." James 5:1-3, NIV.

NOTE.—This age of greatest intellectual and material achievement is marked by a race for money, and vast accumulations of wealth contrasted with misery and poverty.

How does God view the poor?

"Listen, my dear brothers: Has not God chosen those who are poor in the eyes of the world to be rich in faith and to inherit the kingdom he promised those who love him?" James 2:5, NIV.

How did James rebuke Christians for their treatment of the poor and favoritism to the rich?

"My brothers, as believers in our glorious Lord Jesus Christ, don't show favoritism. Suppose a man comes into your meeting wearing a gold ring and fine clothes, and a poor man in shabby clothes also comes in. If you show special attention to the man wearing fine clothes and say, 'Here's a good seat for you,' but say to the poor man, 'You stand there' or 'Sit on the floor by my feet,' have you not discriminated among yourselves and become judges with evil thoughts?" Verses 1-4, NIV.

Why did James criticize the rich?

"Is it not the rich who are exploiting you? Are they not the ones who are dragging you into court? Are they not the ones who are slandering the noble name of him to whom you belong?" Verses 6, 7, NIV.

What scriptural command did James point Christians to as a guideline for behavior?

"If you really keep the royal law found in Scripture, 'Love your neighbor as yourself,' you are doing right. But if you show favoritism, you sin and are convicted by the law as lawbreakers." Verses 8, 9, NIV.

NOTE.—James is quoting Leviticus 19:18.

Who gives us the power to get wealth?

"But remember the Lord your God, for *it is he who gives you the ability to produce wealth*." Deuteronomy 8:18, NIV.

"Moreover, when *God gives any man wealth and possessions*, and enables him to enjoy them, to accept his lot and be happy in his work—*this is a gift of God*." Ecclesiastes 5:19, NIV.

Why did the master in the parable of the talents reprove the servant who failed to put to good use the money entrusted to him?

"His master replied, 'You wicked, lazy servant! So you knew that I harvest where I have not sown and gather where I have not scattered seed? Well then, you should have put my money on deposit with the bankers, so that when I returned I would have received it back with interest.' " Matthew 25:26, 27, NIV.

NOTE.—God entrusts us with resources to be used for Him, and to test us to see if we will be worthy of being entrusted with things of greater value in another realm. Our wealth is to be used to bless others.

In Jesus' parable of the rich fool, what did God say to the rich man who decided to build larger barns in which to store his goods?

"But God said to him, *'You fool! This very night your life will be demanded from you*. Then who will get what you have prepared for yourself?' " Luke 12:20, NIV.

Where should we place our priorities?

"Now listen, you who say, 'Today or tomorrow we will go to this or that city, spend a year there, carry on business and make money.'

Why, you do not even know what will happen tomorrow. What is your life? You are a mist that appears for a little while and then vanishes. Instead, you ought to say, 'If it is the Lord's will, we will live and do this or that.' As it is, you boast and brag. All such boasting is evil. Anyone, then, who knows the good he ought to do and doesn't do it, sins." James 4:13-17, NIV.

NOTE.—"As James comes to the end of the first of two concurrent diatribes against the rich, he throws in a maxim which does not seem to fit well with the rest of the passage. He writes: 'Anyone, then, who knows the good he ought to do and doesn't do it, sins' (James 4:17, NIV). The 'then' indicates that James intends this to be a concluding statement for these verses. When placed in the context of the merchants, it is possible that James is pointing out that these business schemers know better and fail to do accordingly. Thus their actions are sinful.

"Too often we have relegated the sin of omission to a minor place in our hierarchy of errors. Thus a person who neglects to do something has merely missed an opportunity for obedience. For James, he or she has sinned. This is true especially when it has to do with the social realities of the poor. In James, the failure to do is significant, as the indictment in 2:14-26 clearly indicated. Faith without works is dead. Having faith, but omitting to house and feed the poor, still places one in the category of sinner." Pedrito Maynard-Reid, *The Abundant Life Bible Amplifier: James* (Boise, Idaho: Pacific Press, 1996), pp. 182, 183.

How have the rich defrauded laborers?

"Look! *The wages you failed to pay the workmen who mowed your fields are crying out against you*. The cries of the harvesters have reached the ears of the Lord Almighty." James 5:4, NIV.

How does James condemn the greed of the rich?

"You have lived on earth in luxury and self-indulgence. You have fattened yourselves in the day of slaughter. You have condemned and murdered innocent men, who were not opposing you." James 5:5, 6, NIV.

NOTE.—Some have lived in luxury and for pleasure, heedless of their responsibility to God or to others. Heartless greed disregards the rights, the welfare, and even the lives of those affected by its merciless schemes and machinations. But the righteous do not resist this unjust treatment with force.

"Three groups of wealthy persons are singled out for special mention in James's epistle. In 2:6, 7 they are the financiers and bankers.

. . . In 4:13-17 they are the merchants, and in 5:1-6 they are rich agriculturalists. We must be aware, however, that these classes are not distinct. The activities are different functions of the same individual or group of individuals. But in this final outburst, James attacks the rich from the perspective of two different spheres of their existence. As they operate within these spheres, they bring suffering upon the poor. It is for this reason that James attacks and opposes them.

"In the first part of his remarks (4:13-17), he zeroes in on the financiers who desire to carry on business as usual without concern for anyone—neither God nor the poor. Then in the second section (5:1-6), he lambasts the rich agriculturalist and big landlords because of their luxurious living. It is only after he has laid low the economically powerful that James can admonish the economically marginal to be patient (verse 7)." Pedrito Maynard-Reid, *The Abundant Life Bible Amplifier: James* (Boise, Idaho: Pacific Press, 1996), p. 177.

How does James encourage Christians in light of oppression in the world?

"Be patient, then, brothers, until the Lord's coming. See how the farmer waits for the land to yield its valuable crop and how patient he is for the autumn and spring rains. You too, be patient and stand firm, because the Lord's coming is near. Don't grumble against each other, brothers, or you will be judged. The Judge is standing at the door!

"Brothers, as an example of patience in the face of suffering, take the prophets who spoke in the name of the Lord. As you know, we consider blessed those who have persevered. You have heard of Job's perseverance and have seen what the Lord finally brought about. The Lord is full of compassion and mercy." James 5:7-11, NIV.

How should poor and oppressed Christians relate to such maltreatment?

"But I tell you, *Do not resist an evil person*. If someone strikes you on the right cheek, turn to him the other also. And if someone wants to sue you and take your tunic, let him have your cloak as well." Matthew 5:39, 40, NIV.

NOTE.—Hebrews 10:34 commends those Christians who "joyfully accepted the confiscation of your property, because you knew that you yourselves had better and lasting possessions" (NIV).

NOTE.—Jesus' principle of turning the other cheek gives power back to the oppressed. The oppressor is no longer in control of the situation, and the oppressed is no longer in a subordinate position. The oppressor is exposed to the true nature of their actions, for to strike again is to realize how unjust one has been. Leaders like Gandhi and

Martin Luther King understood the transforming power of "passive resistance," which, while nonviolent, is scarcely "passive" at all, for it actively seeks to draw out, expose, and vanquish oppression. It requires much discipline and strength of character, but it is the only way to cause true change. It is such peacemakers that Jesus commends (Matthew 5:9).

What did Jesus say to one individual who focused too much on money?

"Someone in the crowd said to him, 'Teacher, tell my brother to divide the inheritance with me.' Jesus replied, 'Man, who appointed me a judge or an arbiter between you?' Then he said to them, 'Watch out! *Be on your guard against all kinds of greed; a man's life does not consist in the abundance of his possessions.*' " Luke 12:13-15, NIV.

What was the advice of John the Baptist to the Roman soldiers, who were known for their extortion?

"Don't extort money and don't accuse people falsely—be content with your pay." Luke 3:14, NIV.

NOTE.—Labor unions, strikes, etc., may improve conditions temporarily, but they cannot eradicate the deep-seated evil greed in the heart. Nothing but conversion—a change of the heart—can eradicate the sin of selfishness, which is a failure to love one's neighbor as oneself. The struggle between capital and labor is inevitable as long as sin and selfishness are in the world. And near the end of time it becomes more intense.

In the twentieth century labor unions rose to prominence, often resorting to the use of force to accomplish their will. That century also fell under the blight of Communism, a philosophy that exploits the struggle between the higher and lower classes. While professing to elevate the masses (the "proletariat"), urging them to rise up against the wealthy and assume their rightful position, Communism in fact enslaved the masses, creating a new tyranny of the privileged few. Between 1915 and 1990, under such dictators as Josef Stalin and Mao Tse-tung, Communist countries were responsible for the deaths of approximately 100 million people—all victims in the struggle between capital and labor.

What experience of the early Christian church shows that Jesus is the solution to the class struggle?

"All the believers were one in heart and mind. No one claimed that any of his possessions was his own, but *they shared everything they had. . . .* There was no needy person among them. For from time to time those who owned lands or houses sold them, brought the money from the sales and put it at the apostles' feet, and *it was distributed to anyone as he had need.*" Acts 4:32-35, NIV.

NOTE.—The early Christians practiced voluntary communism, based on their love for Jesus. To some degree this practice continued into the second century A.D. One early Christian document dating to the beginning of the second century prescribed: "You shall not turn away from someone in need, but shall share everything with your brother, and not claim that anything is your own" (*Didache* 4:8). Speaking of the first half of the second century, Eusebius writes: "For most of the disciples at that time . . . had first fulfilled the Savior's precept by distributing their substance to the needy. Afterwards leaving their country, they performed the office of evangelists to those who had not yet heard the faith" (*Ecclesiastical History* 3. 37). Will Durant remarks: "Lucian, about 160, described 'those imbeciles,' the Christians, as 'disdaining things terrestrial, and holding these as belonging to all in common' (*Peregrinus Proteus*). A generation later Tertullian declared that 'we' (Christians) 'have all things in common except our wives' . . . (*Apologeticus* 39. 11)." *Caesar and Christ: A History of Roman Civilization and of Christianity From Their Beginnings to A.D. 325* (New York: Simon and Schuster, 1944), p. 597.

Jesus makes people generous, and even though it is not always necessary in affluent societies to sell our property to meet the basic needs of our brothers and sisters in Christ, still God calls for our sacrifice to enable the church to meet the needs of the less fortunate.

What did John the Baptist command in light of the nearness of the judgment?

" 'The ax is already at the root of the trees, and every tree that does not produce good fruit will be cut down and thrown into the fire'

" 'What should we do then?' the crowd asked.

"John answered, *'The man with two tunics should share with him who has none, and the one who has food should do the same.'* " Luke 3:9-11, NIV.

What will finally happen to the rich oppressors of God's people?

"Terrified at her torment, they will stand far off and cry: 'Woe! Woe, O great city, O Babylon, city of power! In one hour your doom has come!' The merchants of the earth will weep and mourn over her because no one buys their cargoes any more—cargoes of gold, silver, precious stones and pearls; fine linen, purple, silk and scarlet cloth; every sort of citron wood, and articles of every kind made of ivory, costly wood, bronze, iron and marble; cargoes of cinnamon and spice, of incense, myrrh and frankincense, of wine and olive oil, of fine flour and wheat; cattle and sheep; horses and carriages; and bodies and souls of men. They will say, 'The fruit you longed for is gone from you. All your riches and splendor have vanished, never to be recovered.' The merchants who sold these things and gained their wealth from her will stand far off, terrified at her torment. They will weep and mourn and cry out: 'Woe! Woe, O great city, dressed in fine linen, purple and scarlet, and glittering with gold, precious stones and pearls! *In one hour such great wealth has been brought to ruin!*' " Revelation 18:10-17, NIV.

INTERNATIONAL TURMOIL

Why did Christ reprove the Pharisees and Sadducees?

"You know how to interpret the appearance of the sky, but you cannot interpret the signs of the times." Matthew 16:3, NIV.

What did the disciples ask about Christ's second coming?

"As Jesus was sitting on the Mount of Olives, the disciples came to him privately. 'Tell us,' they said, 'when will this happen, and *what will be the sign of your coming and of the end of the age?*'" Matthew 24:3, NIV.

What critical situation was to characterize the nations?

"On the earth, nations will be in *anguish and perplexity* at the roaring and tossing of the sea." Luke 21:25, NIV.

What emotions would reign in the hearts of people?

"Men will faint from terror, apprehensive of what is coming on the world, for the heavenly bodies will be shaken." Verse 26, NIV.

NOTE.—In spite of the end of the cold war, nuclear destruction on a limited scale is now even more likely than before, for terrorists are seeking to acquire nuclear weapons, and terrorists cannot be deterred by the threat of massive retaliation.

What does the Bible point to as the cause of the world's peril in the last days?

"But mark this: *There will be terrible times in the last days*. People will be *lovers of themselves*, lovers of money, boastful, proud, abusive, disobedient to their parents, ungrateful, unholy, slanderous, without self-control, brutal, not lovers of the good, treacherous, rash, conceited, lovers of pleasure rather than lovers of God—having a form of godliness but denying its power." 2 Timothy 3:1-5, NIV.

NOTE.—The trouble is within people themselves.

How does Scripture describe the cataclysm with which the world will end?

"But the day of the Lord will come like a thief. *The heavens will disappear with a roar; the elements will be destroyed by fire, and the earth and everything in it will be laid bare.* . . . That day will bring about the destruction of the heavens by fire, and the elements will melt in the heat." 2 Peter 3:10-12, NIV. (See also Isaiah 13:6-11.)

What do all these warnings mean to us?

"Since everything will be destroyed in this way, what kind of people ought you to be? *You ought to live holy and godly lives as you look forward to the day of God and speed its coming.* That day will bring about the destruction of the heavens by fire, and the elements will melt in the heat." 2 Peter 3:11, 12, NIV.

What may we expect to follow this destruction?

"But in keeping with his promise we are looking forward to *a new heaven and a new earth*, the home of righteousness. So then, dear friends, since you are looking forward to this, make every effort to be found spotless, blameless and at peace with him. Bear in mind that our Lord's patience means salvation." Verses 13-15, NIV.

THE WORLD'S CONVERSION

How did Jesus describe world conditions in the last days?

"Just as it was in the days of Noah, so also will it be in the days of the Son of Man." Luke 17:26, NIV. (See also verses 27-30, and Matthew 24:37-39.)

What was the condition of things in the days of Noah?

"The Lord saw how great man's wickedness on the earth had become, and that every inclination of the thoughts of his heart was only evil all the time. . . . Now the earth was corrupt in God's sight and was full of violence." Genesis 6:5-11, NIV.

NOTE.—Today wickedness is billboarded and advertised as entertainment. Addictions and debauchery are epidemic. Selfishness and pride fill hearts while righteousness is neglected. Civilization is repeating the sins of the days of Noah.

According to the parable of the wheat and the tares, how long are the good and bad to remain together?

"The field is the world, and the good seed stands for the sons of the kingdom. The weeds are the sons of the evil one, and the enemy who sows them is the devil. The harvest is the end of the age, and the harvesters are angels." Matthew 13:38, 39, NIV. "Let both grow together *until the harvest*. At that time I will tell the harvesters: First collect the weeds and tie them in bundles to be burned; then gather the wheat and bring it into my barn." Verse 30, NIV.

NOTE.—The wicked (the weeds) live with the righteous (the wheat) till the end of the world. There is, then, no time before Christ's coming for a sinless state, in which everyone will be converted and turn to God.

Did Christ say that worldwide preaching of the gospel will result in world conversion?

"And this gospel of the kingdom will be preached in the whole world *as a testimony to all nations*, and then the end will come." Matthew 24:14, NIV.

NOTE.—Jesus did say the gospel would be preached everywhere, but He did not say that all would receive it.

Does Scripture portray the last days as an era of faith or an era of disbelief?

"First of all, you must understand that in the last days *scoffers* will come, scoffing and following their own evil desires. They will say, 'Where is this "coming" he promised? Ever since our fathers died, everything goes on as it has since the beginning of creation.' " 2 Peter 3:3, 4, NIV.

How did Paul characterize the last days?

"Evil men and impostors will go from bad to worse, deceiving and being deceived." 2 Timothy 3:13, NIV.

What are people saying while preparing for war?

"They dress the wound of my people as though it were not serious. *'Peace, peace,'* they say, when there is no peace." Jeremiah 6:14, NIV.

NOTE.—World leaders talk of peace and at the same time prepare for war. The world has endured numerous local conflicts and major struggles; it has stood by and ignored genocide in such nations as Bosnia, Cambodia, Rwanda, and China, where the followers of Mao Tse-tung killed some 70 million people. There is no cure for human hatred short of the second coming of Christ.

What does the apostle Paul say concerning this?

"You know very well that the day of the Lord will come like a thief in the night. *While people are saying, 'Peace, and safety,' de-*

struction will come on them suddenly, as labor pains on a pregnant woman, and they will not escape." 1 Thessalonians 5:2, 3, NIV.

How should Christians relate to the world's uncertainty?

"But you, brothers, are not in darkness so that this day should surprise you like a thief. You are all sons of the light and sons of the day. We do not belong to the night or to the darkness. So then, let us not be like others, who are asleep, but let us be alert and self-controlled. For those who sleep, sleep at night, and those who get drunk, get drunk at night. But since we belong to the day, let us be self-controlled, putting on faith and love as a breastplate, and the hope of salvation as a helmet. For God did not appoint us to suffer wrath but to receive salvation through our Lord Jesus Christ. He died for us so that, whether we are awake or asleep, we may live together with him. Therefore encourage one another and build each other up, just as in fact you are doing." Verses 4-11, NIV.

NOTE.—Those in darkness are looking for a time of peace and safety, while those not in darkness are looking for the day of the Lord, a day of destruction—the end of the world and the coming of Christ. (See Jeremiah 7:1-19; Daniel 12:1; Joel 2:1-11; Zephaniah 1; Matthew 25:31-46; Galatians 5:16-21.) The world, heedless of the signs of the times, is approaching the day of the Lord unprepared. As a thief in the night, this day will take unawares all who are not looking, watching, and waiting for their Lord's return. Instead of looking for the world's conversion, we should be looking for Christ's coming.

How did Jesus encourage us to relate to the end-times?

"When these things begin to take place, *stand up and lift up your heads*, because your redemption is drawing near." Luke 21:28, NIV.

CHRIST'S SECOND COMING

With what words did Jesus promise to return?

"Do not let your hearts be troubled. Trust in God; trust also in me. In my Father's house are many rooms; if it were not so, I would have told you. I am going there to prepare a place for you. And if I go and prepare a place for you, *I will come back* and take you to be with me that you also may be where I am." John 14:1-3, NIV.

What follows the signs of Christ's coming?

"At that time they will see *the Son of Man coming in a cloud with power and great glory.*" Luke 21:27, NIV.

At His ascension, how was Christ's return promised?

"They were looking intently up into the sky as he was going, when suddenly two men dressed in white stood beside them. 'Men of Galilee,' they said, 'why do you stand here looking into the sky? This same Jesus, who has been taken from you into heaven, will come back *in the same way you have seen him go into heaven*.'" Acts 1:10, 11, NIV.

How does Paul give expression to this hope?

"Our citizenship is in heaven. *And we eagerly await a Savior* from there, the Lord Jesus Christ." Philippians 3:20, NIV.

"We wait for the blessed hope—the glorious appearing of our great God and Savior, Jesus Christ." Titus 2:13, NIV.

What is Peter's testimony regarding it?

"We did not follow cleverly invented stories when we told you about the power and coming of our Lord Jesus Christ, but *we were eyewitnesses of his majesty*." 2 Peter 1:16, NIV.

How will the world respond to His coming?

"At that time the sign of the Son of Man will appear in the sky, *and all the nations of the earth will mourn*." Matthew 24:30, NIV.

"Look, he is coming with the clouds, and every eye will see him, even those who pierced him; and *all the peoples of the earth will mourn because of him*." Revelation 1:7, NIV.

Why will many be unready for this event?

"But *suppose that servant is wicked and says to himself, 'My master is staying away a long time*,' and he then begins to beat his fellow servants and to eat and drink with drunkards. The master of that servant will come on a day when he does not expect him and at an hour he is not aware of. He will cut him to pieces and assign him a place with the hypocrites, where there will be weeping and gnashing of teeth." Matthew 24:48-51, NIV.

What will everyday life be like when Christ comes?

"Just as it was in the days of Noah, so also it will be in the days of the Son of Man. *People were eating, drinking, marrying and being given in marriage* up to the day Noah entered the ark. Then the flood came and destroyed them all. It was the same in the days of Lot. *People were eating and drinking, buying and selling, planting and building*. But the day Lot left Sodom, fire and sulfur rained down from heaven and destroyed them all." Luke 17:26-29, NIV.

NOTE.—These texts do not teach that it is wrong to eat, drink, marry, buy, sell, plant, or build. But they warn against becoming so preoccupied with the routine affairs of life that we give little thought to the future life and make no plans or preparation to meet Jesus when He comes.

Who blinds human beings to the gospel of Christ?

"The god of this age [Satan] has blinded the minds of unbelievers, so that they cannot see the light of the gospel of the glory of Christ, who is the image of God." 2 Corinthians 4:4, NIV.

NOTE.—Dwight L. Moody wrote: "To my mind this precious doctrine—for such I must call it—of the return of the Lord to this earth is taught in the New Testament as clearly as any other doctrine in it; yet I was in the Church fifteen or sixteen years before I ever heard a sermon on it. There is hardly any church that doesn't make a great deal of baptism, but in all of Paul's epistles I believe baptism is only spoken of thirteen times, while it speaks about the return of our Lord fifty times; and yet the Church has had very little to say about it. Now, I can see a reason for this; the devil does not want us to see this truth, for nothing would wake up the Church so much. The moment a man takes hold of the truth that Jesus Christ is coming back again to receive His followers to Himself, this world loses its hold upon him. . . . His heart is free, and he looks for the blessed appearing of his Lord, who, at His coming, will take him into His blessed Kingdom." *The Second Coming of Christ* (Revell), pp. 6, 7.

When will the saved become like Jesus?

"Dear friends, now we are children of God, and what we will be has not yet been made known. But we know that *when he appears, we shall be like him*, for we shall see him as he is." 1 John 3:2.

Will Christ's coming be a time of reward?

"For the Son of Man is going to come in his Father's glory with his angels, and *then he will reward each person according to what he has done*." Matthew 16:27, NIV.

"Behold, I am coming soon! *My reward is with me*, and I will give to everyone according to what he has done." Revelation 22:12, NIV.

To whom is salvation promised at Christ's appearing?

"So Christ was sacrificed once to take away the sins of many people; and he will appear a second time, not to bear sin, but to bring salvation to *those who are waiting for him*." Hebrews 9:28, NIV.

How does this hope influence us?

"We know that when he appears, we shall be like him, for we shall see him as he is. *Everyone who has this hope in him purifies himself*, just as he is pure." 1 John 3:2, 3, NIV.

To whom is a crown of righteousness promised?

"For I am already being poured out like a drink offering, and the time has come for my departure. I have fought the good fight, I have finished the race, I have kept the faith. Now there is in store for me the crown of righteousness, which the Lord, the righteous Judge, will award to me on that day—and not only to me, but also *to all who have longed for his appearing*." 2 Timothy 4:6-8, NIV.

What will the waiting ones say when Jesus comes?

"In that day they will say, *'Surely this is our God; we trusted in him, and he saved us. This is the Lord, we trusted in him; let us rejoice and be glad in his salvation.'*" Isaiah 25:9, NIV.

Has the exact time of Christ's coming been revealed?

"No one knows about that day or hour, not even the angels in heaven, nor the Son, but only the Father." Matthew 24:36, NIV.

How should we live in view of this?

"Therefore keep watch, because you do not know on what day your Lord will come." Verse 42, NIV.

NOTE.—"To the secure and careless He will come as a thief in the night: to His own, as their Lord." Henry Alford, *The New Testament for English Readers*, vol. 1, part 1, p. 170.

What warning has Christ given so that this great event might not take us by surprise?

"Be careful, or your hearts will be weighed down with dissipation, drunkenness and the anxieties of life, and that day will close on you unexpectedly like a trap. For it will come upon all those who live on the face of the whole earth. *Be always on the watch, and pray* that you may be able to escape all that is about to happen, and that you may be able to stand before the Son of Man." Luke 21:34-36, NIV.

What Christian grace are we urged to exercise in our expectant longing for this event?

"Be patient, then, brothers, until the Lord's coming. See how the farmer waits for the land to yield its valuable crop and how patient he is for the autumn and spring rains. You too, be patient and stand firm, because the Lord's coming is near." James 5:7, 8, NIV.

MANNER OF CHRIST'S RETURN

Is Christ coming again?

"I will come *again*." John 14:3.

Did the early disciples equate the second coming of Christ with death?

"When Peter saw him [John], he asked, 'Lord, what about him?'

"Jesus answered, *'If I want him to remain alive until I return, what is that to you?* You must follow me.'

"Because of this, the rumor spread among the brothers *that this disciple would not die*. But Jesus did not say that he would not die; he only said, 'If I want him to remain alive until I return, what is that to you?' " John 21:21-23, NIV.

NOTE.—From this it is evident that the early disciples regarded death and the coming of Christ as two separate events. Dwight L. Moody wrote, " 'Therefore be ye also ready: for in such an hour as ye think not the Son of man cometh.' Some people say that means death; but the Word of God does not say it means death. Death is our enemy, but our Lord hath the keys of Death; He has conquered death, hell and the grave. . . . Christ is the Prince of Life; there is no death where He is; death flees at His coming; dead bodies sprang to life when He touched them or spoke to them. His coming is not death; He is the resurrection and the life; when He sets up His kingdom there is to be no death, but life forevermore." *The Second Coming of Christ* (Revell), pp. 10, 11.

The common Christian teaching that Christians go to heaven at death arose early in the second century. In the middle of the second century A.D., Justin Martyr, in his *Dialogue With Trypho* (80), wrote, "If you have fallen in with some who are called Christians, but who . . . venture to blaspheme the God of Abraham, and the God of Isaac, and the God of Jacob; who say there is no resurrection of the dead, and that their souls, when they die, are taken to heaven; do not imagine that they are Christians." Likewise with another of the Church Fathers, Ireneaus: "For the heretics . . . affirm that immediately upon their death they shall pass above the heavens." *Against Heresies* 5. 31.

How did Jesus Himself say He would come?

"For the Son of Man is going to come *in his Father's glory with his angels*." Matthew 16:27, NIV.

"At that time the sign of the Son of Man will appear in the sky, and all the nations of the earth will mourn. They will see the Son of Man coming *on the clouds of the sky, with power and great glory*." Matthew 24:30, NIV.

"If anyone is ashamed of me and my words, the Son of Man will be ashamed of him when he *comes in his glory and in the glory of the Father and of the holy angels*." Luke 9:26, NIV.

"When the Son of Man comes in his glory, and *all the angels with him*, he will sit on his throne *in heavenly glory*." Matthew 25:31, NIV.

How many will see Jesus when He comes?

"Look, he is coming with the clouds, and every eye will see him, even those who pierced him." Revelation 1:7, NIV.

NOTE.—Jesus' second coming will be as real as was His first, as visible as His ascension, and far more glorious. To merely "spiritualize" Jesus' return is to pervert the obvious meaning of His promise "I will come again," and nullify the whole plan of redemption, for the reward of the faithful of all ages is to be given at this most glorious of all events.

What demonstration will accompany His coming?

"For the Lord himself will come down from heaven, with a *loud command*, with the *voice of the archangel* and with the *trumpet call of God*, and the dead in Christ will rise first." 1 Thessalonians 4:16, NIV.

NOTE.—This passage is supposed by some to refer to what is known as a "secret rapture," an event in which God's people are stolen away and others are left behind for several years. The idea of God's people leaving earth in secret contradicts the blatant, unrestrained nature of the event described in this verse.

What warning did Christ give concerning false views?

"At that time if anyone says to you, *'Look, here is the Christ!'* or, *'There he is!' do not believe it.* For false Christs and false prophets will appear and perform great signs and miracles to deceive even the elect—if that were possible. See, I have told you ahead of time. So if anyone tells you, 'There he is, out in the *desert*,' do not go out; or 'Here he is, in the *inner rooms*,' do not believe it." Matthew 24:23-26, NIV.

How visible will Jesus' return be?

"For *as lightning that comes from the east is visible even in the west*, so will be the coming of the Son of Man." Verse 27, NIV.

OBJECT OF JESUS' RETURN

For what purpose did Christ say He would come again?

"In my Father's house are many rooms; if it were not so, I would have told you. I am going there to prepare a place for you. And if I go and prepare a place for you, *I will come back and take you to be with me* that you also may be where I am." John 14:2, 3, NIV.

What part will the angels have in this event?

"And he will send his angels with a loud trumpet call, and *they will gather his elect* from the four winds, from one end of the heavens to the other." Matthew 24:31, NIV.

What takes place at the sounding of the trumpet?

"For the Lord himself will come down from heaven, with a loud command, with the voice of the archangel and with the trumpet call of God, and *the dead in Christ will rise first*." 1 Thessalonians 4:16, NIV.

What happens to the righteous living?

"After that, we who are still alive and are left *will be caught up together with them in the clouds* to meet the Lord in the air. And so we will be with the Lord forever." Verse 17, NIV.

In what way will the saved be transformed at that moment?

"Listen, I tell you a mystery: We will not all sleep, but we will all be changed—in a flash, in the twinkling of an eye, at the last trumpet. For the trumpet will sound, the dead will be raised imperishable, and we will be changed. *For the perishable must clothe itself with the imperishable, and the mortal with immortality*." 1 Corinthians 15:51-53, NIV.

When did Jesus say the saved will be rewarded?

"You will be repaid *at the resurrection of the righteous*." Luke 14:14, NIV.

Have the saved from ages past already received their heavenly reward?

"These were all commended for their faith, yet *none of them received what had been promised*. God had planned something better for us so that *only together with us would they be made perfect*." Hebrews 11:39, 40, NIV.

When did Paul expect to receive his crown?

"From now on there is reserved for me the crown of righteousness, which the Lord, the righteous judge, will give me *on that day*, and not only to me but also to all who have longed for *his appearing.*" 2 Timothy 4:8, NRSV.

NOTE.—In other words, all of the saved will receive their reward, not at death, but at the day of Jesus' appearing—a clear reference to the Second Coming (compare 2 Thessalonians 2:3; 2 Timothy 1:12, 18).

How is Jesus' return related to judgment?

"He comes to judge the earth. He will judge the world in righteousness and the peoples in his truth." Psalm 96:13, NIV.

What did Enoch say about the judgment?

"Enoch, the seventh from Adam, prophesied about these men: 'See, the Lord is coming with thousands upon thousands of his holy ones to judge everyone.' " Jude 14, 15, NIV.

THE RESURRECTION OF THE JUST

What question does Job ask and answer about life after death?

"If a man dies, will he live again? All the days of my hard service I will wait for my renewal to come. *You will call and I will answer you*; you will long for the creature your hands have made." Job 14:14, 15, NIV.

Why did Job wish that his words were permanent?

"Oh, that my words were recorded, that they were written on a scroll, that they were inscribed with an iron tool on lead, or engraved in rock forever! *I know that my Redeemer lives*, and that in the end he will stand upon the earth. And after my skin has been destroyed, yet *in my flesh I will see God; I myself will see him with my own eyes—I, and not another. How my heart yearns within me!"* Job 19:23-27, NIV.

What does Christ proclaim Himself to be?

"I am the resurrection and the life. He who believes in me will live, even though he dies; and whoever lives and believes in me will never die." John 11:25, 26, NIV.

"I am the Living One; I was dead, and behold I am alive for ever and ever! And I hold the keys of death and Hades." Revelation 1:18, NIV.

What will be the destiny of the resurrected?

"A time is coming when all who are in their graves will hear his voice and come out—*those who have done good will rise to live, and those who have done evil will rise to be condemned.*" John 5:28, 29, NIV.

Upon what one fact does Paul base the Christian hope?

"But if it is preached that Christ has been raised from the dead, how can some of you say that there is no resurrection of the dead? *If there is no resurrection of the dead, then not even Christ has been raised. And if Christ has not been raised, our preaching is useless and so is your faith.* More than that, we are then found to be false witnesses about God, for we have testified about God that he raised Christ from the dead. But he did not raise him if in fact the dead are not raised. For if the dead are not raised, then Christ has not been raised either. And if Christ has not been raised, your faith is futile; you are still in your sins. Then those also who have fallen asleep in Christ are lost. If only for this life we have hope in Christ, we are to be pitied more than all men." 1 Corinthians 15:12-19, NIV.

What positive declaration does Paul then make?

"But *Christ has indeed been raised from the dead*, the first-fruits of those who have fallen asleep. For since death came through a man, the resurrection of the dead comes also through a man. For as in Adam all die, so in Christ all will be made alive." Verses 20-22, NIV.

NOTE.—The resurrection of Christ is the most significant fact in history. It is the great and impregnable foundation and hope of the Christian church. Every fundamental truth of Christianity is involved in the resurrection of Christ. If this could be overthrown, every essential doctrine of Christianity would be invalidated. The resurrection of Christ is the pledge of our resurrection and future life.

How should we relate to death?

"Brothers, we do not want you to be ignorant *about those who fall asleep*, or to grieve like the rest of men, who have no hope." 1 Thessalonians 4:13, NIV.

NOTE.—Death is frequently referred to in Scripture as a sleep. (See Job 14:10, 12; Psalm 13:3; John 11:1-14; Matthew 27:52; 1 Corinthians 11:30; 1 Thessalonians 4:13-16.)

What is the basis for Christians' hope and comfort?

"We believe that Jesus died and rose again and so we believe *that God will bring with Jesus those who have fallen asleep in him.*" 1 Thessalonians 4:14, NIV. "We know that the one who raised the

Lord Jesus from the dead will also raise us with Jesus and present us with you in his presence." 2 Corinthians 4:14, NIV.

What is said of those raised in the first resurrection?

"Blessed and holy are those who have part in the first resurrection. The second death has no power over them, but *they will be priests of God and of Christ and will reign with him for a thousand years."* Revelation 20:6, NIV.

When will this resurrection of the saved take place?

"According to the Lord's own word, we tell you that we who are still alive, who are left till *the coming of the Lord*, will certainly not precede those who have fallen asleep. *For the Lord himself will come down from heaven*, with a loud command, with the voice of the archangel and with the trumpet call of God, *and the dead in Christ will rise first."* 1 Thessalonians 4:15, 16, NIV.

What will then take place?

"After that, *we who are still alive and are left will be caught up together with them in the clouds* to meet the Lord in the air. And so we will be with the Lord forever." Verse 17, NIV.

How should we apply this truth to our lives?

"Therefore *encourage each other* with these words." Verse 18, NIV.

How does Paul say the saved will be raised?

"Listen, I tell you a mystery: We will not all sleep, but we will all be changed—in a flash, in the twinkling of an eye, at the last trumpet. For the trumpet will sound, *the dead will be raised imperishable, and we will be changed."* 1 Corinthians 15:51, 52, NIV.

How will their bodies be transformed?

"So will it be with the resurrection of the dead. The body that is sown is perishable, it is *raised imperishable*; it is *sown in dishonor*, it is *raised in glory*; it is *sown in weakness*, it is *raised in power*; it is *sown a natural body*, it is *raised a spiritual body."* Verses 42-44, NIV.

What else has God promised to do?

"He will wipe every tear from their eyes. There will be no more death or mourning or crying or pain, for the old order of things has passed away." Revelation 21:4, NIV. (See pp. 631-646.)

THE GATHERING OF ISRAEL

What judgment came upon the ancient Israelites of Judah because of their disobedience?

" 'Because you have not listened to my words, I will summon all the peoples of the north and my servant Nebuchadnezzar king of Babylon,' declares the Lord, 'and I will bring them against this land and its inhabitants and against all the surrounding nations. I will completely destroy them and make them an object of horror and scorn, and an everlasting ruin. . . . This whole country will become a desolate wasteland, and these nations will serve the king of Babylon seventy years.' " Jeremiah 25:8-11, NIV.

What prophecy spoke of their return from captivity?

" 'For I know the plans I have for you,' declares the Lord, 'plans to prosper you and not to harm you, plans to give you hope and a future. Then you will call upon me and come and pray to me, and I will listen to you. You will seek me and find me when you seek me with all your heart. I will be found by you,' declares the Lord, 'and will bring you back from captivity. I will gather you from all the nations and places where I have banished you,' declares the Lord, 'and will bring you back to the place from which I carried you into exile.' " Jeremiah 29:11-14. (See also Jeremiah 23:3.)

NOTE.—The first dispersion of the Jews occurred under Nebuchadnezzar, king of Babylon, who conquered Jerusalem and deported many captives. After Babylon was conquered by Persia, the Persian kings Cyrus and Artaxerxes allowed large numbers of Jews to return to their homeland in Palestine. This was the first gathering of Israel. However, many remained dispersed among the nations, and so Israel looked forward to a greater gathering to come. But this gathering was conditional upon searching for God with all their heart (compare Deuteronomy 30:1-5).

What did Moses warn would happen if they were unfaithful to God?

"The Lord will bring a nation against you from far away, like an eagle swooping down . . . They will lay siege to all the cities throughout your land until the high fortified walls in which you trust fall down. They will besiege all the cities throughout the land the Lord your God is giving you." Deuteronomy 28:49-52, NIV. "Then the Lord will scatter you among all nations, from one end of the earth to the other." Verse 64, NIV.

NOTE.—When Jesus stood on the Mount of Olives, weeping over Jerusalem with the sad lament "How often have I longed to gather your children together," He said, "Look, your house is left to you desolate." Matthew 23:37, 38. In A.D. 70, about 40 years later, the Roman armies besieged and destroyed Jerusalem under the Roman general Titus, son of the emperor Vespasian.

With what striking symbol was all this foretold?

"This is what the Lord says: 'Go and buy a clay jar from a potter.' " Jeremiah 19:1, NIV. "Then break the jar while those who go with you are watching, and say to them, 'This is what the Lord Almighty says: *I will smash this nation and this city just as this potter's jar is smashed and cannot be repaired.*' " Verses 10, 11, NIV.

What did Jesus say would happen to Jerusalem?

"They will fall by the sword and will be taken as prisoners to all the nations. *Jerusalem will be trampled on by the Gentiles until the times of the Gentiles are fulfilled.*" Luke 21:24, NIV.

What will terminate the "times" allotted to the Gentiles?

"And this gospel of the kingdom will be preached in the whole world as a testimony to all nations, and then the end will come." Matthew 24:14, NIV.

NOTE.—The gospel was first preached in Jerusalem and Judea, but in A.D. 34, beginning at the stoning of Stephen, the Christians were scattered, and went everywhere preaching the word (Acts 8:1, 4). Paul and Barnabas later said to the Jews at Antioch, "We had to speak the word of God to you first. Since you reject it and do not consider yourselves worthy of eternal life, we now turn to the Gentiles" Acts 13:46, NIV.

According to James, why was the gospel to be preached to the Gentiles?

"Simon has described to us how God at first showed his concern by taking from the Gentiles a people for himself. The words of the prophets are in agreement with this, as it is written: 'After this I will return and rebuild David's fallen tent. Its ruins I will rebuild, and I will restore it, that the remnant of men may seek the Lord, and all the Gentiles who bear my name, says the Lord, who does these things' that have been known for ages." Acts 15:14-18, NIV.

NOTE.—James is quoting Amos 9:11, 12.

What promise did God once make to Abraham?

"The promise *that he would be heir of the world.*" Romans 4:13, NIV.

Since this promise was never fulfilled to Abraham or his descendants, how will it be fulfilled?

"The promises were spoken to Abraham and to his seed. The Scripture does not say 'and to seeds,' meaning many people, but 'and to your seed,' meaning one person, who is Christ." Galatians 3:16, NIV.

Who are Abraham's seed?

"If you belong to Christ, then you are Abraham's seed, and heirs according to the promise." Verse 29, NIV.

"A man is not a Jew if he is only one outwardly. . . . No, a man is a Jew if he is one inwardly . . . by the Spirit, not by the written code. Such a man's praise is not from men, but from God." Romans 2:28, 29, NIV.

"For not all who are descended from Israel are Israel. Nor because they are his descendants are they all Abraham's children. . . . But it is the children of the promise who are regarded as Abraham's offspring." Romans 9:6-8, NIV.

NOTE.—Here is a key that unlocks, not merely one, but many otherwise mysterious passages of the Sacred Scriptures. The gathering of Israel to their own land is not a regathering of Abraham's literal descendants to Old Jerusalem, but a gathering in faith of the spiritual seed to the New Jerusalem, the city for which Abraham looked, "whose builder and maker is God." Hebrews 11:10. (See pp. 632, 633.)

When will the gathering finally come?

"Let both grow together until *the harvest*. At that time I will tell the harvesters: First collect the weeds and tie them in bundles to be burned; then *gather* the wheat and bring it into my barn." Matthew 13:30, NIV.

Who are the reapers?

"And he will send *his angels* with a loud trumpet call, and they will *gather* his elect from the four winds, from one end of the heavens to the other." Matthew 24:31, NIV.

When does this harvest take place?

"When the Son of Man comes in his glory, and all the angels with him, he will sit on his throne in heavenly glory. All the nations will be *gathered* before him, and he will separate the people one from another as a shepherd separates the sheep from the goats." Matthew 25:31, 32, NIV.

"Concerning the *coming of our Lord Jesus Christ* and our being *gathered* to him." 2 Thessalonians 2:1, NIV.

Who will inherit the earth?

"But *the meek* will inherit the land and enjoy great peace." Psalm 37:11, NIV. "Blessed are the meek, for they will inherit the earth." Matthew 5:5, NIV.

THE MILLENNIUM

What passage speaks of a millennium?

"I saw thrones on which were seated those who had been given *authority to judge*. And I saw the souls of those who had been beheaded because of their testimony for Jesus and because of the word of God. They had not worshiped the beast or his image and had not received his mark on their foreheads or their hands. *They came to life and reigned with Christ a thousand years*." Revelation 20:4, NIV.

NOTE.—Although only those who were beheaded are mentioned, it is clear that all of the redeemed are included (see Daniel 7:27; Revelation 15:2). Only a tiny fraction of Christians were beheaded; in New Testament times this penalty was reserved for Roman citizens, such as Paul. Note that these once-persecuted saints are given thrones to sit on, and so they become the judges of those who have judged and condemned them to death.

Whom does Paul say the saints are to judge?

"If any of you has a dispute with another, dare he take it before the ungodly for judgment instead of before the saints? *Do you not know that the saints will judge the world? . . . Do you not know that we will judge angels?*" 1 Corinthians 6:1-3, NIV.

What did Jesus tell His disciples would be their destiny?

"Jesus said to them, 'I tell you the truth, at the renewal of all things, when the Son of Man sits on his glorious throne, *you who have followed me will also sit on twelve thrones, judging the twelve tribes of Israel.*'" Matthew 19:28, NIV.

What role awaits those raised in the first resurrection?

"Blessed and holy are those who have part in the first resurrection. The second death has no power over them, but *they will be priests of God and of Christ and will reign with him for a thousand years*." Revelation 20:6, NIV.

What does Jesus have planned for the saved when He comes?

"And if I go and prepare a place for you, I will come back and take you to be with me that you also may be where I am." John 14:3, NIV.

NOTE.—In other words, Christ will take the saved to heaven, there to live and reign with Him during the 1,000 years.

Where did John, in vision, see the saved?

"After this I looked and there before me was a great multitude that no one could count, from every nation, tribe, people and language, *standing before the throne* and in front of the Lamb." Revelation 7:9, NIV.

NOTE.—This scripture shows plainly that Jesus will take the righteous to heaven immediately after the first resurrection, as He promised in John 14:1-3. Peter desired to accompany Jesus to those mansions; but Jesus answered, "Where I am going, you cannot follow now, but *you will follow later*." John 13:36, NIV. This makes it clear that when Jesus returns to earth to receive His people, He takes them to the Father's house in heaven.

What becomes of the living wicked when Christ comes?

"Just as it was in the days of Noah, so also will it be in the days of the Son of Man. People were eating, drinking, marrying and being given in marriage up to the day Noah entered the ark. Then the flood came and *destroyed them all.* It was the same in the days of Lot. . . . The day Lot left Sodom, fire and sulfur rained down from heaven and *destroyed them all.* It will be just like this on the day the Son of Man is revealed." Luke 17:26-30, NIV.

What does the apostle Paul say concerning this?

"While people are saying, 'Peace and safety,' *destruction will come on them suddenly, . . . and they will not escape*." 1 Thessalonians 5:3, NIV.

NOTE.—When Christ comes, the righteous will be delivered and taken to heaven, and all the living wicked will be suddenly destroyed, as they were at the Flood. (See also 2 Thessalonians 1:7-9; Revelation 6:14-17; 19:11-21; Jeremiah 25:30-33.) There will be no general resurrection of the wicked until the end of the 1,000 years. This will leave the earth desolate and without human inhabitants during this period.

How long is Satan to be imprisoned on this earth?

"And I saw an angel coming down out of heaven, having the key to the Abyss and holding in his hand a great chain. He seized the dragon, that ancient serpent, who is the devil, or Satan, and bound him for *a thousand years*. He threw him into the Abyss, and locked and sealed it over him, to keep him from deceiving the nations anymore until the thousand years were ended." Revelation 20:1-3, NIV.

NOTE.—Earth will be the dreary prison of Satan during this period. Satan will have opportunity to reflect upon the results of his rebellion against God.

The righteous dead are raised at Christ's second coming. When will the rest of the dead, the wicked, be raised?

"The rest of the dead did not come to life *until the thousand years were ended*." Verse 5, NIV.

NOTE.—From this we see that the beginning and the close of the millennium, or one thousand years, are marked by the two resurrections. The word "millennium" is from two Latin words, *mille*, meaning a thousand, and *annus*, year—a thousand years. Its beginning is marked by the close of probation, the pouring out of the seven last plagues, the second coming of Christ, the binding of Satan, the resurrection of the righteous dead, and their translation to heaven. It closes with the descent of the New Jerusalem from heaven to earth, the loosing of Satan from his prison, the resurrection of the wicked, and their final destruction in the lake of fire.

During the 1,000 years that the earth lies desolate, Satan and his angels are confined there; and the saints, with Christ, pass judgment on the wicked, which determines their allotted punishment (compare Luke 12:47, 48). At the end, when the wicked dead are raised and Satan is loosed, the wicked, under Satan's command, surround the Holy City with the saints inside and attempt to attack it, but God brings fire down from heaven that devours them (Revelation 20:7-10). This fire cleanses the earth, which is then renewed, and this new earth becomes the eternal home of the saints.

What happens to Satan at the close of the 1,000 years?

"After that, *he must be set free for a short time*." Verse 3, NIV.

NOTE.—At the close of the 1,000 years Christ, accompanied by the saints, comes to the earth again, to execute judgment upon the wicked, and to prepare the earth, by a re-creation, to be the eternal home of the righteous. At this time the wicked dead of all ages awake to life. This is the second resurrection, the resurrection unto damnation. The wicked come forth with the same rebellious spirit that possessed them in this life. Satan now has followers to work with, and hence he is released from his long period of captivity and inactivity.

As soon as the wicked are raised, what will Satan proceed to do?

"When the thousand years are over, Satan will be released from his prison and will go out to *deceive the nations* in the four corners of the earth—Gog and Magog—*to gather them for battle*. In number they are like the sand of the seashore." Verses 7, 8, NIV.

Against whom do the wicked go to make war, and what is the outcome?

"They marched across the breadth of the earth and surrounded *the camp of God's people, the city he loves. But fire came down from heaven and devoured them*." Verse 9, NIV.

NOTE.—This is the last act in the great controversy between Christ and Satan. The whole human race meet for the first and last time. The eternal separation of the righteous from the wicked occurs as God's judgment is executed upon the wicked in the lake of fire. This is the second death. This ends the great rebellion against God and His government. Now is heard the voice of God as He sits upon His throne, speaking to the saints, and saying, "I am making everything new!" Revelation 21:5, NIV. God creates "a new heaven and a new earth," (verse 1, NIV), in which the redeemed shall find an everlasting inheritance and dwelling place.

THE DAY OF THE LORD

What is the character of "the day of the Lord"?

"Alas for that day! For the day of the Lord is near; it will come *like destruction* from the Almighty." Joel 1:15, NIV.

"Blow the trumpet in Zion; sound the alarm on my holy hill. Let all who live in the land tremble, for the day of the Lord is coming. It is close at hand—a day of darkness and gloom, a day of clouds and blackness." Joel 2:1, 2, NIV.

"The day of the Lord is great; it is dreadful. Who can endure it?" Verse 11, NIV.

"The great and dreadful day of the Lord." Verse 31, NIV.

"That day will be a day of wrath, a day of distress and anguish, a day of trouble and ruin, a day of darkness and gloom, a day of clouds and blackness, a day of trumpet and battle cry against the fortified cities and against the corner towers." Zephaniah 1:15, 16. (See also Jeremiah 30:7; Isaiah 13:6-13.)

How solemn is the warning concerning "the day of the Lord"?

"Woe to you who long for the day of the Lord! Why do you long

for the day of the Lord? *That day will be darkness, not light."* Amos
5:18, NIV. (See also Joel 1:14, 15; 2:1; 3:14.)

What signs will indicate that "the day of the Lord" is near?

"I will show wonders in the heaven above and signs on the earth
below, blood and fire and billows of smoke. The *sun* will be *turned
to darkness* and the *moon* to *blood* before the coming of the great
glorious day of the Lord." Acts 2:19, 20, NIV.

NOTE.—Peter is quoting Joel 2:30, 31. (See also Isaiah 13:6, 10;
Joel 2:10, 11; 3:14-16; Zephaniah 1:14; Matthew 24:29; Revelation
6:12, 13.)

How do the people react to "the day of the Lord"?

"For the great day of their wrath has come, and *who can stand?"*
Revelation 6:17, NIV.

"The day of the Lord is great; it is dreadful. Who can endure it?"
Joel 2:11, NIV.

NOTE.—One class of people—the unprepared—cry out to the
mountains and rocks, "Fall on us and hide us from the face of him
who sits on the throne and from the wrath of the Lamb!" Revelation
6:16. (See also Zephaniah 1:14.) Another class of people—the prepared—in that day will say, "Surely this is our God; we trusted in
him, and he saved us. This is the Lord, we trusted in him; let us rejoice and be glad in his salvation." Isaiah 25:9, NIV.

To whom should we turn for help in "the day of the Lord"?

"Seek the *Lord,* all you humble of the land, you who do what he
commands. Seek righteousness, seek humility; perhaps you will be
sheltered on the day of the Lord's anger." Zephaniah 2:3, NIV.

"Trust in the Lord forever, for the Lord, the Lord, is the Rock eternal." Isaiah 26:4, NIV. (See also Joel 2:12, 13, 32; 3:16, 17; Isaiah
26:20.)

What is God's personal appeal to us?

"Since everything will be destroyed in this way, what kind of people ought you to be? You ought to live holy and godly lives as you
look forward to the day of God and speed its coming. That day will
bring about the destruction of the heavens by fire, and the elements
will melt in the heat. But in keeping with his promise we are looking
forward to a new heaven and a new earth, the home of righteousness.
So then, dear friends, since you are looking forward to this, *make
every effort to be found spotless, blameless and at peace with him."*
2 Peter 3:11-14, NIV.

ELIJAH THE PROPHET

What does God promise concerning Elijah?

"See, I will send you the prophet Elijah before that great and dreadful day of the Lord comes. *He will turn the hearts of the fathers to their children, and the hearts of the children to their fathers.*" Malachi 4:5, 6, NIV.

Whom did Christ indicate as fulfilling this prophecy?

"Jesus replied, 'To be sure, Elijah comes and will restore all things. But I tell you, *Elijah has already come*, and they did not recognize him, but have done to him everything they wished. In the same way the Son of Man is going to suffer at their hands.' Then the disciples understood that he was talking to them about *John the Baptist.*" Matthew 17:11-13, NIV.

When John the Baptist was asked if he were Elijah, what did he say?

"He said, *'I am not.'*" John 1:21, NIV. "John replied in the words of Isaiah the prophet, *'I am the voice of one calling in the desert*, "Make straight the way for the Lord."'" Verse 23, NIV.

In what sense was John the Baptist Elijah?

"Many of the people of Israel will he bring back to the Lord their God. And he will go on before the Lord, *in the spirit and power of Elijah*, to turn the hearts of the fathers to their children and the disobedient to the wisdom of the righteous—to make ready a people prepared for the Lord." Luke 1:16, 17, NIV.

NOTE.—John went forth "in the spirit and power of Elijah," and, in preparing a people for Christ's first coming, did a work similar to that done by Elijah the prophet in Israel centuries before (see 1 Kings 17 and 18). In this sense he was the Elijah of Malachi 4:5.

How did the ancient prophet Elijah answer the accusation that he was a troublemaker?

"Ahab went to meet Elijah. When he saw Elijah, he said to him, 'Is that you, troubler of Israel?'

" '*I have not made trouble for Israel,*' Elijah replied. '*But you and your father's family have. You have abandoned the Lord's commands and have followed the Baals.*'" 1 Kings 18:16-18, NIV.

NOTE.—Israel had forsaken God and gone off into idolatry. Jezebel, Ahab's wicked and idolatrous wife, who supported the prophets of Baal, had killed the Lord's prophets (verse 4), and was seeking to slay Elijah. So Elijah had called for a famine on the land, and said to Ahab, "As the Lord, the God of Israel, lives, whom I serve, there will be neither dew nor rain in the next few years except at my word." 1 Kings 17:1, NIV. This was why he was considered a troublemaker. However, he was simply bearing God's message of rebuke. Elijah's message, like that of John the Baptist, was a call to repentance and obedience to God's commandments.

With what mandate did Elijah confront Israel?

"Elijah went before the people and said, 'How long will you waver between two opinions? *If the Lord is God, follow him; but if Baal is God, follow him.*'" 1 Kings 18:21, NIV.

NOTE.—As a result of the test by fire that followed on Mount Carmel (read the remainder of this chapter), there was a great turning to God, the people saying, "The Lord—he is God." Verse 39, NIV.

What was the burden of the message of John the Baptist?

"Repent, for the kingdom of heaven is near." Matthew 3:2, NIV. *"Produce fruit* in keeping with repentance." Verse 8, NIV.

What was the result of this message?

"People went out to him from Jerusalem and all Judea and the whole region of the Jordan. Confessing their sins, *they were baptized by him* in the Jordan river." Verses 5, 6, NIV.

NOTE.—There was a genuine work of repentance and reform. John was not satisfied with a mere profession of religion. He told the Pharisees and Sadducees who came to his baptism: "Produce fruit in keeping with repentance." He wished to see religion in the life, the heart, the home. Thus he prepared a people for Christ's first coming. And those who heeded his message submitted to the rite of baptism as a sign of their faith.

When did the prophecy say Elijah was to come?

"See, I will send you the prophet Elijah before that great and dreadful day of the Lord comes." Malachi 4:5, NIV.

How is this day described?

" 'Surely the day is coming; it will burn like a furnace. All the arrogant and every evildoer will be stubble, and that day that is coming will set them on fire,' says the Lord Almighty. 'Not a root or a branch will be left to them.' " Verse 1, NIV.

NOTE.—This "great and dreadful day of the Lord" is yet future. Therefore, the work done by John the Baptist at Christ's first advent cannot be all that was contemplated in the prophecy concerning the sending of Elijah the prophet. There must be another and greater fulfillment of it, to precede Christ's second advent, and to prepare, or "make ready," a people for that great event.

What is the threefold message of Revelation 14:6-10?

" 'Fear God and give him glory, because *the hour of his judgment has come*. Worship him who made the heavens, the earth, the sea and the springs of water.' . . . *'Fallen! Fallen is Babylon the Great, which made all the nations drink the maddening wine of her adulteries.'* . . . *'If anyone worships the beast and his image and receives his mark on the forehead or on the hand*, he, too, will drink of the wine of God's fury, which has been poured full strength into the cup of his wrath." Revelation 14:7-10, NIV.

NOTE.—Like the messages of Elijah and John the Baptist, this is a call to repentance and reform—to forsake false, idolatrous worship, and to turn to God, and worship Him alone. The first part of this threefold message describes God in language that echoes the fourth commandment, which calls us to remember the seventh-day Sabbath. This message, now due, is today being proclaimed throughout the world (see pp. 212-226.) Those who proclaim these messages constitute the Elijah for this time, as John the Baptist did at the time of Christ's first coming.

What is the result of this threefold message?

"Here is a call for the endurance of the saints, those who keep the commandments of God and hold fast to the faith of Jesus." Verse 12, NRSV.

NOTE.—This message produces a people who will be ready to meet Jesus when He comes because they have heeded the call of last-day Elijah to repentance and reform. They have become concerned, not only for their own salvation, but for the conversion of their friends and relatives. By this message the hearts of the fathers are turned to the children, and the hearts of the children to their fathers, each burdened for the conversion and salvation of the other. True spirituality cannot exist in the heart of one who does not care for the eternal interests of loved ones. When this message has done its work, God will usher in the great day of the Lord.

CHAPTER 8

The Law of God

THE LAW OF GOD

How did God proclaim His law to the Israelites?

"Then the Lord spoke to you out of the fire. . . . He declared to you his covenant, the Ten Commandments, which he commanded you to follow and then *wrote them on two stone tablets*." Deuteronomy 4:12, 13, NIV. (See also Nehemiah 9:13, 14; for the Ten Commandments, see Exodus 20:2-17.)

What is the nature of God's law?

"So then, the law is holy, and the commandment is *holy, righteous, and good*. . . . We know that the law is spiritual; but I am unspiritual, sold as a slave to sin." Romans 7:12-14, NIV.

NOTE.—In His comments on the sixth and seventh commandments (Matthew 5:21-28) Christ demonstrated the spiritual nature of the law, showing that it relates not merely to outward actions, but also to the thoughts and intents of the heart. (See Hebrews 4:12.) The tenth commandment forbids all unlawful desire (Romans 7:7). Obedience to this law, therefore, requires not merely an outward compliance but genuine heart service. This can be rendered only by a regenerated soul. "The law of the Lord is perfect, reviving the soul." Psalm 19:7, NIV.

How comprehensive are these commandments?

"Fear God and keep his commandments; for *this is the whole duty of man*." Ecclesiastes 12:13, NIV.

NOTE.—Notice that the commandments are carefully arranged in a certain sequence, which gives us a set of priorities. We find in the commandments a hierarchy of values: God is first (first through fourth commandments); family is next (fifth and seventh commandments); then others (sixth and ninth commandments); and last of all come material things (eighth and tenth commandments).

What inspired tribute does Psalms pay to the law of God?

"*The law of the Lord is perfect*, reviving the soul. The statutes of the Lord are trustworthy, making wise the simple. The precepts of the Lord are right, giving joy to the heart." Psalm 19:7, 8, NIV.

NOTE.—"Its *perfection* is a proof of its divinity. No human lawgiver could have given forth such a law as that which we find in the decalogue. It is a perfect law; for all human laws that are right are to be found in that brief compendium and epitome of all that is good and excellent toward God, or between man and man." Charles H. Spurgeon, *Sermons*, series 2 (1857), p. 280.

How does James describe the law?

"But those who look into *the perfect law, the law of liberty*, and persevere, being not hearers who forget but doers who act—they will be blessed in their doing." James 1:25, NIV.

NOTE.—Liberty is possible only because of law. The law of gravity, for example, is rather confining. It doesn't allow us to fly without help, and many who run afoul of it die. What a harsh law! But take away gravity, and we couldn't drive a car down the highway. We would all go floating off into space. The earth's atmosphere would disappear, and we would suffocate. The law of gravity gives us freedom.

Who hasn't heard an orchestra tuning up before a concert? The members are doing their own thing. That pandemonium is the sound of lawlessness. But when the orchestra submits itself to the absolute rule of the director, something wonderful begins to happen. Obedience to the laws of music and the direction of the conductor creates beauty. Without law, the orchestra has a sort of freedom—the freedom of chaos and anarchy—but it is not free to produce symphonies. When we surrender our lives to God's rule, He makes music out of us.

The law brings liberty. Those who keep the law are kept by the law from the slavery of sin and addiction, for "a man is a slave to whatever has mastered him." 2 Peter 2:19, NIV.

Does the law enslave us or liberate us?

"I will walk about in freedom, for I have sought out your precepts." Psalm 119:45, NIV.

NOTE.—God's law is like an owner's manual for a new car. With all its do's and don'ts, the manual tells how to keep the car in tip-top condition. If rightly used, the manual will prolong the life of the car and increase the freedom of the driver. It would be highly irresponsible to discard the manual and rejoice in our freedom from "all those nitpicking rules and regulations"! If we want to drive in security and avoid breakdown, we must follow the manual.

What is the essential principle of the law of God?

"Let no debt remain outstanding, except the continuing debt to love one another, for he who loves his fellowman has fulfilled the law. The commandments, 'Do not commit adultery,' 'Do not murder,'

'Do not steal,' 'Do not covet,' and whatever other commandment there may be, are summed up in this one rule: 'Love your neighbor as yourself.' Love does no harm to its neighbor. Therefore *love* is the fulfillment of the law." Romans 13:8-10, NIV.

NOTE.—Does this mean that as long as we have love, we can break the commandments as we please? Of course not. It means that as long as we are motivated by love, we will naturally fulfill the law. Love is not a substitute for obedience; it is the source of obedience.

"It is a basic tenet of nineteenth-century theological liberalism that in Christianity the law was completely superseded by love. Whatever else may be said of this view, it is not one that squares with the New Testament data." Gerard S. Sloyan, *Is Christ the End of the Law?* (Philadelphia: Westminster Press, 1978), p. 56. Love results in obedience; it does not replace it.

What two commandments sum up the law of God?

"Jesus replied: 'Love the Lord your God with all your heart and with all your soul and with all your mind.' This is the first and greatest commandment. And the second is like it: 'Love your neighbor as yourself.' All the Law and the Prophets hang on these two commandments." Matthew 22:37-40, NIV.

NOTE.—Those who love God with all their heart will keep the first table of the law (first through fourth commandments); those who love their neighbor as themselves will keep the second (fifth through tenth commandments). The love commandment—"Love the Lord with all your heart, and your neighbor as yourself "—is a shorthand summary of the law. If we were unfallen beings, we would need only one commandment: "Always love." But since our minds are darkened by sin, God had to spell out what love means by breaking it down into 10 separate commands.

What is revealed in God's law?

"If you know *his [God's] will* and approve of what is superior because you are instructed by the law." Romans 2:18, NIV.

Why should we fear God and keep His commandments?

"Fear God and keep his commandments, for this is the whole duty of man. *For God will bring every deed into judgment*, including every hidden thing, whether it is good or evil." Ecclesiastes 12:13, 14, NIV.

What will be the standard in the judgment?

"So speak and so act as those who are to be *judged by the law of liberty*." James 2:12, NRSV.

NOTE.—This is James's expression for the Ten Commandments (compare verse 11).

How many of the commandments is it necessary to break in order to be a transgressor of the law?

"For whoever keeps the whole law but fails in one point has become accountable for all of it. For the one who said, 'You shall not commit adultery,' also said, 'You shall not murder.' Now if you do not commit adultery but if you murder, you have become a transgressor of the law." James 2:10, 11, NIV.

NOTE.—"The ten commandments are not ten different laws; they are one law. If I am being held up in the air by a chain with ten links and I break one of them, down I come, just as surely as if I break the whole ten. If I am forbidden to go out of an enclosure, it makes no difference at what point I break through." Dwight L. Moody, *Weighed and Wanting* (1898), p. 119. "The ten words of Sinai were not ten separate commandments," said G. Campbell Morgan, "but ten sides of the one law of God."—*The Ten Commandments* (Revell, 1901), p. 11. "As he [a Methodist] loves God, so he keeps his commandments; not only some, or most of them, but all, from the least to the greatest. He is not content to 'keep the whole law, and offend in one point'; but has, in all points, 'a conscience void of offence towards God and towards man.' " John Wesley, "The Character of a Methodist," in *Works* (1830), vol. 8, p. 344.

How is sin defined by the law?

"Everyone who commits sin is guilty of lawlessness; *sin is lawlessness.*" 1 John 3:4, NIV.

How do we come to a knowledge of sin?

"Therefore no one will be declared righteous in his sight by observing the law; rather, *through the law* we become conscious of sin." Romans 3:20, NIV. (See Romans 7:7.)

For what did Christ reprove the Pharisees?

"Jesus replied, 'And why do you break the command of God for the sake of your tradition? For God said, "Honor your father and mother" and "Anyone who curses his father or mother must be put to death." But you say that if a man says to his father or mother, "Whatever help you might otherwise have received from me is a gift devoted to God," he is not to "honor his father" with it. Thus you nullify the word of God for the sake of your tradition.' " Matthew 15:3-6, NIV.

NOTE.—Tradition is not necessarily bad as long as it does not contradict Scripture. Some traditions are good (2 Thessalonians 2:15; 3:6). But Jesus here condemns any human tradition that conflicts with God's law. The specific Jewish tradition He mentions here was one that, in effect, released children from the obligation to support their aged parents financially if they donated their money to the Temple. The children were then free to use the money as long as they lived, but since it was pledged to the Temple at their death, they could not spend it on needy parents. It was "holy money." This apparent act of piety had a selfish motive, and amounted to setting aside the fifth commandment.

Consequently, how did Christ value their worship?

"You hypocrites! Isaiah was right when he prophesied about you: 'These people honor me with their lips, but their hearts are far from me. *They worship me in vain*; their teachings are but rules taught by men.' " Matthew 15:9, NIV.

NOTE.—Jesus is here quoting Isaiah 29:13, a condemnation of the ancient people of Jerusalem.

Can one know God and not keep His commandments?

"We know that we have come to know him if we obey his commands. The man who says, 'I know him,' but does not do what he commands is a liar, and the truth is not in him. But if anyone obeys his word, God's love is truly made complete in him. This is how we know we are in him: *Whoever claims to live in him must walk as Jesus did*." 1 John 2:4-6, NIV.

What was Christ's attitude toward God's will as expressed in His law?

"Then I said, 'Here I am, I have come—it is written about me in the scroll. I *desire to do your will, O my God; your law is within my heart*.' " Psalm 40:7, 8. (See how the book of Hebrews uses this text in Hebrews 10:5, 7, NIV.)

Who did Jesus say would enter the kingdom of heaven?

"Not everyone who says to me, 'Lord, Lord,' will enter the kingdom of heaven, but only *he who does the will of my Father* who is in heaven." Matthew 7:21, NIV.

How will we be rated in relation to God's commandments?

"Anyone who breaks one of the least of these commandments and teaches others to do the same will be called least in the kingdom of heaven, but *whoever practices and teaches these commands will be called great in the kingdom of heaven*." Matthew 5:19, NIV.

What did Christ say was a condition of entering into life?

"If you want to enter life, obey the commandments." Matthew 19:17, NIV.

How does Paul contrast a mind controlled by the Spirit with a mind controlled by the sinful nature?

"The mind of sinful man is death, but the mind controlled by the Spirit is life and peace; the sinful mind is hostile to God. It does not submit to God's law, nor can it do so. Those controlled by the sinful nature cannot please God." Romans 8:6-8, NIV.

Can we keep the law in our own strength, without Christ?

"I am the vine; you are the branches. If a man remains in me and I in him, he will bear much fruit; *apart from me you can do nothing*." John 15:5, NIV. (See Romans 7:14-19.)

What provision has been made to enable us to keep God's law?

"For what the law was powerless to do in that it was weakened by the sinful nature, *God did by sending his own Son in the likeness of sinful man to be a sin offering*. And so he condemned sin in sinful man, *in order that the righteous requirements of the law might be fully met in us*, who do not live according to the sinful nature but according to the Spirit." Romans 8:3, 4, NIV.

How does the renewed heart regard God's law?

"This is love for God: to obey his commands. And *his commands are not burdensome*, for everyone born of God overcomes the world." 1 John 5:3, 4, NIV.

How does God regard those who walk in His law?

"*Blessed* are they whose ways are blameless, who walk according to the law of the Lord." Psalm 119:1, NIV.

How are those who keep God's commandments blessed?

"The fear of the Lord is pure, enduring forever. The ordinances of the Lord are sure and altogether righteous. They are more precious than gold, than much pure gold; they are sweeter than honey, than honey from the comb. By them is your servant warned; *in keeping them there is great reward*." Psalm 19:9-11, NIV.

What gift comes to those who love God's law?

"Great peace have they who love your law, and nothing can make them stumble." Psalm 119:165, NIV.

How would God have blessed the ancient Israelites if they'd kept His commandments?

"If only you had paid attention to my commands, *your peace would have been like a river, your righteousness like the waves of the sea*." Isaiah 48:18, NIV.

What other blessing attends commandment keeping?

"The fear of the Lord is the beginning of *wisdom*; all who follow his precepts have good *understanding*." Psalm 111:10, NIV.

In what does a blessed person delight?

"Blessed is the man who does not walk in the counsel of the wicked or stand in the way of sinners or sit in the seat of mockers. But *his delight is in the law of the Lord, and on his law he meditates day and night*." Psalm 1:1, 2, NIV. (See Romans 7:22.)

NOTE.—"Divine mercy . . . makes conformity to Divine will, and obedience to Divine commands, if sometimes difficult, at least at all times delightful, and engraves, on the living tablets of human hearts now, the Law written long ago by the finger of God on tables of stone." John Burr, *Studies on the Ten Commandments* (1935), pp. 8, 9.

THE LAW'S CONTINUING OBLIGATION

How many lawgivers are there?

"There is only *one Lawgiver* and Judge, the one who is able to save and destroy." James 4:12, NIV.

How does God describe the stability of His character?

"I the Lord *do not change*." Malachi 3:6, NIV.

How enduring are His commandments?

"The works of his hands are faithful and just; all his precepts are trustworthy. *They are steadfast for ever and ever*, done in faithfulness and uprightness." Psalm 111:7, 8, NIV.

Did Christ come to abolish or to destroy the law?

"Do not think that I have come to abolish the Law or the Prophets; I have not come to abolish them but to fulfill them. I tell you the truth, until heaven and earth disappear, not the smallest letter, nor the least stroke of a pen, will by any means disappear from the Law until everything is accomplished." Matthew 5:17, 18, NIV.

What does "fulfill" mean in this verse?

"But John tried to deter him, saying, 'I need to be baptized by you, and do you come to me?' Jesus replied, 'Let it be so now; it is proper for us to do this to fulfill all righteousness.' Then John consented." Matthew 3:14, 15, NIV.

NOTE.—To "fulfill" prophecy is to accomplish, to bring to pass, as in Matthew 4:14, "to fulfill what was said through the prophet Isaiah" (NIV). To "fulfill" the law is to carry it out, keep it, act in accordance with it; as in Galatians 6:2, "Carry each other's burdens, and in this way you will fulfill the law of Christ." In Matthew 3:15 Jesus urges John to baptize Him "to *fulfill* all righteousness," i.e., to carry out righteousness. This does not, of course, mean to abolish righteousness. Jesus fulfilled the law, He kept it, and carried out its demands; He did not abolish it.

How did Christ treat His Father's commandments?

"I have *obeyed* my Father's commands and remain in his love." John 15:10, NIV.

If we profess to abide in Christ, how ought we to walk?

"Whoever claims to live in him must walk *as Jesus did.*" 1 John 2:6, NIV.

What is sin?

"Everyone who sins breaks the law; in fact, *sin is lawlessness.*" 1 John 3:4, NIV.

NOTE.—If sin is defined as lawlessness, then the law is still in force in the gospel dispensation. The text does not say "sin *was* lawlessness."

In what condition are we all?

"For *all have sinned* and fall short of the glory of God." Romans 3:23, NIV.

"We have already made the charge that *Jews and Gentiles* alike *are all under sin.*" Verse 9, NIV.

What proves us all guilty?

"Now we know that *whatever the law says*, it says to those who are under the law, so that every mouth may be silenced and the whole world held accountable to God." Verse 19, NIV.

Does faith in God make void the law?

"Do we, then, nullify the law by this faith? *Not at all! Rather, we uphold the law.*" Verse 31, NIV.

How does the death of Christ prove the perpetuity and immutability of the law of God?

"For God so loved the world that he gave his only Son, so that everyone who believes in him may not perish but may have eternal life." John 3:16, NRSV. "Christ died for our sins." 1 Corinthians 15:3.

NOTE.—If sin could have been dealt with by doing away with the law, then Christ would not have needed to come and die for our sins. The gift of Christ, therefore, more than all else, proves the immutability of the law of God. Christ must come and die, and satisfy the claims of the law, or the world must perish. The law could not give way. The fact that the law is to be the standard in the judgment is another proof of its enduring nature. (See Ecclesiastes 12:13, 14; James 2:8-12.)

What attitude toward the law brings us blessing?

"But the man who looks intently into the perfect law that gives freedom, and continues to do this, *not forgetting what he has heard, but doing it*—he will be blessed in what he does." James 1:25, NIV.

How may we know that we have passed from death to life?

"We know that we have passed from death to life, *because we love our brothers.* Anyone who does not love remains in death." 1 John 3:14, NIV.

And how may we know that we love the brethren?

"This is how we know that we love the children of God: *by loving God and carrying out his commands.*" 1 John 5:2, NIV.

NOTE.—Our efforts to obey God's law are never the cause or basis of our salvation, but the result of it. Holy living is the fruit and not the root of salvation. But our behavior is the test of whether we truly believe. Only those who love their brothers and sisters in Christ—even the unlovable ones—are truly converted.

What is the love of God?

"This is love for God: *to obey his commands.*" Verse 3, NIV.

How does the book of Revelation describe those who will prepare for the coming of Christ?

"Here is a call for the endurance of the saints, those who keep the commandments of God and hold fast to the faith of Jesus." Revelation 14:12, NRSV.

THE LAW GIVEN AT SINAI

How does Nehemiah describe the giving of the law at Sinai?

"You came down on Mount Sinai; you spoke to them from heaven. *You gave them regulations and laws that are just and right, and decrees and commands that are good.* You made known to them your holy Sabbath and gave them commands, decrees and laws through your servant Moses." Nehemiah 9:13, 14, NIV.

What advantage did the Jews possess?

"What advantage, then, is there in being a Jew . . . ? Much in every way! First of all, *they have been entrusted with the very words of God.*" Romans 3:1, 2, NIV.

NOTE.—God honored Israel by making them the guardians and keepers of His law, to be held by them as a sacred trust for the whole world. God's law brings moral and intellectual vigor to those who honor it, and these effects continue for generations.

"The Jewish ethic, which was the foundation of the Christian ethic, was itself founded on the Ten Commandments. But these commandments might well be called the universal foundation, not only of Jewish ethics, but of all ethics. They contain the basic laws of human conduct in society, laws which are not so much particularly and exclusively Jewish, but which are the starting point of life for all men who have agreed to live together in any community." William Barclay, *The Ten Commandments for Today* (New York: Harper & Row, 1973), p. 11.

Before receiving the law at Sinai, how did Moses judge?

"Whenever they have a dispute, it is brought to me, and I decide between the parties and inform them of *God's decrees and laws.*" Exodus 18:16, NIV.

Before He gave the law at Sinai, how did God rebuke the people for going out to gather manna on the seventh day?

"Then the Lord said to Moses, 'How long will you refuse to keep my commands and my instructions?' " Exodus 16:28, NIV.

Had the Lord previously spoken of the Sabbath?

"He said to them, 'This is what the Lord commanded: "Tomorrow is to be a day of rest, a holy Sabbath to the Lord." ' " Verse 23, NIV.

NOTE.—It is therefore evident that the Sabbath and the law of God existed before the law was given at Sinai. That is why the fourth commandment begins by telling us to "remember" the Sabbath.

Was sin in the world before the law was given on Mount Sinai?

"For before the law was given, sin was in the world. But sin is not taken into account when there is no law." Romans 5:13, NIV.

How does this prove that the law existed in Eden?

"Through the disobedience of the one man the many were made sinners." Romans 5:19, NIV. "And where there is no law there is no transgression." Romans 4:15, NIV. "Everyone who sins breaks the law; in fact, sin is lawlessness." 1 John 3:4, NIV.

NOTE.—The fact that sin was imputed before the law was given at Sinai proves that the law existed before that event. If there had been no law prior to Sinai, then there could have been no sinners prior to Sinai, since sin is the transgression of the law.

"God gave to Adam a law, as a covenant of works, by which he bound him and all his posterity to personal, entire, exact, and perpetual obedience; promised life upon the fulfilling, and threatened death upon the breach of it; and endued him with power and ability to keep it. This law, after his fall, continued to be a perfect rule of righteousness; and, as such, was delivered by God upon mount Sinai in ten commandments, and written in two tables; the first four commandments containing our duty towards God, and the other six our duty to man." Westminster Confession of Faith, chap. 19, in Philip Schaff, *The Creeds of Christendom* (Scribner's), vol. 3, p. 640.

How was the law reaffirmed at Sinai?

"And God spoke all these words: . . . 'You shall have no other gods before me.'" Exodus 20:1-3, NIV.

How did God present the law to Israel in permanent form?

"When the Lord finished speaking to Moses on Mount Sinai, he gave him the two tablets of the Testimony, the tablets of stone inscribed by the finger of God." Exodus 31:18, NIV.

NOTE.—The law of God, as well as the knowledge of creation, the plan of redemption, and the experiences of the early patriarchs, had been handed down from father to son until this time, but not in written form. God wrote the Ten Commandments upon two tables of stone with His own finger.

What did Moses do when he discovered that the children of Israel had broken their covenant with God?

"When Moses approached the camp and saw the calf and the dancing, his anger burned and *he threw the tablets out of his hands, breaking them to pieces* at the foot of the mountain." Exodus 32:19, NIV.

How did God reproduce the tables of the law to replace the broken ones?

"The Lord wrote on these tablets what he had written before, the Ten Commandments he had proclaimed to you on the mountain, out of the fire, on the day of the assembly. And the Lord gave them to me." Deuteronomy 10:4, NIV.

Where did Moses place these two tables of stone?

"Then I came back down the mountain and *put the tablets in the ark* I had made, as the Lord commanded me." Verse 5, NIV.

NOTE.—The law was placed in the ark of the tabernacle in the Holy of Holies. Above the ark, in which rested the law, the presence of God was manifested in the glory of the Shekinah. Thus the Lord would teach Israel the sacredness of those immutable principles that are the foundation of His government. The purpose of making known this law was twofold: First, the law was to govern in the lives of God's people. "But those who look into the perfect law, the law of liberty, and persevere, being not hearers who forget but doers who act—they will be blessed in their doing." James 1:25, NRSV. Israel covenanted to be obedient to this law. Second, "through the law comes the knowledge of sin." Romans 3:20, NRSV. It was above the law and on the mercy seat of the ark that the high priest sprinkled the blood of atonement, once in the year. "The wages of sin is death" (Romans 6:23), and the blood of the victim was typical of the blood of Christ, shed in satisfaction of the holy law.

What other law was given at this time?

"Moses finished writing in a book the words of this law from beginning to end." Deuteronomy 31:24, NIV.

NOTE.—Besides the ten-commandment law, God gave Moses instruction concerning the sanctuary service, which was ceremonial, and certain civil laws regulating the subjects of the nation. Moses wrote these laws in a book, called the law of Moses, whereas the other law was written on tables of stone with the finger of God. For a further study of these laws, see pp. 323-327.)

Why did the Lord take His people out of Egypt?

"He brought out his people with rejoicing, his chosen ones with shouts of joy; he gave them the lands of the nations, and they fell heir to what others had toiled for—*that they might keep his precepts and observe his laws.*" Psalm 105:43-45, NIV.

How were they to teach the law to their children?

"Recite them to your children and talk about them when you are at home and when you are away, when you lie down and when you rise. Bind them as a sign on your hand, fix them as an emblem on your forehead, and write them on the doorposts of your house and on your gates." Deuteronomy 6:7-9, NRSV.

NOTE.—Here is the origin of the symbol of a mark on the hand or the forehead. God's law was to be stamped on their mind, shaping their belief, and on their hand, shaping their practice. This was to be accomplished by daily diligence in teaching their children the precepts of God.

What promise to Israel hinged on keeping the law?

"Now if you obey me fully and keep my covenant, then *out of all nations you will be my treasured possession.* Although the whole earth is mine, you will be for me a kingdom of priests and a holy nation." Exodus 19:5, 6, NIV.

Was this promise made to the Israelites alone?

"The Lord had said to Abram, 'Leave your country, your people and your father's household and go to the land I will show you. I will make you into a great nation and I will bless you; I will make your name great, and you will be a blessing. I will bless those who bless you, and whoever curses you I will curse; and *all peoples on earth will be blessed through you.*' " Genesis 12:1-3, NIV. "If you belong to Christ, then you are Abraham's seed, and heirs according to the promise." Galatians 3:29, NIV.

NOTE.—These texts show that God did not make one provision of grace and one law for the Jew and another means of salvation and another law for the Gentile; but the plan was that through Abraham's seed all the families of the earth should be recipients of divine grace and should receive the blessing through obedience.

What shows that the ten-commandment law, spoken and written at Mount Sinai, is the Christian law?

"For whoever keeps the whole law and yet stumbles at just one point is guilty of breaking all of it. *For he who said, 'Do not commit adultery,' also said, 'Do not murder.'* If you do not commit adultery but do commit murder, you have become a lawbreaker. Speak and act as those who are going to be judged by *the law that gives freedom*." James 2:10-12, NIV.

NOTE.—James, years after the Christian Era began, emphasizes the obligation of the Christian to keep the law of ten commandments, not merely one precept, but all, and sets forth this law as the standard by which men will be judged in the great day of God. To us, as Christians, God has committed the blessed law in writing, as He did to ancient Israel. This law points out sin to us, that we may confess it and find forgiveness. The Decalogue also becomes to us the law of life, and we find the blessings for those who live in harmony with its holy precepts. Hence James calls this law the "law that gives freedom," or "the law of liberty" (NRSV).

THE PENALTY FOR TRANSGRESSION

What is the wages of sin?

"The wages of sin is *death*." Romans 6:23. "When you eat of it you will surely die." Genesis 2:17, NIV. "The soul who sins is the one who will die." Ezekiel 18:4, NIV.

How did death enter the world?

"Therefore, just as sin entered the world through one man, and *death through sin*, and in this way death came to all men, because all sinned." Romans 5:12, NIV.

God is merciful, but does this clear the guilty?

"The Lord is slow to anger, abounding in love and forgiving sin and rebellion. *Yet he does not leave the guilty unpunished*." Numbers 14:18, NIV. (See also Exodus 34:5-7.)

What is the result of willful sin?

"If we deliberately keep on sinning after we have received the knowledge of the truth, *no sacrifice for sins is left, but only a fearful expectation of judgment and of raging fire that will consume the enemies of God*. Anyone who rejected the law of Moses died without mercy on the testimony of two or three witnesses. How much more severely do you think a man deserves to be punished who has trampled the Son of God under foot, who has treated as an unholy thing the blood of the covenant that sanctified him, and who has insulted the Spirit of grace?" Hebrews 10:26-29, NIV.

NOTE.—The verb is in the present continuous tense, hence the

NIV translates, "If we deliberately keep on sinning." This passage does not mean that a single fall into sin after baptism is fatal. It means that we cannot choose to continue in willful sin and presume to be covered by the atonement.

What presumptuous course do many pursue?

"When the sentence for a crime is not quickly carried out, *the hearts of the people are filled with schemes to do wrong.*" Ecclesiastes 8:11, NIV.

What warning message does God send to His children?

"Tell the righteous *it will be well with them*, for they will enjoy the fruit of their deeds. *Woe to the wicked! Disaster is upon them!* They will be paid back for what their hands have done." Isaiah 3:10, 11, NIV.

How can we escape the penalty for sin?

"For the wages of sin is death, but *the gift of God is eternal life in Christ Jesus our Lord.*" Romans 6:23, NIV.

NOTE.—"God threatens to punish all who transgress these commandments: we should, therefore, fear His anger, and do nothing against such commandments. But He promises grace and every blessing to all who keep them: we should, therefore, love and trust in Him, and gladly obey His commandments." *Luther's Small Catechism*, in Philip Schaff, *The Creeds of Christendom* (Scribner's), vol. 3, p. 77.

"Through the atonement of Christ more honor is done to the law, and consequently the law is more established, than if the law had been literally executed, and all mankind had been condemned." Jonathan Edwards, *Works* (1842), vol. 2, p. 369.

To whom is the gift of eternal life given?

"For God so loved the *world* that he gave his one and only Son, that whoever believes in him shall not perish but have eternal life." John 3:16, NIV.

How is the gift received?

"Whoever *believes* in him is not condemned, but whoever does not believe stands condemned already because he has not believed in the name of God's one and only Son." John 3:18, NIV. "Yet to all who received him, to those who *believed* in his name, he gave the right to become children of God." John 1:12, NIV.

THE LAW OF GOD IN THE NEW TESTAMENT

What did Jesus say of His attitude toward the law?

"Do not think that I have come to abolish the Law or the Prophets; *I have not come to abolish them but to fulfill them.*" Matthew 5:17, NIV.

NOTE.—Christ fulfilled both the law and the prophets. The ceremonial types and shadows contained in the books of Moses He fulfilled as their great antitype. The moral law, the basic fabric underlying all Moses' writings, Christ fulfilled by perfect obedience. The prophets He fulfilled in His advent as the foretold Messiah, Prophet, Teacher, and Savior.

What did Jesus teach concerning the stability of the law?

"I tell you the truth, until heaven and earth disappear, not the smallest letter, not the least stroke of a pen, *will by any means disappear from the Law* until everything is accomplished." Verse 18, NIV.

NOTE.—The New Testament assumes the perpetuity of the moral law. The third commandment provides a good test case. Taking the Lord's name in vain always has been and always will be wrong. Yet the commandment against taking the Lord's name in vain *is not repeated anywhere in the New Testament.* It is taken for granted. God's standard of righteousness does not change from age to age. God says, "I am the Lord; I change not."

How did Jesus stress the importance of keeping the law?

"Anyone who breaks one of the least of these commandments and teaches others to do the same will be called least in the kingdom of heaven, but whoever practices and teaches these commands will be called great in the kingdom of heaven." Verse 19, NIV.

NOTE.—"Our King has not come to abrogate the law, but to confirm and reassert it. His commands are eternal; and if any of the teachers of it should through error break His law, and teach that its least command is nullified, they will lose rank, and subside into the lowest place. The peerage of His kingdom is ordered according to obedience. . . . The Lord Jesus does not set up a milder law, nor will He allow any one of His servants to presume to do so. Our King fulfills the ancient law, and His Spirit works in us to will and to do of God's good pleasure as set forth in the immutable statutes of righteousness." Charles H. Spurgeon, *The Gospel of the Kingdom* (1893), p. 48.

The statement about the perpetuity of the law in Matthew 5:17-

19 is illustrated by the entire rest of the chapter, in which Jesus cites several of the commandments and proceeds to broaden them—that is, to make them even more stringent by applying them even to the hidden emotions of the heart. The new Torah is more demanding than the old; and hence it defines a righteousness that exceeds that of the scribes and Pharisees (verse 20). Jesus did not intend to abolish the law in this age; He broadened it, making it more full.

What did Christ tell the rich young man to do in order to enter into life?

"If you want to enter life, *obey the commandments*." Matthew 19:17, NIV.

When asked which commandments, what did Jesus say?

" 'Do not murder, do not commit adultery, do not steal, do not give false testimony, honor your father and mother,' and 'love your neighbor as yourself.' " Verses 18, 19.

NOTE.—While not quoting all 10 commandments, Jesus quoted sufficient to identify the moral law. The last command, to love one's neighbor, was the one that the rich young man was violating.

How is sin defined?

"Everyone who sins breaks the law; in fact, sin is lawlessness." 1 John 3:4, NIV.

Does faith void the law?

"Do we, then, nullify the law by this faith? *Not at all! Rather, we uphold the law*." Romans 3:31, NIV.

What is more important than any outward ceremony?

"Circumcision is nothing and uncircumcision is nothing. *Keeping God's commands is what counts*." 1 Corinthians 7:19, NIV.

NOTE.—This shows that while certain ritual parts of the law were done away with, such as circumcision, the moral law is still binding. Paul makes a similar distinction between circumcision and the moral requirements of the law in Romans 2:25-27: "Circumcision has value if you observe the law, but if you break the law, you have become as though you had not been circumcised. If those who are not circumcised keep the law's requirements, will they not be regarded as though they were circumcised? The one who is not circumcised physically and yet obeys the law will condemn you who, even though you have the written code and circumcision, are a lawbreaker" (NIV).

What kind of mind is not subject to the law of God?

"The sinful mind is hostile to God. It does not submit to God's law, nor can it do so." Romans 8:7, NIV.

How is the law fulfilled?

"Let no debt remain outstanding, except the continuing debt to love one another, for *he who loves his fellowman has fulfilled the law.* The commandments, 'Do not commit adultery,' 'Do not murder,' 'Do not steal,' 'Do not covet,' and whatever other commandment there may be, are summed up in this one rule: 'Love your neighbor as yourself.' Love does no harm to its neighbor. Therefore *love is the fulfillment of the law."* Romans 13:8-10, NIV.

How may we know that we love the children of God?

"This is how we know that we love the children of God: *by loving God and carrying out his commands."* 1 John 5:2, NIV.

What is the love of God declared to be?

"This is love for God: *to obey his commands."* Verse 3, NIV.

How is the church of the last days described?

"Then the dragon was enraged at the woman and went off to make war against the rest of her offspring—*those who obey God's commandments and hold to the testimony of Jesus."* Revelation 12:17, NIV. "This calls for patient endurance on the part of the saints *who obey God's commandments and remain faithful to Jesus."* Revelation 14:12, NIV.

THE MORAL AND CEREMONIAL LAWS

The laws that God gave can be grouped under three general categories. One is similar to what people today would describe as "civil law." It involved such things as what to do if an ox gores someone (Exodus 21:28-32) or the requirement that a homeowner build a parapet around the roof to keep people from falling off it (Deuteronomy 22:8). The second type of law we often call "moral law." It involves the relationship between us and God and with our fellow human beings (e.g., the Ten Commandments [Exodus 20:3-17]). The third type of law, ceremonial, regulates religious practices, such as the sacrifices and the definitions of what is clean and unclean (e.g., purification after childbirth [Leviticus 12]). People often especially confuse the moral and ceremonial laws.

What title of distinction is given the moral law of God?

"If you really keep the *royal law* found in Scripture, 'Love your neighbor as yourself,' you are doing right." James 2:8, NIV.

How does the law inform us of our sin?

"What shall we say, then? Is the law sin? Certainly not! Indeed I would not have known what sin was except through the law. For I would not have known what coveting really was if the law had not said, *'Do not covet.'* " Romans 7:7, NIV.

NOTE.—This is the tenth commandment, so the law in question is the Ten Commandments.

What law will judge us in the end?

"The end of the matter; all has been heard. Fear God, and keep his commandments; for that is the whole duty of everyone. For God will bring every deed into judgment, including every secret thing, whether good or evil." Ecclesiastes 12:13, 14, NRSV. "So speak and so act as those who are to be judged by *the law of liberty*." James 2:12, NRSV.

NOTE.—"The law of liberty," which says, "Do not commit adultery" and "Do not murder" (verse 11, NIV), is the Ten Commandments, which James also calls "the royal law." This is the law by which all are to be judged.

In contrast, what was the function of the sacrificial system of the Old Testament?

"The law is only a shadow of the good things that are coming— not the realities themselves. For this reason it can never, by the same sacrifices repeated endlessly year after year, make perfect those who draw near to worship." Hebrews 10:1, NIV.

NOTE.—These ritual sacrifices were made necessary by sin, and served to foreshadow the coming of a Savior.

What part of the old covenant law was done away with after the resurrection of Christ?

"Now the *first covenant had regulations for worship and also an earthly sanctuary. . . .* This is an illustration for the present time, indicating that the gifts and sacrifices being offered were not able to clear the conscience of the worshiper. They are only a matter of food and drink and various ceremonial washings—external regulations *applying until the time of the new order.*" Hebrews 9:1-10, NIV.

NOTE.—Verses 2-8 of this passage describes the sacrificial service in some detail. Clearly, the laws that have become obsolete are those pertaining to the Temple and its sacrifices, including food and drink offerings. (See Leviticus 23:13, 18, 37, etc.) These ritual, or ceremonial, laws of Moses became obsolete because they were only a foreshadowing of the reality of the atoning work of Christ, and once the reality came, the shadow was no longer necessary. Hebrews 8:13 says of these laws: "By calling this covenant 'new,' he has made the first one obsolete; and what is obsolete and aging will soon disappear" (NIV). It is also important to realize that the law given to Moses served as the constitution and bylaws of the nation of Israel. But the Jews were no longer an independent nation in New Testament times, so their civic laws were obsolete. It is only the great moral principles of the law contained in the Ten Commandments that are eternal.

Notice how this is phrased in chapter 19 of the Westminster Confession of Faith: "Beside this law, commonly called moral, God was pleased to give to the people of Israel as a church under age, ceremonial laws, containing several typical ordinances, partly of worship, prefiguring Christ, His graces, actions, sufferings, and benefits; and partly holding forth divers instructions of moral duties. All which ceremonial laws are now abrogated under the New Testament. To them also, as a body politic, He gave sundry judicial laws, which expired together with the state of that people." Philip Schaff, *The Creeds of Christendom* (Scribner's), vol. 3, p. 641.

What is another reason for setting aside the old ceremonial law?

"For when there is a change of the priesthood, there must also be a change of the law. . . . *The former regulation is set aside because it was weak and useless (for the law made nothing perfect)*, and a better hope is introduced, by which we draw near to God." Hebrews 7:12-19, NIV.

NOTE.—It was because the law made nothing perfect that the sacrifices had to be repeated over and over (Hebrews 10:1, 2, 11). Hence the law of the Levitical priesthood had to be set aside to allow for the high priesthood of Jesus, whose perfect sacrifice atoned for sin once and for all; for Jesus was not of the tribe of Levi, as required by the old law.

By whom was the ten-commandment law proclaimed?

"Then *the Lord* spoke to you out of the fire. You heard the sound of words but saw no form; there was only a voice. He declared to you his covenant, the Ten Commandments, which he commanded you to follow and then wrote them on two stone tablets." Deuteronomy 4:12, 13, NIV.

How was the ceremonial law made known to Israel?

"The Lord called to Moses. . . . He said, *'Speak to the Israelites* and say to them: "When any of you brings an offering to the Lord . . ."' " Leviticus 1:1, 2, NIV.

"These, then, are the regulations for the burnt offering, the grain offering, the sin offering, the guilt offering, the ordination offering and the fellowship offering, which the Lord gave Moses on Mount Sinai on the day he commanded the Israelites to bring their offerings to the Lord, in the Desert of Sinai." Leviticus 7:37, 38, NIV.

Were the Ten Commandments alone a complete law?

"These are the commandments the Lord proclaimed in a loud voice to your whole assembly there on the mountain from out of the fire, the cloud and the deep darkness; and *he added nothing more. Then he wrote them on two stone tablets* and gave them to me." Deuteronomy 5:22, NIV. (See also Exodus 24:12.)

On what did God write the Ten Commandments?

"He declared to you his covenant, the Ten Commandments, which he commanded you to follow and then wrote them on *two stone tablets.*" Deuteronomy 4:13, NIV.

In what were the laws of sacrifices written?

"They set aside the burnt offerings to give them to the subdivisions of the families of the people to offer to the Lord, as is written in *the Book of Moses.*" 2 Chronicles 35:12, NIV.

What is the nature of the moral law?

"The law of the Lord is *perfect,* reviving the soul." Psalm 19:7, NIV. "We know that the law is *spiritual.*" Romans 7:14.

NOTE.—"The law of God is a divine law, holy, heavenly, perfect. Those who find fault with the law, or in the least degree depreciate it, do not understand its design, and have no right idea of the law itself Paul says, 'The law is holy, but I am carnal; sold under sin.' In all we ever say concerning justification by faith, we never intend to lower the opinion which our hearers have of the law, for the law is one of the most sublime of God's works. There is not a commandment too many; there is not one too few; but it is so *incomparable,* that its *perfection* is a proof of its divinity." Charles H. Spurgeon, *Sermons,* 2nd series (1857), p. 280.

What was the nature of the ceremonial law?

"The former regulation is set aside because it was weak and useless (for the law made nothing perfect), and a better hope is introduced, by which we draw near to God." Hebrews 7:18, 19, NIV.

NOTE.—The blood of bulls and goats was incapable of washing away sin.

Were the ceremonial gifts and sacrifices capable of clearing the conscience?

"The gifts and sacrifices being offered *were not able to clear the conscience of the worshiper.*" Hebrews 9:9, NIV.

Until what time was the ceremonial law imposed?

"They are only a matter of food and drink and various ceremonial washings—external regulations applying *until the time of the new order.*" Verse 10, NIV.

When was this time of the new order?

"When Christ came as a high priest of the good things that have come, then through the greater and perfect tent (not made with hands, that is, not of this creation), he entered once for all into the Holy Place, not with the blood of goats and calves, but with his own blood, thus obtaining eternal redemption." Verses 11, 12, NRSV.

How did Christ's death affect the ceremonial law?

"Having canceled the written code, with its regulations, that was against us and that stood opposed to us; he took it away, nailing it to the cross." Colossians 2:14, NIV.

"By *abolishing* in his flesh *the law with its commandments and regulations.*" Ephesians 2:15, NIV.

What signified that the sacrificial system was ended?

"And when Jesus had cried out again in a loud voice, he gave up his spirit. At that moment *the curtain of the temple was torn* in two from top to bottom." Matthew 27:50, 51, NIV.

In what words had the prophet Daniel foretold the end of the sacrificial system?

"He will confirm a covenant with many for one 'seven.' *In the middle of the 'seven' he will put an end to sacrifice and offering.*" Daniel 9:27, NIV.

How enduring is the moral law?

"His commandments . . . stand fast for ever and ever." Psalm 111:7, 8.

THE TWO COVENANTS

What two covenants does the Bible contrast?

"By calling this covenant *'new,'* he has made the *first* one obso-

The Two Laws Contrasted

The Moral Law	The Ceremonial Law
Is *called the "royal law."* James 2:8.	Is *called "the law . . . contained* in ordinances." Ephesians 2:15.
Was *spoken by God.* Deuteronomy 4:12, 13.	Was *spoken by Moses.* Leviticus 1:1-3.
Was *written by God on tables of stone.* Exodus 24:12.	Was *"the handwriting of ordinances."* Colossians 2:14.
Was *written "with the finger of God"* on stone. Exodus 31:18.	Was *written by Moses in a book.* 2 Chronicles 35:12.
Was *placed in the ark.* Exodus 40:20; 1 Kings 8:9; Hebrews 9:4.	Was *placed in the side of the ark.* Deuteronomy 31:24-26.
Is *"perfect."* Psalm 19:7.	*"Made nothing perfect."* Hebrews 7:19.
Is to *"stand fast for ever and ever."* Psalm 111:7, 8.	Was *nailed to the cross.* Colossians 2:14.
Was *not destroyed by Christ.* Matthew 5:17.	Was *abolished by Christ.* Ephesians 2:15.
Was to be *magnified by Christ.* Isaiah 42:21.	Was *taken out of the way by Christ.* Colossians 2:14.
Gives *knowledge of sin.* Romans 3:20; 7:7.	Was *instituted in consequence of sin.* Leviticus 3-7.

lete, and what is obsolete and aging will soon disappear." Hebrews 8:13, NIV.

By what other terms are these covenants designated?

"For if that *first covenant* had been faultless, there would have been no need to look for a *second* one." Verse 7, NRSV.

When was the old covenant made?

"Not like the covenant that I made with their ancestors, on the day *when I took them by the hand to lead them out of the land of Egypt;* for they did not continue in my covenant, and so I had no concern for them, says the Lord." Verse 9, NRSV. (See Exodus 19:3-8.)

When God was about to proclaim His law to Israel, of what did He tell Moses to remind them?

"Then Moses went up to God, and the Lord called to him from the mountain and said, 'This is what you are to say to the house of Jacob and what you are to tell the people of Israel: "You yourselves have seen what I did to Egypt, and how I carried you on eagles' wings and brought you to myself." ' " Exodus 19:3, 4, NIV.

NOTE.—Thus even the old covenant began with grace. In other words, God was saying, "Here is what I have done for you. Now here is what I want you to do for Me."

What proposition did He submit to them?

"Now *if you obey me fully and keep my covenant, then out of all nations you will be my treasured possession.* Although the whole earth is mine, you will be for me a kingdom of priests and a holy nation." Verses 5, 6, NIV.

What response did the people make to this proposition?

"The people all responded together, *'We will do everything the Lord has said.'* " Verse 8, NIV.

What covenant obligation was imposed upon Israel?

"Now if you *obey me fully and keep my covenant.*" Verse 5, NIV.

Upon what was this covenant with God based?

"He declared to you his covenant, the Ten Commandments, which he commanded you to follow and then wrote them on two stone tablets." Deuteronomy 4:13, NIV.

After the law had been proclaimed from Sinai, what did the people again say?

"When Moses went and told the people all the Lord's words and laws, they responded with one voice, *'Everything the Lord has said we will do.'* " Exodus 24:3, NIV.

What did Moses do to prevent misunderstanding?

"Moses then *wrote down everything the Lord had said.* . . . Then he took the Book of the Covenant and read it to the people." Verses 4-7, NIV.

How was this covenant then confirmed and dedicated?

"He sent young men of the people of Israel, who offered burnt offerings and sacrificed oxen as offerings of well-being to the Lord. Moses took half of the blood and put it in basins, and half of the blood he dashed against the altar. Then he took the book of the covenant, and read it in the hearing of the people; and they said, 'All that the Lord has spoken we will do, and we will be obedient.' *Moses took the blood and dashed it on the people, and said, 'see the blood of the covenant that the Lord has made with you in accordance with all these words.*'" Verses 5-8, NRSV.

How does Paul describe this ratification of the covenant?

"For when every commandment had been told to all the people by Moses in accordance with the law, he took the blood of calves and goats, with water and scarlet wool and hyssop, and *sprinkled both the scroll itself and all the people*, saying, 'This is the blood of the covenant that God has ordained for you.'" Hebrews 9:19, 20, NIV.

NOTE.—God promised to make them His special people on condition that they would keep His commandments. Again they promised to obey. The agreement was then ratified, or sealed, with blood. This is the old covenant.

Less than 40 days after making this covenant, while Moses communed with God on the mountain, what did the Israelites say to Moses' brother Aaron?

"When the people saw that Moses was so long in coming down from the mountain, they gathered around Aaron and said, *'Come, make us gods who will go before us.* As for this fellow Moses who brought us up out of Egypt, we don't know what has happened to him.'" Exodus 32:1, NIV.

When Moses came down from Sinai, what did he see?

"When Moses approached the camp and saw *the calf* and *the dancing*, his anger burned and he threw the tablets out of his hands, breaking them to pieces at the foot of the mountain." Verse 19, NIV.

NOTE.—The breaking of the tables of the law signified that the terms of the covenant had been broken. Almost immediately after their pledge to keep the covenant the people had begun to commit idolatry, breaking their oath and violating the covenant. This incident therefore served to teach the people their weakness, and their inability to keep the law without God's help. The violation of the old covenant led them to feel their need of the provisions of the new covenant.

Today we have to learn the same lesson. We cannot keep our

promises. There is no salvation for anyone while trusting in self. Unaided, no one can keep the law. Only in Christ is there remission of sins or power to keep from sinning.

What did God do about the broken tables of the law?

"The Lord said to Moses, 'Chisel out two stone tablets like the first ones, and I will write on them the words that were on the first tablets, which you broke.' " Exodus 34:1, NIV. "Moses was there with the Lord forty days and forty nights, without eating bread or drinking water. And he wrote on the tablets the words of the covenant—the Ten Commandments." Verse 28, NIV.

NOTE.—God is patient and forgiving. He gives His people a second chance. He restores what they have ruined. God still gives us another chance today when we fail Him.

What reason is given for making the new covenant?

"For if there had been nothing wrong with that first covenant, no place would have been sought for another. But God found fault with the people and said: 'The time is coming, declares the Lord, when I will make a new covenant' " Hebrews 8:7, 8, NIV.

NOTE.—The chief fault in connection with the old covenant lay with the people. They were not able, in themselves, to fulfill their part of it.

How does the new covenant differ from the old?

"But the ministry Jesus has received is as superior to theirs as the covenant of which he is mediator *is superior to the old one, and it is founded on better promises*." Verse 6, NIV.

What are the new covenant's "better promises"?

" 'This is the covenant I will make with the house of Israel after that time,' declares the Lord. *'I will put my law in their minds and write it on their hearts. . . . For I will forgive their wickedness and will remember their sins no more.' "* Jeremiah 31:33, 34, NIV. (See also Hebrews 8:8-12.)

NOTE.—"The difference between the Old and New Covenants is that under the former that law is written on tables of stone, confronting man as an external ordinance and condemning him because of his failure through sin to obey its commandments, whereas under the latter the Law is written internally within the redeemed heart by the dynamic regenerating work of the Holy Spirit, so that through faith in Christ, the only law-keeper, and inward experience of His power man no longer hates but loves God's

Law and is enabled to fulfill its precepts." Philip Edgcumbe
Hughes, *Paul's Second Epistle to the Corinthians, The New International Commentary on the New Testament* (Grand Rapids:
William B. Eerdmans, 1962), p. 94.

The commandments that God writes on the heart are the same
ones He wrote on tables of stone. "And I will put my Spirit in you
and move you to follow my decrees and be careful to keep my
laws." Ezekiel 36:27, NIV. It is not the regulations that are new; it
is the regulatee that is renewed. The law is not weakened; the heart
is strengthened.

How was help promised as soon as sin entered?

"So the Lord God said to the serpent, '. . . I will put enmity between you and the woman, and between your offspring and hers; he
will crush your head, and you will strike his heal.' " Genesis 3:14,
15, NIV.

NOTE.—The covenant of grace dates from the foundation of the
world. God promised that the offspring (descendant; i.e., Christ) of
the woman would fight against the serpent, or Satan.

To whom was this covenant promise later renewed?

"Then God said, 'Yes, but your wife Sarah will bear you a son,
and you will call him Isaac. I will establish my covenant with him as
an everlasting covenant for his descendants after him.' " Genesis
17:19, NIV.

"I will make your descendants as numerous as the stars in the sky
. . . , and *through your offspring all nations on earth will be blessed.*"
Genesis 26:4, NIV.

Who was the seed here referred to?

"The promises were spoken to Abraham and to his seed. The
Scripture does not say 'and to seeds,' meaning many people, but
'and to your seed,' meaning one person, who is *Christ.*" Galatians
3:16, NIV.

What shows that the new, or second, covenant and the Abrahamic covenant are virtually the same?

"If you belong to Christ, then you are Abraham's seed, and heirs
according to the promise." Verse 29, NIV.

What is necessary where there is a covenant?

"In the case of a will, it is necessary to prove the death of the one who
made it, because a will is in force only when somebody has died; it never

takes effect while the one who made it is living." Hebrews 9:16, 17, NIV.

With whose blood was the new covenant dedicated?

"And he did the same with the cup after supper, saying, 'This cup that is poured out for you is the new covenant in my blood.' " Luke 22:20, NRSV.

What power is there in the blood of this covenant?

"May the God of peace, who through the blood of the eternal covenant brought back from the dead our Lord Jesus, that great Shepherd of the sheep, *equip you with everything good* for doing his will." Hebrews 13:20, 21, NIV.

Through which covenant only is there remission of sins?

"How much more will the blood of Christ, who through the eternal Spirit offered himself without blemish to God, purify our conscience from dead works to worship the living God! For this reason he is the mediator of a *new covenant,* so that those who are called may receive the promised eternal inheritance, because a death has occurred that redeems them from the transgression under the first covenant" Hebrews 9:14, 15, NRSV.

NOTE.—The fact that Christ, as mediator of the second covenant, died for the remission of the transgressions that were under the first covenant shows that there was no permanent forgiveness by virtue of the first covenant.

What unites all believers under the new covenant?

"Therefore, remember that formerly you who are Gentiles by birth and called 'uncircumcised' by those who call themselves 'the circumcision' (that done in the body by the hands of men)—remember that at that time you were separate from Christ, excluded from citizenship in Israel and foreigners to the covenants of the promise, without hope and without God in the world. But now in Christ Jesus you who once were far away have been brought near through the blood of Christ." Ephesians 2:11-13, NIV.

WHAT DID CHRIST ABOLISH?

How did Christ's death affect the sacrificial system?

"After the sixty-two 'sevens' the Anointed One will be cut off. . . . He will confirm a covenant with many for one 'seven.' *In the middle of the 'seven' he will put an end to sacrifice and offering."* Daniel 9:26, 27, NIV.

The Two Covenants

Similarities Between the Two Covenants

1. Both are called covenants.
2. Both were ratified with blood.
3. Both were made concerning the law of God.
4. Both were made with the people of God.
5. Both were established upon promises.

Dissimilarities Between the Two Covenants

Old Covenant	New Covenant
A temporary compact.	An everlasting covenant.
Dedicated with the blood of animals.	Ratified with the blood of Christ.
Was faulty.	Is a better covenant.
Was established upon the promises of the people.	Is established upon the promises of God.
Had no mediator.	Has a mediator.
No provision for forgiveness.	Has provision for forgiveness.
Law was written on tables of stone.	Law is written on the heart.

What did Christ nail to His cross and thus abolish?

The debt of our sin.

"When you were dead in your sins and in the uncircumcision of your sinful nature, God made you alive with Christ. He forgave us all our sins, having canceled the *written code,* with its regulations, that was against us and that stood opposed to us; he took it away, *nailing it to the cross."* Colossians 2:14, NIV.

"For he himself is our peace, who has made the two one and has destroyed the barrier, the dividing wall of hostility, by abolishing in his flesh the *law with its commandments and regulations.* His purpose was to create in himself one new man out of the two, thus making peace, and in this one body to reconcile both of them to God through the cross, by which he put to death their hostility." Ephesians 2:14-16, NIV.

NOTE.—Colossians 2 is addressing the removal of the writing of condemnation against us, which is not the law itself.

"God has not only removed the debt; he has also destroyed the document on which it was recorded. . . . A common thought in Judaism was that of God keeping accounts of man's debt, calling in the debt through angels and imposing a just judgment based on the records kept in the ledger. . . .

"Like an IOU it contained penalty clauses. (See Job 5:3; Philemon 19.) The Jews had contracted to obey the law, and in their case the penalty for breach of this contract meant death (Deut. 27:14-26; 30:15-20). Paul assumes that the Gentiles were committed, through their consciences, to a similar obligation, to the moral law inasmuch as they understood it (cf. Romans 12:14, 15). Since the obligation had not been discharged by either group the 'bond' remained against us. . . .

"The metaphorical language is not to be pressed. God has cancelled the bond by nailing it to the cross—this is a vivid way of saying that because Christ was nailed to the cross our debt has been completely forgiven. (There may also be an allusion to the custom of affixing to the cross the 'inscription' . . . bearing the crime of the evildoer, Mark 15:26. God nails the accusation against us to the cross of Jesus, just as his accusation had been nailed there.)" Peter T. O'Brien, *Word Biblical Commentary: Colossians, Philemon* (Waco, Tex.: Word Books, 1982), pp. 124-126.

"Those who had once been spiritually dead in their trespasses and sinful nature God had made alive. The Colossians had come to life with Christ who was dead and rose again. Their new life, then, was a sharing in the life which he received when he rose from the dead. God had forgiven them as Gentiles, along with Paul and other Jewish Christians, all their trespasses. Indeed, he had not only canceled the debt but also destroyed the document on which it was recorded. This he did by blotting out the bond with its damning indictment against us and nailing it to the cross when Christ died." *Ibid.*, p. 133.

Did Christ's death change the Christian's attitude toward any religious practices?

"Therefore do not let anyone judge you by what you eat or drink, or with regard to a religious festival, a New Moon celebration or a Sabbath day. These are *a shadow of the things that were to come;* the reality, however, is found in Christ." Colossians 2:16, 17, NIV.

NOTE.—At first glance Colossians 2:16, 17 seems to say that Christ's death abolishes the weekly Sabbath or at least makes it of no significance. But we need to consider another passage as well:

"The law is only a *shadow of the good things that are coming*—not the realities themselves. For this reason it can never, by the same *sacrifices* repeated endlessly year after year, make perfect those who draw near to worship. . . . Therefore, when Christ came into the world, he said: 'sacrifice and offering you did not desire, but a *body* you prepared for me.' . . He sets aside the first to establish the second." Hebrews 10:1-9, NIV.

Both passages use the same phrases. The whole subject is the sacrificial system (which included sacrifices on the seventh-day Sabbath [Numbers 28:9, 10], but not seventh-day Sabbath rest), and how Christ's "body" has made it obsolete. This is just a longer way of saying "these are a *shadow* of the things that were to come; the *reality*, however, is found in Christ."

Why did Paul object to the Colossians observation of these practices?

"See to it that no one takes you captive through philosophy and empty deceit, according to human tradition, according to *the elemental spirits of the universe*, and not according to Christ." Colossians 2:8, NRSV.

NOTE.—Like the pagans, the Colossians believed they needed to worship other powers (angels or other beings) in addition to God and follow certain ascetic practices that would please those powers. They thought that such practices had some kind of value or merit toward their salvation. But Paul emphasizes again and again that salvation only comes through Christ and His death. Not only can no other power save us, it cannot aid us in the slightest degree.

Why did Paul oppose their dietary practices? "Paul is probably not referring directly to the Old Testament food laws since the Torah contained no prohibitions respecting drinks, except in a few special cases (e.g., of priests ministering in the tabernacle, Leviticus 10:9; Numbers 6:3 . . .). Nor is he directing attention to abstentions similar to those enjoined in the apostolic letter of Acts 15:23-29 in which Gentiles without compromising their Christian liberty were to behave considerately to their 'weaker brethren' of Jewish birth. Rather, these are more stringent regulations of an ascetic nature apparently involving the renunciation of animal flesh and of wine and strong drink, after a Nazirite fashion. They follow from the demand of 'severe treatment of the body' (verse 23), whereby abstinence from certain food is required (verse 21; cf. 1 Timothy 4:3).

"There are various reasons why abstinence from food and drink was practiced in the ancient world: the belief in the transmigration of souls might prevent a person from eating meat. Some practiced asceticism since it was bound up with their views of purity. Others thought that by fasting one served the deity, came closer to him or prepared oneself for receiving a divine revelation, a point that is important in the light of verse 18. . . . The observance of taboos and sacred times in the Colossian 'philosophy' seems to have related to obedient submission to the 'elemental spirits of the universe' (cf. verse 20)." Peter T. O'Brien, *Word Biblical Commentary: Colossians, Philemon,* (Waco, Tex.: Word Books, 1982), pp. 138, 139.

Did Paul oppose the celebration of religious holy days? No. "The author of Colossians is not advising his readers not to allow the other teachers to impose on them the observance of the Sabbath because to do so would be to deal with shadows rather than with Christ. Rather, he insists that since they have died with Christ (2:20) and have been circumcised of the flesh (2:11-13), they have been forgiven (1:14). On matters of food, drink, a festival, a new moon, or a Sabbath, no one should judge them for doing such things, which are a shadow of things to come. In other words, he approves their practices in manners of eating and Sabbath keeping. He defends the value of liturgical rhythms and dietary prescriptions, even as he qualifies their role. In 2:16 he tells them that they should not allow others to judge them for doing what they are doing. Then in 2:18 he tells them that they should not allow others to disqualify them for not doing what others think they should be doing. The other teachers promise access to ultimate reality by means of asceticism, worship with angels, and visions. In this connection they impose regulations as to what can be handled (2:14, 20). In opposition, the author of Colossians insists the ultimate reality is in the future, when the 'things to come' come. According to him, the gospel brings 'hope' (1:24). Those nonsurgically circumcised in Christ have 'the hope of glory' (1:27). In the meantime Sabbath observance, among other things, is quite valuable as a 'shadow' of that glorious future.

"The contrast in this text is not between 'shadow' and 'body.' The contrast is between 'shadow' and 'what is to come.' The shadow of what is to come does not refer to shadows of the Christ who has already come and made these observances obsolete. In this case the 'shadow' is the present blurred manifestation of a hoped-for reality. In its shadow the expected future is seen as coming." Harold Weiss, *A Day of Gladness: The Sabbath among Jews and Christians in Antiquity,* (Columbia, S.C.: University of South Carolina Press, 2003), pp. 135, 136.

Why was the sacrificial system to end at Christ's death?

"First he said, *'sacrifices and offerings, burnt offerings and sin offerings* you did not desire, nor were you pleased with them' (although the law required them to be made). Then he said, 'Here I am, I have come to do your will.' *He sets aside the first to establish the second."* Hebrews 10:8, 9, NIV.

NOTE.—In other words, the sacrificial offerings were set aside and replaced by the all-sufficient blood of Christ, the only sacrifice that could take away sin. To have continued the offering of animals after the cross would have been a denial that the Lamb of God, whom the offerings prefigured, had come.

How did Jesus suggest to the woman at Jacob's well that the ceremonial system of worship would be abolished?

"Jesus declared, 'Believe me, woman, a time is coming when you will worship the Father neither on this mountain nor in Jerusalem.' " John 4:21, NIV.

NOTE.—The Jewish worship centered in the ritual service of the temple "in Jerusalem," while the Samaritans had instituted a rival service "on this mountain," Mount Gerizim. Jesus therefore indicated that the time was near when the whole Temple system would pass away.

How did the question of the ritual law confront the apostles?

"Some men came down from Judea to Antioch and were teaching the brothers: *'Unless you are circumcised, according to the custom taught by Moses, you cannot be saved.' "* Acts 15:1, NIV.

"We have heard that some went out from us without our authorization and disturbed you, troubling your minds by what they said." Verse 24, NIV.

NOTE.—The false teachers were saying that the Christians had to be circumcised and keep the ceremonial law.

To what group of leaders was the dispute submitted for a decision?

"This brought Paul and Barnabas into short dispute and debate with them. So Paul and Barnabas were appointed, along with some other believers, to go up to Jerusalem to see the *apostles and elders* about this question." Verse 2, NIV.

After a lengthy discussion, what decision was reached by the apostles?

"It seemed good to the Holy Spirit and to us not to burden you with anything beyond the following requirements: *You are to abstain from food sacrificed to idols, from blood, from the meat of strangled animals and from sexual immorality.* You will do well to avoid these things." Verses 28, 29, NIV.

NOTE.—Interestingly, this decision scarcely references the Ten Commandments. Why? There are two possibilities. Either all parties agreed that the Ten Commandments were obsolete and it was now perfectly proper for Christians to worship other gods, bow down to idols, take the Lord's name in vain, break the Sabbath, kill, steal, lie, etc., or *all parties took for granted that the Ten Commandments were still binding;* there was never any debate on that issue. The debate was over which portions of the ceremonial law were binding on non-Jewish Christians.

Here is how the apostles solved this problem: under the direction of the Holy Spirit they waived the ceremonial rite of circumcision, but retained (in addition to the Ten Commandments) those statutes of Moses that applied not only to the Jews but also to the aliens living among them, as decreed in Leviticus 17 (see verses 8, 10, 12, 13, 15). Notice how the list in Acts 15:29 follows Leviticus: "You are to abstain from food sacrificed to idols [see Leviticus 17:7-9], from blood [see verses 10-14], from the meat of strangled animals [see verses 15, 16] and from sexual immorality [see Leviticus 18]" (NIV).

Of what was Stephen accused concerning the Mosaic law?

"They set up *false witnesses,* who said, 'This man never stops say- ing things against this holy place and the law; for we have heard him say that this Jesus of Nazareth will destroy this place and *will change the customs that Moses handed on to us.*'" Acts 6:13, 14, NRSV.

What similar charge was brought against Paul?

"'This man,' they charged, 'is persuading the people to worship God in ways contrary to the law.'" Acts 18:13, NIV.

How did Paul defend himself?

"However, I admit that I worship the God of our fathers as a fol- lower of the Way, which they call a sect. *I believe everything that agrees with the Law and that is written in the Prophets.*" Acts 24:14, NIV.

"I have done nothing wrong *against the law of the Jews* or against the temple or against Caesar." Acts 25:8, NIV.

NOTE.—The charge against Stephen and Paul was not based upon any violation of the moral law, but upon their teaching that the cere- monial law was obsolete; and Paul's admission that he was guilty of what they called heresy meant simply that he differed from them as to the obligation to observe any longer the ceremonial law, which was im- posed upon them "until the time of reformation" (Hebrews 9:10).

In what way is Christ the end of the law?

"Christ is the end of the law *so that there may be righteousness* for everyone who believes." Romans 10:4, NIV.

NOTE.—The word "end" is from the Greek word *telos. Telos* sometimes means "end" in the sense of termination, but more often it means goal, purpose, result, outcome (as in our expression "to what end?"). That is the meaning here. This is clear from other texts in the New Testament that use the same word. James 5:11 reads, "You have heard of the endurance of Job, and have seen the *purpose [telos]* of the Lord, how the Lord is compassionate and merciful" (NIV). Obviously this does not mean the termination of the Lord, but the outcome. First Peter 1:9 talks about "receiving the *outcome [telos]* of your faith; the salvation of your souls" (NRSV). That is, the goal or result of faith is salvation. First Timothy 1:5 says, "The *end [telos]* of the commandment is charity out of a pure heart." The NIV translation reads, "The *goal* of this command is love, which comes from a pure heart." Love is not the termination of law; it is the goal of it, the fulfillment of it.

So Romans 10:4 means that righteousness is the goal of the law. Even if *telos* here meant "end," the text still does not merely say that Christ is the end of the law, but that He is the end of the law *for righteousness.* Once a person comes to Christ, they no longer rely on lawkeeping for righteousness, for righteousness is a gift, not an achievement.

THE LAW AND THE GOSPEL

What role does the law have in preparing the heart for the gospel?

"We have already made the charge that Jews and Gentiles *alike are under sin* . . . Now we know that whatever the law says, it says to those who are *under the law,* so that *every mouth may be silenced* and the whole world held accountable to God." Romans 3:9-19, NIV.

NOTE.—Notice that all are "under sin" and hence "under the law"—that is, under the condemnation of the law. By condemning us as sinners, the law convicts us of sin. Dwight L. Moody wrote: "God, being a perfect God, had to give a perfect Law, and the Law was given not to save men, but to measure them. I want you to understand this clearly, because I believe hundreds and thousands stumble at this point. They try to save themselves by trying to keep the law; but it was never meant for men to save themselves by. . . . Ask Paul what it was given for. Here is his answer, 'That every mouth may be stopped, and all the world may become guilty before God' (Romans 3:19). . . . The law stops every man's mouth. . . . I can always tell a man who is near the kingdom of God; his mouth is stopped. . . . This, then is what God gives us the law for—to show us ourselves in our true colors." *Select Sermons* (Chicago: Moody Press, 1881), pp. 25, 26.

What is the purpose of the law?

"Therefore no one will be declared righteous in his sight by observing the law; rather, *through the law we become conscious of sin.*" Romans 3:20, NIV.

NOTE.—Without the law there is no sense of sin, for sin is defined as transgression of the law (1 John 3:4), and "where there is no law, there is no transgression" (Romans 4:15, NIV).

The law is like a plumb line, which shows when a wall is crooked. No matter how you use it, a plumb line can't make a crooked wall straight. The law is God's plumb line, designed to show us that we are crooked, or sinful. It was never intended to straighten out our lives. Only the Carpenter can do that.

Again, the law is like a thermometer. It tells us when we are sick, but it can never make us well. Only the Physician can do that. The thermometer merely reveals our departure from God's norm.

No one has ever been set right by the law. The law is only a sin detecter, an early-warning system, that motivates us to seek help elsewhere. As such, it has an essential role to play. Solving the sin problem by abolishing the moral law would be like trying to solve the problem of a crooked wall by throwing away the plumb line, or trying to reduce a fever by breaking the thermometer. We do not correct the defect by abolishing the standard, but the standard is incapable of correcting the defect. Only Jesus saves. In other words, "We know that the law is good, if one uses it properly." 1 Timothy 1:8, NIV.

What is the result of this knowledge of sin?

"The law of the Lord is perfect, converting the soul." Psalm 19:7.

NOTE.—The law cannot save us; that is not its function. Instead, it convicts us of sin, making us desire salvation.

God used the law to convert the seventeenth-century author John Bunyan. In his autobiography *Grace Abounding to the Chief of Sinners,* he shares his conversion experience. Bunyan lists a number of judgments and gracious providences of God in his life that should have impressed him but didn't. "None of these things awakened my soul to righteousness, so I kept on sinning and grew more and more rebellious against God and careless of my own salvation. . . . I never considered that sin would damn me, no matter what religion I followed, unless I was found in Christ. . . . But one day it happened that, among the various sermons our parson preached, his subject was 'the

Sabbath day' and the evil of breaking it either with work or sports or in any other way. Then my conscience began to prick me, and I thought that he had preached this sermon on purpose to show me my evil ways. That was the first time I can remember that I felt guilty and very burdened, for the moment at least, and I went home when the sermon was ended with a great depression upon my spirit."

What is the gospel declared to be?

"I am not ashamed of the gospel, because it is *the power of God for the salvation of everyone who believes."* Romans 1:16, NIV.

What is the significance of the name Jesus?

"She will give birth to a son, and you are to give him the name *Jesus, because he will save his people from their sins."* Matthew 1:21, NIV.

In whom is this power to save from sin revealed?

"We preach . . . *Christ the power of God,* and the wisdom of God" 1 Corinthians 1:23, 24.

What does Christ promise to do for us under the new covenant?

"But the ministry Jesus has received is as superior to theirs as the covenant of which he is mediator is superior to the old one, and is founded on better promises. For if there had been nothing wrong with that first covenant, no place would have been sought for another. But God found fault with the people and said: . . . 'This is the covenant I will make with the house of Israel after that time, declares the Lord. *I will put my laws in their minds and write them on their hearts.'* " Hebrews 8:6-10, NIV.

What must we do in order to benefit by Christ's work?

"For it is with your heart that you *believe* and are justified, and it is with your mouth that you *confess* and are saved." Romans 10:10, NIV.

For what did the apostle Paul trust Christ?

"I consider everything a loss compared to the surpassing greatness of knowing Christ Jesus my Lord, for whose sake I have lost all things. I consider them rubbish, that I may gain Christ and be found in him, *not having a righteousness of my own that comes from the law,* but that which is through faith in Christ—*the righteousness that comes from God and is by faith."* Philippians 3:8, 9, NIV.

What relation does the law sustain to this righteousness?

"But now a righteousness from God, apart from law, has been made known, to *which the Law and the Prophets testify.*" Romans 3:21, NIV.

NOTE.—This righteousness is something that comes apart from the law, but the law and the prophets bore witness of it.

Does the faith that brings righteousness nullify the law?

"Do we, then, nullify the law by this faith? Not at all! Rather, we *uphold the law.*" Verse 31, NIV.

NOTE.—In the gospel, the law, first written in the heart of Christ, becomes "the law of the Spirit of life in Christ Jesus," and is thus transferred to the heart of the believer, where Christ dwells by faith. Thus the new covenant promise is fulfilled. This is righteousness by faith—a righteousness that is witnessed by the law, and revealed in the life in harmony with the law. Such faith, instead of making void the law, establishes it in the heart of the believer.

"The law demands obedience, but cannot produce it; it is holy in itself, but it cannot make us holy; it convinces of sin, but it cannot cure it; it reveals the disease, but it cannot provide the remedy; while the gospel both requires and enables, saves and sanctifies (Romans 3:19-22; 4:15; 5:20, 21; 7:7-13; 2 Corinthians 3:7-9; Galatians 3:21-24; 1 Timothy 1:8-11). . . .

"The gospel shows us the Savior whom we need, and declares that He has fully obeyed the precepts of the law by His spotless life as our great representative, as well as completely exhausted its penalties through His atoning death as our great substitute (2 Corinthians 5:21). . . .

"It is the aim alike of the law and of the gospel to secure obedience, but the law compels us to it as a duty, making it irksome and distasteful, while the gospel constrains us to it as a privilege, rendering it easy and delightful The law sets obedience before us as a means of salvation, and makes blessing strictly conditional upon it. The gospel reveals it as the natural consequence of redemption, and enjoins obedience as the necessary result of blessing." William C Procter, in *Moody Bible Institute Monthly,* November 1933, pp. 107, 108. Used by permission.

What did Christ, by His death, abolish or take away?

"Look, the Lamb of God, who takes away *the sin of the world!*" John 1:29, NIV.

What else has Christ abolished?

"This grace was given us in Christ Jesus before the beginning of time, but it has now been revealed through the appearing of our Savior, Christ Jesus, who has *destroyed death* and has brought life and immortality to life through the gospel." 2 Timothy 1:9, 10, NIV.

NOTE.—"Man . . . needs to be solemnly reminded that the law of the spirit of life in Christ sets him free from the law of sin and death, but not from the law of God." G. Campbell Morgan, *The Ten Commandments* (Revell, 1901 ed.), p. 12.

What change is brought about through the gospel?

"And we, who with unveiled faces all reflect the Lord's glory, are being transformed into his likeness with ever-increasing glory, which comes from the Lord, who is the Spirit." 2 Corinthians 3:18, NIV.

NOTE.—It is sometimes claimed that Christ changed, abolished, or took away the law, and put the gospel in its place; but this shows a misapprehension of the real work of Christ. The individual believer is changed by beholding the glory revealed in the gospel (2 Corinthians 4:4; John 1:14); death has been abolished through the death of Christ; and sin has been taken away by the great Sin Bearer; but the law of God still remains unchanged as the very foundation of His throne.

What spiritual interpretation did Christ give to the sixth and seventh commandments?

"You have heard that it was said to the people long ago, 'Do not murder, and anyone who murders will be subject to judgment.' But I tell you that *anyone who is angry with his brother* will be subject to judgment" Matthew 5:21, 22, NIV.

"You have heard that it was said, 'Do not commit adultery.' But I tell you that *anyone who looks at a woman lustfully has already committed adultery with her in his heart."* Verses 27, 28, NIV.

NOTE.—Far from doing away with the commandments, the words of Jesus make them all the more demanding, governing even the thoughts of the heart.

Of what prophecy was this teaching a fulfillment?

"It pleased the Lord for the sake of his righteousness *to make his law great and glorious."* Isaiah 42:21, NIV.

NOTE.—Christ not only gave a spiritual interpretation to the law and observed it Himself, but showed the holiness and the immutable nature of the law by dying on the cross to pay the penalty of its transgression. In this way, above all, He magnified the law.

In what promise was the gospel preached to Abraham?

"The Scripture foresaw that God would justify the Gentiles by faith, and announced *the gospel* in advance to Abraham: *'All nations will be blessed through you.' "* Galatians 3:8, NIV.

On what basis was Abraham accounted righteous?

"What does the Scripture say? *'Abraham believed God, and it was credited to him as righteousness.' "* Romans 4:3, NIV.

NOTE.—Paul is quoting Genesis 15:6.

What hope can we have of being justified by our good works?

"Therefore *no one will be declared righteous in his sight* by observing the law; rather, through the law we become conscious of sin. But now a righteousness from God, apart from law, has been made known, to which the Law and the Prophets testify. This righteousness from God comes through faith in Jesus Christ to all who believe." Romans 3:20-22, NIV.

In what way are all believers in Jesus justified?

"Justified freely by his grace through the redemption that came by Christ Jesus." Verse 24, NIV.

Is the believer expected to go on in sin after this?

"What shall we say, then? Shall we go on sinning so that grace may increase? By no means! We died to sin; how can we live in it any longer?" Romans 6:1, 2, NIV.

What was Christ's personal attitude toward the law?

"Do not think that I have come to abolish the Law or the Prophets; *I have not come to abolish them but to fulfill them."* Matthew 5:17, NIV.

"If you obey my commands, you will remain in my love, just *as I have obeyed my Father's commands* and remain in his love." John 15:10, NIV.

NOTE.—The New Testament is *for* law as a standard of behavior, but *against* law as a method of salvation.

What text shows that God's end-time people will understand the proper relation between law and gospel?

"This calls for patient endurance on the part of the saints *who obey God's commandments and remain faithful to Jesus."* Revelation 14:12, NIV.

CHAPTER 9

The Sabbath

INSTITUTION OF THE SABBATH

When and by whom was the Sabbath made?

"Thus the heavens and the earth were completed in all their vast array. *By the seventh day God had finished the work* he had been doing; *so on the seventh day he rested from all his work."* Genesis 2:1, 2, NIV.

Why did God create the Sabbath?

"And God blessed the seventh day and made it holy, *because on it he rested from all the work of creating that he had done. This is the account of the heavens and the earth when they were created."* Genesis 2:3, 4, NIV.

NOTE.—To keep the seventh-day Sabbath is to follow God's example. "That God rested on the seventh day, and blessed and sanctified it, is the first divine action which man is privileged to witness; and that he himself may keep the Sabbath with God, completely free of work, is the first Word spoken to him, the first obligation laid on him." Karl Barth, *Church Dogmatics* (Edinburgh: T. & T. Clark, 1958), vol. 3, p. 219.

God established the Sabbath in the beginning as a regular reminder of His care for and sovereignty over us. The Sabbath declares that God is our Creator and Lord. It is a "tree of life" to the Christian, bringing refreshment and restoration among the cares of life. Like the tree of life in the Garden of Eden, it was given to humanity before we sinned, but unlike the tree of life, it has never been taken away from us.

What reason did God give at Sinai for keeping the Sabbath day holy?

"For in six days the Lord made the heavens and the earth, the sea, and all that is in them, but he rested on the seventh day. Therefore the Lord blessed the Sabbath day and made it holy." Exodus 20:11, NIV.

NOTE.—The Sabbath is the memorial of creation, the sign of God's creative power. God designed that through observing it humanity should forever remember Him as the true and living God, the

Creator of all things.

Did Jesus have anything to do with creation of the Sabbath?

"In the beginning was the Word [Jesus], and the Word was with God, and the Word was God. He was with God in the beginning. *Through him all things were made.*" John 1:1-3, NIV.

"He [Christ] is the image of the invisible God, the firstborn over all creation. *For by him all things were created;* things in heaven and on earth, visible and invisible, whether thrones or powers or rulers or authorities; all things were created by him and for him." Colossians 1:15, 16, NIV.

After resting on the seventh day, what did God do?

"And God *blessed the seventh day and made it holy,* because on it he rested from all the work of creating that he had done." Genesis 2:3, NIV.

NOTE.—By three distinct acts, then, was the Sabbath made: God rested on it; He blessed it; He made it holy.

For whom did Jesus say the Sabbath was made?

"Then he said to them, 'The Sabbath was made for humankind, and not humankind for the Sabbath.' " Mark 2:27, NRSV.

NOTE.—God instituted the Sabbath to be a source of benefit and blessing to the human family. The Sabbath is not to be observed for its own sake, in a rigid, legalistic manner, but as a celebration of God's faithfulness and good work. It is not to impair or inhibit life, but to enhance it.

"The seventh-day Sabbath may well be called the 'alpha' of God's covenant relationship with humankind. The Protestant Reformers overlooked this particular truth, assuming that God had merely blessed his own 'rest,' which 'rest' could be detached from the specific seventh day of the week. . . .

"Christian believers need to take into account Christ's view of the Creation account in order to learn Christ's view of the Sabbath. Jesus accepted the Creation narratives of Genesis 1 and 2 as possessing unquestionable authority. Hence to Him the Sabbath was of paramount importance. The Sabbath is seen to be of great importance when it comes to restoring true worship in 'spirit and truth' (John 4:24, NASB), and for saving 'what was lost' (Luke 19:10, NIV).

"To Jesus the purpose of the Sabbath was to be a blessing for the human 'from the beginning' when *'the Sabbath was made for man'* (Mark 2:27, NASB). Among other things, Jesus came to restore what had been lost: human beings themselves and the true worship of the covenant God. The Sabbath is a symbol of that return. Revelation assures the church that the Sovereign Ruler of the universe will restore paradise on earth again: 'Behold, I am making all things new!'

"This promise includes the full restoration of the Sabbath rest in the new earth that awaits the redeemed (Revelation 22:1, 2; cf. 22:19; Isaiah 66:22-24). This ultimate fulfillment represents the 'omega' of God's faithfulness to His creation covenant through Christ Jesus (see Revelation 21:6; 22:12-14)!" Hans K. LaRondelle, "The Sabbath: God's Everlasting Covenant," *Ministry,* March 2004, pp. 14, 15.

When did God bless and sanctify the seventh day?

At the climax of creation week. "God saw all that he had made, and it was very good. And there was evening, and there was morning—the sixth day. Thus the heavens and the earth were completed in all their vast array. By the seventh day God had finished the work he had been doing; so on the seventh day he rested from all his work. And God blessed the seventh day and made it holy, because on it he rested from all the work of creating that he had done." Genesis 1:31-2:3, NIV.

NOTE.—"Genesis ties the Sabbath inseparably to God's act of creation. (Genesis 1 and 2). The writer of Genesis sees it as an integral part of Creation It is the climactic point, following a six-day work of creation. God 'rested on the seventh day,' 'blessed the Sabbath day and made it holy' (Exodus 20:11, NASB).

"Three acts of God are described in connection with the Sabbath: God rested, blessed, and made it holy. . . . God 'blessed the seventh day' (Genesis 2:3; Exodus 20:11) and made it a beneficial day for all humankind. Humans were made to live in a loving and joyful fellowship with their Maker on the seventh day, so that 'the Sabbath is one of the greatest blessings bestowed upon men by a loving Creator' [*The Seventh-day Adventist Bible Commentary,* vol. 4, p. 307]." Hans K. LaRondelle, "The Sabbath: God's Everlasting Covenant," *Ministry,* March 2004, p. 14.

"If we had no other passage than this of Genesis 2:3, there would be no difficulty in deducing from it a precept for the universal observance of a Sabbath, or seventh day, to be devoted to God as holy time, by all of that race for whom the earth and its nature were specially prepared. The first men must have known it. The words 'He hallowed it' can have no meaning otherwise. They would be a blank unless in reference to some who were required to keep it holy." John Peter Lange, *A Commentary on the Holy Scriptures,* on Genesis 2:3, vol. 1, p. 197.

"The Sabbath was designed as a holy rest day, set apart as a sacred time for uninterrupted fellowship with the Maker. It was designed by God to be a time for people to contemplate their creatureliness, dignity, and dependence on their heavenly Father and to enjoy the Creator's invigorating and transforming presence (see Psalms 8; 92). In short, the Sabbath was made as the abiding *sacrament* through which human beings could sustain their relationship with God. It reminded humanity of the sacredness of life and it renewed in human beings their (our) sense of accountability to the Creator. The Creation account and the Decalogue are inextricably connected through the fourth commandment." Hans K. LaRondelle, "The Sabbath: God's Everlasting Covenant," *Ministry*, March 2004, pp. 14, 15.

What does the Sabbath commandment require?

"Remember the Sabbath day by keeping it holy. Six days you shall labor and do all your work, but the seventh day is a Sabbath to the Lord your God. *On it you shall not do any work,* neither you, nor your son or daughter, nor your manservant or maidservant, nor your animals, nor the alien within your gates." Exodus 20:8-10, NIV.

NOTE.—About Exodus 16:4, 22-30 Martin Luther wrote, "Hence you can see that the Sabbath was before the law of Moses came, and has existed from the beginning of the world. Especially have the devout, who have preserved the true faith, met together and called upon God on this day." Translated from *Auslegung des Alten Testaments (Commentary on the Old Testament), in Sammtliche Schriften (Collected Writings),* edited by J. G. Walch, vol. 3, col. 950.

What kind of activity did Jesus declare "lawful" on the Sabbath?

"It is lawful *to do good* on the Sabbath." Matthew 12:12, NIV.

How did God demonstrate His constant care to the children of Israel during their 40 years in the wilderness, and train them to follow and trust Him?

"Then the Lord said to Moses, *'I will rain down bread from heaven for you.* The people are to go out each day and gather enough for that day. *In this way I will test them and see whether they will follow my instructions.' "* Exodus 16:4, NIV.

On which day was a double portion of manna to be gathered?

"On the *sixth day* they are to prepare what they bring in, and that is to be twice as much as they gather on the other days." Verse 5, NIV.

Why was no manna to be gathered on the seventh day of the week?

"He said to them, 'This is that which the Lord commanded: *"Tomorrow is to be a day of rest, a holy Sabbath to the Lord." '* " Verse 23, NIV.

What did some of the people do on the seventh day?

"Nevertheless, some of the people *went out on the seventh day to gather* it, but they found none." Verse 27, NIV.

How did God reprove their disobedience?

"Then the Lord said to Moses, '*How long will you refuse to keep my commands and my instructions?*'" Verse 28, NIV.

Why was double manna given on the sixth day?

"*Bear in mind that the Lord has given you the Sabbath; that is why on the sixth day he gives you bread for two days.*" Verse 29, NIV.

How, then, did the Lord test the people?

Over the keeping of the Sabbath.

NOTE.—The Sabbath commandment was a part of God's law before this law was spoken from Sinai, for this incident occurred before Israel came to Sinai. Both the Sabbath and the law existed from creation.

GOD'S MEMORIAL

After the Israelites crossed the Jordan River into Canaan, their Promised Land, Joshua instructed 12 men to each gather a stone for a monument. What was this monument declared to be?

"And *these stones shall be for a memorial* to the children of Israel forever." Joshua 4:7, NKJV.

What were these stones to commemorate?

"And Joshua set up at Gilgal the twelve stones they had taken out of the Jordan. He said to the Israelites, 'In the future when your descendants ask their fathers, "What do these stones mean?" tell them, *"Israel crossed the Jordan on dry ground."*'" Verses 20-22, NIV.

NOTE.—These stones were to be a standing memorial, or reminder, of Israel's miraculous crossing of the Jordan river.

What was the Passover called?

"So *this day shall be to you a memorial;* and you shall keep it as a feast to the Lord throughout your generations. You shall keep it as a feast by an everlasting ordinance." Exodus 12:14, NKJV.

NOTE.—The Passover was an annual memorial, to be observed on the fourteenth day of the first month of each year, commemorating the Israelites' deliverance from slavery. A seven-day feast of unleavened bread followed it. (See Exodus 13:39.)

What did God command the Israelites to observe in memory of His work of creation?

"Remember the Sabbath day by keeping it holy. . . . For in six days the Lord made the heavens and the earth, the sea, and all that is in them, but he rested on the seventh day. Therefore the Lord blessed the Sabbath day and made it holy." Exodus 20:8-11, NIV.

Of what was this memorial to be a sign?

"Keep my Sabbaths holy, that they may be a sign between us. Then you will know that I am the Lord your God." Ezekiel 20:20, NIV.

What besides Creation were the people of Israel to remember when they kept the Sabbath?

"Remember that you were slaves in Egypt and that the Lord your God brought you out of there with a mighty hand and an outstretched arm. Therefore the Lord your God has commanded you to observe the Sabbath day." Deuteronomy 5:15, NIV.

NOTE.—The memory of their oppression in Egypt was an additional incentive for keeping the Sabbath. Besides being a memorial of creation, the Sabbath was a memorial of their deliverance from bondage through God's great power. As Egypt symbolizes our slavery to sin, so we should keep the Sabbath as a memorial of our deliverance from sin by the mighty power of God through Christ.

Of what else does God say He gave the Sabbath to His people to be a sign, or reminder?

"Also I will give them my Sabbaths as a sign between us, so they would know that I the Lord made them holy." Ezekiel 20:12, NIV.

NOTE.—Sanctification is a work of redemption—of making sinners holy. Like the work of creation itself, this requires creative power. (See Psalm 51:10; John 3:3, 6; Ephesians 2:10.) And as the Sabbath is the appropriate sign, or memorial, of the creative power of God, so it is of God's re-creative power. This will be one great reason for the saints' keeping it throughout eternity. It will remind them not only of their own creation and the creation of the universe, but also of their redemption.

Through whom do we have sanctification?

"But of Him you are in Christ Jesus, who became for us wisdom from God—and righteousness and sanctification and redemption." 1 Corinthians 1:30, NKJV.

NOTE.—The Sabbath is a sign, or memorial, that it is God who sanctifies us. As Christ is the one through whom our sanctification is accomplished, the Sabbath is a memorial that we are united with Christ. God designed the Sabbath to link His children with Christ.

REASONS FOR SABBATHKEEPING

How is the true God distinguished from all false gods?

"The Lord is the true God; he is the living God, the eternal King. . . . 'Tell them this: *These gods, who did not make the heavens and the earth,* will perish from the earth and from under the heavens.' ' *But God made the earth by his power;* he founded the world by his wisdom and stretched out the heavens by his understanding." Jeremiah 10:10-12, NIV.

How did Paul describe God to the idolatrous Athenians?

"Now what you worship as something unknown I am going to proclaim to you. *The God who made the world and everything in it is the Lord of heaven and earth.*" Acts 17:23, 24, NIV.

What did the apostles say to the idolaters at Lystra?

"We are bringing you good news, telling you to turn from these worthless things *to the living God, who made heaven and earth and sea and everything in them.*" Acts 14:15, NIV. (See also Revelation 10:6; 14:6, 7.)

The words in Revelation 14:6,7 are an evident allusion to which commandment?

"Then I saw another angel flying in mid-heaven, with an eternal gospel to proclaim to those who live on the earth—to every nation and tribe and language and people. He said in a loud voice, 'Fear God and give him glory, for the hour of his judgment has come; and *worship him who made heaven and earth, the sea and the springs of water.*'" Revelation 14:6, 7, NRSV.

"Remember the sabbath day, and keep it holy. For six days you shall labor and do all your work. But the seventh day is a sabbath to the Lord your God; you shall not do any work—you, your son or your daughter, your male or female slave, your livestock, or the alien resident in your towns. For in six days the Lord *made heaven and earth, the sea, and all that is in them,* but rested the seventh day; therefore the Lord blessed the Sabbath day and consecrated it." Exodus 20:8-11, NRSV.

What reason is given in the fourth commandment for keeping the Sabbath day holy?

"For in six days the Lord made the heavens and the earth, the sea, and all that is in them, and rested the seventh day." Exodus 20:11, NKJV.

The Fourth Commandment in Revelation

Although the book of Revelation is filled with references to the Old Testament, it never quotes the Old Testament. It merely alludes to it with a word here and a phrase there. Figuring out what Old Testament texts the revelator is referring to at a given point can be a complex matter . . . Only in a handful of places in Revelation can you find as many as four, five, or six words in common with an Old Testament source. These are, of course, among the clearest allusions to the Old Testament in the Apocalypse. One of these places is the last part of Revelation 14:7: 'Worship him who made the heavens, the earth, the sea, and the springs of water' (NIV). . . .

"What is the significance of this quotation? Simply this: seven times in chapters 13 and 14 the word 'worship' is applied to the unholy trinity. 'They worshiped the dragon.' 'Worship the beast.' 'Worship the image of the beast.' Only one time in this whole section is there a call to worship the true God. If true versus false worship is the central issue at the end, *this passage (Revelation 14:7) is the central text of the section, perhaps of the entire book. When Revelation finally gets around to calling on people to worship the true God, it does so in the context of the fourth commandment, the Sabbath command. In a special sense, therefore, the author of Revelation understood the Sabbath to be the crucial issue in the final crisis.*

"In both texts (Revelation 14:7 and Exodus 20:8-11) the call to worship takes place in the context of Creation. One of the best reasons to worship God is the fact that He created us (this is also the theme of Revelation 4:9-11). As the memorial of creation, the Sabbath points continually to God as the object of worship. The issue in the final crisis, therefore, is not limited to the Sabbath, but the Sabbath is an integral part of the issue." Jon Paulien, *What the Bible Says About the End-time* (Hagerstown, Md.: Review and Herald, 1994), pp. 125, 126.

What is the Sabbath to those who keep it holy?

"Keep my Sabbaths holy, that *they may be a sign between us. Then you will know that I am the Lord your God.*" Ezekiel 20:20, NIV.

How important is it that we know God?

"Now *this is eternal life:* that they may know you, the only true God, and Jesus Christ, whom you have sent." John 17:3, NIV.

Is there any danger of God's people forgetting Him?

"Be careful that you do not forget the Lord your God, failing to observe his commands, his laws and his decrees that I am giving you this day." Deuteronomy 8:11, NIV.

What other reason did God give Israel for keeping the Sabbath?

"Say to the Israelites, 'You must observe my Sabbaths. This will be a sign between me and you for the generations to come, *so you may know that I am the Lord, who makes you holy.*'" Exodus 31:13, NIV.

NOTE.—To sanctify is to make holy, to set apart for a holy use. The sanctification of sinful people can be accomplished only by the creative power of God through Christ by the Holy Spirit. In 1 Corinthians 1:30 we are told that Christ is made unto us "sanctification"; and in Ephesians 2:10 it is said that "we are God's workmanship, created in Christ Jesus to do good works" (NIV). The Sabbath is thus a sign of sanctification, and of what Christ is to the believer, because it reminds us of God's creative power restoring us. It is the sign of the power of God in both creation and redemption.

What special reason did Israel have for Sabbathkeeping?

"Remember that you were slaves in Egypt and that the Lord your God brought you out of there with a mighty hand and an outstretched arm. Therefore the Lord your God has commanded you to observe the Sabbath day." Deuteronomy 5:15, NIV.

NOTE.—As slaves the Israelites had lost much of the knowledge of God, and departed from His precepts. In consequence of the oppression, especially the rigorous exactions made upon them by the Pharaoh of the Exodus, Sabbath observance was made apparently impossible. (See Exodus 5:1-19.) Moses and Aaron had shown them that obedience to God was the first condition of deliverance. Their efforts to restore the observance of the Sabbath among the Israelites brought Pharaoh's accusation, "' Moses and Aaron, why do you take the people from their work? Get back to your labor.' . . . 'Look, the people of the land are many now, and you make them rest [Hebrew, *shabbath*] from their labor!'" Exodus 5:4, 5, NKJV. Deliverance from this oppression was therefore an additional reason for their keeping the Sabbath. But Egyptian bondage simply represents the bondage of sin. (See Revelation 11:8; Hosea 11:1; Matthew 2:15; Zechariah 10:10.) Everyone who is delivered from sin has the same reason for keeping the Sabbath as the Israelites who were released from Egyptian bondage.

Why did God lead His people from Egypt to Canaan?

"He brought out his people with rejoicing, his chosen ones with shouts of joy; he gave them the lands of the nations, and they fell heir to what others had toiled for—*that they might keep his precepts and observe his laws.*" Psalm 105:43-45, NIV.

NOTE.—Their deliverance from Egyptian bondage was a reason for the keeping not only of the fourth commandment, but of every precept of God's law. This is indicated by the preamble to the law as given on Sinai: "I am the Lord your God, who brought you out of Egypt, out of the land of slavery," prefacing "You shall have no other gods before me." Exodus 20:2, 3, NIV (see also Leviticus 19:35-37; Deuteronomy 10:19; 15:12-15; 24:17, 18). Likewise, God calls everyone who, through Christ, has been delivered from the bondage of sin, to keep not only the Sabbath but every precept of His holy law. "Blessed is the man who does this, the man who holds it fast, who keeps the Sabbath without desecrating it, and keeps his hand from doing any evil." Isaiah 56:2, NIV.

What is the meaning of the word "sabbath"?

Rest.

NOTE.—Prior to the Fall, God designed that people's time should be occupied with pleasant, invigorating labor (Genesis 2:15). Wearisome toil came in consequence of sin (Genesis 3:17-19). Since the Fall the Sabbath may bring physical rest to both humans and beasts of burden (Exodus 23:12), but physical rest was not its original and primary design or purpose. God asks us to rest from our ordinary labors, not because these are sinful in themselves, but that we might have a regular period to contemplate God and His works.

Under the gospel, the Sabbath is a sign of spiritual rest and freedom from sin. "There remains, then, a Sabbath-rest for the people of God; for anyone who enters God's rest also rests from his own work, just as God did from his." Hebrews 4:9, 10, NIV.

Was the Sabbath intended as a day for public worship?

"There are six days when you may work, but the seventh day is a Sabbath of rest, a day of sacred assembly." Leviticus 23:3, NIV.

A Day of Rest

The command is that the day is to be a *rest* day. God rested during Creation week on the seventh day. He blessed that day then and made it holy, and we are commanded to do the same.

"Why is rest so important? To begin with, we can say that physically, emotionally, and socially, people who work hard need it. The Sabbath also symbolizes that God is the One who does the really important things in this world. Our rest shows that all things—especially the things that matter, such as creation and salvation—come from Him. We can't earn them but can simply rest in His good gifts.

"The day is *humanitarian*. Not only do Israelites rest, but their children, servants, animals, and visiting aliens all rest as well. All humans and animals are blessed by a day off.

"The Sabbath is thus *egalitarian*. Young and old, male and female, slave and free, Israelite and Gentile, rich and poor—all get a rest. God shows no favorites in this beautiful gift of the Sabbath.

"The Sabbath commandment as it appears in Deuteronomy 5:12-15 differs somewhat from the Exodus version. Deuteronomy says, 'Observe the Sabbath' (NIV), while Exodus says, 'Remember the Sabbath' (NIV). More important than this, Deuteronomy gives a different rationale for Sabbath observance. Exodus says we keep it because God rested from His work of creation, while Deuteronomy gives the Exodus from Egypt as the reason. One need not ask which one is right, because both are. Humans didn't create and neither did they accomplish the Exodus. God did. The only way we can respond is by resting on the day God commanded as a memorial to both creation and redemption. This demonstrates that the commandment did not change, but the rationale and explanation for it could be broadened. The order to rest remains constant, but the reason for resting can grow and be enriched as time passes.

"If there is any command hurried and hassled modern people need, it is the Sabbath. We are so busy trying to create meaning in our own life and serving ourselves that we forget that God is the only One who can give meaning to our lives. We show our 'resting' in Him by resting on His day." Jon L. Dybdahl, *The Abundant Life Bible Amplifier: Exodus* (Boise, Idaho: Pacific Press, 1994), pp. 185, 186.

KEEPING THE SABBATH

What is first commanded in the Sabbath commandment?
"Remember the sabbath day." Exodus 20:8.

Which day is the Sabbath?
"The *seventh* day is the Sabbath." Verse 10.

For what purpose are we to remember the Sabbath day?
"Remember the sabbath day, to keep it holy." Verse 8.

NOTE.—All through the week we are to "remember the sabbath day, to keep it holy." This means that all our plans are to be laid and all our business adjusted with reference to the Sabbath, the object of which is to remind us that God is the Creator of all things. This is just as essential to spiritual growth during the six working days as upon the Sabbath itself. We are to remember that day, also, that when it comes we may not be tempted by circumstances of our own creating to treat it, or any part of it, as secular, or common, time. Thus the Sabbath commandment is to be obeyed every day, though the Sabbath itself can be kept, or observed, only upon the seventh day, for "the seventh day is the sabbath."

Who made the Sabbath day holy?
"Therefore the *Lord* blessed the Sabbath day, and made it holy." Verse 11, NIV.

NOTE.—God made the Sabbath day holy; we are to keep it holy.

What is it that makes a thing holy?
God's *presence* in it. (See Exodus 3:5; 29:43-46; Joshua 5:13-15.)

To keep the Sabbath day holy, we must recognize what?
God's *presence* in the day, His *blessing* upon it, and His *sanctification* of it.

When does the Bible say a day begins?
"And there was *evening*, and there was morning—the first day." Genesis 1:5, NIV.

NOTE.—The Bible marks the beginning and end of days at sunset.

What kind of labor is to be done through the week?
"Six days you shall labor and do *all your work.*" Exodus 20:9, NIV.

Is any of this kind of work to be done on the Sabbath?

"On it you shall not do any work." Verse 10, NIV.

NOTE.—If the Sabbath is to be kept "holy," mere physical rest one day in seven cannot be the great purpose of the Sabbath institution.

What is the day to prepare for the Sabbath?

"It was Preparation Day, and the Sabbath was about to begin." Luke 23:54, NIV. (See also Exodus 16:22, 23.)

NOTE.—In order to keep the Sabbath day holy, we must remember it all through the week; and on the sixth day, Friday, the day just before the Sabbath, special preparation should be made *to be ready* to welcome and observe the day when it comes.

During their wilderness journey, how did the Israelites prepare for the Sabbath?

"On the sixth day, they gathered twice as much [manna]." Exodus 16:22, NIV.

How does the prophet Isaiah describe true Sabbathkeeping?

"If you [turn back your foot from] the Sabbath, from pursuing your affairs on My holy day; if you call the Sabbath 'delight,' the Lord's holy day 'honored'; and if you honor it and go not your ways nor look to your affairs, nor strike bargains—then you can seek the favor of the Lord. I will set you astride the heights of the earth, and let you enjoy the heritage of your father Jacob—for the mouth of the Lord has spoken." Isaiah 58:13, 14, Tanakh.

A Rest From "Business as Usual"

Some modern English translations of Isaiah 58:13, 14 have caused some confusion over how we should observe the Sabbath. God's call in Isaiah 58:13, 14 to avoid "doing your pleasure" (verse 13, NKJV) on the Sabbath resonates with us, but what does it mean?

The fourth commandment does not forbid pleasure on Sabbath, but only work. The Hebrew word translated 'you shall labor,' *ta'abd,* is 'sweat of your brow' work, like that done by an *'ebed,* a servant or slave. The Hebrew word translated 'your work,' *m^{c}la'kttek,* especially suggests occupations, such as

A Rest From "Business as Usual" CONTINUED

shopkeeper or artisan, the work of commerce, though it also
means work. The Old Testament says very little about Sabbath
worship, but it strongly emphasizes Sabbath rest. The Hebrew
word for Sabbath, *šabbat*, is a noun. The verb it is derived from,
šabbat, means 'to cease,' primarily from work. . . .

"God asks us to call the Sabbath a delight. . . . That means
learning to find it delightful, or doing on it what is delightful.
The Hebrew word translated 'delight,' found twice in verses 13
and 14, is *'oneg,* which means 'exquisite delight,' 'dainty,' 'soft,'
and 'delicate.' It sometimes refers to luxury, what is rich and
delicious, like Sabbath dinner. That's God's intention for the
Sabbath! It should be the most exquisite, luxuriously delightful
day of the week! Isn't that better than 'your own pleasure'? But
if the Sabbath is an 'exquisite delight' for us, are we not taking
pleasure in it? . . .

" ' From the Sabbath.' . . . The first question stems from the
faulty parallelism introduced by translators: 'If you turn your
foot away from the Sabbath, . . . and call the Sabbath a delight
. . .' If we turn away our feet from the Sabbath, why would we
call the Sabbath a delight? As translated, this makes no sense.
. . . In Hebrew, the phrase 'from the Sabbath' is one word,
mišabbat. That *mi* is short for *min*, which is usually translated
'from.' Several dozen times, however, it means not 'from,' but
'on account of,' or 'because of.' That's the correct translation
here, as well. . . .

"So the text is talking about turning away from something
'on account of' the Sabbath, because observing the Sabbath requires this turning away. It doesn't mean turning away 'from'
the Sabbath.

" ' *Turn away.*' Second, what does it mean to 'turn away your
foot'? Does it mean to stop trampling on the Sabbath? No, it
doesn't. It's an idiomatic expression.

" ' Turning away the foot' means stopping whatever one is
doing and returning to where one came from. The Hebrew word
translated 'turn away' is related to the Hebrew word *sh b,* 'return.' That is God's Old Testament word for repentance. . . .

"Turning away from our daily activities and returning to Sabbathkeeping is our own choice. It's not automatic, it's not a forced
decision, and it's not an accident. God asks us to make that choice.

A Rest From "Business as Usual" CONTINUED

"Sabbath pleasures? Third, what is meant by 'your own pleasure'? . . . If we take delight in the Sabbath, isn't that pleasure? . . .

"There is another valid way of translating the verse that better fits the fourth commandment's prohibition of work on the seventh day.

" '*Pleasure*' is the most common meaning of the Hebrew noun *hepes,* but not the only meaning. . . .

"The word also means 'business,' 'affair,' and 'matter.' It occurs in Ecclesiastes 3:1 and 17, in the phrase 'a time for every purpose' (NKJV), which we never translate as 'a time for every pleasure.' . . .

"Thus God is not speaking against pleasure here, but against working, doing business on Sabbath. 'Finding your own pleasure' should actually be translated 'finding business,' or 'looking for customers.'

"Silence on Sabbath? Fourth, in the New King James Version italicized words are not in the original. 'Not *speaking your own words'* reads, literally, not 'speaking words.' Are we to remain silent on the Sabbath? The New International Version changes this to not 'speaking idle words,' which makes sense, but it's not what the Hebrew says.

"In Hebrew, the expression is *dav r d v r,* 'the speaking of a word.' Is God asking for silence on Sabbath? No, He's not. The noun *d v r* is usually translated 'word,' as in 'the word of the Lord,' but it seldom means an actual word. It's more likely to mean a 'statement,' a 'message,' a 'speech,' a 'report,' an 'edict,' or even a 'thing.'

"However, more significantly, *d v r* sometimes means a 'matter' or 'affair' or 'business' or 'occupation.' In 1 Samuel 21:8 it's translated 'business' In 2 Samuel 19:29 we also find the words *dav r . . . d v r.* There they are translated 'speak . . . of your matters' (NKJV), as in 'business matters.'

"We find, thus, that God is asking us to refrain not only from 'finding business,' but from 'talking business' or making deals on Sabbath. Does this mean that if I invite people over for lunch on Sabbath, I shouldn't ask them how their work is going? I don't think so. But spending the afternoon discussing work does not fill us with delight. It isn't refreshing. . . .

A Rest From "Business as Usual" CONTINUED

" ' *Doing your own ways.*' Fifth, we're familiar with the phrase 'going your own way,' but both the Hebrew and the New King James Version read '*doing* your own ways.' . . .

"The Hebrew word *derek* usually means 'road' or 'way.' . . .

" ' Doing' your way or road doesn't make sense, so we should look for another meaning of *derek*. We find the word also means what is 'customary,' our usual 'undertaking' or way of doing business. So, again the text speaks against working on Sabbath, this time not against 'finding' or 'talking,' but against 'doing.'

" ' Finding your own pleasure' actually means 'finding business,' looking for potential customers. 'Speaking words' actually means 'talking business.' 'Doing your own ways' actually means 'doing business as usual.'

"Translating these phrases this way fits nicely with the fourth commandment as well, as it forbids both field labor and commerce.

"But was working on Sabbath a serious problem for the Israelites? Wasn't the Sabbath always precious to them? Nehemiah writes, in Nehemiah 13:15, 'In those days I saw men in Judah treading winepresses on the Sabbath and bringing in grain and loading it on donkeys, together with wine, grapes, figs and all other kinds of loads. And they were bringing all this into Jerusalem on the Sabbath. Therefore I warned them against selling food on that day" (NIV).

"Was this happening in Isaiah's time, as well? In verse 18 Nehemiah says, 'Didn't your forefathers do the same things, so that our God brought all this calamity upon us and upon this city?' In Isaiah 58, God is trying to get those forefathers to avoid the coming catastrophe by putting aside their daily work and not treating the Sabbath as a normal business day. . . .

"The passage doesn't mean 'Don't do what you please on Sabbath.' It means 'Don't do what you please if what pleases you is working.' Remember too that the Sabbath is not only a deliverance from work, but a symbol of deliverance from our own works.

"This doesn't mean Sabbath is for doing whatever we feel like doing. But *pleasure* is not forbidden. . . . If it is not our ordinary work, if it delights us, and if we can share that delight

---

A Rest From"Business as Usual" CONTINUED

with God without rationalizing our behavior, then God smiles on us. . . .

"Conversely, if what we do makes the Sabbath a misery to us or to our children, if it makes us hate Sabbath, if it makes us long for Sabbath to be over, we're going the wrong way. In a sense, whatever we do on Sabbath that is not delightful in a God-honoring way breaks the Sabbath. Ed Christian, *Joyful Noise* (Hagerstown, Md.: Review and Herald, 2003), pp. 166-171.

What is the nature of God, and how only can He be truly worshipped?

"God is Spirit: and those who worship Him must worship in spirit and truth." John 4:24, NKJV.

NOTE.—Attempts to encourage Sabbathkeeping by human laws is altogether out of place. Such laws can never foster true devotion to God's law, for that is *spiritual*, and must be of the *mind* and from the *heart*, not *perfunctory, mechanical*, or by force.

What is one thing of which the Sabbath is a sign?

That it is God who *sanctifies* His people, or *makes them holy.* (See Exodus 31:13; Ezekiel 20:12; and p. 351.)

What does the "psalm for the Sabbath day" suggest as proper themes for Sabbath thought and action?

"It is good to *praise the Lord and make music to your name,* O Most High, to proclaim *your love* in the morning and *your faithfulness* at night, to the music of the ten-stringed lyre and the melody of the harp. For you make me glad by your deeds, O Lord; I sing for joy at the work of your hands. How great are your works, O Lord; I sing for joy at the works of your hands. *How great are your works, O Lord, how profound your thoughts!"* Psalm 92:15, NIV.

What do the works of God declare?

"The heavens declare *the glory of God;* the skies proclaim *the work of his hands.* Day after day they pour forth speech; night after night they display *knowledge.* . . . Their voice goes out into all the earth, their words to the ends of the world." Psalm 19:13, NIV.

NOTE.—God designed that the Sabbath should direct our minds to

His created works, and through these to Him, the Creator. Nature itself speaks to our senses, telling us that there is a God, the Creator and Supreme Ruler of the universe. The Sabbath, ever pointing to God through nature, was designed to keep the Creator constantly in mind.

What evidence is there that the Sabbath was designed to be a day for public worship?

"There are six days when you may work, but the seventh day is a Sabbath of rest, *a day of sacred assembly."* Leviticus 23:3, NIV.

What was Jesus' custom on the Sabbath day?

"He went to Nazareth, where he had been brought up, and on the Sabbath day *he went into the synagogue, as was his custom."* Luke 4:16, NIV.

What else did Jesus do on the Sabbath?

He healed people. "Now the day on which Jesus had made the mud and opened the man's eyes was a Sabbath." John 9:14, NIV.

NOTE.—A large share of Christ's ministry consisted of miracles and acts of mercy performed for the relief of suffering humanity, and many of these were done on the Sabbath. On this day, as on other days, He "went about doing good." See next reading.

With what words did Jesus justify acts of mercy on the Sabbath?

"He said to them, 'If any of you has a sheep and it falls into a pit on the Sabbath, will you not take hold of it and lift it out? How much more valuable is a man than a sheep! Therefore *it is lawful to do good on the Sabbath."* Matthew 12:11, 12, NIV.

NOTE.—Much of Jesus' earthly ministry was devoted to uplifting the Sabbath, and showing the beneficial character of the Sabbath institution. It was not meant to be a day of sorrow, austerity, or gloom. Acts of love and mercy are always in place on the Sabbath. *Lawful* means "according to law."

Often when Jesus healed people, He urged them to not tell anyone (e.g., Luke 5:14), but when Jesus healed on the Sabbath, he did it in as public a way as possible (e.g., Mark 3:3). In so doing, Jesus emphasized the Sabbath's important role as a day of restoration of mind, body, and spirit.

JESUS AND THE SABBATH

What authoritative relationship did Jesus claim to the Sabbath?

"At that time Jesus went through the grain fields on the Sabbath.

His disciples were hungry and began to pick some heads of grain and eat them. When the Pharisees saw this, they said to him, 'Look! Your disciples are doing what is unlawful on the Sabbath.'

"He answered, 'Haven't you read what David did when he and his companions were hungry? He entered the house of God, and he and his companions ate the consecrated bread—which was not lawful for them to do, but only for the priests. Or haven't you read in the Law that on the Sabbath the priests in the temple desecrate the day and yet are innocent? I tell you that one greater than the temple is here. If you had known what these words mean, 'I desire mercy, not sacrifice,' you would not have condemned the innocent. For the Son of Man is *Lord of the Sabbath.*" Matthew 12:1-8, NIV. (See also Mark 2:28.)

NOTE.—Jesus here quotes Hosea 6:6 about mercy being more important than ritual.

"The priests actually worked harder on the Sabbath than on any other day of the week. But their work was not sinful, because it was in the service of God. Their priestly service was justifiable work, because it was sacred, not secular.

"The argument based on this example rests on a famous principle of hermeneutics termed *qal wahomer*, that is, 'the light and the weighty,' applied to an actual precept of the law. The Christological statement in Matthew 12:6 is indeed significant: 'I tell you, something greater than the temple is here' (RSV). It is an assertion that our Lord is superior to the Jewish regulations of worship. He is greater than the Temple and its cultus. It was to Him and His work as both priest and sacrifice that the Temple services pointed forward. He came to earth as the Redeemer of the world. His disciples were associated with Him in the great work of redeeming mankind, a work that was sacred, not secular. Hence it was right for them to satisfy their physical hunger to receive strength to carry on their work further.

"The real nature of the Sabbath was often gravely misunderstood. Mere cessation of labor was not the essence of the Sabbath. It was never God's intention that the Sabbath be made a day of useless inactivity. The Sabbath was to be a day when man forsook his secular pursuits and devoted the day to worship and to the service of God.

"According to Matthew, Jesus also referred to some well-known words of the prophet Hosea: 'And if you had known what this means, "I desire mercy, and not sacrifice," you would not have condemned the guiltless' (Matt. 12:7, RSV). Jesus had come to establish the rule of the kingdom of God. In the eyes of a gracious God, mercy is of far more importance than a legalistic obedience to the law. Hence on another occasion our Lord accused the scribes and Pharisees of neglecting the weightier matters such as 'justice and mercy and faith,' while meticulously tithing 'mint and dill and cumin' ([Matt.] 23:23, RSV).

"In Mark's account (chap. 2:27), Jesus then raised the issue of the purpose of the Sabbath. The Sabbath was not an end in itself. 'The Sabbath was made for man, and not man for the Sabbath' (RSV). It was designed to be a blessing to man, a day of physical rest, but also a day devoted to spiritual exercises. The Pharisees treated the day as though man were created to serve the Sabbath, rather than the Sabbath meeting the needs of man. . . .

"All three of the Synoptic Gospels record the concluding statement, 'The Son of man is lord even of the Sabbath' (Mark 2:28, RSV; Matt 12:8; Luke 6:5). This statement asserts Christ's sovereignty over the Sabbath. He, after all, was with our heavenly Father when the Sabbath was made (John 1:1-3). Therefore He, rather than the scribes and Pharisees, has the authority to state what is lawful and not lawful to do on the day of rest. It was not the Sabbath law itself that Jesus' disciples had violated, but the man-made pharisaical regulations regarding Sabbath observance. Jesus on more than one occasion completely ignored the oral law so dear to the Pharisees." Walter F. Specht, "The Sabbath in the New Testament," *The Sabbath in Scripture and History,* ed. Kenneth A. Strand (Washington, D.C.: Review and Herald, 1982), pp. 96, 97.

How did Jesus reaffirm and expand the Sabbath's significance through personal example?

"Going on from that place, he went into their synagogue, and a man with a shriveled hand was there. Looking for a reason to accuse Jesus, they asked him, 'Is it lawful to heal on the Sabbath?'

"He said to them, 'If any of you has a sheep and it falls into a pit on the Sabbath, will you not take hold of it and lift it out? How much more valuable is a man than a sheep! Therefore it is lawful to do good on the Sabbath'

"Then he said to the man, 'Stretch out your hand.' So he stretched it out and it was completely restored, just as sound as the other" Matthew 12:8-13, NIV.

"On a Sabbath Jesus was teaching in one of the synagogues, and a woman was there who had been crippled by a spirit for eighteen years. She was bent over and could not straighten up at all. When Jesus saw her, he called her forward and said to her, 'Woman, you are set free from your infirmity.' Then he put his hands on her, and immediately she straightened up and praised God." Luke 12:10-13, NIV.

"Some time later, Jesus went up to Jerusalem for a feast of the Jews. Now there is in Jerusalem near the Sheep Gate a pool, which in Aramaic is called Bethesda and which is surrounded by five covered colonnades. Here a great number of disabled people used to lie—the blind, the lame, the paralyzed. One who was there had been an invalid for thirty-eight years. When Jesus saw him lying there and learned that he had been in this condition for a long time, he asked him, 'Do you want to get well?'

" ' Sir,' the invalid replied, 'I have no one to help me into the pool when the water is stirred. While I am trying to get in, someone else goes down ahead of me.'

"Then Jesus said to him, 'Get up! Pick up your mat and walk' At once the man was cured; he picked up his mat and walked.

"The day on which this took place was a Sabbath, and so the Jews said to the man who had been healed, 'It is the Sabbath; the law forbids you to carry your mat.'

"But he replied, 'The man who made me well said to me, "Pick up your mat and walk." ' "

"So they asked him, 'Who is this fellow who told you to pick it up and walk?'

"The man who was healed had no idea who it was, for Jesus had slipped away into the crowd that was there.

"Later Jesus found him at the temple and said to him, 'See, you are well again. Stop sinning or something worse may happen to you.' The man went away and told the Jews that it was Jesus who made him well." John 5:1-15, NIV.

NOTE.—As God established the Sabbath by His personal example of resting on the seventh day of Creation , so Jesus confirmed the Sabbath's significance by His personal example. That Christ went to such lengths to reform people's understanding and observance of the Sabbath shows that He was seeking to maintain it, not to set it up for abandonment.

Although the Lord, the Maker, and a keeper of the Sabbath, how was Jesus watched and spied upon on this day?

"The Pharisees and the teachers of the law were looking for a reason to accuse Jesus, so *they watched him closely to see if he would heal on the Sabbath.*" Luke 6:7, NIV.

How did Christ counter their false ideas of Sabbathkeeping and emphasize the Sabbath's true purpose?

"Then Jesus said to them, *'I ask you, which is lawful on the Sabbath: to do good or to do evil, to save life or to destroy it?' "* Verse 9, NIV.

"One Sabbath, when Jesus went to eat in the house of a prominent Pharisee, he was being carefully watched. There in front of him was a man suffering from dropsy. Jesus asked the Pharisees and experts in the law, 'Is it lawful to heal on the Sabbath or not?' But they remained silent. So taking hold of the man, he healed him and sent him away.

"Then he asked them, 'If one of you has a son or an ox that falls into a well on the Sabbath day, will you not immediately pull him out?' And they had nothing to say." Luke 14:1-6, NIV.

How did the religious leaders respond when Jesus healed a man with a withered hand on a Sabbath?

"But they were furious and began to discuss with one another what they might do to Jesus." Luke 6:11, NIV.

"Then the Pharisees went out and began to plot with the Herodians how they might kill Jesus." Mark 3:6, NIV.

NOTE.—Although the miracle Christ performed had demonstrated that He was from God, they were angry because He had *shown their views of Sabbathkeeping to be wrong.* Their wounded pride, obstinacy, and malice combined to fill them with madness; and they went out immediately and held counsel with the Herodians—their political enemies—to see how they could have Jesus killed.

Because Jesus healed a man on the Sabbath day, and told him to take up his bed and walk, what did the Jewish religious leaders do?

"So, because Jesus was doing these things on the Sabbath, the Jews persecuted him." John 5:16, NIV.

NOTE.—Jesus' approach to Sabbath observance was prominent among the reasons the religious leaders sought to kill Him. Prophecy points to a similar conflict over Sabbath observance at the end of time.

How did Jesus answer them?

"Jesus said to them, 'My Father is always at his work to this very day, and I, too, am working.' " Verse 17, NIV.

NOTE.—The ordinary operations of nature, as manifested in God's almighty, overseeing, and healing power, continue on the Sabbath. To cooperate with God and nature in the work of healing on the Sabbath is not, therefore, out of harmony with God's Sabbath law.

What effect did this answer have upon the Jewish leaders?

"For this reason the Jews *tried all the harder to kill him; not only was he breaking the Sabbath, but he was even calling God his own Father, making himself equal with God."* Verse 18, NIV.

What did the Pharisees say when they spied Jesus' disciples plucking a few heads of grain on the Sabbath to satisfy their hunger?

"The Pharisees said to him, 'Look, why are they doing what is unlawful on the Sabbath?' " Mark 2:24, NIV.

What pointed statement did Jesus make to counter legalistic views of the Sabbath?

" 'The Sabbath was made for man, not man for the Sabbath.' " Verses 27, NIV.

NOTE.—Many have viewed the Sabbath as a burden for people to endure, as largely a test of our ability to restrain ourselves for God. Jesus' words here turn that idea on its head. Jesus tells us that we were not created for the Sabbath's benefit—the Sabbath was created for ours. Jesus invites us to discover the blessing He intended for us when He created the Sabbath. He bids us to find restoration, renewal, and re-creation in the Sabbath—and to share those blessings with others in need.

What argument did a religious leader give against Jesus' healing a woman one Sabbath?

"Indignant because Jesus had healed on the Sabbath, the synagogue ruler said to the people, 'There are six days for work. So come and be healed on those days, not on the Sabbath.' " Luke 13:14, NIV.

What was Christ's answer?

"You hypocrites! Doesn't each of you on the Sabbath untie his ox or donkey from the stall and lead it out to give it water? Then should not this woman, a daughter of Abraham, whom Satan has kept bound for eighteen long years, be set free on the Sabbath day from what bound her?" Verses 15, 16, NIV.

NOTE.—For too many people the Sabbath has been a day of self-ishness. Jesus calls us to follow His example and make the Sabbath a day of love and faith in action.

What effect did Christ's answers have upon the people?

"All his opponents were humiliated, but *the people were delighted* with all the wonderful things he was doing." Verse 17, NIV.

What dispute did Jesus' miracles cause?

"Some of the Pharisees said, 'This man is not from God, for he does not keep the Sabbath.' But others asked, 'How can a sinner do such miraculous signs?' So they were divided." John 9:16, NIV.

THE SABBATH IN THE NEW TESTAMENT

What day do the gospels tell us precedes the first day of the week?

"The next day, the one after Preparation Day, the chief priests and the Pharisees went to Pilate. 'Sir,' they said, 'we remember that while he was still alive that deceiver said, 'After three days I will rise again' '" . . . After *the Sabbath,* at dawn on the first day of the week, Mary Magdalene and the other Mary went to look at the tomb." Matthew 27:62-28:1, NIV.

NOTE.—According to the New Testament, the Sabbath had passed when the first day of the week began. Matthew emphasizes the two Marys' observation of the Sabbath, drawing a sharp contrast to the political maneuvering that consumed the Pharisees' Sabbath. This indicates that Matthew's readers still observed the Sabbath decades after Jesus' resurrection. Writing for a Gentile audience, Mark matter-of-factly states, "It was Preparation Day (that is, the day before the Sabbath. . . . Mary Magdalene and Mary the mother of Joses saw where he was laid. When the Sabbath was over, Mary Magdalene, Mary the Mother of James, and Salome bought spices so that they might go to anoint Jesus' body." Mark 15:42-16:1, NIV.

After the Crucifixion, what day was kept by the women who followed Jesus?

"Then they went home and prepared spices and perfumes. But they rested on the Sabbath in obedience to the commandment." Luke 23:56, NIV.

What day of the week is the Sabbath "in obedience to the commandment"?

"But the seventh day is the sabbath of the Lord thy God." Exodus 20:10.

In what instruction to His disciples did Christ recognize the existence of the Sabbath long after His ascension?

"Pray that your flight will not take place in winter or *on the Sabbath"* Matthew 24:20, NIV.

NOTE.—The flight of the Christians took place late in October, A.D. 66, three and one-half years before the fall of Jerusalem. Jesus "instructed them to pray at that time of crisis they would not find it necessary to flee on the Sabbath. But the implication is that conditions could be such as to make instant flight necessary even on the day of rest. But the fear, bustle, and confusion that a hasty flight on Sabbath would bring were not in harmony with the worship, peace, and joy that should characterize the sacred day of rest. Hence, Jesus' followers were urged to pray that the flight would occur on a different day of the week." Walter F. Specht, "The Sabbath in the New Testament," *The Sabbath in Scripture and History,* ed. Kenneth A. Strand, (Washington, D.C.: Review and Herald, 1982), p. 103.

On what day did Paul and Barnabas preach at Antioch?

"From Perga they went on to Pisidian Antioch. *On the Sabbath* they entered the synagogue and sat down." Acts 13:14, NIV.

When did the Gentiles ask Paul to repeat his sermon?

"As Paul and Barnabas were leaving the synagogue, the people invited them to speak further about these things *on the next Sabbath.*" Verse 42, NIV.

On what day did Paul preach to the women at Philippi?

"On the Sabbath we went outside the city gate to the river, where we expected to find a place of prayer. We sat down and began to speak to the women who had gathered there." Acts 16:13, NIV.

NOTE.—These verses confirm the early Christian church continued to call the seventh day the Sabbath, just as the Jews did.

On what day did Paul speak to the Jews at Thessalonica?

"They came to Thessalonica, where there was a synagogue of the Jews. As his custom was, Paul went in to the synagogue, and on three Sabbaths he reasoned with them from the Scriptures." Acts 17:1, 2, NIV.

NOTE.—It was Paul's manner, as it was Jesus' custom (Luke 4:16), to attend religious services on the Sabbath.

How did Paul spend the working days of the week when at Corinth, and what did he do on the Sabbath?

"There he met a Jew named Aquila, a native of Pontus, who had recently come from Italy with his wife Priscilla, because Claudius had ordered all the Jews to leave Rome. Paul went to see them, and because he was a tentmaker as they were, he stayed and worked with them. Every Sabbath he reasoned in the synagogue, trying to persuade Jews and Greeks." Acts 18:2-4, NIV.

NOTE.—"He continued there a year and six months, teaching the word of God among them." Verse 11. These texts do not definitely prove that the apostle held seventy-eight Sabbath meetings in Corinth, but they show conclusively that it was his custom to observe that day by devoting it to religious purposes. The careful student will note that his reasoning in the synagogue every Sabbath applies only to the comparatively brief time during which he was permitted the use of the synagogue. But the history of the apostle's work in the book of Acts fully warrants us in believing that wherever he was, Paul utilized to the full every opportunity to pursue his gospel work on the Sabbath. The same is true, not only of the apostles, but of most Christians during the first three centuries.

On what day was John in the Spirit?

"I was in the Spirit *on the Lord's day.*" Revelation 1:10.

Who is Lord of the Sabbath?

"The Son of man is Lord also of the sabbath." Mark 2:28.

What, through Isaiah, does the Lord call the Sabbath?

"If you keep your foot from breaking the Sabbath, and from doing as you please *on my holy day,* if you call the Sabbath a delight and *the Lord's holy day* honorable . . ." Isaiah 58:13, NIV.

Why does the Lord call the Sabbath His day?

"For in six days the Lord made the heavens and the earth, the sea, and all that is in them, but *he rested on the seventh day.* Therefore the Lord *blessed* the Sabbath day *and made it holy.*" Exodus 20:11, NIV.

Through whom did God create the world?

"In these last days [God] has spoken to us by *His Son,* whom he appointed heir of all things, and through whom he made the universe." Hebrews 1:1, 2, NIV.

NOTE.—The Bible recognizes but one weekly Sabbath—the day upon which God rested in the beginning; which was made known to Israel at Sinai (Nehemiah 9:13, 14); was observed by Christ and His apostles; and is to be kept by the redeemed in the new earth (Isaiah 66:22, 23).

"The sacred name of the seventh day is Sabbath. This fact is too clear to require argument. The truth is stated in concise terms: 'The seventh day is the Sabbath of the Lord thy God.' This utterance is repeated in Exodus 16:26; 23:12; 31:15; 35:2; Leviticus 23:3; and Deuteronomy 5:14. On this point the plain teaching of the word has been admitted in all ages. Except to certain special sabbaths appointed in Levitical law, and these invariably governed by the month rather than the week, the Bible in all its utterances never, no, not once, applies the name Sabbath to any other day." J. J. Taylor, *The Sabbatic Question* (Revell), pp. 16, 17.

The first day of the week is mentioned but eight times in the

New Testament, six of which are found in the four Gospels, and refer to the day on which Christ arose from the dead. (See Matthew 28:1; Mark 16:2, 9; Luke 24:1; John 20:1, 19.) The other two (Acts 20:7; 1 Corinthians 16:2) refer to the only religious meeting held on the first day of the week after the ascension recorded in the New Testament, and to a systematic accounting and laying by in store at home on that day for the poor saints in Judea and Jerusalem.

It is therefore evident that the Sabbath of the New Testament is the same as the Sabbath of the Old Testament, and that the New Testament does not set aside the seventh-day Sabbath, replacing it with the first day of the week.

Some have argued that Jesus' salvific work finished the weekly Sabbath's role. As the Sabbath was established before Adam and Eve sinned, however, Jesus' work saving us from sin would not impact it.

THE CHANGE OF THE SABBATH

Of what is the Sabbath commandment a part?

The law of God. (See Exodus 20:8-11.)

In His most famous sermon, the Sermon on the Mount, what did Jesus say about the law?

"Do not think that I have come to abolish the Law or the Prophets; I have not come to abolish them but to fulfill them." Matthew 5:17, NIV.

How enduring did He say the law is?

"I tell you the truth, until heaven and earth disappear, not the smallest letter, not the least stroke of a pen, will by any means disappear from the Law until everything is accomplished." Verse 18, NIV.

What did He say of those who should break one of the least of God's commandments, and teach people to do so?

"Anyone who breaks one of the least of these commandments and teaches others to do the same will be called least in the kingdom." Verse 19, NIV.

NOTE.—It is evident that all ten commandments are binding in the Christian dispensation, and that Christ had no thought of changing any of them. (See readings on pp. 312, 334, 335, 345.) One of these commands the observance of the seventh day as the Sabbath. But most Christians keep the first day of the week instead.

Many believe that Christ changed the Sabbath. But, from His own words, we see that He came for no such purpose. The responsibility for this change must therefore be looked for elsewhere. Those who believe that Jesus changed the Sabbath base it only on a supposition.

What did God, through the prophet Daniel, say the power represented by the "little horn" would think to do?

"And he shall speak words against the most High, and shall wear out the saints of the most High, and think to change the times and the laws." Daniel 7:25.

NOTE.—For an explanation of this symbolism, see pp. 179-181.

What did the apostle Paul say the "man of sin" would do?

"Don't let anyone deceive you in any way, for that day will not come until the rebellion occurs and the man of lawlessness is revealed, the man doomed to destruction. He will oppose and will exalt himself over everything that is called God or is worshiped, so that he sets himself up in God's temple, proclaiming himself to be God." 2 Thessalonians 2:3, 4, NIV.

NOTE.—There is only one way by which any power could exalt itself above God, and that is by assuming to change the law of God, and to require obedience to its own law instead of God's law.

Why did God command Israel to hallow the Sabbath?

"Keep my Sabbaths holy, that they may be a sign between us. Then you will know that I am the Lord your God." Ezekiel 20:20, NIV.

NOTE.—As the Sabbath was given that man might keep God in mind as Creator, it can be readily seen that a power endeavoring to exalt itself above God could do this in no other way so effectually as by setting aside God's memorial—the.seventh-day Sabbath. Daniel spoke of this work when he said, "He will speak against the Most High and oppress his saints and *try to change the set times and the laws.*" Daniel 7:25, NIV.

How did this change in observance of days come about?

Through a *gradual* transference.

NOTE.—"The Christian Church made no formal, but a *gradual* and almost unconscious, transference of the one day to the other." F. W Farrar, *The Voice From Sinai,* p. 167. This of itself is evidence that there was no divine command for the change of the Sabbath.

For how long a time was the seventh-day Sabbath observed in the Christian church?

For many centuries. In fact, its observance has never wholly ceased in the Christian church.

NOTE.—"A history of the problem shows that in some places, it was really only after some centuries that the Sabbath rest really was entirely abolished, and by that time the practice of observing a bodily rest on the Sunday had taken its place." Vincent J. Kelly, *Forbidden Sunday and Feast-Day Occupations,* p. 15.

Lyman Coleman says: "Down even to the fifth century the observance of the Jewish Sabbath was continued in the Christian church, but with a rigor and a solemnity gradually diminishing until it was wholly discontinued." *Ancient Christianity Exemplified,* chap. 26, sec. 2.

The church historian Socrates, who wrote in the fifth century, says: "Almost all the churches throughout the world celebrate the sacred mysteries on the Sabbath of every week, yet the Christians of Alexandria and at Rome, on account of some ancient tradition, have ceased to do this." *Ecclesiastical History,* book 5, chap. 22, in *A Select Library of Nicene and Post-Nicene Fathers,* 2nd Series, vol. 2, p. 32.

Sozomen, another historian of the same period, writes: "The people of Constantinople, and almost everywhere, assemble together on the Sabbath as well as on the first day of the week, which custom is never observed at Rome or at Alexandria" *Ecclesiastical History,* book 7, chap. 19, in the same volume as the above quotation.

All this would have been inconceivable had there been a divine command given for the change of the Sabbath. The last two quotations also show that Rome led in the apostasy and in the change of the Sabbath.

How did Sunday observance originate?

As a voluntary celebration of the resurrection, a custom without pretense of divine authority.

NOTE.—"Opposition to Judaism introduced the particular festival of Sunday very early, indeed, into the place of the Sabbath. . . . The festival of Sunday, like all other festivals, was always only a human ordinance, and it was far from the intentions of the apostles to establish a Divine command in this respect, far from them, and from the early apostolic Church, to transfer the laws of the Sabbath to Sunday. Perhaps, at the end of the second century a false application of this kind had begun to take place; for men appear by that time to have considered laboring on Sunday as a sin." Augustus Neander, *The History of the Christian Religion and Church* (Rose's translation from the first German edition), p. 186.

"The observance of the Sunday was at first supplemental to that of the Sabbath, but in proportion as the gulf between the Church and the Synagogue widened, the Sabbath became less and less important and ended at length in being entirely neglected." L. Duchesne, *Christian Worship: Its Origin and Evolution* (translated from the 4th French ed. by M. L. McClure, London, 1910), p. 47.

Who first enforced Sundaykeeping by law?

The Roman emperor Constantine the Great.

NOTE.—"(1) That the Sunday was in the beginning not looked on as a day of bodily repose; nor was an analogy drawn between the Jewish Sabbath and the Christian Sunday, except as days of worship. . . .

"(3) The keeping of the Sunday rest arose from the custom of the people and the constitution of the Church. . . .

"(5) Tertullian was probably the first to refer to a cessation of worldly affairs on the Sunday; the Council of Laodicea issued the first conciliar legislation for that day; Constantine I issued the first civil legislation; St. Martin of Braga was probably the first to use the term 'servile work' in its present theological sense." Vincent J. Kelly, *Forbidden Sunday and Feast-Day Occupations,* p. 203.

"The earliest recognition of the observance of Sunday as a legal duty is a constitution of Constantine in 321 A.D., enacting that all courts of justice, inhabitants of towns, and workshops were to be at rest on Sunday (*venerabili die solis*), with an exception in favor of those engaged in agricultural labor." *Encyclopaedia Britannica,* 11th ed., art. "Sunday." (See p. 417.)

"On the venerable day of the sun let the magistrates and people residing in cities rest, and let all workshops be closed. In the country, however, persons engaged in agriculture may freely and lawfully continue their pursuits; because it often happens that another day is not so suitable for grain sowing or for vine planting; lest by neglecting the proper moment for such operations the bounty of heaven should be lost. (Given the 7th day of March, Crispus and Constantine being consuls each of them for the second time.)" *Codex Justinianus,* book 3, title 12, section 3; translated in Philip Schaff, *History of the Christian Church,* (Scribner's, 1902 ed.), vol. 3, p. 380.

This edict, issued by Constantine, who first opened the way for the union of church and state in the Roman Empire, in a manner supplied the lack of a divine command for Sunday observance. It was one of the important steps in bringing about and establishing the change of the Sabbath.

What testimony does Eusebius bear on this subject?

"All things whatsoever that it was duty to do on the Sabbath, these *we* [the church] have transferred to the Lord's day." Translated from Eusebius, *Commentary on the Psalms,* in Migne, *Patrologia Graeca,* vol. 23, cols. 1171, 1172.

NOTE.—The change of the Sabbath was the result of the combined efforts of church and state, and it took centuries to accomplish it. Eusebius of Caesarea (270-338) was a noted bishop of the church, biographer and flatterer of Constantine, and the reputed father of ecclesiastical history.

By what church council was the observance of the seventh day forbidden, and Sunday observance enjoined?

The Council of Laodicea, in Asia Minor, in the fourth century.

NOTE.—Canon 29 reads: "Christians shall not Judaize and be idle on Saturday [*sabbato*, the Sabbath], but shall work on that day; but the Lord's day they shall especially honor, and, as being Christians, shall, if possible, do no work on that day. If, however, they are found Judaizing, they shall be shut out [*anathema*] from Christ." Charles Joseph Hefele, *A History of the Councils of the Church* (1896 English ed.), vol. 2, p. 316.

The Puritan William Prynne said (1655) that "the Council of Laodicea . . . first set[t]led the observation of the Lords-day, and prohibited . . . . the keeping of the Jewish Sabbath under an Anathema." *A Briefe Polemicall Dissertation Concerning . . . the Lords-day-Sabbath,* p. 44.

What was done at the Council of Laodicea was but one of the steps by which the change of the Sabbath was effected. It was looked back upon as the first church council to forbid Sabbath observance and enjoin Sunday rest as far as possible, but it was not so strict as later decrees. Different writers give conflicting dates for this Council of Laodicea. The exact date is unknown, but may be placed "generally somewhere between the years 343 and 381" (Hefele, vol. 2, p. 298).

What determines who we serve?

"Don't you know that when you offer yourselves to someone to obey him as slaves, *you are slaves to the one whom you obey?*" Romans 6:16, NIV.

When asked to bow to Satan, Christ replied how?

"Jesus said to him, 'Away from me, Satan! For it is written: *"Worship the Lord your God, and him only." '*" Matthew 4:10, NIV.

What kind of worship does the Savior call that which is not according to God's commandments?

"They worship me in vain; their teachings are but *rules taught by men.*" Matthew 15:9, NIV.

What appeal did the prophet Elijah make to the ancient nation of Israel?

"How long will you waver between two opinions? If the Lord is God, follow him; but if Baal is God, follow him." 1 Kings 18:21, NIV.

NOTE.—Speaking of idol worship, which substituted human-made gods for God, Paul told the people of Athens, "In the past God overlooked such ignorance, but now he commands all people everywhere to repent." Acts 17:30, NIV. God winks at that which otherwise would be sin if people had spiritual light, but when light comes He commands us to repent and follow Him.

Integrating Covenant, Law, and the Sabbath

Many Christians believe that when the Old Covenant of the Old Testament gave way to the New Covenant of the New Testament, Old Covenant law became obsolete and therefore literal Sabbath observance—as it is actually expressed in the fourth commandment—is no longer relevant.

"This approach has been adopted by a broad spectrum of Christians, from those who hold that Christians are not bound to keep any particular day to those who slide aspects of the Old Testament Sabbath over to Sunday to make it 'Christian.' . . .

"Standing back from Scripture and viewing the big picture, one sees that the divine covenants are unified and function as phases of development in God's overall plan. Each is a part of a single, unified program of revelation. The enactment or primacy of one does not nullify or subordinate another. None of these covenants replaces the one before it; instead, each supplements what has come before.

"In the new covenant prophesied in Jeremiah 31, all of God's covenant purposes—preservation, promise, and law—climax in Jesus Christ, who is Priest (Hebrews 7-10; like Phinehas) and King (Revelation 19:11-16; like David).

"Thus we see that cumulative phases of God's unified ever-

Integrating Covenant, Law, and the Sabbath CONTINUED

lasting covenant bring wave upon wave of gracious divine initiative throughout Old Testament times and on into the New Testament, where the comprehensive culmination in the ultimate revelation and only truly effective sacrifice of Jesus Christ washes over the human race in a tidal wave of grace.

"Like the new covenant, the Old Testament covenants were based on grace rather than law. For example, only after God delivered Noah and his family did He formalize or ratify a covenant with them, in the process of which He stated some stipulations or laws (Genesis. 8:20-9:17).

"So the laws were for people who were *already* saved by grace, that is, by God's own effective intervention (compare Exodus 19:3-6; 20:2). Ever since the Fall, the only way to salvation has been by grace through faith (Ephesians 2:8) in the *seed* of Eve (Genesis 3:15), that is, Jesus Christ (Galatians 3:16).

"Paul's distinction between *under law* and *under grace* in Romans 6:14, 15, has to do with states of persons who are *under condemnation by the law* or *freed from condemnation through Christ.* This distinction is not between two different dispensations. Both of these states could characterize people within the Old Testament *or* New Testament eras.

"Yet, according to Paul, Christ has eclipsed the Mosaic Torah in the sense that He is a more glorious, effective, complete, and adequate revelation of God's character (2 Corinthians 3). Christ did not replace God's holy, righteous, good, and spiritual law (Romans 7:12, 14) as a means of salvation from sin because God has never offered salvation on the basis of law.

"Both within the Bible and elsewhere in ancient Near Eastern covenants and treaties, law operates within the framework of covenant. If we accept God as the authority behind the whole Bible (e.g., 2 Timothy 3:15-17) and recognize that His covenants are cumulative, it's clear that laws given in connection with the Old Testament covenant phases should in some way inform our conduct.

"Some biblical laws, such as the Ten Commandments and many of the *civil laws* (such as Deuteronomy 22:8—protecting people from falling off your flat roof), can be applied today in a straightforward or fairly straightforward manner, except that church discipline replaces the civil penalties administered under the ancient Israelite judicial system. Many laws are applicable

Integrating Covenant, Law, and the Sabbath CONTINUED

in principle even when the culturally dependent specifics do not apply (e.g., Exodus 1:33, 34).

Some biblical laws we cannot keep if we no longer have the social institutions they regulated, such as levirate marriage (Deuteronomy 25:5-10). The ritual laws, dependent and centered upon the function of the earthly sanctuary and the temple as the dwelling place of God, no longer apply because that institution is gone.

"Since the ascension of Christ, our worship has been focused toward God's sanctuary in heaven (Hebrews 8-10). However, we can greatly enrich our comprehension of God's relationship to human beings through study of the Old Testament ritual laws as they relate to the Hebrew sanctuary.

"Although circumcision was a ritual law (Genesis 17), it predated the sanctuary or temple system and was not dependent on it. So loss of the temple in the first century A.D. does not remove the possibility that circumcision could be an ongoing requirement. Cessation of this requirement is based on another principle: Membership in the 'new covenant' phase no longer requires membership in ethnic Israel (Acts 15).

"Is there a single criterion that can be used to determine whether a law should or should not be kept today? I propose the following rule of thumb: *A biblical law should be kept to the extent that its principle can be applied unless the New Testament removes the reason for its application.* . . .

"Categories such as moral, health, civil, and ceremonial laws, which imply the extent to which a given law remains applicable, are postbiblical analytical classifications, and a law may fit in more than one of these categories. Nothing in the biblical text explicitly places the Sabbath laws in one category or another, and we must allow for the possibility that they belong to more than one category. In fact, various laws involving Sabbath can be viewed as pertaining to all four:

"1. *Moral.* In Exodus 20:8-11 and Deuteronomy 5:12-15, God commands cessation from work on the seventh-day Sabbath within the context of His Ten Commandments. The other nine commandments are clearly moral in nature, and there is no compelling reason to single out Sabbath rest as essentially ceremonial.

Integrating Covenant, Law, and the Sabbath CONTINUED

"2. *Health*. In Exodus 23:12, the benefit of Sabbath rest must include a physical component because it is for animals as well as for human beings.

"3. *Civil*. Under the Israelite theocracy, a man who flagrantly violated the Sabbath by gathering firewood on this day was stoned to death by the community at God's command (Numbers 15:32-36).

"4. *Ceremonial*. At the ancient Israelite sanctuary, special rituals performed on the Sabbath quite understandably honored its holiness (Leviticus 24:8; Numbers 28:9, 10).

"We have found that Sabbath is involved with laws belonging to all four categories The moral and health roles of Sabbath rest are timeless and remain even when civil penalties and ceremonial performances pass away. So it appears that ceasing from work on the seventh-day Sabbath *should be kept to the extent that its principle can be applied*. We will test this provisional conclusion by considering some potential objections.

"*Objection 1: Seventh-day Sabbath observance was commanded only for literal Israelites.*

There is no *explicit* biblical record that the requirement for Sabbath observance *was expressly formulated as a law* before God commanded the Israelites to honor it (Exodus 16; 20). But who says that a divinely mandated duty does not exist until/unless God commands it in the form of a law? If this were true, why would God have held Cain accountable for murdering his brother (Genesis 4)?

"In the early chapters of Genesis, where Sabbath is first mentioned (see below), God was concerned with setting up the ideal order of relationships rather than commanding protection of existing relationships.

"On the seventh day of the Creation week, God by His example, instituted the refreshing cessation from work for the benefit of all human beings (Genesis 2:2, 3; compare Exodus 31:17). Jesus confirmed this when He said that the Sabbath was made for humankind (*anthropos*) and not humankind for the Sabbath (Mark 2:27).

"The seventh-day Sabbath is the 'birthday of the world,' which cannot be changed because it celebrates a historical event

Integrating Covenant, Law, and the Sabbath CONTINUED

that occurred at a point of time in the past, long before the nation of Israel existed. Thus nothing that human beings do or do not do can affect the holiness of the Sabbath itself. Sabbath also signifies dependence upon the One who created and sanctifies people (Exodus 31:13, 17), and who keeps all human beings alive (Daniel 5:23; Job 12:10; Psalm 114:14, 15; 145:15, 16). Because God will always be our Creator and Sustainer, the basic meaning of seventh-day Sabbath rest, which encapsulates this divine-human relationship, cannot become obsolete as long as human beings inhabit planet Earth

" ' Neither antinominianism nor dispensationalism may remove the obligation of the Christian today to observe the creation ordinance of the Sabbath. The absence of any explicit command concerning Sabbath observance prior to Moses does not relegate the Sabbath principle to temporary legislation of the law-epoch. . . . God blessed man through the Sabbath by delivering him from slavery to work' [O. Palmer Robertson, *The Christ of the Covenants* (Phillipsburg, N.J.: Presbyterian and Reformed, 1980), pp. 68, 69].

"Objection 2: Literal seventh-day Sabbath observance is no longer relevant because it was a temporary type/symbol of Christian 'rest.'

"Some see support for this approach in Hebrews 4, where Sabbath rest symbolizes a life of gospel rest, involving all days of the week, which results from believing in God. However, a historical/horizontal type like the Israelite sacrificial system prefigures something in the future, which constitutes its antitype.

"When the antitype commences, the type becomes obsolete. In Hebrews 4, God's 'rest' has not suddenly become available for Christians; it was available all along and was not fully appropriated in Old Testament times only because of unbelief. Because it was available *at the same time* the weekly Sabbath was in operation for the Israelites, the weekly Sabbath cannot merely be a historical type of the life of rest.

"Colossians 2:16, 17 reads: 'Therefore do not let anyone condemn you in matters of food and drink or of observing festivals, new moons, or sabbaths. These are only a shadow of what is to come, but the substance belongs to Christ' (NRSV).

Integrating Covenant, Law, and the Sabbath CONTINUED

"In verse 17, 'shadow' (*skia*) has been taken to mean 'temporary type.' So interpreters have commonly supposed that the 'sabbaths' mentioned in verse 16 function as temporary types. However, at issue here is the problem that in spite of Christ's victory and removal of condemnation against sinners through the cross (cf. verses 13-15), some early Christians were prone to judge others (cf. Romans 14:3) for not engaging in ascetic practices, which involved matters of diet and observance of holy times, in accordance with their philosophy.

"Whatever the precise meaning of *sabbaton*, 'S/sabbath(s)' in Colossians 2:16, may be, it seems clear that Paul was not addressing straightforward observance of Mosaic Torah, but its misuse within the framework of a misguided philosophy.

" ' For Israel the keeping of these holy days was evidence of obedience to God's law and a sign of her election among the nations. At Colossae, however, the sacred days were to be kept for the sake of the 'elemental spirits of the universe,' those astral powers who directed the course of the stars and regulated the order of the calendar.

"'So Paul is not condemning the use of sacred days or seasons as such; it is the wrong motive involved when the observance of these days is bound up with the recognition of the elemental spirits' [Peter T. O'Brien, *Word Biblical Commentary: Colossians, Philemon* (Waco, Tex.: Word Books, 1982), p. 139].

Besides, the literal seventh-day Sabbath enjoined in the fourth commandment cannot be a temporary type because God instituted it *before the Fall* (Genesis 2:2, 3). Thus, it was not one of the temporary post-lapsarian types/symbols set up to lead human beings to salvation from sin.

Objection 3: Sabbath is like circumcision (compare Acts 15) in that the New Testament has removed the reason for its application.

"To the contrary, the nonceremonial Sabbath principle of rest on the seventh day is not mentioned as abrogated or altered in Acts 15 or anywhere else in the New Testament. Moreover, by restoring internalized holiness and obedience through God's Holy Spirit (Jeremiah 31:31-34; Ezekiel 36:25-28) the New Covenant restores the Sabbath to its true significance.

"Sabbath points to a living reality: People who are allowing

Integrating Covenant, Law, and the Sabbath CONTINUED

God to sanctify them honor or keep holy the sanctified day. Because their sanctification means that they emulate the character of holy God, who is love (Leviticus 19:2, 18; 1 Thessalonians 3:12, 13; 1 John 14:8), the fact that Sabbath is a sign of sanctification (compare Exodus 31:13, 17; Ezekiel 20:12) implies that it is a celebration of holy love! . . .

"[It has been argued that every moral principle contained in the Ten Commandments was reiterated by the apostles except the commandment to keep the Sabbath. This misses the fact that the Sabbath is special.] It was reiterated in the New Testament not merely by an apostolic exhortation, but by records of Christ's repeated example!

"Jesus risked controversy and danger by making a point of healing people on the Sabbath (e.g., Mark 3:1-6; John 5:2-18; 9:1-41), thereby giving rest from suffering and showing that the real purpose of the Sabbath was for humankind (Mark 2:27). His re-creative healing reveals the heart of the New Covenant and agrees with the emphasis on redemption in the motive clause of the Sabbath command in the Deuteronomy version of the Decalogue (Deuteronomy 5:15).

"Jesus said that because Sabbath was made for man, 'the Son of Man is Lord even of the Sabbath' (Mark 2:28, NIV). This divine lordship over the Sabbath was part of His claim to be the Messiah.

"Because the Sabbath was made for people and not vice versa, people cannot determine it or use it as they please. Thus, in this statement that Christians commonly take today as liberating them from sabbatical law, Christ actually bound His followers to it more definitely.

"During His ministry, Jesus showed Christians how to live under the New Covenant. Why would He claim the seventh-day Sabbath as His and reform its observance if He was about to do away with it? That would make as much sense as remodeling a house just before demolishing it!

"The New Covenant ratified by Christ's blood culminates God's initiative to restore an intimate relationship with human beings. It fulfills God's long-range plan of grace rather than radically repealing everything that has gone before.

"Divine law is for the benefit of parties involved in covenant

Integrating Covenant, Law, and the Sabbath CONTINUED

relationships. The divine command to rest from work on the seventh day of the week embodies a principle that protects the divine-human relationship, as shown by its inclusion in the Ten Commandments. At the same time, Sabbath rest provides an ongoing physical, mental, and spiritual health benefit.

"That modern Christians should continue to observe rest on the seventh-day Sabbath as part of their New Covenant experience is supported by three major factors:

"1. The Sabbath is universal rather than limited to Israel [because it originated before the Israelites existed as a people].

"2. The Sabbath is timeless rather than a temporary type/symbol [because God instituted it before the need for such types].

"3. The 'new covenant' confirms and restores the heart of Sabbath and its true observance." Roy Gane, "Justly Integrating Covenant, Law, and Sabbath," *Ministry,* February 2004, pp. 6-11. Reprinted with permission from *Ministry.*

THE SEAL OF GOD AND THE MARK OF APOSTASY

What is the purpose of a sign, or seal?

"Now, O king, *establish* the decree and *sign the writing, so that it cannot be changed.*" Daniel 6:8, NKJV.

NOTE.—That is, affix the signature of royalty, that it may have the proper authority. Ancient kings used a seal ring, containing the name, initials, or monogram, for this purpose. Jezebel, the wife of King Ahab, "wrote letters in Ahab's name, and sealed them with his seal" (1 Kings 21:8). Of a Persian decree it is said that "in the name of King Ahasuerus it was written, and sealed with the king's ring." Esther 3:12, NKJV.

What are the three essentials of an official seal?

The seal of a lawgiver must show three things: (1) his name; (2) his official position, title, or authority, and so his right to rule; and (3) the extent of his dominion and jurisdiction.

Where is God's seal to be found?

"Bind up the testimony, *seal the law among my disciples.*" Isaiah 8:16.

Which commandment alone of the Decalogue reveals the name, authority, and dominion of the Author of this law?

"Remember the Sabbath day by keeping it holy. Six days you shall labor and do all your work, but the seventh day is a Sabbath to the Lord your God. On it you shall not do any work, neither you, nor your son or daughter, nor your manservant or maidservant, nor your animals, nor the alien within your gates. For in six days the Lord made the heavens and the earth, the sea, and all that is in them, but he rested on the seventh day. Therefore the Lord blessed the Sabbath day and made it holy." Exodus 20:8-11, NIV.

NOTE.—In six days, (1) the Lord (name); (2) made (office, Creator); (3) heaven and earth (dominion). This commandment alone, therefore, contains "the seal of the living God." This commandment shows God's authority to enact all the commandments, and shows all other gods to be false gods. The Sabbath commandment, therefore, contains the seal of God; and the Sabbath itself, which is enjoined by the commandment, is inseparably connected with this seal; it is to be kept in memory of God's creation of all things; and it is itself called a "sign" of the knowledge of this great truth (Exodus 31:17; Ezekiel 20:20).

Why did God declare the Sabbath a sign between Himself and the Israelites?

"It will be a sign between me and the Israelites forever, for in six days the Lord made the heavens and the earth, and on the seventh day he abstained from work and rested." Exodus 31:17, NIV.

NOTE.—The Sabbath is the sign, or mark, or seal, of the Creator.

In what two ways did God tell Israel that the Sabbath is a sign?

1. "Keep my Sabbaths holy, that they may be a sign between us. *Then you will know that I am the Lord your God."* Ezekiel 20:20, NIV.

2. "You must observe my Sabbaths. This will be a sign between me and you for the generations to come, *so you may know that I am the Lord, who makes you holy."* Exodus 31:13, NIV.

NOTE.—The Sabbath is the sign of God's creative power, both in creation and redemption, for redemption is creation—*re*-creation. It requires the same power to *redeem* that it does to *create*. "*Create* in me a clean heart." Psalm 51:10. "We are . . . *created* in Jesus Christ to do good works." Ephesians 2:10, NIV. God designs that each Sabbath shall call Him to mind as the one who created us, and whose grace and sanctifying power are working in us to fit us for His eternal kingdom.

What special sealing work is to take place just before the letting loose of the winds of destruction upon the earth?

"Then I saw another angel coming up from the east, *having the seal of the living God.* He called out in a loud voice to the four angels who had been given power to harm the land and the sea: *'Do not harm the land or the sea or the trees until we put a seal on the foreheads of the servants of our God.* Then I heard the number of those who were sealed: 144,000 from all the tribes of Israel." Revelation 7:2, 3, NIV. (See Ezekiel 9:16.)

How is this same company described a little later?

"Then I looked, and there before me was *the Lamb, standing on Mount Zion, and with him 144,000 who had his name and his Father's name written on their foreheads.*" Revelation 14:1, NIV.

What is said of the character of these sealed ones?

"No lie was found in their mouths; *they are blameless.*" Verse 5, NIV.

What threefold warning does the third angel give?

"A third angel followed them and said in a loud voice, *'If anyone worships the beast and his image* and receives his mark on the forehead or on the hand, *he, too, will drink of the wine of God's fury,* which has been poured full strength into the cup of his wrath.' " Verses 9, 10, NIV.

NOTE.—Over against the seal of God stands the mark of the beast, the mark of apostasy. Against this false and idolatrous worship and the reception of this mark, God sends this solemn warning.

By contrast with the worshippers of the beast, how are the worshippers of God described?

"This calls for *patient endurance* on the part of the saints *who obey God's commandments and remain faithful to Jesus"* Verse 12, NIV.

NOTE.—The keeping of the commandments by the worshippers of God and the violation of those commandments by the worshippers of the beast will constitute the distinction between these two classes of worshippers.

How will the earth beast enforce this mark?

"He was given power to give breath to the image of the first beast, so that it could speak and cause all who refused to worship the image to be killed. He also forced everyone, small and great, rich and poor, free and slave, to receive a mark on his right hand or on his forehead, so that no one could buy or sell unless he had the mark, which is the name of the beast or the number of his name." Revelation 13:15-17, NIV.

NOTE.—The twohorned beast represents a collusion of church and state in the end times.

Over what do the people of God finally gain the victory?

"And I saw what looked like a sea of glass mixed with fire and, standing beside the sea, those who had been victorious *over the beast and his image and over the number of his name*." Revelation 15:2, NIV.

THE LORD'S DAY

From what time was Christ associated with the Father?

"In the beginning was the Word, and the Word was with God, and the Word was God. He was with God in the beginning." John 1:1, 2, NIV. (Compare verse 14.)

By whom were all things created?

"God, who created all things by Jesus Christ." Ephesians 3:9. "In these last days he has spoken to us by *his Son,* whom he appointed heir of all things, and *through whom he made the universe."* Hebrews 1:2, NIV. "For *by him all things were created:* things in heaven and on earth, visible and invisible, whether thrones or powers or rulers or authorities; *all things were created by him* and for him. He is before all things, and in him all things hold together." Colossians 1:16, 17, NIV.

Was anything made without Christ?

"Through him all things were made; *without him nothing was made that has been made."* John 1:3, NIV.

Was the Sabbath "made"?

"The sabbath was *made* for man." Mark 2:27.

Then by whom was the Sabbath made?

By Christ.

NOTE.—This conclusion is inevitable. If all things were made by Christ, and the Sabbath was one of the things that were made, then it follows that the Sabbath must have been made by Christ. This being so, the Sabbath must be *the Lord's day.*

What did God do in the beginning on the seventh day?

"So on the seventh day *he rested* from all his work. And God *blessed the seventh day and made it holy,* because on it he rested from all the work of creating he had done." Genesis 2:2, 3, NIV.

NOTE.—If all things were made by Jesus Christ, then He, with the Father, rested on the first seventh day from His work of creation, blessed the day, and sanctified it.

How much honor is due to Christ?

"All men should *honor the Son just as they honor the Father.*" John 5:23. "I and my Father are *one.*" John 10:30.

NOTE.—Sabbathkeeping, then, honors Christ equally with the Father.

Did Christ keep the Sabbath?

"I have kept My Father's commandments." John 15:10.

Did Christ's followers observe the Sabbath after His resurrection?

"As his custom was, Paul went into the synagogue, and *on three Sabbath days he reasoned with them from the Scriptures."* Acts 17:2, NIV. (See also Acts 13:14, 42-44; 16:13; 18:1-4, 11.)

On what day does John say he was in the Spirit?

"I was in the Spirit on *the Lord's day."* Revelation 1:10.

What day does the commandment say is the Lord's?

"The seventh day is the sabbath of the Lord." Exodus 20:10.

What does the prophet Isaiah, speaking for God, call the seventh-day Sabbath?

"My holy day." Isaiah 58:13.

On what day must John have been in the Spirit?

The seventh, if he referred to a day of the week at all.

NOTE.—No other day of the week in all the Bible is claimed by God as His day. During the early centuries of the Christian Era, apostasy came. Though lacking any biblical command, Christians began to neglect the Sabbath of the commandment, and to honor the first day of the week, on which Christ rose from the dead, calling it "the Lord's day." Finally the Sabbath was almost lost sight of, and Sunday observance generally replaced it. But there was no warrant for this change in the divine and unchangeable law of God. The Bible knows but one

God, one Lawgiver, one Mediator between God and humanity, one
Lord and Savior Jesus Christ, one Spirit, one faith, one baptism, and
one Sabbath. (See Jeremiah 10:10-12; Revelation 14:6, 7; 1 Timothy
2:5; Ephesians 4:4-6; Exodus 20:8-11.) (See pp. 346, 364, 365.)

**What influence do the Bible and history speak of working in the
church immediately after apostolic days?**

"Even from your own number men will arise and distort the truth
in order to draw away disciples after them." Acts 20:30, NIV.

NOTE.—"Between the days of the apostles and the conversion
of Constantine, the Christian commonwealth changed its aspect. . . .
Rites and ceremonies, of which neither Paul nor Peter ever heard,
crept silently into use, and then claimed the rank of divine institutions." W. D. Killen, *The Ancient Church,* pp. xv, xvi.

What did Christ say of worship based on tradition?

"They worship me in vain; their teachings are but rules taught by
men." Matthew 15:9, NIV.

NOTE.—Jesus is quoting Isaiah 29:13.

Whose commands should we obey in all religious matters?

"We must obey God rather than men." Acts 5:29, NIV.

NOTE.—In all matters of religion we as Christians must walk as
Christ walked, think as Christ thought, talk as Christ talked. To His
disciples He said, "Therefore go and make disciples of all nations.
. . . And teaching them to obey everything I have commanded you."
Matthew 28:19, 20, NIV.

THE SABBATH IN HISTORY

When and by what acts was the Sabbath made?

"And on the seventh day God ended His work which He had done;
and He rested on the seventh day from all His work which He had
done. Then God blessed the seventh day, and sanctified it, because in
it He rested from all His work which God had created and made."
Genesis 2:2, 3, NKJV.

What division of time is marked off by the Sabbath?

The week.

NOTE.—The week is "a time unit that, unlike all others, has pro-
ceeded in absolutely invariable manner since what may be called the
dawn of history." *Nature,* June 6, 1931.

In the official League of Nations *Report on the Reform of the Cal-*

endar, published at Geneva, August 17, 1926, are statements from astronomers: "The week . . . has been followed for thousands of years, and therefore has been hallowed by immemorial use." M. Anders Donner, formerly professor of astronomy at the University of Helsingfors, quoted on p. 51.

"I have always hesitated to suggest breaking the continuity of the week, which is without a doubt the most ancient scientific institution bequeathed to us by antiquity." M. Edouard Bailland, director of the Paris Observatory, quoted on p. 52.

Genesis 7:4, 10 and 8:10, 12, show that the week was known at the time of the Flood.

"So far as our knowledge goes the week was used only by the progenitors of the Hebrews, by them and related [Semitic] peoples, and where their influence extended. Since Jesus the extension of Christianity, especially in the last two centuries, has carried with it increasingly the use of the week for time reckoning." W. O. Carver, *Sabbath Observance,* p. 34. Copyright 1940 by the Sunday School Board of the Southern Baptist Convention. Used by permission.

Why did God set apart the seventh day as holy?

"For in six days the Lord made the heavens and the earth, the sea, and all that is in them, but he rested on the seventh day. Therefore the Lord blessed the Sabbath day and made it holy." Exodus 20:11, NIV.

What promise did God make to Israel, through Jeremiah, if they would keep the Sabbath?

"But if you are careful to obey me, declares the Lord, and bring no load through the gates of this city on the Sabbath, but keep the Sabbath day holy by not doing any work on it, *then kings who sit on David's throne will come through the gates of this city with their officials. . . . And this city will be inhabited forever."* Jeremiah 17:24, 25, NIV.

What would happen if they did not keep the Sabbath holy?

"But if you do not obey me to keep the Sabbath day holy by not carrying any load as you come through the gates of Jerusalem on the Sabbath day, *then I will kindle an unquenchable fire in the gates of Jerusalem that will consume her fortresses."* Verse 27, NIV.

What befell Jerusalem in fulfillment of this when it was captured by Nebuchadnezzar, king of Babylon?

"He carried to Babylon all the articles from the temple of God, both large and small, and the treasures of the Lord's temple and the treasures of the king and his officials. They set fire to God's temple and broke down the wall of Jerusalem; they burned all the palaces and destroyed everything of value there. . . . The land enjoyed its Sabbath rests; all the time of its desolation it rested, until the seventy years were completed in fulfillment of the word of the Lord spoken to Jeremiah." 2 Chronicles 36:18-21, NIV.

After Israel's restoration from the Babylonian captivity, what did Nehemiah say was the reason for their punishment?

"Men from Tyre who lived in Jerusalem were bringing in fish and all kinds of merchandise and selling them in Jerusalem on the Sabbath to the people of Judah. I rebuked the nobles of Judah and said to them, 'What is this wicked thing you are doing—desecrating the Sabbath day? Didn't your forefathers do the same things, so that our God brought all this calamity upon us and upon this city?" Nehemiah 13:16-18, NIV.

How did Nehemiah speak of God's giving the Sabbath to Israel?

"You came down on Mount Sinai; you spoke to them from heaven. You gave them regulations and laws that are just and right, and decrees and commands that are good. You made known to them your holy Sabbath and gave them commands, decrees and laws through your servant Moses." Nehemiah 9:13, 14, NIV.

NOTE.—This text does not say that God *made* the Sabbath then, but simply that He made it *known* to Israel then. They had largely forgotten it while in Egypt. (See pp. 351. 354, 355.)

By what did Christ recognize the Sabbath law?

"Therefore it is lawful to do good on the Sabbath." Matthew 12:11, 12, NIV.

NOTE.—"The fact, however, that Christ until His death, and His Apostles at least for a time after Christ's Ascension, observed the Sabbath is evidence enough that our Lord Himself did not substitute the Lord's day for the Sabbath, during His lifetime on earth." Vincent J. Kelly, *Forbidden Sunday and Feast-Day Occupations* (1943), pp. 19, 20.

William Prynne says: "It is certain, that Christ himself, his Apostles, and the Primitive Christians, for some good space of time did constantly observe the seventh day Sabbath."—*A Briefe Polemicall Dissertation, Concerning . . . The Lordsday-Sabbath,* p. 33.

What was one of the first efforts of the Roman church in behalf of the recognition of Sunday?

About A.D. 196, Victor, bishop of Rome, attempted to impose on all the churches the Roman custom of having the Passover, or Easter, as it is commonly called, celebrated every year on Sunday, and presumed to excommunicate the churches of Asia Minor because they observed it annually, regardless of the day of the week.

What was one of the principal questions settled at the Council of Nice [Nicaea], A.D. 325?

"The question relating to the observance of Easter, which was agitated in the time of Anicetus and Polycarp, and afterwards in that of Victor, was still undecided. It was one of the principal reasons for convoking the council of Nice, being the most important subject to be considered after the Arian controversy." Isaac Boyle, *Historical View of the Council of Nice* (1836), p. 23.

NOTE.—The council fixed Easter on the Sunday immediately following the full moon which was nearest after the vernal equinox.

What reason did Constantine give for urging this decree on the churches?

"Let us then, have nothing in common with the detestable Jewish crowd." Eusebius, *The Life of Constantine,* book 3, chap. 8.

What had Constantine already done, in A.D. 321, to help forward Sunday to a place of prominence?

He issued an edict requiring "the magistrates and people residing in the cities" to rest on "the venerable day of the sun" and calling for all workshops to be closed. (See p. 375.)

Who did Eusebius, bishop of Caesarea, and one of Constantine's most ardent supporters, say had transferred the obligations of the Sabbath to Sunday?

"All things whatsoever that it was duty to do on the Sabbath, these WE [the church] have transferred to the Lord's day." Translated from Eusebius, *Commentary on the Psalm,* in Migne, *Patrologia Graeca,* vol. 23, cols. 1171, 1172.

What did Sylvester, bishop of Rome (A.D. 314 to 337), do for the Sunday institution by his "apostolic authority"?

He officially changed the title of the first day, calling it the Lord's day. (See the Venerable Bede, *De Ratione Computi,* in Migne, *Patrologia Graeca,* vol. 90, col. 584.)

What did the Council of Laodicea decree?

Canon 29. "Christians shall not Judaize and be idle on Saturday [*Sabbato*, the Sabbath], but shall work on that day; but the Lord's day they shall especially honour." Charles Joseph Hefele, *A History of the Councils of the Church* (1896 English ed.), vol. 2, p. 316.

How late did Christians keep the Sabbath?

Public worship on both Sabbath and Sunday can be traced down to the fifth century.

NOTE.—"Down even to the fifth century the observance of the Jewish Sabbath was continued in the Christian church." Lyman Coleman, *Ancient Christianity Exemplified,* chap. 26, sec. 2.

Various writers who kept Sunday, and who were not interested in Sabbath observance, nevertheless mention the fact that it was being observed. (See Justin Martyr, *Dialogue With Trypho,* chap. 47; Tertullian, *On Prayer,* chap. 23; Origen, *Homily on Numbers 23,* sec. 4; the anonymous *Constitutions of the Holy Apostles,* book 2, sec. 4, chap. 36; book 2, sec. 7, chap. 59; book 7, sec. 3, chap. 36; book 8, sec. 4, chap. 33; Cassian, *Institutes,* book 3, chap. 12; book 5, chap. 26.) The very Council of Laodicea, whose canon 29 anathematized refraining from labor on the Sabbath, made provision in canon 16 for public Scripture reading on the Sabbath.

How general was this practice in the middle of the fifth century?

"Although almost all churches throughout the world celebrate the sacred mysteries on the sabbath of every week, yet the Christians of Alexandria and at Rome, on account of some ancient tradition have ceased to do this." Socrates, *Ecclesiastical History,* book 5, chap. 22.

How late was Sabbathkeeping preached in Rome?

In the time of Pope Gregory I (590-604).

NOTE.—Gregory denounced as "preachers of Antichrist" those who in Rome "forbid anything to be done on the Sabbath." (See his epistle to the Roman citizens, book 13, no. 1, in *Nicene and Post-Nicene Fathers,* 2nd series, vol. 13 [1898], p. 92.)

Did observance of the seventh-day Sabbath survive later?

Traces can be found in modified form or in scattered places through the centuries.

NOTE.—"Tracts of seventh-day keepers are found in the times of Gregory I, Gregory VII, and in the twelfth century in Lombardy." McClintock and Strong, *Cyclopedia of Biblical, Theological, and Ecclesiastical Literature,* vol. 1, p. 600.

The Eastern Church through many centuries held church services on both Sabbath and Sunday, and refused to follow the Roman method of disparaging the Sabbath by fasting on it. For example:

Syria: "They keep Saturday holy, nor esteem Saturday fast lawful but on Easter Even. They have solemn service on Saturdays, eat flesh, and feast it bravely like the Jews." Samuel Purchas, *Purchas His Pilgrimes* (London, 1625), part 2, book 8, chap. 6, p. 1269.

Ethiopia (1534): "It is not, therefore, in imitation of the Jews, but in obedience to Christ and His holy apostles, that we observe that day [the Sabbath]." Michael Geddes, *Church History of Ethiopia* (London, 1696), pp. 87, 88.

Celtic Church of Scotland: "The Celts used a Latin Bible unlike the Vulgate, and kept Saturday as a day of rest, with special religious services on Sunday." A. C. Flick, *The Rise of the Mediaeval Church* (Putnams, 1909), p. 237.

Waldenses: Some of the Waldenses were observers of the Sabbath. We have no evidence of this practice in the main body represented by the modern inhabitants of the Waldensian valleys of the Italian Alps, yet among the widespread groups embraced under the term *Waldenses* in the broad sense, there were Sabbathkeepers. The Passagii, or Passaginians, classified by Perrin as a branch of the Waldenses, kept the seventh day. (See Jean Perrin, *History of the Vaudois,* book 1, chap. 3.) Also the "Waldensian Picards"—Bohemian Brethren, who had procured ordination from a Waldensian bishop—are described thus in a Catholic manuscript:

"They do not hear the masses of Christians [i.e., Catholics] . . . they flee the image of the Crucifix as the devil, they do not celebrate the feasts of the divine Virgin Mary and of the Apostles; certain ones the Lord's day only. *Some indeed celebrate the Sabbath with the Jews."* Translated from the Latin text printed by J.J.I. von Doellinger, *Beitraege zur Sektengeschichte des Mittelalters,* vol. 2, no. 61, p. 662.

Who among the early Reformers raised this question of Sabbath observance?

Andreas Carlstadt, a colleague of Luther.

NOTE.—Carlstadt held to the divine authority of the Sabbath from the Old Testament, but he was uncertain about which day ought to be kept. He wrote: "Concerning Sunday one is uneasy that men have instituted it. Concerning Saturday, it is still under dispute. It is clear, however, that you should celebrate the seventh day and allow your servants to do so as often as they have worked six days." Translated from his *Von dem Sabbat und gebotten feyertagen* (1524), chap. [10]. Luther's noted Catholic opponent, Eck, later taunted the Lutherans for observing Sunday: "The Scripture teaches: Remember that you keep holy the Sabbath day; . . . yet the [Catholic] church has changed the Sabbath to the Lord's day by its own authority, upon which you have no Scripture" Translated from Johann Eck, *Enchiridion Locorum Communium Adversus Lutheranos* (Handbook of Commonplaces Against the Lutherans) (1533), folios 4 verso, 5 recto.

What was a new development in post-Reformation England?

The hybrid "Puritan Sabbath" (Sunday).

NOTE.—In the English Reformation, "Sundays and holydays stood much on the same footing as days on which no work except for good cause was to be performed," but later "the more scrupulous party, while they slighted the Church-festivals as of human appointment, prescribed a stricter observance of the Lord's day." Henry Hallam, *The Constitutional History of England* (New York, 1873), p. 227.

"The use of the word Sabbath instead of Sunday became in that age a distinctive mark of the Puritan party." *Ibid.*, p. 229.

Was the seventh-day Sabbath observed at this time?

During this battle between the Reformation Sunday and the "Sabbatarian" Sunday, the observers of the seventh day increased.

NOTE.—In Europe and in England many found the truth of the Bible Sabbath, and persecutions resulted.

SABBATH REFORM

What commandment had the Pharisees made void?

"For God said, 'Honor your father and mother.' . . . But you say that if a man says to his father or mother, 'Whatever help you might otherwise have received from me is a gift devoted to God,' he is not to 'honor his father' with it. Thus you nullify the word of God for the sake of your tradition." Matthew 15:46, NIV.

NOTE.—The Pharisees taught that by a gift of property to the Temple service a person might be freed from the duties required by the fifth commandment.

What answer did Jesus give when asked, "Do you know that the Pharisees were offended when they heard this?"

"He replied, *'Every plant that my heavenly Father has not planted will be pulled up by the roots.' "* Verse 13, NIV.

NOTE.—What is true of the fifth commandment is true of every other commandment. If through tradition men set aside any other of God's commandments. these words are equally applicable to them. They are guilty of making void the commandment of God, and of instituting vain worship.

How did the ancient Israelites break God's law relative to the Sabbath?

"Her priests do violence to my law and profane my holy things; they do not distinguish between the holy and the common; they teach that there is no difference between the unclean and the clean; and *they shut their eyes to the keeping of my Sabbaths,* so that I am profaned among them." Ezekiel 22:26, NIV.

How did Israel's false prophets justify their actions?

"Her prophets whitewash these deeds for them by false visions and lying divinations. They say, 'This is what the Sovereign Lord says'—when the Lord has not spoken." Verse 28, NIV.

NOTE.—Thus it is with the reasons advanced today for not keeping the Bible Sabbath, the seventh day. They are not only unsound and untenable in themselves, but are utterly inconsistent, contradictory, and destructive one of the other, among themselves. They are like the witnesses employed by the Jewish leaders to condemn Christ. Of these the record says: "The chief priests and the whole Sanhedrin were looking for evidence against Jesus so that they could put him to death, but they did not find any. Many testified falsely against him, but their statements did not agree." Mark 14:55, 56, NIV. The lack of agreement among them was evidence in itself of the *falseness* of their testimony. In nothing, perhaps, is a lack of agreement better illustrated than in the reasons assigned for Sundaykeeping. Note the following:

One says the Sabbath has been *changed* from the seventh to the first day of the week.

Another says that the Sabbath commandment requires only one day of rest after six of labor, and *hence there has been no change*.

Some reason that all ought to keep Sunday, because although, as they affirm, God did not appoint a *particular* day, yet *agreement* is necessary; and to have any or every day a sabbath would be equal to no sabbath at all.

Others, to avoid the claims of God's law, assert that the Sabbath precept is one of those ordinances which was *against us, contrary to us, blotted out, and nailed to the cross.* Still, they admit that a day of rest and convocation is necessary, and therefore the day of Christ's resurrection, they say, has been chosen.

Another class say they believe it is impossible to know which is the *seventh day,* although they have no difficulty in locating the *first.*

Some are so bold as to declare that *Sunday is the original seventh day.*

Others, with equal certainty, say that those who keep the seventh day are endeavoring to be *justified by the law,* and are *fallen from grace.*

Another class say that everyone should be fully persuaded in his own mind, whether he keep this day, or that, or none at all.

Still again, as if having found the missing link in the argument, some declare that it is *impossible to keep the seventh day on a round world.*

Last, some, like King Herod slaying all of Bethlehem's babies in order to make sure of killing Christ, go so far as to teach that *all ten commandments have been abolished.*

Said Christ, "Do not think that I have come to abolish the Law or the Prophets; I have not come to abolish them but to fulfill them. I tell you the truth, until heaven and earth disappear, not the smallest letter, not the least stroke of a pen, will by any means disappear from the Law until everything is accomplished. Anyone who breaks one of the least of these commandments and teaches others to do the same will be called least in the kingdom of heaven, but whoever practices and teaches these commands will be called great in the kingdom of heaven." Matthew 5:17-19, NIV.

When, and by whom, was the Sabbath "planted"?

"For in six days *the Lord* made heaven and earth, the sea, and all that is in them, but rested on the seventh day. Therefore the Lord blessed the Sabbath day and made it holy." Exodus 20:11, NIV.

When will God's people receive final salvation?

"Who through faith are shielded by God's power until the coming of the salvation that is ready to be revealed *in the last time.*" 1 Peter 1:5, NIV.

When God's salvation is "close at hand," upon whom does He pronounce a blessing?

"This is what the Lord says: 'Maintain justice and do what is right, for my salvation is close at hand and my righteousness will soon be revealed. Blessed is the man who does this, the man who holds it fast, who keeps the Sabbath without desecrating it, and keeps his hand from doing evil.' " Isaiah 56:1, 2, NIV.

Is this promised blessing confined to any one class?

"And foreigners who bind themselves to the Lord to serve him, to love the name of the Lord, and to worship him, all who keep the Sabbath without desecrating it and who hold fast to my covenant—these I will bring to my holy mountain and give them joy in my house of prayer." Verses 6, 7, NIV.

A Day of Liberation

The Sabbath presents to us our intrinsic worth apart from profession, past, or appearance. It is a day of grace. At the end of a consuming week, Sabbath disengages us from the belittling belief that we are worth what we earn and produce and look like. We are reminded again that god loves and appreciates us because of who we *are*—His children.

" ' I gave them my Sabbaths," God says in *Ezekiel*, chapter 20, 'as a sign between us, so they would know that I the Lord made them holy' [verse 12, NIV]. God assures us that the way to achieve holiness—wholeness—is to celebrate not our creations but His creations.

"In this context Sabbath creates a counterpoint to legalism, the foundation for most of the world's religions. Legalism teaches that we can somehow earn our way to salvation (or nirvana, paradise, enlightenment, harmony) by what we do. Unfortunately, legalism lies at the base of pride, the root of our separation from God and from each other; hence our need of 'connectedness.'

"God in effect assures us every Sabbath, 'You are a human being, not a human doing or a human done. You are valued, even if you produce nothing—you are worth an infinite amount. You are priceless because I have paid infinity for you. You are my child. "I will never forget you. Your name is graven on the palms of my hand" [see Isaiah 49: 15, 16].'

"The Sabbath is a day of delight. . . . Saving extraordinary surprises for the Sabbath day enhances how we view it: a longed-for book, a luscious raspberry dessert, the company of a close friend, or a hike to wild alpine forget-me-nots. Jesus pronounces, 'The Sabbath was made for people, not people for the Sabbath.' However we choose to rejoice each Sabbath, we honor it first when we delight in it. . . ."

"A young fighter pilot once maintained that he didn't really require an oxygen mask up to twenty thousand feet. He could

A Day of Liberation CONTINUED

function fine without it, thank you. His superiors, deciding to *show* him, placed him in a low-oxygen chamber that stimulated air at twenty thousand feet and asked him, after a few minutes, to write on a pad of paper his full name, address, family's names, Social Security number, and phone number.

"Upon exiting, the pilot grinned. He felt fine—no problem. Then he looked at what he had written and stared slack-jawed. The last three items were total gibberish, incomprehensible scrawling. He hadn't known his state at all. Like the pilot, we function each week in rarefied, depleted air. The life-giving oxygen masks of prayer, the Bible, and Sabbath enable us to legibly live God's love.

"Modern society suffers from acrophobia—a fear of high ideals and lofty thoughts Bombarded by amusements, we lose time for thoughtful reflection. In a famous passage, Henry David Thoreau writes, 'I went to the woods because I wished to live deliberately, to front only the essential facts of life, and see if I could not learn what it has to teach, and not, when I came to die, discover that I had not lived.' Admirable and virtuous, surely , but realistically, with our responsibilities, can we leave and do what Thoreau did?

"Sabbath is our woods, our Walden Pond. Each week Sabbath engages us and lifts our sights. . . . If our thoughts never rise above the level of humanity, if we never contemplate infinite wisdom and love, we will sink lower and lower.

"God proclaims Sabbath a day of liberation. In *Genesis* the Sabbath is tied to Creation, but in *Deuteronomy* God connects Sabbath to freedom: 'Remember that you were slaves in Egypt, and that the Lord your God brought you out of there with a mighty hand and an outstretched arm. Therefore the Lord your God has commanded you to observe the Sabbath day' [Deuteronomy 5:15, NIV].

"Jesus goes out of His way to liberate on the Sabbath. On one Sabbath He heals 'a man blind from his birth' [John 9:1, NIV], and a few Pharisees denounce Him, saying, 'This man is not from God, for he does not keep the Sabbath' [verse 16, NIV]. Jesus pays them no heed.

"On other occasions, He responds directly. Walking through a wheat field, He confronts His inquisitors, the traveling truth

A Day of Liberation CONTINUED

squad. 'If you had known what this means, "I desire mercy, and not sacrifice," you would not have condemned the guiltless. For the Son of man is lord of the sabbath' [Matthew 12:7, 8, RSV]. Sabbath—the Lord's day—is for mercifully setting people free. Jesus makes His point even more decisively another Sabbath. He approaches a painfully hunched woman—for eighteen years she has been unable to stand straight—suffering probably from rheumatoid arthritis, and says, 'Woman, you are freed from your infirmity' [Luke 13:12, RSV]. He touches her. 'Immediately she is made straight, and she praises God' [verse 13, RSV].

"The ruler of the synagogue, however, is irate. 'There are six days to do work. Come and be healed on those days—not on the sabbath' [verse 14, NIV].

"Jesus responds, 'You hypocrites! Each Sabbath every one of you unties your cow or donkey from the stall and leads it to water. Then shouldn't this woman, whom Satan has tied up for eighteen years, be freed on this Sabbath day?' [see verses 15, 16]. His adversaries are put to shame, and the people rejoice.

"The Sabbath liberates every living being on earth. In *Exodus*, chapter twenty, examine who is set free: you, your children, your servants, your animals, and the 'sojourner within your gates' [verse 10, RSV], strangers. To the freed slaves who were brought out from Egypt, God says, 'As I set you free, on this day set each other free.' Our human hierarchies disappear as we experience our equal status before God.

"The exhortation to treat people with dignity, allowing them to delight in rest, extends to us today. . . .

"The Sabbath liberates the planet as well. In a time of global environmental concerns, it's good to know that God cares for the well-being of animals and His entire creation—not only for humans. At the opening of *Genesis*, when Sabbath first appears, God calls us to be caretakers of the earth. Later, in *Leviticus*, God institutes a sabbatical year: 'Six years you shall sow your field, and six years you shall prune your vineyard, and gather in its fruits; but in the seventh year there shall be a sabbath of solemn rest for the land, a sabbath to the Lord; you shall not sow your field or prune your vineyard' [Leviticus 25:3, 4, RSV].

A Day of Liberation CONTINUED

"Niels-Erik Andreason says, 'Every week on the Sabbath, as we contemplate God's created works, we do not turn away from the material world, but *toward* it. We affirm this as our God-given environment, where life is nurtured, sustained, provided for, and made secure.'

"In addition, Sabbath liberates us from the effects of over-stimulation. Blaming the complexity of our lives on the complexity of our environment, we may dream of flying to some remote island to relish the simple life, but the problem is not entirely our environment. The problem is in our anxious, disjointed selves. 'We are tendencies, or rather symptoms,' Emerson sighs. 'We touch and go, and sip the foam of many lives.' We are fragmented. We are torn and aching. Life doesn't work for us because we are without Jesus. The simplicity of Sabbath brings wholeness.

"Sabbath is a day for all of us wrapped up in materialistic values. Establishing God's priorities sets us free. Judy Duncan tells a story of her little brother carrying to school two baby scorpions. 'These scorpions,' he said to the class, 'are worth more than a big bar of gold.' A hiss of skepticism rose from his classmates. 'Yes, they are!' he emphatically exclaimed. 'It's because they have *life*.'

"Sabbath also liberates us from *boxes*. We may eat from a box, work in a box, type into a box, fill in the boxes, drive home in a box, live in a box, throw trash into boxes, be entertained by a box (yearning for box tickets), sleep in a box, and fittingly, be buried in a box. No wonder we feel unnaturally boxed in. At the end of the week the boxed lies, that we are ultimately in control of the universe and the universe *owes* us, are hauled out and dumped; in grateful humility we acknowledge the freeing truth that every good thing comes from God. God Himself breaks out of the tiny, moldy boxes we've placed Him in and speaks to us so because we are listening for the voice, the heartbeat. We experience God in the leaping dolphin, the cypress limbs, the moon rising over an open field. . . .

"Sabbbath frees us for time to reflect. The difference between a parent who hits a child and a parent who doesn't is about ten seconds. We clear our minds, like rinsing brushes and rollers after painting, because we know the next job won't be as

A Day of Liberation CONTINUED

good if we don't clean our tools thoroughly. This clearing time
for reflection makes us more effective.

"Though we are hounded by time, the Sabbath liberates us
to enjoy the eternal present. We no longer live in the past or the
more debilitating future—wishing, wondering, and trembling.
C. S. Lewis reveals in *The Screwtape Letters,* 'The Present is
the point at which time touches eternity . . . The Future is, of all
things, the thing *least like* eternity. . . . Nearly all vices are
rooted in the Future. Gratitude looks to the Past and love to the
Present; fear, avarice, lust, and ambition look ahead. . . . [God's
enemies] want a whole race perpetually in pursuit of the rainbow's end, never honest, nor kind, nor happy *now.*"

"Best of all, the Sabbath frees us to fall in love with God
again and again. Now.

"The Sabbath window enlightens; looking through it we receive new eyes. Seeing Jesus hanging on the cross, we see ourselves as we are and as we can be, without excuse and with real
hope. We give in to grace. Dispelling darkness and spiritual
rigor mortis, we enter the fray again, renewed and emboldened
by rest, assurance, and clarity. Rather than contributing to boxes
of people plague, we stay distinctly and fully human. Instead of
adding to the madness, we pull back and lift our sights to reflect
on larger questions: where we came from, why we're here, and
where we're going.

"The Sabbath places our lives again on a higher plane. We
experience transcendent love, knowing that we are accepted in
the Beloved, feeling the rightness of being, and doing what will
rejuvenate us for the week ahead.

"Sabbath is the cool side of the pillow on a hot night.

"God is restful." Chris Blake, *Searching for a God to Love*
(Nashville: Word Publishing, 2000), pp. 198-206.

CHAPTER 10

Christian Liberty

THE AUTHOR OF LIBERTY

How is Israel's slavery in Egypt described?

"The Israelites *groaned* in their slavery and *cried* out, and their cry for help because of their slavery went up to God." Exodus 2:23, NIV. Compare with James 5:1-4.

Who heard their cries?

"God heard their groaning and he remembered his covenant with Abraham, with Isaac and with Jacob." Exodus 2:24, NIV.

What covenant promise had God made to Israel's ancestor Abraham?

"As the sun was setting, Abram fell into a deep sleep, and a thick and dreadful darkness came over him. Then the Lord said to him, 'Know for certain that your descendents will be strangers in a country not their own, and they will be enslaved and mistreated four hundred years. But I will punish the nation they serve as slaves, and afterward they will come out with great possessions.'" Genesis 15:12-14, NIV.

What reason did God give for setting the Israelites free?

"And now the cry of the Israelites has reached me, and *I have seen the way the Egyptians are oppressing them.* So now, go. I am sending you to Pharaoh to bring my people the Israelites out of Egypt." Exodus 3:9, 10, NIV.

How did God protect the nation of Israel against the terrible effects of slavery?

"If a fellow Hebrew, a man or a woman, sells himself to you and serves you six years, *in the seventh year you must let him go free.* And when you release him, *do not send him away empty-handed.* Supply him liberally from your flock, your threshing floor and your winepress. Give to him as the Lord your God has blessed you. *Remember that you were slaves in Egypt* and the Lord your God redeemed you. That is why I give you this command today." Deuteronomy 15:12-15, NIV.

"Do not mistreat an alien or oppress him, for you were aliens in Egypt." Exodus 22:21, NIV. (See 2 Corinthians 1:3, 4.)

What was one reason Israel should keep the Sabbath?

"Remember that you were slaves in Egypt and that the Lord your God brought you out of there with a mighty hand and an outstretched arm. *Therefore the Lord your God has commanded you to observe the Sabbath day."* Deuteronomy 5:15, NIV.

NOTE.—This suggests that they had difficulty observing the Sabbath in Egypt. From the accusation brought against Moses and Aaron by Pharaoh—"You make them rest [Hebrew, *shabbath*] from their labor" (Exodus 5:5)—it seems they had previously been required to work on the Sabbath, but now Moses and Aaron were teaching them to keep it. Where individual rights and religious liberty are recognized, Sabbath observance must not be denied by civil authority.

What was to be proclaimed in Israel every 50 years?

"Consecrate the fiftieth year and proclaim liberty throughout the land to all its inhabitants. It shall be a jubilee for you; each one of you is to return to his family property and each to his own clan." Leviticus 25:10, NIV.

NOTE.—The year of jubilee was a unique institution found in no other religion. It was a sort of exalted sabbatical year that was to be kept every fiftieth year, being announced at the sound of the trumpet on the Day of Atonement. During this year all slaves who were Hebrews were to be liberated, and all lands restored to the former owners.

Did Israel follow God's jubilee plan?

"Then the word of the Lord came to Jeremiah: 'This is what the Lord, the God of Israel, says: I made a covenant with your forefathers when I brought them out of Egypt, out of the land of slavery. I said, "Every seventh year each of you must free any fellow Hebrew who has sold himself to you. After he has served you six years, you must left him go free." *Your fathers, however, did not listen to me or pay attention to me.* Recently you repented and did what is right in my sight: Each of you proclaimed freedom to his countrymen. You even made a covenant before me in the house that bears my Name. But now you have turned around and profaned my name; each of you has taken back the male and female slaves you had set free to go where they wished. You have forced them to become your slaves again." Jeremiah 34:12-16, NIV.

Did Israel keep the Sabbath faithfully?

"This is what the Lord says: Be careful not to carry a load on the Sabbath day or bring it through the gates of Jerusalem. Do not bring a load out of your houses or do any work on the Sabbath, but keep the Sabbath day holy, as I commanded your forefathers. Yet they did not listen or pay attention; they were stiff-necked and would not listen or re-spond to this discipline." Jeremiah 17:21-23, NIV.

Because Israel failed to do this, became oppressive, and disre-garded and misused the Sabbath, what did God do?

"Therefore, this is what the Lord says: You have not obeyed me; you have not proclaimed freedom for your fellow countrymen. So I now proclaim 'freedom' for you, declares the Lord—'freedom' to fall by the *sword, plague and famine.* I will make you abhorrent to all the kingdoms of the earth." Jeremiah 34:17, NIV. (See also Jeremiah 17:24-27; 2 Chronicles 36:19-21.)

What fault did God find with Israel's fasting?

"Yet on the day of your fasting, *you do as you please and exploit all your workers.* Your fasting ends in *quarreling and strife,* and in *strik-ing each other with wicked fists.* You cannot fast as you do today and expect your voice to be heard on high." Isaiah 58:3, 4, NIV.

What kind of fasting was God looking for from His children?

"Is not this the kind of fasting I have chosen: *to loose the chains of injustice* and *untie the cords of the yoke,* to *set the oppressed free* and *break every yoke*? Is it not to *share your food with the hungry* and to *provide the poor wanderer with shelter*—when you see the naked, to *clothe him,* and not to turn away from your own flesh and blood?" Verses 6, 7, NIV.

NOTE.—All this shows that God loves liberty and hates bondage.

What promise does God give if we will follow him in this?

"Then *your light will break forth like the dawn*, and *your healing will quickly appear*; then *your righteousness will go before you*, and *the glory of the Lord will be your rear guard*. Then you will call, and *the Lord will answer*; you will cry for help, and *he will say: Here am I.* If you do away with the yoke of oppression, with the pointing finger and malicious talk, and if you spend yourselves in behalf of the hungry and satisfy the needs of the oppressed, then *your light will rise in the dark-ness, and your night will become like noonday*.

"The Lord will guide you always; he will satisfy your needs in a sun-scorched land and will strengthen your frame. You will be like a well-watered garden, like a spring whose waters never fail." Verses 8-11, NIV.

What prophetic words of Isaiah did Jesus claim as His mission?

"He went to Nazareth, where he had been brought up, and on the

Sabbath day he went into the synagogue, as was his custom. And he stood up to read. The scroll of the prophet Isaiah was handed to him. Unrolling it, he found the place where it is written:

" ' The Spirit of the Lord is on me, because he has anointed me to *preach good news to the poor.* He has sent me to proclaim *freedom for the prisoners* and *recovery of sight for the blind,* to *release the oppressed,* to *proclaim the year of the Lord's favor.*' " Luke 4:16-18, NIV.

In what condition are those who commit sin?

"Whoever commits sin is a *slave of sin.*" John 8:34, NKJV. "The evil deeds of a wicked man *ensnare him*; the cords of his sin hold him fast." Proverbs 5:22, NIV.

Why were Mary and Joseph to name their Son Jesus?

"And you shall call His name Jesus, for *He will save His people from their sins.*" Matthew 1:21, NKJV.

Who alone, then, can give real freedom?

"Therefore if *the Son* makes you free, you shall be free indeed." John 8:36, NKJV.

By what scripture is the equality of rights clearly shown?

"You shall love your neighbor as yourself." Leviticus 19:18, NKJV.

What rule did Jesus lay down in harmony with this?

"So in everything, *do to others what you would have them do to you.*" Matthew 7:12, NIV.

What did Peter proclaim about salvation in Christ?

"*Salvation is found in no one else*, for there is no other name under heaven given to men by which we must be saved." Acts 4:12, NIV.

What was Jesus' attitude toward unbelievers?

"And if anyone hears My words and does not believe, *I do not judge him*; for I did not come to judge the world but to save the world." John 12:47, NIV.

What spirit did Christ say should control His disciples?

"Jesus called them together and said, 'You know that those who are regarded as rulers of the Gentiles lord it over them, and their high officials exercise authority over them. Not so with you. Instead, whoever wants to become great among you must be your servant, and whoever wants to be first must be slave of all. *For even the Son of Man did not come to be served, but to serve*, and to give his life as a ransom for many.' " Mark 10:42-45, NIV.

What is present where the Spirit of the Lord is?

"Now the Lord is that Spirit; and where the Spirit of the Lord is, there is liberty." 2 Corinthians 3:17.

What kind of worship does God desire?

"Yet a time is coming and has now come when the true worshipers will worship the Father *in spirit and truth*, for they are the kind of worshipers the Father seeks. God is spirit, and his worshipers must worship in spirit and in truth." John 4:23, 24, NIV.

THE POWERS THAT BE

Who should be subject to civil government?

"*Everyone* must submit himself to the governing authorities, for there is no authority except that which God has established." Romans 13:1, NIV.

By whom are the powers that be ordained?

"The authorities that exist have been established by *God*." Verse 1, NIV.

What does one who resists civil authority resist?

"Consequently, he who rebels against the authority is rebelling against *what God has instituted*, and those who do so will bring judgment on themselves." Verse 2.

NOTE.—"That is, they who rise up against government itself; who seek anarchy and confusion; who oppose the regular execution of the laws. It is implied, however, that those laws shall not be such as to violate the rights of conscience, or oppose the laws of God." Albert Barnes, on Romans 13:2.

What are the proper sphere and work of civil authority?

"For rulers hold no terror for those who do right, but for those who do *wrong*. Do you want to be free from fear of the one in authority? Then do what is right and he will commend you. For he is God's servant to do you good. But if you do wrong, be afraid, for he does not bear the sword for nothing. He is God's servant, *an agent of wrath to bring punishment on the wrongdoer*." Verses 3, 4, NIV.

For whom is law made?

"We also know that law is made not for the righteous but for *lawbreakers and rebels*." 1 Timothy 1:9, NIV.

How are Christians admonished to respect civil authority?

"Remind the people to be subject to rulers and authorities, to be obedient, to be ready to do whatever is good." Titus 3:1, NIV.

"Submit yourselves for the Lord's sake to every authority instituted among men: whether to the king, as the supreme authority, or to governors, who are sent by him to punish those who do wrong and to commend those who do right. For it is God's will that by doing good you should silence the ignorant talk of foolish men. Live as free men, but do not use your freedom as a cover-up for evil; live as servants of God. Show proper respect to everyone: Love the brotherhood of believers, fear God, honor the king." 1 Peter 2:13-17, NIV.

"This is also why you pay taxes, for the authorities are God's servants, who give their full time to governing. Give everyone what you owe him: If you owe taxes, pay taxes; if revenue, then revenue; if respect, then respect; if honor, then honor." Romans 13:6, 7, NIV.

In what words does Jesus show that there is another realm outside of Caesar's, or civil government?

"Give to Caesar what is Caesar's, *and to God what is God's*." Matthew 22:21, NIV.

To whom alone did He say worship is to be rendered?

"You shall worship the Lord your God, and Him only you shall serve." Matthew 4:10, NKJV.

Sometime after he conquered Jerusalem and brought selected Hebrews to Babylon, King Nebuchadnezzar had a huge golden idol set up on the plain of Dura. What did he command the people to do?

"Then the herald loudly proclaimed, 'This is what you are commanded to do, O peoples, nations and men of every language: As soon as you hear the sound of the horn, flute, zither, lyre, harp, pipes and all kinds of music, you must *fall down and worship the image* of gold that King Nebuchadnezzar has set up. Whoever does not fall down and worship will immediately be thrown into a blazing furnace." Daniel 3:4-6, NIV.

NOTE.—This decree was in direct conflict with the second commandment of God's law, which forbids making, bowing down to, and serving images. It was religious, idolatrous, and persecuting in character.

Shadrach, Meschach, and Abednego, friends of the prophet Daniel, attended this gathering, but their faith would not let them participate. What answer did they give to the king's decree, even after he gave them a second chance to bow down?

"Shadrach, Meshach, and Abednego replied to the king, 'O Nebuchadnezzar, we do not need to defend ourselves before you in this matter. If we are thrown into the blazing furnace, the God we serve is able to save us from it, and he will rescue us from your hand, O king. But even if he does not, we want you to know, O king, that *we will not serve your gods or worship the image of gold you have set up*." Verses 16-18, NIV.

What did Nebuchadnezzar then do?

"Then Nebuchadnezzar was furious with Shadrach, Meshach, and Abednego, and his attitude toward them changed. He ordered the furnace heated seven times hotter than usual and commanded some of the strongest soldiers in his army to tie up Shadrach, Meshach, and Abednego and *throw them into the blazing furnace*." Verses 19-21, NIV.

God miraculously delivered the three friends from the furnace, unharmed by the flames. What did Nebuchadnezzar say?

"Then Nebuchadnezzar said, 'Praise be to the God of Shadrach, Meshach and Abednego, who has sent his angel and rescued his servants! They trusted in him and defied the king's command and were willing to give up their lives rather than serve or worship any god except their own God." Verse 28, NIV.

NOTE.—By preserving these men in the fire, God demonstrated that religion is a realm outside the legitimate sphere of civil authority; and that every individual should be left free to worship, or not to worship, according to the dictates of their own conscience.

Many years later, after the Persians conquered Babylon, the prophet Daniel was appointed an administrator over the kingdom under King Darius. Daniel's new colleagues looked for something they could accuse Daniel of in order to destroy him, but found nothing in his actions. What did they settle on instead?

"Finally these men said, 'We will never find any basis for charges against this man Daniel unless it has *something to do with the law of his God.*' " Daniel 6:5, NIV.

What decree did they push Darius to make?

"That anyone who prays to any god or man during the next

thirty days, except to you, O king, shall be thrown into the lions' den." Verse 7, NIV.

NOTE.—Unlike the decree of Nebuchadnezzar, this decree forbade the worship of the true God, and was in direct conflict with the first commandment, which forbids the worship of any other god.

How did Daniel respond to this decree?

"Now when Daniel learned that the decree had been published, he went home to his upstairs room where the windows opened toward Jerusalem. *Three times a day he got down on his knees and prayed, giving thanks to his God, just as he had done before.*" Verse 10, NIV.

What happened to Daniel?

"So the king gave the order, and *they brought Daniel and threw him into the lions' den.*" Verse 16, NIV.

What did Darius say when he came to the lions' den the next day?

"When he came near the den, he called to Daniel in an anguished voice, 'Daniel, servant of the living God, has your God, whom you serve continually, been able to rescue you from the lions?' " Verse 20, NIV.

How did Daniel reply?

"Daniel replied, 'O king, live forever! My God sent His angel, and he shut the mouths of the lions. They have not hurt me, because I was found innocent in his sight. Nor have I ever done any wrong before you, O king." Verses 21, 22, NIV.

NOTE.—Here again God demonstrated by a miracle that no government should attempt to force or prohibit religious observance.

What parting command did Jesus give His disciples?

"Go into all the world and preach the good news to all creation." Mark 16:15, NIV.

What countercommand did the Jewish religious authorities soon give them?

"So they called them and commanded them *not to speak at all nor teach in the name of Jesus.*" Acts 4:18, NKJV.

What reply did Peter and John make?

"*Whether it is right in the sight of God to listen to you more than to God, you judge.* For we cannot but speak the things which we have seen and heard." Verses 19, 20, NKJV.

What happened to the disciples as a result of their continuing to preach?

"Then the high priest rose up, and all those who were with him (which is the sect of the Sadducees), and they were filled with indignation, and *laid their hands on the apostles and put them in the common prison.*" Acts 5:17, 18, NKJV.

What did an angel of God then do?

"But at night an angel of the Lord *opened the prison doors and brought them out, and said, 'Go, stand in the temple and speak to the people all the words of this life.'*" Verses 19, 20, NKJV.

NOTE.—Here once again is demonstrated the fact that government has no right to interfere with the free exercise of religion, and that when earthly laws conflict with the law and word of God, we are to obey God, whatever the consequences may be.

When the apostles were called before the council again, what question did the high priest ask them?

"*Did we not strictly command you not to teach in this name?* And look, you have filled Jerusalem with your doctrine, and intend to bring this Man's blood on us!" Verse 28, NKJV.

What reply did the apostles make?

"*We ought to obey God rather than men.*" Verse 29, NKJV.

NOTE.—"Obedience is to be rendered to all human governments, in subordination to the will of God. These governments are a recognized necessity, in the nature of the case, and their existence is manifestly in accordance with the divine will. Hence the presumption is always in favor of the authority of civil law; and any refusal to obey, must be based on the moral proof that obedience will be sin. . . . It is too obvious to need discussion, that the law of God, the great principle of benevolence, is supreme, and that 'we ought to obey God, rather than men,' in any case of conflict between human law and the divine." James H. Fairchild, *Moral Philosophy* (1869), pp. 178-181.

In religious matters, whom alone should we call Father?

"Do not call anyone on earth your father; *for One is your Father, He who is in heaven.*" Matthew 23:9, NIV.

When tempted to bow to Satan, what did Jesus reply?

"Jesus said to him, 'Away from me, Satan! For it is written: "Worship the Lord your God, and serve Him only."'" Matthew 4:10, NIV. (See Deuteronomy 6:13; 10:30.)

To whom alone, then, is each one accountable in religion?

"So then, each of us will give an account of himself *to God.*" Romans 14:12, NIV.

NOTE.—In his 1789 reply to the Virginia Baptists, George Washington wrote: "Every man, conducting himself as a good citizen, and being accountable to God alone for his religious opinions, ought to be protected in worshipping the Deity according to the dictates of his own conscience." *Writings of George Washington,* ed. J. C. Fitzpatrick, vol. 30, p. 321.

"Religious matters are to be separated from the jurisdiction of the state not because they are beneath the interests of the state, but, quite to the contrary, because they are too high and too holy and thus are beyond the competence of the state." Isaac Backus, *An Appeal to the Religious Liberty* (1773).

Why is it wrong to force people in the name of religion?

It is putting oneself in the place of God, and contradicting God's character, which never forces anyone to follow Him. (See 2 Thessalonians 2:3, 4.)

Whom are we responsible to in matters of faith and worship?

"Who are you to judge someone else's servant? *To his own master he stands or falls.* And he will stand, for *the Lord* is able to make him stand." Romans 14:4, NIV.

Whose servants are we not to be?

"You were bought at a price; do not become *slaves of men.*" 1 Corinthians 7:23, NIV.

NOTE.—"Satan's methods ever tend to one end—to make men the slaves of men," and thus separate them from God, destroy faith in God, and so expose men to temptation and sin. Christ's work is to set men free, to renew faith, and to lead to willing and loyal obedience to God. Martin Luther wrote:

"Concerning God's Word and eternal matters God does not permit such a submission of one man to another . . . because faith, submission, and humility is the real worship which . . . should not be rendered to any creature, . . . since to trust any creature in things pertaining to eternal life means the same as giving honor to a created being, an honor which belongs to God alone." Translated from Martin Luther, Letter to the Emperor Charles V, April 28, 1521, in his *Sammtlich Schriften* (Walch ed.), vol. 15, col. 1897.

Where must all finally appear to render up their account?

"For we must all appear *before the judgment seat of Christ*, that each one may receive what is due him for the things done while in the body, whether good or bad." 2 Corinthians 5:10, NIV.

NOTE.—Religion is a personal, individual matter. Each of us must give account of ourselves to God. No one should be forced to observe religion a certain way. "He that complies against his will is of his own opinion still" (Samuel Butler), and enforced religion is an affront to personal spirituality. Coerced religion is not true religion.

UNION OF CHURCH AND STATE

What element was already at work in the church in Paul's day?

"For the *mystery of lawlessness* is already at work." 2 Thessalonians 2:7, NKJV.

What class did he say would arise in the church?

"I know that after I leave, *savage wolves* will come in among you and will not spare the flock. *Even from your own number men will arise and distort the truth in order to draw your disciples after them.*" Acts 20:29, 30, NIV.

How was this "falling away" from the truth shown?

By the adoption of pagan beliefs and practices, such as the immortality of the soul and prayers to the dead.

NOTE.—Tertullian, about A.D. 200, mentions many unscriptural practices as already traditional in his day, such as triple immersion in baptism, thus "making a somewhat ampler pledge than the Lord has appointed in the Gospel"; offerings for the dead as birthday honors; the prohibition of "fasting or kneeling in worship on the Lord's day", "also from Easter to WhitSunday"; a special reverence for bread and wine; and the tracing of the sign of the cross on the forehead "at every forward step and movement, at every going in and out, when we put on our clothes and shoes, when we bathe, when we sit at table, when we light the lamps, on couch, on seat, in all the ordinary actions of daily life." *De Corona*, chap. 3, in *The Ante-Nicene Fathers* (1918), vol. 3, pp. 94, 95.

What did church bishops determine to do?

"This theocratical theory was already the prevailing one in the time of Constantine; and . . . the bishops voluntarily made themselves dependent on him by their disputes, and by their determination to make use of the power of the state for the furtherance of their aims." Augustus Neander, *General History of the Christian Religion and Church* (Torrey's Translation), vol. 2, p. 132.

NOTE.—The "theocratic theory," that of a government administered by God through the bishops, was confronted by the actuality of the pagan system under which the emperor had been pontifex maximus, or chief priest, of the pagan state religion. After his recognition of Christianity, Constantine regarded himself as a sort of bishop of the external affairs of the church, and the church as a sort of department of the government. The ideal of the bishops, that of a government guided by God through the church, was pursued with variable but increasing success in Western Europe. Under Constantine's successor official paganism was abolished, and Christianity made the only legal religion of the state.

How did this elevation of the church begin?

Through the *patronage* and *religious legislation* of Constantine.

NOTE.—Authorities differ as to when—or whether—Constantine was converted to Christianity, and whether he favored the church more from religious or political motives. The outline of events follows:

A.D. 306—Constantine's accession as one of four rulers of the empire, with jurisdiction over the Prefecture of Gaul.

312—His victory over Maxentius, which made him sole ruler of the west, and which he attributed to the aid of the God of the Christians, whom he had invoked after a supposed vision of a cross in the sky.

313—The so-called Edict of Milan, issued jointly with his colleague Licinius, granting religious liberty to all, of whatever religious belief, and particularly mentioning the Christians. Hereafter Constantine surrounded himself with bishops, gave preference to the Christians, and issued legislation in their favor, without renouncing or persecuting paganism.

321—His Sunday law, which served to unite his Christian and pagan subjects in the observance of "the venerable day of the Sun."

323 or 324—His attainment of sole rule of the whole empire by the defeat of his last rival, the pagan Licinius, who had resumed persecution of Christians in the east; his open espousal and promotion of Christianity about this time, and the subsequent disappearance of the sun god and other pagan symbols from his coinage.

325—His convening of the Council of Nicaea, which he dominated, in order to secure unity in the church; subsequently, his enforcement of that unity against heretical Christians in favor of the Catholic Church.

337—His long-deferred baptism during his last illness.

For the principal facts about Constantine, see Philip Schaff, *History of the Christian Church,* vol. 3, pp. 12-36; for shorter treatment, see A. C. Flick, *The Rise of the Mediaeval Church*, pp. 115-122; A.E.R. Boak, *A History of Rome to 565 A.D.*, pp. 347-350.

What kinds of religious legislation united church and state?

Laws granting privileges and patronage, and those enforcing church dogmas, practices, or disciplinary decrees, or suppressing paganism and heresy.

NOTE.—Constantine's earliest Christian legislation "exempted the Christian clergy from military and municipal duty (March 313); abolished various customs and ordinances offensive to the Christians (315); facilitated the emancipation of Christian slaves (before 316); legalized bequests to catholic churches (321); enjoined the civil observance of Sunday, though not as dies Domini [Lord's day], but as dies Solis [the Sun's day], . . . and in company with an ordinance for the regular consulting of the haruspex [soothsayer] (321)." Philip Schaff, *History of the Christian Church* (Scribner's, 1902), vol. 3, p. 31. For Sunday legislation, see the following reading.

How did Constantine initiate state supervision of the church?

Having achieved political unity in the empire, he sought to gain church unity through church councils.

NOTE.—The first ecumenical, or general, council at Nicaea, in 325, was called and presided over by Constantine. "The ecumenical councils," Schaff wrote, "have not only an ecclesiastical significance, but bear also a *political* or state-church character. The very name refers to . . . the empire. . . . The Christian Graeco-Roman *emperor* is indispensible to an ecumenical council in the ancient sense of the term; its temporal head and its legislative strength. . . . Upon this Byzantine precedent, and upon the example of the kings of Israel, the Russian Czars and the Protestant princes of Germany, Scandinavia, and England—be it justly or unjustly—build their claim to a similar and still more extended supervision of the church in their dominions." Philip Schaff, *History of the Christian Church*, vol. 3, pp. 334, 335.

What were the principal questions discussed at Nicaea?

First the Arian controversy; next, the date of Easter.

NOTE.—"It appears that the churches of Syria and Mesopotamia continued to follow the custom of the Jews, and celebrated Easter on the fourteenth day of the moon, whether falling on Sunday or not. All the other churches observed that solemnity on Sunday only, viz.: those of Rome, Italy, Africa, Lydia, Egypt, Spain, Gaul and Britain; and all Greece, Asia, and Pontus." Isaac Boyle, *Historical View of the Council of Nice* (1836), p. 23. By this council Easter was fixed on the Sunday immediately following the full moon that was nearest after the vernal equinox.

What does Neander say of the securing of religious laws?

"In this way, the church received help from the state for the furtherance of her ends. *General History of the Christian Religion and Church* (Torrey's translation, 1852), vol. 2, p. 301.

NOTE.—Church and state were united. The church gained control of the civil power, which it later used as a means of carrying on most bitter and extensive persecutions. In this way the church denied Christ and the power of godliness, and demanded that civil power should be exerted to compel citizens to serve God as the church should dictate.

SABBATH LEGISLATION

Who made the Sabbath?

"For in six days *the Lord* made the heavens and the earth, the sea, and all that is in them, but he rested on the seventh day. Therefore *the Lord* blessed the Sabbath day and made it holy." Exodus 20:11, NIV.

To whom does the Sabbath belong?

"The seventh day is a Sabbath to *the Lord your God.*" Verse 10, NIV.

To whom, then, should its observance be rendered?

"Give to Caesar what is Caesar's and *to God what is God's.*" Mark 12:17, NIV.

NOTE.—When people make laws based on religious doctrine, they require observance to be rendered to the *government*, or to God *through the government*, which amounts to the same thing.

In religious things, to whom alone are we accountable?

"So then, each of us will give an account of himself to *God.*" Romans 14:12, NIV.

NOTE.—Laws requiring religious observance try to make citizens accountable to the government instead of God.

How does God show the holiness of the Sabbath day?

"Remember the sabbath day, to keep it holy." Exodus 20:8. "The seventh day is a Sabbath of rest, *a day of sacred assembly.*" Leviticus 23:3, NIV. Since the Sabbath is holy, is to be kept holy, and is a day for holy gatherings, it must be religious.

What, then, must be the nature of all Sabbath legislation?

It is *religious legislation*.

What has generally been the result of religious legislation, or a union of religion and state?

Religious intolerance and persecution grows, while true spirituality is diminished.

What was the first Sunday law?

Constantine's Sunday law of March 7, 321.

NOTE.—"On the venerable day of the sun let the magistrates and people residing in cities rest, and let all workshops be closed. In the country, however, persons engaged in agriculture may freely and lawfully continue their pursuits; because it often happens that another day is not so suitable for grain sowing or for vine planting; lest by neglecting the proper moment for such operations the bounty of heaven should be lost. (Given the 7th day of March, Crispus and Constantine being counsuls each of them for the second time.)" *Codex Justinianus*, vol. 3, title 12, section 3; translated by Philip Schaff, *History of the Christian Church* (Scribner's, 1902), vol. 3, p. 380.

What church council required Sunday observance and forbade Sabbath observance?

The Council of Laodicea decreed that Christians should keep the Sunday, and that if they persisted in resting on the seventh-day Sabbath, "they shall be shut out from Christ." Charles Joseph Hefele, *A History of the Councils of the Church* (1896 English ed.), vol. 2, p. 316.

Was there further imperial Sunday legislation?

"Constantine's decrees marked the beginning of a long, though intermittent series of imperial decrees in support of Sunday rest." Charles Joseph Hefele, *A History of the Councils of the Church* (1896 English ed.), vol. 2, p. 29.

NOTE.—"By a law of the year 386 [Theodosius I], those older changes effected by the emperor Constantine were more rigorously enforced, and, in general, civil transactions of every kind on Sunday were strictly forbidden. . . .

"In the year 425 [Theodosius the Younger], the exhibition of spectacles on Sunday, and on the principal feast days of the Christians, was forbidden, in order that the devotion of the faithful might be free from all disturbance. . . .

"In this way, the church received help from the state for the furtherance of her ends. . . . But had it not been for that confusion of spiritual and secular interests, had it not been for the vast number of mere outward conversions thus brought about, she would have needed no such help." Augstus Neander, *General History of the Christian Religion and Church* (1852), vol. 2, pp. 300, 301.

The decrees of later emperors between 364 and 467 added other prohibitions and exemptions from time to time. Justinian's code collected the laws of the empire on the subject, and from the time when Charlemagne, king of the Franks, was crowned emperor (800), this code was in effect all over what later became the "Holy Roman Empire." The medieval decrees and canons of popes and councils concerning Sunday observance were enforced by the civil power. (See *The New Schaff-Herzog Encyclopedia of Religious Knowledge*, vol. 11, p. 147.)

Later the church councils had an influence to some extent throughout the former Roman Empire, for the church maintained a large degree of unity. The Council of Laodicea (fourth century) ordered men to work on the Sabbath and rest if possible on Sunday. "The Council of Orleans (538), while protesting against excessive Sabbatarianism, forbade all field work under pain of censure; and the Council of Macon (585) laid down that the Lord's Day 'is the day of perpetual rest, which is suggested to us by the type of the seventh day in the law and the prophets,' and ordered a complete cessation of all kinds of business. How far the movement had gone by the end of the sixth century is shown by a letter of Gregory the Great (pope 590-604) protesting against prohibition of baths on Sunday." James Hastings, "Decrees of Church Councils," *Encyclopedia of Religion and Ethics*, vol. 12, pp. 105, 106, art.

Law of Charlemagne 789: "And, we decree according to what the Lord commanded also in the law, that servile work shall not be done on the Lord's days, and just as my father of blessed memory commanded in his synodal edicts, that is, that men shall not carry on rural work, neither in cultivating the vine, nor in plowing in the fields [etc.]. . . . Likewise the women shall not do weaving [etc.]. . . in order that in every way the honor and rest of the Lord's day may be kept. But let them come together from everywhere to the church to the celebration of the mass, and praise God in all the good things which He has done for us on that day." Translated from Charlemagne, *Admonitio Generalis,* in *Monumenta Germaniae Historica, Leges*, sect. 2, tome 1, p. 61, par. 81.

In England, according to Lord Mansfield (*Swann vs. Browne*, 3 Burrow, 1599), William the Conqueror and Henry II declared the codes of Justinian on Sunday observance to be the law of England. A succession of Parliamentary acts regulated Sunday observance in England. (See *The New Schaff-Herzog Encyclopedia of Religious Knowledge*, vol. 11, pp. 147, 148.)

The first Sunday law in force in America, Virginia, 1610:

"Every man and woman shall repair in the morning to the divine service, and sermons preached upon the Sabbath day, and in the afternoon to divine service, and catechizing, upon pain for the first fault to lose their provision and the allowance for the whole week following, for the second to lose the said allowance and also be whipped, and for the third to suffer death." *For the Colony in Virginea Britannia, Lavves, Morall and Martiall, &c*, in Peter Force, *Tracts Relating to the Colonies in North America* (Washington, 1844), vol. 3, no. 2, p. 10.

Law of Charles II, twenty-ninth year, 1676-1677: "Be it enacted . . . that all and every Person and Persons whatsoever, shall on every Lord's Day apply themselves to the Observation of the same, by exercising themselves thereon in the Duties of Piety and true Religion, publickly and privately; and that no . . . Person whatsoever, shall do or exercise any worldly Labour, Business, or Work of their ordinary Callings, upon the Lord's Day, or any Part thereof (Works of Necessity and Charity only excepted;) . . . and that no Person or Persons whatsoever, shall publickly cry, shew forth, or expose to Sale, any Wares, Merchandizes," etc. *British Statutes at Large*, twenty-ninth year of Charles II, chap. 7.

Modeled somewhat after the Puritan laws of 1644 to 1658, but much shorter and milder, it further forbids travel, but does not mention sports and pastimes, and makes the same exception for food and milk.

The importance of this act is that it stood, with modifications, as the basic Sunday law of England for nearly 200 years (see *Encyclopaedia Britannica* [1945], vol. 21, p. 565), and was followed as a model for many of the subsequent Sunday laws in various American colonies, and thus somewhat set the pattern for America's state laws.

PERSECUTION

Because Jesus had not kept the Sabbath according to their beliefs, how was He treated?

"The man went away and told the Jews that it was Jesus who had made him well. Therefore the Jews started persecuting Jesus, because he was doing such things on the sabbath." John 5:16, NRSV.

Why did Cain kill Abel?

"This is the message you heard from the beginning: We should love one another. Do not be like Cain, who belonged to the evil one and murdered his brother. And why did he murder him? *Because his own actions were evil and his brother's righteous."* 1 John 3:11, 12, NIV.

Commenting upon the treatment of Isaac, the son of Sarah, by Ishmael, the son of a slave, what principle does the apostle Paul lay down?

"At that time *the son born in the ordinary way persecuted the son born by the power of the Spirit. It is the same now."* Galatians 4:29, NIV.

NOTE.—Other instances of persecution mentioned in the Bible are:

a. Esau, who sold his birthright, persecuted Jacob, who vowed his loyalty to God. Genesis 25:29-34; 27:41; 32:6. *

b. The wayward and envious sons of Jacob persecuted Joseph, who feared God. Genesis 37; Acts 7:9.

c. The idolatrous Egyptians persecuted the Hebrews, who worshipped the true God. Exodus 1 and 5.

d. The Hebrew who did his neighbor wrong thrust Moses, as mediator, aside. Exodus 2:13, 14; Acts 7:26, 27.

e. Saul, who disobeyed God, persecuted David, who feared God. 1 Samuel 15, 19, 24.

f. Israel, in their apostasy, persecuted Elijah and Jeremiah, who were prophets of God. 1 Kings 19:9, 10; Jeremiah 36:20-23; 38:1-6.

g. Nebuchadnezzar, while an idolater, persecuted the three Hebrew captives for refusing to worship idols. Daniel 3.

h. The envious and idolatrous princes under Darius persecuted Daniel for daring to pray to the God of heaven. Daniel 6.

i. The apostles were persecuted for preaching Christ. Acts 4 and 5.

j. Paul, before his conversion, persecuted the church of God. Acts 8:1; 9:1, 2; 22:4, 5, 20; 26:9-11; Galatians 1:13; 1 Timothy 1:12, 13.

The history of all the religious persecutions since Bible times is but a repetition of this same story. And thus it will continue to be until the conflict between good and evil is ended. (See Psalm 37:12, 14, 32.)

Who does Paul say shall suffer persecution?

"In fact, *everyone who wants to live a godly life in Christ Jesus will be persecuted."* 2 Timothy 3:12, NIV.

Since persecution is invariably wrong, what must be true of persecuting governments?

They likewise must be in the wrong.

NOTE.—"There are many who do not seem to be sensible that all violence in religion is irreligious and that whoever is wrong, the persecutor cannot be right." Thomas Clarke, *History of Intolerance* (1819), vol. 1, p. 3.

"It is now no more that toleration is spoken of as if it was by the indulgence of one class of the people that another enjoyed the exercise of their inherent natural rights, for, happily, the government of the United States, which gives to bigotry no sanction, to persecution no assistance, requires only that they who live under its protection should demean themselves as good citizens in giving it on all occasions their effectual support." President George Washington, to the congregation of Touro Synagogue, Newport, Rhode Island, August 1790.

God never forces the will or the conscience, but Satan has no such qualms. To accomplish his purpose, he works through religious and secular rulers, influencing them to enact and enforce human laws in defiance of the law of God.

What self-deception did Jesus say would motivate persecutors?

"All this I have told you so that you will not go astray. They will put you out of the synagogue; in fact, a time is coming when *anyone who kills you will think he is offering a service to God*." John 16:1, 2, NIV.

Who is the original murderer?

"You belong to your father, *the devil*, and you want to carry out your father's desire. *He was a murderer from the beginning*, not holding to the truth, for there is no truth in him. When he lies, he speaks his native language, for he is a liar and the father of lies." John 8:44, NIV.

When James and John wished to call fire from heaven to consume the Samaritans who did not receive Jesus, what did Jesus say?

"But He turned and rebuked them, and said, '*You do not know what manner of spirit you are of. For the Son of Man did not come to destroy men's lives but to save them.*'" Luke 9:55, 56, NIV.

What divine precepts, if received and obeyed, would do away with all oppression and persecution?

"You shall love your neighbor as yourself." Matthew 22:39, NKJV. "Therefore, whatever you want men to do to you, do also to them." Matthew 7:12, NKJV.

What relationship does love have with the law?

"Love does no harm to its neighbor. Therefore *love is the fulfillment of the law*." Romans 13:10, NIV.

What promise does Jesus give those who are persecuted?

"Blessed are those who are persecuted because of righteousness,

Freedom of Religion

The doctrine which, from the very first origin of religious dissensions, has been held by all bigots of all sects, when condensed into a few words, and stripped of rhetorical disguise, is simply this: I am in the right, and you are in the wrong. When you are the stronger, you ought to tolerate me; for it is your duty to tolerate truth. But when I am the stronger, I shall persecute you; for it is my duty to persecute error." "Sir James Mackintosh" in *Critical and Historical Essays* (1865), vol. 1, pp. 333, 334.

"When a religion is good, I conceive that it will support itself; and, when it cannot support itself, and God does not take care to support, so that its professors are obliged to call for the help of the civil power, it is a sign, I apprehend, of its being a bad one." Letter to Dr. Price, Oct. 9, 1780, in *The Writings of Benjamin Franklin*, ed. Albert Henry Smyth, vol. 8, p. 154.

"Condemn no man for not thinking as you think: Let every one enjoy the full and free liberty of thinking for himself: Let every man use his own judgment, since every man must give an account of himself to God. Abhor every approach, in any kind or degree, to the spirit of persecution. If you cannot reason or persuade a man into the truth, never attempt to force him into it. If love will not compel him to come, leave him to God, the Judge of all." John Wesley, "Advice to the People Called Methodists," *Works* (1830), vol. 8, p. 357.

for theirs is the kingdom of heaven. Blessed are you when people insult you, persecute you and falsely say all kinds of evil against you because of me. Rejoice and be glad, because great is your reward in heaven, for in the same way they persecuted the prophets who were before you." Matthew 5:10-12, NIV. (See also Revelation 2:10; 6:9-11.)

NOTE.—The world hates righteousness and loves sin. This is what caused the hostility to Jesus when He lived on earth. Those who do not accept the love of God will find Christianity a disturbing element and will sooner or later war against the truth and its representatives. Fellowship with God brings enmity with the world.

CHAPTER 11

Life, Death, and the Supernatural

THE ORIGIN, HISTORY, AND DESTINY OF SATAN

Have any other than human beings sinned?

"God did not spare angels when they sinned." 2 Peter 2:4, NIV.

Who led the angels to sin?

"Then he will say to those on his left, 'Depart from me, you who are cursed, into the eternal fire prepared for *the devil and his angels.*' " Matthew 25:41, NIV.

NOTE—The devil is also known as "the great dragon," "that old serpent," "Satan," "Lucifer" (Revelation 12:9; Isaiah 14:12).

What was Satan's condition when created?

"You were blameless in your ways from the day you were created till wickedness was found in you." Ezekiel 28:15, NIV.

NOTE.—Peter speaks of "the angels that sinned" (2 Peter 2:4), and Jude refers to "the angels who did not keep their positions of authority" (Jude 6); both of which show that these angels were once in a state of sinlessness and innocence.

Satan is described in Ezekiel 28: "You were the model of perfection, full of wisdom and perfect in beauty. You were in Eden, the garden of God; every precious stone adorned you. . . . You were anointed as a guardian cherub, for so I ordained you. You were on the holy mount of God." Verses 12-14, NIV. Evidently Satan was an exalted angel before he fell, a perfect masterpiece of wisdom and beauty. Since this angel is called a "guardian cherub," he evidently stood in the immediate presence of God, as suggested by the golden cherubim whose wings overshadowed the mercy seat in the earthly sanctuary (Exodus 25:16-22; Hebrews 9:3-5; Psalm 99:1).

Much of what we know about the origin of Satan comes from Isaiah 14 and Ezekiel 28. But if the subject is Satan, then why do these passages refer explicitly to the kings of Babylon (Isaiah 14:4, 22) and Tyre (Ezekiel 28:12)? It is obvious that the extravagant language of the passage cannot refer merely to any human king (For example, the king of Tyre was never in Eden [verse 13]). The reason is this: Initially the prophets focus on the human king, but their attention is soon drawn to the *power behind the power*, the de-

monic spirit who empowered the pagan gods of the kingdom. Just
as God was the true king of Israel (Isaiah 41:21; Zephaniah 3:15),
so Satan was the true king of Babylon and Tyre, and earthly kings
were only representatives of these heavenly powers. These two lev-
els of reality are mentioned in Isaiah 24: "The Lord will punish
the powers in the heavens above and the kings on the earth below."
These demonic heavenly powers are also mentioned in Ephesians
6:12; Colossians 1:16; 2:15; and 1 Peter 3:22. Satan, the leader of
these beings, was the ultimate power behind the powers of Babylon and Tyre.

What led to Satan's downfall?

"Your heart became proud on account of your beauty, and you
corrupted your wisdom because of your splendor. So I threw you
to the earth; I made a spectacle of you before kings." Ezekiel
28:17, NIV.

NOTE.—This sort of daring, arrogant pride, or hubris, is a fault
to which the extremely gifted are prone. Solomon, with all his
riches and wisdom, experienced a similar downfall, and he wrote,
"Pride goes before destruction, a haughty spirit before a fall."
Proverbs 16:18, NIV. First Timothy 3:6 warns that those who become "lifted up with pride" will "fall into the condemnation of the
devil."

In contrast to Satan, Jesus "humbled himself" (Philippians 2:8).
Satan sought to ascend, and pulled many down when he fell; Christ
sought to descend, and lifted many up when He rose. Satan demonstrated the sad results of the love of power; Christ demonstrated the
wonderful results of the power of love.

How does the prophet Isaiah describe Satan's fall?

"How you have fallen from heaven, O morning star, son of the
dawn! You have been cast down to the earth, you who once laid low
the nations!" Isaiah 14:12, NIV.

Why was Satan expelled from his high position?

"Through your widespread trade you were filled with violence,
and *you* sinned. So I drove you in disgrace from the mount of God,
and I expelled you, O guardian cherub, from among the fiery stones."
Ezekiel 28:16, NIV.

What happened when God expelled Satan from heaven?

"And there was war in heaven. Michael and his angels fought
against the dragon, and the dragon and his angels fought back. But

he was not strong enough, and they lost their place in heaven. The great dragon was hurled down—that ancient serpent called the devil, or Satan, who leads the whole world astray. *He was hurled to the earth, and his angels with him.*" Revelation 12:7-9, NIV.

Where did Satan and his angels finally establish themselves?

"And the great dragon was cast out . . . *into the earth*, and his angels were cast out with him." Revelation 12:9.

What was Satan's domain?

"One day the angels came to present themselves before the Lord, and *Satan also came with them*. The Lord said to Satan, 'Where have you come from?' Satan answered the Lord, 'From roaming through the earth and going back and forth in it.'" Job 1:6, 7.

NOTE—In 2 Corinthians 4:4 Satan is called "the god of this world."

What has been the character of Satan since his fall?

"The devil has sinned from the beginning." 1 John 3:8, NKJV. "He was a murderer from the beginning, not holding to the truth, for there is no truth in him. When he lies, he speaks his native language, for he is a liar and the father of lies." John 8:44, NIV.

NOTE.—Satan is the original apostate, rebel, renegade, traitor, and mutineer.

What did God tell Adam and Eve would happen if they sinned by eating the forbidden fruit?

"And the Lord God commanded the man, saying, 'Of every tree of the garden you may freely eat; but of the tree of knowledge of good and evil you shall not eat, for in the day that you eat of it *you shall surely die*." Genesis 2:16, 17, NKJV.

What did Satan say to Eve through the serpent?

"You will not surely die." Genesis 3:4, NKJV.

NOTE.—As far as we know from the Scriptures, this was the first lie—a direct denial of the word of God.

By deception Satan led our first parents to commit sin; and since "the wages of sin is death," he caused their death, and so became the first murderer. A lie is the father of murder, and is hateful to God, the "God of truth" (see Proverbs 6:16-19, 12:19). "All liars shall have their part in the lake which burns with fire and brimstone: which is the second death." Revelation 21:8. (See also Revelation 21:27; 22:15.)

What has been the result of sin's entrance into the world?

"By one man sin entered into the world, and death by sin . . . by one man's disobedience *many were made sinners*." Romans 5:12-19. "The whole world lies under the sway of the wicked one." 1 John 5:19, NKJV. "In Adam *all die*." 1 Corinthians 15:22, NKJV.

What sort of encounter did Christ have with Satan?

"He was there in the wilderness forty days, *tempted of Satan*." Mark 1:13, NKJV (See also Matthew 4:1-11).

How severely was Christ tempted of Satan?

"For we do not have a high priest who is unable to sympathize with our weaknesses, but we have one who has been tempted *in every way, just as we are—yet was without sin*." Hebrews 4:15, NIV.

What is now the special object of Satan's hatred?

"When the dragon saw that he had been hurled to the earth, *he pursued the woman [the church]*. . . Then the dragon was enraged at the woman and went off to make war against the rest of her off-spring—those who obey God's commandments and hold to the testimony of Jesus." Revelation 12:13-17, NIV.

How will Satan deceive people in the last days?

"And deceiveth them that dwell on the earth *by the means of those miracles* which he had power to do." Revelation 13:14.

NOTE—Miracles are no proof of the divine. They may indicate the presence of the demonic. According to 2 Thessalonians 2:9, Satan can work "with all power and signs and lying wonders."

What will miracle-working spirits accomplish?

"They are spirits of demons performing *miraculous signs*, and they go out to the kings of the whole world, to gather them for the battle on the great day of God Almighty." Revelation 16:14, NIV.

What will happen to Satan at the second coming of Christ?

"And I saw an angel coming down out of heaven, having the key to the Abyss and holding in his hand a great chain. He seized the dragon, that ancient serpent, who is the devil, or Satan, and *bound him for a thousand years*. He threw him into the Abyss, and locked and sealed it over him, to keep him from deceiving the nations any-more until the thousand years were ended. After that, he must be set free for a short time." Revelation 20:1-3, NIV.

What happens after Satan's thousand years of imprisonment?

"When the thousand years are over, *Satan will be released from his prison and will go out to deceive the nations* in the four corners of the earth—Gog and Magog—to gather them for battle. In number they are like the sand on the seashore." Verses 7, 8, NIV.

NOTE.—Satan's evil career began in rebellion against God in heaven, and ends in rebellion against Him on earth.

What will be the final fate of Satan and his followers?

"They marched across the breadth of the earth and surrounded the camp of God's people, the city he loves. But *fire came down from heaven and devoured them*. And the devil, who deceived them, was thrown into the lake of burning sulfur, where the beast and the false prophet had been thrown." Verses 9, 10, NIV. "By your many sins and dishonest trade you have desecrated your sanctuaries. So I made a fire come out from you, and it consumed you, and *I reduced you to ashes* on the ground in the sight of all who were watching. All the nations who knew you are appalled at you; *you have come to a horrible end and will be no more*." Ezekiel 28:18, 19, NIV.

How did Christ win the right to destroy the devil?

"Since the children have flesh and blood, he too shared in their humanity so that *by his death* he might destroy him who holds the power of death—that is, the devil—and free those who all their lives were held in slavery by their fear of death." Hebrews 2:14, NIV.

Is it possible for Christians to resist the devil?

"Be self-controlled and alert. Your enemy the devil prowls around like a roaring lion looking for someone to devour. *Resist him, standing firm in the faith*." 1 Peter 5:8, 9, NIV. "*Resist the devil*, and he will flee from you." James 4:7, KJV.

How did Christ resist Satan?

"It is written." (See Matthew 4:4-10.)

NOTE.—When Satan tempted Jesus, Jesus quoted Scripture. His weapon was God's Word. The Word of God is the "sword of the Spirit" (Ephesians 6:17). If Christ met and vanquished the enemy this way, so may we.

Why will some people fall under the delusion of Satan?

"They perish *because they refuse to love the truth* and so be saved. *For this reason God sends them a powerful delusion, so that they will believe the lie* and so that all will be condemned who have not believed the truth but have delighted in wickedness." 2 Thessalonians 2:10-12, NIV.

THE NATURE OF HUMANITY

Of what was the first human being formed?

"God formed man of the *dust* of the ground." Genesis 2:7.

NOTE.—Other creatures were also formed out of the ground: "And out of the ground the Lord God formed every beast of the field, and every fowl of the air." Verse 19.

What act made him a living soul?

"And [God] breathed into his nostrils the breath of life; and man *became* a living soul." Verse 7.

NOTE.—The Hebrew word for soul is *nephesh*. In the King James Version *nephesh* is translated more than 400 times as "soul," more than 100 times as "life," and approximately 30 times as "person," and is occasionally rendered by other words, such as "mind," "heart," "creature," "body," etc.

Notice that Adam *became* a soul; he did not *acquire* one. The soul is the person. Here we have a simple equation that defines the composition of the soul: body (dust) + breath (life principle) = soul (person). Take away either of the two elements on the left side of the equation, and the soul ceases to exist.

Here is a useful analogy: bulb + electricity = light. If you break the bulb, or turn off the electricity, what happens to the light? It simply goes out. It ceases to exist.

Are animals also "living souls"?

"So God created the great creatures of the sea and every living [*nephesh chaiyah*, 'living soul'] and moving thing with which the water teems, and according to their kinds, and every winged bird according to its kind." Genesis 1:21, NIV. "The sea . . . became as the blood of a dead man: and every *living soul* died in the sea." Revelation 16:3.

NOTE.—The Greek word translated "souls" in Revelation 16:3 is the word *psyche*, usually translated either "soul" or "life" in the New Testament. The word is equivalent to the Latin *anima*, spirit. Here it is used of fish. Both the first and last books of the Bible call fish "souls."

It is commonly believed that human beings alone possess a soul, and that this constitutes their uniqueness. But this is not supported by the Genesis creation account, where both animals and human beings are called "souls." The Hebrew word for soul, *nephesh*, refers to animals in Genesis 1:21, 24; 2:19; 9:10, 15, 16, etc., where it is translated "living creature," and this is the same expression applied to human beings in Genesis 2:7. According to commentator Adam Clarke, this phrase *nephesh chaiyah* in Hebrew is "a general term to express all creatures endued with animal life."

Do other animals also have the "breath of life"?

"Every living thing that moved on the earth perished—birds, livestock, wild animals, all the creatures that swarm over the earth, and all mankind. *Everything on dry land that had the breath of life in its nostrils died.*" Genesis 7:21, 22, NIV. "Man's fate is like that of the animals; the same fait awaits them both: As one dies, so does the other. All have the same breath; man has no advantage over the animal." Ecclesiastes 3:19, NIV.

What is another term for that which God breathed into human nostrils?

"All the while my breath is in me, and the spirit of God is in my nostrils." Job 27:3.

NOTE.—"Breath" and "spirit" are synonymous terms (see also Genesis 7:22, Job 32:8, 33:4). In fact, they are both translations of the same Hebrew word, *ruach*. In the King James Version *ruach* is rendered more than 200 times as "spirit," nearly 100 times as "wind," and almost 30 times as "breath." This "breath" is more than just air; it is the "electricity" of life; the life force.

When human beings give up this spirit, what becomes of it?

"The dust returns to the ground it came from, and *the spirit returns to God* who gave it." Ecclesiastes 12:7, NIV.

NOTE.—This verse describes the decomposition of the soul (the person); the undoing of the process of creation described in Genesis 2:7. The spirit or breath returns to God who gave it; the body returns to dust; and the soul (which is the body plus the spirit) vanishes. The individual no longer exists as a living, conscious, thinking being, except as he exists in the mind, plan, and purpose of God through Christ and the resurrection. The spirit, or breath, or life force, which is on loan from God, at death goes back to the great Author of life. Having come from Him, it belongs to God, and man can have it eternally only as a gift from God, through Jesus Christ (Romans 6:23).

Note how the decomposition of the soul in death is described in Psalm 146:4: "His spirit departs, he returns to the earth; in that very day his thoughts perish." Verse 4, NASB. Note that it is the spirit not the soul, that returns to God. "No biblical text authorizes the statement that the 'soul' is separated from the body at the moment of death." E. Jacob, "Death," *The Interpreter's Dictionary of the Bible*, vol. 1, p. 802).

Where did Jesus' spirit go when He died?

"Jesus called out with a loud voice, 'Father, *into your hands* I commit my spirit.' When he had said this, he breathed his last." Luke 23:46, NIV.

What did Jesus, after His resurrection, say about where He had been?

"Jesus said, 'Do not hold on to me, for I have not yet returned to the Father.' " John 20:17, NIV.

NOTE.—This shows that the spirit/breath that returns to God cannot be the conscious self, for although Jesus' breath returned to God at His death, yet after His resurrection He claimed He had not yet been to see His Father (John 20:17).

How then do human beings differ from animals?

"Then God said, 'Let us make man in our image, in our likeness, and let them rule over the fish of the sea and the birds of the air, over the livestock, over all the earth, and over all the creatures that move along the ground.' *So God created man in his own image*, in the image of God he created him; male and female he created them." Genesis 1:26, 27, NIV.

NOTE.—Only human beings are made in the image of God. The Hebrew word for "image" refers primarily to the physical being—which includes the brain and its facilities of speech and reason and worship. However, there is no logical reason to assume that creatures made in the image of God must be inherently immortal. God is also omniscient and omnipresent, but no one assumes creatures made in the image of God must be omniscient or omnipresent. No passage of Scripture teaches that human beings are inherently immortal.

Are human beings mortal or immortal by nature?

"Shall *mortal* man be more just than God?" Job 4:17.

What is God's nature?

"Now to the King, *eternal, immortal, invisible, the only God*, be honor and glory for ever and ever. Amen." 1 Timothy 1:17, NIV.

NOTE.—The Bible never applies the adjective "immortal" to

human beings. The redeemed will receive immortality as a gift at the Second Coming (1 Corinthians 15:54, 55).

In what condition was Adam created?
"What is man that you are mindful of him, the son of man that you care for him? You made him *a little lower than the angels*." Hebrews 2:6, 7, NIV.

What will be the state of the righteous in the world to come?
"*They can no longer die; for they are like the angels*. They are God's children, for they are children of the resurrection." Luke 20:36, NIV.

How will our resurrected bodies differ from our earthly bodies?
"So will it be with the resurrection of the dead. The body that is sown is *perishable*, it is raised *imperishable*; it is sown in *dishonor*, it is raised in *glory*; it is sown in *weakness*, it is raised in *power*; it is sown a *natural* body, it is raised a *spiritual* body." 1 Corinthians 15:42-44, NIV.

NOTE.—If the righteous go to heaven at death, then a resurrection would not be needed, since the saints would have already received their reward. Why would these glorified spirits have any interest in recovering their earthly bodies which had long since rotted into dust? Even if resurrected bodies are freed from all pollution and limitations, whatever could be the point of a fleshly resurrection out of the dirt for ethereal spirits? Only if there is no human existence apart from the body, and the righteous are asleep in the grave, does physical resurrection make sense.

Who only have eternal life?
"*He who has the Son* has life; he who does not have the Son does not have life." 1 John 5:12, NIV.

NOTE.—Only the righteous have, by faith, eternal life. Unsaved sinners have no such thing: "No murderer has eternal life in him" (1 John 3:15, NIV). Jesus' statement in John 10:28, "I give them eternal life, and they shall never perish" (NIV), refers to the righteous, and this is a gift, not a birthright. One of the greatest mistakes of the church has been to insist that the *wicked* have eternal life in hell, and never perish.

Why was Adam driven from Eden and the tree of life?
"And the Lord God said, 'The man has now become like one of us, knowing good and evil. *He must not be allowed to reach out his*

hand and take also from the tree of life and eat, and live forever.' So the Lord God banished him from the Garden of Eden to work the ground from which he had been taken. After he drove the man out, he placed on the east side of the Garden of Eden cherubim and a flaming sword flashing back and forth to guard the way to the tree of life." Genesis 3:22-24, NIV.

What is the natural state of humanity?

"All of us also lived among them at one time, gratifying the cravings of our sinful nature and following its desires and thoughts. Like the rest, we were *by nature objects of wrath.*" Ephesians 2:3, NIV.

If the wrath of God abides on us, of what are we deprived?

"Whoever believes in the Son has eternal life, but whoever rejects the Son *will not see life*, for God's wrath remains on him." John 3:36, NIV.

Through whom can we be saved from wrath and given immortality?

"Since we have now been justified by his blood, how much more shall we be saved from God's wrath *through him!*" Romans 5:9, NIV. "Our Savior, *Christ Jesus*, who has destroyed death and has brought life and immortality to light through the gospel." 2 Timothy 1:10, NIV.

Who only possesses inherent immortality?

"God, the blessed and only Ruler, the King of kings and Lord of lords, *who alone is immortal* and who lives in unapproachable light, whom no one has seen or can see." 1 Timothy 6:15, 16, NIV.

NOTE.—God is the only being who possesses original life or immortality in Himself. All others must receive it from God. (See John 5:26; 6:27; 10:10, 27, 28; Romans 6:23; 1 John 5:11.)

To whom is eternal life promised?

"To *those who* by persistence in doing good *seek glory, honor, and immortality*, he will give eternal life." Romans 2:7, NIV.

NOTE.—One does not need to seek for a thing already possessed. The fact that we are to seek for immortality is proof that we do not now possess it.

When will the faithful become immortal?

"Listen, I tell you a mystery: We will not all sleep, but we will all be changed—in a flash, in the twinkling of an eye, at the last trumpet. For the trumpet will sound, the dead will be raised imperishable, and we will all be changed. For the perishable must clothe itself with the imperishable, and the mortal with immortality. When the perishable has been clothed with the imperishable, and the mortal with immortality, then the saying that is written will come true: 'Death is swallowed up in victory.'" 1 Corinthians 15:51-54, NIV.

NOTE.—The final trumpet is blown at the Second Coming (Matthew 24:31; 1 Thessalonians 4:16).

THE INTERMEDIATE STATE

What term for death is frequently used in the Bible?

"Give light to my eyes, or I *will sleep* in death." Psalm 13:3, NIV. "We do not want you to be ignorant about those who fall *asleep*, or to grieve like the rest of men, who have no hope. We believe that Jesus died and rose again and so we believe that God will bring with Jesus those who have fallen asleep in him. According to the Lord's own word, we tell you that we who are still alive, who are left till the coming of the Lord, will certainly not precede those who have fallen asleep. For the Lord himself will come down from heaven, with a loud command, with the voice of the archangel and with the trumpet of God, and the dead in Christ will rise first." 1 Thessalonians 4:13-16, NIV.

How did Jesus refer to Lazarus after he died?

"After he had said this, he went on to tell them, 'Our friend Lazarus has fallen asleep; but I am going there to wake him up' His disciples replied, 'Lord, if he sleeps, he will get better.' Jesus had been speaking of his death, but his disciples thought he meant natural sleep. So then he told them plainly, 'Lazarus is dead.' " John 11:11-14, NIV.

NOTE.—Many, though not all, Jews in Jesus' day believed the intermediate state to be one of suspended animation, as taught in the religious literature of the day. The apocryphal book of 2 Baruch says, "Our fathers went to rest without grief and, behold, the righteous sleep at rest in the earth. For they did not know this anguish, nor did they hear that which has befallen us" (2 Baruch 11:4, 5). Second Baruch 21:24 speaks of "Abraham, Isaac, and Jacob and all those who were like them, who sleep in the earth." Sirach 17:27-30 echoes the claim of Psalm 115:17 that the dead do not praise the Lord. *The Testament of the 12 Patriarchs* describes the death of the patriarchs as an "eternal sleep" (Test. Issachar 7:9; Test. Dan 7:1), yet expects their resurrection: "Those who died on account of the Lord shall be wakened to life" (Test. Judah 25:4; cf. Test. Zebulun 10:1; Test. Benjamen 10:7). First Enoch, a book that was almost certainly familiar to every New Testament writer, says in 91:10 and 92:3 that the righteous arise from their sleep. First Enoch 100:5 says, "Though the righteous sleep a long sleep, they have nothing to fear."

These statements, which were written in the first century B.C. to first century A.D., are very similar to the language in the New Testament, which says that death is a sleep (John 11:11-14; Acts 7:60; 13:36; 1 Corinthians 11:30; 15:6, 18, 20; 1 Thessalonians 4:13, 14; 5:10), and the dead are in their graves (John 5:28; Acts 2:29, 34). Clearly, the apostles were not speaking merely in metaphor. That was standard Jewish teaching.

Where do the dead sleep?

"And many of those who sleep *in the dust of the earth* shall awake." Daniel 12:2, NKJV. "All go to one place: all are from the dust, and *all return to dust*." Ecclesiastes 3:20, NKJV. "Why do you not pardon my offenses and forgive my sins? For I will soon lie down *in the dust*; you will search for me, but I will be no more." Job 7:21, NIV.

How long will they sleep there?

"But man dies and is laid low; he breathes his last and is no more. As water disappears from the sea or a riverbed becomes parched and dry, so man lies down and does not rise; *till the heavens are no more*, men will not awake or be roused from their sleep." Job 14:10-12, NIV.

Where, for example, was King David sleeping, after the resurrection of Jesus?

"I can tell you confidently that the patriarch David died and was buried, and his tomb is here to this day. . . . For *David did not ascend to heaven*." Acts 2:29-34, NIV.

What does a dead person know about their family?

"If his sons are honored, *he does not know it*; if they are brought low, he does not see it." Job 14:21, NIV.

Do the dead know anything?

"For the living know that they will die, but *the dead know nothing*; they have no further reward, and even the memory of them is forgotten. Their love, their hate and their jealousy have long since vanished; never again will they have a part in anything that happens under the sun." Ecclesiastes 9:5, 6, NIV.

NOTE.—In death one loses all the attributes of mind—love, hatred, envy, etc. Thus it is plain that human consciousness ceases, and there is no further contact with the things of this world. But if, as some teach, those who die go directly to heaven or hell at death, what then is the need of a future judgment, or of a resurrection, or of the second coming of Christ?

Are the dead aware of God?

"Turn, O Lord, and deliver me; save me because of your unfailing love. *No one remembers you when he is dead.* Who praises you from the grave?" Psalm 6:4, 5, NIV.

NOTE.—The Bible everywhere represents death as an unconscious sleep, with no remembrance of God. If the dead were in heaven or hell, would Jesus have said, "Our friend Lazarus has fallen asleep"? John 11:11, NIV. If Lazarus was in heaven, then why call him back to life on this earth and rob him of heaven's bliss?

Are the righteous dead in heaven praising God?

"*It is not the dead who praise the Lord*, those who go down to silence." Psalm 115:17, NIV. "For *the grave cannot praise you, death cannot sing your praise*; those who go down to the pit cannot hope for your faithfulness." Isaiah 38:18, NIV.

What must take place before the dead can praise God?

"But *your dead will live*; their bodies will rise. You who dwell in the dust, wake up and shout for joy. Your dew is like the dew of the morning; the earth will give birth to her dead." Isaiah 26:19, NIV.

If there were no resurrection of the dead, what would be the fate of those fallen asleep in Christ?

"For if the dead are not raised, then Christ has not been raised either. . . . Then *those* also *who have fallen asleep in Christ are lost*." 1 Corinthians 15:16-18, NIV.

Have the righteous dead of the past ages received their reward?

"These were all commended for their faith, yet *none of them received what had been promised*. God had planned something better for us so that only together with us would they be made perfect." Hebrews 11:39, 40, NIV.

When will the resurrection of the righteous take place?

"*For the Lord himself will come down from heaven*, with a loud command, with the voice of the archangel and with the trumpet call of God, *and the dead in Christ will rise first*." 1 Thessalonians 4:16, NIV.

NOTE.—If the dead are unconscious, then they do not experience the passing of time, and it will seem to them when they awake that it has been but an instant since they died. It is comforting to know that, regardless of how long the sleep of death lasts, it will seem as if the moment of parting were followed instantly by a glad reunion at the Second Coming. For those who are anxious about deceased loved ones who persisted in sin, it is comforting to know that they are not now in torment, but are quietly sleeping in their graves. God's way is best: that consciousness should cease at death, and that all should wait till the resurrection for their future life and eternal reward (see Hebrews 11:39, 40).

THE TWO RESURRECTIONS

What promise of resurrection did God give through Hosea?

"I will ransom them from the power of the grave; *I will redeem them from death*. Where, O death, are your plagues? Where, O grave, is your destruction?" Hosea 13:14, NIV.

Through whom will this redemption come?

"For since death came through a man, the resurrection of the dead comes also through a man. For as in Adam all die, *so in Christ all will be made alive*." 1 Corinthians 15:21, 22, NIV.

Why did God give His only begotten Son to the world?

"For God so loved the world that he gave his one and only Son, that whoever believes in him shall not perish but have eternal life." John 3:16, NIV.

What did the Sadducees of Jesus' day believe about the resurrection?

"Some of the Sadducees, *who say there is no resurrection*, came to Jesus with a question." Luke 20:27, NIV.

NOTE.—The Sadducees accepted only the books of Moses as authoritative Scripture, and denied any doctrine not taught by Moses. Thus they did not believe in the resurrection, since it is not explicitly taught in the Pentateuch (the five books of Moses). There are several very clear passages on the resurrection in the Old Testament, such as Daniel 12:2, but Jesus did not use these texts, as the Sadducees did not accept their authority. Jesus met them on their own ground, pointing out the hidden implications of a passage from the Pentateuch that they had missed.

How did Christ prove the resurrection from the books of Moses?

"But in the account of the bush, even Moses showed that the dead rise, for he calls the Lord 'the God of Abraham, and the God of Isaac, and the God of Jacob.' He is not the God of the dead, but the living, for to him all are alive." Luke 20:37, 38, NIV.

NOTE.—That is, all are alive *as far as God is concerned*, because "God who gives life to the dead . . . calls things that are not as though they were" (Romans 4:17). Christ speaks here proleptically of the future resurrection as if it were already a reality. Note that the point under discussion is not that "the dead are alive," but that "the dead rise." This passage proves nothing about the state of the dead, but everything about the certainty of the resurrection for those who love God.

To what is the resurrection compared?

"What you sow does not come to life unless it dies." 1 Corinthians 15:36, NIV. "I tell you the truth, unless a kernel of wheat falls to the ground and dies, it remains only a single seed. But if it dies, it produces many seeds." John 12:24, NIV.

NOTE.—The seed dies to spring forth into new life. In this we are taught the lesson of the resurrection. All who love God will spring forth to life, and live again at the resurrection of the just at Christ's return.

What two groups will be resurrected?

"There will be a resurrection of both the *righteous* and the *wicked*." Acts 24:15, NIV.

How did Christ describe the two resurrections?

"Do not be amazed at this, for a time is coming when all who are in their graves will hear his voice and comes out—those who have done good will rise to live, and those who have done evil will rise to be condemned." John 5:28, 29, NIV.

When will the resurrection of the just occur?

"For *the Lord himself will come down from heaven*, with a loud command, with the voice of an archangel and with the trumpet call of God, and *the dead in Christ will rise first*." 1 Thessalonians 4:16, NIV. (See also 1 Corinthians 15:23.)

How will our resurrection body differ from our present one?

"So will it be with the resurrection of the dead. The body that is sown is *perishable*, it shall be raised *imperishable*; it is sown in *dis-*

honor, it is raised in *glory*; it is sown in *weakness*, it is raised in *power*; it is sown a *natural* body, it is raised a *spiritual* body." 1 Corinthians 15:42-44, NIV.

Whose body will our resurrected body resemble?

"Our citizenship is in heaven. And we eagerly await a Savior from there, the Lord *Jesus Christ,* who, by the power that enables him to bring everything under his control, will transform our lowly bodies so that they will be like *his glorious body*." Philippians 3:20, 21, NIV.

What will the righteous do upon rising from the grave?

"But your dead will live; their bodies will rise. You who dwell in the dust, wake up and *shout for joy*. Your dew is like the dew of the morning; the earth will give birth to her dead." Isaiah 26:19, NIV.

What poetic words does Paul use to describe the victory of the righteous over death?

"Where, O death, is your victory? Where, O death, is your sting?" 1 Corinthians 15:55, NIV.

When will the unrighteous be raised?

"I saw thrones on which were seated those who had been given authority to judge. And I saw the souls of those who had been beheaded because of their testimony for Jesus and because of the word of God. They had not worshiped the beast or his image and had not received his mark on their foreheads or hands. They came to life and reigned with Christ a thousand years. *(The rest of the dead did not come to life until the thousand years were ended.)* " Revelation 20:4, 5, NIV.

What is to be their fate?

"They marched across the breadth of the earth and surrounded the camp of God's people, the city he loves. But *fire came down from heaven and devoured them*." Verse 9, NIV.

What is the last enemy to be destroyed?

"The last enemy to be destroyed is *death*." 1 Corinthians 15:26, NIV. (See Revelation 20:13, 14.)

How does Jesus describe the transformed righteous in eternity?

"Then *the righteous will shine like the sun* in the kingdom of their Father." Matthew 13:43, NKJV.

FATE OF THE TRANSGRESSOR

What does the Bible say is the wages of sin?
"The wages of sin is *death.*" Romans 6:23.

What will happen to those who do not repent?
"Unless you repent, you too will all *perish.*" Luke 13:3, NIV.

To what are the wicked in their punishment compared?
"But the wicked will perish: The Lord's enemies will be like *the beauty of the fields,* they will vanish—vanish like smoke." Psalm 37:20, NIV.

What will be the character of this death?
"This will happen when the Lord Jesus is revealed from heaven in blazing fire with his powerful angels. He will punish those who do not know God and do not obey the gospel of our Lord Jesus. They will be punished with *everlasting destruction* and shut out from the presence of the Lord and from the majesty of his power." 2 Thessalonians 1:7-9, NIV.

How does John the Baptist describe this destruction?
"His winnowing fork is in his hand, and he will clear his threshing floor, gathering his wheat into the barn and burning up the chaff with *unquenchable fire.*" Matthew 3:12, NIV.

NOTE.—Not just burn them, but burn them *up.* The Bible says the wicked will die, be destroyed, perish. All of these words indicate total and complete annihilation of existence.

Unquenchable fire is fire that cannot be put out. Of course, it goes out by itself when its fuel is exhausted (compare Jeremiah 7:20 with 2 Chronicles 36:19 and Nehemiah 2:3).

For whom was this fire originally prepared?
"Then he will say to those on his left, 'Depart from me, you who are cursed, into the eternal fire prepared for *the devil and his angels.*' " Matthew 25:41, NIV.

NOTE.—This fire is called eternal or "everlasting" (*aionion,* Greek, "age lasting"), not because it lasts forever, but because its results last forever.

What Old Testament cities were burned with eternal fire?
"In a similar way, *Sodom and Gomorrah* and the surrounding towns gave themselves up to sexual immorality and perversion. They

serve as an example of those who suffer the punishment of eternal
fire." Jude 7, NIV. "He condemned the cities of Sodom and Gomorrah by burning them to ashes, and made them an example of what is
going to happen to the ungodly." 2 Peter 2:6, NIV.

NOTE.—Sodom and Gomorrah are given as an example of what
will happen to the wicked. These cities were reduced to ashes, yet
the text says they were burned with "eternal fire." Yet Sodom is not
still burning now. It was the result, not the process, that made the fire
eternal. The "eternal fire" of hell will likewise go out, but its results
(annihilation) will last forever.

Notice these expressions where "eternal" refers to the result, not
the process: "eternal salvation" (Hebrews 5:9); "eternal judgment"
(Hebrews 6:2); "eternal sin" (Mark 3:29, NIV); "eternal punishment"
(Matthew 25:46, NIV); "eternal destruction" (2 Thessalonians 1:9,
NRSV). It is not the *process* (the saving, the judging, the sinning, the
punishing, and the destroying) that is eternal—it is the *result* (salvation, judgment, sin, punishment, destruction). When Scripture speaks
of "eternal punish*ment*" or "eternal destruc*tion*" it does not mean
eternal punish*ing* or destroy*ing*. The penalty is eternal death (punish*ment*), not eternal torment (punish*ing*).

Like Sodom, the wicked will be burned with eternal fire, which
will reduce them to ashes and then go out. That is what "eternal destruction" means.

Matthew 25:46 says that the wicked "will go away to eternal punishment, but the righteous to eternal life" (NIV). Those who believe
in an eternally burning hell suggest that the "eternal punishment"
here must last just as long as the "eternal life" mentioned alongside
it. They are quite correct: the penalty of eternal death does last just
as long as the reward of eternal life. Remember: punish*ment,* not punish*ing*; eternal extinction, not eternal torture. Result, not process.

Will any part of the wicked be left?

"Surely the day is coming; it will burn like a furnace. All the arrogant and every evildoer will be stubble, and that day that is coming will set them on fire,' says the Lord Almighty. '*Not a root or a
branch will be left* to them.' " Malachi 4:1, NIV.

How completely will the wicked be destroyed in hell?

"Do not be afraid of those who kill the body but cannot kill the
soul. Rather, be afraid of the One who can destroy *both soul and body*
in hell." Matthew 10:28, NIV.

NOTE.—Hell destroys the entire person, leaving nothing behind to suffer. Scripture never says that the soul is immortal, in-

destructible, but says that "the soul who sins is the one who will die." Ezekiel 18:4, NIV.

In the King James Version's New Testament, "hell" is translated from three Greek words:

Gehenna, 12 times. Matthew 5:22, 29, 30; 10:28; 18:9; 23:15, 33; Mark 9:43, 45, 47; Luke 12:5; James 3:6. This is an allusion to the Valley of Hinnom, the place outside Jerusalem for burning refuse, dead animals, and the bodies of criminals. This valley became a place of judgment (Jeremiah 7:29-34, 19:1-7). Incompletely burned bodies were devoured by worms. So long as the fires were never quenched and the worms did not die (see Job 17:14; 21:26; 24:19, 20, Isaiah 14:11; 51:8), the result of being cast into Gehenna was utter destruction. The flames of Gehenna do not preserve, but consume, whatever they feed on.

Hades, 10 times. Matthew 11:23; 16:18; Luke 10:15; 16:23; Acts 2:27, 31; Revelation 1:18; 6:8; 20:13, 14. (Hades is also "grave" once, [1 Corinthians 15:55].) Hades (the lower world, place of the dead, the grave) is the equivalent of sheol. It is used in Acts 2:27, 31, to translate from Psalm 16:10.

Tartaroo occurs only in 2 Peter 2:4. Tartaroo is a verb, meaning "to cast down to Tartarus." This is an allusion to the Tartarus of Greek mythology, an abyss deeper than Hades, the prison of the Titans, who fought against the gods.

What parable of Jesus' talks about hell?

"There was a rich man who was dressed in purple and fine linen and lived in luxury every day. At his gate was laid a beggar named Lazarus, covered with sores and longing to eat what fell from the rich man's table. Even the dogs came and licked his sores. The time came when the beggar died and the angels carried him to Abraham's side. The rich man also died and was buried. In hell, where he was in torment, he looked up and saw Abraham far away, with Lazarus by his side. So he called to him, 'Father Abraham,' have pity on me and send Lazarus to dip the tip of his finger in water and cool my tongue, because I am in agony in this fire.'

"But Abraham replied, 'Son, remember that in your lifetime you received your good things, while Lazarus received bad things, but now he is comforted here and you are in agony. And besides all this, between us and you a great chasm has been fixed, so that those who want to go from here to you cannot, nor can anyone cross over from there to us.'

"He answered, 'Then I beg you, father, send Lazarus to my father's house, for I have five brothers. Let him warn them, so that they will not also come to this place of torment.'

"Abraham replied, 'They have Moses and the Prophets; let them listen to them.'

" ' No, father Abraham,' he said, 'but if someone from the dead goes to them, they will repent.'

"He said to him, 'If they do not listen to Moses and the Prophets, they will not be convinced even if someone rises from the dead.' " Luke 16:19-31, NIV.

NOTE.—The story of the rich man and Lazarus has been misunderstood as teaching that hell is burning now. But this story is clearly a parable since Luke's introductory wording is always used for parables ("certain," Greek *tis* [Luke 14:16; 15:11; 16:1; 18:2; 19:12]). It is hazardous to base a theological belief on the incidental details of a parable. For example, the parable about talking plants in Judges 9 does not prove that plants can talk. Likewise, Jesus did not tell this parable to show that the dead can suffer. The essential elements of the story of the rich man and Lazarus were already part of popular Jewish folklore in the first century A.D. Jesus borrowed them to make a point about the use of money and how it affects our destiny. The righteous dead are not literally in Abraham's bosom any more than they are literally under an altar (Revelation 6:9-11). Obviously, through this metaphor Scripture says the dead are sleeping in the grave (Daniel 12:2; John 5:28; 11:11-14; 1 Corinthians 15:6, 18, 20).

If hell is already burning now, then why should God take sinners out of this fire at the end of time just so that they can be judged and cast back into it?

When will the wicked be punished?

"By the same word the present heavens and earth are reserved for fire, being kept *for the day of judgment and destruction* of ungodly men." 2 Peter 3:7, NIV. "As the weeds are pulled up and burned in the fire, so it will *be at the end of the age.* The Son of Man will send out his angels, and they will weed out of his kingdom everything that causes sin and all who do evil." Matthew 13:40, 41, NIV.

What will be the result of the fires of the last day?

"But the day of the Lord will come like a thief. The heavens will disappear with a roar; *the elements will be destroyed by fire, and the earth and everything in it will be laid bare.* Since everything will be destroyed in this way, what kind of people ought you to be? You ought to live holy and godly lives as you look forward to the day of God and speed its coming. That day will bring about the destruction of the heavens by fire, and the elements will melt in the heat." 2 Peter 3:10-12, NIV.

When are the wicked dead raised for final punishment?

"The rest of the dead did not come to life until *the thousand years were ended.*" Revelation 20:5, NIV.

What is the origin of this fire?

"They [the unrighteous] marched across the breadth of the earth and surrounded the camp of God's people, the city he loves. But fire came down *from heaven* and devoured them." Verse 9, NIV.

NOTE.—In Isaiah 28:21 this work of destruction is called God's "strange act" and His "strange work," because it seems so contrary to His character of love. But by this means God will once and forever cleanse the universe of sin and all its sad results.

What symbolism is used to emphasize the horror of God's retribution?

"A third angel followed them and said in a loud voice: 'If anyone worships the beast and his image and receives his mark on the forehead or on the hand, he, too, will drink of the wine of God's fury, which has been poured full strength into the cup of his wrath. He will be tormented with burning sulfur in the presence of the holy angels and of the Lamb. And *the smoke of their torment rises for ever and ever.* There is no rest day or night for those who worship the beast and his image, or for anyone who receives the mark of his name.'" Revelation 14:9-11, NIV.

NOTE.—The book of Revelation specializes in symbols. The wine and the cup in this passage are obviously symbolical, and so is the smoke ascending forever. This is shown by an examination of the Old Testament source of the metaphor.

This language is borrowed from Isaiah 34: "Edom's streams will be turned into pitch, her dust into burning sulfur; her land will become blazing pitch! It will not be quenched night and day; its smoke will rise forever." Verses 9, 10, NIV. This is part of a long passage depicting the destruction of the land of Edom by fire and its eventual restoration (Isaiah 34:5–35:10). Even though Isaiah says this fire will burn "forever," and no one will ever pass through the land "for ever and ever," yet the following verses indicate that wild plants will grow and that wild animals will live there; and the following chapter describes the restoration of this very same land (compare 34:13 with 35:7, 9) and its repopulation by the righteous! So even the biblical expression "for ever and ever" clearly means only a limited period of time.

The Greek and Hebrew words translated "eternal" and "for ever" in the Bible tend to have the meaning "indefinitely." The sprinkling of blood at the Passover is said to be "for ever" (Exodus 12:24). So were the Aaronic priesthood (Exodus 29:9; 40:15; Leviticus 3:17), Caleb's inheritance (Joshua 14:9), Solomon's Temple (1 Kings 8:12, 13), and Gehazi's leprosy (2 Kings 5:27). Yet none of these things still continue today. "For ever" can mean "as long as life lasts" (1 Samuel 1:22, 28; Exodus 21:6). It can be used of a very short period (Jonah 2:6). The expression "burn for ever" (Jeremiah 17:4) may refer to a temporary burning (Jeremiah 23:20; Ezekiel 5:13). There is no word in Scripture that necessarily implies absolute endlessness.

A more concise example of "eternal" destruction followed by restoration is Isaiah 32:14-15, NIV, which says the land "will become a wasteland *forever,* . . . till the Spirit is poured upon us from on high, and the desert becomes a fertile field." This is what is going to happen to Planet Earth, according to Revelation 20:11–21:4. The fire that destroys the impenitent will be followed by the renewal of this planet. Indeed, death and hell itself will be cast into this fire (Revelation 20:14). Afterward the earth will be created anew, and there will be *no more death* or pain (Revelation 21:4). In other words, *everything* cast into the fire, including even death and hell itself, eventually ceases to exist.

Neither in Greek or in Hebrew does any word translated "forever" necessarily imply absolute endlessness.

What will be left of the wicked?

" ' Then you will trample down the wicked; they will be *ashes* under the soles of your feet on the day when I do these things,' says the Lord Almighty." Malachi 4:3, NIV.

NOTE.—The wicked are to be utterly destroyed—consumed away into smoke, brought to ashes. Through sin they have forfeited the right to life and an immortal existence. Their destruction will, in fact, be an act of love and mercy on the part of God; for to perpetuate their lives would only be to perpetuate sin and suffering.

What is this final destruction of the wicked called?

"This is *the second death.*" Revelation 20:14, NIV.

NOTE.—The term "second death" is found in Egyptian sources, such as the Book of the Dead, where it clearly refers to *total extinction* of existence, both body and soul. The phrase is also found in the Targums. Most often cited is Targum Isaiah 65:5, 6: "Their punishment shall be in Gehenna where the fire burns all the day. Behold, it is written before me: 'I will not give them respite during (their) life but will render to them the punishment of their transgressions and will deliver their bodies to the second death.' " Note that the punishment in Gehenna *precedes* the second death. Cf. Targum Isaiah

65:15: "The Lord God will slay you with the second death, but his servants, the righteous, he shall call by a different name"; Targum Jeremiah 51:39, 57: "And they shall die the second death, and shall not live for the world to come, says the Lord." Cessation of existence is implied.

What will happen afterward?

"Then I saw *a new heaven and a new earth,* for the first heaven and the first earth had passed away, and there was no longer any sea." Revelation 21:1, NIV. "But in keeping with his promise we are looking forward to a new heaven and a new earth, the home of righteousness." 2 Peter 3:13, NIV.

How will the righteous be recompensed in the new earth?

"Blessed are the meek: for they shall inherit the earth." Matthew 5:5. "Then shall the righteous shine forth as the sun in the kingdom of their Father." Matthew 13:43.

NOTE.—In due time Jesus will cleanse this world from sin and sinners, restore it to Edenic perfection, and give it to the saints for an everlasting possession (Daniel 7:18, 22, 27).

How will God comfort the redeemed who have lost loved ones in the final destruction?

"They will be his people, and God himself will be with them and be their God. He will wipe every tear from their eyes. There will be no more death or mourning or crying or pain, for the old order of things has passed away." Revelation 21:3, 4, NIV.

What is the essence and nature of God?

"God is love." 1 John 4:16.

NOTE.—There are overwhelming logical and philosophical difficulties with the concept of a God who subjects His finite creatures to infinite torture for their faults. We would not think very highly of a king who tortured his lame subjects because they could not keep up in the royal races, and it would not help matters at all if the king made exceptions only for friends of his son! In comparison with a God of endless torment, Adolf Hitler was a paragon of tender mercy.

By now it should be evident that Scripture does not teach that the lost will be tortured forever by a God whose unfathomable love is matched only by His insatiable cruelty. Christians must bury this monstrous dogma, and apologize to the world for so misrepresenting the character of the God they serve.

Ten Important Principles for Bible Study

Bible study presents many challenges, especially in doctrines such as the state of the dead. Here are 10 principles to guide your study.

"*1. Always read with the guidance of the Holy Spirit.* The fact that so many people come up with radically different interpretations of the same passage shows that we cannot depend upon human reason alone to understand the Bible. We need the aid of the Holy Spirit to grasp spiritual things (1 Corinthians 2:9-14).

"It is normal to read and interpret through the perspectives and biases of our own culture and experiences. God's people have always lived in a world that takes some kind of afterlife for granted. It is hard to accept the idea that people really cease to exist. Those whom we have known and loved—they cannot possibly be no more. So we come to divine revelation with a predisposition to want to believe that the image of God in humanity includes natural immortality—that the good go immediately to their reward and that the wicked receive the unending punishment which we would like to inflict on them if we had any choice in the matter.

"The Bible student who wants to rise above the mind-sets of our world must pray for divine guidance. Paul prayed for the Ephesians 'that the God of our Lord Jesus Christ, the Father of glory, may give you a spirit of wisdom and revelation as you come to know him, so that, with the eyes of your heart enlightened, you may know what is the hope to which he has called you, what are the riches of his glorious inheritance among the saints, and what is the immeasurable greatness of his power for us who believe' (Ephesians 1:17-19, NRSV).

"Bible study is not just an intellectual pursuit or exercise. Since we are dealing with concepts and issues beyond human experience, we need the Holy Spirit, 'the spirit of truth' (John 15:26, NRSV). 'When the Spirit of truth comes,' Jesus promised, 'he will guide you into all the truth' (John 16:13, NRSV).

"*2. Search for the commonsense meaning of the passage.* Those who approach Scripture from the Protestant tradition

Ten Important Principles for Bible Study CONTINUED

usually assume that the true meaning of a passage lies in its literal interpretation. As David H. Kelsey put it: '*Literal* needs to be understood carefully. What they [the Protestant Reformers] had in mind was the "natural" sense of the passage. So if stylistic and grammatical analysis shows that a passage would have been seen as a moral parable or as an allegory by its original readers, then its literal sense would be its moral or allegorical sense. It would be absurd to insist that it be taken in a flat-footed or unimaginatively "literal" way.' [David H. Kelsey, "Protestant Attitudes Regarding Methods of Biblical Interpretation," in Frederick E. Greenspahn, ed., *Scripture in the Jewish and Christian Traditions: Authority, Interpretation, Relevance* (Nashville: Abingdon, 1982), p. 140].

"Few would argue that Scripture presents Christ as a literal lamb, door, lion, light, or other metaphorical ways He is portrayed. Most of us instantly recognize such things as figures of speech. But metaphorical language can be more subtle. . . .

"If a passage consists largely of symbolic or metaphorical language, or employs many literary devices, be cautious about pulling a specific detail out of it and treating that detail as literal. Even worse, don't build a doctrine around the detail. . . .

"[Some] feel that it if we admit that something is metaphorical, we are at the same time declaring that it presents no real objective, historical reality. But often the most real things in the world can be told only through metaphorical language. Literal language simply won't do. For example, what color is love? What shape is it? Does it have a specific density? We can describe it only through symbolic language, even though it is one of the most important realities of life. . . . One can accept the truth, authority, and accuracy of Scripture without literalizing everything.

"*3. Reconstruct as far as possible how the first listeners or readers understood a passage.* Don't read into it later ideas, experiences, or concepts until you first understand what it originally meant. Try to find out the customs and thought patterns of the biblical world. What the passage said to its first audience can act as a touchstone to keep you from going off into flights of fancy. It guides you as you apply later revelation or understandings and interpretations.

Ten Important Principles for Bible Study CONTINUED

"For example, unlike modern Western cultures, with orientation toward the future, the biblical world's time view focused on the present and the past. We expect things to get better over time, whereas the ancients wanted to continue the best of the past into the present. The present was most important.

"John J. Pilch and Bruce J. Malina show how the book of Luke develops its 'prophecy-fulfillment' material from this focus on the present: 'Luke most dramatically expresses his present time orientation with the emphatic comment "Today." ' 'They cite as examples Luke 2:11; 4:21; 19:9, and conclude with '*Today* you will be with me in Paradise' (Luke 23:43). The two scholars stress that the 'basic time orientation is on "today" and not the distant future.' [John J. Pilch and Bruce J. Malina, eds., *Biblical Social Values and Their Meaning: A Handbook* (Peabody, Mass.: Hendrickson Publishers, 1993), pp. xxv, xxvi].

"Thus Jesus in Luke emphasizes that salvation has already come to the dying thief. Verse 43 is not meant as a proof text for the idea that people immediately go to heaven when they die.

"*4. Look for the context of a passage.* Because for centuries printed Bibles presented each verse separate from those preceding and following, it is easy to treat each verse as an isolated statement independent of all others. We sometimes treat a verse as if it were a self-contained aphorism. But the surrounding verses help explain the meaning by modifying, limiting, or expanding the thought. A modern translation that arranges the verses in paragraph form helps us to see the relationships of ideas in Scripture much more clearly.

"The context of a passage includes more than the verses before or after it. It may include whole chapters, books of the Bible, or the totality of Scripture itself. . . . The context of the parable of the rich man and Lazarus consisted of its inclusion in a series of parables and sayings on the believer's relationship to wealth. The fact that the parable is part of a long section tied together by the theme of wealth and possessions strongly suggests that Christ did not intend as its purpose a discussion about the afterlife. Rather it was an illustration of how almost nothing can change the materialistic mind-set of those determined to cling to their possessions.

Ten Important Principles for Bible Study CONTINUED

"*5. See how the immediate context uses a particular term.*
Don't assume that the Bible uses a word exactly the same each
time. Words usually have a range of meanings, and a specific
passage will generally focus on one particular shade of meaning.

"*Sheol,* for example, depending on the context, can refer to
the grave, death, or what we would call the realm or state of the
dead.

"*Nephesh* has . . . a broad range of meaning. If at all possible, we must let context determine meaning, and not read the
shade of meaning employed in one passage into all other passages that use the same term. And naturally we should avoid
extrabiblical definitions of Bible terms.

"' Everlasting' can indicate that something will continue
forever or that it has eternal consequences. We must determine
that by examining how the rest of Scripture treats whatever the
passage labels as 'everlasting.'

"*6. Don't elevate a minor aspect of a passage to major importance.* If something seems to be mentioned just in passing
or is a detail to flesh out a story, don't make a major doctrine
of it—especially if removing the element from the passage
would not alter it or undermine the conclusion or theme.

"Some have misused this principle, however, by arguing that
we should not put too much emphasis on the Old Testament re-
strictions on the dead, especially those that appear in the book
of Ecclesiastes. Protesting that its tone is pessimistic, they claim
that we should not put too much stress on the author's allusions
to the dead. But if the dead are not really unconscious and unaware of life on earth (Ecclesiastes 9:5, 6), if both the righteous
and wicked do not share the same fate at death (Ecclesiastes
6:6; 9:2), and if human beings and animals do not have the
same condition at death (Ecclesiastes 3:19-21), then his arguments collapse. These details are not minor elements that we
can ignore. They are pivotal to the author's reasoning.

"*7. Watch for literary patterns or structures that could give
clues as to how to interpret a passage that is otherwise written
in literal language.* Saul's visit to the sorceror of Endor is a historical event written in narrative style. . . . The way the author
presents the end of Saul's kingship mirrors his rise. A true

Ten Important Principles for Bible Study CONTINUED

prophet from God revealed that the young man would be king, then honored him with a meal. But at Endor another prophecy told Saul that his kingdom was lost and that death was his only fate. Then the woman—who practices rites forbidden by God Himself—urges him to eat, and prepares him a meal. Since the meal was hardly an honor and Saul's fate was death, we would hardly conclude that the being that the woman claimed to have presented the message was a prophet from God. The mirror image here is an evil one, a reverse of the good that Saul once experienced.

"*8. Search for the whole Bible teaching on a topic.* Don't emphasize either the Old or the New Testament over each other, but remember that both had one source. The Old Testament was the Bible of the first Christians. The New Testament Scriptures do not replace or supersede the Old. Although revelation is progressive, it does not invalidate what God has already presented. It builds upon what has come before without contradicting it.

"Those who protest that the New Testament has a clearer presentation on death and the afterlife really want to ignore the Old Testament teaching on the subject. Especially those definite boundaries on the dead, boundaries that are indirectly supported by what science is learning about the relationship of consciousness and the brain. (On the other hand, while the New Testament reveals much more about the Messiah, many . . . are not as quick to downplay the Old Testament passages on the subject as they are toward Old Testament teaching on death.)

"At the same time, when we search for all that Scripture has to say about a particular topic, we must not homogenize those passages. We must not throw them into a spiritual blender and destroy their unique emphases and perspectives. For example, each Gospel writer tells an incident from the life of Christ from a specific perspective or to bring out a specific theological point. If we combine all parallel accounts into one single version, we lose those unique themes and stresses each writer gives to his own Gospel.

"The books of Samuel/Kings and the books of Chronicles parallel each other. Each set presents the same historical events. But they do so from different perspectives, bringing out different lessons. To blend all the accounts into one is to destroy their

Ten Important Principles for Bible Study CONTINUED

individual messages, to erase part of God's broader gift.

"We must keep the whole Bible teaching on death and the nature of human existence together and in balance. If the Old Testament categorically states that the dead cannot do certain things and a passage appears to contradict that, then we must check to see if the passage is using metaphorical language or some other literary device. In our search for harmony, we must find the commonsense meaning, not the literalistic one. Thus the prophet in Isaiah 14 is mocking the king of Babylon, not expounding on the nature of the afterlife.

"*9. Recognize that the Bible may use imagery familiar to the original audience but reject some or all of the concepts behind it.* In Numbers 21 the Israelites complained against God and Moses. 'Why have you brought us up out of Egypt to die in the wilderness? For there is no food and no water, and we detest this miserable food' (verse 5, NRSV). God sends poisonous serpents as a punishment (verse 6). The people rush to Moses and admit that 'we have sinned by speaking against the Lord and against you; pray to the Lord to take away the serpents from us' (verse 7, NRSV).

"After Moses' prayer God tells him, 'Make a poisonous serpent, and set it on a pole; and everyone who is bitten shall look at it and live' (verse 8, NRSV). The Hebrew leader casts a bronze snake and prominently mounts it upon a pole (verse 9).

"The snake was a common religious symbol in Egypt and Palestine. The uraeus, or serpent on the Pharaoh's crown, was a symbol of his power and divine protection. Fiery serpents even protected the sun god Re. The Egyptians worshiped the snake god Apophis and presented prayers and offerings to the serpent goddess Reneutet Meretseger to avoid or cure snakebites. They especially worshiped the cobra goddess Meretseger during the 'new kingdom' (1550-1069 B.C.), the period of the Exodus. Archaeologists have found a number of copper images of snakes as well as many ceramic ones. Egypt apparently also used some copper snakes as magic wands. But most important of all, the ancients worshiped the images. In fact, the image and the standard it was mounted on were a manifestation of the god depicted. 'Egyptian texts so identify the poles with the deities that they often use the words *standards*

Ten Important Principles for Bible Study CONTINUED

and *gods* interchangeably.' The Hebrews could not have been unaware of the pagan connotations of the serpent image, yet God chose to use it as a symbol for Himself anyway.

"Why God would employ an object that surrounding cultures worshiped to represent His saving power naturally puzzles us. It had clear and undeniable pagan connotations. Perhaps He expected His people to remember His equally clear commands against worshiping images and thus interpret His use of the snake imagery through those commands. They would then see that the object was only an illustration to communicate His power, that it had none of its own. . . .

"In the same way Scripture employs imagery echoing pagan concepts of afterlife and divine punishment while expecting us to interpret them within the clear boundaries of what God has said about the dead. We must not go beyond what God intended for that imagery. The bronze serpent was an illustration of God's power and care. It has no power or authority in and of itself.

"Unfortunately God's people kept forgetting His power and their relationship to Him. Eventually the bronze serpent became such an object of veneration that Hezekiah had to destroy it (2 Kings 18:4). Yet Jesus still used it as an illustration of His crucifixion (John 3:14, 15). Clearly God was willing to borrow pagan imagery as a teaching device if people were familiar with it. But that did not mean He approved of everything associated with it. Sometimes it is vital to know *why* biblical writers said something before we can understand *what* they meant by it.

"And today we must be careful not to go beyond the restricted way that Scripture employs that imagery. We must not make a passage say more than God intended. Just because the New Testament alludes to the imagery of eternally burning fire does not mean that it actually exists. It is emphasizing the fact that He will punish the wicked, not necessarily how long He will do it.

"*10. Scripture must be the final criterion and authority behind any doctrine.* We must avoid projecting popular belief, philosophy, science, or anything else into biblical teaching." Gerald Wheeler, *Beyond Life: What God Says About Life, Death, and Immortality* (Hagerstown, Md.: Review and Herald, 1998), pp. 125-132.

THE MINISTRY OF GOD'S ANGELS

Of what family does Paul speak in Ephesians?

"For this reason I kneel before the Father, from whom *his whole family in heaven and on earth* derives its name." Ephesians 3:14, 15, NIV.

By what name are the members of this family called?

"Now there was a day when *the sons of God* came to present themselves before the Lord." Job 1:6. "How great is the love the Father has lavished on us, that we should be called children of God! And that is what we are!" 1 John 3:1, NIV.

NOTE.—Although angels are a different order of beings than humanity, redeemed human beings are still children of God and members of the family of heaven.

By what name do we know the family in heaven?

"Then I looked and heard the voice of many *angels,* numbering thousands upon thousands, and ten thousand times ten thousand." Revelation 5:11, NIV.

Are angels of a higher order of beings than human beings?

"What is man that you are mindful of him, the son of man that you care for him? You made him *a little lower than the heavenly beings.*" Psalm 8:5, NIV.

NOTE.—There are different orders of angels: "Cherubim" (see Genesis 3:24; Exodus 25:18); "Seraphim" (see Isaiah 6:2, 6); "Archangel" (see 1 Thessalonians 4:16; Jude 9).

Did angels exist before the death of any human beings?

"*After he drove the man out, he placed* on the east side of the Garden of Eden *cherubim* and a flaming sword flashing back and forth to guard the way to the tree of life." Genesis 3:24, NIV.

NOTE.—Cherubim are a type of angel (the word cherubim is plural: Hebrew forms the plural by adding -im, just as English does by adding -s). These angels were present in Eden, before the first human being ever died. Therefore angels are a separate creation; they are not the spirits of dead people.

What does the book of Hebrews say of their number?

"But you have come to Mount Zion, to the heavenly Jerusalem, the city of the living God. You have come to *thousands upon thousands* of angels in joyful assembly." Hebrews 12:22, NIV. (See also Daniel 7:10.)

To whose authority are the angels subject?

"*Jesus Christ,* who has gone into heaven and is at God's right hand—with angels, authorities and powers in submission to him." 1 Peter 3:21, 22, NIV.

What does Scripture say about the worship of angels?

"Do not let anyone who delights in false humility and the worship of angels disqualify you for the prize." Colossians 2:18, NIV.

NOTE.—Holy angels never accept worship. Worship is due only to God. Only evil spirits demand or accept worship.

When John the revelator fell in worship at the feet of his guiding angel, how did the angel protest?

"At this I fell at his feet to worship him. But he said to me, *'Do not do it!'* I am a fellow servant with you and with your brothers who hold to the testimony of Jesus. *Worship God!'"* Revelation 19:10, NIV.

NOTE.—In fact, John made the same mistake again in Revelation 22:8, 9, and again the angel said, in essence, "Stop! I'm just one of your brothers, a servant of God like you." It is heartwarming to know that angels consider themselves our brothers. They humble themselves; they exalt Jesus Christ and worship Him (Hebrews 1:6). Only once in Scripture does an angel introduce himself by name: Gabriel (Luke 1:19), and in this case the purpose was to identify with a name already known from Scripture (Daniel 8:16; 9:21). Beware of stories involving modern encounters with a spirit who likes to talk about himself, his power, his knowledge, or even his name.

Why does the book of Hebrews encourage us to be hospitable to strangers?

"Do not forget to entertain strangers, *for by so doing some people have entertained angels* without knowing it." Hebrews 13:2, NIV.

What is said of the strength and character of the angels?

"Praise the Lord, you his angels, *you mighty ones who do his bidding, who obey his word.*" Psalm 103:20, NIV.

In what work are angels engaged?

"Are not all angels *ministering spirits sent to serve* those who will inherit salvation?" Hebrews 1:14, NIV.

In his dream at Bethel, what did Jacob see?

"He had a dream in which he saw *a stairway resting on the earth, with its top reaching to heaven, and the angels of God were ascending and descending on it."* Genesis 28:12, NIV.

Does each child of God have an accompanying angel?

"See that you do not look down on one of these little ones. For I tell you *their angels* in heaven always see the face of my Father in heaven." Matthew 18:10, NIV.

NOTE.—Christians who live in the light of God's countenance are always accompanied by unseen angels, and these holy beings leave behind them a blessing in our homes.

How do angels watch over us?

"The angel of the Lord *encamps around those who fear him, and he delivers them."* Psalm 34:7, NIV. "For he will command his angels concerning you to guard you in all your ways; *they will lift you up in their hands, so that you will not strike your foot against a stone."* Psalm 91:11, 12, NIV.

How was Daniel saved from death in the lions' den?

"My God sent *his angel,* and he *shut the mouths of the lions."* Daniel 6:22, NIV.

What did Elisha do when surrounded by the Syrian army?

" ' *Don't be afraid,' the prophet answered. 'Those who are with us are more than those who are with them.'* And Elisha prayed, *'O Lord, open his eyes so he may see.'* Then the Lord opened the servant's eyes, and *he looked and saw the hills full of horses and chariots of fire all around Elisha."* 2 Kings 6:16, 17, NIV.

When threatened by the Assyrians, King Hezekiah prayed for deliverance. What was the result?

"Then *the angel of the Lord went out and put to death a hundred and eighty-five thousand* men in the Assyrian camp. When the people got up the next morning—there were all the dead bodies!" Isaiah 37:36, NIV.

NOTE.—Holy angels are not always sweetness and light. Though they usually preserve life, sometimes they are authorized to take it. Normally agents of God's mercy, they are also agents of His wrath. The seven angels of the apocalypse are given the command to pour out the seven bowls of God's wrath on the earth (Revelation 16:1) near the end of time.

Sometimes angels gird on their armor and fight as warriors of the Lord. The scriptural phrase "the Lord of hosts" is a military term meaning "the commander of the armies." Joel implored God to "Bring down your warriors, O Lord!" (Joel 3:11, NIV). "The chariots of God," writes the Psalmist, "are tens of thousands and thousands of thousands" (Psalm 68:17, NIV). Against the Egyptians God unleashed "a band of destroying angels" (Psalm 78:49, NIV). These destroying angels are pictured with sword in hand in 2 Samuel 24:16, 17; 1 Chronicles 21:15-30; and Numbers 22:23, 31.

Awesome is the power of the forces that are on our side. An angel struck down wicked King Herod (Acts 12:23). God promised to send an angel before the Israelites to drive out their enemies (Exodus 33:2). But sometimes retribution was directed, not at Israel's enemies, but at Israel itself in times of apostasy. Paul in 1 Corinthians 10 reminded the Christians in Corinth not to grumble like some of the Israelites did. They "were killed by the destroying angel" (verse 10, NIV).

By what means were the apostles delivered from prison?

"But *during the night an angel of the Lord opened the doors of the jail* and brought them out." Acts 5:19, NIV.

How was Peter delivered later?

"Suddenly *an angel of the Lord appeared* and a light shone in the cell. He struck Peter on the side and woke him up. 'Quick, get up!' he said, and the chains fell off Peter's wrists.

"Then the angel said to him, 'Put on your clothes and sandals.' And Peter did so. 'Wrap your cloak around you and follow me,' the angel told him. Peter followed him out of the prison, but he had no idea that what the angel was doing was really happening; he thought he was seeing a vision. They passed the first and second guards and came to the iron gate leading to the city. It opened for them by itself, and they went through it. When they had walked the length of the street, suddenly the angel left him." Acts 12:7-10, NIV.

NOTE.—Walls form no barrier to angels.

How was Elijah strengthened for a 40-days' journey?

"The *angel of the Lord* came back a second time and *touched him and said, 'Get up and eat,* for the journey is too much for you.' So he got up and ate and drank. *Strengthened by that food, he traveled* forty days and forty nights *until he reached Horeb,* the mountain of God." 1 Kings 19:7, 8, NIV.

After His 40-days' temptation, how was Christ strengthened?

"Then the devil left him, and *angels came and attended him.*" Matthew 4:11, NIV.

NOTE.—Even though angels are sent to minister to us, they are under God's direction, not ours. It is a mistake to pray to angels. After all, why speak to the underlings when you can speak directly to the Boss? In the Bible, angels are *sent* (Daniel 3:28; 6:22; 10:11; Luke 1:19, 26) by God, they do not simply *come* on their own initiative, and cannot be *summoned* by human beings by any ritual. We pray only to God, and sometimes He sends an angel to answer that prayer.

How was Jesus strengthened in Gethsemane?

"*An angel* from heaven appeared to him and *strengthened him*." Luke 22:43, NIV.

Are the angels interested in the plan of salvation?

"Concerning this salvation, the prophets, who spoke of the grace that was to come to you, searched intently and with the greatest care, trying to find out the time and circumstances to which the Spirit of Christ in them was pointing when he predicted the sufferings of Christ and the glories that would follow. It was revealed to them that they were not serving themselves but you, when they spoke of the things that have now been told you by those who have preached the gospel to you by the Holy Spirit sent from heaven. *Even angels long to look into these things*." 1 Peter 1:12, NIV. "In the same way, I tell you, there is rejoicing in the presence of the angels of God over one sinner who repents." Luke 15:10, NIV.

Do angels play a role in the judgment?

"*Thousands upon thousands attended him;* ten thousand times ten thousand stood before him. The court was seated, and the books were opened." Daniel 7:10, NIV.

What role will angels play in the Second Coming?

"For the Son of man shall come in the glory of His Father *with His angels*." Matthew 16:27.

"And he will send his angels with a loud trumpet call, and *they will gather his elect* from the four winds, from one end of the heavens to the other." Matthew 24:31, NIV.

THE OPPRESSION OF EVIL ANGELS

Where did Satan and his evil angels come from?

"And there was war in heaven. Michael and his angels fought against the dragon, and the dragon and his angels fought back. But he was not strong enough, and they lost their place in *heaven*. The great dragon was hurled down—that ancient serpent, called the devil, or Satan, who leads the whole world astray. He was hurled to the earth, and his angels with him." Revelation 12:7-9, NIV.

What is Satan's position now?

"The *prince of this world*." John 14:30. "*The ruler of the kingdom of the air,* the spirit who is now at work in those who are disobedient." Ephesians 2:2, NIV.

What is the chief occupation of Satan and his angels?

"And he was there in the wilderness forty days, *tempted of Satan*." Mark 1:13. "Be self-controlled and alert. Your enemy the devil prowls around like a roaring lion *looking for someone to devour*." 1 Peter 5:8, NIV. (See Revelation 16:14.)

What are we admonished not to do?

" ' In your anger do not sin.': Do not let the sun go down while you are still angry, and do not give the devil a foothold." Ephesians 4:26, 27, NIV.

NOTE.—Those who give vent to anger or refuse to let go of old grudges give place to the devil; that is, they give the devil an opportunity to work through them; they give him an advantage over them. This is also true of other indulgences. We should therefore close every avenue to Satan and his angels. We should be gentle, sober, and watchful, and close the door on every prompting to sin.

The Christian life is a battle. Against whom are we fighting?

"For our struggle is not against flesh and blood, but *against the rulers, against the authorities, against the powers of this dark world and against the spiritual forces of evil* in the heavenly realms." Ephesians 6:12, NIV.

Who has conquered these demonic powers?

"And having disarmed the powers and authorities, *he [Jesus]* made a public spectacle of them, triumphing over them by the cross." Colossians 2:15, NIV. "Who has gone into heaven and is at God's right hand—with angels, authorities and powers in submission to him." 1 Peter 3:22, NIV.

Why is there no need to fear these demonic powers?

"No, in all these things we are more than conquerors through him who loved us. For I am convinced that neither death nor life, neither

angels nor demons, neither the present nor the future, nor any powers, neither height nor depth, nor anything else in all creation, will be
able to separate us from the love of God that is in Christ Jesus our
Lord." Romans 8:37-39, NIV.

What spiritual affliction was common in Jesus' day?

"News about him spread all over Syria, and people brought to him
all who were ill with various diseases, those suffering severe pain,
the *demon-possessed,* those having seizures, and the paralyzed, and
he healed them." Matthew 4:24, NIV.

NOTE.—Evil angels at times take possession of those whose
minds and bodies they can gain control. Only through Christ can this
demonic captivity be broken. Until this is done, one in this condition
is led captive by Satan "at his will." Their self-control and power to
resist temptation are gone. (See 2 Timothy 2:26.)

What authority did Jesus give His disciples?

"He called his twelve disciples to him and gave them authority *to
drive out evil spirits and to heal every disease and sickness.*"
Matthew 10:1, NIV.

How did Jesus extend this authority to all believers?

"And these signs will accompany those who believe: In my name
they will drive out demons." Mark 16:17, NIV.

How did the disciples use this authority after the ascension of Jesus?

"People brought the sick into the streets and laid them on beds
and mats so that at least Peter's shadow might fall on some of them
as he passed by. Crowds gathered also from the towns around
Jerusalem, bringing their sick and those tormented by evil spirits,
and all of them were healed." Acts 5:15, 16, NIV.

As we near the close of earth's history, may we expect an increase in demonic manifestations?

"Woe to the earth and the sea, because the devil has gone down
to you! *He is filled with fury, because he knows that his time is short.*"
Revelation 12:12, NIV.

NOTE.—Acquainted, as they are, with the laws of nature, Satan
and his angels scatter disease and death as far as they can, and they
likewise pervert the truth and disseminate error as far as possible.
They know that the end of all things is fast approaching, and that
their time to work is short.

What deception will characterize the last days?

"The Spirit clearly says that in later times some will abandon the faith and follow *deceiving spirits and things taught by demons.*" 1 Timothy 4:1, NIV.

THE OCCULT

How does God feel about those who dabble in the occult?

"Let no one be found among you who sacrifices his son or daughter in the fire, who practices divination or sorcery, interprets omens, engages in witchcraft, or casts spells, or who is a medium or spiritist or who consults the dead. *Anyone who does these things is detestable to the Lord.*" Deuteronomy 18:10-12, NIV.

NOTE.—Satan can harass and oppress those who venture onto his ground. Because, there are many doorways into occult darkness. These include Ouija boards, tarot, fortunetelling, astrology, palmistry, hypnotism, astral projection, spells, curses, voodoo, spiritualism, séances, and other forms of witchcraft. Also to be avoided are items that have been "blessed" or dedicated to some spirit, and that thereafter serve as a focus of occult power, such as carved idols, amulets, fetishes, talismans, and charms. Most curios and souvenirs sold are harmless because they have never been "blessed," but those that have carry a curse. The same is true of certain occult literature and media. These can also bring one under the influence of the demonic.

Anyone who experiments with or seeks to benefit from paranormal powers is dancing on a minefield, because Satan's ultimate goal is not to save but to destroy. He is a cunning foe, however; he may first bestow benefits, and only later bring ruin. He may seemingly bring healing to the body, only to curse the soul.

What does Paul say to those who are guilty of witchcraft?

"Idolatry, *witchcraft,* hatred, . . . *they which do such things shall not inherit the kingdom of God.*" Galatians 5:20, 21. "But the cowardly, the unbelieving, the vile, the murderers, the sexually immoral, those who practice magic arts, the idolaters and all liars—their place will be in the fiery lake of burning sulfur. This is *the second death.*" Revelation 21:8, NIV.

How did the new converts at Ephesus renounce their dabbling in the occult?

"Many of those who believed now came and openly confessed their evil deeds. A number who had practiced sorcery *brought their scrolls [books on the occult] together and burned them publicly.*

When they calculated the value of the scrolls, the total came to fifty thousand drachmas." Acts 19:18, 19, NIV.

How does God regard those who traffic in the occult?

"So *do not listen* to your prophets, your diviners, your interpreters of dreams, your mediums or your sorcerers. . . . They prophesy lies to you that will only serve to remove you far from your lands." Jeremiah 27:9, 10, NIV. "So I will come near to you for judgment. I will be quick to testify against sorcerers, adulterers and perjurers." Malachi 3:5, NIV.

What if some fortunetellers demonstrate a genuine ability to predict the future?

"If a prophet, or one who foretells by dreams, appears among you and announces to you a miraculous sign or wonder, and if the sign or wonder of which he has spoken takes place, and he says, 'Let us follow other gods' (gods you have not known) 'and let us worship them,' *you must not listen to the words of that prophet or dreamer.* The Lord your God is testing you to find out whether you love him with all your heart and with all your soul. It is the Lord your God you must follow, and him you must revere. Keep his commands and obey him; serve him and hold fast to him." Deuteronomy 13:1-4, NIV.

What can we learn from Paul's encounter with a fortuneteller?

"Once when we were going to the place of prayer, we were met by a slave girl who had a spirit by which she predicted the future. She earned a great deal of money for her owners by fortune-telling. This girl followed Paul and the rest of us, shouting, 'These men are servants of the Most High God, who are telling you the way to be saved.' She kept this up for many days. Finally Paul became so troubled that he turned around and said to the spirit, 'In the name of Jesus Christ I command you to come out of her!' At that moment the spirit left her." Acts 16:16-18, NIV.

NOTE.—The girl proclaimed truth, yet she was using the power of Satan. Her predictive powers came from being possessed by a demon. Satan's agents may tell the truth when it suits their purpose, and have some ability to predict the future.

What instruction does the apostle John give touching this subject?

"Dear friends, do not believe every spirit, but *test the spirits to see whether they are from God,* because many false prophets have gone out into the world." 1 John 4:1, NIV.

By what standard should we try the spirits?

"To the law and to the testimony! If they do not speak according to this word, they have no light of dawn." Isaiah 8:20, NIV.

What is spiritualism, or spiritism?

Spiritualism, or spiritism, is the belief that the spirits of the dead communicate with us, usually through individuals known as mediums or channellers. The practice of consulting the dead is called necromancy. It often involves a gathering known as a séance. But does the Bible teach this?

Should the living ever consult the dead?

"When men tell you to consult mediums and spiritists, who whisper and mutter, should not a people inquire of their God? *Why consult the dead on behalf of the living?*" Isaiah 8:19, NIV.

How much do the dead know of what is going on among men?

"You overpower him once for all, and he is gone; you change his countenance and send him away. *If his sons are honored, he does not know it; if they are brought low, he does not see it.*" Job 14:20, 21, NIV.

Can the dead interact with the living?

"For the living know that they will die, but *the dead know nothing;* they have no further reward, and even the memory of them is forgotten. Their love, their hate and their jealousy have long ago vanished; never again will they have a part in anything that happens under the sun." Ecclesiastes 9:5, 6, NIV.

Can spirits haunt places?

"As a cloud vanishes and is gone, so *he who goes down to the grave does not return. He will never come to his house again; his place will know him no more.*" Job 7:9, 10, NIV.

What does the law of Moses say concerning mediums and spiritists?

"Do not allow a sorceress to live." Exodus 22:18, NIV. "A man or woman who is a medium or spiritist among you must be put to death." Leviticus 20:27, NIV.

NOTE.—This practice was so dangerous in God's sight that it was punished by death under the laws of the nation of Israel.

Who was the "spirit" called Samuel that appeared when Saul consulted the witch of Endor (1 Samuel 28:11-14)?

"So Saul died for his unfaithfulness which he had committed

against the Lord, because he did not keep the word of the Lord, and also because he consulted a medium for guidance." 1 Chronicles 10:13, 14, NKJV.

NOTE.—First Samuel 28:13 says that the spirit called up in this séance was an *elohim,* a Hebrew word that is never used of the dead. It is the normal Hebrew word for a supernatural being, divine or demonic.

To inquire of Samuel would have been to inquire of the Lord (1 Samuel 9:9 says that to "go to the seer" was to "inquire of God"). So this "spirit" could not have been the real Samuel. The Lord had refused to answer Saul by the prophets (1 Samuel 28:6). If God would not speak through a living prophet, why would He speak through a dead one—particularly since communication with the dead was explicitly forbidden?

The Bible writer calls the spirit "Samuel" in accordance with its appearance. This is quite common in Scripture: Genesis 18 and 19 consistently refer to the angels who destroyed Sodom as "men" in accordance with their appearance; Gabriel is called a "man" in Daniel 9:21, though Luke 1:19, 26 calls him an angel; and the two angels of Luke 24:23 are called "men" in Luke 24:4.

It is clear from the story in 1 Samuel 28 that both Saul and the medium of Endor believed that the spirit was actually Samuel, which demonstrates how persuasive the satanic deception can be. But in the end the spirit's words betray him. He told Saul "tomorrow . . . you will be with me" (1 Samuel 28:19, NIV) in some subterranean region (compare verses 13, 15). But surely righteous Samuel would not be with wicked Saul after death! Only a demon would say, "You're coming down to be with me!"

How does Satan transform himself to deceive?

"And no wonder, for Satan himself *masquerades as an angel of light.*" 2 Corinthians 11:14, NIV.

NOTE.—If Satan can transform himself into an angel of light, he can surely transform himself into somebody's dead relative. As invisible witnesses, demons are privy to our deepest secrets. If a human actor can impersonate the voice and characteristics of others in a crude way, how much more can demons impersonate the deceased perfectly, with flawless inflections, gestures, and secret knowledge. "For they are the spirits of devils, working miracles." Revelation 16:14.

It is now clear why God forbade communication with the dead: the beings in question are really lying spirits working under false pretenses to deceive the gullible into believing that they bring priceless wisdom from beyond. This occult phenomenon includes the hundreds of appearances of the virgin Mary that have been documented around the world during the past century. God does not communicate with human beings through the spirits of the dead.

Poet Rudyard Kipling warns intruders who seek to traffic with spirits that they are entering on a dangerous path.

Oh the road to Endor is the oldest road
And the craziest road of all.
Straight it runs to the Witch's abode,
As it did in the days of Saul.
And nothing has changed of the sorrow in store
For such as go down on the road to Endor!

How will Satan work just before Christ's second coming?

"The coming of the lawless one will be in accordance with the work of Satan displayed in all kinds of *counterfeit miracles, signs and wonders,* and in every sort of evil that deceives those who are perishing. They perish because they refused to love the truth and so be saved." 2 Thessalonians 2:9, 10, NIV.

How will Satan and his agents attempt to counterfeit the coming of Christ?

"At that time if anyone says to you, 'Look, here is the Christ!' or, 'There he is!' do not believe it. For *false Christs and false prophets will appear and perform great signs and miracles to deceive even the elect*—if that were possible." Matthew 24:23, 24, NIV.

What will be one of the last great signs performed by this means, to deceive the world?

"And he performed great and miraculous signs, even *causing fire to come down from heaven to earth* in full view of men. Because of the signs he was given power to do on behalf of the first beast, he deceived the inhabitants of the earth." Revelation 13:13, 14, NIV.

"These miraculous signs performed by the beast remind one of the signs and wonders that the Holy Spirit worked through the apostles in the book of Acts (cf. 2:43; 4:30; 5:12-16). Just as through miraculous signs the Holy Spirit convinced people to accept Jesus Christ and worship Him, so this counterfeit Christ 'deceives those living on the earth by means of the signs' (Revelation 13:13).

"The bringing of fire down from heaven to the earth might be a counterfeit to the day of Pentecost when the tongues of fire came down from heaven upon the disciples (Acts 2:3). However, this fire bears a stronger allusion to the fire that the prophet Elijah called down from heaven (1 Kings 18:38), which demonstrated that Yahweh was the true God of Israel and the only one to be worshiped. Thus, in the second case, the earth beast functions as the counterfeit of Elijah, who, by bringing fire down from heaven, misleads people into worshiping the false god. Whatever this fire might represent, it is effective in counterfeiting the truth and the gospel. All of this is designed to deceive people and persuade them that these great and miraculous signs are the manifestations of divine power.

"The strategy of this end-time miracle worker seems to be effective. Through great miraculous signs, the earth beast *deceives those living on the earth by means of the signs.* This deceit is satanic, because the authority to perform these signs was *given* to the beast by Satan. This idea recalls Paul's prophecy of the lawless one whose coming would be 'in accord with the activity of Satan, with all power and signs and false wonders, and with all the deception of wickedness for those who perish, because they did not receive the love of the truth so as to be saved' (2 Thessalonians 2:8-10. NASB)." Ranko Stefanovich, *The Revelation of Jesus Christ: Commentary on the Book of Revelation* (Berrien Springs, Mich.: Andrews University Press, 2002), pp. 420, 421.

While many will be deceived by these wonders, what will those who have maintained their love for the truth, and patiently waited for Christ's return, say?

"In that day they will say, 'Surely this is our God; we trusted in him, and he saved us. This is the Lord, we trusted in him; let us rejoice and be glad in his salvation.'" Isaiah 25:9, NIV.

CHAPTER 12

Christian Growth and Experience

GROWTH IN GRACE

How does the apostle Peter close his Second Epistle?

"But *grow in grace,* and in the knowledge of our Lord and Saviour Jesus Christ." 2 Peter 3:18.

How may grace and peace be multiplied in believers?

"Grace and peace be yours in abundance *through the knowledge of God, and of Jesus our Lord.*" 2 Peter 1:2, NIV.

What is implied in a knowledge of God and Jesus Christ?

"Now *this is eternal life*: that they may know you, the only true God, and Jesus Christ, whom you have sent." John 17:3, NIV.

How can we be partakers of the divine nature?

"Through these *he has given us his very great and precious promises, so that through them you may participate in the divine nature* and escape the corruption in the world caused by evil desires." 2 Peter 1:4, NIV.

What graces are we to add in our character building?

"For this very reason, make every effort to add to your faith *goodness;* and to goodness, *knowledge;* and to knowledge, *self-control;* and to self-control, *perseverance;* and to perseverance, *godliness;* and to godliness, *brotherly kindness;* and to brotherly kindness, *love.*" Verses 5-7, NIV.

NOTE.—*Faith* is the first round in the Christian ladder, the first step Godward. "Anyone who comes to [God] must *believe.*" Hebrews 11:6, NIV.

But an inoperative faith is useless. "Faith without *works* is dead." James 2:20. To be of value, faith must be coupled with *virtue,* or *moral excellence.*

To moral excellence there needs to be added knowledge; otherwise, one may have a zeal, but "*not based on knowledge.*" Romans 10:2, NIV. Fanaticism is the result of such courage, or zeal. Knowledge, therefore, is an essential to healthy Christian growth.

To knowledge there needs to be added *self-control.* To know to do good, and not do it, is as useless as is faith without works. "Anyone, then, who knows the good he ought to do and doesn't do it, sins." James 4:17, NIV.

Perseverance naturally follows *self-control.* It is nearly impossible for an intemperate person to be *patient.*

Having gained control of oneself, and become patient, one is in a condition to manifest *godliness,* or *Godlikeness.*

Kindness to others, or *brotherly kindness,* follows godliness.

Love for *all,* even our *enemies,* is the crowning grace, the highest step, the eighth round, in the Christian ladder.

The order of these graces is by no means accidental or haphazard, but logical and sequential, each following the other in natural, necessary order.

What does the Bible say about love?

"Love is patient, love is kind. It does not envy, it does not boast, it is not proud. It is not rude, it is not self-seeking, it is not easily angered, it keeps no record of wrongs. Love does not delight in evil but rejoices with the truth. It always protects, always trusts, always hopes, always perseveres." 1 Corinthians 13:4-7, NIV.

"Above all, love each other deeply, because love covers over a multitude of sins." 1 Peter 4:8, NIV.

"Hatred stirs up dissension, but love covers over all wrongs." Proverbs 10:12, NIV.

How does love tie everything together?

"Therefore, as God's chosen people, holy and dearly loved, clothe yourselves with compassion, kindness, humility, gentleness, and patience. Bear with each other and forgive whatever grievances you may have against one another. Forgive as the Lord forgave you. *And over all these virtues put on love, which binds them all together in perfect unity.*" Colossians 3:12-14, NIV.

What is the result of cultivating these eight graces?

"For if you possess these qualities in increasing measure, *they will keep you from being ineffective and unproductive in your knowledge of our Lord Jesus Christ.*" 2 Peter 1:8, NIV.

What is the condition of one who lacks these graces?

"But if anyone does not have them, he is nearsighted and blind, and has forgotten that he has been cleansed from his past sins." Verse 9, NIV.

What is promised those who add grace to grace?

"Therefore, my brothers, be all the more eager to make your calling and election sure. For if you do these things, *you will never fall,* and you will receive a rich welcome into the eternal kingdom of our Lord and Savior Jesus Christ." Verse 10, NIV.

Love

If I speak in the tongues of men and of angels, but have not love, I am only a resounding gong or a clanging cymbal.

"If I have the gift of prophecy and can fathom all mysteries and all knowledge, and if I have a faith that can move mountains, but have not love, I am nothing.

"If I give all I possess to the poor and surrender my body to the flames, but have not love, I gain nothing.

"Love is patient, love is kind. It does not envy, it does not boast, it is not proud.

"It is not rude, it is not self-seeking, it is not easily angered, it keeps no record of wrongs.

"Love does not delight in evil but rejoices with the truth.

"It always protects, always trusts, always hopes, always perseveres.

"Love never fails. But where there are prophecies, they will cease; where there are tongues, they will be stilled; where there is knowledge, it will pass away.

"For we know in part and we prophesy in part, but when perfection comes, the imperfect disappears.

"When I was a child, I talked like a child, I thought like a child, I reasoned like a child. When I became a man, I put childish ways behind me.

"Now we see but a poor reflection as in a mirror; then we shall see face to face. Now I know in part; then I shall know fully, even as I am fully known.

"And now these three remain: faith, hope and love. But the greatest of these is love." 1 Corinthians 13, NIV.

THE CHRISTIAN ARMOR

What power makes war upon the remnant people prior to the Second Coming?

"Then *the dragon* [Satan] was enraged at the woman and went off to make war against the rest of her offspring—those who obey God's commandments and hold to the testimony of Jesus." Revelation 12:17, NIV.

What reward is promised to those who achieve victory?

"To him who overcomes, I will give *the right to eat from the tree of life,* which is in the paradise of God." Revelation 2:7, NIV. (See also Revelation 2:11, 17, 26-28; 3:5, 12, 21.) "He who overcomes will inherit all this, and *I will be his God and he will be my son.*" Revelation 21:7, NIV.

Through whom are we able to conquer the power that wars against us?

"No, in all these things we are more than conquerors through him who loved us." Romans 8:37, NIV.

Who was the invisible leader of the armies of Israel?

"Now when Joshua was near Jericho, he looked up and saw a man standing in front of him with a drawn sword in his hand. Joshua went up to him and asked, 'Are you for us or for our enemies?'

" ' Neither,' he replied, 'but as *commander of the army of the Lord* I have now come.' " Joshua 5:13, 14, NIV. (See also 1 Corinthians 10:1-4.)

NOTE.—In the spiritual realm the question is not whether God is on our side, but whether we're on His.

What is the character of the Christian's weapons of warfare?

"The weapons we fight with are *not the weapons of the world. On the contrary, they have divine power to demolish strongholds.*" 2 Corinthians 10:4, NIV.

What are these weapons able to conquer?

"We demolish *arguments* and *every pretension that sets itself up against the knowledge of God,* and we take captive every thought to make it obedient to Christ." Verse 5, NIV.

What spiritual armor should we wear?

"*Put on the full armor of God* so that you can take your stand against the devil's schemes." Ephesians 6:11, NIV.

What kind of forces do we contend with?

"For our struggle is not against flesh and blood, but against *the rulers,* against *the authorities,* against *the powers of this dark world*

and against *the spiritual forces of evil in the heavenly realms.* Therefore put on the full armor of God, so that when the day of evil comes,
you may be able to stand your ground, and after you have done everything, to stand." Verses 12, 13, NIV.

What are the first essentials of the needed armor?

"Stand firm then, with the *belt of truth* buckled around your waist,
with the *breastplate of righteousness* in place." Verse 14, NIV.

With what are the feet to be shod?

"And with your feet fitted with the *readiness that comes from the
gospel of peace.*" Verse 15, NIV. (See also Ephesians 2:14; James 3:18.)

What piece of armor is next mentioned as necessary?

"In addition to all this, take up *the shield of faith,* with which you
can extinguish all the flaming arrows of the evil one." Ephesians 6:16,
NIV. (See 1 John 5:4; Hebrews 11:6.)

What armor is the Christian to put on as a protection to the head?

"Take the *helmet of salvation.*" Ephesians 6:17, NIV.

NOTE.—In 1 Thessalonians 5:8 the helmet is called "the hope of
salvation." The helmet was worn to protect the head. So the hope of
salvation will preserve the courage, and thus aid in protecting the
spiritual life of the Christian pilgrim when attacked by the enemy.

What is the sword of the Christian soldier?

"The *sword of the Spirit,* which is the word of God." Ephesians
6:17, NIV.

NOTE.—By this Christ defeated the enemy. (See Matthew 4:1-
11; Luke 4:1-13.) But no one can *use this sword* who does not *know
it.* Hence, the importance of studying and knowing the Bible.

In what words are the courage, faithfulness, and loyalty of the church expressed?

"They overcame him by the blood of the Lamb and by the word
of their testimony; they did not love their lives so much as to shrink
from death." Revelation 12:11, NIV.

Will Christ's loyal soldiers be victorious under Him?

"And I saw what looked like a sea of glass mixed with fire and,
standing beside the sea, those who had been victorious over the beast
and his image and over the number of his name." Revelation 15:2, NIV.

WALKING IN THE LIGHT

How important is it that we walk in the light when it comes to us?

"Walk while you have the light, before darkness overtakes you. The man who walks in the dark does not know where he is going. Put your trust in the light while you have it, so that you may become sons of light." John 12:35, 36, NIV.

NOTE.—It is important to settle a plain question of duty at once, and not delay obedience under the excuse of waiting for more light. Nor should we, like those who refused to believe in Jesus, seek a sign from heaven to convince us that we ought to obey the Written Word. See 1 Kings 22:1-36; Ezekiel 14:1-5.

How may we be cleansed of sin?

"*But if we walk in the light,* as he is in the light, we have fellowship with one another, and the blood of Jesus, his Son, purifies us from all sin." 1 John 1:7, NIV.

Who is the light of the world?

Jesus. "I am the light of the world. Whoever follows me will never walk in darkness, but will have the light of life." John 8:12, NIV.

How are we to walk in Christ?

"As you received Christ Jesus as Lord, continue to live in him, rooted and built up in him, strengthened in the faith as you were taught, and overflowing with thankfulness." Colossians 2:6, 7, NIV.

What has God given to guide our feet in the path of truth and duty?

"Your *word* is a lamp to my feet and a light to my path." Psalm 119:105, NKJV. (See Proverbs 6:23.)

How does Bible study affect our spiritual lives?

"The unfolding of your words gives light; it gives understanding to the simple." Psalm 119:130, NIV.

Who does Christ say will be blessed through the prophecies of the book of Revelation?

"Blessed is the one who reads the words of this prophecy, and blessed are those who hear it and take to heart what is written in it, because the time is near." Revelation 1:3, NIV.

NOTE.—We are in the last days, when the book's warning message is to be proclaimed. (See Revelation 14:6-10; 18:1-5.)

How long may the righteous expect increased light to shine upon their pathway?

"The path of the righteous is like the first gleam of dawn, shining ever brighter till the full light of day." Proverbs 4:18, NIV.

How did God respond to Cornelius' sincerity of worship?

"At Caesarea there was a man named Cornelius, a centurion in what was known as the Italian Regiment. He and all his family were devout and God-fearing; he gave generously to those in need and prayed to God regularly. One day at about three in the afternoon he had a vision. He distinctly saw an angel of God, who came to him and said, 'Cornelius!'

"Cornelius stared at him in fear. 'What is it, Lord?' he asked.

"The angel answered, 'Your prayers and gifts to the poor have come up as a memorial offering before God.' " Acts 10:1-4, NIV.

Was God's commendation evidence that Cornelius had nothing more to learn or do?

"Now send men to Joppa, and send for Simon whose surname is Peter. He is staying with Simon, a tanner, whose house is by the sea. *He will tell you what you must do.*" Verses 5, 6, NIV.

NOTE.—God favored Cornelius with a visit from one of His angels, not because Cornelius knew the way of salvation perfectly, but because God saw in him a sincere desire for more light, and a mind willing to comply with every known requirement. That spirit pleased God. All may now receive advanced light, if, like Cornelius, they seek it, and are willing to walk in it when it comes to them. If they neglect the light they are guilty before God, and are in danger of the enemy's attacks.

What happens to our light if we fail to walk in it?

"Your eye is the lamp of your body. When your eyes are good, your whole body also is full of light. But when they are bad, your body also is full of darkness. *See to it, then, that the light within you is not darkness.*" Luke 11:34, 35, NIV.

Why did the sin of those who rejected Jesus remain?

"Jesus said, 'If you were blind, you would not be guilty of sin; but *now that you claim you can see, your guilt remains.*' " John 9:41, NIV. (See also John 15:22.)

NOTE.—With advanced light comes increased responsibility. Duty is always in proportion to one's light and privileges. Present truth always brings with it present duty. (See pp. 99-103.)

Why are those who do not come to the light condemned?

"This is the verdict: Light has come into the world, *but men loved darkness instead of light because their deeds were evil.*" John 3:19, NIV.

What will one who is really seeking the truth do?

"But whoever lives by the truth *comes into the light,* so that it may be seen plainly that what he has done has been done through God." Verse 21, NIV.

What will those who reject light and truth finally be led to believe?

"For this reason God sends them a powerful delusion so that *they will believe the lie* and so that all will be condemned who have not believed the truth but have delighted in wickedness." 2 Thessalonians 2:11, 12, NIV.

NOTE.—The opposite of light is darkness; the opposite of truth is a lie. For those who reject light and truth, only darkness and error remain. The Bible shows God allowing people to reap the results of their own choices. (See Psalm 81:12; 1 Kings 22:20-23; Romans 1:21-28.)

On what condition do we share in Christ?

"We have come to share in Christ *if we hold firmly till the end the confidence we had at first.*" Hebrews 3:14, NIV. (See Matthew 10:22; 24:12, 13; Hebrews 10:35-39.)

SAVING FAITH

What is faith?

"Now faith is *being sure of what we hope for* and certain of what we do not see." Hebrews 11:1, NIV.

How important is faith? What must one believe about God?

"And *without faith it is impossible to please God,* because anyone who comes to him must believe that he exists and that he rewards those who earnestly seek him." Verse 6, NIV.

What is the only true way to know God?

"No one knows the Son except the Father, and no one knows the Father except the Son and *those to whom the Son chooses to reveal him.*" Matthew 11:27, NIV.

In whom must we believe in order to be saved?

"For God so loved the world that he gave *his one and only Son,*

that whoever believes in him shall not perish but have eternal life."
John 3:16, NIV.

How only can we be justified? Since the law cannot justify a sinner, is it without value?

"Therefore, since we have been justified *through faith,* we have peace with God through our Lord Jesus Christ." Romans 5:1, NIV. "Therefore no one will be declared righteous in his sight by observing the law; rather, *through the law we become conscious of sin.*" Romans 3:20, NIV.

What challenge does the apostle James make as to the evidence that one has genuine faith?

"Show me your faith without deeds, and I will show you my faith by what I do." James 2:18, NIV.

How did Abraham show that he had perfect faith in God?

"Was not our ancestor Abraham considered righteous for what he did *when he offered his son Isaac on the altar?* You see that his faith and his actions were working together, and his faith was made complete by what he did." Verses 21, 22, NIV.

What practical example does James give to illustrate the difference between genuine, living faith and a dead faith?

"Suppose a brother or sister is without clothes and daily food. If one of you says to him, 'Go, I wish you well; keep warm and well fed,' but does nothing about his physical needs, what good is it?" Verses 15, 16, NIV.

How necessary are works in maintaining living faith?

"Do you want evidence that *faith without deeds is useless?* . . . As the body without the spirit is dead, so faith without deeds is dead." Verses 20-26, NIV.

NOTE.—The apostle was not here arguing for justification or salvation by faith *and* works, but for a living faith—a faith *that* works.

"There are two errors against which the children of God—particularly those who have just come to trust in His grace—especially need to guard. The first . . . is that of looking to their own works, trusting to anything they can do, to bring themselves into harmony with God. He who is trying to become holy by his own works in keeping the law is attempting an impossibility. All that man can do without Christ is polluted with selfishness and sin. It is the grace of Christ alone, through faith, that can make us holy. The opposite and no less dangerous error is that belief in Christ releases men from keeping the law of God; that since by faith alone we become partakers of the grace of Christ, our works have nothing to do with our redemption. . . . Obedience—the service and allegiance of love—is the true sign of discipleship. . . . Instead of releasing man from obedience, it is faith, and faith only, that makes us partakers of the grace of Christ, which enables us to render obedience. We do not earn salvation by our obedience; for salvation is the free gift of God, to be received by faith. But obedience is the fruit of faith. . . . That so-called faith in Christ which professes to release men from the obligation of obedience to God is not faith, but presumption." Ellen G. White, *Steps to Christ*, pp. 59-61.

"If it is He alone that taketh away our sins, it cannot be ourselves and our own works. But good works follow redemption, as the fruit grows on the tree." Martin Luther, in Merle d'Aubigne, *History of the Reformation,* book 2, chap. 6.

What does the hope of salvation lead one to do?

"We know that when he appears, we shall be like him, for we shall see him as he is. Everyone who has this hope in him *purifies himself,* just as he is pure." 1 John 3:2, 3, NIV.

Upon what conditions has God promised us cleansing and the forgiveness of our sins?

"But *if we walk in the light,* as he is in the light, we have fellowship with one another, and the blood of Jesus, his Son, purifies us from all sin. . . . *If we confess our sins,* he is faithful and just and will forgive us our sins and purify us from all unrighteousness." 1 John 1:7-9, NIV.

NOTE.—Intelligent faith as to what God will do for us touching any matter must be gained by what God's Word says concerning that point. No one can consistently hope for that which God has not promised. To expect that God will do that which He has never promised to do is only presumption. Faith is distinct from presumption. To have abiding confidence in the promise of God is faith; but presumption may rest entirely on feeling or desire. Feeling cannot be relied on in the matter of faith. Faith is a pure belief, a confiding trust in the promises of God, irrespective of feeling. This perfect trust enables one to surmount difficulties under the most trying circumstances, even when our feelings are depressed or nearly crushed.

Upon what is genuine, saving faith based?

"Faith comes from hearing the message, and the message is heard through *the word of God.*" Romans 10:17, NIV.

Why did Peter sink after he started walking out to meet Jesus on the stormy sea?

"Immediately Jesus reached out his hand and caught him. 'You of little faith,' he said, 'why did you have doubt?' " Matthew 14:31, NIV.

NOTE.—Peter's fear of the boisterous sea caused him to doubt the strength of Christ's word, "Come."

What does God give us when we trust Him?

"May the God of hope fill you with *all joy and peace* as you trust in him, so that you may overflow with *hope* by the power of the Holy Spirit." Romans 15:13, NIV.

Faith may be strengthened by daily exercise. It is not some great thing, done once for all, that gives us faith; but an everyday, simple, childlike trust in God, and an implicit obedience to His Word. Some make faith a more difficult matter than God would have them, because they try to embrace too much at one time. They take on the burdens of tomorrow or next week, when the Lord supplies strength only for today. *When tomorrow comes, grapple with its duties, but not until it does come. We should remember the precious promise, "As your days, so shall your strength be." Deuteronomy 33:25, NKJV.*

SUFFERING AND TRIALS

What does Peter say about spiritual trials?

"Dear friends, *do not be surprised at the painful trial you are suffering,* as though something strange were happening to you. But *rejoice that you participate in the sufferings of Christ,* so that you may be overjoyed when his glory is revealed." 1 Peter 4:12, 13, NIV.

How important is the trial of our faith?

"These have come so that your faith—of greater worth than gold, which perishes even though refined by fire—may be proved genuine and may result in praise, glory and honor when Jesus Christ is revealed." 1 Peter 1:7, NIV.

What reason did Paul give for glorying in tribulations?

"Not only so, but we also rejoice in our sufferings, because *we know that suffering produces perseverance; perseverance, character;* and *character, hope. And hope does not disappoint us,* because God has poured out his love into our hearts by the Holy Spirit, whom he has given us." Romans 5:3-5, NIV.

What, according to the prophecy of Daniel, was to befall the people of God down through the ages?

"Those who are wise will instruct many, though for a time *they will fall by the sword or be burned or captured or plundered.*" Daniel 11:33, NIV.

Why was this to be?

"Some of the wise will stumble, *so that they may be refined, purified and made spotless until the time of the end,* for it will still come at the appointed time." Verse 35, NIV.

Looking forward to the conflicts through which His followers must pass, Jesus sent what encouraging message?

"*Do not be afraid of what you are about to suffer.* I tell you, the devil will put some of you in prison to test you, and you will suffer persecution for ten days. *Be faithful, even to the point of death, and I will give you the crown of life.* He who has an ear, let him hear what the Spirit says to the churches. *He who overcomes will not be hurt at all by the second death.*" Revelation 2:10, 11, NIV. (See pp. 245, 246, 269-271.)

How many does Paul say will suffer persecution?

"Everyone who wants to live a godly life in Christ Jesus will be persecuted." 2 Timothy 3:12, NIV.

What description does Paul give of the sufferings endured by some of God's people in former ages?

"Others were *tortured* and refused to be released, so that they might gain a better resurrection. Some *faced jeers* and *flogging,* while still others were *chained* and *put in prison.* They were *stoned;* they were *sawed in two;* they were *put to death by the sword.* They went about in sheepskins and goatskins, destitute, *persecuted* and mistreated—the world was not worthy of them. They *wandered in deserts and mountains, and in caves and in holes in the ground.*" Hebrews 11:35-38, NIV.

Does God willingly afflict His children?

"For men are not cast off by the Lord forever. Though he brings grief, he will show compassion, so great is his unfailing love. *For he does not willingly bring affliction or grief to the children of men.*" Lamentations 3:31-33, NIV.

Why does God permit hardship?

"Endure hardship as discipline; God is treating you as sons. For what son is not disciplined by his father? If you are not disciplined (and everyone undergoes discipline), then you are illegitimate children and not true sons. Moreover, we have all had human fathers who disciplined us and we respected them for it. How much more should we submit to the Father of our spirits and live! Our fathers disciplined us for a little while as they thought best; but God disciplines us for our good, *that we may share in his holiness.*

"No discipline seems pleasant at the time, but painful. Later on, however, *it produces a harvest of righteousness and peace* for those who have been trained by it." Hebrews 12:7-11, NIV.

What was Jesus' prayer for Peter before the Crucifixion?

"Simon, Simon, Satan has asked to sift you as wheat. But I have prayed for you, Simon, *that your faith may not fail.* And when you have turned back, strengthen your brothers." Luke 22:31, 32, NIV.

What cheering promise is made to those who endure the trials and temptations of this life?

"Blessed is the man who perseveres under trial, because when he has stood the test, *he will receive the crown of life* that God has promised to those who love him." James 1:12, NIV.

NOTE.—"Our sorrows do not spring out of the ground. God 'doth not afflict willingly nor grieve the children of men.' Lamentations 3:33. When He permits trials and afflictions, it is 'for our profit, that we might be partakers of His holiness.' Hebrews 12:10. If received in faith, the trial that seems so bitter and hard to bear will prove a blessing. The cruel blow that blights the joys of earth will be the means of turning our eyes to heaven. How many there are who would never have known Jesus had not sorrow led them to seek comfort in Him! The trials of life are God's workmen, to remove the impurities and roughness from our character. Their hewing, squaring, and chiseling, their burnishing and polishing, is a painful process; it is hard to be pressed down to the grinding wheel. But the stone is brought forth prepared to fill its place in the heavenly temple." Ellen G. White, *Thoughts From the Mount of Blessing,* p. 10.

OVERCOMING

Who can overcome the world?

"Everyone who believes that Jesus is the Christ is born of God, and everyone who loves the Father loves his child as well. This is how we know that we love the children of God: by loving God and carrying out his commands. This is love for God: to obey his commands. And his commands are not burdensome, for *everyone born of God* overcomes the world. This is the victory that has overcome the world, even our faith. Who is it that overcomes the world? Only he who believes that Jesus is the Son of God." 1 John 5:1-5, NIV.

In whose victory may the Christian ever rejoice and take courage?

The victory of Jesus. "I have told you these things, so that in me you may have peace. In this world you will have trouble. But take heart! *I have overcome the world.*" John 16:33, NIV.

Through whom do we obtain the victory?

"But thanks be to God! He gives us the victory through *our Lord Jesus Christ.*" 1 Corinthians 15:57, NIV. "No, in all these things we are more than conquerors through him who loved us." Romans 8:37, NIV.

How did Christ overcome when tempted?

By the Word of God. (See Matthew 4:1-11.)

How do the Scriptures say the saints overcame the enemy?

"They overcame him *by the blood of the Lamb and by the word of their testimony;* they did not love their lives so much as to shrink from death." Revelation 12:11, NIV.

How can we overcome evil?

"Do not repay anyone evil for evil. Be careful to do what is right in the eyes of everybody. If it is possible, as far as it depends on you, live at peace with everyone. Do not take revenge, my friends, but leave room for God's wrath, for it is written, 'It is mine to avenge; I will repay,' says the Lord. On the contrary:

" 'If your enemy is hungry, feed him; if he is thirsty, give him something to drink. In doing this, you will heap burning coals on his head.' Do not be overcome by evil, but *overcome evil with good.*" Romans 12:17-21, NIV.

NOTE.—Paul is quoting Deuteronomy 32:35 and Proverbs 25:21, 22.

Why did God change Jacob's name to Israel?

"Then the man said, 'Your name will no longer be Jacob, but Israel, *because you have struggled with God and with men and have overcome.*' " Genesis 32:28, NIV.

Exceeding Great and Precious Promises

To him who overcomes, I will give the right to eat from the tree of life, which is in the paradise of God." Revelation 2:7, NIV.

"He who overcomes will not be hurt at all by the second death." Verse 11, NIV.

"To him who overcomes I will give some of the hidden manna." Verse 17, NIV.

"To him who overcomes and does my will to the end, I will give authority over the nations." Verse 26, NIV.

"He who overcomes will, like them, be dressed in white. I will never blot out his name from the book of life, but will acknowledge his name before my Father and his angels." Revelation 3:5, NIV.

"Him who overcomes I will make a pillar in the temple of my God." Verse 12, NIV.

"To him who overcomes, I will give the right to sit with me on my throne, just as I overcame and sat down with my Father on his throne." Verse 21, NIV.

"He who overcomes will inherit all this, and I will be his God and he will be my son." Revelation 21:7, NIV.

The Way to Win

The victory is not won without much earnest prayer, without the humbling of self at every step. Our will is not to be forced into cooperation with divine agencies, but it must be voluntarily submitted. Were it possible to force upon you with a hundredfold greater intensity the influence of the Spirit of God, it would not make you a Christian, a fit subject for heaven. The stronghold of Satan would not be broken. The will must be placed on the side of God's will. You are not able, of yourself, to bring your purposes and desires and inclinations into submission to the will of God; but if you are 'willing to be made willing,' God will accomplish the work for you." Ellen G. White, *Thoughts From the Mount of Blessing,* p. 142.

COMFORT IN AFFLICTION

Why did Solomon say that it is better to go to the house of mourning than to the house of feasting?

"It is better to go to a house of mourning than to go to a house of feasting, *for death is the destiny of every man;* the living should take this to heart." Ecclesiastes 7:2, NIV.

Why did Solomon say that sorrow is better than laughter?

"Sorrow is better than laughter, *because a sad face is good for the heart.*" Verse 3, NIV.

NOTE.—"Many of the loveliest songs of peace and trust and hope which God's children sing in this world have been taught in the hushed and darkened chambers of sorrow. . . . Afflictions, sanctified, soften the asperities of life. They tame the wildness of nature. They temper human ambitions. They burn out the dross of selfishness and worldliness. They humble pride. They quell fierce passions. They reveal to men their own hearts, their own weaknesses, faults, blemishes, and perils. They teach patience and submission. They discipline unruly spirits. They deepen and enrich our experiences." J. R. Miller, *Week-Day Religion,* pp. 90, 91.

Are God's follower's spared this world's afflictions?

"*A righteous man may have many troubles,* but the Lord delivers him from them all." Psalm 34:19, NIV.

Does God discipline us to discourage us?

"*Blessed is the man whom God corrects;* so do not despise the discipline of the Almighty." Job 5:17, NIV.

What promise does Christ bring to those who suffer?

"The Spirit of the Sovereign Lord is on me, because the Lord has anointed me to preach good news to the poor. He has sent me *to bind up the brokenhearted, to proclaim freedom for the captives and release from darkness for the prisoners, to proclaim the year of the Lord's favor and the day of vengeance of our God, to comfort all who mourn, and provide for those who grieve in Zion—to bestow on them a crown of beauty* instead of ashes, the *oil of gladness* instead of mourning, and *a garment of praise* instead of a spirit of despair. They will be called oaks of righteousness, a painting of the Lord for the display of his splendor." Isaiah 61:1-3, NIV.

Whom does the Lord discipline?

"My son, do not despise the Lord's discipline, and do not resent his rebuke, because the Lord disciplines *those he loves,* as a father the son he delights in." Proverbs 3:11, 12, NIV.

How should we relate to discipline?

"No discipline seems pleasant at the time, but painful. Later on, however, *it produces a harvest of righteousness and peace* for those who have been trained by it." Hebrews 12:11, NIV.

What, aside from sin, causes more sorrow than all else?

Death.

What comfort may Christians have in the face of death?

"Brothers, we do not want you to be ignorant about those who fall asleep, or to grieve like the rest of men, who have no hope. We believe that Jesus died and rose again and so *we believe that God will bring with Jesus those who have fallen asleep in him.*" 1 Thessalonians 4:13, 14, NIV.

NOTE.—God can use tragedy in our lives to draw us closer to Him. (See Psalm 119:71; Isaiah 26:9.)

Who is the author of disease and death?

"Then should not this woman, a daughter of Abraham, *whom Satan has kept bound* for eighteen long years, be set free on the Sabbath day from what bound her?" Luke 13:16, NIV.

"To keep me from becoming conceited because of these surpassingly great revelations, there was given me a thorn in my flesh, a messenger of *Satan,* to torment me." 2 Corinthians 12:7, NIV.

"Since the children have flesh and blood, he [Jesus] too shared in their humanity so that by his death he might destroy *him who holds the power of death—that is, the devil.*" Hebrews 2:14, NIV.

NOTE.—It should be remembered that suffering and death come from Satan, the one who "sowed weeds among the wheat" (Matthew 13:25, NIV). But God overrules the devices of the enemy for the good of those who put their trust in Him. He works all things for good to them that love Him (Romans 8:28).

What has God promised to be to those in trouble?

"God is *our refuge and strength, an ever-present help in trouble.* Therefore we will not fear, though the earth give way and the mountains fall into the heart of the sea, though its water roar and foam and the mountains quake with their surging." Psalm 46:1-3, NIV.

How does God feel about His children?

"As a father has compassion on his children, so *the Lord has com-*

passion on those who fear him; for he knows how we are formed, he remembers that we are dust." Psalm 103:13, 14, NIV.

What has the Lord promised to be to the oppressed?

"The Lord is *a refuge* for the oppressed, a stronghold in times of trouble. Those who know your name will trust in you, for you, Lord, have never forsaken those who seek you." Psalm 9:9, 10, NIV.

What has God promised His children when they experience trials and afflictions?

"When you pass through the waters, *I will be with you;* and when you pass through the rivers, they will not sweep over you. When you walk through the fire, you will not be burned; the flames will not set you ablaze." Isaiah 43:2, NIV.

What did King David say with reference to his being afflicted?

"*It was good for me to be afflicted* so that I might learn your decrees." Psalm 119:71, NIV.

What did David pray for when he was afflicted?

"Turn to me and be gracious to me, for I am lonely and afflicted. The troubles of my heart have multiplied; free me from my anguish. *Look upon my affliction and my distress and take away all my sins.*" Psalm 25:16-18, NIV.

Before he was afflicted, what did he do?

"Before I was afflicted *I went astray,* but now I obey your word." Psalm 119:67, NIV.

What did Jesus learn through suffering?

"Although he was a son, he learned *obedience* from what he suffered." Hebrews 5:8, NIV.

How should God's comfort motivate us to reach out to others?

"Praise be to the God and Father of our Lord Jesus Christ, the Father of compassion and the God of all comfort, who comforts us in all our troubles, so that we can comfort those in any trouble with the comfort we ourselves have received from God. For just as the sufferings of Christ flow over into our lives, so also through Christ our comfort overflows." 2 Corinthians 1:3-5, NIV.

NOTE.—One who has passed through an affliction himself, and received comfort from God, is better able to minister to others facing life's problems.

Whom does God comfort?

"God . . . comforts the downcast." 2 Corinthians 7:6, NIV.

What promise is given to those that mourn?

"Blessed are those who mourn, for *they will be comforted.*" Matthew 5:4, NIV.

How should we sympathize with others?

"Rejoice with those who rejoice; *mourn with those who mourn.*" Romans 12:15, NIV. "A despairing man should have the devotion of his friends, even though he forsakes the fear of the Almighty." Job 6:14, NIV.

Does Jesus sympathize with us in our afflictions?

"For we do not have a high priest who is unable to sympathize with our weaknesses, but we have one who has been tempted in every way, just as we are—yet was without sin." Hebrews 4:15, NIV.

How did Jesus share in the sorrow of Mary and her friends over the death of Lazarus?

"When Jesus saw her weeping, and the Jews who had come along with her also weeping, he was deeply moved in spirit and troubled. 'Where have you laid him?' he asked. 'Come and see, Lord,' they replied. *Jesus wept.*" John 11:33-35, NIV.

Whatever may come, what blessed assurance does everyone who loves God share?

"And we know that in all things God works for the good of those who love him, who have been called according to his purpose." Romans 8:28, NIV.

NOTE.—Those who love God may rest assured that good will come out of every trial and affliction.

What may Christians take courage in when faced with grief and loss?

"Brothers, we do not want you to be ignorant about those who fall asleep, or to grieve like the rest of men, who have no hope. We believe that Jesus died and rose again and so we believe that God will bring with Jesus those who have fallen asleep in him. According to the Lord's own word, we tell you that we who are still alive, who are left till the coming of the Lord, will certainly not precede those who have fallen asleep. For the Lord himself will come down from heaven, with a loud command, with the voice of the archangel and with the trumpet call of God, and the dead in Christ will rise first. After that, we who are still alive and are left will be caught up together with them in the clouds to meet the Lord in the air. And so we will be with the Lord forever. *Therefore encourage each other with these words.*" 1 Thessalonians 4:13-18, NIV.

What did Christ say would be the experience of His people in this world?

"I tell you the truth, you will weep and mourn while the world rejoices. You will grieve, but your grief will turn to joy. A woman giving birth to a child has pain because her time has come; but when her baby is born she forgets the anguish because of her joy that a child is born into the world. So with you: *Now is your time of grief, but I will see you again and you will rejoice,* and no one will take away your joy. . . . I have told you these things, so that in me you may have peace" John 16:20-33, NIV.

What promise does the Bible give to those who suffer in this life?

"*Those who sow in tears will reap with songs of joy.* He who goes out weeping, carrying seed to sow, will return with songs of joy, carrying sheaves with him." Psalm 126:5, 6, NIV.

TRUSTING IN JESUS

What did the prophet Isaiah predict of Christ?

"In that day the Root of Jesse will stand as a banner for the peoples; *the nations will rally to him, and his place of rest will be glorious.*" Isaiah 11:10, NIV.

NOTE.—Paul renders this, "The Gentiles will hope in him." Romans 15:12, NIV.

Why does God wish us to trust in Jesus?

"In him we were also chosen, having been predestined according to the plan of him who works out everything in conformity with the purpose of his will, in order that we, who were the first to hope in Christ, might be *for the praise of his glory.*" Ephesians 1:11, 12, NIV.

How does God regard one who abandons his faith?

"He who is coming will . . . not delay. But my righteous one will live by faith. And if he shrinks back, *I will not be pleased with him.* But we are not of those who shrink back and are destroyed, but of those who believe and are saved." Hebrews 10:37-39, NIV.

Is there danger of believers losing their hold on Christ?

"*Because of the increase of wickedness, the love of most will grow cold,* but he who stands firm to the end will be saved." Matthew 24:12, 13, NIV.

How did hearing the gospel affect the Ephesians?

"*You also were included in Christ* when you heard the word of truth, the gospel of your salvation. Having believed, *you were marked in him with a seal, the promised Holy Spirit,* who is a deposit guaranteeing our inheritance until the redemption of those who are God's possession—to the praise of his glory." Ephesians 1:13, 14, NIV.

NOTE.—To trust in Jesus is to believe in Him, to have abiding and unbounded confidence in Him. When such trust exists, we are sealed by the Holy Spirit of promise.

What is the gospel to everyone that believes?

"I am not ashamed of the gospel, because it is *the power of God for the salvation of everyone* who believes." Romans 1:16, NIV.

By what does one gain the victory over the world?

"This is the victory that has overcome the world, even our *faith.*" 1 John 5:4, NIV.

What encouragement does Jesus give us to meet the troubles and trials of life cheerfully?

"I have told you these things, so that in me you may have peace. In this world you will have trouble. But *take heart! I have overcome the world.*" John 16:33, NIV.

What has this firm trust in Jesus led many to do?

"They overcame him by the blood of the Lamb and by the word of their testimony; *they did not love their lives so much as to shrink from death.*" Revelation 12:11, NIV.

"Some faced jeers and flogging, while still others were chained and put in prison. They were stoned; they were sawed in two; they were put to death by the sword. They went about in sheepskins and goatskins, destitute, persecuted and mistreated—the world was not worthy of them. They wandered in deserts and mountains, and in caves and holes in the ground." Hebrews 11:36-38, NIV.

What did Moses' trust in God lead him to do?

"By faith Moses, when he had grown up, *refused to be known as the son of Pharaoh's daughter. He chose to be mistreated along with the people of God rather than to enjoy the pleasures of sin for a short time.* He regarded disgrace for the sake of Christ as of greater value than the treasures of Egypt, because he was looking ahead to his reward. By faith he left Egypt, not fearing the king's anger; he persevered because he saw him who is invisible." Hebrews 11:24-26, NIV.

What is promised those who put their complete trust in Jesus?

"No one who has left home or brothers or sisters or mother or father or children or fields for me and the gospel will fail to receive *a hundred times as much in this present age* (homes, brothers, sisters, mothers, children and fields—and with them, persecutions) and *in the age to come, eternal life.*" Mark 10:29, 30, NIV.

How does God wish to aid us when sin and trouble threaten us?

"To him who is able *to keep you from falling* and to present you before his glorious presence without fault and with great joy—to the only God our Savior be glory, majesty, power and authority, through Jesus Christ our Lord, before all ages, now and forevermore! Amen." Jude 24, 25, NIV.

What does the Bible say about patience?

"The end of a matter is better than its beginning, and *patience is better than pride.*" Ecclesiastes 7:8, NIV. "Be patient with everyone." 1 Thessalonians 5:14, NIV. "By standing firm you will gain life." Luke 21:19, NIV.

What virtue is there in patience?

"A patient man has *great understanding,* but a quick-tempered man displays folly." Proverbs 14:29, NIV.

What did James say about the importance and value of patience?

"Be patient, then, brothers, until the Lord's coming. See how the farmer waits for the land to yield its valuable crop and how patient he is for the autumn and spring rains. You too, be patient and stand firm, because the Lord's coming is near. Don't grumble against each other, brothers, or you will be judged. The Judge is standing at the door!

"Brothers, as an example of patience in the face of suffering, take the prophets who spoke in the name of the Lord. As you know, *we consider blessed those who have persevered.* You have heard of Job's perseverance and have seen what the Lord finally brought about. The Lord is full of compassion and mercy." James 5:7-11, NIV.

What do life's trials develop in us?

"The testing of your faith develops *perseverance.*" James 1:3, NIV. "Not only so, but we also rejoice in our sufferings, because we know that suffering produces *perseverance.*" Romans 5:3, NIV.

How should we grow spiritually beyond our initial faith?

"For this very reason, make every effort to add to your faith goodness; and to goodness, knowledge; and to knowledge, self-control; and to self-control, *perseverance*; and to perseverance, godliness; and to godliness, brotherly kindness; and to brotherly kindness, love." 2 Peter 1:6, NIV.

NOTE.—Patience naturally follows temperance. Hence the importance of right living—of gaining control over the appetites and passions.

Why does James urge patience?

"Consider it pure joy, my brothers, whenever you face trials of many kinds, because you know that the testing of your faith develops perseverance. *Perseverance must finish its work so that you may be mature and complete,* not lacking anything." James 1:2-4, NIV.

How are we exhorted to run the Christian race?

"Let us run *with perseverance* the race marked out for us. *Let us fix our eyes on Jesus,* the author and perfecter of our faith." Hebrews 12:1, 2, NIV.

What encouragement did Jesus give for people persecuted for their faith?

"He who stands firm to the end will be saved." Matthew 10:22, NIV.

What will be one characteristic of God's remnant?

"This calls for *patient endurance* on the part of the saints who obey God's commandments and remain faithful to Jesus." Revelation 14:12, NIV.

What does Psalm 130 say about waiting on God through life's trials?

"Out of the depths I cry to you, O Lord; O Lord, hear my voice. Let your ears be attentive to my cry for mercy. If you, O Lord, kept a record of sins, O Lord, who could stand? But with you there is forgiveness; therefore you are feared. I wait for the Lord, my soul waits, and in his word I put my hope. My soul waits for the Lord more than watchmen wait for the morning . . . . O Israel, put your hope in the Lord, for with the Lord is unfailing love and with him is full redemption. He himself will redeem Israel from all their sins." Psalm 130:1-8, NIV.

What will the saved say when God rescues and restores them?

"In that day they will say, '*Surely this is our God; we trusted in him, and he saved us.* This is the Lord, we trusted in him; *let us rejoice and be glad in his salvation.*' " Isaiah 25:9, NIV.

What does Paul say is great gain?

"But *godliness with contentment* is great gain. For we brought nothing into the world, and we can take nothing out of it." 1 Timothy 6:6, 7, NIV.

With what are we encouraged to be content?

"Keep your lives free from the love of money and *be content with what you have,* because God has said, 'Never will I leave you; never will I forsake you.' " Hebrews 13:5, NIV. "But if we have *food and clothing,* we will be content with that." 1 Timothy 6:8, NIV.

NOTE.—The author of Hebrews is here quoting Deuteronomy 31:6.

What does Jesus tell us not to be anxious about?

"So do not worry, saying, '*What shall we eat?*' or '*What shall we drink?*' or '*What shall we wear?*' For the pagans run after all these things, and your heavenly Father knows that you need them." Matthew 6:31, 32, NIV.

What evils befall those who are determined to be rich?

"People who want to get rich *fall into temptation and a trap and into many foolish and harmful desires* that plunge men into ruin and destruction. For the love of money is a root of all kinds of evil. *Some people,* eager for money, *have wandered from the faith and pierced themselves with many griefs.*" 1 Timothy 6:9, 10, NIV.

By what illustrations did Christ teach contentment?

"Then Jesus said to his disciples: 'Therefore I tell you, do not worry about your life, what you will eat; or about your body, what you will wear. Life is more than food, and the body more than clothes. *Consider the ravens:* They do not sow or reap, they have no storeroom or barn; yet God feeds them. And how much more valuable you are than birds! Who of you by worrying can add a single hour to his life? Since you cannot do this very little thing, why do you worry about the rest? *Consider how the lilies grow*. They do not labor or spin. Yet I tell you, not even Solomon in all his splendor was dressed like one of these." Luke 12:22-28, NIV.

What lesson in contentment did Paul say he had learned?

"I have learned to be content whatever the circumstances." Philippians 4:11, NIV.

What ancient promise should lead to contentment?

"As long as the earth endures, seedtime and harvest, cold and heat, summer and winter, day and night will never cease." Genesis 8:22, NIV.

Why should we give our cares to God?

"Cast all your anxiety on him *because he cares for you*." 1 Peter 5:7, NIV.

CHEERFULNESS AND CHRISTIAN COURTESY

What encouraging message did Jesus give to His disciples before leaving them?

"I have told you these things, so that in me you may have peace. In this world you will have trouble. But *take heart! I have overcome the world.*" John 16:33, NIV.

What were some of the cheering words He said to them?

"Do not let your hearts be troubled. Trust in God; trust also in me. In my Father's house are many rooms; if it were not so, I would have told you. *I am going there to prepare a place for you.* And if I go and prepare a place for you, *I will come back and take you to be with me* that you also may be where I am." John 14:1-3, NIV.

In what spirit should we serve the Lord?

"Serve the Lord with *gladness:* come before his presence with singing." Psalm 100:2.

What effect does a cheerful attitude have on our health?

"A cheerful heart is *good medicine,* but a crushed spirit dries up the bones." Proverbs 17:22, NIV.

NOTE.—The mind has a great influence over the body. Cheerfulness is conducive to life and health; sorrow, care, anxiety, and worry tend to disease and death.

What effect do helpful, cheerful words have on us?

"An anxious heart weighs a man down, but *a kind word cheers him up*." Proverbs 12:25, NIV.

By what temporal blessings does God fill our hearts with gladness?

"Yet he has not left himself without testimony: He has shown kindness by giving you *rain from heaven and crops in their seasons;* he provides you with *plenty of food* and fills your hearts with joy." Acts 14:17, NIV.

Why and for what may every child of God rejoice?

"I delight greatly in the Lord; my soul rejoices in my God. For *he has clothed me with garments of salvation and arrayed me in a robe of righteousness,* as a bridegroom adorns his head like a priest, and as a bride adorns herself with her jewels." Isaiah 61:10, NIV.

What lesson about attitude did Paul highlight from the Israelites' wilderness journey?

"And *do not grumble,* as some of them did—and were killed by the destroying angel." 1 Corinthians 10:10, NIV.

What did Jesus tell us to do even when we are persecuted?

"Blessed are you when men hate you, when they exclude you and insult you and reject your name as evil, because of the Son of Man. *Rejoice in that day and leap for joy,* because great is your reward in heaven." Luke 6:22, 23, NIV.

How did the apostles respond when they were beaten for preaching Christ?

"The apostles left the Sanhedrin, *rejoicing* because they had been counted worthy of suffering disgrace for the Name." Acts 5:41, NIV.

What did Paul and Silas, after severe whippings and with their feet chained to stocks, do while in prison?

"About midnight Paul and Silas were *praying and singing hymns to God,* and the other prisoners were listening to them." Acts 16:25, NIV.

What encouragement does Paul give us in the face of life's hardships?

"And we know that in all things *God works for the good of those who love him,* who have been called according to his purpose." Romans 8:28, NIV.

What attitude should we always keep in our hearts?

"*Rejoice in the Lord always.* I will say it again: Rejoice!" Philippians 4:4, NIV.

How should Christians relate to each other?

"Finally, all of you, *live in harmony with one another;* be sympathetic, love as brothers, be compassionate and humble." 1 Peter 3:8, NIV.

Who deserves our respect?

"Show proper respect to *everyone:* Love the brotherhood of believers, fear God, honor the king." 1 Peter 2:17, NIV.

Whom should we be friendly with?

"And if you greet only your brothers, what are you doing more than others? Do not even pagans do that?" Matthew 5:47, NIV.

What respect should we show the aged?

"*Rise* in the presence of the aged, show respect for the elderly and revere your God. I am the Lord." Leviticus 19:32, NIV. (See 2 Kings 2:23, 24.)

Whom especially should children honor?

"Honor your *father* and your *mother.*" Exodus 20:12, NKJV.

How should faithful gospel ministers be regarded?

"The elders who direct the affairs of the church well are *worthy of double honor,* especially those whose work is preaching and teaching." 1 Timothy 5:17, NIV.

What is the basis of true Christian courtesy?

"*Love* is patient, love is kind. It does not envy, it does not boast, it is not proud. It is not rude, it is not self-seeking, it is not easily angered, it keeps no record of wrongs." 1 Corinthians 13:4, 5, NIV.

NOTE.—Genuine Christian courtesy is the outgrowth of love, and manifests itself in thoughtful consideration for others.

CONFESSING FAULTS AND FORGIVING ONE ANOTHER

What has God promised to do when we confess our sins?

"If we confess our sings, *he is faithful and just and will forgive us our sins* and purify us from all unrighteousness." 1 John 1:9, NIV.

How is it that our sins can be forgiven?

"If anybody does sin, we have one who speaks to the Father in our defense—Jesus Christ, the Righteous One. *He is the atoning sacrifice for our sins,* and not only for ours but also for the sins of the whole world." 1 John 2:1, 2, NIV.

When we do wrong, what is the natural thing for us to do?

Excuse it, seek to hide it, or blame someone else for it. (See Genesis 3:12-14; 4:9.)

After David's adultery and murder had been pointed out to him, what did he say?

"I have sinned against the Lord." 2 Samuel 12:13, NIV. "I know my transgressions." Psalm 51:3, NIV.

Is it ever right to tell someone of their faults?

"Do not hate your brother in your heart. *Rebuke your neighbor frankly* so you will not share in his guilt." Leviticus 19:17, NIV.

How should we relate to those who wrong us?

"*Do not seek revenge or bear a grudge* against one of your people, but *love your neighbor as yourself.*" Verse 18, NIV.

What guidelines should we follow when sinned against?

"If your brother sins against you, go and show him his fault, just between the two of you. If he listens to you, you have won your brother over. But if he will not listen, take one or two others along, so that 'every matter may be established by the testimony of two or three witnesses.' If he refuses to listen to them, tell it to the church; and if he refuses to listen even to the church, treat him as you would a pagan or a tax collector." Matthew 18:15-17, NIV.

NOTE.—Jesus says that if we are unable to reconcile with those who have sinned against us, we should treat them "as you would a pagan or a tax collector." What example did Jesus give in His treatment of pagans and tax collectors? With grace and love He worked to win their hearts.

"Confess your sins to God, who only can forgive them, and your faults to one another. If you have given offense to your friend or neighbor you are to acknowledge your wrong, and it is his duty freely to forgive you. Then you are to seek the forgiveness of God because the brother whom you have wounded is the property of God, and in injuring him you sinned against his Creator and Redeemer." Ellen G. White, *Testimonies for the Church,* vol. 5, p. 639.

To confess one's faults is not an easy thing to do; in fact, it is one of the hardest lessons to learn, for it requires the grace of humility as well as that of sorrow and true repentance. It has been said that the four hardest words to pronounce in the English language are, "I made a mistake."

The confession should be not only complete, but as broad and as public as was the offense. Private offenses should be confessed in private.

In what spirit should this kind of work be done?

"Brothers, if someone is caught in a sin, *you who are spiritual should restore him gently.* But watch yourselves, or you also may be tempted." Galatians 6:1, NIV.

NOTE.—It is much easier to tell *someone else* of a person's faults than it is to tell *that person* of them; but this is not the Christian way to proceed. The first efforts should be made with the offender *in person* and *alone.* But it is easier even to tell people of *their* faults than it is to confess *our own.* This is a hard lesson to learn, the one Christian duty difficult to perform. Only humility and the grace of God will enable one to do it.

How does our attitude of resentment or forgiveness affect our prayer life?

"And when you stand praying, if you hold anything against anyone, *forgive him, so that your Father in heaven may forgive you your sins.*" Mark 11:25, NIV.

If we do not forgive others, what will God not do?

"But *if you do not forgive, neither will your Father* who is in heaven *forgive your sins.*" Verse 26, NIV. (See, for illustration, Christ's parable recorded in Matthew 18:23-35.)

What words of Joseph to his brothers show that he forgave them for selling him into slavery?

"And now, *do not be distressed and do not be angry with yourselves for selling me here,* because it was to save lives that God sent me ahead of you. . . . But *God sent me ahead of you to preserve for you a remnant on earth* and to save your lives by a great deliverance." Genesis 45:5-8, NIV.

What was Jesus' reply to Peter's question of how forgiving we should be?

"Then Peter came to [Jesus] and said, 'Lord, how often shall my brother sin against me and I forgive him? Up to seven times?' Jesus said to him, *I do not say to you, up to seven times, but seventy times seven.*' " Matthew 18:21, 22, NKJV.

NOTE.—That is, an unlimited number. We must forgive offenses against us though ever so often done; we must forgive to the end.

What spirit did Jesus manifest toward those who nailed Him to the cross?

"Jesus said, '*Father, forgive them,* for they do not know what they are doing.' " Luke 23:34, NIV.

How did Stephen manifest the same spirit toward those who stoned him?

"While they were stoning him, Stephen prayed, 'Lord Jesus, receive my spirit.' Then he fell on his knees and cried out, 'Lord, do not hold this sin against them.' When he had said this, he fell asleep." Acts 7:59, 60, NIV. (See also 1 Peter 4:8.)

THE DUTY OF ENCOURAGEMENT

When 10 explorers brought back a despairing report on the land of Canaan, what did Caleb say?

"Then Caleb silenced the people before Moses and said, '*We should go up and take possession of the land, for we can certainly do it.*' " Numbers 13:30, NIV.

What did the 10 explorers say?

"But the men who had gone up with him said, '*We can't attack those people; they are stronger than we are.*' " Verse 31, NIV.

What effect did this report have upon the people?

"That night *all the people* of the community *raised their voices and wept aloud.* All the Israelites grumbled against Moses and Aaron, and the whole assembly said to them, 'If only we had died in Egypt! Or in this desert! Why is the Lord bringing us to this land only to let us fall by the sword? Our wives and children will be taken as plunder. Wouldn't it be better for us to go back to Egypt?' And they said to each other, '*We should choose a leader and go back to Egypt.*' " Numbers 14:1-4, NIV.

With what words did Moses encourage Joshua as Joshua prepared to take over leadership?

"Then Moses summoned Joshua and said to him in the presence of all Israel, '*Be strong and courageous . . . The Lord himself goes before* you and will be with you; he will never leave you nor forsake you. Do not be afraid; do not be discouraged.'" Deuteronomy 31:7, 8, NIV.

In his final charge to Joshua, what did Moses, speaking for God, say to him?

"The Lord gave this command to Joshua son of Nun: '*Be strong and courageous,* for you will bring the Israelites into the land I promised them on oath, and I myself will be with you.'" Verse 23, NIV.

After Moses' death, how did God encourage Joshua?

"The Lord said to Joshua, son of Nun, Moses' aide: . . . 'No one will be able to stand against you all the days of your life. As I was with Moses, so I will be with you; I will never leave you nor forsake you. *Be strong and courageous,* because you will lead these people to inherit the land I swore to their forefathers to give them.'" Joshua 1:1-6, NIV.

When Sennacherib, king of Assyria, came against Jerusalem, what did King Hezekiah say to Israel?

"*Be strong and courageous. Do not be afraid or discouraged* because of the king of Assyria and the vast army with him, for there is a greater power with us than with him. With him is only the arm of flesh, but with us is the Lord our God to help us and to fight our battles." 2 Chronicles 32:7, 8, NIV.

What effect did these words have upon the people?

"*And the people gained confidence* from what Hezekiah king of Judah said." Verse 8, NIV.

How did King Josiah seek to promote the worship of God?

"He *appointed the priests to their duties and encouraged them* in the service of the Lord's temple." 2 Chronicles 35:2, NIV.

By what message, through the prophet Haggai, did God seek to encourage the people to rebuild the Temple?

"'But now be strong, O Zerubbabel,' declares the Lord. 'Be strong, O Joshua son of Jehozadak, the high priest. Be strong, all you people of the land,' declares the Lord, 'and work. For I am with you,' declares the Lord Almighty. 'This is what I covenanted with you when you came out of Egypt. And my Spirit remains among you. Do not fear.' " Haggai 2:4, 5, NIV.

What encouraging message has Jesus left us?

"But take heart! *I have overcome the world.*" John 16:33, NIV.

UNITY OF BELIEVERS

What relation do the Father and the Son sustain to each other?

"I and my Father are one." John 10:30.

In what does this oneness consist?

"By myself I can do nothing; I judge only as I hear, and my judgment is just, for *I seek not to please myself but him who sent me.*" John 5:30, NIV.

NOTE.—Their oneness, therefore, consists in their having the same nature, mind, will, and purpose.

What did Jesus pray the Father in behalf of His disciples?

"*That they may be one,* even as we are one." John 17:22. (See also verses 11 and 23.)

Why did Jesus desire this oneness, or unity, to exist among His followers?

"My prayer is not for them alone. I pray also for those who will believe in me through their message, that all of them may be one Father, just as you are in me and I am in you. May they also be in us *so that the world may believe that you have sent me.*" Verses 20, 21, NIV.

How will the world recognize us as Jesus' followers?

"By this all men will know that you are my disciples, *if you love one another.*" John 13:35, NIV.

NOTE.—"God has united believers in church capacity in order that one may strengthen another in good and righteous endeavor. The church on earth would indeed be a symbol of the church in heaven if the members were of one mind and of one faith. It is those who are not moved by the Holy Spirit that mar God's plan. Another spirit takes possession of them, and they help to strengthen the forces of darkness. Those who are sanctified by the precious blood of Christ will not become the means of counterworking the great plan which God has devised. They will not bring human depravity into things small

or great. They will do nothing to perpetuate division in the church."
Ellen G, White, *Testimonies for the Church,* vol. 6, pp. 238, 239.

When there is disunion among believers, the world concludes that
they cannot be the people of God, because they are working against
one another. When believers are one with Christ, they will be united
among themselves.

How did Paul show his concern in this matter?

"*I appeal to you,* brothers, in the name of our Lord Jesus Christ,
*that all of you agree with one another so that there may be no divi-
sions among you* and that you may be perfectly united in mind and
thought." 1 Corinthians 1:10, NIV.

What was a prominent cause of division in the early church?

"I know that after I leave, savage wolves will come in among you
and will not spare the flock. *Even from your own number men will
arise and distort the truth* in order to draw away disciples after them."
Acts 20:29, 30, NIV.

What was already at work in the church in Paul's day?

"For *the secret power of lawlessness* is already at work; but the
one who now holds it back will continue to do so till he is taken out
of the way." 2 Thessalonians 2:7, NIV.

Before Christ should come, what did Paul say was to take place?

"Don't let anyone deceive you in any way, for that day will not
come until *the rebellion occurs and the man of lawlessness is revealed,* the man doomed to destruction. He will oppose and will exalt
himself over everything that is called God or is worshiped, so that he
sets himself up in God's temple, proclaiming himself to be God."
Verses 3, 4, NIV.

Together, what do believers in Christ form?

"Now you are *the body of Christ,* and each one of you is a part of
it." 1 Corinthians 12:27, NIV.

What else do we, being members of Christ's body, belong to?

"So in Christ we who are many form one body, and each member
belongs to all the others." Romans 12:5, NIV.

NOTE.—In Christ we are united in one group, and are thus caretakers and supporters of each other.

As members of one another, what is the duty of each?

"So that there should be no division in the body, but that its parts should have equal *concern for each other.* If one part suffers, every part suffers with it; if one part is honored, every part rejoices with it." 1 Corinthians 12:25, 26, NIV.

What should they endeavor to keep?

"As a prisoner for the Lord, then, I urge you to live a life worthy of the calling you have received. Be completely humble and gentle; be patient, bearing with one another in love. *Make every effort to keep the unity of the Spirit through the bond of peace.*" Ephesians 4:1-3, NIV.

What unity of faith is finally to exist among God's watchmen?

"Listen! Your watchmen lift up their voices; *together they shout for joy.* When the Lord returns to Zion, they will see it with their own eyes." Isaiah 52:8, NIV.

What solemn message, just before the Lord's coming, will unite God's people?

" ' Fear God and give him glory, because the hour of his judgment has come. Worship him who made the heavens, the earth, the sea and the springs of water.' . . . 'Fallen! Fallen is Babylon the Great, which made all the nations drink the maddening wine of her adulteries.' . . . 'If anyone worships the beast and his image and receives his mark on the forehead or on the hand, he, too, will drink of the wine of God's fury, which has been poured full strength into the cup of his wrath.' " Revelation 14:7-10, NIV. (See Revelation 18:1-5.)

How are those who receive this message described?

"This calls for patient endurance on the part of *the saints who obey God's commandments and remain faithful to Jesus.*" Verse 12, NIV.

When the Lord comes, what will be the united cry of God's people?

"In that day they will say, '*Surely this is our God; we trusted in him, and he saved us.* This is the Lord, we trusted in him; let us rejoice and be glad in his salvation.' " Isaiah 25:9, NIV.

MEEKNESS AND HUMILITY

What promise is made to the meek?

"Blessed are the meek: for *they shall inherit the earth.*" Matthew 5:5.

NOTE.—Meek: The Greek word thus translated means "gentle," "humble," and "considerate."

What did Christ say of His own character?

"Come to me, all you who are weary and burdened, and I will give you rest. Take my yoke upon you and learn from me, for *I am gentle and humble in heart,* and you will find rest for your souls. For my yoke is easy and my burden is light." Matthew 11:28-30, NIV.

Of what is meekness a fruit?

"But the fruit *of the Spirit* is love, joy, peace, patience, kindness, goodness, faithfulness, gentleness and self-control." Galatians 5:22, 23, NIV.

With whom does God dwell?

"For this is what the high and lofty One says—he who lives forever, whose name is holy: 'I live in a high and holy place, but also *with him who is contrite and lowly in spirit,* to revive the spirit of the lowly and to revive the heart of the contrite.'" Isaiah 57:15, NIV.

How does Jesus dwell in our hearts?

"I pray that out of his glorious riches he may strengthen you with power through his Spirit in your inner being, so that Christ may dwell in your hearts *through faith.* And I pray that you, being rooted and established in love, may have power, together with all the saints, to grasp how wide and long and high and deep is the love of Christ, and to know this love that surpasses knowledge—that you may be filled to the measure of all the fullness of God." Ephesians 3:16-19, NIV.

Whom will God guide in righteousness?

"Good and upright is the Lord; therefore he instructs *sinners* in his ways. He guides *the humble* in what is right and teaches them his way." Psalm 25:8, 9, NIV.

What does Jesus say about those who exalt themselves?

"For *everyone who exalts himself will be humbled,* and he who humbles himself will be exalted." Luke 14:11, NIV.

NOTE.—The spirit of self-exaltation is of Satan. (See Isaiah 14:12-14; Ezekiel 28:17.) Christ humbled Himself, made Himself lowly, and became obedient even to the death on the cross. (See Philippians 2:5-8.)

How did Jesus illustrate true humility?

"He called a little child and had him stand among them. And he said: 'I tell you the truth, unless you change and become like little children, you will never enter the kingdom of heaven. Therefore, *whoever humbles himself like this child is the greatest in the kingdom of heaven.'*" Matthew 18:2-4, NIV.

NOTE.—Humility is "freedom from pride and arrogance; lowliness of mind; a modest estimate of one's own worth." It implies a sense of one's own unworthiness through imperfection and sinfulness, and consists in rating our *claims* low, in being willing to *waive our rights,* and to *take a lower place than might be our due.* It does not require that we underrate ourselves or our lifework. The humility of Christ was perfect, yet He had a true sense of the importance of His life and mission.

How will humility lead us to esteem others?

"Do nothing out of selfish ambition or vain conceit, but *in humility consider others better than yourselves.*" Philippians 2:3, NIV.

When we are asked a reason for our hope, in what spirit should we answer?

"But in your hearts set apart Christ as Lord. Always be prepared to give an answer to everyone who asks you to give the reason for the hope that you have. But do this *with gentleness and respect,* keeping a clear conscience, so that those who speak maliciously against your good behavior in Christ may be ashamed of their slander." 1 Peter 3:15, 16, NIV.

Who should labor for one caught in a sin, and in what spirit?

"Brothers, if someone is caught in a sin, you who are spiritual should restore him gently. But watch yourself, or you may also be tempted." Galatians 6:1, NIV.

What is more important to God—our outside appearance or our inner character?

"Your beauty should not come from outward adornment, such as braided hair and the wearing of gold jewelry and fine clothes. Instead, it should be that of your inner self, the *unfading beauty of a gentle and quiet spirit,* which is of great worth in God's sight." 1 Peter 3:3, 4, NIV.

What are the meek urged to seek?

"Seek the Lord, all you humble of the land, you who do what he commands. *Seek righteousness, seek humility."* Zephaniah 2:3, NIV.

NOTE.—Sanctification, the development of a godly character, is a progressive work.

Why are we exhorted to humble ourselves?

"All of you, clothe yourselves with humility toward one another, because, 'God opposes the proud but gives grace to the humble.' *Humble yourselves,* therefore, under God's mighty hand, *that he may lift you up in due time.* Cast all your anxiety on him because he cares for you." 1 Peter 5:5-7, NIV.

NOTE.—Peter is here quoting Proverbs 3:34.

"The higher a man is in grace, the lower he will be in his own esteem." Charles Spurgeon.

With what will the Lord crown the humble?

"For the Lord takes delight in his people; *he crowns the humble with salvation."* Psalm 149:4, NIV.

What inheritance is promised the meek?

"A little while, and the wicked will be no more; though you look for them, they will not be found. But *the meek will inherit the land and enjoy great peace."* Psalm 37:10, 11, NIV.

DIGNITY AND SELF-CONTROL

To what extent did Solomon test the pleasures of this world?

"I thought in my heart, 'Come now, I will test you with pleasure to find out what is good.' But that also proved to be meaningless. 'Laughter,' I said, 'is foolish. And what does pleasure accomplish?' I tried cheering myself with wine, and embracing folly—my mind still guiding me with wisdom. I wanted to see what was worthwhile for men to do under heaven during the few days of their lives. I undertook great projects: I built houses for myself and planted vineyards. I made gardens and parks and planted all kinds of fruit trees in them. I made reservoirs to water groves of flourishing trees. I bought male and female slaves and had other slaves who were born in my house. I also owned more herds and flocks than anyone in Jerusalem before me. I amassed silver and gold for myself, and the treasure of kings and provinces. I acquired men and women singers, and a harem as well—the delights of the heart of man. I became greater by far than anyone in Jerusalem before me. In all this my wisdom stayed with me. I denied myself nothing my eyes desired; *I refused my heart no pleasure.* My heart took delight in all my work, and this was the reward for all my labor." Ecclesiastes 2:1-10, NIV.

How much true enjoyment did such a course provide Solomon?

"Yet when I surveyed all that my hands had done and what I had toiled to achieve, *everything was meaningless, a chasing after the wind;* nothing was gained under the sun." Verse 11, NIV.

What does Solomon exhort young people to keep in mind?

"Be happy, young man, while you are young; and let your heart give you joy in the days of your youth. Follow the ways of your heart and whatever your eyes see, *but know that for all these things God will bring you to judgment.*" Ecclesiastes 11:9, NIV.

How does the grace of God teach us that we should live?

"For the grace of God that brings salvation has appeared to all men. It teaches us to say 'No' to ungodliness and worldly passions, and to *live self-controlled, upright and godly lives in this present age.*" Titus 2:11, 12, NIV.

How are we to learn self-control?

"*Teach the older men* to be temperate, worthy of respect, self-controlled, and sound in faith, in love and in endurance. *Likewise, teach the older women* to be reverent in the way they live, not to be slanderers or addicted to much wine, but to teach what is good. *Then they can train the younger women* to love their husbands and children, to be self-controlled and pure, to be busy at home, to be kind, and to be subject to their husbands, so that no one will malign the word of God. *Similarly, encourage the young men* to be self-controlled." Verses 2-6, NIV.

What similar advice is given in the Epistle to the Romans?

"*Let us behave decently,* as in the daytime, not in orgies and drunkenness, not in sexual immorality and debauchery, not in dissension and jealousy." Romans 13:13, NIV.

What should characterize a Christian's speech?

"Nor should there be obscenity, foolish talk or coarse joking, which are out of place, but rather *thanksgiving.*" Ephesians 5:4, NIV.

Why are self-control and vigilance especially necessary?

"Be self-controlled and alert. *Your enemy the devil prowls around like a roaring lion looking for someone to devour.*" 1 Peter 5:8, NIV.

How should we prepare for the last days?

"Therefore, *prepare your minds for action; be self-controlled; set your hope fully on the grace to be given you when Jesus Christ is revealed.* As obedient children, do not conform to the evil desires you had when you lived in ignorance. But just as he who called you is holy, so be holy in all you do; for it is written: 'Be holy, because I am holy.' " 1 Peter 1:13-16, NIV.

"The end of all things is near. Therefore be *clear minded and self-controlled* so that you can pray." 1 Peter 4:7, NIV.

TRUE WISDOM

Why are we told to seek wisdom?

"Wisdom is supreme; therefore get wisdom. Though it cost all you have, get understanding." Proverbs 4:7, NIV.

NOTE.—Wisdom implies the ability to judge soundly and deal sagaciously. It is knowledge, with the capacity to make due use of it. One may have an abundance of *knowledge* yet possess little *wisdom.*

Of how much value is wisdom?

"She is more precious than rubies; nothing you desire can compare with her." Proverbs 3:15, NIV.

Who gives wisdom?

"For *the Lord* gives wisdom, and from his mouth come knowledge and understanding." Proverbs 2:6, NIV.

How may it be obtained?

"If any of you lacks wisdom, he should *ask God,* who gives generously to all without finding fault, and it will be given to him." James 1:5, NIV.

When Solomon became king, what did he ask the Lord to give him?

"Give me *wisdom* and *knowledge,* that I may lead this people." 2 Chronicles 1:10, NIV. (See also 1 Kings 3:9.)

How did the Lord regard this request?

"The Lord was *pleased* that Solomon had asked for this." 1 Kings 3:10, NIV.

How was Solomon's prayer answered?

"So God said to him, 'Since you have asked for this and not for long life or wealth for yourself, nor have you asked for the death of your enemies but for discernment in administering justice, *I will do what you have asked. I will give you a wise and discerning heart,* so that there will never have been anyone like you, nor will there ever be. *Moreover, I will give you what you have not asked for—both riches and honor*—so that in your lifetime you will have no equal among kings." Verses 11-13, NIV.

What is the beginning of wisdom?

"*The fear of the Lord* is the beginning of wisdom; all who follow his precepts have good understanding. To him belongs eternal praise." Psalm 111:10, NIV.

How did King David become wiser than his enemies?

"*You, through commandments,* make me wiser than my enemies; for they are ever with me." Psalm 119:98, NKJV.

Why did his understanding exceed that of his teachers?

"I have more insight than all my teachers, for *I meditate on your statutes.*" Verse 99, NIV.

What blessings follow the attainment of wisdom?

"Esteem her, and *she will exalt you;* embrace her, and *she will honor you.* She will set a garland of grace on your head and present you with a crown of splendor." Proverbs 4:8, 9, NIV.

How does wisdom affect our attitude?

"Who is like the wise man? Who knows the explanation of things? *Wisdom brightens a man's face and changes its hard appearance.*" Ecclesiastes 8:1, NIV.

In what did Christ say the children of this world excel the children of light?

"For the children of this world are in their generation wiser than the children of light." Luke 16:8.

NOTE.—That is, they show more prudence, more cunning, and more intelligence about their business than do Christians concerning the things of God's kingdom. "They show more skill, study more plans, contrive more ways, to provide for themselves than the children of light do to promote the interests of religion." Albert Barnes.

What advice did Paul give about our relationship to the world?

"I want you to be wise about what is good, and innocent about what is evil." Romans 16:19, NIV.

How many kinds of wisdom are there?

"We do, however, speak *a message of wisdom among the mature,* but not the wisdom of this age or of the rulers of this age, who are coming to nothing. No, we speak of *God's secret wisdom, a wisdom that has been hidden and that God destined for our glory* before time began." 1 Corinthians 2:6, 7, NIV.

How does God regard the world's wisdom?

"For the wisdom of this world is *foolishness* in God's sight." 1 Corinthians 3:19, NIV.

What is the character of that wisdom which comes from God?

"But the wisdom that comes from heaven is first of all *pure;* then *peace-loving, considerate, submissive, full of mercy and good fruit, impartial and sincere.*" James 3:17, NIV.

What wisdom are the Scriptures able to give?

"From infancy you have known the holy Scriptures, which are able to make you *wise for salvation* through faith in Christ Jesus." 2 Timothy 3:15, NIV.

DILIGENCE IN LABOR

What general command has God given concerning labor?

"Six days you shall labor and do all your work." Exodus 20:9, NKJV.

Instead of living off the earnings of others, what instruction is given?

"*He* who has been stealing must steal no longer, but *must work, doing something useful with his own hands,* that he may have something to share with those in need." Ephesians 4:28, NIV.

What general rule does Paul lay down upon this subject?

"For even when we were with you, we gave you this rule: '*If a man will not work, he shall not eat.*'" 2 Thessalonians 3:10, NIV.

In what language does he condemn idleness?

"We hear that some among you are idle. They are not busy; they are busybodies. *Such people we command and urge in the Lord Jesus Christ to settle down and earn the bread they eat.*" Verses 11, 12, NIV.

What example did Paul himself set in this matter?

"We were not idle when we were with you, nor did we eat anyone's food without paying for it. On the contrary, *we worked day and night, laboring and toiling so that we would not be a burden* to any of you. We did this, not because we do not have the right to such help, but in order to make ourselves a model for you to follow." Verses 7-9, NIV.

What labor was appointed man in consequence of the Fall?

"By the sweat of your brow you will eat your food." Genesis 3:19, NIV.

NOTE.—A life of laborious and perpetual toil, in a world cursed with weeds, thorns, and thistles, was appointed to us in consequence of the entrance of sin. This was a part of the curse. And yet even this was appointed in love, and, under existing circumstances, is a blessing in disguise.

What are some of the results of industry?

"*He who works his land will have abundant food,* but the one who chases fantasies will have his fill of poverty." Proverbs 28:19, NIV. "Lazy hands make a man poor, but *diligent hands bring wealth.*" Proverbs 10:4, NIV. "The sluggard craves and gets nothing, but *the desires of the diligent are fully satisfied.*" Proverbs 13:4, NIV.

What does Solomon say concerning diligence in business?

"*Whatever your hand finds to do, do it with all your might.*" Ecclesiastes 9:10, NIV. "Be sure to know the condition of your flocks, *give careful attention to your herds.*" Proverbs 27:23, NIV. "*He who gathers crops in summer is a wise son,* but he who sleeps during harvest is a disgraceful son." Proverbs 10:5, NIV.

What does Solomon say of the industrious woman?

"*She watches over the affairs of her household and does not eat the bread of idleness.* Her children arise and call her blessed; her husband also, and he praises her." Proverbs 31:27, 28, NIV.

What results from slackness and indolence in business?

"*Lazy hands make a man poor,* but diligent hands bring wealth." Proverbs 10:4, NIV. "*The sluggard craves and gets nothing,* but the desires of the diligent are fully satisfied." Proverbs 13:4, NIV.

How does Solomon describe the slothful?

"I went past the field of the sluggard, past the vineyard of the man who lacks judgment; thorns had come up everywhere, the ground was covered with weeds, and the stone wall was in ruins." Proverbs 24:30, 31, NIV.

What has Paul said of the professed Christian who does not provide for his own family?

"If anyone does not provide for his relatives, and especially for his immediate family, *he has denied the faith and is worse than an unbeliever.*" 1 Timothy 5:8, NIV.

In spiritual matters, what is also necessary?

"But also for this very reason, *giving all diligence,* add to your faith virtue, to virtue knowledge, to knowledge, self-control, to self-control perseverance, to perseverance godliness, to godliness brotherly kindness, and to brotherly kindness love. For if these things are yours and abound, you will be neither barren nor unfruitful in the knowledge of our Lord Jesus Christ. For he who lacks these things is shortsighted, even to blindness, and has forgotten that he was cleansed from his old sins. Therefore, brethren, *be even more diligent* to make your call and election sure." 2 Peter 1:5-10, NKJV.

NOTE.—Lazy people fail to take advantage of life's opportunities, while the industrious seize each one.

PERFECTION OF CHARACTER

Why are we exhorted to patience?

"Perseverance must finish its work *so that you may be mature and complete, not lacking anything.*" James 1:4, NIV.

How should our Christian faith progress?

"Therefore *let us* leave the elementary teachings about Christ and *go on to maturity.*" Hebrews 6:1, NIV.

In what is the Christian to grow?

"But grow in grace, and in the knowledge of our Lord and Saviour Jesus Christ." 2 Peter 3:18.

How may one grow in grace?

"Giving all diligence, *add to your faith virtue; . . . knowledge; . . . temperance; . . . patience; . . . godliness; . . . brotherly kindness; . . . charity.*" 2 Peter 1:5-7.

Why does Christ desire this growth in His followers?

"Christ loved the church and gave himself up for her to make her holy, cleansing her by the washing with water through the word, and *to present her to himself as a radiant church, without stain or wrinkle or any other blemish, but holy and blameless.*" Ephesians 5:25-27, NIV.

What will cause the Christian to grow?

"Like newborn babies, crave *pure spiritual milk,* so that by it you may grow up in your salvation, now that you have tasted that the Lord is good." 1 Peter 2:2, 3, NIV.

In order to grow by the Word of God, what must one do?

"*I have hidden your word in my heart* that I might not sin against you." Psalm 119:11, NIV.

"*Let the word of Christ dwell in you richly* as you teach and admonish one another with all wisdom, and as you sing psalms, hymns and spiritual songs with gratitude in your hearts to God." Colossians 3:16, NIV.

What does God's Word then become to the believer?

"When your words came, I ate them; they were *my joy and my heart's delight,* for I bear your name." Jeremiah 15:16, NIV.

Why are the Scriptures given?

"All Scripture is God-breathed and is useful for teaching, rebuking, correcting and training in righteousness, *so that the man of God may be thoroughly equipped for every good work.*" 2 Timothy 3:16, 17, NIV.

How may we gain the wisdom we lack?

"If any of you lacks wisdom, he should *ask God,* who gives generously to all without finding fault, and it will be given to him." James 1:5, NIV.

In how many things may we ask help from God?

"Do not be anxious about anything, but *in everything,* by prayer and petition, with thanksgiving, *present your requests to God.*" Philippians 4:6, NIV.

What is an evidence of perfection?

"We all stumble in many ways. *If anyone is never at fault in what he says, he is a perfect man,* able to keep his whole body in check." James 3:2, NIV.

What prescription does Paul give for the Christian life?

"As God's chosen ones, holy and beloved, clothe yourselves with compassion, kindness, humility, meekness, and patience. Bear with one another and, if anyone has a complaint against another, forgive each other; just as the Lord has forgiven you, so you also must forgive. Above all, *clothe yourselves with love,* which binds everything together in perfect harmony. And let the peace of Christ rule in your hearts, to which indeed you were called in the one body. And be thankful. Let the word of Christ dwell in you richly; teach and admonish one another in all wisdom; and with gratitude in your hearts sing psalms, hymns, and spiritual songs to God. And whatever you do, in word or deed, do everything in the name of the Lord Jesus, giving thanks to God the Father through him." Colossians 3:12-17, NRSV. (See Philippians 3:13, 14; Hebrews 12:14.)

How perfect would God have us become?

"May the God of peace himself *sanctify you entirely;* and *may your spirit and soul and body be kept sound and blameless* at the coming of our Lord Jesus Christ." 1 Thessalonians 5:23, NRSV.

SOWING AND REAPING

What does Paul say regarding sowing and reaping?

"Do not be deceived; God is not mocked, for *you reap whatever you sow.*" Galatians 6:7, NRSV.

How is the same truth expressed by Christ?

"Do not judge, and you will not be judged; do not condemn, and you will not be condemned. Forgive, and you will be forgiven; give, and it will be given to you. A good measure, pressed down, shaken together, running over, will be put into your lap; for *the measure you give will be the measure you get back.*" Luke 6:37, 38, NRSV.

How does King David apply the law to the wicked?

"He loved to pronounce a curse—may it come on him; he found no pleasure in blessing—may it be far from him." Psalm 109:17, NIV.

According to what was judgment called upon ancient Babylon?

"Repay her for her deeds; *do to her as she has done.*" Jeremiah 50:29, NIV.

Why did Jesus tell Peter to put away his sword when He was arrested in the garden of Gethsemane?

" ' Put your sword back in its place,' Jesus said to him, '*for all who draw the sword will die by the sword.*' " Matthew 26:52, NIV.

Why was the power represented by the sea beast of Revelation to go into captivity?

"*If anyone is to go into captivity, into captivity he will go.* If anyone is to be killed with the sword, with the sword he will be killed." Revelation 13:10, NIV.

What punishment did God pronounce to ancient Jerusalem when they betrayed the freedom of their Hebrew slaves, enslaving them again?

"Therefore, this is what the Lord says: You have not obeyed me; you have not proclaimed freedom for your fellow countrymen. So I now proclaim 'freedom' for you, declares the Lord— *'freedom' to fall by the sword, plague, and famine.*" Jeremiah 34:17, NIV.

What is to be the punishment of spiritual Babylon?

"*Give back to her as she has given;* pay her back double for what she has done." Revelation 18:6, NIV.

What did David say will come to the persecutor?

"He who digs a hole and scoops it out falls into the pit he has made. The trouble he causes recoils on himself; *his violence comes down on his own head.*" Psalm 7:15, 16, NIV.

"The nations have fallen into the pit they have dug; their feet are caught in the net they have hidden." Psalm 9:15, NIV.

On what condition does Christ say God will forgive us?

"For *if you forgive men when they sin against you,* your heavenly Father will also forgive you. But if you do not forgive men their sins, your Father will not forgive your sins." Matthew 6:14, 15, NIV. (See also Matthew 18:23-35.)

CHAPTER 13

Prayer and Public Worship

THE IMPORTANCE OF MEDITATION AND PRAYER

By what title does David address God in Psalm 65?

"O *you who hear prayer,* to you all men will come." Psalm 65:2, NIV.

NOTE.—"Prayer is the opening of the heart to God as to a friend." Ellen G. White, *Testimonies for the Church*, vol. 4, p. 533. God does not require elegant language but sincerity of heart. Just tell God honestly what you are thinking.

Of whom does the Bible teach that God is a rewarder?

"He rewards *those who earnestly seek him.*" Hebrews 11:6, NIV.

How willing is God to hear and answer prayer?

"If you, then, though you are evil, know how to give good gifts to your children, how much more will your Father in heaven give good gifts to those who ask him!" Matthew 7:11, NIV.

What above all else shows God's willingness to do this?

"*He who did not spare his own Son,* but gave him up for us all—how will he not also, along with him, graciously give us all things?" Romans 8:32, NIV.

Upon what conditions are we promised needed blessings?

"Ask and it will be given to you; seek and you will find; knock and the door will be opened to you. For everyone who asks receives; he who seeks finds; and to him who knocks, the door will be opened." Matthew 7:7, 8, NIV.

NOTE.—Prayer is not the overcoming of God's reluctance; it is the taking hold of God's willingness.

From whom do all good and perfect gifts come?

"Every good and perfect gift is from above, coming down from the *Father of the heavenly lights,* who does not change like shifting shadows." James 1:17, NIV.

If one lacks wisdom, what is he told to do?

"If any of you lacks wisdom, he should *ask God*, who gives generously to all without finding fault, and it will be given to him." Verse 5, NIV.

How must one ask in order to receive?

"But when he asks, *he must believe and not doubt,* because he who doubts is like a wave of the sea, blown and tossed by the wind. That man should not think he will receive anything from the Lord; he is a double-minded man, unstable in all he does." Verses 6-8, NIV. (See Mark 11:24.)

Under what condition does the Lord not hear prayer?

"*If I had cherished sin in my heart,* the Lord would not have listened, but God has surely listened and heard my voice in prayer. Praise be to God, who has not rejected my prayer or withheld his love from me!" Psalm 66:18-20, NIV. (See Isaiah 59:1, 2; James 4:3.)

NOTE.—All Christians stumble and fall from time to time. These sins, confessed, do not shut us out from God. This text is speaking of cherished sin.

What actions and attitudes separate us from God's blessings?

"*If anyone turns a deaf ear to the law,* even his prayers are detestable." Proverbs 28:9, NIV.

"What causes fights and quarrels among you? Don't they come from your desires that battle within you? You want something but don't get it. You kill and covet, but you cannot have what you want. You quarrel and fight. You do not have, because you do not ask God. When you ask, you do not receive, because you ask with wrong motives, that you may spend what you get on your pleasures." James 4:1-3, NIV.

NOTE.—Sin creates a barrier between God and humanity. Isaiah wrote, "Surely the arm of the Lord is not too short to save, nor his ear too dull to hear. But your iniquities have separated you from your God; your sins have hidden his face from you, so that he will not hear." Isaiah 59:1, 2, NIV.

How can marital strife hinder one's prayer life?

"Husbands, in the same way be considerate as you live with your wives, and treat them with respect as the weaker partner and as heirs with you of the gracious gift of life, *so that nothing will hinder your prayers.*" 1 Peter 3:7, NIV.

Should we pray only for people we love?

"But I tell you: Love your enemies and pray for those who persecute you." Matthew 5:44, NIV.

NOTE.—We cannot hate those for whom we pray sincerely.

When we are praying, what must we do in order to be forgiven?

"And when you stand praying, *if you hold anything against anyone, forgive him,* so that your Father in heaven may forgive you your sins." Mark 11:25, NIV.

What did Jesus say concerning secret prayer?

"But when you pray, *go into your room, close the door and pray to your Father, who is unseen.* Then your Father, who sees what is done in secret, will reward you." Matthew 6:6, NIV.

To what place did Jesus retire for private devotion?

"After he had dismissed them, he went up *on a mountainside* by himself to pray." Matthew 14:23, NIV.

With what should our prayers be blended?

"Do not be anxious about anything, but in everything, by prayer and petition, *with thanksgiving,* present your requests to God." Philippians 4:6, NIV.

How often should we pray?

"And *pray in the Spirit on all occasions* with all kinds of prayers and requests. With this in mind, be alert and always keep on praying for all the saints." Ephesians 6:18, NIV. "*Pray continually.*" 1 Thessalonians 5:17, NIV. "*Every day* I will praise you and extol your name for ever and ever." Psalm 145:2, NIV.

NOTE.—"Pray continually" does not mean to pray without pause; it means "never stop praying." We need not be constantly bowed before God in prayer, but we should ever be in a prayerful frame of mind, even when walking by the way or engaged in the duties of life—ever ready to send up our petitions to heaven for help in time of need.

In whose name did Christ teach us to pray?

"And I will do whatever you ask in *my name.*" John 14:13, NIV. "Until now you have not asked for anything in my name. Ask and you will receive, and your joy will be complete." John 16:24, NIV.

What practice goes along with prayer?

"Let me understand the teaching of your precepts; then I will *meditate* on your wonders." Psalm 119:27, NIV.

NOTE.—Meditation is to the soul what digestion is to the body. It makes personal and practical that which has been seen, heard, or read.

How does Psalm 119 describe meditating on God's word?

"Teach me, O Lord, to follow your decrees; then I will keep them to the end. Give me understanding, and I will keep your law and obey it with all my heart. Direct me in the path of your commands, for there I find delight. Turn my heart toward your statutes and not toward selfish gain. Turn my eyes away from worthless things; preserve my life according to your word. Fulfill your promise to your servant, so that you may be feared. Take away the disgrace I dread, for your laws are good. How I long for your precepts! Preserve my life in your righteousness. . . .

"I will speak of your statutes before kings, and will not be put to shame, for I delight in your commands because I love them. I lift up my hands to your commands, which I love, and I meditate on your decrees. . . .

"Oh, how I love your law! I meditate on it all day long. Your commands make me wiser than my enemies, for they are ever with me. I have more insight than all my teachers, for I meditate on your statutes." Psalm 119:33-99, NIV.

How will such meditation be to one who loves God?

"May my meditation be *pleasing to him,* as I rejoice in the Lord." Psalm 104:34, NIV.

PRAYER AND WATCHFULNESS

How can we prepare ourselves for Jesus' return?

"Be on guard! Be alert! You do not know when that time will come. It's like a man going away: He leaves his house and puts his servants in charge, each with his assigned task, and tells the one at the door to keep watch. Therefore keep watch because you do not know when the owner of the house will come back—whether in the evening, or at midnight, or when the rooster crows, or at dawn. If he comes suddenly, do not let him find you sleeping. What I say to you, I say to everyone: 'Watch!' " Mark 13:33-37, NIV. (See also Luke 21:36.)

How should we maintain our prayer lives?

"The end of all things is near. Therefore *be clear minded and self-controlled* so that you can pray." 1 Peter 4:7, NIV.

NOTE.—We should couple with our prayers a spirit of watchfulness, thus cooperating with God in answering them.

What is one of the petitions of the Lord's Prayer?

"Lead us not into temptation." Matthew 6:13.

How can we escape temptation?

"Watch and pray so that you will not fall into temptation." Matthew 26:41, NIV.

How does Paul describe this necessity?

"Devote yourselves to prayer, *being watchful* and thankful." Colossians 4:2, NIV.

How faithful should we be in this matter?

"And pray in the Spirit on all occasions with all kinds of prayers and requests. With this in mind, be alert and always keep on praying for all the saints." Ephesians 6:18, NIV.

How should we keep watch for Jesus' return?

"Therefore keep watch, because you do not know on what day your Lord will come. But understand this: If the owner of the house had known at what time of night the thief was coming, he would have kept watch and would not have let his house be broken into. So you also must be ready, because the Son of Man will come at an hour when you do not expect him." Matthew 24:42-44, NIV.

What is promised those who wait upon the Lord?

"Even youths grow tired and weary, and young men stumble and fall; but *those who hope in the Lord will renew their strength. They will soar on wings like eagles; they will run and not grow weary, they will walk and not be faint."* Isaiah 40:30, 31, NIV.

What did Habakkuk say he would watch for?

"I will stand at my watch and station myself on the ramparts; I will look *to see what he will say to me."* Habakkuk 2:1, NIV.

NOTE.—Some are concerned that God should hear them when they pray, but are indifferent as to what He says in reply.

How may we escape the evils coming on the world?

"Be always on the watch, and pray that you may be able to escape all that is about to happen, and that you may be able to stand before the Son of Man." Luke 21:36, NIV.

NOTE.—Vigilance, as well as prayer, is necessary if we would escape the evils, deceptions, and calamities of the last days.

What will be the result of not watching?

"But suppose the servant says to himself, 'My master is taking a long time in coming,' and he then begins to beat the menservants and maidservants and to eat and drink and get drunk. *The master of that servant will come on a day when he does not expect him and at an hour he is not aware of. He will cut him to pieces and assign him a place with the unbelievers.*" Luke 12:45, 46, NIV.

What will Christ's servants be doing when He comes?

"Be dressed ready for service and keep your lamps burning, like men waiting for their master to return from a wedding banquet, so that when he comes and knocks they can immediately open the door for him. It will be good for those servants whose master finds them *watching* when he comes." Verses 35-37, NIV.

ANSWERS TO PRAYER

How does God anticipate the needs of His children?

"*Before they call I will answer;* while they are still speaking I will hear." Isaiah 65:24, NIV.

Is there any limit to God's ability to help?

"Now to him who is *able to do immeasurably more than all we ask or imagine,* according to his power that is at work within us." Ephesians 3:20, NIV.

How fully has God promised to supply our needs?

"*My God will meet all your needs* according to his glorious riches in Christ Jesus." Philippians 4:19, NIV.

How does the Holy Spirit aid us in prayer?

"In the same way, the Spirit helps us in our weakness. We do not know what we ought to pray for, but the Spirit himself intercedes for us with groans that words cannot express. And he who searches our hearts knows the mind of the Spirit, because the Spirit intercedes for the saints in accordance with God's will." Romans 8:26, 27, NIV.

Does God always see fit to grant our petitions?

"To keep me from becoming conceited because of these surpassingly great revelations, there was given me a thorn in my flesh, a messenger of Satan, to torment me. Three times I pleaded with the Lord to take it away from me. But he said to me, 'My grace is sufficient for you, for my power is made perfect in weakness.' Therefore I will boast all the more gladly about my weaknesses, so that Christ's power may rest on me. That is why, for Christ's sake, I delight in weaknesses, in insults, in hardships, in persecutions, in difficulties. For when I am weak, then I am strong." 2 Corinthians 12:8-10, NIV.

NOTE.—Paul's affliction may have been impaired sight (Acts 9:8, 9, 18; 22:11-13). Such an imperfection would be a constant reminder of his conversion, and hence a blessing in disguise.

If an answer does not come at once, what should we do?

"Be still before the Lord and *wait patiently for him.*" Psalm 37:7, NIV.

What is the lesson of the parable of the persistent widow?

"Then Jesus told his disciples a parable *to show them that they should always pray and not give up.*" Luke 18:1, NIV.

NOTE.—The widow got her request because of her persistence. God wants us to seek Him, and to seek Him earnestly, when we pray. He rewards those who *diligently* seek Him (Hebrews 11:6).

How did Elijah pray before obtaining his request?

"Elijah was a man just like us. *He prayed earnestly* that it would not rain, and it did not rain on the land for three and a half years. Again he prayed, and the heavens gave rain, and the earth produced its crops." James 5:17, 18, NIV. (See Revelation 11:3-6.)

Upon what condition does Christ say we shall receive?

"Therefore I tell you, whatever you ask for in prayer, *believe* that you have received it, and it will be yours." Mark 11:24, NIV.

Will God answer prayer without this faith?

"But when he asks, *he must believe and not doubt,* because he who doubts is like a wave of the sea, blown and tossed by the wind. *That man should not think he will receive anything from the Lord.*" James 1:6, 7, NIV.

What petitions may we confidently expect God to hear?

"This is the confidence we have in approaching God: *that if we ask anything according to his will, he hears us.* And if we know that he hears us—whatever we ask—we know that we have what we asked of him." 1 John 5:14, 15, NIV.

NOTE.—God's will is expressed in His law, His promises, and His word (Psalm 40:8; Romans 2:17, 18; 1 Peter 1:4).

When Daniel and his friends were about to be slain because the wise men of Babylon could not reveal to Nebuchadnezzar his dream, how did God answer their united prayers?

"During the night the mystery was revealed to Daniel in a vision. Then Daniel praised the God of heaven." Daniel 2:19, NIV.

NOTE.—God is sovereign over the rulers of this world. (See Daniel 4:17, 24, 25.)

After Peter was arrested, what did the church do for him?

"So Peter was kept in prison, but *the church was earnestly praying to God for him.*" Acts 12:5, NIV.

How were their prayers answered?

"Suddenly an angel of the Lord appeared and a light shone in the cell. He struck Peter on the side and woke him up. 'Quick, get up!' he said, and the chains fell off Peter's wrists. Then the angel said to him, 'Put on your clothes and sandals.' And Peter did so. 'Wrap your cloak around you and follow me,' the angel told him. Peter followed him out of the prison, but he had no idea that what the angel was doing was really happening; he thought he was seeing a vision. They passed the first and second guards and came to the iron gate leading to the city. It opened for them by itself, and they went through it. When they had walked the length of one street, suddenly the angel left him." Verses 7-10, NIV.

After Peter was delivered from prison in answer to prayer, where did he go?

"He went to the house of Mary, the mother of John, also called Mark, where many people had gathered and were praying. . . . When they opened the door and saw him, they were astonished. Peter motioned with his hand for them to be quiet and described how the Lord had brought him out of prison." Acts 12:12-17, NIV.

NOTE.—There is great power in united prayer. God does not always choose to deliver. But in response to prayer He sometimes does that which He would not have otherwise done (see, for example, 2 Kings 20).

Because Solomon asked for wisdom rather than for long life and riches, what did God give him in addition to wisdom?

"Since you have asked for this and not for long life or wealth for yourself, nor have asked for the death of your enemies but for discernment in administering justice, I will do what you have asked. I will give you a wise and discerning heart. . . . Moreover, I will give you what you have not asked for—both riches and honor." 1 Kings 3:11-13, NIV.

NOTE.—The following are some things we are taught in the Scriptures to pray for:

1. For daily bread. Matthew 6:11.

2. For the forgiveness of sin. 2 Chronicles 7:14; Psalm 32:5, 6; 1 John 1:9; 5:16.

3. For the Holy Spirit. Luke 11:13; Zechariah 10:1; John 14:16.

4. For deliverance in the hour of temptation and danger. Matthew 6:13; John 17:11, 15; Proverbs 3:26; Psalm 91; Matthew 24:20.

5. For wisdom and understanding. James 1:5; 1 Kings 3:9; Daniel 2:17-19.

6. For peaceable and quiet lives. 1 Timothy 2:1, 2.

7. For the healing of the sick. James 5:14, 15; 2 Kings 20:1-11.

8. For the prosperity of the ministers of God and the gospel. Ephesians 6:18, 19; Colossians 4:3; 2 Thessalonians 3:1.

9. For those who suffer for the truth's sake. Hebrews 13:3; Acts 12:5.

10. For kings, rulers, and all in authority. 1 Timothy 2:1, 2; Ezra 6:10.

11. For temporal prosperity. 2 Corinthians 9:10; James 5:17, 18.

12. For our enemies. Matthew 5:44.

13. For all saints. Ephesians 6:18.

14. For all persons. 1 Timothy 2:1.

15. For the Lord to vindicate His cause. 1 Kings 18:30-39.

16. For the coming of Christ and of God's kingdom. Matthew 6:10; Revelation 22:20.

THE POWER OF INTERCESSORY PRAYER

How did Abraham intercede with God for the inhabitants of Sodom?

"Then Abraham approached him and said: 'Will you sweep away the righteous with the wicked? What if there are fifty righteous people in the city? Will you really sweep it away and not spare the place for the sake of the fifty righteous people in it? . . . The Lord said, 'If I find fifty righteous people in the city of Sodom, I will spare the whole place for their sake.' " Genesis 18:23-26, NIV.

NOTE.—Abraham continued to press his case, and God finally agreed to spare the city if there were only 10 righteous citizens (see verse 32). However, not even 10 righteous could be found, and God destroyed the city. But first He delivered Abraham's nephew Lot and his family (see Genesis 19:1-29).

What service did Abraham perform for the pagan king Abimelech?

"Now return the man's wife, for he is a prophet, and *he will pray for you and you will live.* But if you do not return her, you may be sure that you and all yours will die." Genesis 20:7, NIV.

What happened when Abraham prayed for Abimelech?

"Then Abraham prayed to God, and God healed Abimilech, his wife and his slave girls so they could have children again." Verse 17, NIV.

Can God still be influenced by intercession today?

"I the Lord do not change." Malachi 3:6, NIV.

Who is God's appointed mediator between God and man?

"For there is one God and one mediator between God and men, the man Christ Jesus." 1 Timothy 2:5, NIV.

NOTE.—This does not mean that our own intercession for others is not needed, because in the same passage Paul urges as a Christian duty that "requests, prayers, intercession and thanksgiving be made for everyone" (verse 1, NIV).

Who else also makes intercession for the saints?

"In the same way, *the Spirit* helps us in our weakness. We do not know what we ought to pray for, but the Spirit himself intercedes for us with groans that words cannot express." Romans 8:26, NIV.

For what class of people do Jesus and the Holy Spirit intercede?

"And he who searches out our hearts knows the mind of the Spirit, because the Spirit intercedes *for the saints* in accordance with God's will." Verse 27, NIV.

"Therefore he is able to save completely *those who come to God through him,* because he always lives to intercede for them." Hebrews 7:25, NIV.

"Who will bring any charge against *those whom God has chosen*? It is God who justifies. Who is he that condemns? Christ Jesus, who died—more than that, who was raised to life—is at the right hand of God and is also interceding for us." Romans 8:33, 34, NIV.

"I am *not praying for the world, but for those you have given me,* for they are yours." John 17:9, NIV.

NOTE.—Scripture assures us that all who seek God through Jesus enjoy the benefits of the merits and mediation of Jesus, and the intercession of the Holy Spirit. No earthly priest or deceased saint is required to speak on their behalf with God. However, there is a class of people who have no relationship with God, and whom Jesus does not know:

How does Jesus contrast those whom He knows with those whom He does not know?

"My sheep listen to my voice; *I know them, and they follow me.*" John 10:27, NIV. "Then I tell them plainly, 'I never knew you. Away from me, *you evildoers!*' " Matthew 7:23, NIV. (See also Matthew 25:12; 12:47-50.)

NOTE.—When a stranger seeks a favor from a benefactor, he needs a go-between to introduce him and to speak on his behalf. In the passages above, Sodom and Abimelech needed someone to intercede for them because they had no relationship with God. Likewise, our loved ones who do not know God, and do not pray for themselves, need someone to pray for them.

How was a king healed by the intercession of a follower of God?

"Then the king said to the man of God, 'Intercede with the Lord your God and pray for me that my hand may be restored.' *So the man of God interceded with the Lord, and the king's hand was restored and became as it was before.*" 1 Kings 13:6, NIV.

What does James say about intercessory prayer?

"The prayer of a righteous man is powerful and effective." James 5:16, NIV.

NOTE.—This does not mean that God hears only the prayers of those who are sinlessly perfect. In the Bible a righteous man is one who honors God, turns from evil, and is generous to others. God is especially interested in upright leaders who will pray for those under their care.

When God threatened to destroy Israel, how did Moses obtain pardon for them?

" ' In accordance with your great love, *forgive the sin of these people,* just as you have pardoned them from the time they left Egypt until now.' The Lord replied, '*I have forgiven them, as you asked.*' " Numbers 14:19, 20, NIV. (See also Numbers 21:7.)

What did Moses later say about this incident in regards to Aaron?

"I feared the anger and wrath of the Lord, for he was angry enough with you to destroy you. But again the Lord listened to me. And *the Lord was angry enough with Aaron to destroy him, but at that time I prayed for Aaron too.*" Deuteronomy 9:19, 20, NIV.

How did Samuel intercede with God for Israel?

"Then Samuel said, 'Assemble all Israel at Mizpah and *I will intercede with the Lord for you.*'" 1 Samuel 7:5, NIV. "The people all said to Samuel, '*Pray to the Lord your God for your servants so that we will not die.*' . . . Samuel replied, . . . 'As for me, *far be it from me that I should sin against the Lord by failing to pray for you.* And I will teach you the way that is good and right.'" 1 Samuel 12:19-23, NIV.

How did Hezekiah obtain forgiveness for those who partook of the Passover while ritually impure?

"Although most of the many people . . . had not purified themselves, yet they ate the Passover, contrary to what was written. But *Hezekiah prayed for them, saying, 'May the Lord, who is good, pardon everyone who sets his heart on seeking God*—the Lord, the God of his Fathers—even if he is not clean according to the rules of the sanctuary.' *And the Lord heard Hezekiah and healed the people.*" 2 Chronicles 30:18-20, NIV.

What happened when Amos prayed that God would forgive Israel?

"This is what the Sovereign Lord showed me: He was preparing swarms of locusts . . . When they had stripped the land clean, I cried out, 'Sovereign Lord, forgive! How can Jacob survive? He is so small!' *So the Lord relented. 'This will not happen,' the Lord said.*" Amos 7:1-3, NIV.

Whose sins did Nehemiah confess when he interceded for his people?

"Let your ear be attentive and your eyes open to hear the prayer your servant is praying before you day and night for your servants, the people of Israel. *I confess the sins we Israelites, including my father and my father's house, have committed against you.*" Nehemiah 1:6, NIV. (See also Daniel 9:4-19.)

What powerful promise is given to intercessors by John?

"This is the confidence we have in approaching God: that *if we ask anything according to his will, he hears us.* And if we know that he hears us—whatever we ask—*we know that we have what we asked of him.*" 1 John 5:14, 15, NIV.

NOTE.—John is talking about praying, not for material blessings, but for the salvation of souls.

How does Paul commend a coworker who was diligent in intercession?

"Epaphras, who is one of you and a servant of Christ Jesus, sends greetings. *He is always wrestling in prayer for you, that you may stand firm in all the will of God, mature and fully assured.*" Colossians 4:12, NIV.

Whom are we fighting against?

"For our struggle is not against flesh and blood, but against *the rulers,* against *the authorities,* against *the powers of this dark world* and against *the spiritual forces of evil in the heavenly realms.*" Ephesians 6:12, NIV.

How therefore should we fight?

"*And pray in the Spirit on all occasions* with all kinds of prayers and requests. With this in mind, be alert and always keep on praying for *all the saints.*" Verse 18, NIV.

NOTE.—God is pleased when we graduate from prayer focused solely on personal benefit to selfless prayers on behalf of others. Intercession is one of the indicators of spiritual maturity.

What power do our weapons have against evil influences?

"The weapons we fight with are not the weapons of the world. On the contrary, they have *divine power to demolish strongholds.*" 2 Corinthians 10:4, NIV.

Knowing the power of intercessory prayer, what does Paul repeatedly ask the churches to do for him?

"Pray for us." 2 Thessalonians 3:1. (Compare Hebrews 13:18.)

INTERCESSORY PRAYER FOR FRIENDS AND CHILDREN

Why did Job's friends require his intercession?

"After the Lord had said these things to Job, he said to Eliphz the Temanite, 'I am angry with you and your two friends, because you have not spoken of me what is right, as my servant Job has. So now take seven bulls and seven rams and go to my servant Job and sacrifice a burnt offering for yourselves. *My servant Job will pray for you, and I will accept his prayer* and not deal with you according to your folly." Job 42:7, 8, NIV.

What was the result of Job's intercession for his three friends?

"So Eliphaz the Temanite, Bildad the Shuhite and Zophar the Naamathite did what the Lord told them, and the Lord accepted Job's prayers. After Job had prayed for his friends, the Lord made him prosperous again and gave him twice as much as he had before." Verses 9, 10, NIV.

Does God ever extend mercy to wayward children for the sake of Godly parents?

"So the Lord said to Solomon, 'Since this is your attitude and you have not kept my covenant and my decrees, which I commanded you, I will most certainly tear the kingdom away from you and give it to one of your subordinates. Nevertheless, *for the sake of David your father,* I will not do it during your lifetime. I will tear it out of the hand of your son. Yet I will not tear the whole kingdom from him, but will give him one tribe for the sake of David my servant.'" 1 Kings 11:11-13, NIV.

"Nevertheless, *for David's sake* the Lord his God gave him a lamp in Jerusalem by raising up a son to succeed him and by making Jerusalem strong." 1 Kings 15:4, NIV.

"Jehoram was thirty-two years old when he became king. . . . He did evil in the eyes of the Lord. Nevertheless, because of the covenant the Lord had made with David, the Lord was not willing to destroy the house of David. He had promised to maintain a lamp for him and his descendants forever." 2 Chronicles 21:5-7, NIV.

"*For the sake of Jacob my servant,* of Israel my chosen, I summon you by name and bestow on you a title of honor, *though you do not acknowledge me.*" Isaiah 45:4, NIV.

What if one's children come under the influence of an unbelieving spouse?

"For the unbelieving husband has been sanctified through his wife, and the unbelieving wife has been sanctified through her believing husband. Otherwise your children would be unclean, but as it is, they are holy." 1 Corinthians 7:14, NIV.

Is there any hope for the children of God's people who are taken captive by the enemy?

"But this is what the Lord says: 'Yes, captives will be taken from warriors, and plunder retrieved from the fierce; I will contend

with those who contend with you, and *your children I will save.'* "
Isaiah 49:25, NIV.

How did Paul agonize over his children in the faith?

"My dear children, for whom I am again in the pains of childbirth
until Christ is formed in you." Galatians 4:19, NIV.

How may we obtain life for our loved ones?

"This is the confidence we have in approaching God: that if we
ask anything according to his will, he hears us. And if we know that
he hears us—whatever we ask—we know that we have what we asked
of him. *If anyone sees his brother commit a sin that does not lead to
death, he should pray and God will give him life.* I refer to those
whose sin does not lead to death. There is a sin that leads to death. I
am not saying that we should pray about that." 1 John 5:14-16, NIV.

What sin cannot be forgiven?

"And so I tell you, every sin and blasphemy will be forgiven men,
but *the blasphemy against the Spirit will not be forgiven.* Anyone who
speaks a word against the Son of Man will be forgiven, but anyone
who speaks against the Holy Spirit will not be forgiven, either in this
age or the age to come." Matthew 12:31, 32, NIV.

NOTE.—By rejecting the workings of God's Spirit we make it
impossible for God to reach us. The Spirit is Jesus' successor on earth
(John 14:16; 15:26; 16:7). Even those who blaspheme Jesus may still
come under the later influence of the Holy Spirit. But if they resist
God's Spirit, what more can He do? There is no fourth member of the
Godhead.

Are there limits to God's forbearance when grievous sin is involved?

"Son of man, if a country sins against me *by being unfaithful* and
I stretch out my hand against it to cut off its food supply and send
famine upon it and kill its men and their animals, *even if these three
men—Noah, Daniel and Job—were in it, they could save only themselves* by their righteousness, declares the Sovereign Lord." Ezekiel
14:13, 20, NIV.

About this same time, what did God forbid Jeremiah to do for rebellious Israel?

"So do not pray for this people nor offer any plea or petition for
them; do not plead with me, for I will not listen to you." Jeremiah
7:16, NIV.

NOTE.—Just prior to the exile, God told Jeremiah that wicked Israel had passed beyond the boundaries of probation, and further intercession would be futile. But up until that point, Jeremiah "stood before you and spoke in their behalf to turn your wrath away from them" (Jeremiah 18:20). Until God tells us to stop praying for someone, we should continue to pray.

Charles Finney, in his book *Answers to Prayer,* tells how he had been interceding for a prominent man in the community who had come under a sense of conviction. One day he was tearfully pleading with God for his friend, only to find the door of heaven slammed shut in his face. God seemed to be saying, "No, I will not hear. Speak no more of this matter." The next morning Finney saw his friend, a legislator, and brought up the question of submission to God. The man replied that it was out of the question for the time being, as he was politically committed to cast a vote that was incompatible with Christianity. Then Finney understood. The Holy Spirit had gone from the man, and he never again came under conviction.

But unless God demands it, don't give up. Charles Finney himself was converted because the church didn't give up on an unpromising case. Finney learned that "some members of the church had proposed, in a church meeting, to make me a particular subject of prayer, and that Mr. Gale had discouraged them, saying that he did not believe I would ever be converted, that from conversing with me he had found that I was very much informed upon the subject of Christianity, and very much hardened." Fortunately, the church prayed for Finney anyway.

After they had been punished by exile in Babylon, however, what promise did God hold out for the children of Israel?

"This is what the Lord says: 'Restrain your voice from weeping and your eyes from tears, for your work will be rewarded,' declares the Lord '*They will return from the land of the enemy.* So there is hope for your future,' declares the Lord. '*Your children will return to their own land.*' " Jeremiah 31:16, 17, NIV.

"If you return to the Lord, then your brothers and *your children will be shown compassion by their captors and will come back to this land,* for the Lord your God is gracious and compassionate. He will not turn his face from you if you return to him." 2 Chronicles 30:9, NIV.

How do these promises made to the children of Israel apply to our children today?

"If you belong to Christ, then *you are Abraham's seed, and heirs according to the promise.*" Galatians 3:29, NIV.

What are some other promises that faithful parents may claim for blessing on their offspring?

"The children of your servants will live in your presence; their descendants will be established before you." Psalm 102:28, NIV.

"But from everlasting to everlasting the Lord's love is with those who fear him." Psalm 103:17, NIV.

"He will bless those who fear the Lord—small and great alike. May the Lord make you increase, both you and your children." Psalm 115:13, 14, NIV.

"All your sons will be taught by the Lord, and great will be your children's peace." Isaiah 54:13, NIV.

" 'As for me, this is my covenant with them,' says the Lord 'My Spirit, who is on you, and my words that I have put in your mouth will not depart from your mouth, or from the mouths of your children, or from the mouths of their descendants from this time on and forever,' says the Lord." Isaiah 59:21, NIV.

"Their descendants will be known among the nations and their offspring among the peoples. All who see them will acknowledge that they are a people the Lord has blessed." Isaiah 61:9, NIV.

"They will not toil in vain or bear children doomed to misfortune; for they will be a people blessed by the Lord, they and their descendants with them." Isaiah 65:23, NIV.

PUBLIC WORSHIP

How only can God be truly worshipped?

"God is spirit, and his worshipers must worship *in spirit and in truth*." John 4:24, NIV.

How are we instructed to worship the Lord?

"Ascribe to the Lord the glory due his name; *worship the Lord in the splendor of holiness*." Psalm 29:2, NIV.

What attitude is indicative of reverence in worship?

"Come, let us *bow down* in worship, let us *kneel* before the Lord our maker." Psalm 95:6, NIV.

Is singing a part of divine worship?

"Shout for joy to the Lord, all the earth. Worship the Lord with gladness; *come before him with joyful songs.* . . . Enter his gates with thanksgiving and his courts with praise; give thanks to him and praise his name." Psalm 100:1-4, NIV.

How does Psalms describe joyful worship?

Psalm 92: A psalm. A song. For the Sabbath day. "It is good to praise the Lord and make music to your name, O Most High, to proclaim your love in the morning and your faithfulness at night, to the music of the ten-stringed lyre and the melody of the harp." Verses 1-3, NIV.

Psalm 150: "Praise him with the sounding of the trumpet, praise him with the harp and lyre, praise him with tambourine and dancing, praise him with the strings and flute, praise him with the clash of symbols, praise him with resounding cymbals." Verses 3-5, NIV. (See also Psalm 92:13.)

What is promised to those who wait upon the Lord?

"Those who hope in the Lord will renew their strength. They will soar on wings like eagles; they will run and not grow weary, they will walk and not be faint." Isaiah 40:31, NIV.

Is Jesus' presence limited to large congregations?

"For where two or three come together in my name, there am I with them." Matthew 18:20, NIV.

Why should we assemble together to worship?

"Let us not give up meeting together, as some are in the habit of doing, but let us encourage one another—and all the more as you see the Day approaching." Hebrews 10:25, NIV.

Does God still expect His people to offer sacrifices today?

"You also, like living stones, are being built into a spiritual house to be a holy priesthood, *offering spiritual sacrifices* acceptable to God through Jesus Christ." 1 Peter 2:5, NIV.

What sort of sacrifices should we offer to God in worship?

"Therefore, I urge you, brothers, in view of God's mercy, to *offer your bodies as living sacrifices,* holy and pleasing to God—*this is your spiritual act of worship.*" Romans 12:1, NIV.

What traditional part of worship is a sacrifice to God?

"Through Jesus, therefore, let us continually offer to God *a sacrifice of praise—the fruit of lips that confess his name.*" Hebrews 13:15, NIV.

NOTE.—In Christian worship, the songs of praise take the place of the animal sacrifices of ancient times. And so do the offerings.

What other sort of sacrifices please God?

"And do not forget to do good and to *share with others,* for *with such sacrifices God is pleased."* Verse 16, NIV.

"I am amply supplied, now that I have received from Epaphroditus *the gifts you sent. They are a fragrant offering, an acceptable sacrifice, pleasing to God."* Philippians 4:18, NIV.

What day has God specially designed for public worship?

"*The seventh day* is a Sabbath of rest, a day of sacred assembly." Leviticus 23:3, NIV.

How has God commanded us to keep this day?

"Remember the Sabbath day by keeping it holy. . . . On it you shall not do any work." Exodus 20:8-10, NIV. (See Isaiah 58:13, 14.)

Will there be public worship in the world to come?

" 'As the new heavens and the new earth that I make will endure before me,' declares the Lord, 'so will your name and descendants endure. From one New Moon to another and from one Sabbath to another, all mankind will come and bow down before me,' says the Lord.' " Isaiah 66:22, 23, NIV.

CHRISTIAN COMMUNION

What was connected with the worship of God before Jesus' death and resurrection?

"Now the first covenant had regulations for worship and also an earthly sanctuary." Hebrews 9:1, NIV.

NOTE.—Paul says that these ordinances consisted in "food and drink and various ceremonial washings," imposed "until the time of the new order" (verse 10, NIV), and that they were "a shadow of the good things that are coming" (Hebrews 10:1, NIV).

To whom did the sacrificial offerings point?

"And live a life of love, just as Christ loved us and gave himself up for us as a fragrant offering and sacrifice to God." Ephesians 5:2, NIV.

NOTE.—Through the provisions of the sacrificial law, the repentant sinner showed his faith in the coming Redeemer, who was to shed His blood for the sins of mankind. These sacrificial offerings were ordinances which pointed forward to the work of Christ, which they typified. Since the Crucifixion, the ordinances of the Christian church point backward, and are designed to show faith in the work of Christ already accomplished.

What does the Lord desire us to keep in mind?

"By this gospel you are saved, if you hold firmly to the word I preached to you. . . . that *Christ died for our sins according to the Scriptures, that he was buried, and he was raised on the third day* according to the scriptures." 1 Corinthians 15:2-4, NIV.

What ordinance commemorates Christ's burial and resurrection?

"Having been buried with him in baptism and raised with him through your faith in the power of God, who raised him from the dead." Colossians 2:12, NIV.

For what purpose was the Lord's Supper instituted?

"For I received from the Lord what I also passed on to you: The Lord Jesus, on the night he was betrayed, took bread, and when he had given thanks, he broke it and said, '*This is my body, which is for you; do this in remembrance of me.*'" 1 Corinthians 11:23, 24, NIV.

What does the wine signify?

"In the same way, after supper he took the cup, saying, 'This cup is the new covenant in *my blood;* do this, whenever you drink it, in remembrance of me.'" Verse 25, NIV.

What do both the bread and the wine commemorate?

"For whenever you eat this bread and drink this cup, you proclaim *the Lord's death* until he comes." Verse 26, NIV.

What attitude should we bring to this ordinance?

"Therefore, whoever eats the bread or drinks the cup of the Lord in an unworthy manner will be guilty of sinning against the body and blood of the dead. A man ought to examine himself before he eats of the bread and drinks of the cup. For anyone who eats and drinks without recognizing the body of the Lord eats and drinks judgment on himself." Verses 27-29, NIV.

NOTE.—The last expression shows what is meant by eating and drinking unworthily. It is not the one who has a deep sense of their own sinfulness and unworthiness of God's mercy. The people of whom Paul speaks were partaking of the meal in a cavalier and careless fashion, unrepentant, eating with selfish gluttony as they might at a secular banquet.

How should we prepare our hearts for this service?

"If we confess our sins, he is faithful and just and will forgive us our sins and purify us from all unrighteousness." 1 John 1:9, NIV.

What is essential to Christian fellowship and to maintain this cleansing from sin?

"*If we walk in the light, as he is in the light,* we have fellowship with one another, and the blood of Jesus, his Son, purifies us from all sin." Verse 7, NIV.

What still higher fellowship does the Christian enjoy?

"And our fellowship is *with the Father and with his Son, Jesus Christ.*" Verse 3, NIV.

PRAISE AND THANKSGIVING

When did the Psalmist say he would bless the Lord?

"I will extol the Lord *at all times;* his praise will always be on my lips." Psalm 34:1, NIV.

"*Every day* I will praise you and extol your name forever and ever." Psalm 145:2, NIV.

How constantly should we give thanks?

"Give thanks in all circumstances, for this is God's will for you in Christ Jesus." 1 Thessalonians 5:18, NIV.

NOTE.—By thanking God even for unpleasant things, we acknowledge His power to bring good out of evil. What does not destroy us makes us stronger, deepens us, and draws us closer to Christ. So we thank God for everything, just as we pay the doctor even when the treatment is painful, realizing that His blessings in the past and His promises for the future are so sweet that our trials in the present pale in comparison. Thanking God for everything is the surest road to freedom.

How often, and for how much, should we render thanks?

"Speak to one another with psalms, hymns and spiritual songs. Sign and make music in your heart to the Lord, *always giving thanks to God the Father for everything,* in the name of our Lord Jesus Christ." Ephesians 5:20, NIV.

What happens to those who fail to glorify God and be thankful?

"For although they knew God, they neither glorified him as God nor gave thanks to him, but their thinking became futile and *their foolish hearts were darkened.*" Romans 1:21, NIV.

What element should enter into all our worship?

"Do not be anxious about anything, but in everything, by prayer and petition, with thanksgiving, present your requests to God." Philippians 4:6, NIV. (See Colossians 4:2.)

What did David exhort all to do?

"*Glorify the Lord* with me; let us exalt his name together." Psalm 34:3, NIV.

Where does David say he will praise God?

"From you comes the theme of my praise *in the great assembly;* before those who fear you will I fulfill my vows." Psalm 22:25, NIV.

What does he say he will declare in the hearing of all who fear God?

"Come and listen, all you who fear God; let me tell you *what he has done for me.*" Psalm 66:16.

With what exhortation does the Psalmist close his songs of praise?

"Praise the Lord. Praise God in his sanctuary; praise him in his mighty heavens. Praise him for his acts of power; praise him for his surpassing greatness. Praise him with the sounding of the trumpet, praise him with the harp and lyre, praise him with tambourine and dancing, praise him with the strings and flute, praise him with the clash of symbols, praise him with resounding cymbals. Let everything that has breath praise the Lord." Psalm 150, NIV.

THE VALUE OF SONG

How early in the world's history do we hear of singing?

"Where were you when I laid the earth's foundation? . . .Who laid its cornerstone *while the morning stars sang together and all the angels shouted for joy?*" Job 38:4-7, NIV.

How did Israel celebrate when delivered from Egypt?

"Then Moses and the Israelites sang this song to the Lord: 'I will sing to the Lord, for he is highly exalted. . . . The Lord is my strength and my song; he has become my salvation. He is my God, and I will praise him, my father's God, and I will exalt him.'" Exodus 15:1, 2, NIV.

How did the angels manifest their joy at Jesus' birth?

"Suddenly a great company of the heavenly host appeared with the angel, praising God and saying, 'Glory to God in the highest, and on earth peace, good will toward men.'" Luke 2:13, 14.

How are we told to come before the Lord?

"Shout for joy to the Lord, all the earth. Worship the Lord with gladness; *come before him with joyful songs.*" Psalm 100:1, 2, NIV.

How did David say such worship is regarded by God?

"I will praise God's name in *song* and glorify him with *thanksgiving. This will please the Lord more than an ox, more than a bull with its horns and hoofs.*" Psalm 69:30, 31, NIV.

What instruction did Paul give concerning singing?

"Let the word of Christ dwell in you richly as you teach and admonish one another with all wisdom, and as you sing psalms, hymns and spiritual songs with gratitude in your hearts to God." Colossians 3:16, NIV. (See also Ephesians 5:19; James 5:13; Psalm 149:5, 6.)

NOTE.—Music, like poetry and flowers, is elevating and refining in its nature, and should therefore have its place in the worship of God and in the life and experience of God's people. It is adapted to every mood and feeling of the human soul, and reaches hearts when other means have failed. Next to prayer, music seems best adapted to worship. "The history of the songs of the Bible is full of suggestion as to the uses and benefits of music and song. Music is often perverted to serve purposes of evil, and it thus becomes one of the most alluring agencies of temptation. But, rightly employed, it is a precious gift of God, designed to uplift the thoughts to high and noble themes, to inspire and elevate the soul. As the children of Israel, journeying through the wilderness, cheered their way by the music of sacred song, so God bids His children today gladden their pilgrim life. There are few means more effective for fixing words in the memory than repeating them in song. And such song has wonderful power. It has power to subdue rude and uncultivated natures; power to quicken thought and to awaken sympathy, to promote harmony of action, and to banish the gloom and foreboding that destroy courage and weaken effort." Ellen G. White, *Education*, pp. 167, 168.

What song does Revelation depict the redeemed singing in heaven?

"*They . . . sang the song of Moses the servant of God and the song of the Lamb:* 'Great and marvelous are your deeds, Lord God Almighty. Just and true are your ways, King of the ages. Who will not fear you, O Lord, and bring glory to your name? For you alone are holy. All nations will come and worship before you, for your righteous acts have been revealed.' " Revelation 15:2-4, NIV

CHAPTER 14

Christian Service

THE GIFT OF GIVING

What example of giving has God given to the world?

"For God so loved the world that *he gave his one and only Son, that whoever believes in him shall not perish but have eternal life.*" John 3:16, NIV.

What did Christ do to redeem us?

"Who *gave Himself* for our sins." Galatians 1:4. (See also Titus 2:14; 1 Timothy 2:6.)

Why did He lay aside His riches and become poor?

"For you know the grace of our Lord Jesus Christ, that though he was rich, yet for your sakes he became poor, *so that you through his poverty might become rich.*" 2 Corinthians 8:9, NIV.

After Abraham was blessed, what was he to be?

"I will bless you, . . . and you will be *a blessing.*" Genesis 12:2, NIV.

What tested Abraham's faith and devotion?

"By faith Abraham, when God tested him, offered Isaac as a sacrifice. He who had received the promises was about to sacrifice his one and only son, even though God had said to him, 'It is through Isaac that your offspring will be reckoned.' Abraham reasoned that God could raise the dead, and figuratively speaking, he did receive Isaac back from death." Hebrews 11:17-19, NIV.

What generous advice did Jesus give as He sent out His disciples to preach, heal the sick, and raise the dead?

"Freely you have received, *freely give.*" Matthew 10:8, NIV.

Why does God comfort us in our troubles?

NOTE.—All who accept the gospel take upon themselves the obligation to pass its blessings on to others. In this way the work of salvation is extended. God expects all souls reclaimed from sin to join in the same work for others which lifted him up, and placed his feet upon the Rock. The good things of God are not to be selfishly kept to ourselves. We receive to give. Says Whittier, "The soul is lost that's saved alone." And as love prompted God's great gift, so His love in our hearts will prompt us to give, to minister, and to engage in loving service for the welfare and the happiness of others.

What did Jesus say of the blessedness of giving?

"In everything I did, I showed you that by this kind of hard work we must help the weak, remembering the words the Lord Jesus Himself said: '*It is more blessed to give than receive.*' " Acts 20:35, NIV.

NOTE.—The government of God is founded on the principle of benevolence, the desire to bless others. Our richest blessings come as the result of the good things we have passed on to others.

For what was Christ anointed by the Holy Spirit?

"The Spirit of the Sovereign Lord is on me, because the Lord has anointed me *to preach good news to the poor.* He has sent me *to bind up the brokenhearted, to proclaim freedom for the captives and release from darkness for the prisoners.*" Isaiah 61:1, NIV. (See Luke 4:18.)

NOTE.—The Holy Spirit is given to empower God's children for service.

After being anointed by the Holy Spirit, what did Jesus do?

"Jesus . . . *went about doing good.*" Acts 10:38.

What should the people do who claim to be followers of Jesus?

"Whoever claims to live in him must *walk as Jesus did.*" 1 John 2:6, NIV.

What does God require of His children?

"He has showed you, O man, what is good. And what does the Lord require of you? *To act justly and to love mercy and to walk humbly with your God.*" Micah 6:8, NIV.

What does it mean to do justice and love mercy? What promises are made to those who befriend and serve the downtrodden?

"Is not this the kind of fasting I have chosen: to loose the chains of injustice and untie the cords of the yoke, to set the oppressed free and break ever yoke? Is it not to share your food with the hungry and to provide the poor wanderer with shelter—when you see the naked, to clothe him, and not to turn away from your own flesh and blood? Then your light wll break forth like the dawn, and your healing will quickly appear; then your righteousness will go before you, and the glory of the Lord will be your rear guard. Then you will call, and the Lord will answer; you will cry for help, and he will say: Here am I. If you do away with the yoke of oppression, with the pointing finger and malicious talk, and if you spend yourselves in behalf of the hungry and satisfy the needs of the oppressed, then your light will rise in the darkness, and your night will become like the noonday. The Lord will guide you always; he will satisfy your needs in a sun-scorched land and will strengthen your frame. You will be like a well-watered garden, like a spring whose waters never fail." Isaiah 58:6-11, NIV.

NOTE.—If we meet the needs of others, God will meet our needs. Those who bless others will be blessed. We become special by making others special. *The surest road to happiness is to make others happy.*

Why not make good things happen around you? Why not send flowers to difficult people and never let them know? Why not leave a book or other gift with an anonymous note inside on a desk or front porch? At the toll booth pay the toll for the car behind you. Write your mail carrier a thank-you note. Surprise people with grace.

Perhaps someone you know is discouraged. Why not send an anonymous note that says, "God's not the only one that loves you!" For someone in need why not leave a note that says, "God will supply all of your needs with His riches in glory," and include a $20 bill. Find a need and fill it. Make someone's dream come true. Create some good things in someone's life. That's the quickest way to create good in your own.

In the judgment, on what basis does Jesus separate the saved from the lost?

"When the Son of Man comes in his glory, and all the angels with him, he will sit on his throne in heavenly glory. All the nations will be gathered before him, and he will separate the people one from another as a shepherd separates the sheep from the goats. He will put the sheep on his right and the goats on his left. Then the King will say to those on his right, 'Come, you who are blessed by my Father; take your inheritance, the kingdom prepared for you since the creation of the world. For I was hungry and you gave me something to eat, I was thirsty and you gave me something to drink, I was a stranger and you invited me in, I needed clothes and you clothed me, I was sick and you looked after me, I was in prison and you came to visit me.' " Matthew 25:31-36, NIV.

In this parable, when the happy but surprised sheep ask Jesus "When did this happen?" what does Jesus answer?

"Then the righteous will answer him, 'Lord, when did we see you hungry and feed you, or thirsty and give you something to drink? When did we see you a stranger and invite you in, or needing clothes and clothe you? When did we see you sick or in prison and go to visit you?' The King will reply, 'I tell you the truth, whatever you did for one of the least of these brothers of mine, you did for me.' " Verses 37-40, NIV.

NOTE.—Jesus separates the saved from the lost on the basis of how they have treated Him in the person of His suffering brothers and sisters. Every loving deed of mercy is counted as if it were done to Jesus. The haunting eyes of a hungry child or a lonely prisoner are the eyes of Jesus. Jesus comes to each of us, not in glory, but in the guise of a beggar. In the helpless, the hopeless, the suffering, we are given the priceless opportunity to serve Jesus today.

What glorious paradox did Jesus proclaim as the secret of abundant living?

"Then Jesus said to his disciples, 'If anyone would come after me, he must deny himself and take up his cross and follow me. For whoever wants to save his life will lose it, but whoever loses his life for me will find it.' " Matthew 16:24, 25, NIV.

NOTE.—The secret of life is this: Lose yourself in loving service to others, and love will flow back to you. Give yourself away, and the rivulet of your life will open up into an ocean of exciting possibilities and rich relationships. Why not put this philosophy to the test?

Resolve now to put your trust in God, to take risks for Him, to step out in faith. Commit to memory Krister Stendahl's magnificent definition of faith: "Faith is not believing in spite of the evidence. Faith is obeying in spite of the consequences."

What did Jesus promise to those who gave all for Him?

" ' I tell you the truth,' Jesus replied, 'no one who has left home or brothers or sisters or mother or father or children or fields for me and the gospel will fail to receive *a hundred times as much in this present age (homes, brothers, sisters, mothers, children and fields— and with them, persecutions) and in the age to come, eternal life.* But many who are first will be last, and the last first.' " Mark 10:29-31, NIV.

NOTE.—Some banks offer a 6 percent annual return on money invested with them. Jesus promises to repay us 100-fold, which amounts to a 10,000 percent return on investment. What a deal! For every loved one estranged from us because we have chosen to follow Jesus, we receive 100 new brothers and sisters in the faith. Of course, Jesus also warns us that along with this will come persecution.

What should our attitude be when our Christian witness arouses anger and opposition?

"Blessed are those who are persecuted because of righteousness, for theirs is the kingdom of heaven. Blessed are you when people insult you, persecute you and falsely say all kinds of evil against you because of me. *Rejoice and be glad,* because great is your reward in heaven, for in the same way they persecuted the prophets who were before you." Matthew 5:10-12, NIV.

How does God promise to protect us as we minister for His sake?

"But now, this is what the Lord says—he who created you, O Jacob, he who formed you, O Israel: 'Fear not, for I have redeemed you; I have summoned you by name; you are mine. When you pass through the waters, I will be with you; and when you pass through the rivers, they will not sweep over you. When you walk through the fire, you will not be burned; the flames will not set you ablaze.' " Isaiah 43:1, 2, NIV.

NOTE.—As Jesus sent his disciples out to witness for Him, he told them, "I have given you authority to trample on snakes and scorpions and to overcome all the power of the enemy; nothing will harm you. However, do not rejoice that the spirits submit to you, but rejoice that your names are written in heaven." Luke 10:19, 20, NIV.

Ultimately, the Christian cannot lose. While following Jesus brings joy, it may also bring conflict and heartache. We may be wounded in the battle, but in the long run our treasure is secure in heaven. And Jesus has promised us, "Never will I leave you; never will I forsake you." Hebrews 13:5, NIV.

What was Christ's mission on earth?

"For the Son of Man came *to seek and to save what was lost.*" Luke 19:10, NIV.

NOTE.—From the manger to Calvary Jesus followed a lifestyle of selflessness. His was not a life of ease and self-indulgence or self-seeking, but one of complete dedication to one cause, the saving of mankind. He said, "The Son of Man did not come to be served, but to serve, and to give his life as a ransom for many" Matthew 20:28, NIV. This was His magnificent obsession.

What does Jesus say that the Spirit-filled Christian will become?

"*You will be my witnesses* in Jerusalem, and in all Judea and Samaria, and to the ends of the earth." Acts 1:8.

NOTE.—Every Christian is to be an ambassador for Jesus Christ. No longer do we live for ourselves. We live to glorify God by sharing our knowledge of His love and salvation with others. " ' Follow me,' Jesus said, 'and I will make you fishers of men.' " Matthew 4:19, NIV.

NOTE.—A good fisher will know how to entice the fish. Jesus first ministered to the physical needs of the people, then to their spiritual needs. He first won their confidence by His loving concern for their cares and afflictions; then He showed them the way of life.

People need Christ, but they don't really want Him; they only want what He has to offer. They have to be shown the beauty of Christianity. So offer them the love of Jesus. People do not care how much you know until they know how much you care.

What did Jesus ask His followers to do?

"Let your light shine before men, that they may see your good deeds and praise your Father in heaven." Matthew 5:16, NIV.

What was Jesus' parting instruction to His followers?

"Therefore *go and make disciples* of all nations, baptizing them in the name of the Father and of the Son and of the Holy Spirit, and teaching them to obey everything I have commanded you. And surely I am with you always, to the very end of the age." Matthew 28:19, 20, NIV.

NOTE.—Precious promises are made to those who sow the gospel seed by sharing the good news of salvation: "Those who sow in tears will reap with songs of joy. He who goes out weeping, carrying seed to sow, will return with songs of joy, carrying sheaves with him." Psalm 126:5, 6, NIV.

What will be the ultimate state of those who bring others to Jesus?

"Those who are wise will *shine like the brightness of the heavens,* and those who lead many to righteousness, like the stars for ever and ever." Daniel 12:3, NIV.

THE SHEPHERD AND HIS WORK

Who did Jesus say is the good shepherd?

"I am the good shepherd." John 10:11.

What is Jesus elsewhere called?

"The Shepherd and Overseer of your souls." 1 Peter 2:25, NIV. "The Chief Shepherd." 1 Peter 5:4, NIV.

NOTE.—The expression "Chief Shepherd" implies that there are *under*shepherds.

How does the good shepherd manifest his love and care for the sheep?

"The good shepherd *lays down his life for the sheep.*" John 10:11, NIV.

What does the hired hand, or false shepherd, do, and why?

"The man runs away because he is a hired hand and cares nothing for the sheep." Verse 13, NIV.

What example will the true shepherd set before his flock?

"In everything set them an example by doing what is good. In your teaching show integrity, seriousness and soundness of speech that cannot be condemned, so that those who oppose you may be ashamed because they have nothing bad to say about us." Titus 2:7, NIV.

What is the special work of the gospel shepherd?

"Keep watch over yourselves and all the flock of which the Holy Spirit has made you overseers. Be shepherds of the church of God, which he bought with his own blood." Acts 20:28, NIV. "Be shepherds of God's flock that is under your care, serving as overseers—not because you must, but because you are willing, as God wants you to be; not greedy for money, but eager to serve; not lording it over those entrusted to you, but being examples to the flock. And when the Chief Shepherd appears, you will receive the crown of glory that will never fade away." 1 Peter 5:2-4, NIV. (See also John 21:15-17.)

How will the true shepherd feed the flock?

"In the presence of God and of Christ Jesus, who will judge the living and the dead, and in view of his appearing and his kingdom, I give you this charge: *Preach the Word;* to be prepared in season and out of season; correct, rebuke and encourage—with great patience and careful instruction." 2 Timothy 4:1, 2, NIV. "Son of man, I have made you a watchman for the house of Israel; *so hear the word I speak and give them warning from me.*" Ezekiel 33:7, NIV. (See Ezekiel 3:17-21.)

Was there to come a time when people would not listen to plain Bible truth? How should God's shepherds respond?

"*For the time will come when men will not put up with sound doctrine.* Instead, to suit their own desires, they will gather around them a great number of teachers to say what their itching ears want to hear. They will turn their ears away from the truth and turn aside to myths. But you, keep your head in all situations, endure hardship, do the work of an evangelist, discharge all the duties of your ministry." 2 Timothy 4:3-5, NIV.

Instead of the straight testimony, what kind of preaching will such demand?

"They say to the seers, 'See no more visions!' and to the prophets, 'Give us no more visions of what is right! *Tell us pleasant things, prophesy illusions.*' " Isaiah 30:10, NIV.

What test is given by which we may distinguish between true and false shepherds?

"*To the law and to the testimony!* If they do not speak according to this word, they have no light of dawn." Isaiah 8:20, NIV. "For the lips of a priest ought to preserve knowledge, and *from his mouth men should seek instruction*—because he is the messenger of the Lord Almighty." Malachi 2:7, NIV.

What will those servants be doing upon whom Jesus pronounces a blessing when He comes?

"Who then is the faithful and wise servant, whom the master has put in charge of the servants in his household *to give them their food at the proper time?* It will be good for that servant whose master finds him doing so when he returns. I tell you the truth, he will put him in charge of all his possessions." Matthew 24:45-47, NIV.

How does the divine shepherd lead His flock?

"He tends his flock like a shepherd: *he gathers the lambs in his arms and carries them close to this heart; he gently leads those that have young.*" Isaiah 40:11, NIV.

"I will *search for the lost and bring back the strays.* I will *bind up the injured and strengthen the weak,* but the sleek and the strong I will destroy. I will shepherd the flock *with justice.*" Ezekiel 34:16, NIV.

After receiving his commission to preach, how did the apostle Paul feel?

"Yet when I preach the gospel, I cannot boast, for I am compelled to preach. *Woe to me if I do not preach the gospel!* If I preach voluntarily, I have a reward; if not voluntarily, I am simply discharging the trust committed to me What then is my reward? Just this: that in preaching the gospel I may offer it free of charge, and so not make use of my rights in preaching it. Though I am free and belong to no man, I make myself a slave to everyone, to win as many as possible.

To the Jews I became like a Jew, to win the Jews. To those under the law I became like one under the law (though I myself am not under the law), so as to win those under the law. To those not having the law I became like one not having the law (though I am not free from God's law but am under Christ's law), so as to win those not having the law. To the weak I became weak, to win the weak. *I have become all things to all men so that by all possible means I might save some.* I do all this for the sake of the gospel, that I may share in its blessings." 1 Corinthians 9:16-23, NIV.

How faithfully will the true shepherd watch the flock?

"They keep watch over you as *men who must give an account.*" Hebrews 13:17, NIV.

If God's workers fail to warn the wicked, what terrible responsibility will be charged to their account?

"When I say to the wicked, 'O wicked man, you will surely die,' and you do not speak out to dissuade him from his ways, that wicked man will die for his sin, and *I will hold you accountable for his blood.* But if you do warn the wicked man to turn from his ways and he does not do so, he will die for his sin, but you will have saved yourself." Ezekiel 33:8, 9, NIV.

PREACHING THE GOSPEL

Before leaving His disciples, what great commission did Jesus give them?

"He said to them, 'Go into all the world and preach the good news to all creation.' " Mark 16:15, NIV.

NOTE.—The word "gospel" means "good news."

What is the gospel of Christ declared to be?

"I am not ashamed of the gospel, because it is *the power of God for the salvation of everyone who believes.*" Romans 1:16, NIV.

How extensively and until when did Jesus say the gospel should be preached?

"And this gospel of the kingdom will be preached *in the whole world* as a testimony to all nations, and *then the end will come.*" Matthew 24:14, NIV.

What was the object of Jesus' ministry?

"I, the Lord, have called you in righteousness; I will take hold of your hand. I will keep you and will make you to be a covenant for the people and a light for the Gentiles, *to open eyes that are blind, to free captives from prison and to release from the dungeons those who sit in darkness.*" Isaiah 42:6, 7, NIV.

For what purpose did Jesus select Paul, and send him to the Gentiles?

"I have appeared to you to appoint you as a servant and as a witness of what you have seen of me and what I will show you. I will rescue you from your own people and from the Gentiles. I am sending you to *them to open their eyes and turn them from darkness to light, and from the power of Satan to God, so that they may receive forgiveness of sins and a place among those who are sanctified by faith in me.*" Acts 26:16-18, NIV.

Why was the gospel to be preached to the Gentiles?

"Simon has described to us how *God* at first *showed his concern by taking from the Gentiles a people for himself.*" Acts 15:14, NIV.

How are those who preach the gospel described?

"How beautiful on the mountains are the feet of those who bring good news, who proclaim peace, who bring good tidings, who proclaim salvation, who say to Zion, 'Your God reigns!' " Isaiah 52:7, NIV.

What is the Christian minister commanded to preach?

"Preach *the word.*" 2 Timothy 4:2.

Of what did Jesus say the Scriptures testify?

"These are the Scriptures that testify about *me.*" John 5:39, NIV.

NOTE.—Everyone, therefore, who preaches the Word aright will preach Christ. Paul, who faithfully preached God's word, said he was determined not to preach anything "except Jesus Christ, and Him crucified." 1 Corinthians 2:2, NIV.

NOTE.—It is said that a young minister once asked Jonathan Edwards what Edwards thought of a sermon he had just preached. "It was a very poor sermon indeed," said Mr. Edwards.

"Why?" the young minister asked.

"Because," said Mr. Edwards, "there was no Christ in it."

All the great truths of the Scriptures center in Jesus. Rightly understood, all lead to Him. Jesus, therefore, should be presented in every discourse as the alpha and omega, the beginning and the end, of the great plan of salvation.

How does God expect His ministers to preach the word?

"Let the one who has my word speak *it faithfully.*" Jeremiah 23:28, NIV.

How did Christ present the truth to the people?

"With many similar parables Jesus spoke the word to them, *as much as they could understand.*" Mark 4:33, NIV.

NOTE.—Ministers should learn to adapt their labors to those for whom they seek to reach—to meet the people where they are.

How should the servant of God labor?

"And the Lord's servant must not quarrel; instead, he must *be kind to everyone, able to teach, not resentful.* Those who oppose him he must *gently instruct,* in the hope that God will grant them repentance leading them to a knowledge of the truth." 2 Timothy 2:24, 25, NIV.

NOTE.—While the claims of the law of God are presented to the sinner, ministers should never forget that love—the love of God—is the only power that can soften the heart and lead to repentance and obedience, and that to save is their great work.

As a preparation for their work, what did Christ do to the apostles?

"Then *he opened their minds* so they could understand the Scriptures." Luke 24:45, NIV.

Why did Jesus tell them to stay and wait in Jerusalem?

"I am going to send you what my Father has promised; but *stay in the city until you have been clothed with power from on high.*" Verse 49, NIV.

How did the apostles preach the gospel?

"It was revealed to them that they were not serving themselves but you, when they spoke of the things that have now been told you by those who have preached the gospel to you *by the Holy Spirit sent from heaven.*" 1 Peter 1:12, NIV.

What was the result of their preaching?

"But *many* who heard the message *believed,* and the number of men grew to about five thousand." Acts 4:4, NIV. "So the *word* of God *spread.* The *number of disciples* in Jerusalem *increased rapidly,* and a large number of priests became obedient to the faith." Acts 6:7, NIV.

MISSIONARY WORK

What responsibility has Jesus given everyone?

"Be on guard! Be alert! You do not know when that time will come. It's like a man going away: He leaves his house and puts his servants in charge, each with his assigned task, and tells the one at the door to watch." Mark 13:33, 34, NIV.

Besides work, what else has been given everyone?

"To one he gave five *talents* of money, to another two talents, and to another one talent, *each according to his ability.*" Matthew 25:15, NIV.

NOTE.—"Talents" represents all the resources and abilities that God gives.

What are those to whom this work is committed called?

"It will be like a man going on a journey, who called his *servants* and entrusted his property to him." Verse 14, NIV.

In the parable of the talents, what use did these servants make of their resources?

"The man who had received the five talents went at once and put his money to work and gained five more. So also, the one with the two talents gained two more. But the man who had received one talent went off, dug a hole in the ground and hid master's money." Verses 16-18, NIV.

What excuse did the one who hid his talent make?

"Then the one who had received the one talent came. 'Master,' he said, 'I knew that you are a hard man, harvesting where you have not sown and gathering where you have not scattered seed. So *I was afraid* and went out and hid your talent in the ground." Verses 24, 25, NIV.

What did his master say to him?

"His master replied, '*You wicked, lazy servant!*' " Verse 26, NIV.

What did he say the servant should have done?

"You should have *put my money on deposit with the bankers,* so that when it returned I would have received it back with interest." Verse 27, NIV.

What is characteristic of slothful persons?

"The sluggard says, 'There is a lion outside!' or 'I will be murdered in the streets!' " Proverbs 22:13, NIV.

NOTE.—That is, they see great obstacles before them, and are always ready with excuses.

What was the fate of the slothful servant?

"And *throw that worthless servant outside, into the darkness,* where there will be weeping and gnashing of teeth." Matthew 25:30, NIV.

What was said to the servant who increased his talents?

"His master replied, '*Well done,* good and faithful servant! You have been faithful with a few things; I will put you in charge of many things. Come and share your master's happiness!'" Verse 21, NIV.

Why did Christ endure the cruel death on the cross?

"Let us fix our eyes on Jesus, the author and perfecter of our faith, *who for the joy set before him endured the cross,* scorning its shame, and sat down at the right hand of the throne of God." Hebrews 12:2, NIV.

What will bring to the Lord this satisfaction and joy?

"After the suffering of his soul, *he will see the light of life* and be satisfied." Isaiah 53:11, NIV.

What did Paul set forth as his crown of rejoicing?

"For what is our hope, our joy, or the crown in which we glory in the presence of our Lord Jesus when he comes? *Is it not you? Indeed, you are our glory and joy.*" 1 Thessalonians 2:19, 20, NIV.

Since this joy comes to Christ only through His self-denial and suffering for others, in what way must all others partake of that joy?

"Here is a trustworthy saying: If we died with him, we will also live with him; *if we endure, we will also reign with him.*" 2 Timothy 2:11, 12, NIV.

What motive should prompt us to soul-saving labor?

"For *Christ's love* compels us." 2 Corinthians 5:14, NIV.

Whom does every faithful Christian worker represent?

"We are therefore *Christ's ambassadors,* as though God were making his appeal through us." Verse 20, NIV.

What does God do with the unfruitful members?

"I am the true vine, and my Father is the gardener. *He cuts off*

every branch in me that bears no fruit, while every branch that
does bear fruit he prunes so that it will be even more beautiful."
John 15:1, 2, NIV.

Can one occupy a mere neutral position toward Christ?

"*He who is not with me is against me,* and he who does not gather
with me, scatters." Luke 11:23, NIV.

How should we pray for God's work?

"He told them, 'The harvest is plentiful, but the workers are few.
Ask the Lord of the harvest, therefore, *to send out workers into his
harvest field.*' " Luke 10:2, NIV.

How are we cautioned against delaying our work?

"Do you not say, 'Four months more and then the harvest'? I tell
you, open your eyes and look at the fields! They are ripe for harvest."
John 4:35, NIV.

What promise is made to those who sow the gospel seed?

"Those who sow in tears will *reap with songs of joy.* He who goes
out weeping, carrying seed to sow, *will return with songs of joy, carrying sheaves with him.*" Psalm 126:5, 6, NIV.

What promise is made to soul winners?

"The fruit of the righteous is a tree of life, and *he who wins souls
is wise.*" Proverbs 11:30, NIV. "*Those who are wise will shine like the
brightness of the heavens,* and those who lead many to righteousness, like the stars for ever and ever." Daniel 12:3, NIV.

OUR DUTY TO THE POOR

What is God's attitude toward the poor?

"For *he will deliver the needy* who cry out, the afflicted who have
no one to help." Psalm 72:12, NIV.

What was Jesus' mission to the downtrodden?

"The Spirit of the Lord is on me, . . . *to preach good news to the
poor.*" Luke 4:18, NIV.

What did Paul say regarding our duty to the poor?

"In everything I did, I showed you that by this kind of hard work *we
must help the weak,* remembering the words the Lord Jesus himself
said: 'It *is more blessed to give than to receive.*' " Acts 20:35, NIV.

What classes of people are we especially enjoined to help?

"Learn to do right! Seek justice, *encourage the oppressed. Defend the cause of the fatherless, plead the case of the widow.*" Isaiah 1:17, NIV.

How did the patriarch Job treat the poor?

"I was a *father* to the needy; *I took up the case of the stranger.*" Job 29:16, NIV.

What is pure and undefiled religion declared to be?

"Religion that God our Father accepts as pure and faultless is this: *to look after orphans and widows in their distress* and to keep oneself from polluting the world." James 1:27, NIV.

What kind of fast is most acceptable to God?

"Is not this the kind of fasting I have chosen: to loose the chains of injustice and untie the cords of the yoke, to set the oppressed free and break every yoke? *Is it not to share your food with the hungry and to provide the poor wanderer with shelter—when you see the naked, to clothe him, and not to turn away from your own flesh and blood?*" Isaiah 58:6, 7, NIV.

How does the Lord regard kindness shown to the poor?

"He who is kind to the poor lends to the Lord, and *he will reward him* for what he has done." Proverbs 19:17, NIV. "God is not unjust; *he will not forget your work and the love you have shown him* as you have helped his people and continue to help them." Hebrews 6:10, NIV.

What fate awaits those who turn a deaf ear to the poor?

"If a man shuts his ears to the cry of the poor, *he too will cry out and not be answered.*" Proverbs 21:13, NIV.

What promises are made to those who help the weak?

"Blessed is he who has regard for the weak; the Lord delivers him in times of trouble. *The Lord will protect him* and preserve his life; *he will bless him* in the land and not surrender him to the desire of his foes. The Lord will sustain him on his sickbed and restore him from his bed of illness." Psalm 41:1-3, NIV.

What is promised those who do this work?

"Then you will call, and the Lord will answer; you will cry for help, and he will say: Here am I. If you do away with the yoke of oppression, with the pointing finger and malicious talk, and if you spend yourselves in behalf of the hungry and satisfy the needs of the oppressed, then your light will rise in the darkness, and your night will become like the noonday. *The Lord will guide you always*; he will satisfy your needs in a sun-scorched land and will strengthen your frame." Isaiah 58:9-11, NIV.

What did Christ tell the rich young man to do?

"Jesus answered, 'If you want to be perfect, go, *sell your possessions and give to the poor,* and you will have treasure in heaven. Then come, follow me.' " Matthew 19:21, NIV.

NOTE.—From Matthew 25:31-45 we learn that Christ identifies Himself with needy, suffering humanity; and that any neglect shown them He regards as done unto Himself, and any service rendered to them as though done for Him. We are not saved because we help the needy; but if we experience the salvation of Christ, we will love the unfortunate. This is a test of the genuineness of our profession.

CHRISTIAN HELP WORK

What was the character of Christ's work among people?

"He went around *doing good.*" Acts 10:38, NIV.

What will His true followers do?

"Whoever claims to live in him must walk as Jesus did." 1 John 2:6, NIV.

In ministering to the needy, whom are we really serving?

"I tell you the truth, whatever you did for one of the least of these brothers of mine, *you did for me.*" Matthew 25:40, NIV.

What relation do all sustain to God?

"Rich and poor have this in common: *The Lord is the maker of them all.*" Proverbs 22:2, NIV.

What classes should Christians particularly help?

"Religion that God our Father accepts as pure and faultless is this: to look after *orphans and widows* in their distress and to keep oneself from being polluted by the world." James 1:27, NIV.

What parable illustrates practical Christian help work?

"In reply Jesus said: 'A man was going down from Jerusalem to Jericho, when he fell into the hands of robbers. They stripped him of his clothes, beat him and went away, leaving him half dead. A priest happened to be going down the same road, and when he saw the man, he passed by on the other side. So too, a Levite, when he came to the place and saw him, passed by on the other side. But a Samaritan, as he traveled, came where the man was; and when he saw him, he took pity on him. He went to him and bandaged his wounds, pouring on oil and wine. Then he put the man on his own donkey, took him to an inn and took care of him. The next day he took out two silver coins and gave them to the innkeeper. "Look after him," he said, "and when I return, I will reimburse you for any extra expense you may have." Which of these three do you think was a neighbor to the man who fell into the hands of robbers?'

"The expert in the law replied, 'The one who had mercy on him.'

"Jesus told him, 'Go and do likewise.' " Luke 10:30-37, NIV.

When Christ sent out the 70, what did He tell them to do in the cities to which they went?

"*Heal the sick* who are there and *tell them, 'The kingdom of God is near you.'* " Luke 10:9, NIV.

What incentive do Christians have for doing prison work?

"*I was in prison* and you came to visit me." Matthew 25:36, NIV.

NOTE.—In the parable of the sheep and the goats Jesus tells us that whatever we do for those in need, including prisoners, we are doing for Him.

Who hears the groans of the prisoner?

"*The Lord* looked down from his sanctuary on high, from heaven he viewed the earth, to hear the groans of the prisoners, and release those condemned to death." Psalm 102:19, 20, NIV.

Is it our duty always to give what is expected or asked?

"Now a man crippled from birth was being carried to the temple gate called Beautiful, where he was put every day to beg from those going into the temple courts. When he saw Peter and John about to enter, he asked them for money. Peter looked straight at him, as did John. Then Peter said, 'Look at us!' So the man gave them his attention, expecting to get something from them. Then Peter said, 'Silver or gold I do not have, *but what I have I give you.* In the name of Jesus Christ of Nazareth, walk.'

"Taking him by the right hand, he helped him up, and instantly the man's feet and ankles became strong. He jumped to his feet and began to walk. Then he went with them into the temple courts, walking and jumping, and praising God." Acts 3:2-8, NIV.

NOTE.—In the story of the man begging at the Temple gate, Peter and John gave him far more than he would ever have thought to ask.

What is one good evidence of genuine repentance?

"Break off your sins by being righteous, and your iniquities by *showing mercy to the poor*." Daniel 4:27, NIV.

What is one evidence that one has a knowledge of God?

" ' *He defended the cause of the poor and needy*, and so all went well. Is that not what it means to know me?' declares the Lord." Jeremiah 22:16, NIV.

What divine law of reciprocity attends giving?

"*Give, and it will be given to you*. A good measure, pressed down, shaken together and running over, will be poured into your lap. *For with the measure you use, it will be measured to you*." Luke 6:38, NIV. (See Psalms 18:25, 26; 109:17; Galatians 6:7.)

What is promised those who give to the poor?

"He who is kind to the poor lends to the Lord, and *he will reward him for what he has done*." Proverbs 19:17, NIV. "*He who gives to the poor will lack nothing*, but he who closes his eyes to them receives many curses." Proverbs 28:27, NIV.

VISITING AND HEALING THE SICK

What is one righteous act for which Jesus will commend the saved?

"I was sick and *you looked after me*." Matthew 25:36, NIV.

Why, in His earthly ministry, did Jesus heal the sick?

"This was *to fulfill what was spoken through the prophet Isaiah*: 'He took up our infirmities and carried our diseases.' " Matthew 8:17, NIV.

NOTE.—Matthew is quoting Isaiah 53:4.

What relief did Jesus bring to Peter's household?

"When Jesus came into Peter's house, *he saw Peter's mother-in-law lying in bed* with a fever. *He touched her hand and the fever left her*, and she got up and began to wait on him." Matthew 8:14, 15, NIV.

How did Peter summarize Jesus' ministry?

"You know what has happened throughout Judea, beginning in Galilee after the baptism that John preached—how God anointed

Jesus of Nazareth with the Holy Spirit and power, and *how he went around doing good and healing all who were under the power of the devil*, because God was with him." Acts 10:38, NIV.

What should we not forget in our ministry for the sick?

"Therefore confess your sins to each other and *pray for each other so that you may be healed*. The prayer of a righteous man is powerful and effective." James 5:16, NIV.

What does the Lord declare Himself to be?

"I am *the Lord, who heals you*." Exodus 15:26, NIV. "Praise the Lord, O my soul, and forget not all his benefits—who forgives all your sins and heals all your diseases, who redeems your life from the pit and crowns you with love and compassion, who satisfies your desires with good things so that your youth is renewed like the eagle's." Psalm 103:2-5, NIV.

What was promised the children of Israel on condition of obedience?

"Therefore, take care to follow the commands, decrees and laws I give you today. If you pay attention to these laws and are careful to follow them, then the Lord your God will keep his covenant of love with you, as he swore to your forefathers. He will love you and bless you and increase your numbers. He will bless the fruit of your womb, the crops of your land—your grain, new wine and oil—the calves of your herds and the lambs of your flocks in the land that he swore to your forefathers to give you. You will be blessed more than any other people; none of your men or women will be childless, nor any of your livestock without young. *The Lord will keep you free from every disease*. He will not inflict on you the horrible diseases you knew in Egypt, but he will inflict them on all who hate you." Deuteronomy 7:11-15, NIV.

When through disobedience Jeroboam's hand was withered, by what means was it restored?

"Then the king said to the man of God, 'Intercede with the Lord your God and *pray for me that my hand may be restored*.' So the man of God interceded with the Lord, and the king's hand was restored and became as it was before." 1 Kings 13:6, NIV.

When Moses' sister, Miriam, was stricken with leprosy, how was she healed?

"So *Moses cried out to the Lord*, 'O God, please heal her!'" Numbers 12:13, NIV.

What mistake did Asa make when physically afflicted?

"In the thirty-ninth year of his reign Asa was afflicted with a disease in his feet. Though his disease was severe, even in his illness *he did not seek help from the Lord*, but only from the physicians." 2 Chronicles 16:12, NIV.

How was Hezekiah's prayer for restoration from sickness answered?

"Go and tell Hezekiah, 'This is what the Lord, the God of your father David, says: *I have heard your prayer and seen your tears; I will add fifteen years to your life.*'" Isaiah 38:5, NIV.

What constituted a large part of Christ's ministry?

"Jesus went throughout Galilee, teaching in their synagogues, preaching the good news of the kingdom, and *healing every disease and sickness among the people.*" Matthew 4:23, NIV.

In doing this, Jesus fulfilled what prophecy?

"When evening came, many who were demon-possessed were brought to him, and he drove out the spirits with a word and healed all the sick. This was to fulfill what was spoken through the prophet Isaiah: '*He took up our infirmities and carried our diseases.*'" Matthew 8:16, 17.

NOTE.—Matthew is quoting Isaiah 53:4. The essence of the gospel is restoration, or healing of body, soul, and spirit. (See John 3:16; Luke 4:17-19; Acts 3:19-21; Romans 8:21-23; 1 Corinthians 15:51-55.)

One of the Bible's greatest stories of faith is that of the healing of the bleeding woman. As Jesus walked to the house of Jairus to heal the ruler's daughter, a woman who had hemorrhaged continually for 12 years reached out and touched the edge of Jesus' cloak. She did it as discreetly as she could, for the Levitical laws of purity declared her unclean on account of her bleeding, and thus a social outcast. She was instantly healed. To what did Jesus credit her healing?

"'Who touched me?' Jesus asked.

"When they all denied it, Peter said, 'Master, the people are crowding and pressing against you.'

"But Jesus said, 'Someone touched me. I know that power has gone out from me.'

"Then the woman, seeing that she could not go unnoticed, came trembling and fell at his feet. In the presence of all the people, she told why she had touched him and how she had been instantly healed.

Then he said to her, 'Daughter, *your faith has healed you.* Go in peace.' " Luke 8:45-48, NIV.

Before sending out the 12, what power did Christ give them?

"When Jesus had called the Twelve together, he gave them *power and authority to drive out all demons and to cure diseases,* and he sent them out to preach the kingdom of God and *to heal the sick.*" Luke 9:1, 2, NIV. (See Matthew 10:1, 7, 8; Luke 10:1, 9.)

What notable miracle did Peter and John perform shortly after the day of Pentecost?

"One day Peter and John were going up to the temple at the time of prayer—at three in the afternoon. Now a man crippled from birth was being carried to the temple gate called Beautiful, where he was put every day to beg from those going into the temple courts. When he saw Peter and John about to enter, he asked them for money. Peter looked straight at him, as did John. Then Peter said, 'Look at us!' So the man gave them his attention, expecting to get something from them. Then Peter said, 'Silver or gold I do not have, but what I have I give you. In the name of Jesus Christ of Nazareth, walk.' . . . *Then he went with them into the temple courts, walking and jumping, and praising God.* When all the people saw him walking and praising God, they recognized him as the same man who used to sit begging at the temple gate called Beautiful, and they were filled with wonder and amazement at what had happened to him." Acts 3:1-10, NIV.

Among others, what gift has God set in the church?

"And in the church God has appointed first of all apostles, second prophets, third teachers, then workers of miracles, also *those having gifts of healing,* those able to help others, those with gifts of administration, and those speaking in different tongues." 1 Corinthians 12:28, NIV.

In sickness, what is every child of God privileged to do?

"Is any one of you sick? *He should call the elders of the church to pray over him and anoint him with oil in the name of the Lord.*" James 5:14, NIV.

What assurance of blessing is given to those who ask according to God's will?

"And *the prayer offered in faith will make the sick person well*; the Lord will raise him up. If he has sinned, he will be forgiven." Verse 15, NIV.

Is healing guaranteed? If we are not healed, is it a sign that we lack faith? What promise does God give us in the face of sickness and death?

"There was given me a thorn in my flesh, a messenger of Satan, to torment me. Three times I pleaded with the Lord to take it away from me. But he said to me, *'My grace is sufficient for you,* for my power is made perfect in weakness.' " 2 Corinthians 12:7-9, NIV.

Can God bless us through our suffering?

"Therefore I will boast all the more gladly about my weaknesses, so that Christ's power may rest on me. That is why, for Christ's sake, I delight in weaknesses, in insults, in hardships, in persecutions, in difficulties. *For when I am weak, then I am strong.*" Verses 9, 10, NIV.

NOTE.—Physical healing may not always be for our good or to the glory of God. Hence we must be ready to pray with Jesus, "Yet not my will, but yours be done." Luke 22:42, NIV. Paul was denied the removal of infirmity, but the Lord assured him, "My grace is sufficient for you." 2 Corinthians 12:9, NIV. It is not a denial of faith to make use of the simple remedial means that God has given, or those ordinary essentials upon which He makes life dependent, such as proper food, pure air, rest, exercise, and sunshine. Medical care may be used of God in restoring health.

Wise Counsel on Visiting the Sick

"It is misdirected kindness, a false idea of courtesy, that leads to much visiting of the sick. Those who are very ill should not have visitors. The excitement connected with receiving callers wearies the patient at a time when he is in the greatest need of quiet, undisturbed rest. To a convalescent or a patient suffering from chronic disease, it is often a pleasure and a benefit to know that he is kindly remembered; but this assurance conveyed by a message of sympathy or by some little gift will often serve a better purpose than a personal visit, and without danger of harm." Ellen G. White, *The Ministry of Healing*, p. 222.

ORDER AND ORGANIZATION

What does Paul say God is the author of?

"For God is not a God of disorder but of *peace*." 1 Corinthians 14:33, NIV.

Why did Paul give instruction to Timothy concerning the duties and qualifications of church leaders?

"I am writing you these instructions so *that . . . you will know how people ought to conduct themselves in God's household*, which is the church of the living God, the pillar and foundation of the truth." 1 Timothy 3:14, 15, NIV.

How should everything pertaining to God's work be done?

"But everything should be done *in a fitting and orderly way*." 1 Corinthians 14:40, NIV.

NOTE.—In the Scriptures Christians are likened to soldiers, and their work to that of a warrior, or to a conqueror going forth to conquer (2 Timothy 2:3, 4; 1 Timothy 1:18; Revelation 6:2). As order, organization, direction, and discipline are necessary in an army, so are they also in the church. The weapons used and the object sought are different in each case (Romans 13:4; 2 Corinthians 10:3, 4); but the necessity for order and organization are the same in both.

That the burden of judging and looking after the affairs of the Israelites might not all rest on Moses, what instruction did Jethro, his father-in-law, give him?

"But select capable men from all the people—men who fear God, trustworthy men who hate dishonest gain—and appoint them as officials over thousands, hundreds, fifties and tens. Have them serve as judges for the people at all times, but have them bring every difficult case to you; the simple cases they can decide themselves. That will make your load lighter, because they will share it with you. If you do this and God so commands, you will be able to stand the strain, and all these people will go home satisfied." Exodus 18:21-23, NIV.

How many apostles did Jesus at first ordain to preach the gospel?

"He appointed 12—designating them apostles—that they might be with him and that he might send them out to preach and to have authority to drive out demons." Mark 3:14, 15, NIV.

How many did He later appoint to this work?

"After this the Lord appointed 72 others and sent them two by two ahead of him to every town and place where he was about to go." Luke 10:1, NIV.

When the number of the disciples multiplied, what instruction did the apostles give the believers, that none might be neglected in the daily ministration of temporal necessities?

"Brothers, choose seven men from among you who are known to be full of the Spirit and wisdom. We will turn this responsibility over to them." Acts 6:3, NIV.

NOTE.—The men thus selected were known as deacons. The lesson to be learned from this is that leaders and people should unite in planning and providing for the necessary organization and officering of the church according to its growth and needs. This cooperation is again shown in the words of Paul: "I will give letters of introduction to the men you approve and send them." 1 Corinthians 16:3, NIV. (See also Acts 15:22.)

What word came through the Spirit to the ministering prophets and teachers laboring at Antioch?

"While they were worshiping the Lord and fasting, the Holy Spirit said, *'Set apart for me Barnabas and Saul for the work to which I have called them.'* So after they had fasted and prayed, they placed their hands on them and sent them off." Acts 13:2, 3, NIV.

What is one of the gifts which God has set in the church?

"Now you are the body of Christ, and each one of you is a part of it. And in the church God has appointed first of all apostles, second prophets, third teachers, then workers of miracles, also those having gifts of healing, those able to help others, *those with gifts of administration*, and those speaking in different kinds of tongues." 1 Corinthians 12:27, 28, NIV.

NOTE.—While God has given His people many different kinds of skills and gifts, we are not all to work independently. God has given to some the gift of organizing and leading people.

What instruction did the apostle Paul give Titus for the direction of matters in the local church?

"The reason I left you in Crete was that you might straighten out what was left unfinished and *appoint elders in every town*, as I directed you." Titus 1:5, NIV.

What advice did Jesus give to those in leadership positions?

"Jesus called them together and said, 'You know that those who are regarded as rulers of the Gentiles lord it over them, and their high officials exercise authority over them. Not so with you. *Instead, whoever wants to become great among you must be your servant*, and whoever wants to be first must be slave of all. For even the Son of Man did not come to be served, but to serve, and to give his life as a ransom for many.' " Mark 10:42-45, NIV. (See 1 Peter 5:5; Hebrews 13:17.)

What instruction and caution are given to elders?

"To the elders among you, I appeal as a fellow elder, a witness of

Christ's sufferings and one who also will share in the glory to be revealed. *Be shepherds of God's flock that is under your care, serving as overseers*—not because you must, but because you are willing, as God wants you to be; not greedy for money, but eager to serve; *not lording it over those entrusted you*, but being examples to the flock." 1 Peter 5:1-3, NIV.

What are the qualifications and duties of church elders?

"Here is a trustworthy saying: If anyone sets his heart on being an overseer, he desires a noble task. Now the overseer must be above reproach, the husband of but one wife, temperate, self-controlled, respectable, hospitable, able to teach, not given to drunkenness, not violent but gentle, not quarrelsome, not a lover of money. He must manage his own family well and see that his children obey him with proper respect. (If anyone does not know how to manage his own family, how can he take care of God's church?) He must not be a recent convert, or he may become conceited and fall under the same judgment as the devil. He must also have a good reputation with outsiders, so that he will not fall into disgrace and into the devil's trap." 1 Timothy 3:1-7, NIV.

"An elder must be blameless, the husband of but one wife, a man whose children believe and are not open to the charge of being wild and disobedient. Since an overseer is entrusted with God's work, he must be blameless—not overbearing, not quick-tempered, not given to drunkenness, not violent, not pursuing dishonest gain. Rather he must be hospitable, one who loves what is good, who is self-controlled, upright, holy, and disciplined. He must hold firmly to the trustworthy message as it has been taught, so that he can encourage others by sound doctrine and refute those who oppose it." Titus 1:6-9, NIV.

How will the world recognize us as disciples of Christ?

"A new command I give you: Love one another. As I have loved you, so you must love one another. By this all men will know that you are my disciples, *if you love one another*." John 13:34, NIV.

What was Jesus' prayer for His disciples on the eve of His death?

"My prayer is not for them alone. I pray also for those who will believe in me through their message, that all of them may be one, Father, just as you are in me and I am in you. May they also be in us so that the world may believe that you have sent me. I have given them the glory that you gave me, so that they may be one as we are one: I in them and you in me. May they be brought to complete unity to let the world know that you sent me and have loved them even as you have loved me." John 17:20-23, NIV.

NOTE.—How God regards rebellion against divinely appointed authority and leadership is illustrated in the expulsion of Satan and his angels from heaven, and in the fate of Korah, Dathan, and Abiram. (See Revelation 12:7-9; Numbers 16.) The unity and harmony which should exist among believers is described in John 13:34, 35; 17:20-23; and Ephesians 4:1-6. The evil of place-seeking in the church is shown in Mark 10:35-45 and Luke 14:7-11; and of ecclesiastical tyranny, in Daniel 7:25; 8:24, 25; 2 Thessalonians 2:3, 4; and John 16:2. The course to be pursued toward offending members, and in cases in which differences arise, is pointed out in Matthew 18:15-18; 5:23, 24; Galatians 6:1; 1 Timothy 5:19, 20; Titus 3:10, 11; 1 Corinthians 5; and Acts 15. And the guide book in all matters of both doctrine and discipline should be the Bible (Isaiah 8:20; 2 Timothy 3:16, 17; 4:1, 2).

What promise does Peter give to faithful church leaders?

"And when the Chief Shepherd appears, you will receive the crown of glory that will never fade away." 1 Peter 5:4, NIV.

SUPPORT OF THE MINISTRY

What is one way in which we are commanded to honor God?

"*Honor the Lord with your wealth, with the firstfruits of all your crops;* then your barns will be filled to overflowing, and your vats will brim over with new wine." Proverbs 3:9, NIV.

What part of one's income has the Lord especially claimed as His?

"*A tithe of everything from the land*, whether grain from the soil or fruit from the trees, belongs to the Lord; it is holy to the Lord." Leviticus 27:30, NIV.

For whose support and for what work was the tithe devoted in Israel?

"I give to the *Levites* all the tithes in Israel as their inheritance in return *for the work they do while serving at the Tent of Meeting.*" Numbers 18:21, NIV.

How does Paul say the gospel ministry is to be supported?

"If we have sown spiritual seed among you, is it too much if we reap a material harvest from you? If others have this right of support from you, shouldn't we have it all the more? . . . Don't you know that those who work in the temple get their food from the temple, and those who serve at the altar share in what is offered on the altar? *In the same way, the Lord has commanded that those who preach the gospel should receive their living from the gospel*." 1 Corinthians 9:11-14, NIV.

Upon what fundamental basis does the requirement of tithe paying rest?

"*The earth is the Lord's*, and everything in it, the world, and all who live in it." Psalm 24:1, NIV.

How did Jesus view tithing?

"Woe to you, teachers of the law and Pharisees, you hypocrites! You give a tenth of your spices—mint, dill and cummin. But you have neglected the more important matters of the law—justice, mercy and faithfulness. You should have practiced the latter, without neglecting the former." Matthew 23:23, NIV.

Who gives us power to get wealth?

"But remember *the Lord your God*, for it is he who gives you the ability to produce wealth, and so confirms his covenant, which he swore to your forefathers, as it is today." Deuteronomy 8:18, NIV.

What statement of Christ's shows that man is not an original owner, but a steward of God's goods?

"Again, it will be like a man going on a journey, who called *his servants and entrusted his property to them*." Matthew 25:14, NIV. (See 1 Corinthians 4:7.)

How early in the history of the world do we read of tithe paying?

"This Melchizedek was king of Salem and priest of God Most High. He met Abraham returning from the defeat of the kings and blessed him, and *Abraham gave him a tenth of everything*." Hebrews 7:1, 2, NIV. (See Genesis 14:17-20.)

What vow did Jacob make at Bethel?

"Then Jacob made a vow, saying, 'If God will be with me and will watch over me on this journey I am taking and will give me food to eat and clothes to wear so that I return safely to my father's house, then the Lord will be my God and this stone that I have set up as a pillar will be God's house, and of *all that you give me I will give a tenth*.' " Genesis 28:20-22, NIV.

Of what is one guilty who withholds the tithe and freewill offerings?

"Will a man rob God? Yet *you rob me*. But you ask, 'How do we rob you?' In tithes and offerings." Malachi 3:8, NIV.

What does the Lord ask us to prove Him regarding, and upon what conditions does He promise great blessings?

"*Bring the whole tithe into the storehouse,* that there may be food in my house. *Test me in this,*' says the Lord Almighty, 'and see if I will not throw open the floodgates of heaven and pour out so much blessing that you will not have enough room for it. I will prevent pests from devouring your crops, and the vines in your fields will not cast their fruit,' says the Lord Almighty." Verses 10, 11, NIV.

FREEWILL OFFERINGS

By what has God ordained that His work be sustained?

"Tithes and offerings." Malachi 3:8.

How are we told to come into His courts?

"Ascribe to the Lord the glory due his name; *bring an offering* and come into his courts." Psalm 96:8, NIV.

NOTE.—Various offerings are mentioned in the Bible, such as thank offerings, peace offerings, sin offerings, and trespass offerings.

In celebrating the three annual feasts, what instruction did God give His people?

"Three times a year you are to celebrate a festival to me. . . . *No one is to appear before me empty-handed.*" Exodus 23:14, 15, NIV.

With what spirit would God have us give?

"Each man should give what he has decided in his heart to give, *not reluctantly or under compulsion, for God loves a cheerful giver.*" 2 Corinthians 9:7, NIV.

What has Christ said regarding giving?

"In everything I did, I showed you that by this kind of hard work we must help the weak, remembering the words the Lord Jesus himself said: '*It is more blessed to give than to receive.*'" Acts 20:35, NIV.

According to what rule should one give?

"Each of you must bring a gift in proportion to the way the Lord your God has blessed you." Deuteronomy 16:17, NIV. (Compare 1 Corinthians 16:2.)

Upon what basis are gifts acceptable to God?

"For if the willingness is there, the gift is acceptable *according to what one has*, not according to what he does not have." 2 Corinthians 8:12, NIV.

What charge was Timothy instructed to give the rich?

"Command those who are rich in this present world not to be arrogant nor to put their hope in wealth, which is so uncertain, but to put their hope in God, who richly provides us with everything for our enjoyment. Command them *to do good, to be rich in good deeds, and to be generous and willing to share*. In this way they will lay up treasure for themselves as a firm foundation for the coming age, so that they may take hold of the life that is truly life." 1 Timothy 6:17-19, NIV.

How does God regard such a course?

"And do not forget to do good and to share with others, *for with such sacrifices God is pleased*." Hebrews 13:16, NIV.

How does God regard the covetous?

"He boasts of the cravings of his heart; *he* blesses the greedy and *reviles the Lord*." Psalm 10:3, NIV. (See also Exodus 18:21.)

What warning did Christ give against covetousness?

"Then he said to them, 'Watch out! *Be on your guard against all kinds of greed*; a man's life does not consist in the abundance of his possessions.' " Luke 12:15, NIV.

What parable did Jesus tell about a covetous man?

"And he told them this parable: 'The ground of a certain rich man produced a good crop. He thought to himself, "What shall I do? I have no place to store my crops." Then he said, "This is what I'll do. I will tear down my barns and build bigger ones, and there I will store all my grain and my goods. And I'll say to myself, 'You have plenty of good things laid up for many years. Take life easy; eat, drink, and be merry.' "

" ' But God said to him, " ' You fool! This very night your life will be demanded from you. Then who will get what you have prepared for yourself?" ' " Verses 16-20, NIV.

What application does Christ make of this parable?

"This is how it will be with anyone who stores up things for himself but is not rich toward God." Verse 21, NIV.

What warning did Paul give about wealth?

"But godliness with contentment is great gain. For we brought nothing into the world, and we can take nothing out of it. But if we have food and clothing, we will be content with that. People who want to get rich fall into temptation and a trap and into many foolish and harmful desires that plunge men into ruin and destruction. *For the love of money is a root of all kinds of evil.* Some people, eager for money, have wandered from the faith and pierced themselves with many griefs." 1 Timothy 6:6-10, NIV.

By what means can we lay up treasure in heaven?

"*Sell your possessions and give to the poor.* Provide purses for yourselves that will not wear out, a treasure in heaven that will not be exhausted, where no thief comes near and no moth destroys." Luke 12:33, NIV. (See also 1 Timothy 6:7.)

What do our priorities tell us about our spiritual state?

"For where your treasure is, there your heart will be also." Luke 12:34, NIV.

WHO IS THE GREATEST?

At their last Passover together, what did Christ say to His disciples?

"And he said to them, 'I have eagerly desired to eat this Passover with you before I suffer. For I tell you, I will not eat it again until it finds fulfillment in the kingdom of God.'" Luke 22:15, 16, NIV.

What had the disciples been arguing about?

"Also a dispute arose among them as to *which of them was considered to be the greatest.*" Verse 24, NIV.

How did Christ rebuke this attitude?

"Jesus said to them, 'The kings of the Gentiles lord it over them; and those who exercise authority over them call themselves Benefactors. But you are not to be like that. Instead, *the greatest among you should be like the youngest, and the one who rules like the one who serves.*'" Verses 25, 26, NIV. (See Mark 10:42-45.)

What did Jesus say of His own position?

"For who is greater, the one who is at the table or the one who serves? Is it not the one who is at the table? *But I am among you as one who serves.*" Verse 27, NIV.

Notwithstanding that He was their Lord and Master, what example of humility and willing service did Christ give?

"So he got up from the meal, took off his outer clothing, and wrapped a towel around his waist. After that, he poured water into a basin and began to wash his disciples' feet, drying them with the towel that was wrapped around him." John 13:4, 5, NIV.

NOTE.—"By putting on an apron, Christ looked like the slave to whom the task of washing the feet of the guests was assigned. Though the disciples realized what Jesus was doing, none of them offered himself for the task. Servanthood was not on their minds. Jesus loved them knowing all about them, including the worst one of them, Judas. All of the disciples knew what needed to be done. All of them could have done it but none of them did. Luke 22:24 gives us a clue to the reason. They were arguing about who was going to be greatest. That kind of thinking will not lead to servant actions (Philippians 2:3, 4). Our actions are the results of our deepest thoughts. Why would Jesus do what He did, that is, take the role of a servant? Because He knew what He knew and thought deeply (verses 1, 3). It didn't intimidate Jesus to take the temporary role of a servant because He knew where He came from and He knew where He was going to and He knew what He was commissioned to do. Thus, Paul urges us, 'Let this mind be in you which was also in Christ Jesus.' " *Nelson's New Illustrated Bible Commentary* (Nashville: Thomas Nelson, Inc., 1999) p. 1344.

What was the ancient custom regarding footwashing?

"Let a little water be brought, and then you may all wash your feet and rest under this tree." Genesis 18:4, NIV.

" ' My lords,' he said, 'please turn aside to your servant's house. You can wash your feet and spend the night and then go on your way early in the morning.' " Genesis 19:2, NIV.

"The steward took the men into Joseph's house, gave them water to wash their feet and provided fodder for their donkeys." Genesis 43:24, NIV. (See also Judges 19:21; 2 Samuel 11:8.)

How did Jesus reprove Simon for misjudging Him in permitting a woman who was a sinner to wash His feet?

"Then he turned toward the woman and said to Simon, 'Do you see this woman? I came into your house. You did not give me any water for my feet, but she wet my feet with her tears and wiped them with her hair.' " Luke 7:44, NIV.

NOTE.—At a feast it was a custom for servants or slaves to wash the feet of guests (see 1 Samuel 25:40, 41). It was not the custom, however, of *equals* to wash the feet of *equals*, much less for *superiors* to wash the feet of *inferiors*. But this is the very thing that Christ did when He washed the disciples' feet and instituted the ordinance of foot washing. In this lies the lesson of humility and willingness to serve that He designed to teach.

What happened when Jesus came to wash Peter's feet?

"He came to Simon Peter, who said to him, 'Lord, are you going to wash my feet?'

"Jesus replied, 'You do not realize now what I am doing, but later you will understand.'

" ' No,' said Peter, 'you shall never wash my feet.'

"Jesus answered, 'Unless I wash you, you have no part with me.'

" ' Then, Lord,' Simon Peter replied, 'not just my feet but my hands and my head as well!'

"Jesus answered, 'A person who has had a bath needs only to wash his feet; his whole body is clean.' " John 13:6-10, NIV.

NOTE.—This ordinance is a symbol of a higher cleansing—the cleansing of the heart from the stain of sin. It is a rebuke to all selfishness and seeking of place and high position among Christ's professed followers, and a witness to the fact that in God's sight it is true humility and loving service that constitute real greatness.

What did Christ, after having washed their feet, say?

"I have set you an example that you should do as I have done for you." Verse 15, NIV.

What did He say about their washing one another's feet?

"When he had finished washing their feet, he put on his clothes and returned to his place. 'Do you understand what I have done for you?' he asked them. 'You call me "Teacher" and "Lord," and rightly so, for that is what I am. Now that I, your Lord and teacher, have washed your feet, *you also should wash one another's feet*.' " Verses 12-14, NIV.

What did Christ say would be their experience in obeying His instruction?

"Now that you know these things, you will be blessed if you do them." Verse 17, NIV.

How does Christ regard an act performed toward the humblest of His disciples?

"I tell you the truth, whatever you did for one of the least of these brothers of mine, you did for me." Matthew 25:40, NIV.

NOTE.—"The foot washing is no ordinary act. Jesus knows who He is (John 13:3), and He knows the character of those He is ministering to (verse 2). It is a deliberate act of divinity in service to sinful, even unregenerate, humanity. Peter, of course, responds with characteristic abruptness. In the Greek, Peter says in the strongest possible language that he will absolutely not (a double negative) permit Jesus to wash his feet, no matter how long he has to think about it (verse 8). The Greek of verse 8 could be translated in modern English, 'No way in all eternity!' Peter is totally appalled at the possibility of Jesus washing his feet.

"Peter no doubt thought that he was protecting Jesus from humiliation. But Jesus' answer to him (verse 8) makes it clear that Peter was actually protecting himself from the humiliation of admitting his need of Jesus' ministry to the lost (Mark 10:45). 'It is not humility to refuse what the Lord deigns to do for us' (R. Jameison, A. R. Fausset, and D. Brown, *Commentary Practical and Explanatory on the Whole Bible,* rev. ed. [Grand Rapids: Zondervan, 1961], p. 1058). The truest humility comes when we accept the self-sacrificing grace of Christ." Jon Paulien, *The Abundant Life Bible Amplifier: John* (Boise, Idaho: Pacific Press, 1995), p. 212.

CHAPTER 15

Admonitions and Warnings

SINFUL PRIDE

What attitudes and actions does God find particularly detestable?

"These six things the Lord hates, yes, seven are an abomination to Him:

"A proud look,

"A lying tongue,

"Hands that shed innocent blood,

"A heart that devises wicked plans,

"Feet that are swift in running to evil,

"A false witness who speaks lies,

"And one who sows discord among brethren." Proverbs 6:16-19, NKJV.

How does God view prideful people?

"*God resists the proud*, but gives grace to the humble." James 4:6, NKJV.

"Blessed is the man who makes the Lord his trust, who does not look to the proud, to those who turn aside to false gods." Psalm 40:4, NIV.

"Whoever slanders his neighbor in secret, him will I put to silence; whoever has haughty eyes and a proud heart, him will I not endure." Psalm 101:5, NIV.

"Though the Lord is on high, he looks upon the lowly, but the proud he knows from afar." Psalm 138:6, NIV.

Why should we not indulge in pride?

"Haughty eyes and a proud heart, the lamp of the wicked, are *sin!*" Proverbs 21:4, NIV.

What sins particularly characterize the world's last days?

"But mark this: There will be terrible times in the last days. People will be lovers of themselves, lovers of money, boastful, proud, abusive, disobedient to their parents, ungrateful, unholy, without love, unforgiving, slanderous, without self-control, brutal, not lovers of the good, treacherous, rash, conceited, lovers of pleasures rather than lovers of God—having a form of godliness but denying its power. Have nothing to do with them." 2 Timothy 3:1-5, NIV.

What are the results of pride?

"*Pride goes before destruction*, a haughty spirit before a fall." Proverbs 16:18, NIV.

"*A man's pride brings him low*, but a man of lowly spirit gains honor." Proverbs 29:23, NIV.

What description from Ezekiel is applied to Satan as the cause of his spiritual downfall in heaven?

"*Your heart became proud* on account of your beauty, and you corrupted your wisdom because of your splendor." Ezekiel 28:17, NIV.

What is to be the ultimate fate of the proud?

" ' For behold, the day is coming, burning like an oven, and *all the proud*, yes, all who do wickedly *will be stubble*. And the day which is coming shall burn them up,' says the Lord of hosts, 'that will leave them neither root nor branch.' " Malachi 4:1, NKJV.

SELFISHNESS

What great commandment excludes selfishness?

"You shall *love your neighbor as yourself*." Matthew 22:39, NKJV.

What sin is forbidden by the tenth commandment?

"You shall not *covet*." Exodus 20:17, NKJV.

How are we admonished with regard to selfishness?

"Nobody should seek his own good, but the good of others." 1 Corinthians 10:24, NIV. "Each of you should look not only to your own interests, but also to the interests of others." Philippians 2:4, NIV. "Even as I try to please everybody in every way. For I am not seeking my own good but the good of many, so that they may be saved." 1 Corinthians 10:33, NIV. "*Each of us should please his neighbor for his good*, to build him up." Romans 15:2, NIV.

How prevalent is the sin of self-seeking?

"For all seek their own, not the things which are Jesus Christ's." Philippians 2:21.

How does Paul describe love's importance and power?

"If I speak in the tongues of men and of angels, but have not love, I am only a resounding gong or a clanging cymbal. If I have the gift of prophecy and can fathom all mysteries and all knowledge, and if I have a faith that can move mountains, but have not love, I am nothing. If I give all I possess to the poor and surrender my body to the flames, but have not love, I gain nothing.

"Love is patient, love is kind. It does not envy, it does not boast, it is not proud. It is not rude, it is not self-seeking, it is not easily angered, it keeps no record of wrongs. Love does not delight in evil but rejoices with the truth. It always protects, always trusts, always hopes, always perseveres.

"Love never fails. But where there are prophecies, they will cease; where there are tongues, they will be stilled; where there is knowledge, it will pass away. For we know in part and we prophesy in part, but when perfection comes, the imperfect disappears. When I was a child, I talked like a child, I thought like a child, I reasoned like a child. When I became a man, I put childish ways behind me. Now we see but a poor reflection as in a mirror; then we shall see face to face. Now I know in part; then I shall know fully, even as I am fully known.

"And now these three remain: faith, hope and love. But the greatest of these is love." 1 Corinthians 13:1-13, NIV.

What does love never do?

"It does not envy, it does not boast, it is not proud. It is not rude, it is not self-seeking, it is not easily angered, it keeps no record of wrongs. Love does not delight in evil but rejoices with the truth. It always protects, always trusts, always hopes, always perseveres." 1 Corinthians 13:4-7, NIV.

What example of unselfishness did Christ leave us?

"For you know the grace of our Lord Jesus Christ, that though he was rich, yet for your sakes he became poor, so that you through his poverty might become rich." 2 Corinthians 8:9, NIV. "Each of us should please his neighbor for his good, to build him up. For even *Christ did not please himself.*" Romans 15:2, 3, NIV.

What commentary does John give on the importance of loving and serving others?

"We know love by this, that he laid down his life for us—and we ought to lay down our lives for one another. How does God's love abide in anyone who has the world's goods and sees a brother or sister in need and yet refuses help? Little children, let us love, not in word or speech, but in truth and action." 1 John 3:16-18, NRSV.

COVETOUSNESS

What warning did Jesus give about covetousness?

"Then he said to them, 'Watch out! *Be on your guard against all kinds of greed*; a man's life does not consist in the abundance of his possessions.'" Luke 12:15, NIV.

What parable did Jesus tell to illustrate this truth?

"And he told them this parable: 'The ground of a certain rich man produced a good crop. He thought to himself, "What shall I do? I have no place to store my crops." Then he said, "This is what I'll do. I will tear down my barns and build bigger ones, and there I will store all my grain and my goods. And I'll say to myself, 'You have plenty of good things laid up for many years. Take life easy; eat, drink and be merry.'"

"'But God said to him, "You fool! This very night your life will be demanded from you. Then who will get what you have prepared for yourself?"

"'This is how it will be with anyone who stores up things for himself but is not rich toward God.'" Verses 16-21, NIV.

What attitude did Jesus tell us to have, rather than worrying?

"Therefore I tell you, do not worry about your life, what you will eat; or about your body, what you will wear. Life is more than food, and the body more than clothes. Consider the ravens: They do not sow or reap, they have no storeroom or barn; yet God feeds them. And how much more valuable you are than birds! Who of you by worrying can add a single hour to his life? Since you cannot do this very little thing, why do you worry about the rest?

"Consider how the lilies grow. They do not labor or spin. Yet I tell you, not even Solomon in all his splendor was dressed like one of these. If that is how God clothes the grass of the field, which is here today, and tomorrow is thrown into the fire, how much more will he clothe you, O you of little faith! And do not set your heart on what you will eat or drink; do not worry about it. For the pagan world runs after all such things, and your Father knows that you need them. But seek his kingdom, and these things will be given to you as well.

"Do not be afraid, little flock, for your Father has been pleased to give you the kingdom. Sell your possessions and give to the poor. Provide purses for yourselves that will not wear out, a treasure in heaven that will not be exhausted, where no thief comes near and no moth destroys. For where your treasure is, there your heart will be also." Verses 22-34, NIV.

What commandment forbids covetousness?

"You shall not covet your neighbor's house; you shall not covet your neighbor's wife, or male or female slave, or ox, or donkey, or anything that belongs to your neighbor." Exodus 20:17, NRSV.

What does Paul call covetousness?

"Put to death, therefore, whatever belongs to your earthly nature: sexual immorality, impurity, lust, evil desires and greed, *which is idolatry*." Colossians 3:5, NIV.

What do these sins bring upon the world?

"Because of these, *the wrath of God* is coming." Verse 6, NIV.

What double service did Christ say is impossible?

"No servant can serve two masters. Either he will hate the one and love the other, or he will be devoted to the one and despise the other. *You cannot serve both God and Money*." Luke 16:13, NIV.

What sin particularly tempted Pharisees?

"*The Pharisees, who loved money*, heard all this and were sneering at Jesus." Luke 16:14, NIV.

What reply did Jesus make?

"He said to them, 'You are the ones who justify yourselves in the eyes of men, but God knows your hearts. *What is highly valued among men is detestable in God's sight*.'" Verse 15, NIV.

What did greed lead Achan to after the battle of Jericho?

"And Achan answered Joshua, 'It is true; I am the one who sinned against the Lord God of Israel. This is what I did: when I saw among the spoil a beautiful mantle from Shinar, and two hundred shekels of silver, and a bar of gold weighing fifty shekels, then *I coveted them and took them*." Joshua 7:20, 21, NRSV.

What did covetousness lead Judas to do?

"Then Judas Iscariot, one of the Twelve, went to the chief priests to *betray Jesus* to them. They were delighted to hear this and *promised to give him money*. So he watched for an opportunity to hand him over." Mark 14:10, 11, NIV.

What parable did Jesus tell to correct the Pharisees' false idea that wealth was a sign of special favor with God?

The parable of the rich man and Lazarus: Luke 16:19-31.

What did Jesus point out as one of the dangers of the possession of wealth?

"Then Jesus looked around and said to His disciples, 'How hard it is for those who have riches to enter the kingdom of God!' And the disciples were astonished at His words. But Jesus answered again. and said to them, 'Children, how hard it is for those who trust in riches to enter the kingdom of God!' " Mark 10:23, 24, NKJV.

NOTE.—And how hard it is for those who have riches not to trust in them!

What class of people often exhibit the strongest faith?

"Listen, my beloved brethren: Has God not chosen *the poor* of this world to be rich in faith and heirs of the kingdom which He promised to those who love Him?" James 2:5, NKJV.

How difficult did Jesus say it is for a rich person to enter the kingdom of God?

"It is easier for a camel to go through the eye of a needle, than for a rich man to enter into the kingdom of God." Mark 10:25.

What advice did Jesus give the rich young man when asked, "What good thing must I do to get eternal life?"

"If you want to be perfect, go, *sell your possessions and give to the poor*, and you will have treasure in heaven. Then come, *follow me*." Matthew 19:21, NIV.

Why was the rich young man unwilling to take Jesus' advice?

"But when the young man heard that saying, he went away sorrowful: *for he had great possessions*." Verse 22.

What advice did Paul give Timothy regarding contentment?

"But *godliness with contentment is great gain*. For we brought nothing into the world, and we can take nothing out of it. But if we have food and clothing, we will be content with that." 1 Timothy 6:6-8, NIV.

What does Paul declare "the root of all kinds of evil"?

"For *the love of money* is a root of all kinds of evil. Some people, eager for money, have wandered from the faith and pierced themselves with many griefs." Verse 10, NIV.

What evils befall those who are anxious to be rich?

"People who want to get rich *fall into temptation and a trap and into many foolish and harmful desires* that plunge men into ruin and destruction." Verse 9, NIV.

Who gives the power to produce wealth?

"You may say to yourself, 'My power and the strength of my hands have produced this wealth for me.' But remember the Lord your God, *for it is he who gives you the ability to produce wealth*." Deuteronomy 8:17, 18, NIV.

How may all, rich and poor, honor God?

"Honor the Lord *with your wealth, with the firstfruits of all your crops*; then your barns will be filled to overflowing, and your vats will brim over with new wine." Proverbs 3:9, 10, NIV.

What caution is given concerning riches?

"Though your riches increase, *do not set your heart on them*." Psalm 62:10, NIV.

What financial evil does Ecclesiastes warn against?

"I have seen a grievous evil under the sun: *wealth hoarded to the harm of its owner*." Ecclesiastes 5:13, NIV.

What charge did Paul give to the rich?

"Command those who are rich in this present world *not to be arrogant nor to put their hope in wealth, which is so uncertain, but to put their hope in God*, who richly provides us with everything for our enjoyment. Command them to *do good*, to be *rich in good deeds*, and to be generous and willing to share. In this way they will lay up treasure for themselves as a firm foundation for the coming age, so that they may take hold of the life that is truly life." 1 Timothy 6:17-19, NIV.

What makes one rich without adding sorrow?

"*The blessing of the Lord* brings wealth, and he adds no trouble to it." Proverbs 10:22, NIV.

How are true riches obtained?

"*Humility* and the *fear of the Lord* bring wealth and honor and life." Proverbs 22:4, NIV.

What did Moses value more than the treasures of Egypt?

"He regarded *disgrace for the sake of Christ* as of greater value than the treasures of Egypt, because he was looking ahead to his reward." Hebrews 11:26, NIV.

What two classes of rich are mentioned in the Bible?

"There is one who makes himself *rich*, yet *has nothing*; and one who makes himself *poor*, yet *has great riches.*" Proverbs 13:7, NKJV.

NOTE.—Luke 12:16-20, the parable of the rich fool, is an example of the first class. Acts 4:32-35 gives an example of the second.

How did the early Christians handle wealth and possessions in their community?

"All the believers were one in heart and mind. *No one claimed that any of his possessions was his own, but they shared everything they had.* With great power the apostles continued to testify to the resurrection of the Lord Jesus, and much grace was upon them all. There were no needy persons among them. For from time to time those who owned lands or houses sold them, brought the money from the sales and put it at the apostles' feet, and it was distributed to anyone who had need." Acts 4:32-35, NIV.

What solemn warning is addressed to the rich who, in the last days, have heaped up treasure, and oppressed the poor?

"Now listen, you rich people, *weep and wail because of the misery that is coming upon you.* Your wealth has rotted, and moths have eaten your clothes. Your gold and silver are corroded. Their corrosion will testify against you and eat your flesh like fire. You have hoarded wealth in the last days. Look! The wages you failed to pay the workmen who mowed your fields are crying out against you. The cries of the harvesters have reached the ears of the Lord Almighty. You have lived on earth in luxury and self-indulgence. You have fattened yourselves in the day of slaughter." James 5:1-5, NIV.

What value is wealth on the day of judgment?

"*Neither their silver nor their gold will be able to save them* on the day of the Lord's wrath. In the fire of his jealousy the whole world will be consumed, for he will make a sudden end of all who live in the earth." Zephaniah 1:18, NIV.

What wisdom does Solomon offer concerning the value of wealth?

"*Ill-gotten treasures are of no value*, but righteousness delivers from death. The Lord does not let the righteous go hungry, but he thwarts the craving of the wicked. Lazy hands make a man poor, but diligent hands bring wealth." Proverbs 11:2-4, NIV.

What picture does Ezekiel paint of the rich in the day of the Lord?

"Every hand will go limp, and every knee will become as weak as water. They will put on sackcloth and be clothed with terror. Their faces will be covered with shame and their heads will be shaved. They will throw their silver into the streets, and their gold will be an unclean thing. Their silver and gold will not be able to save them in the day of the Lord's wrath. They will not satisfy their hunger or fill their stomachs with it, for it has made them stumble into sin." Ezekiel 7:17-19, NIV.

What are we, as stewards of God's gifts, told to do?

"*Each one should use whatever gift he has received to serve others*, faithfully administering God's grace in its various forms." 1 Peter 4:10, NIV.

DANGER OF DEBT

What general rule does the Bible give regarding meeting our obligations?

"*Give everyone what you owe him*: If you owe taxes, pay taxes; if revenue, then revenue; if respect, then respect; if honor, then honor. *Let no debt remain outstanding, except the continuing debt to love one another*, for he who loves his fellowman has fulfilled the law." Romans 13:7, 8, NIV.

In what condition is one who borrows?

"The rich rules over the poor, and *the borrower is servant to the lender*." Proverbs 22:7, NKJV.

Why did the young man in Elisha's time feel so bad about losing an axhead?

"As one of them was cutting down a tree, the iron axhead fell into the water. 'Oh, my lord,' he cried out, '*it was borrowed*!' " 2 Kings 6:5, NIV.

What miracle did Elisha perform to solve this dilemma?

"The man of God asked, 'Where did it fall?' When he showed him the place, Elisha cut a stick and threw it there, and *made the iron float*." Verse 6, NIV.

NOTE.—God is willing to help those who honestly seek to meet their obligations.

How should Christians conduct their business?

"Good will come to him who is generous and lends freely, who conducts his affairs *with justice*." Psalm 112:5, NIV.

What is the fate of one who ignores good advice?

"He who ignores discipline comes to *poverty and shame*, but whoever heeds correction is honored." Proverbs 13:18, NIV.

NOTE.—Those who, from lack of natural business ability, find themselves constantly running into debt should seek advice and counsel from those with more wisdom in such matters.

Which of Christ's parables teaches business discretion?

"For which of you, intending to build a tower, does not sit down first and *count the cost, whether he has enough to finish it*— lest, after he has laid the foundation, and is not able to finish, all who see it begin to mock him, saying, 'This man began to build and was not able to finish.'" Luke 14:28-30, NKJV.

How were funds for building the tabernacle provided?

"And Moses spoke to all the congregation of the children of Israel, saying, 'This is the thing which the Lord commanded, saying: "Take from among you *an offering* to the Lord. Whoever is of a willing heart, let him bring it as an offering to the Lord: gold, silver, and bronze."'" Exodus 35:4, 5 NKJV.

What provision did King David make for building the temple?

"*With all my resources I have provided for the temple of my God*—gold for the gold work, silver for the silver, bronze for the bronze, iron for the iron and wood for the wood." 1 Chronicles 29:2, NIV.

How did the people respond to David's call for contributions?

"Then the leaders of the fathers' houses, leaders of the tribes of Israel, the captains of thousands and of hundreds, with the officers over the king's work, *offered willingly*. They gave for the work of the house of God five thousand talents and ten thousand darics of gold, ten thousand talents of silver, eighteen thousand talents of bronze, and one hundred thousand talents of iron. . . . Then the people rejoiced, for *they had offered willingly, because with a loyal heart they had offered willingly to the Lord*; and King David also rejoiced greatly." Verses 6-9, NKJV.

When King Joash wished to repair the temple, what provision did he make for raising the necessary funds?

"Joash said to the priests, 'Collect all the money that is brought as sacred offerings to the temple of the Lord—the money collected in the census, the money received from personal vows and the money brought voluntarily to the temple. Let every priest receive the money from one of the treasurers, and let it be used to repair whatever damage is found in the temple.' " 2 Kings 12:4, 5, NIV.

When, after 16 years, it was found that these repairs had not yet been made, what was done?

"Jehoiada the priest *took a chest and bored a hole in its lid. He placed it beside the altar, on the right side as one enters the temple of the Lord*. The priests who guarded the entrance put into the chest all the money that was brought to the temple of the Lord." Verse 9, NIV.

What was done with the money thus raised?

"When the amount had been determined, they gave the money to the men appointed to supervise the work on the temple. With it they paid those who worked on the temple of the Lord—the carpenters and builders, the masons and stonecutters. They purchased timber and dressed stone for the repair of the temple of the Lord, and met all the other expenses of restoring the temple." Verses 11, 12, NIV.

NOTE.—These examples furnish good lessons on financing gospel enterprises. In each instance the means were provided before the work of building was begun. No debt, therefore, was created. In all business transactions this plan is an excellent one to follow

RESPECT FOR OTHERS

How does the Bible describe the creation of humanity?

"And the Lord God formed man of the dust of the ground, and breathed into his nostrils the breath of life; and man became a living soul." Genesis 2:7.

Why did Adam name his wife Eve?

"And Adam called his wife's name Eve; *because she was the mother of all living*." Genesis 3:20.

NOTE.—Eve in Hebrew is *chawwah*. "*Chawwah* means 'life,' and is here translated *Zoe* by the Septuagint. It is an old Semitic form, found also in old Phoenician inscriptions, but was no longer used in the Hebrew language by the time the Bible was written. This has been suggested as indicating that Adam spoke an old Semitic language. If Moses had used a contemporary Hebrew equivalent, he would have written the woman's name *chayyah* instead of *chawwah*, but by giving the name in an unusual archaic form he shows that his knowledge goes back into the remote past. In Genesis 4:1 *chawwah* was roughly translated *Eua* by the Septuagint, whence comes our English 'Eve.' " *The Seventh-day Adventist Bible Commentary* (Washington, D.C.: Review and Herald, 1978), vol. 1, p. 235.

In Noah's day a great flood covered the earth. Were there any survivors?

"*Then the Lord said to Noah, 'Come into the ark, you and all your household*, because I have seen that you are righteous before Me in this generation.' " Genesis 7:1, NKJV.

To whom can we all trace our ancestry?

"These are the families of *the sons of Noah*, after their generations, in their nations: and by these were the nations divided in the earth after the flood." Genesis 10:32.

Are all people, regardless of race, related?

"*From one man he made every nation of men*, that they should inhabit the whole earth; and he determined the times set for them and the exact places where they should live." Acts 17:26, NIV.

What revelation came to Peter in vision while he was alone on the housetop?

"He said to them: 'You are well aware that it is against our law for a Jew to associate with a Gentile or visit him. But *God has shown me that I should not call any man impure or unclean.*' " Acts 10:28, NIV.

How did Paul respond when Peter supported those who believed Christians should follow all Jewish customs and practices, including the rite of circumcision?

"When Peter came to Antioch, *I opposed him to his face*, because he was clearly in the wrong. Before certain men came from James, he used to eat with the Gentiles. But when they arrived, he began to draw back and separate himself from the Gentiles because he was afraid of those who belonged to the circumcision group." Galatians 2:11, 12, NIV.

Are some nations or ethnicities cursed by God and condemned to be servants of other groups?

"Then Peter began to speak: 'I now realize how true it is that *God does not show favoritism* but accepts men from every nation who fear him and do what is right.' " Acts 10:34, 35, NIV.

Since all people have one heavenly Father, what must they avoid?

"Have we not all one Father? Did not one God create us? Why do we profane the covenant of our Fathers by *breaking faith with one another*?" Malachi 2:10, NIV.

How seriously does God view snobbery, discrimination, and social ostracism?

"If you really keep the royal law found in Scripture, 'Love your neighbor as yourself,' you are doing right. But if you show favoritism, you sin and are convicted by the law as lawbreakers." James 2:8, 9, NIV.

What prohibitions does the Bible give against favoritism?

"And I charged your judges at that time: Hear the disputes between your brothers and dispute fairly, whether the case is between brother Israelites or between one of them and an alien. *Do not show partiality in judging; hear both small and great alike*. Do not be afraid of any man, for judgment belongs to God." Deuteronomy 1:16, 17, NIV.

"Do not pervert justice; *do not show partiality* to the poor *or favoritism* to the great, but judge your neighbor fairly." Leviticus 19:15, NIV.

"*Blessed is that man* who makes the Lord his trust, *who does not look to the proud*." Psalm 40:4, NIV.

By what illustration is this sin made plain?

"My brothers, as believers in our glorious Lord Jesus Christ, don't show favoritism. Suppose a man comes into your meeting wearing a gold ring and fine clothes, and a poor man in shabby clothes also comes in. If you show special attention to the man wearing fine clothes and say, 'Here's a good seat for you,' but say to the poor man, 'You stand there' or 'Sit on the floor by my feet,' have you not discriminated among yourselves and become judges with evil thoughts?" James 2:1-4, NIV.

What sign identifies the true follower of Jesus?

"A new command I give you: Love one another. As I have loved you, so you must love one another. By this *all men will know that you are my disciples, if you love one another*." John 13:34, 35, NIV.

What two commandments did Jesus identify as the greatest?

"Jesus replied: ' " *Love the Lord your God with all your heart and with all your soul and with all your mind*." This is the first and greatest commandment. And the second is like it: "*Love your neighbor as yourself.*" All the Law and the Prophets hang on these two commandments.' " Matthew 22:37-40, NIV.

Is it possible to love God and hate other people?

"We love because he first loved us. *If anyone says, 'I love God,' yet hates his brother, he is a liar.* For anyone who does not love his brother, whom he has seen, cannot love God, whom he has not seen. And he has given us this command: Whoever loves God must also love his brother." 1 John 4:19-21, NIV.

Where does love for other people originate? How can we come into possession of it?

"Therefore, since we have been justified through faith, we have peace with God through our Lord Jesus Christ, through whom we have gained access by faith into this grace in which we now stand. Not only so, but we also rejoice in our sufferings, because we know that suffering produces perseverance; perseverance, character; and character, hope. And hope does not disappoint us, because *God has poured out his love into our hearts by the Holy Spirit, whom he has given us.*" Romans 5:1-5, NKJV.

What will happen when the Holy Spirit dwells within us?

"But the fruit of the Spirit is love, joy, peace, longsuffering, kindness, goodness, faithfulness, gentleness, self-control." Galatians 5:22, 23, NKJV.

How may we receive such love if it does not come naturally to us?

"*Ask, and it will be given to you; seek, and you will find; knock, and it will be opened to you.* For everyone who asks receives, and he who seeks finds, and to him who knocks it will be opened." Matthew 7:7, 8, NKJV.

Some contend that this love is merely good will. How does it affect our attitude toward other people?

"Be devoted to one another in brotherly love. *Honor one another above yourselves.*" Romans 12:10, NIV.

Why is there such strife and contention between race and nations?

"What causes fights and quarrels among you? *Don't they come from your desires that battle within you?* You want something but don't get it. You kill and covet, but you cannot have what you want. You quarrel and fight. You do not have, because you do not ask God." James 4:1, 2, NIV.

What does God's love make us capable of?

"You have heard that it was said, 'Love your neighbor and hate your enemy.' But I tell you: *Love your enemies and pray for those who persecute you,* that you may be sons of your Father in heaven. He causes his sun to rise on the evil and the good, and sends rain on the righteous and the unrighteous. If you love those who love you, what reward will you get? Are not even the tax collectors doing that? And if you greet only your brothers, what are you doing more than others? Do not even pagans do that? Be perfect, therefore, as your heavenly Father is perfect." Matthew 5:43-48, NIV.

How does God treat people who choose to be His enemies?

"The Lord is gracious and compassionate, slow to anger and rich in love. The Lord is good to all; *he has compassion on all he has made.*" Psalm 145:8, 9, NIV.

In contrast to our view of ourselves and each other, how does God look at us?

"But the Lord said to Samuel, 'Do not consider his appearance or his height, for I have rejected him. The Lord does not look at the things man looks at. Man looks at the outward appearance, but *the Lord looks at the heart.*'" 1 Samuel 16:7, NIV.

Is it profitable, or fair, for us to judge one another?

"*You, therefore, have no excuse, you who pass judgment on someone else,* for at whatever point you judge the other, you are condemning yourself, because you who pass judgment do the same things." Romans 2:1, NIV.

What is the fruit of vicious talk?

"Serve one another in love. The entire law is summed up in a single command: 'Love your neighbor as yourself.' If you keep on biting and devouring each other, watch out or *you will be destroyed by each other.*" Galatians 5:13-15, NIV.

Is Christ partial to some people?

"You are all sons of God through faith in Christ Jesus, for all of you who were baptized into Christ have clothed yourselves with Christ. *There is neither Jew nor Greek, slave nor free, male nor female, for you are all one in Christ Jesus.*" Galatians 3:26-28, NIV.

What basic principle did Christ set forth as applicable to all our relationships?

"So in everything, do to others what you would have them do to you, for this sums up the Law and the Prophets." Matthew 7:12, NIV.

By what standard did Jesus say we should treat other people?

"Love your neighbor as yourself." Matthew 22:39, NIV.

In what specific ways should a person express love for others?

"He has showed you, O man, what is good. And what does the Lord require of you? *To act justly and to love mercy and to walk humbly with your God.*" Micah 6:8, NIV.

What attitude toward others would solve most of the problems that arise between people?

"If you have any encouragement from being united with Christ, if any comfort from his love, if any fellowship with the Spirit, if any tenderness and compassion, then make my joy complete by being like-minded, having the same love, being one in spirit and purpose. *Do nothing out of selfish ambition or vain conceit, but in humility consider others better than yourselves.* Each of you should look not only to your own interests, but also to the interests of others." Philippians 2:1-4, NIV.

GOSSIPING AND BACKBITING

What does the ninth commandment forbid?

"You shall *not bear false witness* against your neighbor." Exodus 20:16, NKJV.

NOTE.—The evident object of this commandment is to guard the rights, interests, and reputation of our neighbor by guarding our conversation, and confining our words to that which is strictly true.

What instruction did John the Baptist give the soldiers who asked his advice regarding the way of life?

"Likewise the soldiers asked him, saying, 'And what shall we do?' So he said to them, 'Do not intimidate anyone or *accuse falsely*, and be content with your wages.' " Luke 3:14, NKJV.

What realistic view of human nature does the apostle James express?

"We all stumble in many ways. If anyone is never at fault in what he says, he is a perfect man, able to keep his whole body in check." James 3:2, NIV.

How did Christ teach the importance of guarding our speech?

"For out of the overflow of the heart the mouth speaks. The good man brings good things out of the good stored up in him, and the evil man brings evil things out of the evil stored up in him. But I tell you that men will have to give account on the day of judgment for every careless word they have spoken. *For by your words you will be acquitted, and by your words you will be condemned.*" Matthew 12:34-37, NIV.

Who knows all our words?

"Before a word is on my tongue *you know it completely, O Lord.*" Psalm 139:4, NIV.

What advice does the Bible give about our words?

"*Do not go about spreading slander among your people.* Do not do anything that endangers your neighbor's life. I am the Lord." Leviticus 19:16, NIV.

To what does Proverbs compare gossip?

"The words of a gossip are like *choice morsels*; they go down to a man's inmost parts." Proverbs 26:22, NIV.

What is their effect?

"He who covers over an offense promotes love, but *whoever repeats the matter separates close friends.*" Proverbs 17:9, NIV.

What is the result when we refrain from gossip?

"Without wood a fire goes out; *without gossip a quarrel dies down.*" Proverbs 26:20, NIV.

Among other things, what did Paul fear he would find in the Corinthian church?

"For I am afraid that when I come I may not find you as I want you to be, and you may not find me as you want me to be. I fear that there may be quarreling, jealousy, outbursts of anger, factions, *slander*, gossip, arrogance and disorder." 2 Corinthians 12:20, NIV.

What result follows backbiting and like evils?

"The entire law is summed up in a single command: 'Love your neighbor as yourself.' *If you keep on biting and devouring each other, watch out or you will be destroyed by each other.*" Galatians 5:14, 15, NIV.

What promise does God give to those who treat their neighbors with love?

"Lord, who *may dwell in your sanctuary*? Who may *live on your holy hill*? He whose walk is blameless and who does what is righteous, who speaks the truth from his heart and has no slander on his tongue, who does his neighbor no wrong and casts no slur on his fellowman, who despises a vile man but honors those who fear the Lord, who keeps his oath even when it hurts, who lends his money without usury and does not accept a bribe against the innocent. He who does these things will never be shaken." Psalm 15:1-5, NIV.

What caution is given in regard to receiving an accusation against a church elder?

"Do not entertain an accusation against an elder *unless it is brought by two or three witnesses*." 1 Timothy 5:19, NIV.

NOTE.—"Many who listen to the preaching of the word of God make it the subject of criticism at home. They sit in judgment on the sermon as they would on the words of a lecturer or a political speaker. The message that should be regarded as the word of the Lord to them is dwelt upon with trifling or sarcastic comment. The minister's character, motives, and actions, and the conduct of fellow-members of the church, are freely discussed. Severe judgment is pronounced, gossip or slander repeated, and this in the hearing of the unconverted. Often these things are spoken by parents in the hearing of their own children. Thus are destroyed respect for God's messengers, and reverence for their message." Ellen White, *Christ's Object Lessons*, pp. 45, 46.

Can we control our speech without the help of God?

"All kinds of animals, birds, reptiles and creatures of the sea are being tamed and have been tamed by man, but no man can tame the tongue. *It is a restless evil, full of deadly poison*." James 3:7, 8, NIV.

What should we pray for to guard against misusing our speech?

"Set a *guard* over my mouth, O Lord; keep watch over the door of my lips." Psalm 141:3, NIV.

What vow did David take against offenses of the tongue?

"I said, 'I will watch my ways and keep my tongue from sin; *I will put a muzzle on my mouth as long as the wicked are in my presence*.'" Psalm 39:1, NIV.

What is a sure cure for backbiting?

"Love your neighbor as yourself." Matthew 22:39, NIV. "So in everything, do to others what you would have them do to you." Matthew 7:12, NIV. "Slander no one . . . be peaceful and considerate." Titus 3:2, NIV.

What advice does James give against slander?

"Brothers, do not slander one another. *Anyone who speaks against his brother or judges him speaks against the law and judges it*. When you judge the law, you are not keeping it, but sitting in judgment on it." James 4:11, NIV.

How does Proverbs describe carefully chosen words?

"A word aptly spoken is like *apples of gold in settings of silver*." Proverbs 25:11, NIV.

HEALING SHAKEN FAITH

What encouragement does Hebrews give to those who might struggle with their faith?

"So do not throw away your confidence; it will be richly rewarded. You need to persevere so that when you have done the will of God, you will receive what he has promised. For in just a very little while, 'He who is coming will come and will not delay. But my righteous one will live by faith. And if he shrinks back, I will not be pleased with him. But we are not of those who shrink back and are destroyed, but of those who believe and are saved." Hebrews 10:35-39, NIV.

What persistent tendency did the ancient Israelites display?

"My people are determined to turn from me." Hosea 11:7, NIV

What is God's attitude toward those who would abandon Him?

"How can I give you up, Ephraim? How can I hand you over, Israel? How can I treat you like Admah? How can I make you like Zeboiim? My heart is changed within me; *all my compassion is aroused*." Hosea 11:8, NIV.

How can we help each other hold on to faith?

"See to it, brothers, that none of you has a sinful, unbelieving heart that turns away from the living God. But *encourage one another daily*, as long as it called Today, so that none of you may be hardened by sin's deceitfulness We have come to share in Christ if we hold firmly till the end the confidence we had at first." Hebrews 3:12-14, NIV.

How did God view Jerusalem's fickle faith?

"Say to them, 'This is what the Lord says: When men fall down, do they not get up? When a man turns away, does he not return? Why then have these people turned away? . . . They cling to deceit, they refuse to return. I have listened attentively, but they do not say what is right. No one repents of his wickedness, saying, "What have I done?" Each pursues his own course like a horse charging into battle. Even the stork in the sky knows her appointed seasons, and the dove, the swift and the thrush observe the time of their migration. But my people do not know the requirements of the Lord.' " Jeremiah 8:4-7, NIV.

What promise did God give to those who had forsaken Him in the time of Malachi?

" ' Ever since the time of your forefathers you have turned away from my decrees and have not kept them. *Return to me, and I will return to you*,' says the Lord Almighty." Malachi 3:7, NIV.

" ' They will be mine,' says the Lord Almighty, 'in the day when I make up my treasured possession. I will spare them, just as in compassion a man spares his son who serves him. And you will again see the distinction between the righteous and the wicked, between those who serve God and those who do not.' " Verses 17, 18, NIV.

What was one aspect of their relationship that God wished to restore?

"But you ask, 'How are we to return?' Will a man rob God? Yet you rob me. But you ask, 'How do we rob you?' *In tithes and offerings.*" Verses 7, 8, NIV.

What would God do if they'd be faithful to Him in this regard?

" ' Bring the whole tithe into the storehouse, that there may be food in my house. Test me in this,' says the Lord Almighty, 'and see if I will not *throw open the floodgates of heaven and pour out so much blessing that you will not have room enough for it.*' " Verse 10, NIV.

What is especially necessary to prevent faltering faith?

"*Watch and pray* so that you will not fall into temptation. The spirit is willing, but the body is weak." Mark 14:38, NIV.

What are believers urged to do?

"*Examine yourselves* to see whether you are in the faith; test yourselves." 2 Corinthians 13:5, NIV.

What words of instruction and encouragement did Paul leave with the Corinthians, that their faith should not falter?

"Do you not realize that Christ Jesus is in you—unless, of course, you fail the test? And I trust that you will discover that we have not failed the test. Now we pray to God that you will not do anything wrong. Not that people will see that we stood the test but that you will do what is right even though we may seem to have failed. For we cannot do anything against the truth, but only for the truth. We are glad whenever we are weak but you are strong; and our prayer is for your perfection." Verses 5-9, NIV.

NOTE.—"The Corinthians, at least a significant number of them, had been persuaded that genuine strength in an authentic apostle of Christ was to be measured by the standards outlined by the 'super-apostles'—a measurement completely foreign to Paul. Over and over again these two areas of contention surface in Paul's letters to the church at Corinth. Who was, in fact, strong, and who was, in fact, the true apostle of Christ? The Corinthians had been awed by the eloquence and 'wisdom' of the 'super-apostles,' who claimed to be apostles of Christ based on the manner in which they demonstrated their power—even when it was an obvious abuse of power at the Corinthians' expense! (2 Corinthians 11:20). . . . Paul tells the Corinthians that they have misunderstood the concepts of weakness and strength, for Christ Himself is all powerful yet was crucified in weakness (2 Corinthians 13:4). That is, weakness as defined by the 'super-apostles' is false; weakness, paradoxically, is precisely what defines strength (2 Corinthians 12:10). Paul, who came to them in the gentleness and meekness of Christ (2 Corinthians 10:1) is therefore arguing that Christ Himself became weak but now lives by God's power (verse 4; see Philippians 2:8). Paul wants the Corinthians to conclude that just as Christ was crucified in weakness and yet lives by God's power, so his own 'weakness' will result in power (see 2 Corinthians 12:9, 10).

"Paul tells the Corinthians that a true understanding of weakness means obedience to God's will; it has nothing to do with the notions of weakness put forth by the 'super-apostles.' Rather, weakness is best defined by words he used in 2 Corinthians 8:9: 'For you know the grace of our Lord Jesus Christ, that though he was rich, yet for your sakes he became poor, so that you through his poverty might become rich' (NIV)—this is a weakness that spells true strength! And Paul is the spokesman for the Lord, who was weak but is now powerful. This, therefore, is the reason the Corinthians should not take his words lightly: 'On my return I will not spare those who sinned earlier or any of the others' (2 Corinthians 13:2, NIV). Paul hopes, of course, that what he has just written will make a difference in the church and that he will not have to be 'strong' when he arrives." W. Larry Richards, *The Abundant Life Bible Amplifier: 2 Corinthians* (Boise, Idaho: Pacific Press, 1998), pp. 221, 222.

If one has God's law in the heart, what will not occur?

"The law of his God is in his heart; *his feet do not slip*." Psalm 37:31, NIV.

How does God respond when we repent?

"Take words with you and return to the Lord. Say to him: 'Forgive all our sins and receive us graciously, that we may offer the fruit of our lips. . . .'

" '*I will heal their waywardness and love them freely*, for my anger has turned away from them." Hosea 14:2-4, NIV.

NOTE.—"The love of God still yearns over the one who has chosen to separate from Him, and He sets in operation influences to bring him back to the Father's house. . . . A golden chain, the mercy and compassion of divine love, is passed around every imperiled soul." Ellen G. White, *Christ's Object Lessons*, p. 202.

What will be the general spiritual state of many in the last days?

"Because of the increase of wickedness, *the love of most will grow cold*, but he who stands firm to the end will be saved." Matthew 24:12, NIV.

How can we be prepared for such times?

"Be careful, or your hearts will be weighed down with dissipation, drunkenness and the anxieties of life, and that day will close on you unexpectedly like a trap. For it will come upon all those who live on the face of the whole earth. *Be always on the watch, and pray* that you may be able to escape all that is about to happen, and that you may be able to stand before the Son of Man." Luke 21:34-36, NIV.

UNBELIEF AND DOUBT

How does God sometimes shape our characters?

"My son, do not despise the Lord's discipline and do not resent his rebuke, because *the Lord disciplines those he loves*, as a father the son he delights in." Proverbs 3:11, 12, NIV.

How can we avoid the fate of the ancient Israelites, who fell short of God's promised land?

"Therefore, since the promise of entering his rest still stands, let us be careful that none of you be found to have fallen short of it. For we also have had the gospel preached to us, just as they did; but the message they heard was of no value to them, because those who heard did not *combine it with faith*." Hebrews 4:1, 2, NIV.

What did Jesus, when told of the disciples' failure to heal an afflicted son, say of that generation?

" '*O unbelieving generation*,' Jesus replied, *'how long shall I stay with you?* How long shall I put up with you? Bring the boy to me.' " Mark 9:19, NIV.

What did Jesus say to Thomas because he did not believe the others' testimony concerning His resurrection?

"Then he said to Thomas, 'Put your finger here; see my hands. Reach out your hand and put it into my side. *Stop doubting and believe*.' " John 20:27, NIV.

NOTE.—The Lord rebuked Thomas for his unbelief, because he would not accept the testimony of so many credible witnesses who had seen Him.

The Gospel of John was written to encourage the "second generation" of Christians, those who neither knew Jesus personally nor knew those who had walked with Him. " ' Doubting Thomas' represents all those in the Gospel whose belief depended on physical signs and wondrous experiences. The greater experience is reserved for that generation who will come to believe through the testimony of others, through the living Word of the Gospel." Jon Paulien, *The Abundant Life Bible Amplifier: John* (Boise, Idaho: Pacific Press, 1995), p. 271.

"It is probably unfair to speak in terms of 'doubting Thomas.' On at least one occasion, he showed exceptional faith and courage (John 11:7-16). The only difference between him and the other disciples in chapter 20 is that he didn't have the opportunity to see Jesus as they had. The disciple who expressed doubts even when Jesus was present was Philip (6:5-7; 14:8-11), but the Gospel does not make a major issue out of Philip's doubts. It is clear from the Thomas incident that Jesus does not reject people who have doubts, as long as those doubts are honest and the person has not rejected all avenues by which Jesus can reach him or her. Doubt can play an important role in the process of rethinking difficult issues. It is probably better to doubt out loud, as Thomas did, than to slide into silent disbelief (Bruce Barton, ed., *Life Application Bible* [Wheaton, Ill.: Tyndale House Publishers, 1991], p. 1927). [William] Barclay notes (*The Gospel of John*, The Daily Study Bible, revised edition [Philadelphia: Westminster Press,

1975], vol. 2, p. 277) that there is more faith in a person who insists on being sure than in someone who glibly repeats what he or she has never thought out." Jon Paulien, *The Abundant Life Bible Amplifier: John* (Boise, Idaho: Pacific Press, 1995), p. 272.

What blessing did Jesus then pronounce after Thomas declared his belief?

"Then Jesus told him, 'Because you have seen me, you have believed; *blessed are those who have not seen and yet have believed.*' " John 20:29, NIV.

What is impossible without faith?

"And without faith it is impossible *to please God*, because anyone who comes to him must believe that he exists and that he rewards those who earnestly seek him." Hebrews 11:6, NIV.

How only can we be justified?

"Being justified by *faith*, we have peace with God through our Lord Jesus Christ." Romans 5:1.

By what do the just live?

"Now the just shall live by *faith*." Hebrews 10:38.

Why did Israel not attain to the standard of righteousness?

"What then shall we say? That the Gentiles, who did not pursue righteousness, have obtained it, a righteousness that is by faith; but Israel, who pursued a law of righteousness, has not attained it. Why not? *Because they pursued it not by faith but as if it were by works.*" Romans 9:30-32, NIV.

NOTE.—We cannot achieve salvation by our own efforts. Salvation is God's ready gift to us and can be attained only through faith.

When God made a promise to Abraham that seemed impossible to fulfill, how did the patriarch receive it?

"Yet he did not waver through unbelief regarding the promise of God, but was strengthened in his faith and gave glory to God, being fully persuaded that God had power to do what he had promised. This is why '*it was credited to him as righteousness.*' The words 'it was credited to him' were written not for him alone, but also for us, to whom God will credit righteousness—for us who believe in him who raised Jesus our Lord from the dead. He was delivered over to death for our sins and was raised to life for our justification." Romans 4:20-25, NIV.

How did God credit Abraham's faith?

"What does the Scripture say? 'Abraham believed God, and it was credited to him as *righteousness.*' Now when a man works, his wages are not credited to him as a gift, but as an obligation. However, to the man who does not work but trusts God who justifies the wicked, his *faith is credited as righteousness.*" Verses 3-5 NIV.

How should we pray when we struggle with doubt?

"I do believe; help me overcome my unbelief!" Mark 9:24, NIV.

What is promised those who believe when they pray?

"Therefore I tell you, *whatever you ask for in prayer*, believe that you have received it, and *it will be yours.*" Mark 11:24, NIV.

How should we relate to those who struggle with doubt?

"Be merciful to those who doubt; snatch others from the fire and save them; to others show mercy, mixed with fear—hating even the clothing stained by corrupted flesh." Jude 22, 23, NIV.

NOTE.—This is reminiscent of Zechariah 3. "Then he showed me Joshua the high priest standing before the angel of the Lord, and Satan standing at his right side to accuse him. The Lord said to Satan, 'The Lord rebuke you, Satan! The Lord, who has chosen Jerusalem, rebuke you! Is not this man a burning stick snatched from the fire?'

"Now Joshua was dressed in filthy clothes as he stood before the angel. The angel said to those who were standing before him, 'Take off his filthy clothes.'

"Then he said to Joshua, 'See, I have taken away your sin, and I will put rich garments on you.'" Verses 1-4, NIV.

What does the book of Hebrews, after speaking of numerous examples of faith, urge us to do?

"Therefore, since we are surrounded by such a great cloud of witnesses, let us *throw off everything that hinders and the sin that so easily entangles*, and let us run with perseverance the race marked out for us. Let us fix our eyes on Jesus, the author and perfecter of our faith, who for the joy set before him endured the cross, scorning its shame, and sat down at the right hand of the throne of God. Consider him who endured such opposition from sinful men, so that you will not grow weary and lose heart." Hebrews 12:1-3, NIV.

NOTE.—The "everything that hinders" here spoken of includes those traits of character and habits of life that retard or hinder our running successfully the Christian race. These are to be laid aside. But there is another thing referred to here: a sin, one that easily overwhelms us all—the sin of unbelief.

HYPOCRISY AND REWARD

Of what sin were the Pharisees particularly guilty?

"Jesus began to speak first to his disciples, saying: 'Be on your guard against the yeast of the Pharisees, which is *hypocrisy.*'" Luke 12:1, NIV.

NOTE.—Hypocrisy is pretending to be what one is not; a concealment of one's real character or motives, especially the assuming of a false appearance of virtue or religion.

How did the Pharisees demonstrate their hypocrisy?

"Then some Pharisees and teachers of the law came to Jesus from Jerusalem and asked, 'Why do your disciples break the tradition of the elders? They don't wash their hands before they eat!'

"Jesus replied, 'And why do you break the command of God for the sake of your tradition? For God said, "Honor your father and mother" and "Anyone who curses his father or mother must be put to death." But you say that if a man says to his father or mother, "Whatever help you might otherwise have received from me is a gift devoted to God," he is not to "honor his father" with it. Thus you nullify the word of God for the sake of your tradition. You hypocrites! Isaiah was right when he prophesied about you: *"These people honor me with their lips, but their hearts are far from me. They worship me in vain; their teachings are but rules taught by men."*'" Matthew 15:1-9, NIV.

How did Jesus describe the prayers of hypocrites?

"And when you pray, do not be like the hypocrites, *for they love to pray standing in the synagogues and on the street corners to be seen by men.* I tell you the truth, they have received their reward in full. But when you pray, go into your room, close the door and pray to your Father, who is unseen. Then your Father, who sees what is done in secret, will reward you." Matthew 6:5, 6, NIV.

What does Christ call those who readily see the faults of others but do not see or correct their own?

"You *hypocrite*, first take the plank out of your own eye, and then you will see clearly to remove the speck from your brother's eye." Matthew 7:5, NIV.

What did David say he would not do?

"I do not sit with deceitful men, *nor do I consort with hypocrites*; I abhor the assembly of evildoers and refuse to sit with the wicked." Psalm 26:4, 5, NIV.

How does Paul describe love in action?

"Love must be *sincere*. Hate what is evil; cling to what is good. Be devoted to one another in brotherly love. Honor one another above yourselves." Romans 12:9, 10, NIV.

How did James describe heavenly wisdom?

"For where you have envy and selfish ambition, there you find disorder and every evil practice. But the wisdom that comes from heaven is *first of all pure; then peace-loving, considerate, submissive, full of mercy and good fruit, impartial and sincere*. Peacemakers who sow in peace raise a harvest of righteousness." James 3:16-18, NIV.

What is the spiritual law of cause and effect?

"For we must all appear before the judgment seat of Christ, that each one may receive *what is due him* for the things done while in the body, whether good or bad." 2 Corinthians 5:10, NIV.

"God 'will give to each person *according to what he has done*.' To those who by persistence in doing good seek glory, honor and immortality, he will give eternal life. But for those who are self-seeking and who reject the truth and follow evil, there will be wrath and anger. There will be trouble and distress for every human being who does evil: first for the Jew, then for the Gentile; but glory, honor and peace for everyone who does good: first for the Jew, then for the Gentile. For God does not show favoritism." Romans 2:6-11, NIV.

"Do not be deceived: God cannot be mocked. *A man reaps what he sows*. The one who sows to please his sinful nature, from that nature will reap destruction; the one who sows to please the Spirit, from the Spirit will reap eternal life. Let us not become weary in doing good, for at the proper time we will reap a harvest if we do not give up. Therefore, as we have opportunity, let us do good to all people, especially to those who belong to the family of believers." Galatians 6:7-10, NIV.

MEASURE FOR MEASURE

How does the Bible describe the spiritual law of cause and effect?

"Do not judge, or you too will be judged. For in the same way you judge others, you will be judged, and *with the measure you use, it will be measured to you.*" Matthew 7:1, 2, NIV. "With the merciful You will show Yourself merciful; With a blameless man You will show Yourself blameless; with the pure You will show Yourself pure; and with the devious You will show Yourself shrewd." Psalm 18:25, 26, NKJV.

In view of this, what are we warned not to do?

"Repay no one evil for evil." Romans 12:17, NKJV. *"Do not repay evil with evil* or insult with insult, *but with blessing*, because to this you were called so that you may inherit a blessing." 1 Peter 3:9, NIV.

What is said of those who return evil for good?

"Evil will not depart from the house of one who returns evil for good." Proverbs 17:13, NRSV.

What principle of justice should govern us in our dealings?

"Do not withhold good from those to whom it is due, when it is in the power of your hand to do so." Proverbs 3:27, NKJV.

What may we be sure that God, in giving out the final awards, will do?

"Shall not the Judge of all the earth do *right?*" Genesis 18:25. "Righteousness and justice are the foundation of your throne; love and faithfulness go before you." Psalm 89:14, NIV.

CHAPTER 16

Home and Family

MARRIAGE

What did God, after creating Adam, say?

"The Lord God said, 'It is not good for the man to be alone. I will make a helper suitable for him.' " Genesis 2:18, NIV.

NOTE.—Adam's companion, or help, was to correspond to him. God made each one suited to meet the other's needs.

How did God create the first woman?

"So the Lord God caused the man to fall into a deep sleep; and while he was sleeping, he took one of the man's ribs and closed up the place with flesh. Then *the Lord God made a woman from the rib he had taken out of the man, and he brought her to the man.*" Verses 21, 22, NIV.

NOTE.—How beautiful is this simple but evocative story. God did not go to the lower animals to create our first human. Rather, God created Adam—and thus the human race—"in His own image."

And with the beauty of symbolism God created Eve from the flesh and bone of Adam. Taking a rib from His sleeping son, God created woman to stand at his side as his equal. The myriad facets of their minds and personalities would combine together to make "the image of God."

What did Adam say when God introduced him to Eve?

"The man said, *'This is now bone of my bones and flesh of my flesh; she shall be called 'woman,' for she was taken out of man.'*" Verse 23, NIV.

What does Genesis say about marriage?

"For this reason a man will leave his father and mother and be united to his wife, and *they will become one flesh.*" Verse 24, NIV.

NOTE: — To be "one flesh" is to be as closely united as two sheets of paper glued together. It is impossible to remove one sheet from the other without damage and tearing. To be truly "one flesh" is a journey of a lifetime.

How did Jesus respond to a question about divorce?

"Some Pharisees came to him to test him. They asked, 'Is it lawful for a man to divorce his wife for any and every reason?'

" ' Haven't you read,' he replied, 'that at the beginning the Creator "made them male and female," and said, "For this reason a man will leave his father and mother and be united to his wife, and the two will become one flesh"? So they are no longer two, but one. Therefore what God has joined together, let man not separate.'

" ' Why then,' they asked, 'did Moses command that a man give his wife a certificate of divorce and send her away?'

"Jesus replied, 'Moses permitted you to divorce your wives because your hearts were hard. But it was not this way from the beginning. I tell you that anyone who divorces his wife, except for marital unfaithfulness, and marries another woman commits adultery.'

"The disciples said to him, 'If this is the situation between a husband and wife, it is better not to marry.'

"Jesus replied, 'Not everyone can accept this word, but only those to whom it has been given. For some are eunuchs because they were born that way; others were made that way by men; and others have renounced marriage because of the kingdom of heaven. The one who can accept this should accept it.' " Matthew 19:3-12, NIV.

NOTE.—In Jesus' day, many people were divided into two camps on the subject of divorce. Interpreting Deuteronomy 24:1, many (following the teachings of Rabbi Shammai) maintained that adultery was the only grounds for divorce, while others (following the teachings of Rabbi Hillel) believed that divorce should be easy to obtain for a variety of offenses. The Pharisees sought to entrap Jesus by forcing Him to take a stand that would turn one group or the other against Him. But Jesus refused to be taken in by their sophistry. Jesus quoted two Old Testament texts, Genesis 1:27 and Genesis 2:24, but did not directly answer the question. Instead He emphasized that what God has blessed should not be broken, a fundamental truth on which all could agree.

"Michael Green (*Matthew for Today* [Dallas: Word, 1989], pp. 181, 182) points out that Jesus made six strong points about marriage in His reply to the Pharisees. First, marriage was designed by God. It is a God-given ordinance, rather than a mere social contract.

"Second, marriage is an ordinance between the sexes. God 'made them male and female.' God's intention was not a unisex world. . . .

"Third, marriage is intended to be permanent: 'The two will become one flesh.' It was never intended that the marriage relationship ever be broken by any 'indecency.' . . . Any deviation from the perpetuity of marriage is a declension from the ideal.

"Fourth, marriage is exclusive. . . . One man and one woman are to be joined together. That ideal rules out the convenient 'affairs' of so many modern people and the polygamy of the ancients. Apparently, God's allowance for polygamy in the Old Testament was a less-than-ideal concession to entrenched custom and human weakness. Beyond that, it provided security for females in cultures where they had no rights as independent citizens and where there were not enough males to go around.

"Fifth, marriage creates a nuclear family unit. It includes both leaving one's parents and uniting with a spouse. Thus marriage becomes the strongest and most important of all human relationships.

"Sixth, marriage is not for everybody. That is implied in verses 10 to 12. The disciples are shocked by the rigor of Jesus' exposition on the nature of marriage. He has been tougher than even Shammai. Therefore, the disciples suggest that if it is impossible to get out of marriage, perhaps it is best not to get into it in the first place.

God's Plan for Marriage

It was in Eden—before sin entered the world—that God created marriage, joining the hands and hearts of our first parents in a lifetime bond. And just as couples today struggle with problems and tragedy, Adam and Eve faced the same. Even in those first precious years of life it would have been easy for either Adam or Eve to blame the other for the thorns and sweat and—most tragic of all—the loss of personal fellowship with the God who kissed them awake. And few of us weep, as they surely did, at the raw grave of one of our sons, murdered by his older brother. And they knew that the serpent had spoken truth when he enticed Eve to eat the forbidden fruit with the promise that she would become as the gods, knowing good *and* evil!

Just as God established the Sabbath at the end of creation week, so, too, He established the ordinance of marriage. The lifelong unity of one man and woman was ordained, not only to people the earth, but to promote social order and human happiness. Committed wholly to one another in marriage, generation after generation of families would transmit the love, joy, and peace that comes to those devoted to God. When the divine origin of marriage is recognized and the divine principles controlling it are obeyed, marriage is indeed a blessing. When these principles are disregarded, untold heartache, confusion, and even tragedy follow. Used rightly, the union of a woman and a man is one of life's greatest blessings.

"While Jesus does not forthrightly deny this suggestion, He does say that not everyone can accept it. Then He adds that some will renounce their right to marriage 'because of the kingdom of heaven' (verse 12). Such was the status of Jesus Himself, John the Baptist, and apparently Paul in his mature years." George Knight, *The Abundant Life Bible Amplifier: Matthew* (Boise, Idaho: Pacific Press, 1994), pp. 197-199.

The Pharisees of Jesus' day justified their selfish divorces (with the intent to remarry another who better suited their current desires) by appealing to Deuteronomy 24. Yet Jesus condemned them as committing adultery as surely as anyone (Matthew 19:9).

By what commands has God guarded marriage?

"You shall not commit adultery." Exodus 20:14, NKJV. "You shall not covet your neighbor's wife." Verse 17, NKJV.

What counsel does the book of Hebrews give regarding marriage?

"Marriage should be honored by all, and the marriage bed kept pure, for God will judge the adulterer and all the sexually immoral." Hebrews 13:4, NIV.

NOTE.—It is a tragedy that even some Christian couples enter into marriage thinking that if it doesn't "work," they can always get a divorce. That men and women who are uncommitted to each other bring children into the world creates problems that roll on through generation after generation. The truth that marriage was given by God in Eden often seems quaint, at best, to modern people. Many of these have no knowledge of its potential for personal fulfillment and its influence for good or evil. And often even those who marry in a church have little idea of its responsibilities and sacred obligations.

How does Scripture use marriage as a symbol of the relationship between God and His people?

"On that day, says the Lord, you will call me 'my husband,' . . . *and I will take you for my wife forever*; I will take you for my wife in righteousness and in justice, in steadfast love, and in mercy. I will take you for my wife in faithfulness, and you shall know the Lord." Hosea 2:16-20, NRSV.

" ' Let us rejoice and exult and give him the glory, for *the marriage of the Lamb has come, and his bride has made herself ready*; to her it has been granted to be clothed with fine linen, bright and pure'—for the fine linen is the righteous deeds of the saints." Revelation 19: 7, 8, NRSV.

"For *your Maker is your husband*—the Lord Almighty is his

name—the Holy One of Israel is your Redeemer; he is called the God of all the earth." Isaiah 54:5, NIV.

" 'Return, faithless people,' declares the Lord, 'for I am your husband. I will choose you—one from a town and two from a clan— and bring you to Zion." Jeremiah 3:14, NIV.

What marriage metaphor does Isaiah use to describe God's future celebration of His children's salvation?

"As a bridegroom rejoices over his bride, so will your God rejoice over you." Isaiah 62:5, NIV.

What covenant language does the Bible use to describe marriage?

"My beloved is mine, and I am his." Song of Solomon 2:16, NRSV.

"Another thing you do: You flood the Lord's altar with tears. You weep and wail because he no longer pays attention to your offerings or accepts them with pleasure from your hands. You ask, 'Why?' *It is because the Lord is acting as the witness between you and the wife of your youth, because you have broken faith with her, though she is your partner, the wife of your marriage covenant.*" Malachi 2:13, 14, NIV.

In the book of Malachi, what stand does God take against divorce?

"Has not the Lord made them one? In flesh and spirit they are his. And why one? Because he was seeking godly offspring. *So guard yourself in your spirit, and do not break faith with the wife of your youth.* 'I hate divorce,' says the Lord God of Israel, 'and I hate a man's covering himself with violence as well as with his garment,' says the Lord Almighty. So guard yourself in your spirit, and do not break faith." Verses 15, 16, NIV.

How does Proverbs warn against adultery?

"For the lips of an adulteress drip honey, and her speech is smoother than oil; but in the end she is bitter as gall, sharp as a double-edged sword. Her feet go down to death; her steps lead straight to the grave. She gives no thought to the way of life; her paths are crooked, but she knows it not." Proverbs 5:3-6, NIV.

"My son, keep your father's commands and do not forsake your mother's teaching. Bind them upon your heart forever; fasten them around your neck. When you walk, they will guide you; when you sleep, they will watch over you; when you awake, they will speak to you. For these commands are a lamp, this teaching is a light, and the corrections of discipline are the way to life, keeping you from the immoral woman, from the smooth tongue of the wayward wife. Do not lust in your heart after her beauty, or let her captivate you with her eyes, for the prostitute reduces you to a loaf of bread, and the adulteress preys upon your very life. Can a man scoop fire into his lap without his clothes being burned? Can a man walk on hot coals without his feet being scorched? So is he who sleeps with another man's wife; no one who touches her will go unpunished." Proverbs 6:20-29, NIV.

How does Proverbs suggest we guard against adultery?

"Drink water from your own cistern, running water from your own well. Should your springs overflow in the streets, your streams of water in the public squares? Let them be yours alone, never to be shared with strangers. May your fountain be blessed, and may you rejoice in the wife of your youth. A loving doe, a graceful deer—may her breasts satisfy you always, may you ever be captivated by her love." Proverbs 5:15-19, NIV.

How did Jesus expand the definition of adultery—marital unfaithfulness—beyond a mere physical act?

"You have heard that it was said, 'You shall not commit adultery.' But I say to you that *everyone who looks at a woman with lust has already committed adultery with her in his heart.*" Matthew 5:27, 28, NRSV.

NOTE.—Adultery is not limited to extramarital sexual relations. Adultery begins in the heart, and is anything that betrays the sacred marital bond. Thus adultery can include such careless acts of selfishness and misplaced priorities as valuing one's career above that of the marriage partnership, ignoring one's spouse's personal needs, and such stark offences as physical violence and sexual assault.

Marriage is God's sacred institution, and should be entered into and maintained with the utmost care and commitment. In all cases much grace and dedication are called for.

What thoughts does Paul share about marriage?

"Now for the matters you wrote about: It is good for a man not to marry. But since there is so much immorality, each man should have his own wife, and each woman her own husband. The husband should fulfill his marital duty to his wife, and likewise the wife to her husband. The wife's body does not belong to her alone but also to her husband. In the same way, the husband's body does not belong to him alone but also to his wife. Do not deprive each other except by mutual consent and for a time, so that you may devote yourselves to prayer. Then come together again so that Satan will not tempt you because of your lack of self-control. I say this as a concession, not as a command. I wish that all men were as I am. But each man has his own gift from God; one has this gift, another has that.

"Now to the unmarried and the widows I say: It is good for them to stay unmarried, as I am. But if they cannot control themselves, they should marry, for it is better to marry than to burn with passion." 1 Corinthians 7:1-9, NIV.

What thoughts does Paul share about tensions relating to marriage?

"To the married I give this command (not I, but the Lord): . . . If any brother has a wife who is not a believer and she is willing to live with him, he must not divorce her. And if a woman has a husband who is not a believer and he is willing to live with her, she must not divorce him. For the unbelieving husband has been sanctified through his wife, and the unbelieving wife has been sanctified through her believing husband. Otherwise your children would be unclean, but as it is, they are holy.

"But if the unbeliever leaves, let him do so. A believing man or woman is not bound in such circumstances; God has called us to live in peace. How do you know, wife, whether you will save your husband? Or, how do you know, husband, whether you will save your wife?

"Nevertheless, each one should retain the place in life that the Lord assigned to him and to which God has called him. This is the rule I lay down in all the churches. Was a man already circumcised when he was called? He should not become uncircumcised. Was a man uncircumcised when he was called? He should not be circumcised. Circumcision is nothing and uncircumcision is nothing. Keeping God's commands is what counts." Verses 10-19, NIV.

What instruction does Paul give regarding partnership with those with different spiritual beliefs, which may be applied to marriage?

"Do not be yoked together with unbelievers. For what do righteousness and wickedness have in common? Or what fellowship can light have with darkness? What harmony is there between Christ and Belial? What does a believer have in common with an unbeliever? What agreement is there between the temple of God and idols? For we are the temple of the living God. As God has said: 'I will live with them and walk among them, and I will be their God, and they will be my people.' " 2 Corinthians 6:14-16, NIV.

NOTE.—While Paul's advice is not limited to marriage, its principles certainly apply to it. A shared spiritual vision in marriage is one of the most crucial components for health and happiness. Our personal picture of God determines how we view and approach life. Our view of God as caring or cruel, loving or legalistic, exacting or embracing, colors every aspect of life, including our relationships. A relationship not united by a positive shared view of God's character is one in danger of failing. Even people of the same faith background can have such different views of God and/or of personal standards that they are not compatible.

King Solomon viewed marriage to wives from surrounding pagan nations as a political obligation. Even so the man often called "the wisest man who ever lived" was influenced by the false gods and idols of his wives. "As Solomon grew old, his wives turned his heart after other gods, and his heart was not fully devoted to the Lord his God, as the heart of David his father had been." 1 Kings 11:4, NIV. To forge a spiritually unequal union is to place one's self on perilous ground. Good sense should teach us that faith can best be maintained, and domestic happiness best ensured, by a husband and wife sharing the same faith outlook.

What counsel did Peter give to women married to unbelievers?

"Wives, in the same way be submissive to your husbands so that, if any of them do not believe the word, they may be won over without words by the behavior of their wives, when they see the purity and reverence of your lives." 1 Peter 3:1, 2, NIV.

NOTE.—"It is clear that Peter has unbelieving husbands in mind, for they need to be won. Then, even more than now, Christian congregations included a large proportion of women who had unbelieving husbands. The basic principle is stated in 3:1, 2. Try to win your husbands by your behavior, not by words." Robert M. Johnston, *The Abundant Life Bible Amplifier: Peter and Jude* (Boise, Idaho: Pacific Press, 1995), p. 85.

For how long does marriage bind the contracting parties?

"By law *a married woman is bound to her husband as long as he is alive*, but if her husband dies, she is released from the law of marriage." Romans 7:2, NIV.

"A woman is bound to her husband as long as he lives. But if her husband dies, she is free to marry anyone she wishes, but he must belong to the Lord." 1 Corinthians 7:39, NIV.

How does Paul describe the love that should characterize marriage?

"Love is patient; love is kind; love is not envious or boastful or arrogant or rude. It does not insist on its own way; it is not irritable or resentful; it does not rejoice in wrongdoing, but rejoices in the truth. It bears all things, believes all things, hopes all things, endures all things." 1 Corinthians 13:4-7, NRSV.

SEXUALITY

How does the Song of Solomon celebrate romantic love?

"[The Beloved] Let him kiss me with the kisses of his mouth—

for your love is more delightful than wine. Pleasing is the fragrance of your perfumes; your name is like perfume poured out. No wonder the maidens love you! Take me away with you—let us hurry! Let the king bring me into his chambers." Song of Solomon 1:1-4, NIV.

"[Lover] I liken you, my darling, to a mare harnessed to one of the chariots of Pharaoh. Your cheeks are beautiful with earrings, your neck with strings of jewels. We will make you earrings of gold, studded with silver.

"[Beloved] While the king was at his table, my perfume spread its fragrance. My lover is to me a sachet of myrrh resting between my breasts. My lover is to me a cluster of henna blossoms from the vineyards of En Gedi.

"[Lover] How beautiful you are, my darling! Oh, how beautiful! Your eyes are doves.

"[Beloved] How handsome you are, my lover! Oh, how charming! And our bed is verdant." Verses 9-16, NIV.

"[Beloved] He has taken me to the banquet hall, and his banner over me is love. Strengthen me with raisins, refresh me with apples, for I am faint with love. His left arm is under my head, and his right arm embraces me. Daughters of Jerusalem, I charge you by the gazelles and by the does of the field: Do not arouse or awaken love until it so desires." Song of Solomon 2:4-7, NIV.

"[Lover] How beautiful you are, my darling! Oh, how beautiful! Your eyes behind your veil are doves. . . . Your lips are like a scarlet ribbon; your mouth is lovely. Your temples behind your veil are like the halves of a pomegranate. Your neck is like the tower of David, built with elegance; on it hang a thousand shields, all of them shields of warriors. Your two breasts are like two fawns, like twin fawns of a gazelle that browse among the lilies. Until the day breaks and the shadows flee, I will go to the mountain of myrrh and to the hill of incense. All beautiful you are, my darling; there is no flaw in you. . . . You have stolen my heart, my sister, my bride; you have stolen my heart with one glance of your eyes, with one jewel of your necklace. How delightful is your love, my sister, my bride! How much more pleasing is your love than wine, and the fragrance of your perfume than any spice! Your lips drip sweetness as the honeycomb, my bride; milk and honey are under your tongue." Song of Solomon 4:1-11, NIV.

"[Beloved] My lover is radiant and ruddy, outstanding among ten thousand. His head is purest gold; his hair is wavy and black as a raven. His eyes are like doves by the water streams, washed in milk, mounted like jewels. His cheeks are like beds of spice yielding perfume. His lips are like lilies dripping with myrrh. His arms are rods of gold set with chrysolite. His body is like polished ivory decorated

with sapphires. His legs are pillars of marble set on bases of pure gold. His appearance is like Lebanon, choice as its cedars. His mouth is sweetness itself; he is altogether lovely. This is my lover, this my friend, O daughters of Jerusalem." Song of Solomon 5:10-16, NIV.

NOTE.—The Song of Solomon celebrates the love God created to exist between a man and a woman.

How does the lover in Song of Solomon describe his sexual attraction to his bride?

"How beautiful your sandaled feet, O prince's daughter! Your graceful legs are like jewels, the work of a craftsman's hands. Your navel is a rounded goblet that never lacks blended wine. Your waist is a mound of wheat encircled by lilies. Your breasts are like two fawns, twins of a gazelle. Your neck is like an ivory tower. Your eyes are the pools of Heshbon by the gate of Beth Rabbim. Your nose is like the tower of Lebanon looking toward Damascus. Your head crowns you like Mount Carmel. Your hair is like royal tapestry; the king is held captive by its tresses. How beautiful you are and how pleasing, O love, with your delights! Your stature is like that of the palm, and your breasts like clusters of fruit. I said, 'I will climb the palm tree; I will take hold of its fruit.' May your breasts be like the clusters of the vine, the fragrance of your breath like apples, and your mouth like the best wine." Song of Solomon 7:1-8, NIV.

NOTE.—By this point in the narrative the descriptions have become much more erotic, as the characters have entered into marriage.

How does the bride respond to her lover's lavish praise and sexual overtures?

"May the wine go straight to my lover, flowing gently over lips and teeth. I belong to my lover, and his desire is for me. Come, my lover, let us go to the countryside, let us spend the night in the villages. Let us go early to the vineyards, to see if the vines have budded, if their blossoms have opened, and if the pomegranates are in bloom—there I will give you my love. The mandrakes send out their fragrance, and at our door is every delicacy, both new and old, that I have stored up for you, my lover." Verses 9-13, NIV.

With what poetic words does the bride describe the love she shares with her beloved?

"Place me like a seal over your heart, like a seal on your arm; for love is as strong as death, its jealousy unyielding as the grave. It burns like blazing fire, like a mighty flame. Many waters cannot quench love; rivers cannot wash it away." Song of Solomon 8:6, 7, NIV.

How do the lovers' friends describe the need to protect love's sanctity?

"We have a young sister, and her breasts are not yet grown. What shall we do for our sister for the day she is spoken for? If she is a wall, we will build towers of silver on her. If she is a door, we will enclose her with panels of cedar." Verses 8, 9, NIV.

Why does Paul condemn sexual immorality?

" ' Everything is permissible for me'—but not everything is beneficial. 'Everything is permissible for me'—but I will not be mastered by anything. 'Food for the stomach and the stomach for food'—but God will destroy them both. *The body is not meant for sexual immorality, but for the Lord, and the Lord for the body.* By his power God raised the Lord from the dead, and he will raise us also. Do you not know that bodies are members of Christ himself? Shall I then take the members of Christ and unite them with a prostitute? Never! Do you not know that he who unites himself with a prostitute is one with her in body? For it is said, 'The two will become one flesh.' But he who unites himself with the Lord is one with him in spirit. Flee from sexual immorality." 1 Corinthians 6:12-18, NIV.

NOTE—"Every sin is equally sinful. Cultural opinions and the variety of distinctions drawn by speculative theologies have no biblical warrant. God is intolerant toward all sin. But how is it with sexual sin?

"In 1 Corinthians 6:18 Paul writes: 'Flee immorality [*porneia*]. Every other sin that a man commits is outside the body [*soma*], but the immoral man [*o de porneion*] sins against his own body' (NASB). Most commentators agree that here Paul singles out sexual sin as a *sui generic* category and in doing so presents five arguments against fornication and adultery:

"1. The first argument is found in verse 13. Food is meant for the stomach and the stomach for food, but the parallel reasoning that immorality is made for body and the body for immorality does not hold true. Sex is not simply a function of human physiology in the way digestion is.

"2. In the second argument, found in verse 14, Paul maintains that it is not right that the body should be given up to sexual pollution because a Christian has been raised from death with Christ, and should therefore live in harmony with his glorified body.

"3. Paul's third argument (verse 15) insists that we are members of a body that has Christ as the head. Thus when we allow our body to act apart from Christ's impulses, we are in violation of this connective reality.

"4. The fourth argument is the most forceful of the five. To begin with, Paul issues a command, 'Flee immorality.' Albert Barnes comments, 'Man should *escape* from it; he should not stay to *reason* about it; to debate the matter; or even to contend with his propensities, and try the strength of his virtue. There are some sins that a man can *resist*; some about which he can reason without danger of pollution. But this is a sin [sexual sin] where a man is *safe* only when he flies; free from pollution only when he refuses to entertain a thought of it; secure when he seeks victory by flight, and conquest by retreat' [*Notes on the New Testament* (Grand Rapids, Mich.: Baker, 1953), p. 106].

"But Paul does not rest his case on his apostolic authority alone. He gives a reason for the command to flee: 'Every *other* sin that a man commits is outside the body, but the immoral man sins against his own body' (verse 18).

"Of the many alternative interpretations of this passage, two complementary variants seem most accepted. One track argues that Paul is addressing another of the Corinthian slogans which claims that since sin belongs to a spiritual realm, and acts of sex are purely a function of the body, humans can relax all controls over their sexuality. Paul stands firmly against this reasoning, insisting, on the contrary, that this sin defiles the entire person (*soma*), the physical dimension included. This has several important implications.

"First, in sexual sin the essential integrity of the human being is damaged since 'not only the sex organs but the whole personality is involved in the sex relationship; thus human sexual sin goes to the very root of our being. The whole man and the whole woman are affected as the well-known phrase from Genesis has it—"they shall be one flesh" (Gen. 2:24).'

"Sex is not a part of the human being as are the feet, hands, or stomach. It determines much more, involving the heart, mind, and attitude. 'A human being is a male or female and in the sex act, masculinity and femininity are revealed. . . . In free love there is a union of the flesh, but not as the Bible means it. Spirit is not associated with the flesh; there is a disintegration of personality' [Gaston Deluz, *A Companion to First Corinthians* (London: Darton, Longman & Todd, 1963), pp. 74, 75].

"Second, a damaged personhood creates cravings for completeness by pursuing other similar experiences, which in turn result in an ever-increasing cheapening of the person's self-respect. . . .

"Finally, a wounded person injures other innocent and legitimate relationships in his/her search for personal fulfillment. So Paul insists: 'Flee immorality.' The final argument in verse 19 reminds Paul's readers that our body is the shrine of the Holy Spirit, and therefore, when we sin sexually, we are attempting to force the third person of the Trinity to cohabit with our sin. And that is a serious matter indeed." Miroslav Kis, "Sexual Misconduct in Ministry: Unforbidden Fruit," *Ministry*, March 2004, pp. 12, 19.

Why is sexual morality so essential?

"All other sins a man commits are outside his body, but he who sins sexually sins against his own body. Do you not know that your body is a temple of the Holy Spirit, who is in you, whom you have received from God? You are not your own; you were bought at a price. Therefore *honor God with your body*." 1 Corinthians 6:18-20, NIV.

NOTE.—Author Frederick Buechner wrote that "sex is not a sin. . . . It's not salvation either. Like nitroglycerin, it can be used either to blow up bridges or to heal hearts."

What advice on living a holy life did Paul give the Thessalonians?

"It is God's will that you should be sanctified: that you should avoid sexual immorality; that each of you should learn to control his own body in a way that is holy and honorable, not in passionate lust like the heathen, who do not know God; and that in this matter no one should wrong his brother or take advantage of him. The Lord will punish men for all such sins, as we have already told you and warned you. For God did not call us to be impure, but to live a holy life." 1 Thessalonians 4:3-7, NIV.

FAMILY

What did God say to Adam and Eve after creating them?

"God blessed them and said to them, *'Be fruitful and increase in number*; fill the earth and subdue it.' " Genesis 1:28, NIV.

How does Psalms describe the family of a man who follows God?

"Blessed are all who fear the Lord, who walk in his ways. You will eat the fruit of your labor; blessings and prosperity will be yours. Your wife will be like a fruitful vine within your house; your sons will be like olive shoots around your table. Thus is the man blessed who fears the Lord." Psalm 128:1-4, NIV.

What are children declared to be?

"Behold, children are *a heritage from the Lord*." Psalm 127:3, NKJV. "Children's children are *the crown of old men*, and the glory of children is their father." Proverbs 17:6, NKJV.

How should husband and wife relate to one another?

"Submit to one another out of reverence for Christ. Wives, sub-

Making Love

What do you think of when you hear the word *lover* or the words *making love*? When those last two words bump together, they attract attention like the beach attracts waves. We've been brainwashed. 'Making love' implies the sexual act of copulating, and in analyzing the phrase we find we're not really talking about creating or building or shaping love; we're talking about making sex. 'They were making sex' does not sound as romantic, of course. And when two people have made sex outside of marriage, to be truly accurate we sadly need to describe what else they were probably making. They were making tears. They were making lies. They were making regrets. Because these are what accompany the mere making of sex without the responsibility and depth and nourishment of committed love. Sex can be a part of love, but it is not love.

"Somehow we get tricked into thinking that God is keeping the *good stuff* from us, and if we just break free from God, we'll enjoy life more. Don't we know that God desperately wants the absolute best for us? What arrogance to pretend otherwise. C. S. Lewis observes, 'We are half-hearted creatures, fooling about with drink and sex and ambition when infinite joy is offered us, like an ignorant child who wants go on making mud pies in a slum because he cannot imagine what is meant by the offer of a holiday at the sea.'

"How do we make love? In the case of couples, watch him washing dishes for them. He's making love. See how she runs errands for him. She's making love. Look at how the two keep confidences, support, and smile through the trouble they go through. They're making love. Witness his opening up his insecurities to her. He's making love. Hear her confront and encourage him. She's making love. Listen to them discussing the meaning of life. They're making love. The sexual act is designed to be bonding and sweet and luminous, but anyone knows the act is wasted unless the right stage is set and the actors know their parts. . . .

"Marriage furnishes a vibrant metaphor for God the lover. The Bible specifically presents Jesus as a bridegroom to His people, the bride. As with all earthly marriages, trust and com-

Making Love CONTINUED

munication are imperatives with God, and our life together is not all fun and games. Moreover, when we seek spiritual highs and intimacy without commitment, we set ourselves up for counterfeit oneness. Allison Lamon remarks in *View*, 'If we seek emotional gratification from God without committing "for better or for worse," then we are trying to have the spiritual equivalent of premarital sex with God. A fling. Marriage vows do not read "as long as our excitement shall last" because that can and will change.'

"Promiscuous people become consumers in marriage, testing and rejecting while carelessly ripping themselves and others apart. The same is true with promiscuous worship. Note the first of the Ten Commandments: 'You shall have no other gods before me' [Exodus 20:3, RSV]. Whether we worship food, exercise, sex, entertainment, job, art, or money instead of God, according them ultimate honor and loyalty, we are unfaithful. We will inevitably make tears and lies rather than love." Chris Blake, *Searching for a God to Love* (Nashville: Word Publishing, 2000), pp. 96, 97.

mit to your husbands as to the Lord. For the husband is the head of the wife as Christ is the head of the church. . . . Husbands, love your wives, just as Christ loved the church and gave himself up for her to make her holy, cleansing her by the washing with water through the word, and to present her to himself as a radiant church, without stain or wrinkle or any other blemish, but holy and blameless. In this same way, husbands ought to love their wives as their own bodies. He who loves his wife loves himself. After all, no one ever hated his own body, but he feeds and cares for it, just as Christ does the church—for we are members of his body. 'For this reason a man will leave his father and mother and be united to his wife, and the two will become one flesh.' This is a profound mystery—but I am talking about Christ and the church. However, each one of you also must love his wife as he loves himself, and the wife must respect her husband." Ephesians 5:21-33, NIV.

Against what are husbands cautioned?

"Husbands, love your wives and *do not be harsh with them*." Colossians 3:19, NIV.

Why should husbands be considerate of their wives?

"Husbands, in the same way be considerate as you live with your wives, and treat them with respect as the weaker partner and as heirs with you of the gracious gift of life, *so that nothing will hinder your prayers*." 1 Peter 3:7, NIV.

NOTE.—"Husbands are not told [here] to submit to their wives; the words 'in the same way' simply connect this counsel to the preceding series. Peter tells husbands to live considerately with their wives, which may mean sensitivity in sexual relations. But what the Greek literally says is, 'Cohabit according to knowledge,' and includes all aspects of marriage. . . . [Husbands] are to show respect to womankind as the weaker vessel (so says the Greek literally), 'vessel' probably meaning body (2 Corinthians 4:7), but above all, because the two of them are coheirs of the grace of life. The word *life* refers to the eternal life that husband and wife will both enjoy with God at the end of history. With these words, Peter acknowledges that on the spiritual level, the sexes are equal (Galatians 3:28).

"Peter adds yet another reason for treating wives kindly: 'So that nothing will hinder your prayers.' Our horizontal relationships with other people affect our vertical relationship with God (Matthew 5:23, 24). When husband and wife do not treat each other as coheirs and do not agree in their prayers (Matthew 18:19), it is hard for them to pray and hard for God to answer." Robert M. Johnston, *The Abundant Life Bible Amplifier: Peter and Jude* (Boise, Idaho: Pacific Press, 1995), p. 89.

How does Proverbs describe a noble mother?

"She is clothed with strength and dignity; she can laugh at the days to come. She speaks with wisdom, and faithful instruction is on her tongue." Proverbs 31:25, 26, NIV.

How will such a mother be regarded?

"Her children arise and call her *blessed*; her husband also, and he praises her." Verse 28, NIV.

How did God instruct the ancient Israelites to communicate His law to their children?

"You shall love the Lord your God with all your heart, with all your soul, and with all your strength. And these words which I command you today shall be in your heart. *You shall teach them diligently to your children*, and shall talk of them when you sit in your house, when you walk by the way, when you lie down, and when you rise up." Deuteronomy 6:5-7, NKJV.

NOTE.—"The home is the child's first school, and it is here that the foundation should be laid for a life of service. Its principles are to be taught not merely in theory. They are to shape the whole life training. . . . Such an education must be based upon the Word of God. Here only are its principles given in their fullness. The Bible should be made the foundation of study and of teaching. The essential knowledge is a knowledge of God and of Him whom He has sent." Ellen G. White, *The Ministry of Healing*, pp. 400, 401.

What is the great secret of a happy home?

"Better is a dinner of vegetables where *love* is than a fatted ox and hatred with it." Proverbs 15:17, NRSV.

RELIGION IN THE HOME

How well does God know each of us?

"O Lord, you have searched me and you know me. *You know when I sit and when I rise*; you perceive my thoughts from afar. You discern my going out and my lying down; you are familiar with all my ways. Before a word is on my tongue you know it completely, O Lord." Psalm 139:1-4, NIV.

What is the beginning of wisdom?

"*The fear of the Lord* is the beginning of wisdom: all those that practice it have a good understanding." Psalm 111:10, NRSV.

What is the value of proper early instruction?

"Train up a child in the way he should go: and *when he is old, he will not depart from it*." Proverbs 22:6.

NOTE.—"Training a child in the way he should go" (literally "according to the mouth of his way" or "according to his way") refers to the talents and capabilities the child has. Discovering one's vocation or calling based on the abilities God has given to develop is a journey that parents and children can and should pursue together. Even when there is a "bent" or giftedness in a given direction, training is still necessary. The parent who pushes a child to become a physician to fulfill the parent's dream when the child's bent is toward music isn't training a child in the way that child should go.

How early was Timothy taught from the Scriptures?

"*From childhood you have known the Holy Scriptures*, which are able to make you wise for salvation through faith which is in Christ Jesus." 2 Timothy 3:15, NKJV.

NOTE.—Timothy's father was Greek and his mother Jewish. The spirituality which he saw in his home life molded him into a faithful Christian. From an early age his devout mother and grandmother taught him the Hebrew Scriptures. Their teaching qualified him to bear responsibilities and to give faithful service. His home instructors had cooperated with God in preparing him for a life of usefulness. Thus it should be in every home.

Why did God confide in Abraham and commit sacred trusts to him?

"For I know him, *that he will command his children and his household after him,* and they shall keep the way of the Lord, to do justice and judgment." Genesis 18:19.

What was Abraham's practice wherever he went?

"There he *built an altar to the Lord,* and called on the name of the Lord." Genesis 12:8, NIV. (See also Genesis 13:4; 21:33.)

NOTE.—"The manner in which the family worship is conducted is very important. It should be made so pleasant as to be looked forward to with gladness even by the youngest children. Too often it is made tedious, monotonous or burdensome. . . . To make it dull and irksome is treason to true religion. . . . A few minutes given every day to preparation for family worship will serve to make it, as it should be, the most pleasant and attractive incident of the day." J. R. Miller, *Week-Day Religion,* pp. 79-81.

What instruction suggests the giving of thanks for daily food?

"Be joyful always; pray continually; give thanks in all circumstances, for this is God's will for you in Christ Jesus." 1 Thessalonians 5:16-18, NIV.

NOTE.— As a rule, children will reflect the life and principles manifested in their parents. The reason so many children are irreverent, irreligious, and disobedient today is that their parents are so. Like parent, like child. If parents would see a different state of things, they must themselves reform. They must bring God into their homes and make His Word their counselor and guide. They must teach their children the fear of God, and that His Word is the voice of God addressed to them, and is to be implicitly obeyed. . . . "In too many households prayer is neglected. . . . If ever there was a time when every house should be a house of prayer, it is now. Fathers and mothers should often lift up their hearts to God in humble supplication for themselves and their children." Ellen G. White, *Patriarchs and Prophets,* p. 143, 144.

PARENTHOOD

According to Solomon, what is every child known by?

"Even a child is known by his *actions*, by whether his conduct is pure and right." Proverbs 20:11, NIV.

What is a child's duty toward their parents?

"Listen, my son, to *your father's instruction*, and *do not forsake your mother's teaching."* Proverbs 1:8, NIV.

What does the fifth commandment require of children?

"Honor your father and your mother, so that you may live long in the land the Lord your God is giving you." Exodus 20:12, NIV.

NOTE.—To the child too young to know God, the earthly parent takes the place of God. Learning to honor, respect, and obey earthly parents is the child's first and most important lesson in learning to honor, respect, and obey God, the heavenly Parent.

For how long a time should one honor his parents?

"Listen to your father, who gave you life, and do not despise your mother *when she is old."* Proverbs 23:22, NIV.

NOTE.—Children should honor and respect their parents as long as they live. The duty enjoined in the fifth commandment does not cease at maturity, nor when the child leaves home.

What is the character of a child who will not listen to his father's instruction?

"A *fool* spurns his father's discipline, but whoever heeds correction shows prudence." Proverbs 15:5, NIV.

How did the religious leaders in Jesus' day make void the fifth commandment for the sake of gain?

"But you say that if a man says to his father or mother, 'Whatever help you might otherwise have received from me is a gift devoted to God,' he is not to 'honor his father' with it. Thus you nullify the word of God for the sake of your tradition." Matthew 15:5, 6, NIV.

NOTE.—The word translated "gift" in this text means a thing dedicated to the service of God in the Temple. In this way the Jewish teachers, by their traditional law, taught that by saying that their property was dedicated to the Temple or to religious purposes, people were free from the obligation to honor and support their parents, thus making void one of the commandments of God. Christ condemned this.

How would God have parents and children relate?

"*Children, obey your parents in everything*, for this pleases the Lord. Fathers, do not embitter your children, or they will become discouraged." Colossians 3:20, 21, NIV.

What responsibility do parents and children have to each other?

"*Children, obey your parents in the Lord*, for this is right. 'Honor your father and mother'—which is the first commandment with a promise—'that it may go well with you and that you may enjoy long life on the earth.' *Fathers, do not exasperate your children*; instead, *bring them up in the training and instruction of the Lord*." Ephesians 6:1-4, NIV.

How did Jesus honor His parents?

"Then he went down with them and came to Nazareth, and *was obedient to them*." Luke 2:51, NRSV.

What will be the reward of those who honor their parents?

"Honor your father and your mother, so that you may live long in the land the Lord your God is giving you." Exodus 20:12, NIV.

NOTE.—This promise will be fully realized in the life to come, first in heaven, then when God re-creates the earth for all who have followed Him.

How does Paul describe people's hearts in the last days?

"But mark this: There will be terrible times in the last days. People will be *lovers of themselves, lovers of money, boastful, proud, abusive, disobedient to their parents*." 2 Timothy 3:1, 2, NIV.

NOTE.—It is of vital importance that parents share the Bible, lessons of faith, and prayer time with their children. Such regular acts of family devotion, teaching by word and example, lay a critical foundation for Christian character.

What high ideal should be placed before young people?

"Don't let anyone look down on you because you are young, but *set an example for the believers* in speech, in life, in love, in faith and in purity." 1 Timothy 4:12, NIV.

What duty does God require of children to their parents?

"Honor your father and your mother." Exodus 20:12, NKJV.

What are some good fruits of proper child training?

"Discipline your son, and *he will give you peace; he will bring delight to your soul*." Proverbs 29:17, NIV.

NOTE.—No one can claim that child rearing is easy. It's a 24/7 job. Often joyful. Often tedious. Its rewards can be priceless.

Having children exacts a price from the parents. Far more than worry over broken bones and sleepless nights nursing high fevers, it is the God-given responsibility of preparing their souls for eternity that can tax most of all.

Discipline—this teaching and training with love—begins at the mother's breast. It is felt in the warmth of her skin and the gentleness of her touch. Discipline—self-control—is learned through the father's patient guidance teaching his son to ride a bike and his daughter to catch a ball. Through these simple things children sense their heavenly Parent's love as well. As the years pass and the child matures, virtually every word and action of the parent teaches an indelible message about God.

God is love, wholly love. And in His love He has placed laws that guide the universe and must guide the lives of parents and their little ones. Here conflict comes and parents face their toughest challenge. For it is the neglect of parents—and ignorance of those who themselves grew up neglected—to discipline their children properly that reaps both sad and tragic consequences.

It's fun to play with your children, and often it's far easier to say yes than it is to say no. But life is not all play, and a yes today may be the first step on the road to sorrow. Vigilance—daily, hourly vigilance that ultimately enables a child to make God-centered choices—is required.

Whom does Proverbs say that the Lord disciplines?

"Do not despise the Lord's discipline and do not resent his rebuke, because the Lord disciplines *those he loves*, as a father the son he delights in." Proverbs 3:11, 12, NIV.

NOTE.—In their landmark empirical study, *The Altruistic Personality: Rescuers of Jews in Nazi Europe*, Samuel and Pearl Oliner sought to discover the key character traits that distinguished those who risked their lives to save others from those who easily acquiesced to an authoritarian environment. They found that rather than threatening their children, the parents of rescuers disciplined through reasoning, encouraging their children to think for themselves. In *Conscience and Courage: Rescuers of Jews During the Holocaust*, Eva Fogelman writes that rescuers' parents "reasoned rather than threatened. They eschewed what New York University social psychologist Martin Hoffman calls the 'power-assertive' technique of discipline. Hoffman, who has studied parental techniques of discipline and its effects on altruism, found that parents who explained rules and used inductive reasoning instead of harsh punishment tend to have children who care for and about others. After all, parents who voluntarily relinquish the use of force in favor of reasoning send their children a message about how the powerful should treat the weak.

"Rescuers' parents talked to their children about what was acceptable behavior and then clearly laid out rules. . . . Such gentle but firm guidance is far different from an authoritarian parent's habitual, peremptory commands. Swiss author Alice Miller, who has studied authoritarian families in which rules are laid down for the child without discussion or justification, points out that children from these kinds of households have trouble making independent judgments. Given little or no explanation, all directives seem, from the child's perspective, arbitrary and irrational. So they give up and do what they are told.

"The ability to think and act independently was, of course, a key element in rescue activity. Coming to the aid of persecuted people required an independent mind. A person had to be accustomed to reasoning through a problem and coming to a conclusion not based on what others thought or what the laws mandated. Those raised in authoritarian families were not likely to resist the pressure to conform." Eva Fogelman, *Conscience and Courage: Rescuers of Jews During the Holocaust* (New York: Doubleday, 1994), pp. 257, 258.

Personal example is another crucial element in raising children with integrity. As a child John Henry Weidner witnessed his minister father again and again imprisoned for not sending his children to school on the Sabbath. As an adult he helped save the lives of 800 Jews and more than 100 Allied airmen during World War II.

Against what evil should parents guard?

"Fathers, *do not embitter your children*, or they will become discouraged." Colossians 3:21, NIV.

NOTE.—Correction should never be given in anger, for anger in the parents stirs up anger in the child. It is well to pray with a child before giving discipline, and frequently mild but faithful instruction, admonition, and prayer are all the training necessary—are, in fact, the best training that can be given. It is best, generally, that correction should be done in private, as this tends to preserve the self-respect of the child, a very important element in character building. No correction or training should be violent or abusive, or given for the purpose of breaking the will of the child. Rather, parents should direct the will, and help the child realize a sense of what is right and duty.

"The effort to 'break the will' of a child is a terrible mistake. Minds are constituted differently; while force may secure outward submission, the result with many children is a more determined rebellion of the heart. . . . Those who weaken or destroy individuality assume a responsibility that can result only in evil. While under authority, the children may appear like well-drilled soldiers; but when the control ceases, the character will be found to lack strength and steadfastness. Having never learned to govern himself, the youth recognizes no restraint except the requirement of parents or teacher. This removed, he knows not how to use his liberty, and often gives himself up to indulgence that proves his ruin. . . .

"In every youth, every child, lies the power, by the help of God, to form a character of integrity and to live a life of usefulness." Ellen G. White, *Education*, pp. 288, 289.

Why did God reprove Eli the high priest?

"On that day I will fulfill against Eli all that I have spoken concerning this house, from beginning to end. For I have told him that I am about to punish his house forever, for the iniquity that he knew, *because his sons were blaspheming God, and he did not restrain them*." 1 Samuel 3:12, 13, NRSV.

How are the present effects and future results of discipline contrasted?

"No discipline seems pleasant at the time, but *painful*. Later on, however, *it produces a harvest of righteousness and peace* for those who have been trained by it." Hebrews 12:11, NIV.

PROMISES FOR THE CHILDREN

What is said of the commandment to honor parents?

"Honor your father and mother—which is *the first commandment with a promise*." Ephesians 6:2, NIV.

What is promised those who honor their parents?

"Honor your father and your mother, so that *you may live long in the land* the Lord your God is giving you." Exodus 20:12, NIV.

What does God desire that children be taught?

"Come, my children, listen to me; I will teach you *the fear of the Lord*." Psalm 34:11, NIV.

What is the fear of the Lord declared to be?

"The fear of the Lord is *the beginning of wisdom*; all who follow his precepts have good understanding." Psalm 111:10, NIV.

What is said of the poor but wise youth?

"Better a poor but wise youth *than an old but foolish king* who no longer knows how to take warning." Ecclesiastes 4:13, NIV.

How did Jesus show His tender regard for children?

"People were bringing little children to Jesus to have him touch them, but the disciples rebuked them. When Jesus saw this, he was indignant. He said to them, *'Let the little children come to me, and do not hinder them*, for the kingdom of heaven belongs to such as these. I tell you the truth, anyone who will not receive the kingdom of God like a little child will never enter it.' And he took the children in his arms, put his hands on them and blessed them." Mark 10:13-16, NIV.

What peaceful scene did the prophet Zechariah paint of a future Jerusalem?

"This is what the Lord Almighty says: 'Once again *men and women of ripe old age will sit in the streets of Jerusalem*, each with cane in hand because of his age. *The city streets will be filled with boys and girls playing there.*'" Zechariah 8:4, 5, NIV.

What happy conditions will prevail in the next world as compared with those of this life?

"They will not toil in vain or bear children doomed to misfortune; for *they will be a people blessed by the Lord*, they and their descendants with them." Isaiah 65:23, NIV. "The infant will play near the hole of the cobra, and the young child put his hand into the viper's nest. *They will neither harm nor destroy on all my holy mountain*, for the earth will be full of the knowledge of the Lord as the waters cover the sea." Isaiah 11:8, 9, NIV.

TEACHING THE CHILDREN

What should be the prayer of every parent?

"O my Lord, . . . teach us what we shall do for the child who will be born." Judges 13:8, NKJV.

NOTE.—This is a part of the prayer of Manoah, the father of Samson.

What were some of the words of hope God shared with Israel through Isaiah?

"All your children shall be taught by the Lord, and great shall be the peace of your children." Isaiah 54:13, NKJV.

What will happen if a child is not properly instructed?

"A child left to himself *brings shame to his mother.*" Proverbs 29:15, NKJV.

How did Solomon's father teach him as a child?

"When I was a boy in my father's house, still tender, and an only child of my mother, *he taught me and said, 'Lay hold of my words with all your heart; keep my commands and you will live. Get wisdom, get understanding; do not forget my words or swerve from them.'*" Proverbs 4:3-5, NIV.

What motive will inspire all true parents to faithfulness in teaching their children?

"Our sons in their youth will be like well-nurtured plants, and our daughters will be like pillars carved to adorn a palace." Psalm 144:12, NIV.

With what words did Hannah dedicate her son Samuel to God?

"And she made a vow, saying, *'O Lord Almighty, if you will only look upon your servant's misery and remember me, and not forget your servant but give her a son, then I will give him to the Lord for all the days of his life.'*" 1 Samuel 1:11, NIV.

What is said of Jesus' childhood?

"And the child grew and became strong; he was filled with wisdom, and the grace of God was upon Him. . . . And Jesus grew in wisdom and stature, and in favor with God and men." Luke 2:40-52, NIV.

PURITY OF HEART

What did Jesus say of the pure in heart?

"Blessed are the pure in heart, for *they will see God.*" Matthew 5:8, NIV.

What scripture shows that social impurity was one of the chief sins that brought on Noah's flood?

"When men began to increase in number on the earth and daughters were born to them, *the sons of God saw that the daughters of men were beautiful, and they married any of them they chose. . . .* The Lord saw how great man's wickedness on the earth had become, and that every inclination of the thoughts of his heart was only evil all the time. The Lord was grieved that he had made man on the earth, and his heart was filled with pain. So the Lord said, 'I will wipe mankind, whom I have created, from the face of the earth . . . for I am grieved that I have made them.' . . . Now the earth was corrupt in God's sight and was full of violence." Genesis 6:1-11, NIV.

What was the character of the inhabitants of Sodom?

"Now the men of Sodom were *wicked* and were sinning greatly against the Lord." Genesis 13:13, NIV. "Now this was the sin of your sister Sodom: She and her daughters were arrogant, overfed and unconcerned; they did not help the poor and needy. They were haughty and did detestable things before me. Therefore I did away with them as you have seen." Ezekiel 16:49, 50, NIV.

NOTE.—Genesis 19:1-9 and 2 Peter 2:6-8 show that they were exceedingly corrupt in morals.

Against what are the people of God warned?

"But among you there must not be even a hint of *sexual immorality*, or of any kind of *impurity*, or of *greed*, because these are improper for God's holy people. Nor should there be *obscenity, foolish talk* or *coarse joking*, which are out of place, but rather thanksgiving." Ephesians 5:3, 4, NIV.

What does Paul describe as "acts of the sinful nature"?

"The acts of the sinful nature are obvious: *sexual immorality, impurity and debauchery; idolatry and witchcraft; hatred, discord, jealousy, fits of rage, selfish ambition, dissensions, factions and envy; drunkenness, orgies, and the like*." Galatians 5:19-21, NIV.

What is said of those who do such things?

"I warn you, as I did before, that those who live like this will not inherit the kingdom of God." Verse 21, NIV.

What did Jesus say the world would be like at the end of time?

"Just as it was in the days of Noah, so also will it be in the days of the Son of Man. People were eating, drinking, marrying, and being given in marriage up to the day Noah entered the ark. Then the flood came and destroyed them all. *It was the same in the days of Lot*. People were eating and drinking, buying and selling, planting and building. But the day Lot left Sodom, fire and sulfur rained down from heaven and destroyed them all. It will be just like this on the day the Son of Man is revealed." Luke 17:26-30, NIV.

Whom does Paul not warn against associating with?

"I have written you in my letter not to associate with sexually immoral people—not at all meaning *the people of this world who are immoral*, or the greedy and swindlers, or idolaters. In that case you would have to leave this world." 1 Corinthians 5:9, 10, NIV.

NOTE.—Paul does not want us to shun those who do not know God or live according to His commandments. Rather, we must witness to them and show them God's grace.

Whom does Paul warn against associating with?

"But now I am writing you that you must not associate with *anyone who calls himself a brother but is sexually immoral or greedy, an idolater or a slanderer, a drunkard or a swindler*. With such a man do not even eat." Verse 11, NIV.

NOTE.—Paul's focus here is not on those who reject Christ and live in sin, but on hypocrites who claim Christ.

Why does Paul not advise Christians to spend their time condemning sinners in the world?

"What business is it of mine to judge those outside the church? Are you not to judge those inside? *God will judge those outside.* 'Expel the wicked man from among you.'" Verses 12, 13, NIV.

NOTE.—God calls, not Christians to condemn the sins of those outside the church, but to get their own houses in order. God desires us to witness by our righteous example, not by condemning the world.

What is the Bible's spiritual law of cause and effect?

"Do not be deceived: God cannot be mocked. *A man reaps what he sows.* The one who sows to please his sinful nature, from that nature will reap destruction; the one who sows to please the Spirit, from the Spirit will reap eternal life." Galatians 6:7, 8, NIV.

What encouraging words does Paul give to those who seek to serve God?

"Let us not become weary in doing good, for at the proper time we will reap a harvest if we do not give up. Therefore, as we have opportunity, let us do good to all people, especially to those who belong to the family of believers." Verses 9, 10, NIV.

What should we do instead of sanctioning evil?

"For you were once darkness, but now you are light in the Lord. Live as children of light (for the fruit of the light consists in all goodness, righteousness and truth) and find out what pleases the Lord. Have nothing to do with the fruitless deeds of darkness, but rather expose them. For it is shameful even to mention what the disobedient do in secret." Ephesians 5:8-12, NIV.

What advice did the apostle Paul give Timothy?

"Keep yourself pure." 1 Timothy 5:22, NKJV.

"Flee the evil desires of youth, and *pursue righteousness, faith, love, and peace*, along with those who call on the Lord out of a pure heart. Don't have anything to do with foolish and stupid arguments, because you know they produce quarrels. And the Lord's servant must not quarrel; instead, he must *be kind to everyone, able to teach, not resentful*. Those who oppose him he must gently instruct, in the hope that God will grant them repentance leading them to a knowledge of the truth." 2 Timothy 2:22-25, NIV.

How should we treat each other in words and action?

"Let no evil talk come out of your mouths, but only what is useful for building up, as there is need, so that your words may give grace to those who hear. And do not grieve the Holy Spirit of God, with which you were marked with a seal for the day of redemption. Put away from you all bitterness and wrath and anger and wrangling and slander, together with all malice, and be kind to one another, tenderhearted, forgiving one another, as God in Christ has forgiven you. Therefore be imitators of God, as beloved children, and live in love, as Christ loved us and gave himself up for us, a fragrant offering and sacrifice to God." Ephesians 4:29–5:2, NRSV.

What does the Lord call upon the wicked to do?

"Let the wicked *forsake his way*, and the unrighteous man his thoughts: and let him *return unto the Lord*, and he will have mercy upon him; and to our God, for he will abundantly pardon." Isaiah 55:7.

How should we relate to others?

"Do nothing out of selfish ambition or vain conceit, but *in humility consider others better than yourselves*. Each of you should look not only to your own interests, but also to the interests of others. Your attitude should be the same as that of Christ Jesus." Philippians 2:3-5, NIV.

Where should we focus our attention in life?

"Finally, beloved, whatever is *true*, whatever is *honorable*, whatever is *just*, whatever is *pure*, whatever is *pleasing*, whatever is *commendable*, if there is any excellence and if there is anything worthy of praise, think about these things." Philippians 4:8, NRSV.

CHAPTER 17

Health and Temperance

GOOD HEALTH

What did the apostle John wish concerning Gaius?

"Dear friend, I pray that you may enjoy *good health* and that all may go well with you, even as your soul is getting along well." 3 John 2, NIV.

What did God promise the Israelites at Mount Sinai?

"Worship the Lord your God, and his blessing will be on your food and water. *I will take away sickness from among you*, and none will miscarry or be barren in your land. I will give you a full life span." Exodus 23:25, 26, NIV.

Upon what conditions was freedom from disease promised?

"He said, 'If you listen carefully to the voice of the Lord your God and do what is right in his eyes, if you pay attention to his commands and keep all his decrees, I will not bring on you any of the diseases I brought on the Egyptians, for I am the Lord, who heals you.' " Exodus 15:26, NIV.

What does King David say the Lord does for His people?

"Praise the Lord, O my soul, and forget not all his benefits—who *forgives all your sins and heals all your diseases*." Psalm 103:2, 3, NIV.

What constituted a large part of Christ's ministry?

"Jesus went throughout Galilee, teaching in their synagogues, preaching the good news of the kingdom, and *healing every disease and sickness among the people*. News about him spread all over Syria, and people brought to him all who were ill with various diseases, those suffering severe pain, the demon-possessed, those having seizures, and the paralyzed, and he healed them." Matthew 4:23, 24, NIV.

Why should we maintain our health?

"Do you not know that *your body is a temple of the Holy Spirit*, who is in you, whom you have received from God? You are not your own; you were bought at a price. Therefore honor God with your body." 1 Corinthians 6:19, 20, NIV.

What was the original diet prescribed for humanity?

"Then God said, 'I give you *every seed-bearing plant on the face of the whole earth and every tree that has fruit with seed in it*. They will be yours for food.' " Genesis 1:29, NIV.

Why did God restrict the Hebrews in their diet?

"For you are a people holy to the Lord your God. Out of all the peoples on the face of the earth, the Lord has chosen you to be his treasured possession. Do not eat any detestable thing." Deuteronomy 14:2, 3, NIV.

NOTE.—Both mind and body are affected by the food we eat.

What effect does a cheerful attitude have upon our health?

"A cheerful heart is *good medicine*." Proverbs 17:22, NIV.

How did Jesus provide rest for His disciples?

"Then, because so many people were coming and going that they did not even have a chance to eat, he said to them, *'Come with me by yourselves to a quiet place and get some rest*.' " Mark 6:31, NIV.

How are we exhorted to present our bodies to God?

"Therefore, I urge you, brothers, in view of God's mercy, to *offer your bodies as living sacrifices, holy and pleasing to God*—this is your spiritual act of worship." Romans 12:1, NIV.

What high purpose should control our habits of life?

"So whether you eat or drink or whatever you do, *do it all for the glory of God*." 1 Corinthians 10:31, NIV.

What topics did Paul address when speaking to Felix?

"Several days later Felix came with his wife Drusilla, who was a Jewess. He sent for Paul and listened to him as he spoke about faith in Christ Jesus. . . . Paul discoursed on righteousness, *self-control*, and the judgment to come." Acts 24:24, 25, NIV.

Of what is temperance a fruit?

"But the fruit of *the Spirit* is love, joy, peace, longsuffering, gentleness, goodness, faith, meekness, temperance." Galatians 5:22, 23.

NOTE.—"Temperance puts wood on the fire, meal in the barrel, flour in the tub, money in the purse, credit in the country, contentment in the house, clothes on the back, and vigor in the body." Benjamin Franklin.

Where in Christian growth and experience does Peter place temperance?

"Make every effort to add to your faith goodness; and to goodness, knowledge; and to knowledge, self-control; and to self-control, perseverance; and to perseverance, godliness; and to godliness, brotherly kindness; and to brotherly kindness, love." 2 Peter 1:5-7, NIV.

NOTE.—Self-control is rightly placed here as to order. Knowledge is a prerequisite to self-control, and self-control to patience. It is very difficult for an intemperate person to exercise patience.

What did Paul, in running the Christian race, say he did?

"Do you not know that in a race all the runners run, but only one gets the prize? Run in such a way as to get the prize. Everyone who competes in the games goes into strict training. They do it to get a crown that will not last; but we do it to get a crown that will last forever. Therefore *I do not run like a man running aimlessly; I do not fight like a man beating the air. No, I beat my body and make it my slave* so that after I have preached to others, I myself will not be disqualified for the prize." 1 Corinthians 9:24-27, NIV.

Why are rulers admonished to exercise self-control?

"It is not for kings, O Lemuel—not for kings to drink wine, not for rulers to crave beer, *lest they drink and forget what the law decrees, and deprive all the oppressed of their rights.*" Proverbs 31:4, 5, NIV.

Why were priests forbidden to use intoxicating drink while engaged in the sanctuary service?

"Then the Lord said to Aaron, 'You and your sons are not to drink wine or other fermented drink whenever you go into the Tent of Meeting, or you will die. . . . *You must distinguish between the holy and the common, between the unclean and the clean.*" Leviticus 10:8-10, NIV.

Why is indulgence in strong drink dangerous?

"Do not get drunk on wine, *which leads to debauchery.* Instead, be filled with the Spirit." Ephesians 5:18, NIV.

For what should we eat and drink?

"Blessed are you, O land whose king is of noble birth and whose princes eat at a proper time—*for strength and not for drunkenness.*" Ecclesiastes 10:17, NIV.

Why did Daniel refuse the food and wine of the king?

"But *Daniel resolved not to defile himself* with the royal food and wine, and he asked the chief official for permission not to defile himself this way." Daniel 1:8, NIV. (See Judges 13:4.)

Instead of these, what did he request?

"Please test your servants for ten days: Give us nothing but *vegetables* to eat and *water* to drink." Verse 12, NIV.

At the end of the test, how did he and his companions appear?

"At the end of the ten days they looked *healthier and better nourished than any of the young men who ate the royal food.*" Verse 15, NIV.

At the end of their three years' course in the school of Babylon, how did the wisdom of Daniel and his companions compare with that of others?

"At the end of the time set by the king to bring them in, the chief official presented them to Nebuchadnezzar. The king talked with them, and he found none equal to Daniel, Hananiah, Mishael, and Azariah; so they entered the king's service. In every matter of wisdom and understanding about which the king questioned them, *he found them ten times better than all the magicians and enchanters in his whole kingdom.*" Verses 18-20, NIV.

For what did Paul pray?

"May God himself, the God of peace, sanctify you through and through. *May your whole spirit, soul and body be kept blameless* at the coming of our Lord Jesus Christ." 1 Thessalonians 5:23, NIV.

NOTE.—For notable examples of total abstinence in the Bible, see the wife of Manoah, the mother of Samson (Judges 13:4, 12-14); the Rechabites (Jeremiah 35:1-10); and John the Baptist (Luke 1:13-15).

EVILS OF INTEMPERANCE

What do the Scriptures say of wine?

"Wine is a mocker and beer a brawler; whoever is led astray by them is not wise." Proverbs 20:1, NIV.

NOTE.—All intoxicating drinks are deceptive. They seem to give strength, but in reality cause weakness; they seem to create heat, but in fact lower the general temperature; they seem to impart vitality, but really destroy life; they seem to promote happiness, but cause the greatest unhappiness and misery. Much of the world's sorrow may be attributed to intemperance.

With what sins is drunkenness classed?

"The acts of the sinful nature are obvious: *sexual immorality, impurity and debauchery; idolatry and witchcraft; hatred, discord, jealousy, fits of rage, selfish ambition, dissensions, factions and envy; drunkenness, orgies, and the like.* I warn you, as I did before, that those who live like this will not inherit the kingdom of God." Galatians 5:19-21, NIV.

What is one of the tragic results of intemperance?

"Do not join those who drink too much wine or gorge themselves on meat, for *drunkards and gluttons become poor*, and drowsiness clothes them in rags." Proverbs 23:20, 21, NIV.

What are other evil effects of intemperance?

"And these also *stagger* from wine and *reel* from beer: Priests and prophets stagger from beer and are *befuddled* with wine; they reel from beer, they stagger when seeing visions, they *stumble* when rendering decisions." Isaiah 28:7, NIV.

What are common accompaniments of intemperance?

"Who has *woe*? Who has *sorrow*? Who has *strife*? Who has *complaints*? Who has *needless bruises*? Who has *bloodshot eyes*? Those who linger over wine, who go to sample bowls of mixed wine." Proverbs 23:29, 30, NIV.

How do intoxicants serve one in the end?

"Do not gaze at wine when it is red, when it sparkles in the cup, when it goes down smoothly! *In the end it bites like a snake and poisons like a viper.* Your eyes will see strange sights and your mind imagine confusing things. You will be like one sleeping on the high seas, lying on top of the rigging. 'They hit me,' you will say, 'but I'm not hurt! They beat me, but I don't feel it! When will I wake up so I can find another drink?'" Verses 31-35, NIV.

Where does intemperance often begin?

Intemperance often begins in the home.

What will drunkards, with other workers of iniquity, never inherit?

"Neither fornicators, nor idolaters, . . . nor thieves, nor cov-

etous, nor drunkards, . . . shall inherit *the kingdom of God*."
1 Corinthians 6:9, 10.

What admonition against intemperance that is especially applicable at the present time did Jesus give?

"Be careful, or your hearts will be weighed down with dissipation, drunkenness and the anxieties of life, and that day will close in on you unexpectedly like a trap." Luke 21:34, NIV.

TRUE TEMPERANCE REFORM

What was the original food provided for humanity?

"Then God said, 'I give you every *seed-bearing plant* on the face of the whole earth and *every tree that has fruit with seed in it.* They will be yours for food." Genesis 1:29, NIV.

NOTE.—In other words, vegetables, grains, fruits, and nuts.

After the Flood what other food was indicated as permissible?

"Everything that lives and moves will be food for you. Just as I gave you the green plants, I now give you everything." Genesis 9:3, NIV.

NOTE.—From this it is evident that flesh food was not included in the original diet provided for man, but that because of the changed conditions resulting from the Fall and the Flood, its use was permitted. However, Noah understood the difference between the clean and unclean animals, and a larger number of the clean beasts were housed safely in the ark.

When God chose Israel for His people, what kinds of flesh food were excluded from their diet by written instruction?

Those called unclean. (See Leviticus 11 and Deuteronomy 14.)

What special food did God provide for the children of Israel during their forty years' wandering in the wilderness?

"Then the Lord said to Moses, 'I will rain down *bread from heaven* for you.' . . . The Israelites ate manna forty years, until they came to a land that was settled; they ate manna until they reached the border of Canaan." Exodus 16:4-35, NIV.

At the same time, what did God promise to do for them?

"I will *take away sickness* from among you." Exodus 23:25, NIV.

What does King David say about their physical condition?

"And from among their tribes *no one faltered*." Psalm 105:37, NIV.

NOTE.—When they complained at God's dealings with them, and longed for the food of Egypt, God gave them their desires, but sent "a wasting disease." (See Numbers 11; Psalms 106:13-15; 1 Corinthians 10:6.) Like many today, they were not content with a simple but wholesome and nourishing diet.

Where, above all, should true temperance reform begin?

In the home.

NOTE.—Unless fathers and mothers practice temperance, they cannot expect their children to do so.

What people especially should be strictly temperate?

Young Christians. Paul wrote to Timothy, "Don't let anyone look down on you because you are young, but set an example for the believers in speech, in life, in love, in faith and in purity." 1 Timothy 4:12, NIV.

Can the fact that the liquor traffic brings in a large revenue to the state justify the licensing of it?

"Woe to him who builds a city with bloodshed and establishes a town by crime!" Habakkuk 2:12, NIV.

NOTE.—In all the walks and relationships of life, whether in the home, the medical profession, the pulpit, or the legislative assembly, we should stand for temperance. To license the liquor traffic is to legalize and foster it. It cannot exist or thrive without the patronage of each rising generation, a large number of whom it must necessarily ruin, body, soul, and spirit. For the state to receive money from such a source, therefore, must be highly reprehensible. The practice has fittingly been compared to a father catching sharks by baiting his hook with his own children.

CHAPTER 18

The Kingdom Restored

PROMISES TO THE OVERCOMER

How can we overcome evil?

"Do not repay anyone evil for evil. Be careful to do what is right in the eyes of everybody. If it is possible, as far as it depends on you, live at peace with everyone. Do not take revenge, my friends, but leave room for God's wrath, for it is written: 'It is mine to avenge; I will repay,' says the Lord. On the contrary:

" ' If your enemy is hungry, feed him; if he is thirsty, give him something to drink. In doing this, you will heap burning coals on his head.' Do not be overcome by evil, but overcome evil with good." Romans 12:17-21, NIV.

NOTE.—Paul is quoting Deuteronomy 32:35 and Proverbs 25:21, 22.

According to John, how can we overcome the world?

"Everyone born of God overcomes the world. This is the victory that has overcome the world, even our faith." 1 John 5:4, NIV.

How does John define "the world"?

"Do not love the world or anything in the world. If anyone loves the world, the love of the Father is not in him. For everything in the world—*the cravings of sinful man, the lust of his eyes and the boasting of what he has and does*—comes not from the Father but from the world. The world and its desires pass away, but the man who does the will of God lives forever." 1 John 2:15-17, NIV.

What promises does Jesus make to those who overcome?

1. "To him who overcomes I will give *the right to eat of the tree of life*, which is in the paradise of God." Revelation 2:7, NIV.

2. "He who overcomes *will not be hurt at all by the second death*." Verse 11, NIV.

3. "To him who overcomes, *I will give some of the hidden manna*. I will also give him a white stone with a new name written on it, known only to him who receives it." Verse 17, NIV.

4. "To him who overcomes and does my will to the end, *I will give authority over the nations*—'He will rule them with an iron scepter;

he will dash them to pieces like pottery'—just as I have received authority from my Father. *I will also give him the morning star*." Verses 26-28, NIV.

5. "He who overcomes will, like them, be *dressed in white. I will never blot out his name from the book of life, but will acknowledge him before my Father and his angels*." Revelation 3:5, NIV.

6. "Him who overcomes *I will make a pillar in the temple of my God. Never again will he leave it. I will write on him the name of my God and the name of the city of my God*, the new Jerusalem, which is coming down out of heaven from my God; and *I will also write on him my new name*." Verse 12, NIV.

7. "To him who overcomes, *I will give the right to sit with me on my throne*, just as I overcame and sat down with my Father on his throne." Verse 21, NIV.

What one overarching promise sums up all these promises?

"He who overcomes will inherit all this, and I will be his God and he will be my son." Revelation 21:7, NIV.

NOTE.—Here are the exceeding great and precious promises to the overcomer, eight in number. They embrace everything—eternal life, health, happiness, and an everlasting home. What more could be asked?

Why did God give Jacob the new name Israel?

"Then the man said, 'Your name will no longer be Jacob, but Israel, because *you have struggled with God and with men and have overcome.*' " Genesis 32:28, NIV.

NOTE.—*Israel* probably means "one who prevails with God."

Afterward who came to be called by this title?

"Now these are the names of *the children of Israel*, which came into Egypt; . . . Reuben, Simeon, Levi, and Judah, Issachar, Zebulun, and Benjamin, Dan, and Naphtali, Gad, and Asher. . . . Joseph." Exodus 1:15, NIV.

NOTE.—In other words, the descendants of Jacob, the grandson of Abraham, were known as the 12 tribes of Israel.

What special blessings were bestowed on the Israelites?

"Theirs is the *adoption as sons*; theirs *the divine glory, the covenants, the receiving of the law, the temple worship* and *the promises*. Theirs are the patriarchs, and from them is traced *the human ancestry of Christ*, who is God over all, forever praised! Amen." Romans 9:4, 5, NIV.

Who constitute the true Israel, or seed of Abraham?

"It is not as though God's word had failed. For not all who are descended from Israel are Israel. Nor because they are his descendants are they all Abraham's children. On the contrary, 'It is through Isaac that your offspring will be reckoned.' In other words it is not the natural children who are God's children but it is *the children of the promise* who are regarded as God's offspring." Verses 6-8, NIV.

NOTE.—Paul here quotes God's words to Abraham in Genesis 21:12.

What did John the Baptist say to the Pharisees and Sadducees who came to see him?

"And do not think you can say to yourselves, 'We have Abraham as our father.' I tell you that *out of these stones God can raise up children for Abraham.* The ax is already at the root of the trees, and every tree that does not produce good fruit will be cut down and thrown into the fire." Matthew 3:9, 10, NIV.

What determines whether one is a child of Abraham?

"Consider Abraham: 'He believed God, and it was credited to him as righteousness.' Understand, then, that *those who believe* are children of Abraham." Galatians 3:6, 7, NIV.

NOTE.—Paul is quoting Genesis 15:6. Because of unbelief many of the Israelites fell in the wilderness, and were not permitted to enter the Promised Land. (See Numbers 14:27-33; Deuteronomy 1:34-36.)

To whom must one belong in order to be Abraham's seed?

"You are all sons of God through faith in *Christ Jesus,* for all of you who were baptized into Christ have clothed yourselves with Christ. There is neither Jew nor Greek, slave nor free, male nor female, for you are all one in Christ Jesus. If you belong to *Christ,* then you are Abraham's seed, and heirs according to the promise." Galatians 3:26-29, NIV.

In what scripture are Christians recognized as the spiritual Israel?

"May I never boast except in the cross of our Lord Jesus Christ, through which the world has been crucified to me, and I to the world. Neither circumcision nor uncircumcision means anything; what counts is a new creation. Peace and mercy to all who follow this rule, *even to the Israel of God.*" Galatians 6:14-16, NIV.

To whom is the gospel the power of God for salvation?

"I am not ashamed of the gospel, because it is the power of God for the salvation of *everyone who believes*: first for the Jew, then for the Gentile." Romans 1:16, NIV.

To whom did Jesus first send the 12 disciples?

"These twelve Jesus sent out with the following instructions: 'Do not go among the Gentiles or enter any town of the Samaritans. Go rather to *the lost sheep of Israel.*'" Matthew 10:5, 6, NIV.

When the Canaanite woman came to Christ, begging Him to heal her daughter, what did He say?

"He answered, *'I was sent only to the lost sheep of Israel.*'" Matthew 15:24, NIV.

When she persisted in her request, and fell down to worship Him, what did He say?

"He replied, *'It is not right to take the children's bread and toss it to their dogs.*'" Verse 26, NIV.

NOTE.—By her persistent faith, this woman, although a Canaanite, showed that she was really a true child of Abraham.

While dining with Zacchaeus, what did Jesus say?

"Jesus said to him, *'Today salvation has come to this house, because this man, too, is a son of Abraham. For the Son of Man came to seek and to save what was lost.*'" Luke 19:9, NIV.

What did Jesus tell the Samaritan woman about the source of salvation?

"You Samaritans worship what you do not know; we worship what we do know, for *salvation is from the Jews.*" John 4:22, NIV.

When the Jews rejected Paul's preaching of the gospel, what did he and Barnabas say?

"Then Paul and Barnabas answered them boldly: 'We had to speak the word of God to you first. Since you reject it and do not consider yourselves worthy of eternal life, we now turn to the Gentiles.'" Acts 13:46, NIV.

In the book of Romans, what symbolizes the Gentile believers who have become a part of the true Israel of God?

"If some of the branches have been broken off, and you, though *a wild olive shoot*, have been grafted in among the others and now share in the nourishing sap from the olive root, do not boast over those branches." Romans 11:17, 18, NIV.

What warning is given the Gentile grafts so that they will not boast, saying that the Jews were broken off to let them come in?

"But they were broken off because of unbelief, and you stand by faith. *Do not be arrogant*, but be afraid. *For if God did not spare the natural branches, he will not spare you either.*" Verses 20, 21, NIV.

What encouragement is held out concerning the branches that have been broken off?

"And if they do not persist in unbelief, they will be grafted in, for God is able to graft them in again." Verse 23, NIV.

What will be the final result of the gospel?

"And so *all Israel will be saved*, as it is written: 'The deliverer will come from Zion; he will turn godlessness away from Jacob. And this is my covenant with them when I take away their sins.' " Verse 26, NIV.

In what condition were the Gentiles before they became Israelites?

"Therefore, remember that formerly you who are Gentiles by birth . . . remember that at that time you were *separate from Christ, excluded from citizenship in Israel and foreigners to the covenants of the promise, without hope and without God in the world.*" Ephesians 2:11, 12, NIV.

NOTE.—If, in order to be saved, Gentiles must become spiritual Israelites; then when converted, they certainly must have faith in Christ and conform their lives to the moral law that God gave to Israel. Otherwise it would be the commonwealth, not of Israel, but of the Gentiles. The writing of the law in the heart is one of the provisions of the new covenant with true Israel. Jeremiah wrote, " ' The time is coming,' declares the Lord, 'when I will make a new covenant with the house of Israel and with the house of Judah. It will not be like the covenant I made with their forefathers when I took them by the hand to lead them out of Egypt, because they broke my covenant, though I was a husband to them,' declares the Lord.

" ' This is the covenant I will make with the house of Israel after that time,' declares the Lord. 'I will put my law in their minds and write it on their hearts. I will be their God, and they will be my people. No longer will a man teach his neighbor, or a man his brother, saying, "Know the Lord," because they will all know me, from the least of them to the greatest,' declares the Lord. 'For I will forgive their wickedness and will remember their sins no more.' " Jeremiah 31:31-34, NIV.

The New Testament quotes Jeremiah 31:31-34 in Hebrews 8:8-12, proclaiming Jesus the high priest of the new covenant. "Every high priest is appointed to offer both gifts and sacrifices, and so it was necessary for this one also to have something to offer. If he were on earth, he would not be a priest, for there are already men who offer the gifts prescribed by the law. They serve at a sanctuary that is a copy and shadow of what is in heaven. This is why Moses was warned when he was about to build the tabernacle: 'See to it that you make everything according to the pattern shown you on the mountain.' But the ministry Jesus has received is as superior to theirs as the covenant of which he is mediator is superior to the old one, and it is founded on better promises.

"For if there had been nothing wrong with the first covenant, no place would have been sought for another. . . . By calling this covenant 'new,' he has made the first one obsolete; and what is obsolete and aging will soon disappear." Hebrews 8:3-13, NIV.

How does Revelation describe God's remnant people?

"This calls for patient endurance on the part of the saints *who obey God's commandments and remain faithful to Jesus*." Revelation 14:12, NIV.

Whose names are in the foundations of the Holy City?

"The wall of the city had twelve foundations, and on them were *the names of the twelve apostles of the Lamb*." Revelation 21:14, NIV.

Whose names are on the 12 gates of the city?

"It had a great, high wall with twelve gates, and with twelve angels at the gates. On the gates were written *the names of the twelve tribes of Israel*." Verse 12, NIV.

Who will inhabit the city?

"The nations will walk by its light, and *the kings of the earth* will bring their splendor into it." Verse 24, NIV.

NOTE.—The New Jerusalem will be for all the nations of the saved; and yet all who enter will go through gates on which are written the names of the twelve tribes of Israel. All who are saved will belong to Israel. The name *Israel* will be perpetuated in the new earth state, and very appropriately so, because of its meaning. All who share in that future home of the saved will be overcomers—princes and prevailers with God. (See Revelation 3:12; 21:7.) Christ, in selecting His apostles, recognized this division of the saved into 12 nations. He chose 12. He recognized it again when to the 12 He said: "You who have followed me will also sit on twelve thrones, judging the twelve tribes of Israel." Matthew 19:28, NIV.

ETERNAL LIFE

What precious promise has God made to His children?

"And this is what he promised us—even *eternal life*." 1 John 2:25, NIV.

How may we obtain eternal life?

"For God so loved the world that he gave his one and only Son, that *whoever believes in him shall not perish but have eternal life*." John 3:16, NIV.

Who has everlasting life?

"Whoever believes in the Son has eternal life." Verse 36, NIV.

Where can we obtain this eternal life?

"And this is the testimony: God has given us eternal life, and *this life is in his Son*." 1 John 5:11, NIV.

What therefore follows?

"He who has the Son has life; he who does not have the Son of God does not have life." Verse 12, NIV.

What does Christ give His followers?

"I give them *eternal life*, and they shall never perish; no one can snatch them out of my hand." John 10:28, NIV.

Why was humanity shut away from the tree of life after Adam and Eve sinned?

"And the Lord God said, 'The man has now become like one of us, knowing good and evil. *He must not be allowed to reach out his hand and take also from the tree of life and eat, and live forever*.' " Genesis 3:22, NIV.

What has Christ promised those who overcome the world?

"To him who overcomes, I will give *the right to eat from the tree of life*, which is in the paradise of God." Revelation 2:7, NIV.

When will immortality be conferred upon the saints?

"Listen, I tell you a mystery: We will not all sleep, but we will all be changed—*in a flash, in the twinkling of an eye, at the last trumpet*. For the trumpet will sound, the dead will be raised imperishable, and we will be changed. For the perishable must clothe itself with the imperishable, and the mortal with immortality." 1 Corinthians 15:51-53, NIV.

NOTE.—In accepting Christ, the believer receives "that eternal life, which was with the Father" (1 John 1:2), and this eternal life is theirs as long as Christ dwells in the heart by faith. At the resurrection God will confer immortality on those who have fallen asleep in Christ, and thus the possession of eternal life becomes a permanent experience.

THE HOME OF THE SAVED

Why did God create the world?

"For this is what the Lord says—he who created the heavens, he is God; he who fashioned and made the earth, he founded it; he did not create it to be empty, but formed it *to be inhabited*." Isaiah 45:18, NIV.

To whom has God given the earth?

"The highest heavens belong to the Lord, but *the earth he has given to man*." Psalm 115:16, NIV.

What role did God have in mind for us?

"You made him *ruler over the works of your hands*; you put everything under his feet." Psalm 8:6, NIV. (See Genesis 1:26; Hebrews 2:8.)

How did humanity lose their dominion?

Through sin. "Therefore, just as sin entered the world through one man, and death through sin, and in this way death came to all men, because all sinned." Romans 5:12, NIV.

When we lost our dominion, who claimed it?

"They promise them freedom, while they themselves are slaves of *depravity*—for a man is a slave to whatever has mastered him." 2 Peter 2:19, NIV.

NOTE.—Humanity was overcome by Satan, and yielded itself and its possessions into the hands of his captor.

What ownership did Satan, in tempting Christ, claim?

"The devil led him up to a high place and showed him in an instant *all the kingdoms of the world*. And he said to him, 'I will give you all their authority and splendor, for it has been given to me, and

I can give to anyone I want to.'" Luke 4:5, 6, NIV.

What blessing awaits the meek?

"Blessed are the meek, for *they will inherit the earth*." Matthew 5:5, NIV.

NOTE.—This inheritance cannot be realized in this life, for here the truly meek generally have little of earth's good things.

Who seem to have the upper hand in today's world?

"For I envied *the arrogant* when I saw the prosperity of *the wicked*. . . . From their callous hearts comes iniquity; the evil conceits of their minds know no limits." Psalm 73:3-7, NIV.

What promise about land did God make to Abraham?

"The Lord said to Abram after Lot had parted from him, 'Lift up your eyes from where you are and look north and south, east and west. *All the land that you see I will give to you and your offspring forever*.'" Genesis 13:14, 15, NIV.

How much did this promise encompass?

"It was not through law that Abraham and his offspring received the promise that *he would be heir of the world*, but through the righteousness that comes by faith." Romans 4:13, NIV.

How much of the land of Canaan did Abraham own in his lifetime?

"He gave him no inheritance here, *not even a foot of ground*. But God promised him that he and his descendants after him would possess the land, even though at that time Abraham had no child." Acts 7:5, NIV. (See Hebrews 11:13.)

How much of the promised possession did Abraham expect during his lifetime?

"By faith Abraham, when called to go to a place he would later receive as his inheritance, obeyed and went, even though he did not know where he was going. By faith he made his home in the promised land like a stranger in a foreign country; he lived in tents, as did Isaac and Jacob, who were heirs with him of the same promise. For he was looking forward to the city with foundations, whose architect and builder is God." Hebrews 11:8-10, NIV.

Who is the seed to whom this promise was made?

"The promises were spoken to Abraham and to his seed. The Scripture does not say 'and to seeds,' meaning many people, but 'and to your seed,' meaning one person, who is *Christ.*" Galatians 3:16, NIV.

Who are heirs of the promise?

"If you belong to Christ, then you are Abraham's seed, and heirs according to the promise." Verse 29, NIV.

Why did God withhold His promises from such people as Abraham?

"These were all commended for their faith, yet none of them received what had been promised. *God had planned something better for us so that only together with us would they be made perfect.*" Hebrews 11:39, 40, NIV.

What will happen to the earth when Jesus returns?

"But the day of the Lord will come like a thief. The heavens will disappear with a roar; *the elements will be destroyed by fire, and the earth and everything in it will be laid bare.*" 2 Peter 3:10, NIV.

What will follow the end of the world?

"But in keeping with his promise we are looking forward to a new heaven and a new earth, the home of righteousness." Verse 13, NIV.

NOTE.—As shown on pages 298-301, the unsaved will die at the coming of Christ, and the saved will go to heaven to dwell with Christ. At the end of the millennium the wicked will be resurrected for the final judgment, and will be destroyed when the earth is at last re-created. Redeemed from sin, humanity will be restored to its original dominion.

What Old Testament promise is Peter evidently referring to?

"Behold, I will create new heavens and a new earth." Isaiah 65:17, NIV.

NOTE.—John echoes this promise in his description of his vision, writing, "Then I saw a new heaven and a new earth, for the first heaven and the first earth had passed away, and there was no longer any sea." Revelation 21:1, NIV.

What picture did Isaiah paint of life in the new earth?

"They will build houses and dwell in them; they will plant vineyards and eat their fruit. No longer will they build houses and others live in them, or plant and others eat. For as the days of a tree, so will be the days of my people; my chosen ones will long enjoy the works of their hands. They will not toil in vain or bear children doomed to misfortune; for they will be a people blessed by the Lord, they and their descendants with them. Before they call I will answer; while they are still speaking I will hear." Isaiah 65:21-24, NIV.

How did Isaiah describe the earth's future peace?

"The wolf and the lamb will feed together, and the lion will eat straw like the ox, but dust will be the serpent's food." Verse 25, NIV.

What seasons of worship did Isaiah describe in the new earth?

" 'As the new heavens and the new earth that I make will endure before me,' declares the Lord, 'so will your name and descendants endure. *From one New Moon to another and from one Sabbath to another*, all mankind will come and bow down before me,' says the Lord." Isaiah 66:22, 23, NIV.

What did Daniel predict about this kingdom?

"Then the sovereignty, power and greatness of the kingdoms under the whole heaven will be handed over to the saints, the people of the Most High. *His kingdom will be an everlasting kingdom*, and all rulers will worship and obey him." Daniel 7:27, NIV.

THE NEW JERUSALEM

How did Jesus promise to return for His followers?

"In my Father's house are many rooms; if it were not so, I would have told you. I am going there to prepare a place for you. And if I go and prepare a place for you, *I will come back and take you to be with me* that you also may be where I am." John 14:2, 3, NIV.

What does Paul say God has prepared for His people?

"Instead, they were longing for a better country—a heavenly one. Therefore God is not ashamed to be called their God, for *he has prepared a city for them*." Hebrews 11:16, NIV.

Where is this city, and what is it called?

"But the *Jerusalem* that is *above* is free, and she is *our mother*." Galatians 4:26, NIV.

How did Abraham look forward to something greater?

"For *he was looking forward to the city with foundations*, whose architect and builder is God." Hebrews 11:10, NIV.

What assurance has God given believers?

"Instead, they were longing for a better country—a heavenly one. Therefore God is not ashamed to be called their God, for *he has prepared a city for them*." Verse 16, NIV.

How did John describe the heavenly city?

"I saw the Holy City, the new Jerusalem, coming down out of heaven from God, *prepared as a bride beautifully dressed for her husband*." Revelation 21:2, NIV.

How many foundations has this city?

"The wall of the city had *twelve* foundations, and on them were the names of the twelve apostles of the Lamb." Verse 14, NIV.

What is the measurement of the city?

"The city was laid out like a square, as long as it was wide. He measured the city with the rod and found it to be *12,000 stadia in length, and as wide and high as it is long*." Verse 16, NIV.

NOTE.—The measure around it, as the words length and breadth imply, and as was the ancient custom of measuring cities, is 12,000 stadia. This is equal to 1,500 miles, 375 miles on each side, making a perfect square. The area of this city is therefore 140,625 square miles, or 90,000,000 acres, or 3,920,400,000,000 square feet.

How does John describe the wall?

"He measured its wall and it was 144 cubits thick, by man's measurement, which the angel was using. The wall was made of jasper, and the city of pure gold, as pure as glass." Verses 17, 18, NIV.

NOTE.—One hundred forty-four cubits are estimated at 216 feet in our measure.

What adorns the 12 foundations?

"And the foundations of the wall of the city were decorated with every kind of precious stone. The first foundation was jasper, the second sapphire, the third chalcedony, the fourth emerald, the fifth sardonyx, the sixth carnelian, the seventh chrysolyte, the eighth beryl, the ninth topaz, the tenth chrysoprase, the eleventh jacinth, the twelfth amethyst." Verses 19, 20, NIV. (See Exodus 28:15-21; Isaiah 54:11, 12.)

How does John describe the 12 gates?

"The twelve gates were twelve pearls, each gate made of a single pearl." Revelation 21:21, NIV.

What is written on these gates?

"On the gates were written the names of the twelve tribes of Israel." Verse 12, NIV.

How does John describe the streets of the city?

"The great street of the city was of pure gold, like transparent glass." Verse 21, NIV.

Why will this city have no need of outside light?

"The city does not need the sun or the moon to shine on it, for the glory of God gives it light, and the Lamb is its lamp. The nations will walk by its light, and the kings of the earth will bring their splendor into it." Verses 23, 24, NIV. (See Revelation 22:5; Isaiah 60:19, 20.)

Why will its gates always remain open?

"On no day will its gates ever be shut, for there will be no night there." Revelation 21:25, NIV.

What will be excluded from this city?

"Nothing impure will ever enter it, nor will anyone who does what is shameful or deceitful, but only those whose names are written in the Lamb's book of life." Verse 27, NIV.

Who will be permitted to enter it?

"Blessed are *those who do His commandments*, that they may have right to the tree of life, and may enter through the gates into the city." Revelation 22:14.

NOTE.—The New International Version and the Revised Standard Version render this, "Blessed are those who wash their robes," etc. The result is the same, for those who wash their robes serve only Christ, and hence do God's commandments.

What flows through the New Jerusalem?

"Then the angel showed me the river of the water of life, as clear as crystal, flowing from the throne of God and of the Lamb down the middle of the great street of the city." Revelation 22:1, 2, NIV.

What stands on either side of the river?

"On each side of the river stood the tree of life, bearing twelve crops of fruit, yielding its fruit every month. And the leaves of the tree are for the healing of the nations." Verse 2, NIV.

NOTE.—The tree of life, which Adam lost through sin, is to be restored by Christ. Access to this is one of the promises to the overcomer (Revelation 2:7). Its bearing 12 kinds of fruit, a new kind each month, suggests a reason that in the new earth "from one new moon to another," as well as "from one sabbath to another," all people are to come before God to worship, as stated in Isaiah 66:22, 23.

THE CONFLICT ENDED

What does Genesis say about the completion of God's creation?

"Thus the heavens and the earth were *completed* in all their vast array. By the seventh day God had *finished* doing the work he had been doing." Genesis 2:1, 2, NIV.

NOTE.—God's creation was described as "very good" (Genesis 1:31). Had it not been for sin, this first plan of God would not have been followed by the three steps we shall now study.

What did Christ, when dying on the cross, say to indicate that the conflict was ended?

"When he had received the drink, Jesus said, *'It is finished.'* With that, he bowed his head and gave up his spirit." John 19:30, NIV.

NOTE.—Christ came into the world to save sinners. He paid the price, costly though it was. In that final moment He said, "It is finished."

At the pouring out of the seventh plague, what announcement will be made?

"The seventh angel poured out his bowl into the air, and out of the temple came a loud voice from the throne saying, 'It is done!' " Revelation 16:17, NIV.

NOTE.—This outpouring of God's wrath is upon the rejecters of Heaven's mercy. Human probation has closed, and when the great voice cries, "It is done," Christ starts on His way to earth the second time.

When the new heavens and the new earth have appeared, and the Holy City, the New Jerusalem, has descended from God and become the metropolis of the new creation, what announcement will then be made?

"He who was seated on the throne said, 'I am making everything new!' Then he said, 'Write this down, for these words are trustworthy and true.' He said to me, 'It is done. I am the Alpha and the Omega, the Beginning and the End. To him who is thirsty I will give to drink without cost from the spring of the water of life. He who overcomes will inherit all this, and I will be his God and he will be my son.' " Revelation 21:5-7, NIV.

How does Isaiah describe how God will transform the ethos of the world?

"The wolf will live with the lamb, the leopard will lie down with the goat, the calf and the lion and the yearling together; and a little child will lead them. The cow will feed with the bear, their young will lie down together, and the lion will eat straw like the ox. The infant will play near the hole of the cobra, and the young child put his hand into the viper's nest. They will neither harm nor destroy on all my holy mountain, for the earth will be full of the knowledge of the Lord as the waters cover the sea." Isaiah 11:6-9, NIV.

What will finally be the privilege of God's children?

"They will see his face, and his name will be on their foreheads." Revelation 22:4, NIV.

NOTE.—Jesus promised, "Blessed are the pure in heart, for they will see God." Matthew 5:8, NIV. (See also Hebrews 12:14.)

How perfect will be their knowledge of God?

"Now we see but a poor reflection as in a mirror; then we shall see face to face. Now I know in part; then I shall know fully, even as I am fully known." 1 Corinthians 13:12, NIV.

How will we be transformed by meeting Christ?

"Dear friends, now we are children of God, and what we will be has not yet been made known. But we know that *when he appears, we shall be like him, for we shall see him as he is*. Everyone who has this hope in him purifies himself, just as he is pure." 1 John 3:2, 3, NIV.

How does Isaiah describe the change from old to new?

"Behold, I will create new heavens and a new earth. The former things will not be remembered, nor will they come to mind." Isaiah 65:17, NIV.

How will God restore His damaged children?

"He will wipe every tear from their eyes. There will be no more death or mourning or crying or pain, for the old order of things has passed away." Revelation 21:4, NIV.

Will God ever be separated from His children again?

"And I heard a loud voice from the throne saying, 'Now the dwelling of God is with men, and he will live with them. They will be his people, and God himself will be with them and be their God.' " Verse 3, NIV.

What will it mean to dwell in God's presence?

"You have made known to me the path of life; you will fill me with joy in your presence, with eternal pleasures at your right hand." Psalm 16:11, NIV.

What peaceful condition will prevail in the earth made new?

"They will neither harm nor destroy on all my holy mountain, for the earth will be full of the knowledge of the Lord as the waters cover the sea." Isaiah 11:9, NIV.

How does Isaiah describe the ransomed of the Lord upon their triumphant return to Zion?

"And the ransomed of the Lord will return. They will enter Zion with singing; everlasting joy will crown their heads. Gladness and joy will overtake them, and sorrow and sighing will flee away." Isaiah 35:10, NIV.

How long will they possess the future kingdom?

"But the saints of the Most High will receive the kingdom and will possess it forever—yes, for ever and ever." Daniel 7:18, NIV.

INDEX